I0729767

WOMEN STREET ARTISTS

24 Contemporary Graffiti and
Mural Artists from Around the World

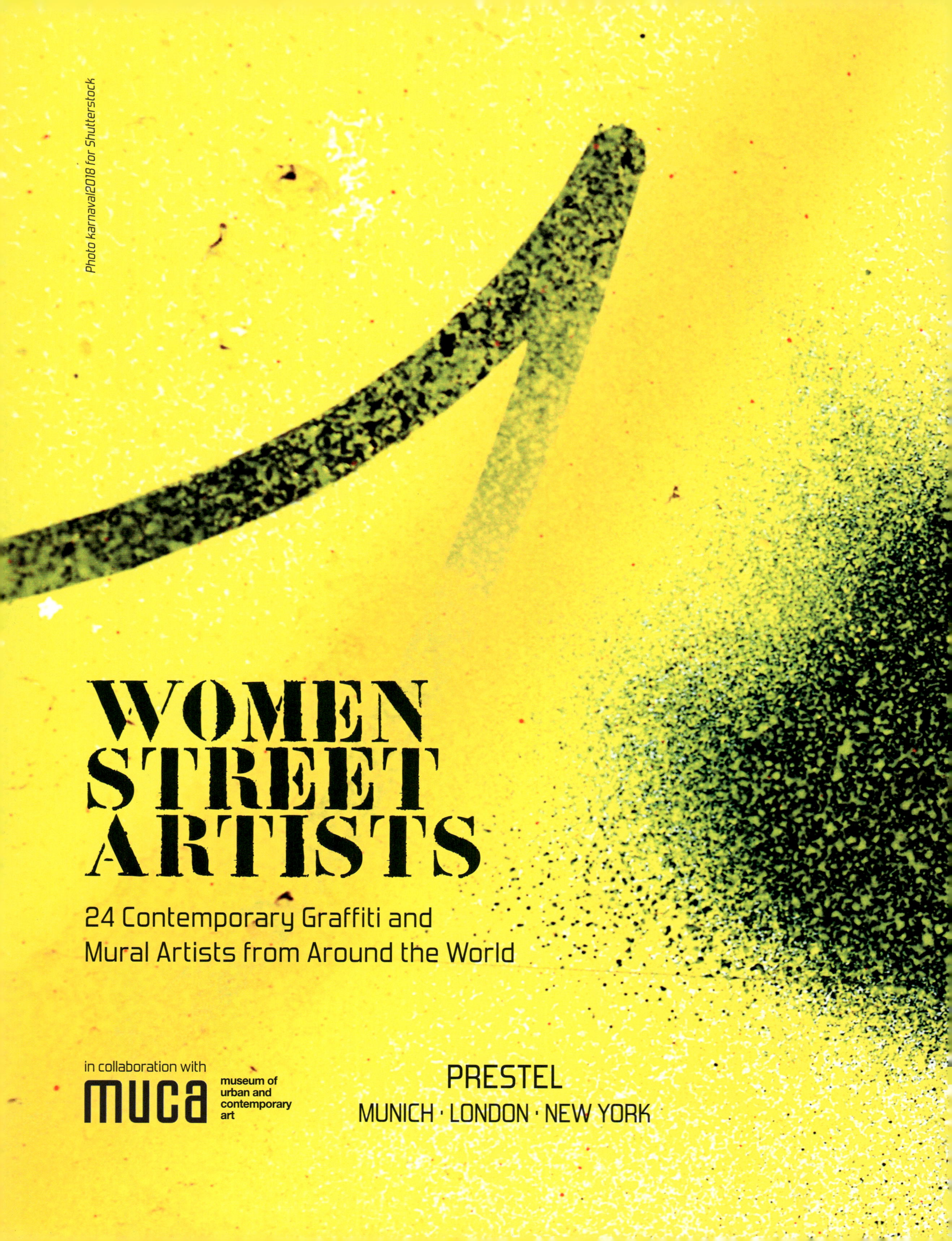

WOMEN STREET ARTISTS

24 Contemporary Graffiti and
Mural Artists from Around the World

in collaboration with

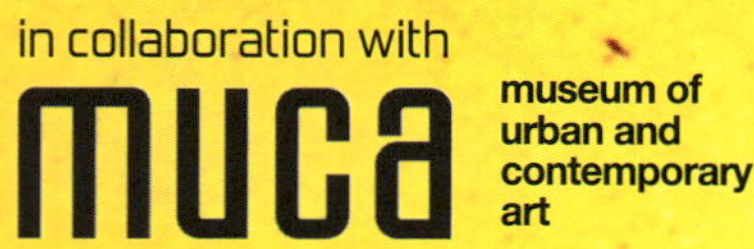

museum of
urban and
contemporary
art

PRESTEL

MUNICH · LONDON · NEW YORK

ALESSANDRA MATTANZA
FOREWORD BY STEPHANIE UTZ

CONTENTS

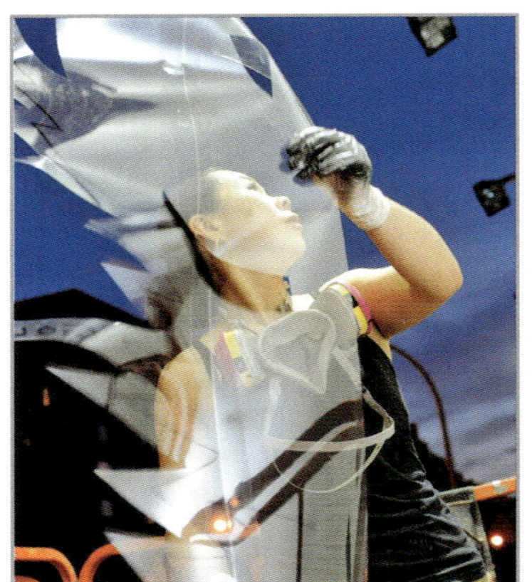

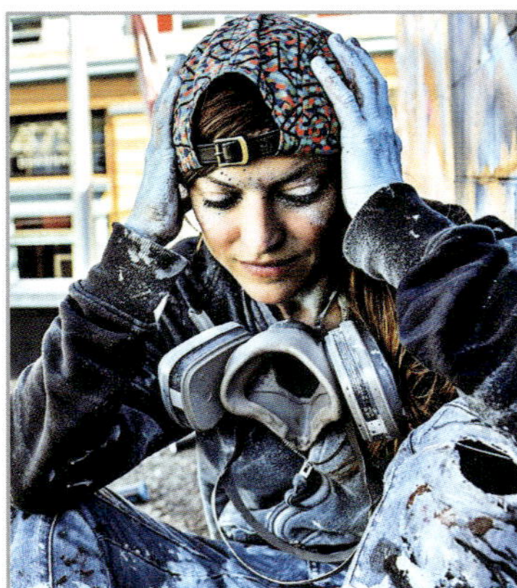

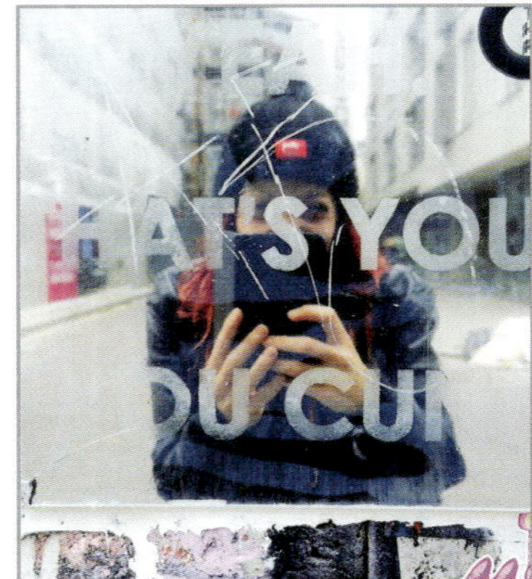

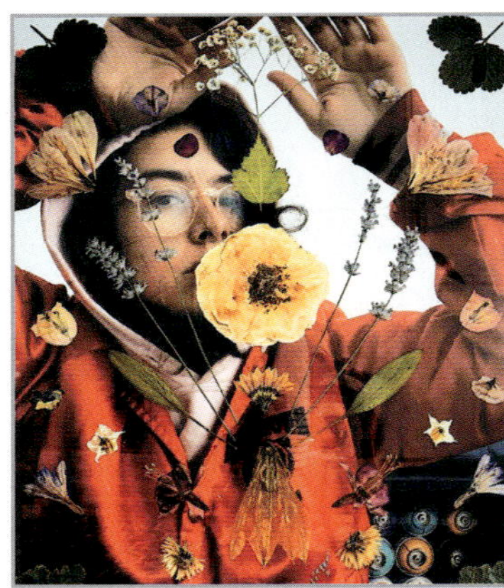

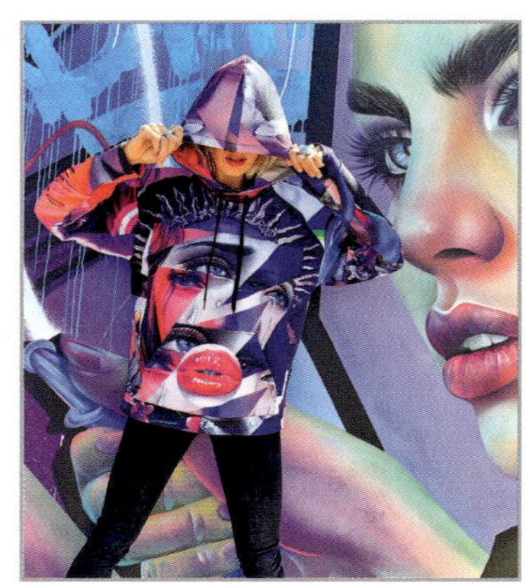

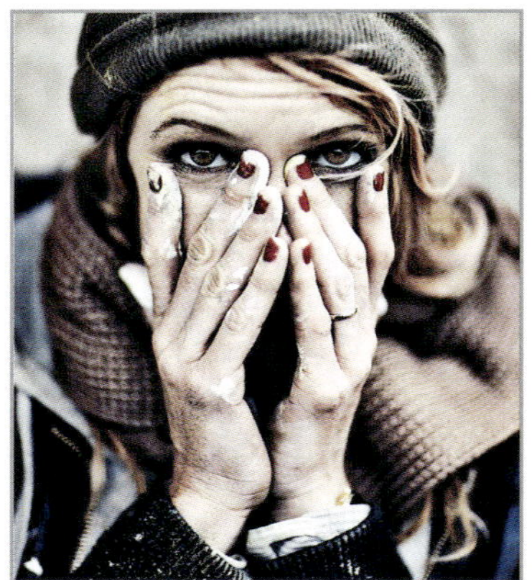

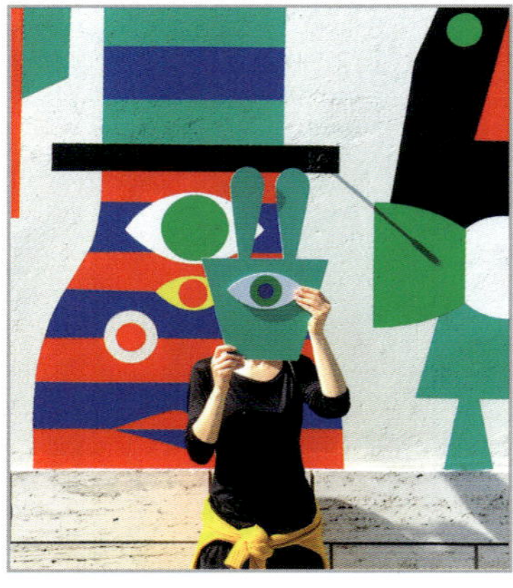

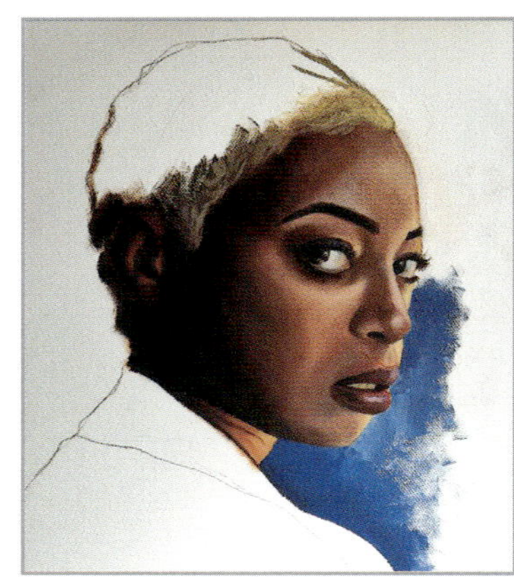

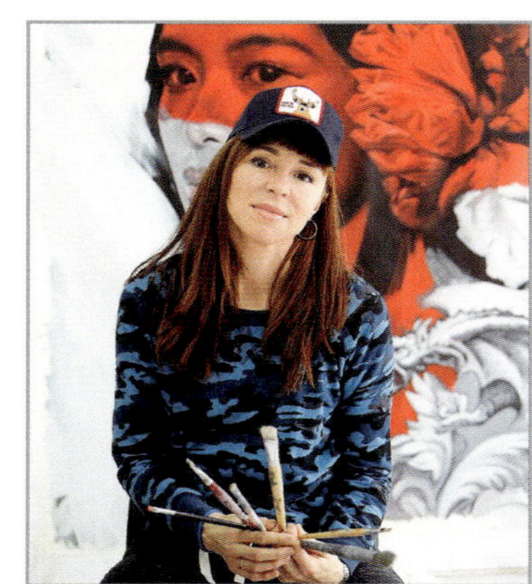

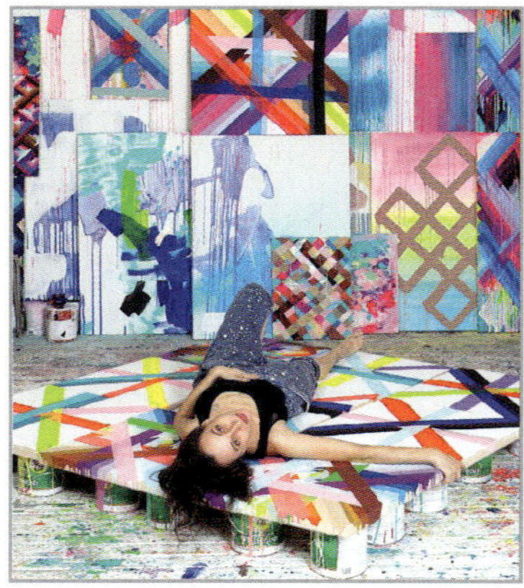

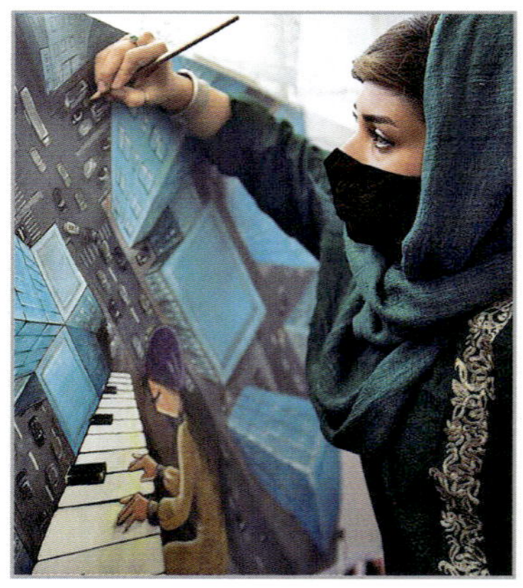

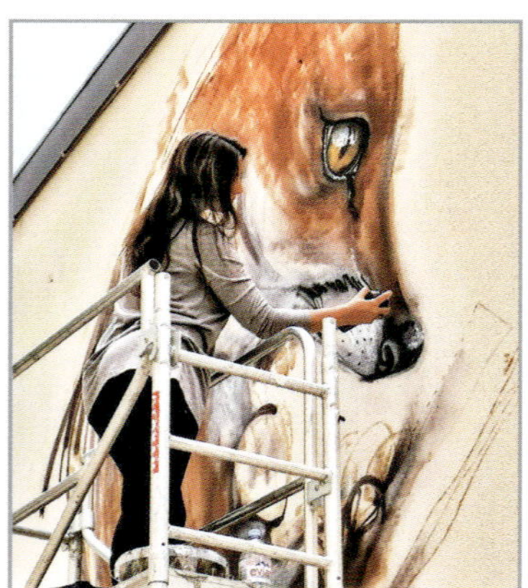

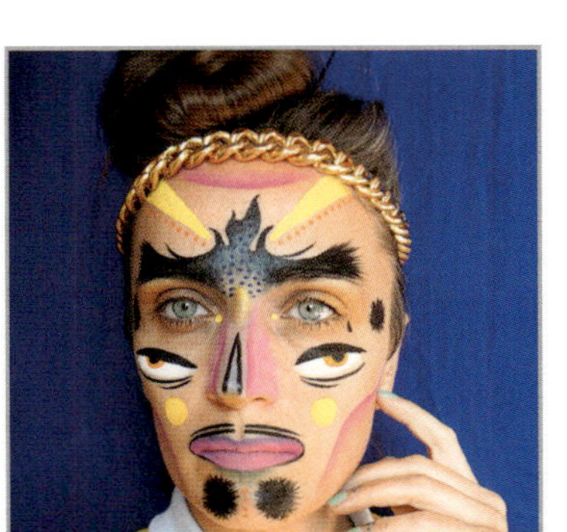

KASHINK

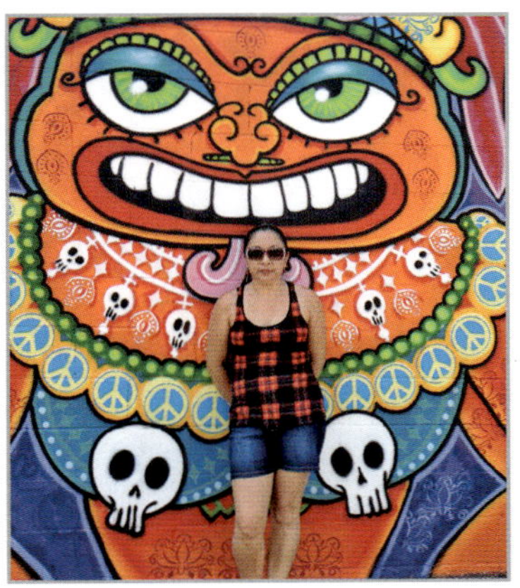

LADY PINK

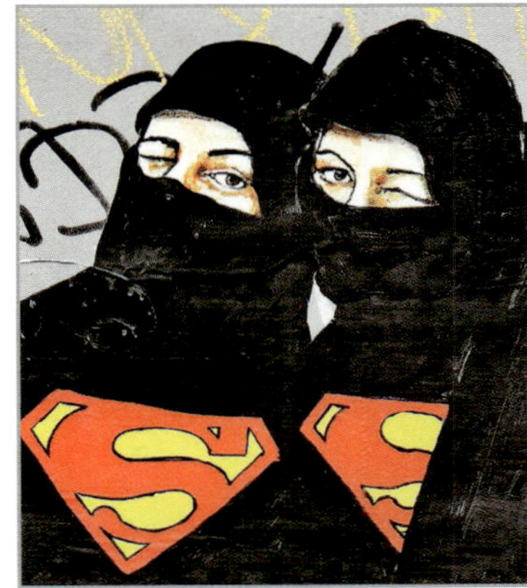

#LEDIESIS

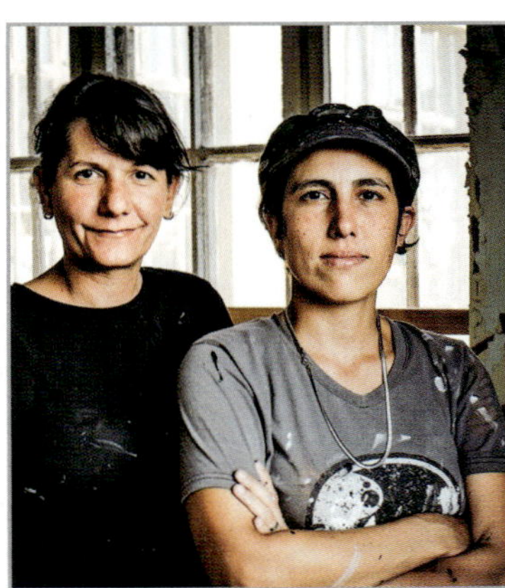

MEDIANERAS

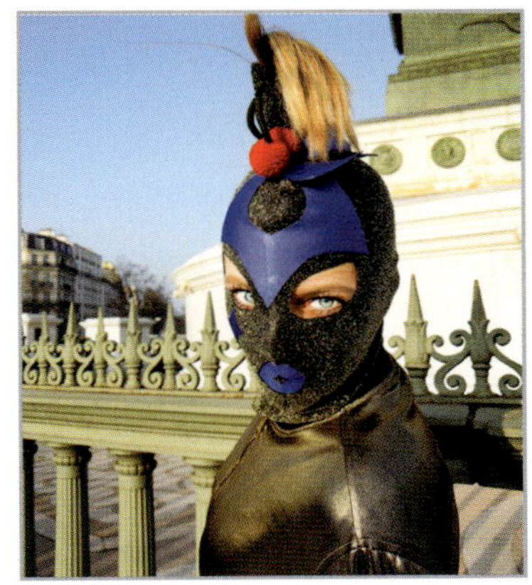

MINA MANIA

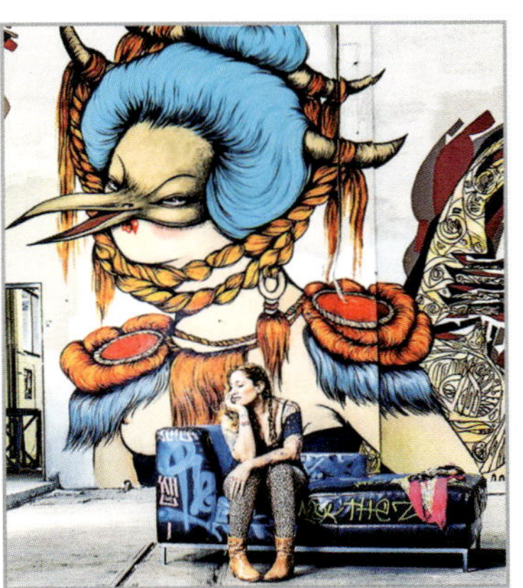

MISS VAN

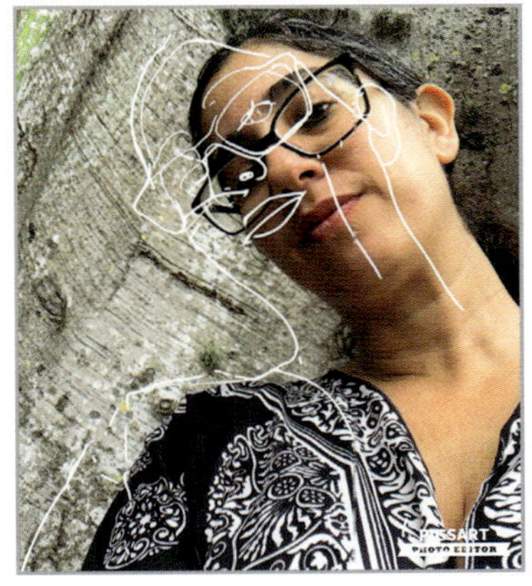

ALICE MIZRACHI

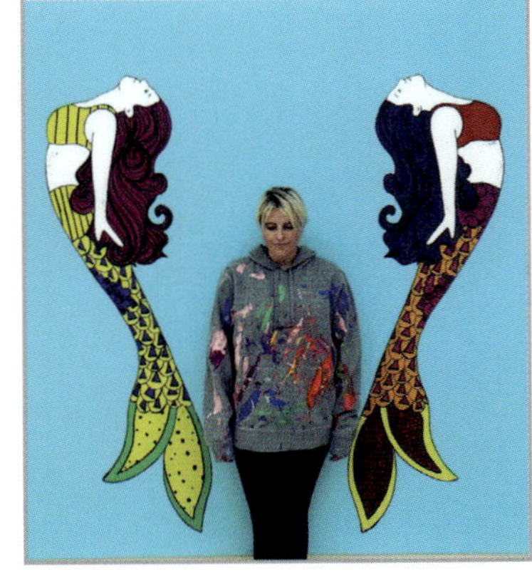

KELSEY MONTAGUE

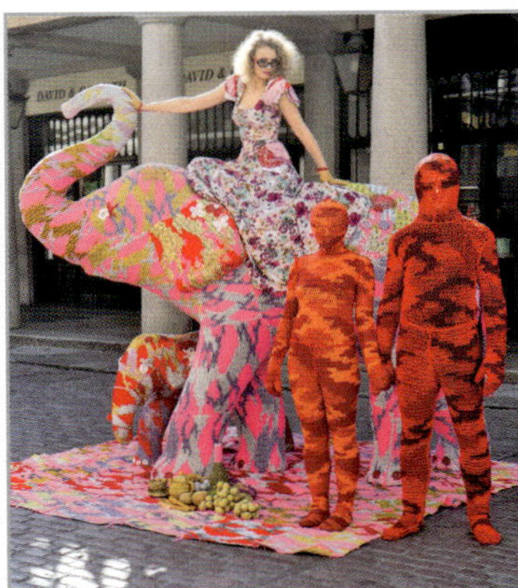

OLEK

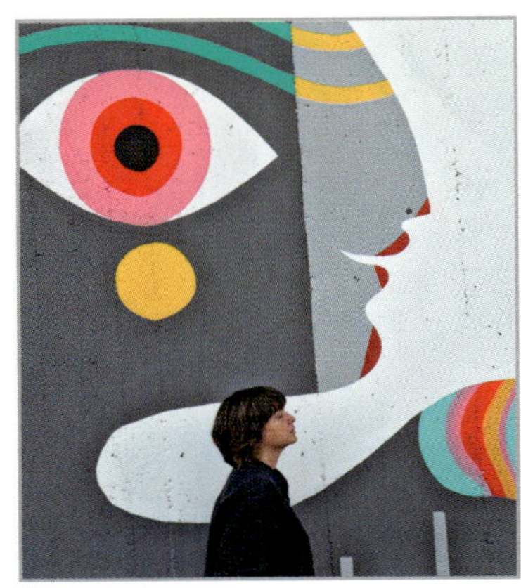

GIO PISTONE

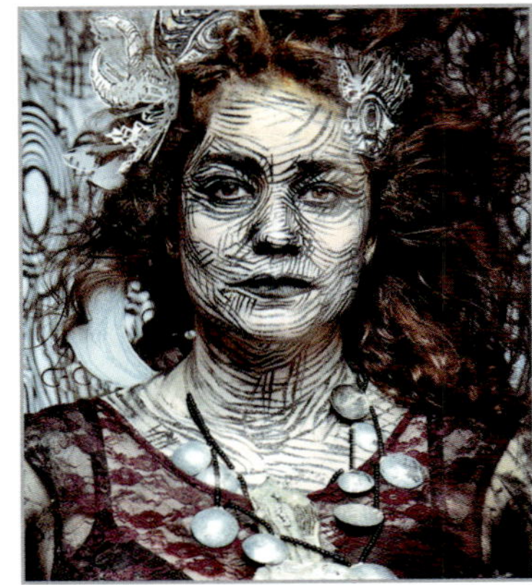

SWOON

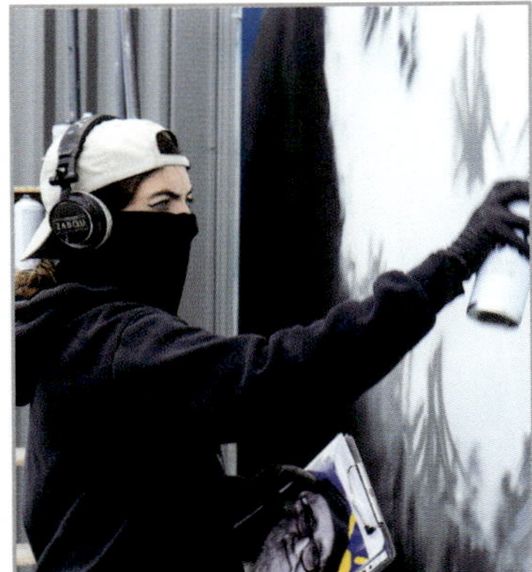

ZABOU

STREET ART IS FEMALE

by Stephanie Utz

Do we have a clear idea of how many talented female artists are out there? Is there really a different unconscious perception when it comes to female art? Or has this discussion already become obsolete?

There is a sharp drop in the proportion of female art graduates versus the number of women represented in galleries and museums. According to the National Museum of Women in the Arts, over half of all visual artists in the US are women, yet only thirty percent of artworks displayed in galleries are by women. Statistics indicate that the problem lies less in a supposed lack of qualified women and more in the need for museums and galleries to reflect on their own curatorial practices, taking active measures to ensure a more balanced representation in collections.

This underlines the importance of exhibiting female street artists. Not only does it dissolve the exclusionary ideal of the male street artist, but it also diversifies the perspectives and techniques to which audiences are exposed.

However, even when women are recognized as talented street artists by established institutions, they face an additional challenge: the art they make is often labeled "feminine." Paradoxically, this risks essentializing a highly diverse cluster of individuals, carving a divide that implies patronizing comparisons: women's success is often defined only relative to their existing male counterparts.

Like many other female street artists, SWOON, for instance, resists gendered interpretations of her work. She is acclaimed as a role model because of her solo career, recognized the world over for her life-sized paper cutouts. Maya Hayuk, known for her large-scale colorful murals, works only with galleries who exhibit a certain percentage of female artists. Faith47's artwork is inspired by social realities translated through a feminine way of painting. AIKO playfully addresses female sexuality in the context of Manga elements, infiltrating male-dominated spaces with recognizably feminine color and content. With her bare-breasted figures, Miss Van shows off the power of femininity in the artistic act.

So, where do we stand today? A lot has changed over the last years. Working in diverse styles, some women consciously advocate feminine elements in street art, while others go beyond gender. They deliberately question and weaponize femininity, neglecting any form of social convention or boundaries. Many artists openly play with their feminine identity, publicly revealing their alias, which has thankfully led to Street Art becoming more and more taken over by women claiming their position in the art scene.

Street Art is no longer an exclusive boys' club. It took some time, but the time has come. Nevertheless, we are still only scratching the surface. There are many more talented female artists out there, paving their way to the front line.

It's about time for women to be recognized for their contributions. The more that women find a platform upon which to exhibit, the more other women will be inspired to paint and find their own identity.

Stephanie Utz, Co-Founder, Museum of Urban and Contemporary Art (MUCA)

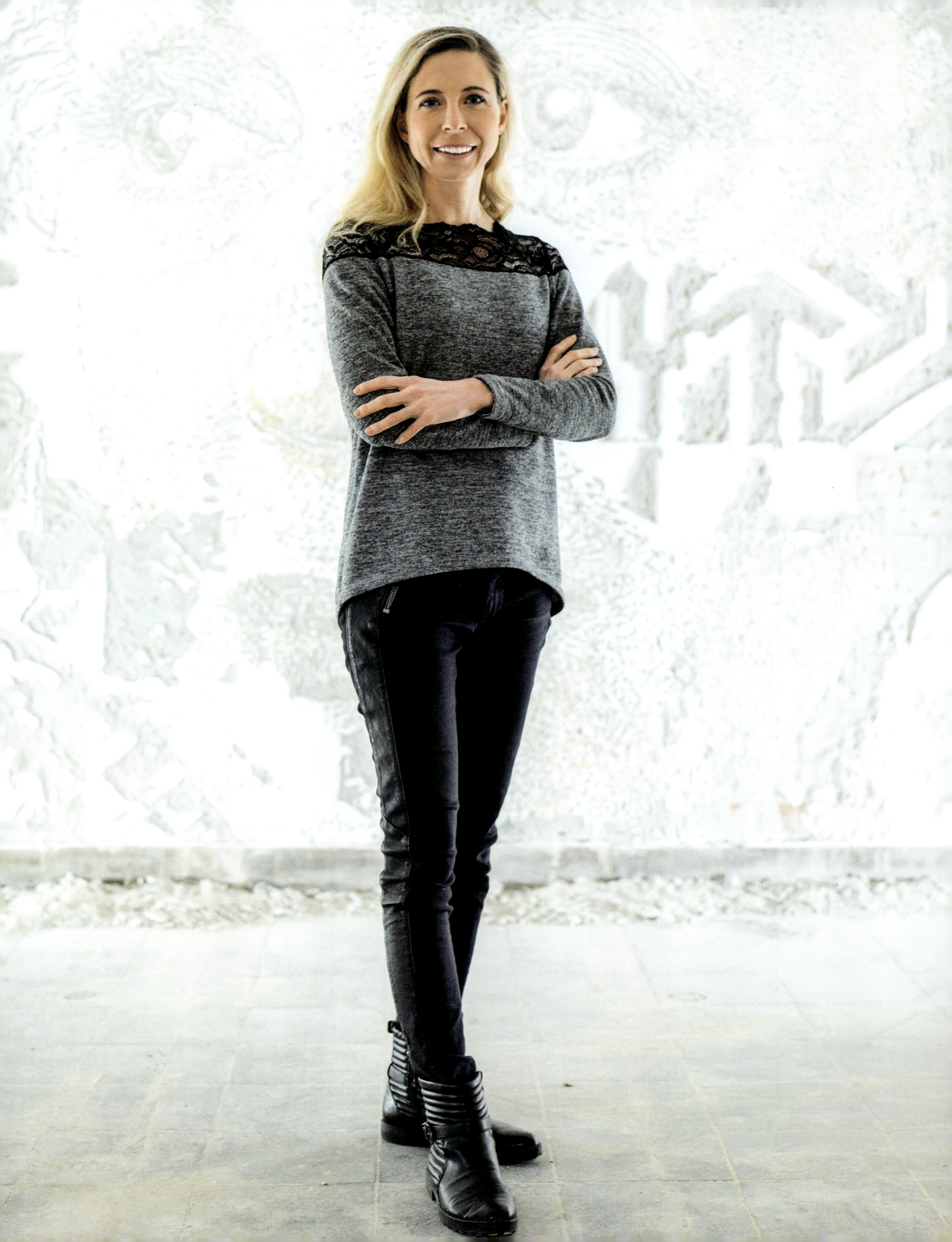

POWER TO WOMEN, POWER TO ART

by Alessandra Mattanza

There are women who remain engraved lifelong in your memory and meeting them becomes fundamental to your existence. Journalist, writer, and activist Gloria Steinem has always been at the forefront of the fight for equality. Getting to know her was a thrill for me, not only because of her vision and thought, but also because of her warm intimacy, her femininity and fervent intellect that transcends the boundaries of gender, space, and time with ideas that intersect the past, present, and future, her leonine grit and courage, and her fearlessness. Gloria is a friend to women, and it is this that touched me profoundly.

"I really admire Gloria for the magnificent human being that she is. She represents all women in their complexity, and is the woman we all want to be. She is endowed with incredible sensitivity and perseverance, as well as inexhaustible patience and an extraordinary will never to give up, to constantly push forward, even when the goal to be reached seems impossible," admits Julianne Moore, who starred in the movie *The Glorias*, directed by another amazing woman, Julie Taymor, who also directed *Frida*. And it was precisely that movie, which skillfully delineated Gloria Steinem's personal path and her struggle for independence and the recognition of fundamental human rights, that prompted me to publish a book dedicated to women street artists, women who operate in a sector that until recently was regarded as purely male, due in part to the free and wild lifestyle with which it is associated, in part to the physical labor it entails, and in part to the dangers that its protagonists sometimes face, especially when working at night, in secrecy. As a street photographer, I feel quite close to them, often sharing their hardships, dangers, and discrimination. Too often, even in my job as journalist, I have found myself in the position of being the only woman at a men's table. Each time, I have asked myself: Why?

All the artists whom I have met in my life have inspired me in some way or another, and I feel honored to have gotten to know these incredible women, who, with perseverance and courage, have sought their place in the world, a place from which they now make their voices heard.

I have been fascinated by extraordinary women ever since my childhood. I have always had the impression that their power unleashed a cathartic energy, one capable of changing the world, precisely because they were often solitary and poorly understood souls, yet always fierce fighters, capable of shining with their light, despite the social canons that tried to keep them invisible. Women who went beyond what was deemed an ordinary life. Women who rebelled and struggled against the rules of quotidian thought while trying to assert their own. Women who did jobs that were usually recognized as male prerogatives. Women who, at times, decided not to be women anymore, who went beyond gender and chose to live life in their own way. Women who had undergone all sorts of abuse but were able to start over, possibly even to help others. Or women who, on their own, had the determination to take over New York City, painting its walls or putting up portraits along its streets.

Lady Pink may have been the first female artist to succeed in an environment that is still largely male, namely that of graffiti, and she used her success to promote everyone's right to equality and equal opportunity, as well as to speak to young people and tell them that dreams must be chased. An attention to the social function of art—as admonition, to denounce injustice—is central to the work of all the street artists I have met.

This is clearly demonstrated by all of Tatyana Fazlalizadeh's works, which address, above all, the condition of women and, in particular, those of African descent. To this end, she conducted the Stop Telling Women to Smile campaign, collecting testimony of women's lived experiences, often of a dramatic and profoundly painful nature. But all the artists who appear in this book are extraordinary, with something special about them. They will make a deep impression on you, touch the depths of your soul, move you with their stories of their myriad experiences, adventures, innovative visions, wild and futuristic activism, and with

their art, which will captivate and inspire you. They will speak to you of their difficult lives, of the inhumane conditions to which many women in the world are subjected, and where they are abused, regarded as little more than animals, without rights, without aspirations, without dreams, to this day. Shamsia Hassani is well aquainted with this harsh reality and can personally testify to the dramatic situation that Afghan women are now experiencing and which, through her art, she can hurl like a boulder at the rest of the world.

This book also aims to be a journey and a wonderful adventure through the infinite universes of these women, these artists, who represent humanity itself as the unstoppable cycle of nature, like the charming spell of shamans that recalls certain aspects represented in the characters of the street artist Swoon, in the primordial instinct of animals and the incessant power of the ocean's waves.

And, as you will discover, thanks to them, new communities of women are arising all over the world, of people who are tired of being invisible, who are no longer afraid to make their voices heard, who support each other in what can only be described as the principle of a true female renaissance. You will also find that women are learning, more and more, that together they will become stronger: *United We Stand*. And remember, this is just the beginning.

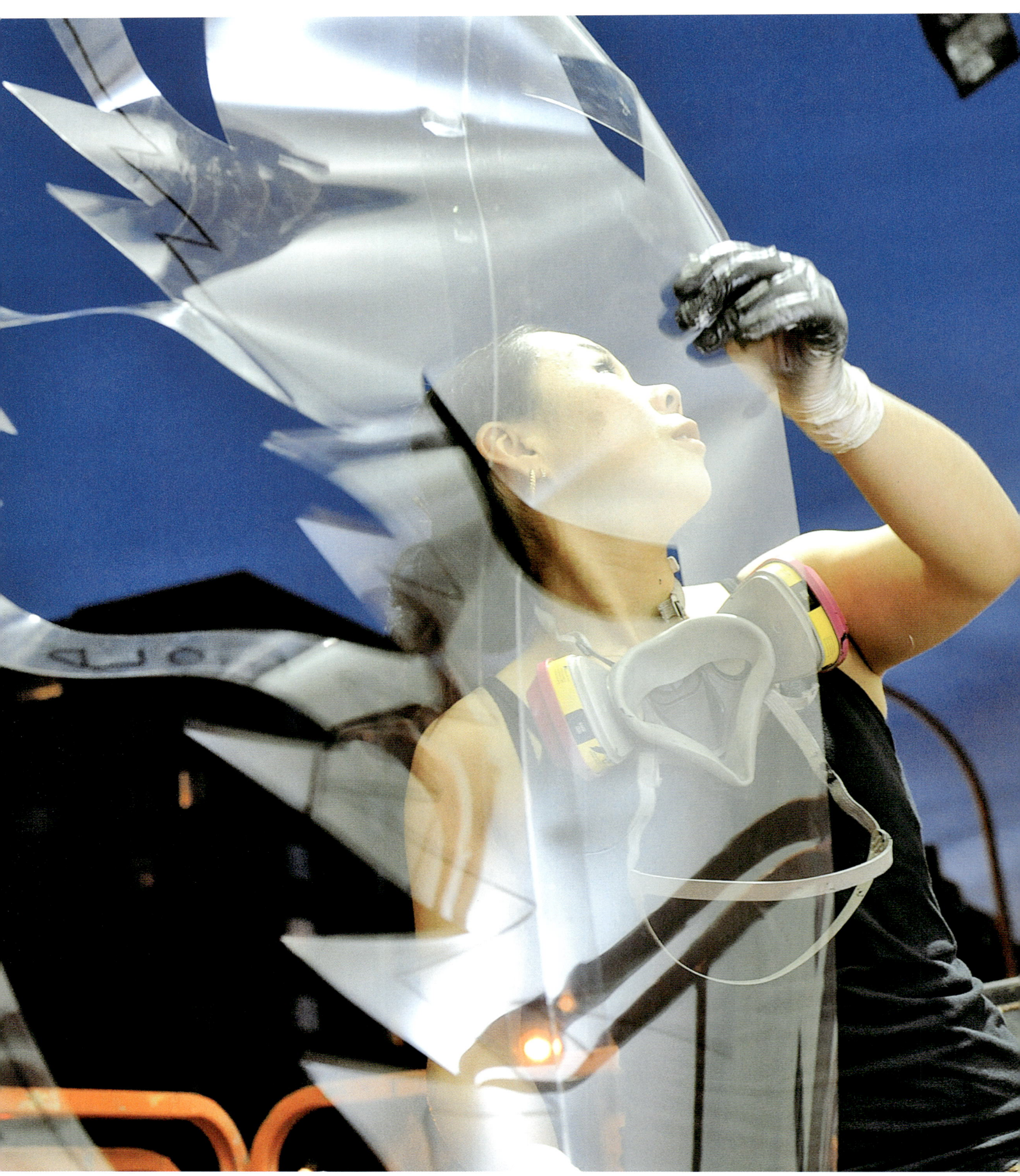

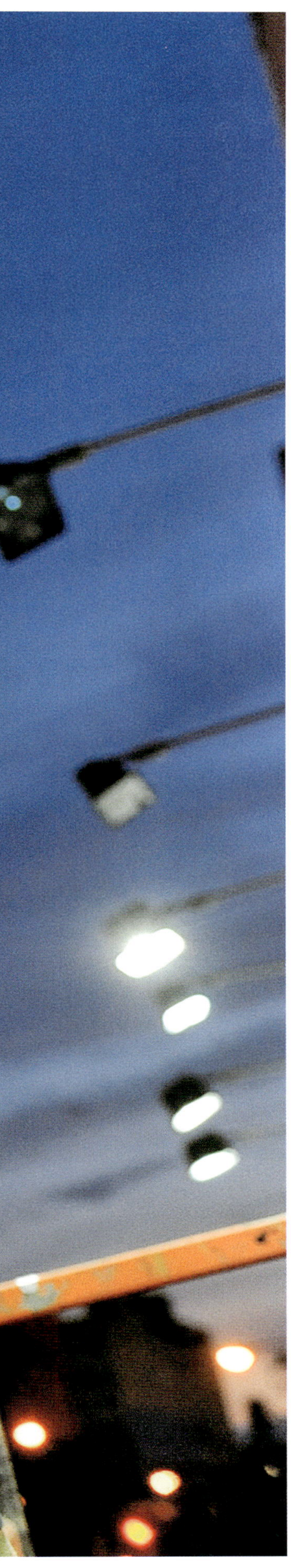

AIKO

THE EXPRESSIONIST OF EASTERN
AND WESTERN SENSUALITY

"What I learned from the outset was that it's hard for a young, foreign woman to enjoy instant success in any society, and certainly in an industry like the art world."

She is a very rare traditional stencil artist. Her stencils are cut and painted by hand, even for large scale walls. Her art stands out from everyone else's because it is a magnificent and seductive encounter of East and West, as well as for its sexy, provocative women, strong in their magnetic instinct, who, like her, are capable of a piercing preliminary gaze. Her murals are unique, often very large, always unforgettable, and able to penetrate deep into the soul. AIKO, aka LADY AIKO, was born in Japan; but from the start, the sexist culture of her native land was too restrictive for her and the reason why she came to New York, which immediately inspired her. "I was born and raised in the middle of the capital city of Tokyo surrounded by a rich culture and beautiful ancient traditions. My childhood was quite fortunate where I had the opportunity to learn a variety of skills such as singing, dancing, writing, painting, and playing music. I spent most of the time expressing my own version of things to entertain the people around me," she recalls with a certain melancholy. "At age three, I was already climbing ladders and happily painting murals alongside my friends in kindergarten, and somehow deep inside I knew this was going to be my purpose in life. To this very day, I have the same joy, passion, and attitude. My family encouraged my eclectic pursuits and were very patient with me as I challenged myself to learn as much as I could about the world. By the time I became a teen in the '80s–'90s, I was fascinated by foreign underground culture, pop art, punk fashion, electro music, and independent films from the West; but due to our limited access I couldn't get enough. I found myself craving more and more. Also, with my interests and attitude, I realized that I didn't fit into the stereotypical Japanese male-dominated society. It was very disappointing. I knew even as a schoolgirl that the patriarchal culture was going to be an obstacle to me becoming a successful artist," she admits.

BOWERY HOUSTON WALL, New York City, New York, USA, 2012, Photo Martha Cooper

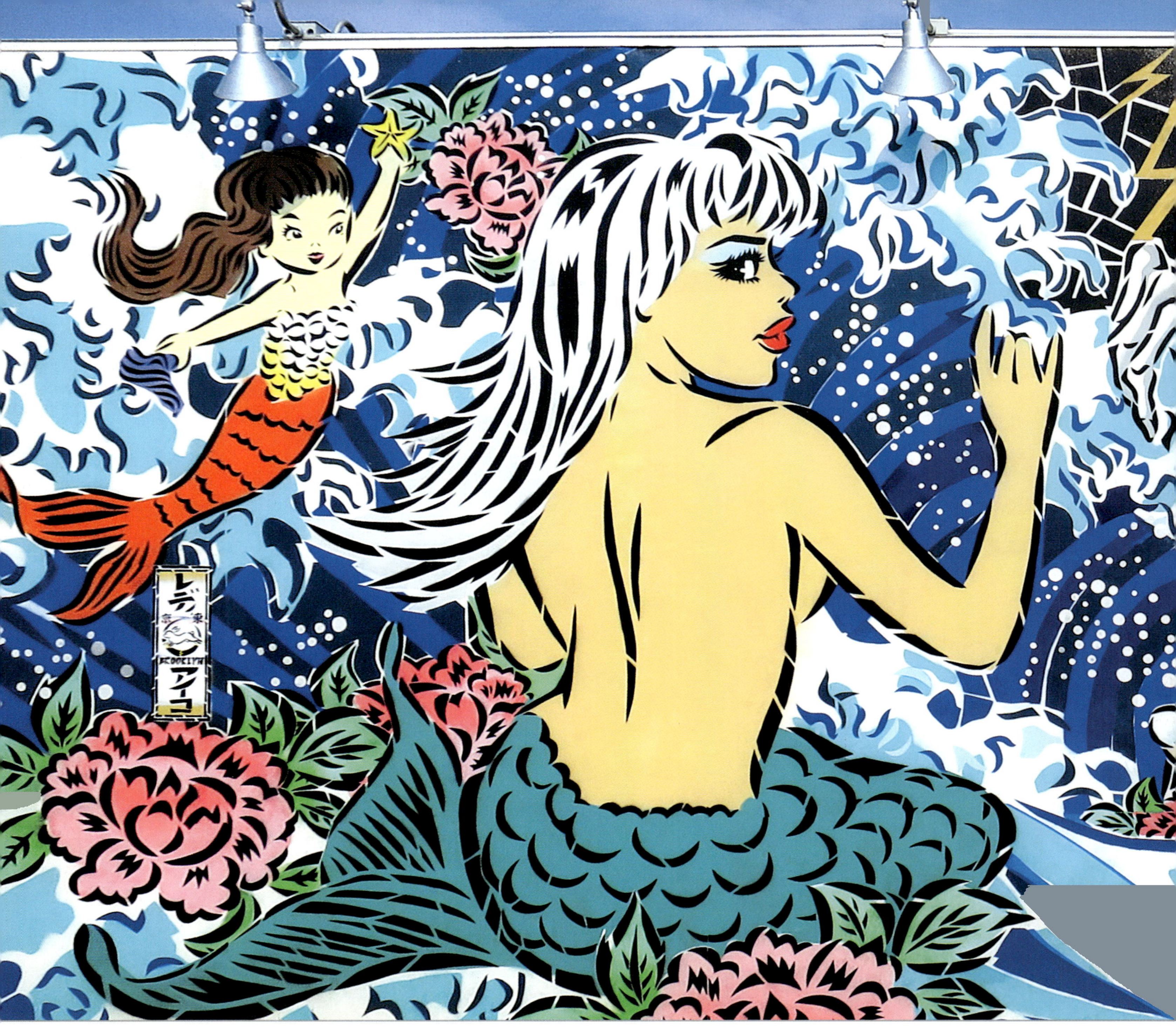

So AIKO left for the United States to pursue her dream: "After finishing art school, where I studied graphic design and filmmaking, I decided to move to New York and seek out my own version of an artist's life in the '90s."

However, things did not go smoothly at first: "It was very difficult for me to begin anew in the US. This was a time before the Internet. I didn't know anyone and I wasn't able to speak English. I only had one suitcase with some clothes, a travel guidebook, and a dictionary. I had absolutely no idea what to expect. So I had to let everything go and start my life in America like a newborn. All of the people I met and places I went were pretty much found by accident. It was a serendipitous time. But inside of me, I knew there was an underlying destiny. I trusted my instincts and listened to my internal voice, which guided my pursuits since childhood," she relates.

She succeeded at finding a job in New York, which allowed her to remain in America. "Not long after arriving, I found a position to assist Takashi Murakami for his first international solo exhibition, *Superflat*, in SoHo in 1998. We had a very small team in a lowly Williamsburg space in Brooklyn with only one work table. I helped by painting his canvases, documenting his process and subsequent exhibitions. Takashi was still very new to the contemporary art world, and I was able to witness the beginning of his career," she recalls.

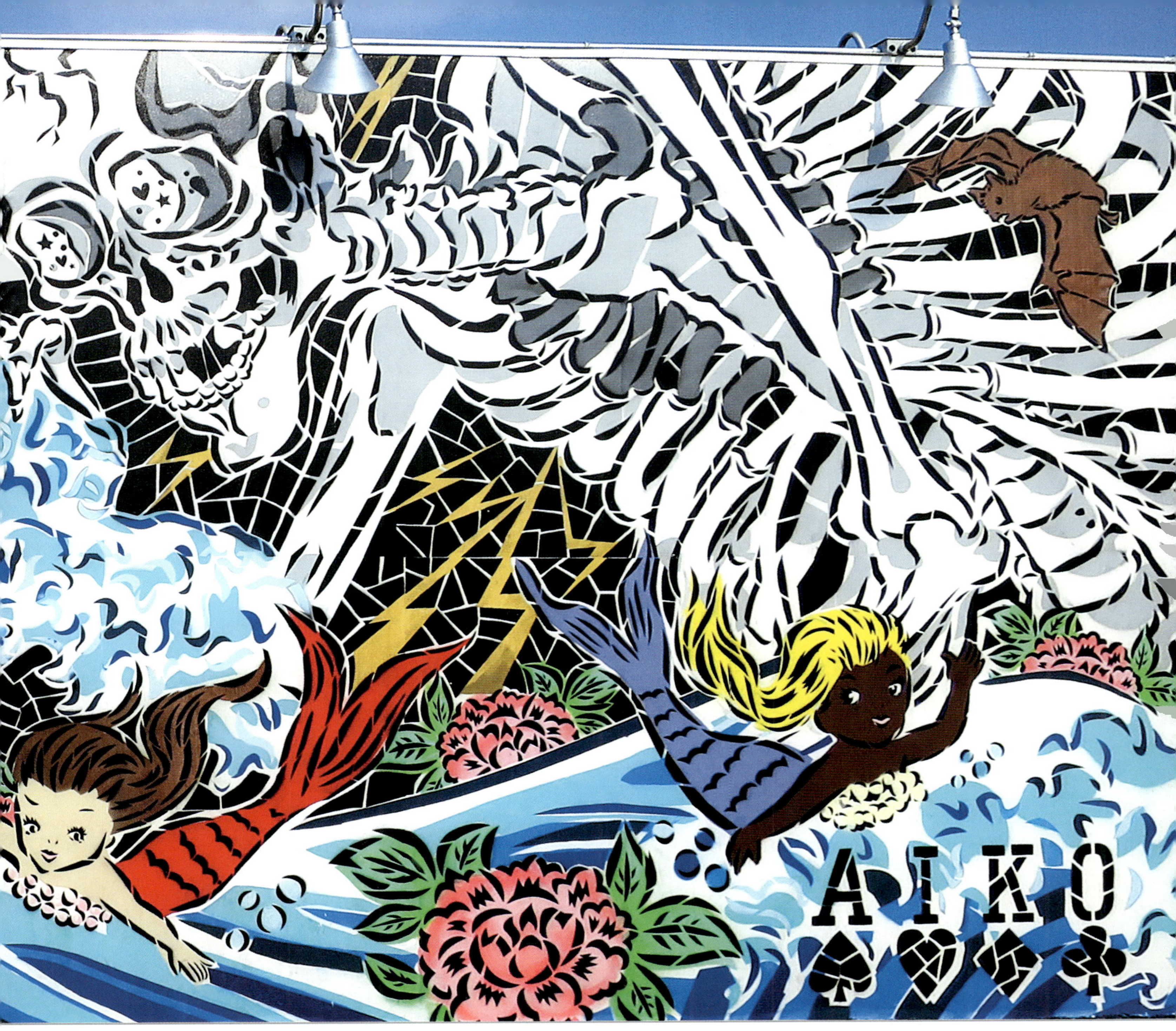

In the meantime, AIKO was busy developing her own personal style: "I spent two years assisting Takashi in his studio while I was applying for graduate school. It was a great way to get to know people, the city, and the larger art world, but I soon realized that I didn't fit into the clean white box spaces with their nicely dressed crowds. I also didn't come to New York to be a studio assistant, and my small salary wasn't enough to live on. I imagined a much grander journey. Meanwhile, I met new local friends who introduced me to graffiti and street art. It was such a rough-and-tumble underground scene with mind-blowing energy. It was far removed from my Japanese home. Takashi once warned me that graffiti was second-class art and didn't make any money: it was not a real art career. But I disagreed, and my passion moved me unbridledly toward creating art in public with my new friends. The adventure was beginning to unfold."

That was a memorable period for AIKO and her development. "What I learned during these early days was that it's hard for a young, foreign woman to enjoy instant success in any society, and certainly in an industry like the art world. To do it alone is even more of an undertaking. The Japanese artist Yayoi

CONEY ART WALL, New York City, New York, USA, 2015, Photo AIKO STUDIO

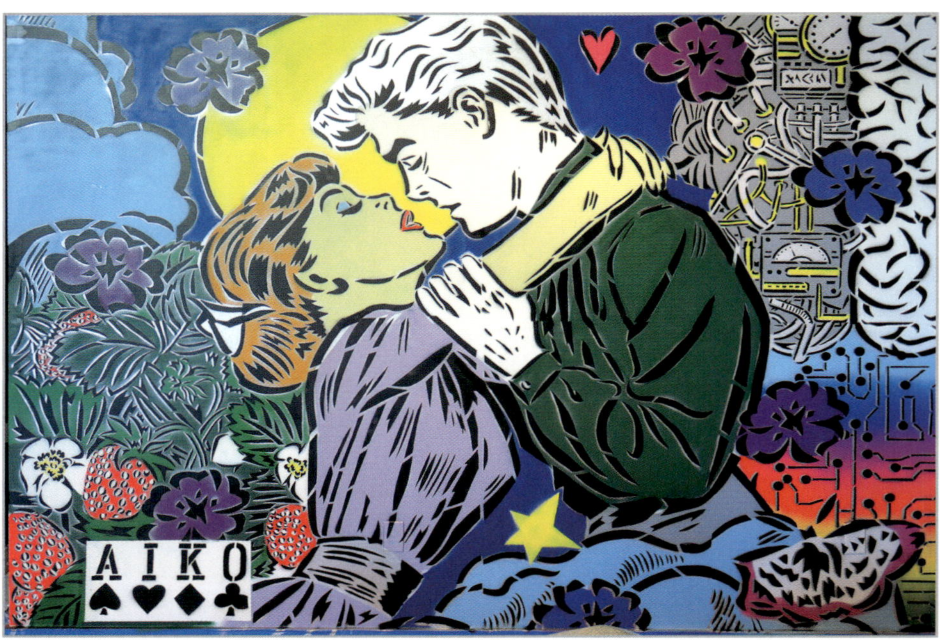

Kusama first came to New York City in 1958 and struggled to draw any crowds. My experience has taken a similar path, and I totally empathize with her. I started the FAILE collective with Patrick McNeil and Patrick Miller around 2000. We were art students in our mid-twenties, living and working together everyday and chasing after every opportunity. We held a lot of shows and did projects for five years until we became very popular. I especially enjoyed making art anonymously and entertaining random audiences on the street with my fellow artist friends like BAST, Banksy, Ben Eine, and Shepard Fairey. We went on numerous missions and traveled like a family," she recalls.

Her collaboration with Banksy took a particularly historical turn: "In 2005, Banksy took me to the major museums in NYC such as The Met, MoMA, and the Brooklyn Museum to install his paintings anonymously. I documented these missions and watched how long they would last (watch *Exit Through the Gift Shop*). It then came out in a huge article on the front page of *The New York Times* and Banksy's name became recognized internationally. I made him into a star, and we created our art market without traditional white boxes. This was a historical moment. It was the beginning of the big graffiti and street art industry for a new generation, and it still continues to grow."

Despite achieving international success, AIKO continued to find the road ahead difficult for a long time: "I barely earned any money or got any credit during this period, but I was able to sleep, eat, and travel all over the world. I spent my time with everyone as a creative free spirit. To discover a variety of intense art styles and strong voices was absolutely inspiring and priceless. But sadly, I had sexual-relationship and business issues with FAILE. I refused to let them become my boss as they insisted on making street art for our crew only. I was told to go back to Japan for using different forms and styles. I was finding my own voice. But I was the girl in their boys' club, and there was simply no room for a woman. I was a threat to their masculinity. It was nonsense, and it left me depressed and angry. But through this grief I had a breakthrough. I decided to continue silently and use my work to exemplify beauty, sexuality, love, freedom, and truth," she confesses with an open heart and complete sincerity.

"With very little support, I had to start again in my thirties. My famous *Bunny with Spray Can* was a symbol of art and freedom. The first bunny stencil was cut and painted at Banksy's

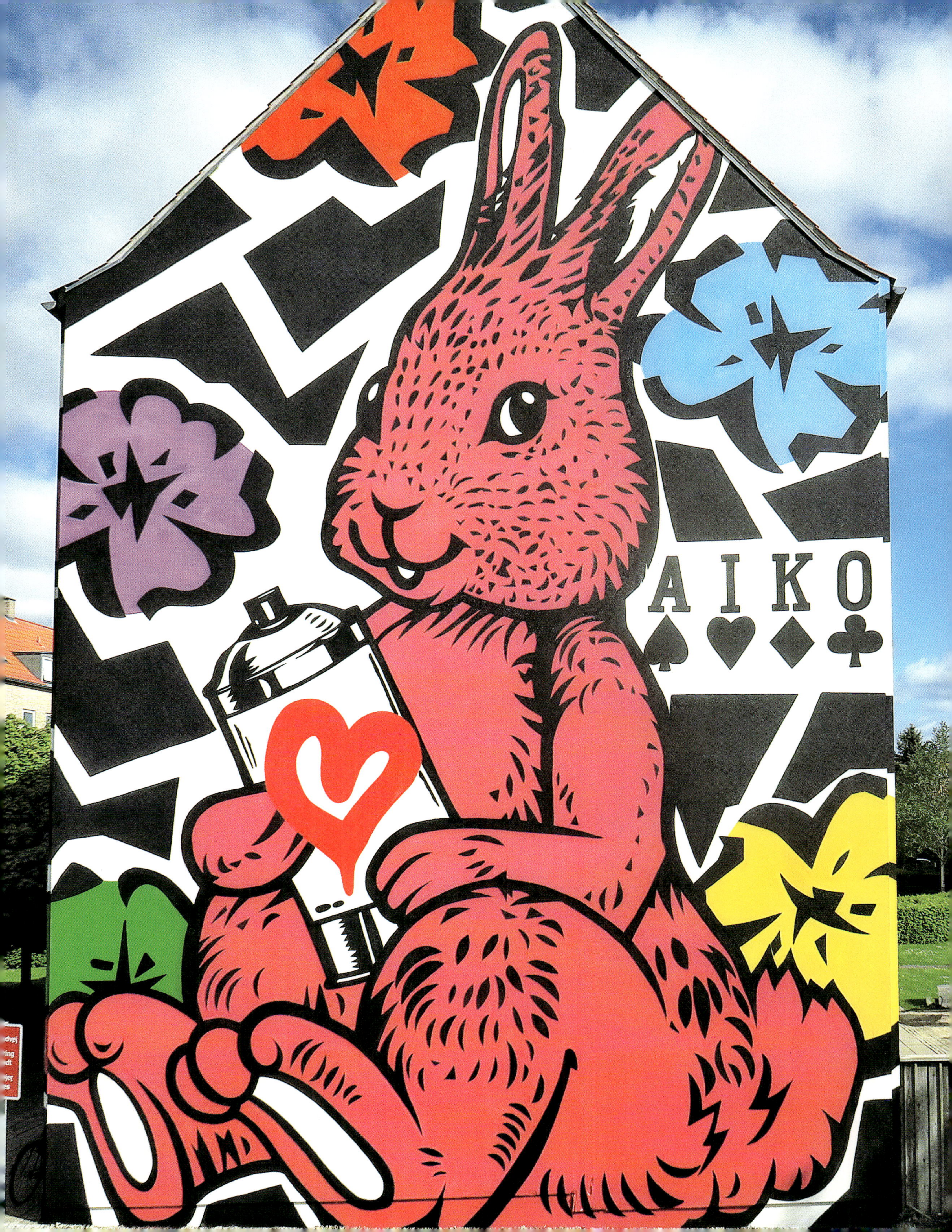

AIKO

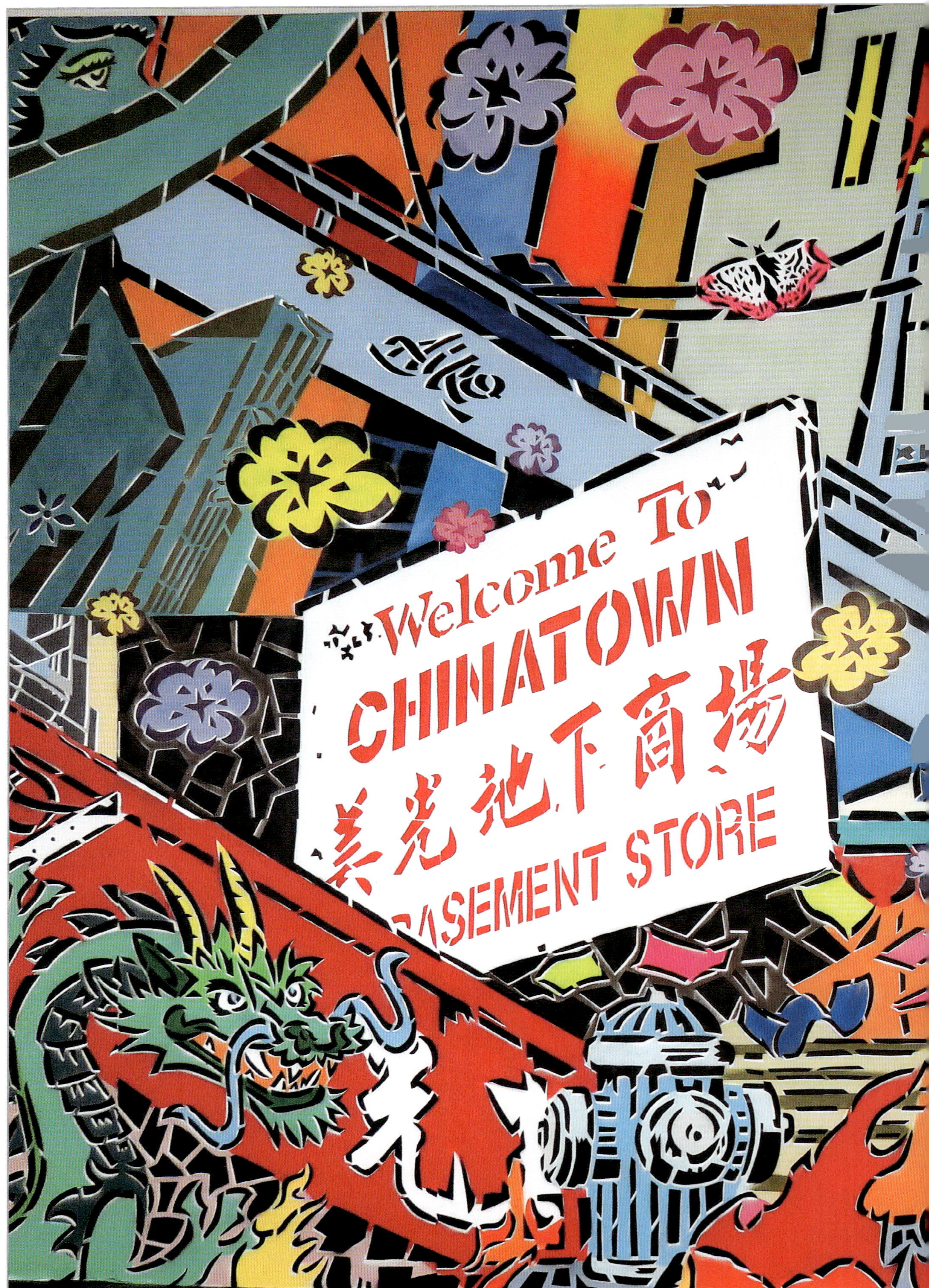

Welcome To
CHINATOWN
美光池下商場
BASEMENT STORE

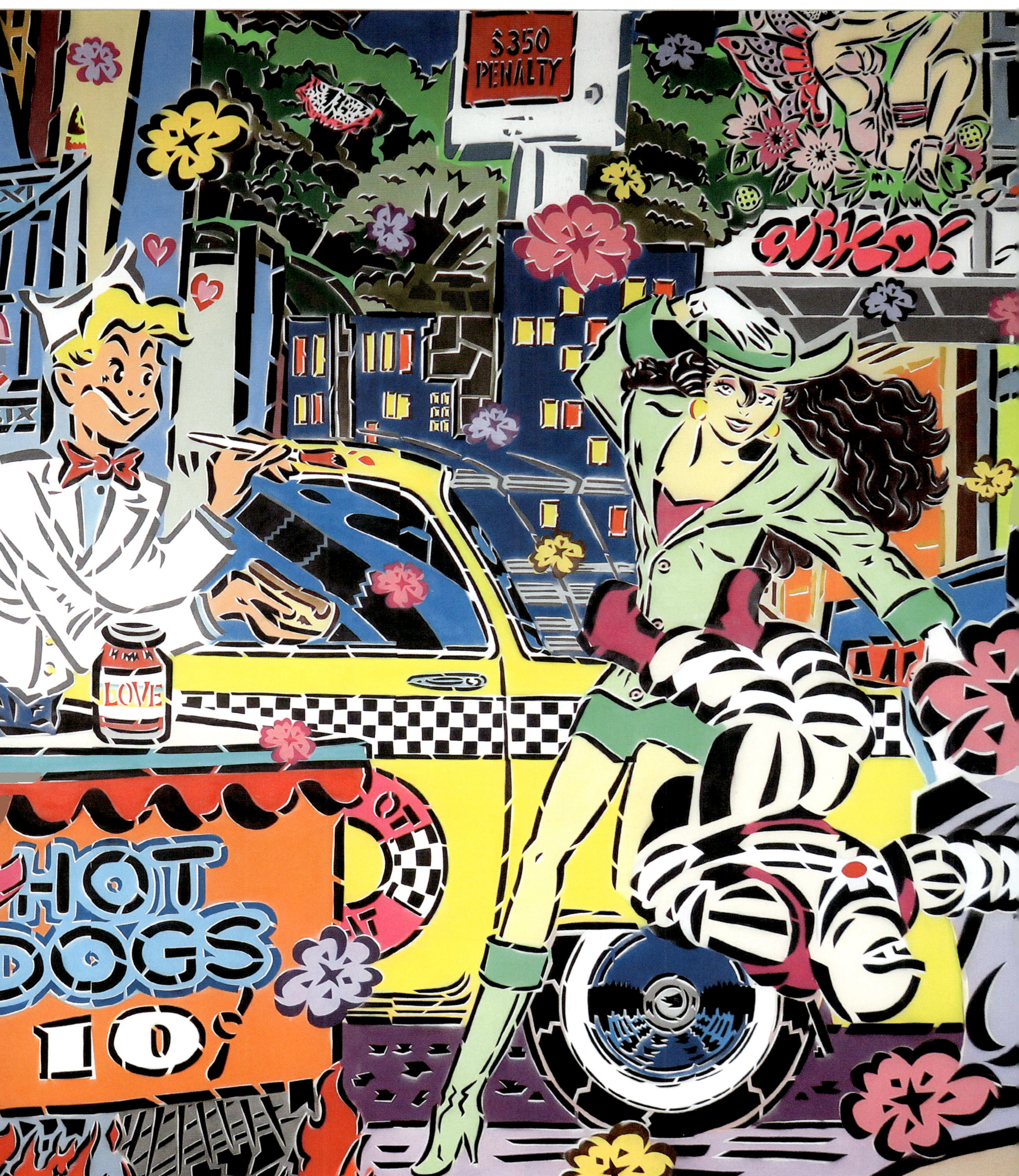

$350
PENALTY
LOVE
HOT
DOGS
10¢

studio in London, and ever since then the Bunny became my calling card. I have been painting it all over the world for the last seventeen years. Combining the Western 'Wild Style' of my young days with my Japanese ancestors' zen spirit created the foundation of AIKO, and I am very thankful to everything and everyone no matter what," she admits.

In the end, AIKO found her own path in New York: "In 2006, I met Martha Cooper and Jeffrey Deitch. They became powerful mentors to me. Martha and I traveled to many different countries for shows and projects. We became great partners in crime. They also introduced me to some old-school subway and street artists like Lady Pink, Crash, Daze, Kenny Scharf, and Futura. I was invited to work on massive shows and other events together. I painted the Wynwood Walls in 2009 and Keith Haring's Bowery Wall in 2012 as the first female artist. I felt I became part of history and my obstacles were finally easing," she explains.

In 2013, she was commissioned by Louis Vuitton to produce a line of limited-edition goods: "I was happy to hear that I was the third Japanese artist to collaborate after Murakami and Kusama. To complete the production, I was invited to the factory in Italy to work with Louis Vuitton's creative team and craftsmen. For me, it was a next-level experience to work alongside a range of talents, high-end skill sets, and extraordinarily beautiful materials. We produced sixty-two color printed silk scarves, which were the most colorful printed products that I and LV had ever made. The scarves sold out immediately. I am very proud of this success, and it brought great satisfaction. Whether it's a commercial or non-commercial project, I prefer working with a variety of talents. It is a challenge to create something that we have never done and seen before," she explains.

How does she envision the future? "The world is heading in a very uncertain direction, and everyone seems to be confused right now. During the pandemic, I had to postpone all of my travels. Instead, I am spending most of my time at my studio in NYC working on canvases and prints. I left 'home' a long time ago, and I've been living like an art monk. As an artist, I would like to spend all of my creative energy for something positive and beautiful at the end of the day. My art is coming from a place of pure love and prayer for the universe and to those who are seeking to heal, to smile, and are wishing for a better future," she concludes.

STREET ART, Vienna, Austria, 2018, Photo AIKO STUDIO

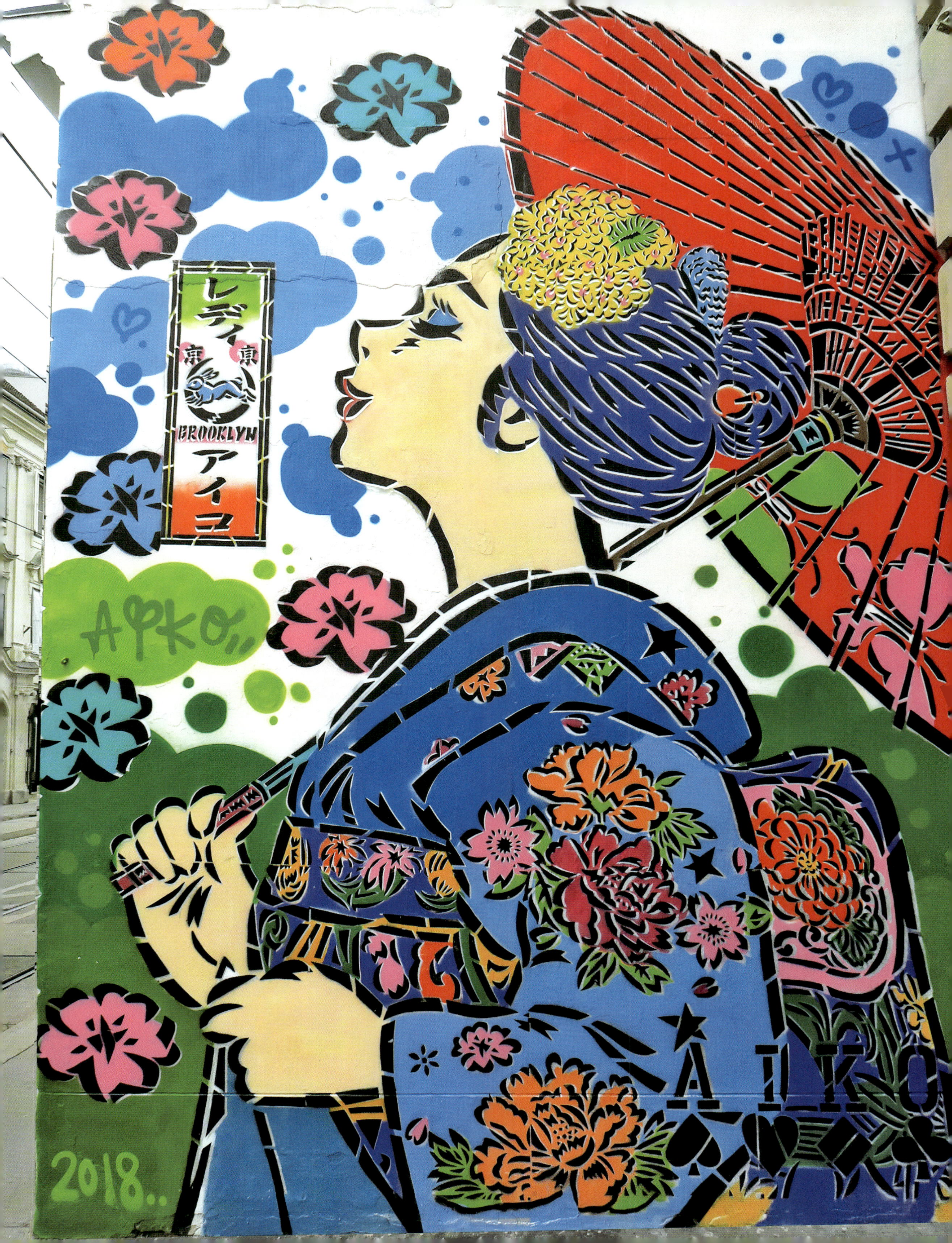

レディ
東京 東京
BROOKLYN
アイコ
AIKO
AIKO
2018..

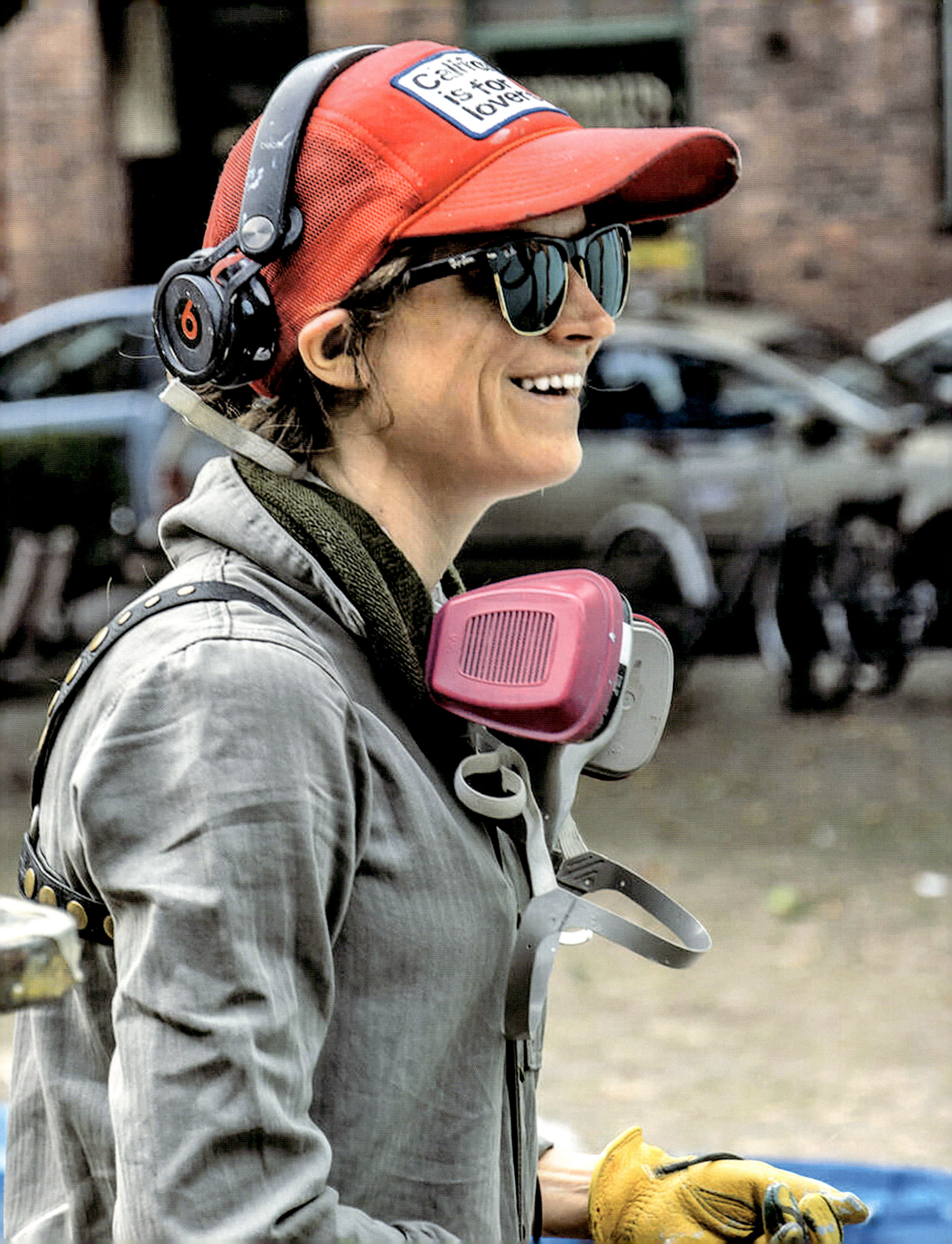
California
is for
lovers

CHRISTINA ANGELINA

THE READER OF THE SOUL
AND SHAMAN OF EMOTIONS

"I'm proud of myself for not having been seduced by the idea that I need to adapt to others' perception of me; I feel that not being possessed by this notion is a success in itself. I'll never know what others think of me; worrying about it would mean preparing myself for a brutal and painful failure. I'm a woman; whether you think I've made it is up to you."

"Fortunate the wayfarer who is briefed by those rare pioneers who chart the uncharted, who brave the depths and spaces of being, and offer future generations the topology of internal states and further spheres."

With this quote by Hazrat Inayat Khan, Christina Angelina begins to speak of herself and to reveal, with the same intensity, her soul as an artist and woman. Also known as "Starfighter," and possessed with the same ardent spirit and a feverish passion for art coursing through her veins, Christina wanders the streets of Venice in Los Angeles, where she grew up and where she feels incredibly part of everything, even if her fame has by now taken her all over the world. "Venice is a palimpsest of opportunities. A collection, a patchwork, of creative expression. Venice has always been and will always be my home. It's a paradise that nurtures my mind, body, and soul," she discloses.

Christina's passion for art emerged when she was quite young. "I began painting while I was a teenager. It was from that point on that I remember letting my instinct take control of my creative process, which in this sense was similar to Jackson Pollock's 'action painting,' though on a far smaller scale. Today I would destroy most of that work, which I regard essentially as a beautiful exercise. It was exhilarating; the results were very different from any of my previous work. The thrill of this purely

PORTRAIT, Malmö, Sweden, 2015, Photo Pacific Press Media Production Corp. / Alamy Stock Photo

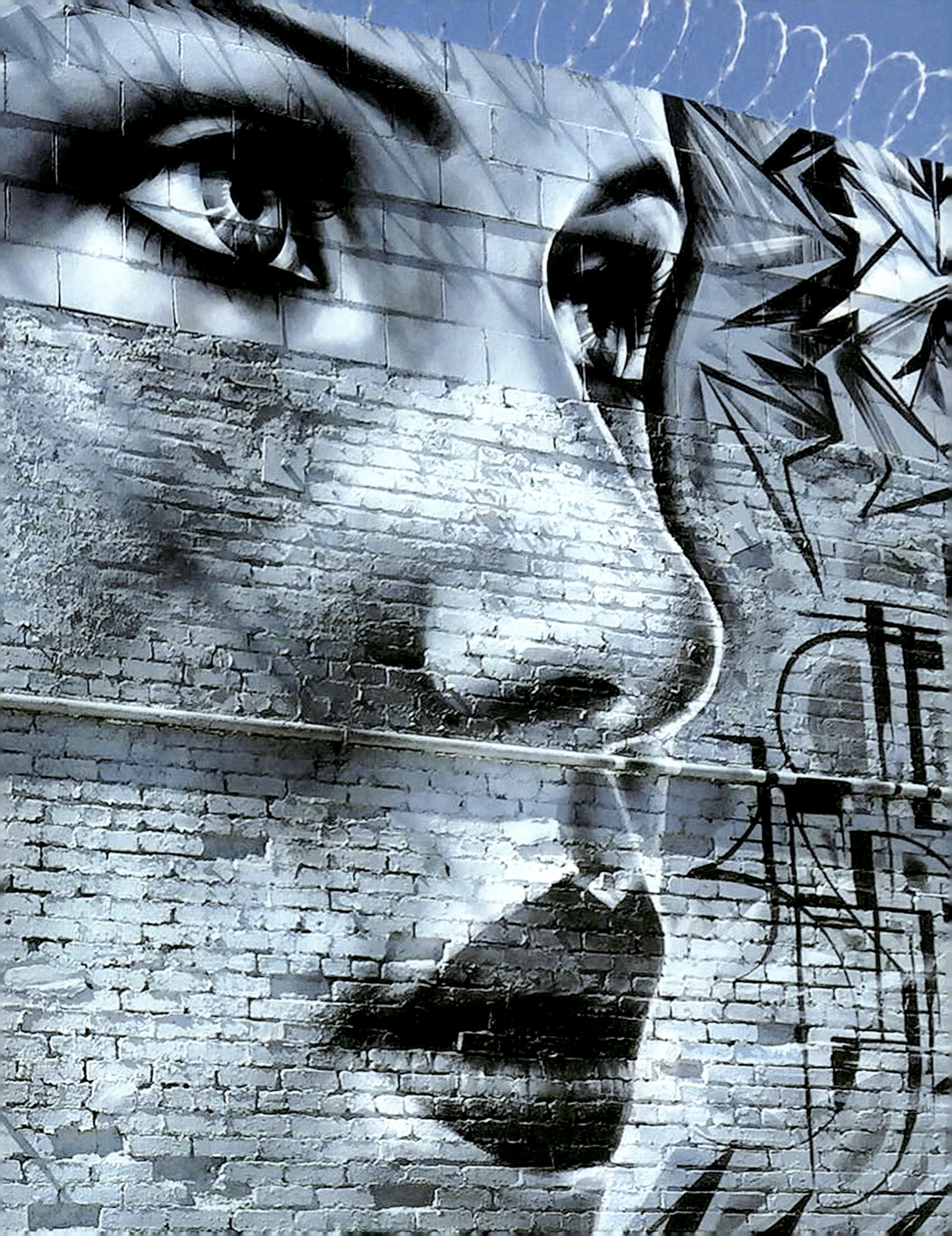

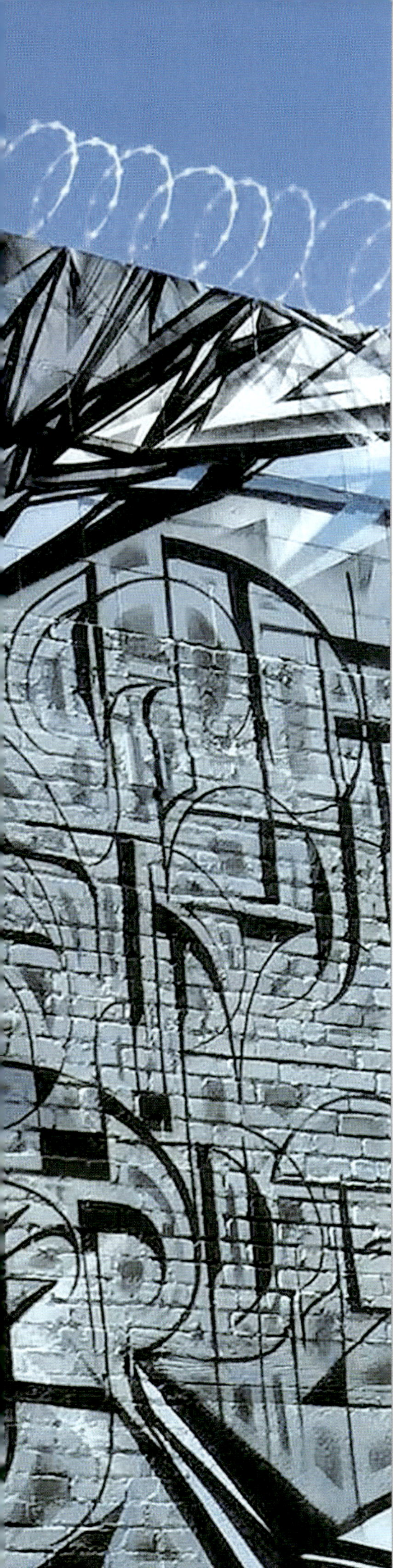

automatic-abstract process, as well as its unexpected myriad results, steered me toward other ideas," she says. "At first I was extremely shy, a slow and precise realist: my work lacked voice, power, scope, and passion," she says, reflecting.

"Human beings can come up with an infinite number of rules: I wanted to be free of the cages that come with submitting or adapting to others. I felt that to endow my art with life, I had to intuit my path. I began by following my feelings and using them as gauges for understanding my work and the boundless nature of the creative process. For example, I would let my hand move automatically, practically by itself, while trying to avoid any thought that might precede or guide its action. This was not an easy road to follow, and it took me a long time to train and transform myself," she recalls.

Location and ambience have made a deep mark on her artistic development. "I observed the art painted on the walls of Venice and everywhere around me, and drew immense inspiration from it. And so, little by little and with care, I began adding my own creations anonymously to these 'conversations.' I still don't sign my work. I don't understand why I should; to me, it seems ridiculous. However, I do understand that writing out their name is extremely important to some people, and I do not intend to take anything away from their experience; it's simply of no value to me. I participate for the sake of collective creation, for the sake of the process," she admits.

As for the essence of street art, Christina follows her own idea, a profoundly philosophical one that she expresses as follows: "A man asked Gautama Buddha, 'I want happiness.' Buddha said, 'First remove *I*; that's Ego. Then remove *want*; that's Desire. See, now you are left with *happiness*.'"

Los Angeles, California, USA, 2016

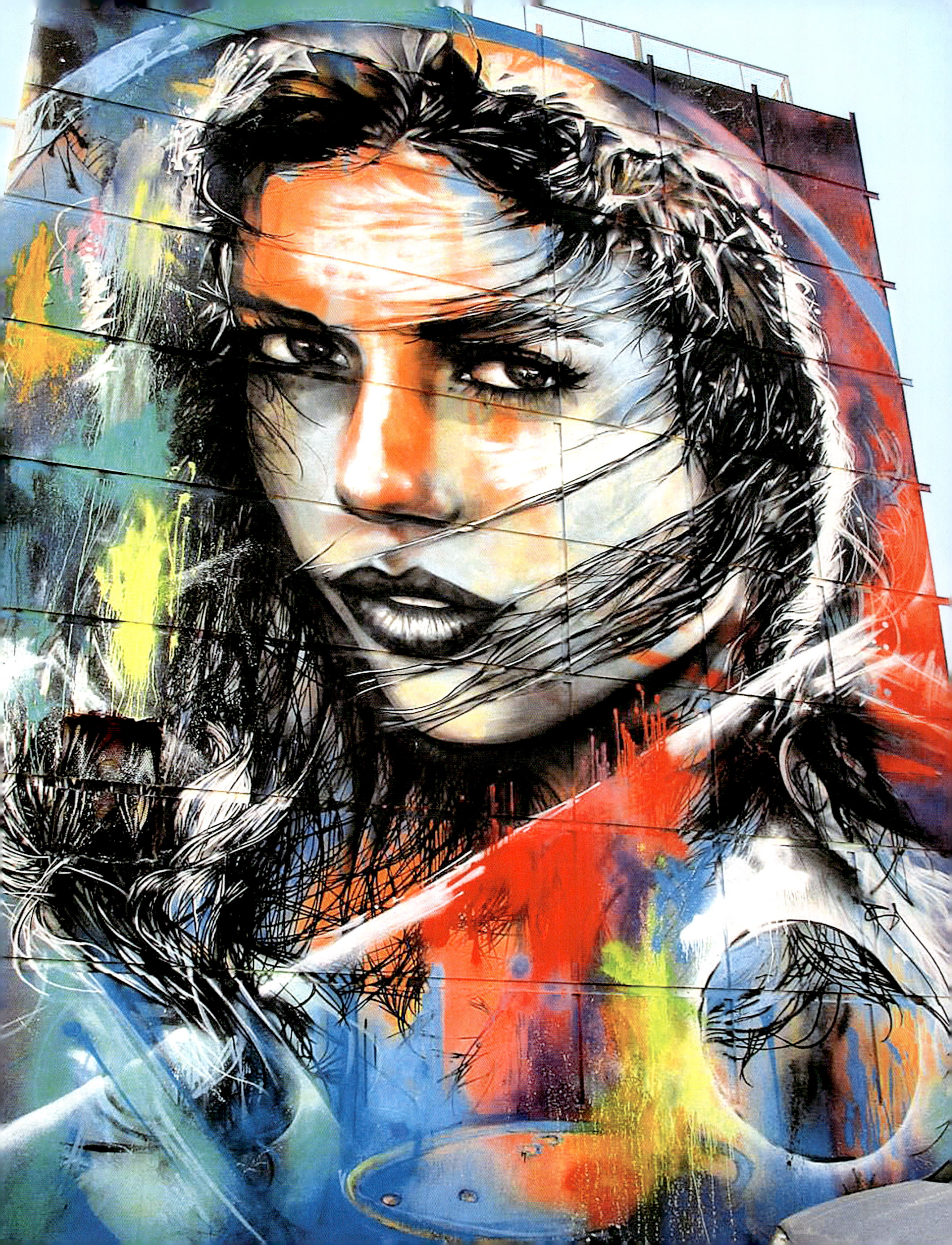

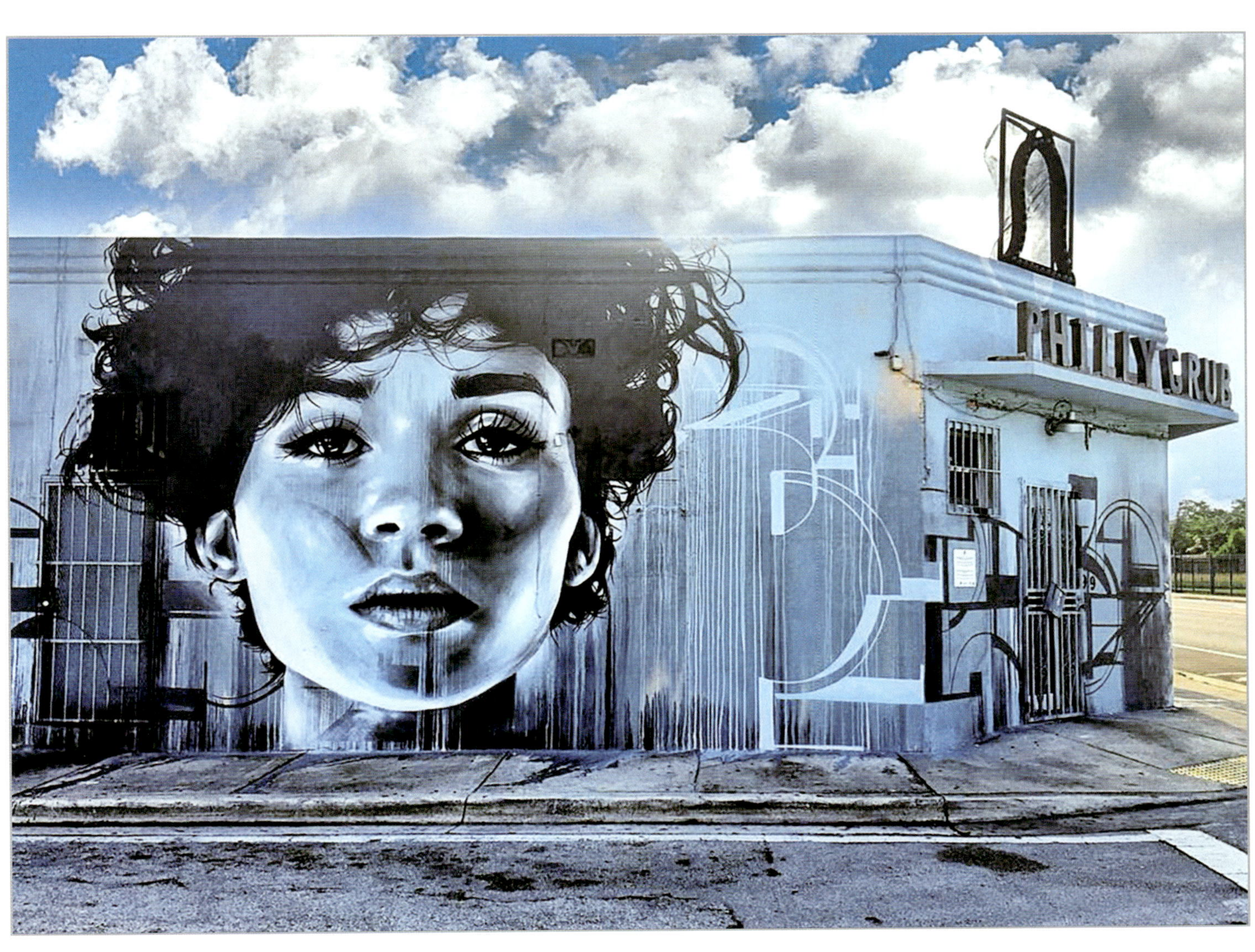

In collaboration with Ease One, Miami, Florida,
USA, 2015

Los Angeles, California, USA, 2016 (left)

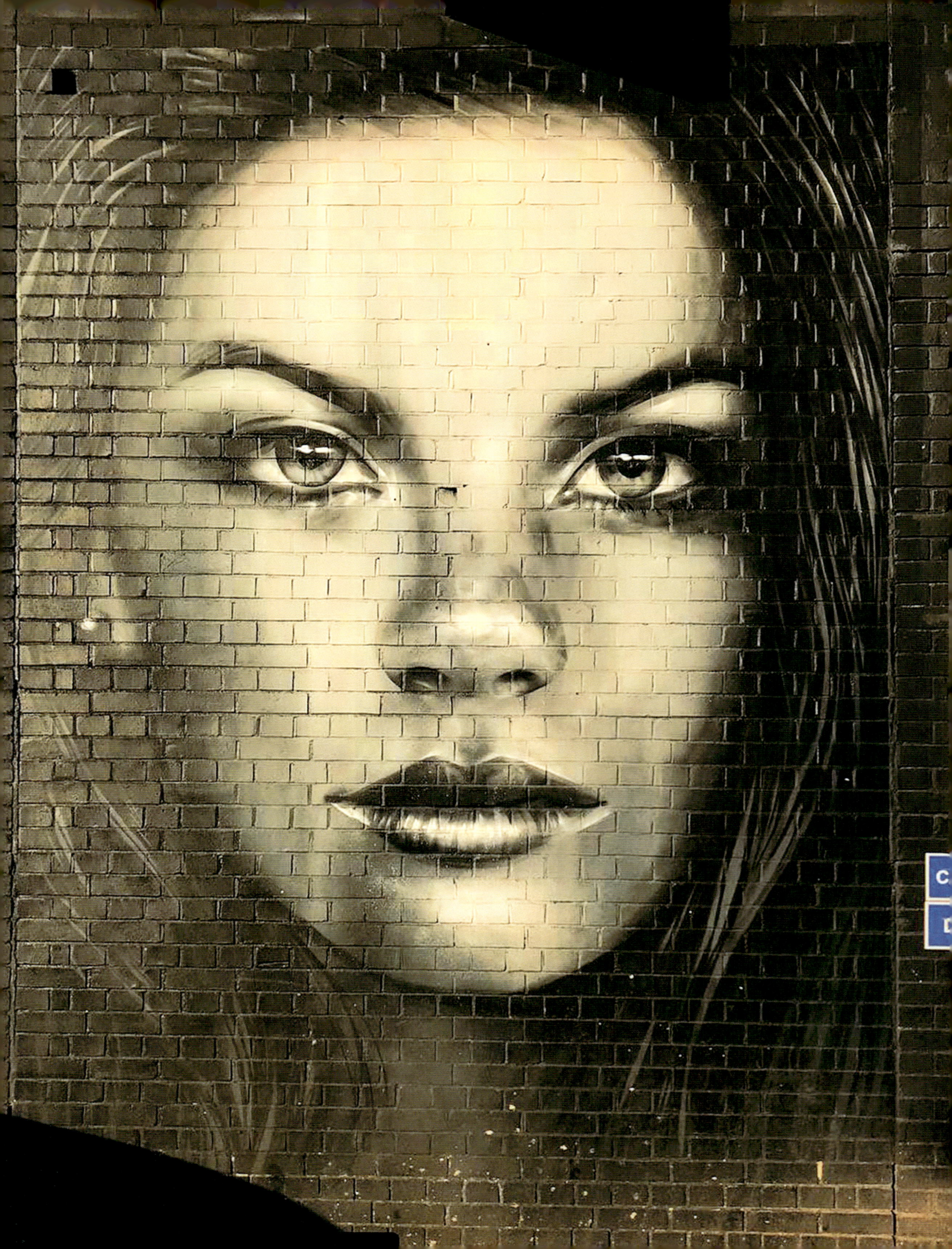
C
D

"Similarly, the idea of the world of street art seems to me an intrinsically constricting one, which is why I always try to get involved and overwhelmed. I try not to lose myself in the creation of worlds within other worlds and in the idea of myself and others being enclosed in shared but intrinsically subjective universes. To allow myself to believe in these 'realities' more than I believe in myself would mean to prepare myself for defeat. I try to create, to get in close touch with my essence, the depth of my soul. I feel that if I constantly challenge myself not to give in to my ego and am able to resist my attraction to ego-based desires, I will be able to truly live up to my mission as an artist and as a human being," she claims.

Christina is also a photographer, and this helps her a great deal in her production of art. "I can't imagine how arduous my artistic process would be without the help of my camera, through which I see the world as if through the eyepiece of a kinetoscope, a visual instrument that well represents my artistic process," she explains. "Windows within windows, constantly unveiling that which is veiled. We're all always teachers, and we're all always students," she adds.

What does art mean to her? "It's genuine romanticism, the momentary encounter of the mortal and the divine. We're all momentary manifestations of divinity, fleeting, fragile, and precious embers. My work is emotional, intuitive, reflective. I am inspired primarily by my own experience: the people, places, and works of art with which I come into contact. My work has matured over time, but its intention has remained the same: to share my thoughts, my feelings, my intuitions; and to communicate. The dust of the universe is within us; it's our blood and bones. I look at the stars, at the most remote corners of that silence and stillness, the infinite expanse of a deceptively luminous space. Each complete work can represent an idea, a question, a series of questions, an abstract narrative.

"In my works, I deliberately leave the storyline incomplete, like a dream that can be developed in infinite ways. Every character is unique, an idea, a conjecture, a thought, a dream, a vision, a moment. I share them, because I feel compelled to do so, hoping that they can serve as a starting point, a platform, a springboard toward something deeper, more meaningful, both

STOP AND STARE, London, UK, 2018

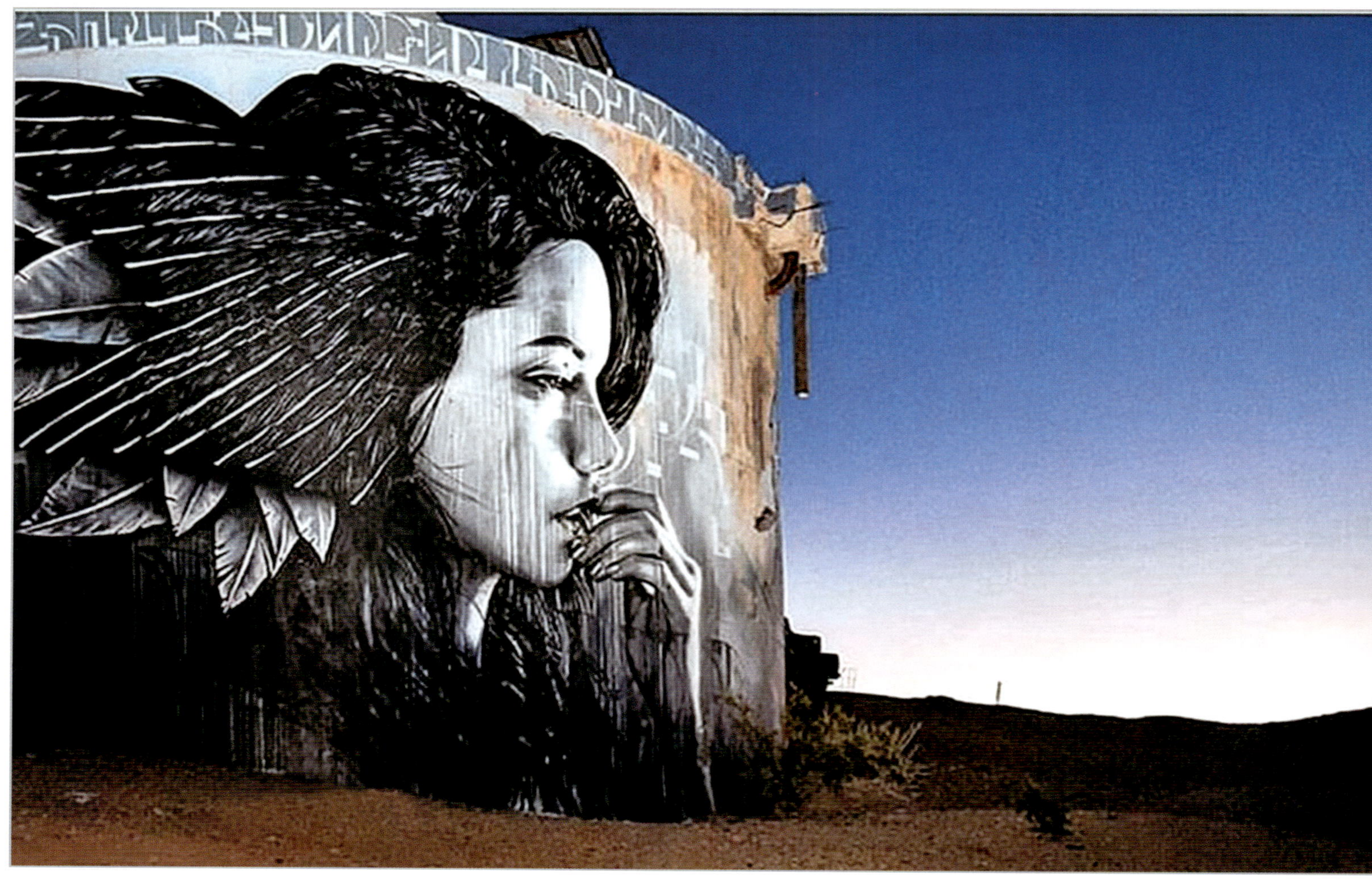

THE TANK, in collaboration with Ease One, Slab City, Salton Sea, California, USA, 2015

to us and others. How the story I began will evolve will depend entirely on who looks at it: the possibilities are endless," she states emphatically.

But her vision is even more profound: "Art is a realm of infinite possibilities in which, through a devout practice, the human being can build a sanctuary within themselves in which the divine and the human can coexist, communicate, and collaborate, at the service of the infinite work of creation. It allows everyone's soul to soar upward and fly along the boundaries of the known and the unknown, challenging them to see without the sense of sight."

It's with this same visionary spirit that Christina creates her characters: "My subjects are a kind of empathic embodiment of my own experience. My process always varies a bit. Sometimes I photograph the people I want to paint; sometimes I put together a complex production with a photo shoot in which I foresee props and depict my subjects in multiple poses."

"Typically, I first make sketches based on the photos, then move on to the mural," she says. "My sensitivity flows and ebbs and merges with whatever surrounds me and with the people I meet. Usually, each face embodies a specific emotion linked to a moment that was instinctively meaningful to me. The subtle connection that binds

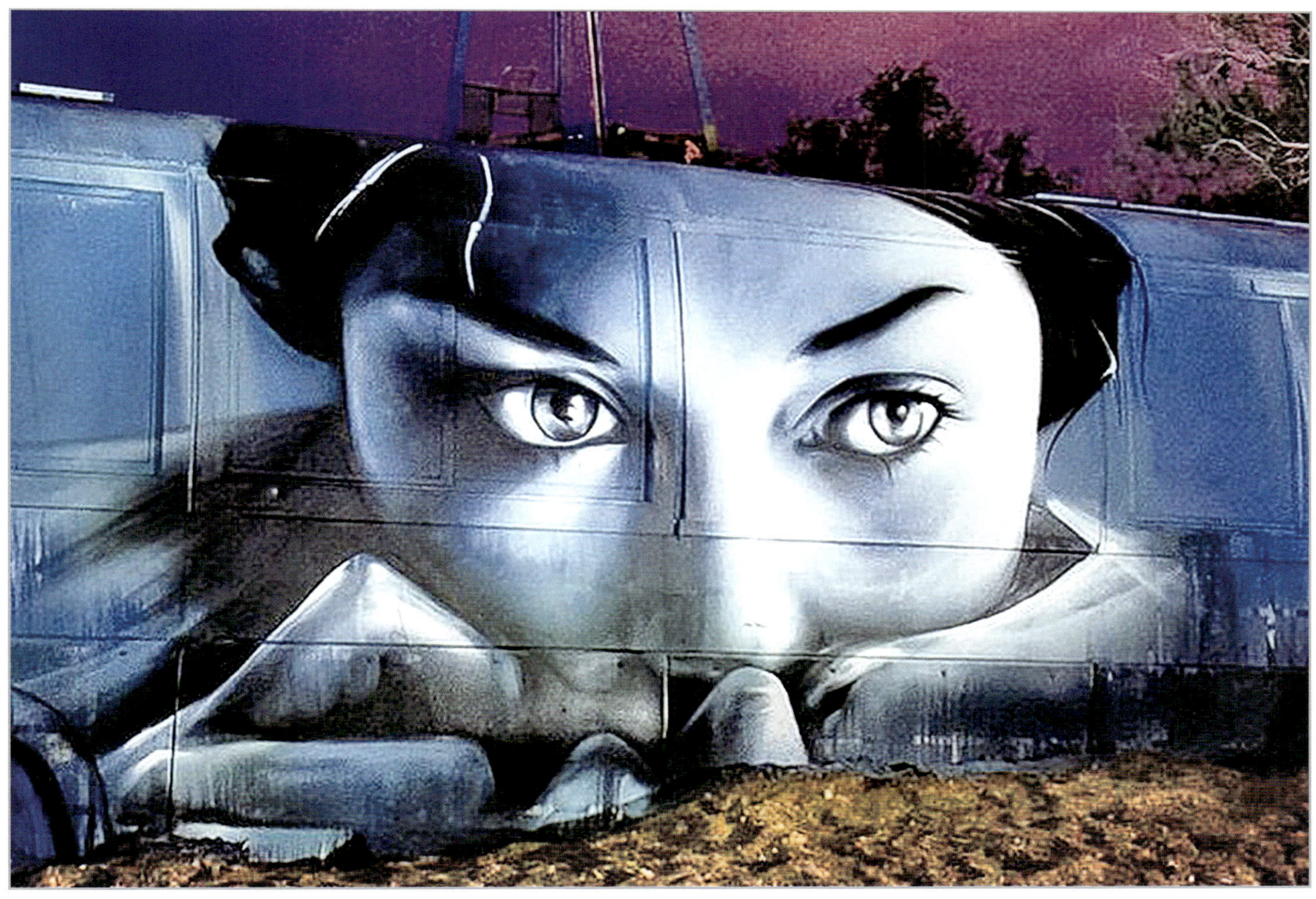

all these moments together generates a sense of 'magic' in its movement, because each shape contributes to the work's natural flow. My constant use of totemic animals, a combination of elements that I've included in my work since I was a child, is deeply representative of my artistic philosophy, which gives life to stories of metamorphosis, transformation, or transfiguration," she maintains.

And, in this respect, the street is her natural environment: "With street art there's a freedom that does not exist anywhere else. I've always wanted my work to be free of constraints, snares, or limitations with regard to this wonderfully brutal physical dimension of a gracefully modeled procession, this 'melting together of sense and non-sense, which produces the supreme meaning,' to cite Carl Jung."

"I want to continue fusing these bits of dreams, visions, mythologies, fantasies, and reality and create artistic spaces that can offer serenity and equilibrium. Toward untraveled romantic roads."

Her hope for a better world?

"Destroy the illusions that blind you."

"Be radiant, reflect and illuminate one another."

"Remember that simple connections can change everything."

WATER, East Jesus, Slab City, Salton Sea, California, USA, 2014

ANNATOMIX

THE MAGIC OF GEOMETRY AND FORMS

"I believe that as a woman, it was easier for me to succeed in art than in music, but I ask myself whether anonymity played a role in all this. . . Because many people still think I'm a man."

"Although my formal education was interrupted when I was eighteen, I still consider myself a student, and will indeed consider myself one for the rest of my life, and I see my art as the product of my studies. Like many artists and philosophers before me, I am fascinated by the human condition and the way we interact with the world around us and with each other. Through my studies I arrived at the conviction that to understand our future and our purpose, we must learn a great deal more about our past," says Annatomix.

"My work is a reflection of how we view nature and our desire to be God: the way in which we literally try to force the natural world into patterns of our own design, choosing those aspects that we like and rejecting those that displease us. I've chosen the fox as the fulcrum of my art because, despite serving as a key symbol in mythology throughout human history around the world, it is often viewed in my country as a parasite and problem that requires a solution. How insanely presumptuous is it of humanity to assume that it enjoys control over the natural world!" she points out.

Annatomix is fascinated by nature and the world of animals, which, fashioned as geometric forms in vibrant colors, stand out from the urban environment with force and intensity, and, thanks to her, assume their own unique personalities. "In school, I studied technical drawing and liked it immensely—so much so that it became the basis of my style. My early works all focused on geometry and models. And 3D cubes quickly became a recurring motif. Initially, I started with a cube and from it created abstract shapes that evolved into spiders and insects, then rabbits, birds, foxes. . ."

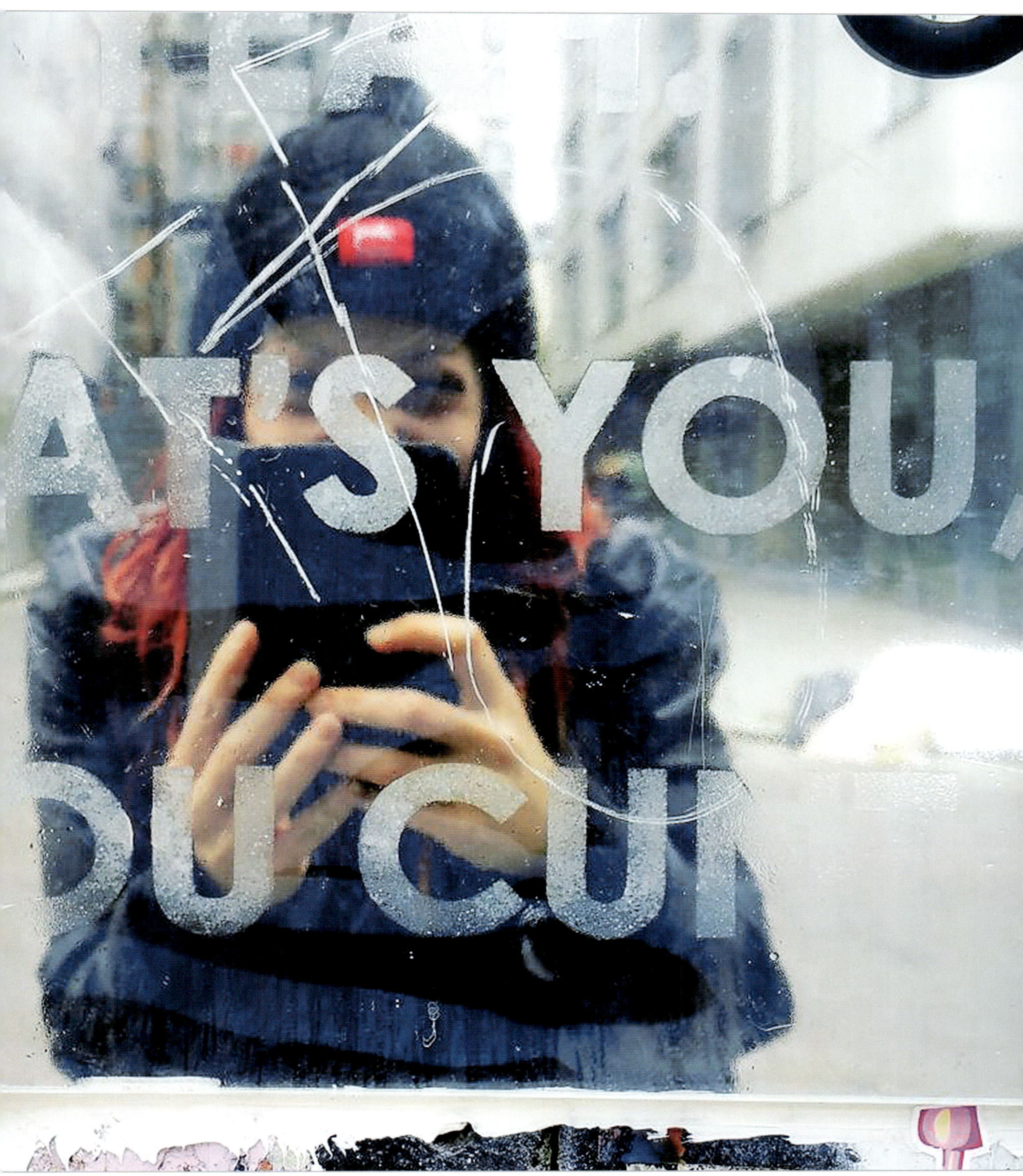
AT'S YOU
DU CUI

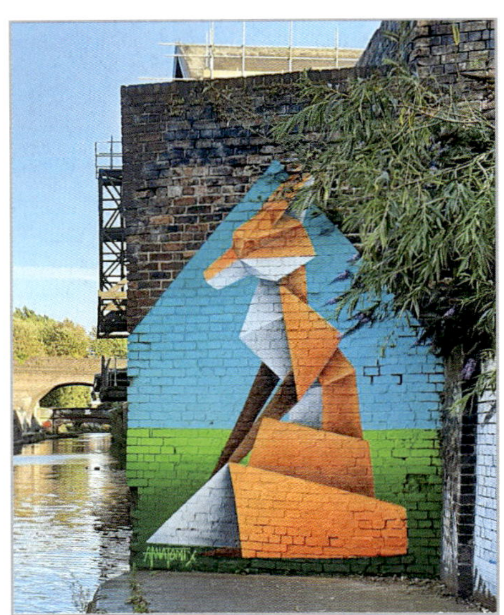 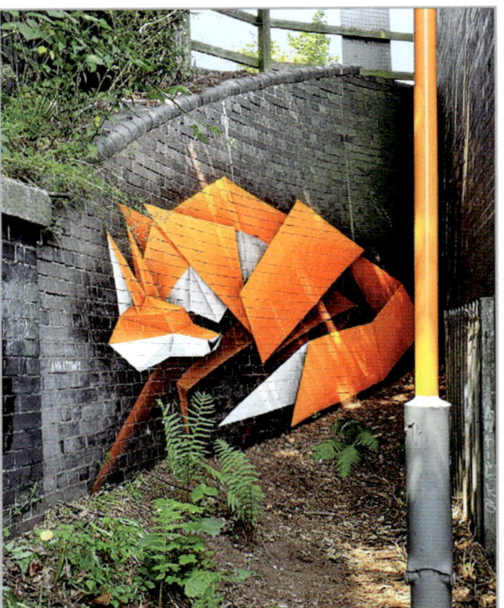

"I wanted to make my animals artificial and aesthetically pleasing, because people prefer seeing nature in that way. For years, I didn't give any of my animals eyes, because we don't care how they see the world or how they see us. My animals," she explains, "represent the false reality that we construct for ourselves."

Annatomix entered the art world by accident, thanks to a series of coincidences and serendipity. Born in Birmingham, she was raised in Stourbridge, a town on the border of Worcestershire, fairly important for its glassworks. "When I was young, in the '80s and '90s, the atmosphere of the city was pretty relaxed and creative. We had a great art school and the local music scene was booming. This made it possible for me to grow up surrounded by really interesting people and the sound of fantastic music. Before moving on to medicine, my mother attended art school, my uncle was a traveling sound engineer, and my grandparents were all highly creative people who taught me everything from woodworking to cooking, sewing, and fixing cars. So I can say that I have always cultivated my creative passion," she recalls. "For the first twenty-five years of my life, my main focus was music, but paired with that was my great love of philosophy, literature, and cinema, especially science fiction.

"Throughout my adolescence, I was also an avid collector of comic books and graphic novels. I always enjoyed drawing, but purely as a hobby, until 2010, when I became a mother. It was then that I began sharing what I was doing on social media, and thus began my artistic career," she explains.

THE RATCATCHER, Digbeth, Birmingham, UK (above, left)

THE FOX AT WYLDE GREEN, Sutton Coldfield, UK (above, right)

A CHANCE ENCOUNTER, Munkfors, Sweden

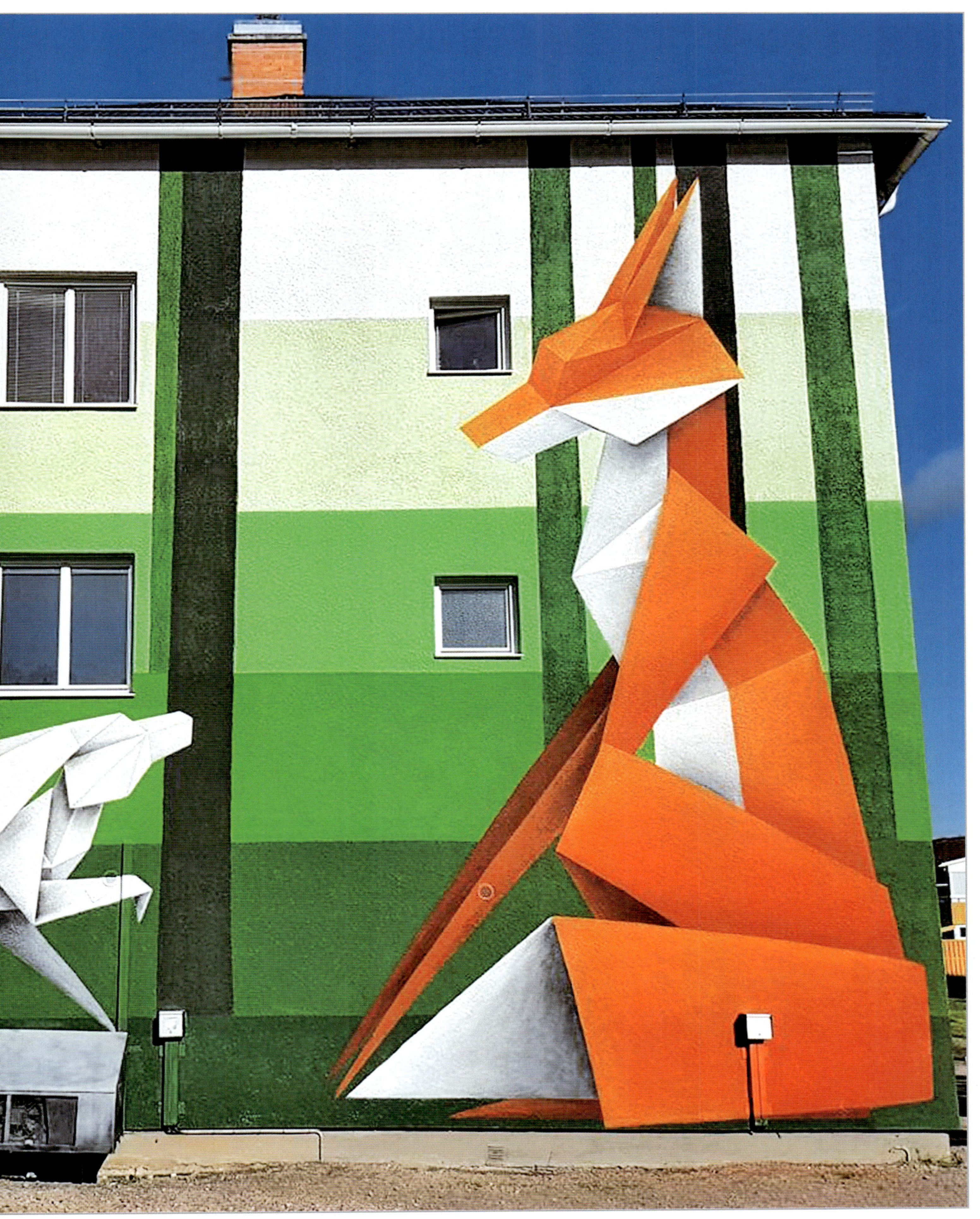

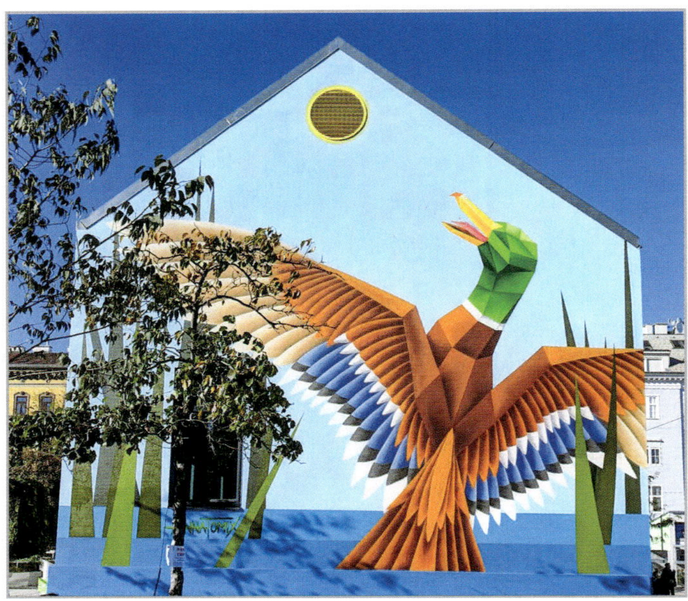

WHAT THE DUCK?, Yppenplatz, Vienna, Austria

From then on, a new microcosmos opened for Annatomix: "I immediately became aware of an entire international community of artists who make only stickers and posters and exchange them with each other, with the objective of exhibiting their own works in cities all over the world. The entire community was inspiring; I was particularly struck by RxSkulls, an artist from Portland, in the US, who was producing some of the most beautiful vinyl stickers I had ever seen and was extremely willing to help other artists. He really encouraged me when I was starting out, and his boundless enthusiasm for street art took total hold of me."

Annatomix began doing street art in 2011: "I made some hand-drawn stickers and put them up all over the streets of Birmingham. They quickly developed into larger posters, and by 2013 I was painting murals.

"I had been surrounded by music since birth. I began taking music lessons at age four, learning how to play the electric organ. My uncle took me to see my first live concert when I was five."

Today, music is still an irreplaceable and infinite source of inspiration for her. Whenever she paints on the street, she brings along a large speaker that allows her to listen to her favorite tracks.

"I never planned on being an artist, but, from the age of twenty, I knew that I definitely wanted to work in a creative environment. I was thinking of remaining in the music world, of making my way through the field, of having my own recording studio; but when the recession hit in 2008, I was forced to leave all that behind. I was a woman, and there was no room for me. I worked for various theater companies until the birth of my son."

As one may imagine, becoming a mother did not make her work as an artist any easier. "In my experience, the art world does not assist artists who are parents, especially single parents. These days, my son shows a keen interest in what I do; I've taken him with me when painting in the street several times, and I imagine he will gradually want to get involved as he grows up," she predicts.

"Until recently, there were very few photos of me online. And even now, never having seen a picture of me, various people presume that I'm a man. Strangely, I take this as a compliment, because I think it indicates that there is nothing overtly feminine about my work. And I'm happy about that. . . Interesting to note, however, I've been attacked by male artists several times—something I never experienced in music.

WHAT THE DUCK?, Yppenplatz, Vienna, Austria

REDSHANK, Belfast, Northern Ireland, UK

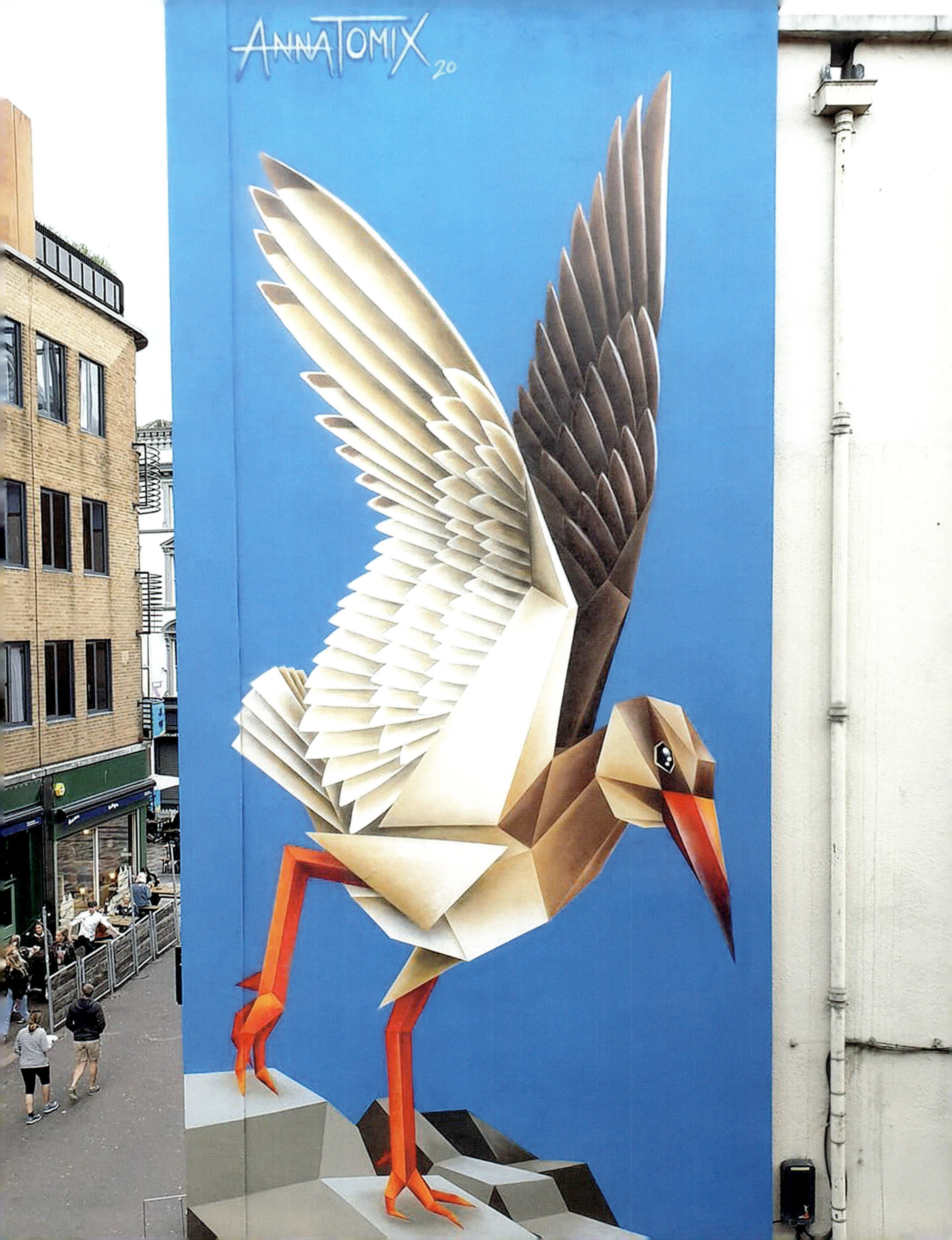

AnnaTomix
20

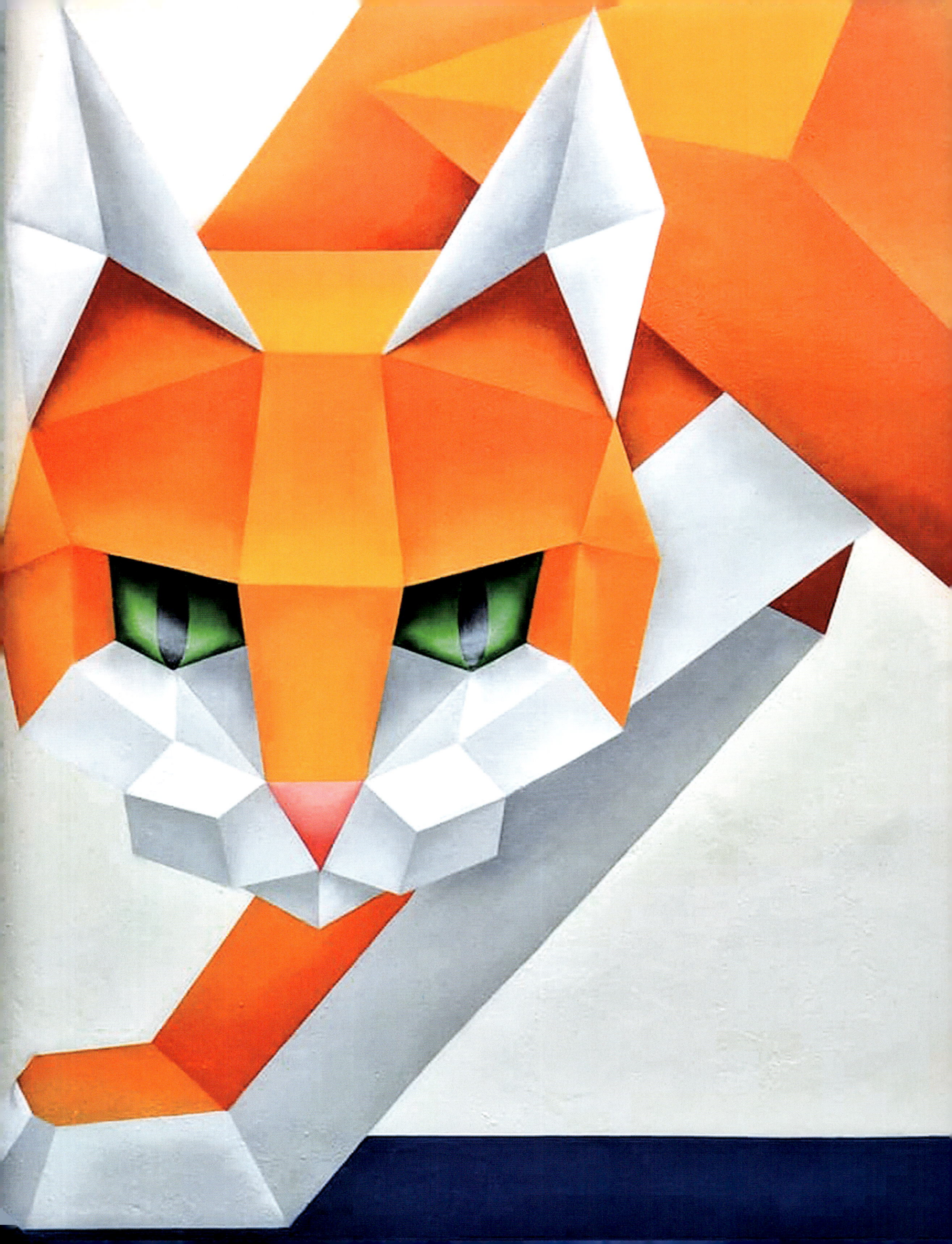

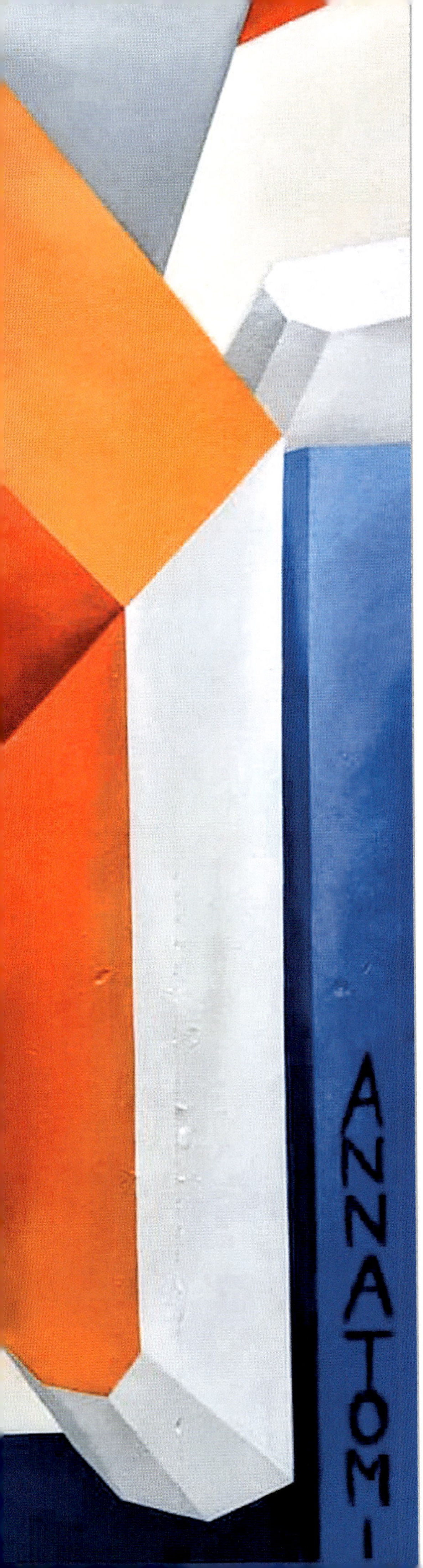

"Their resentment has to do with my style and success, and their threats are meant to destroy my work or career. This can be intimidating, especially since I work alone, but I'm usually able to laugh it off," she muses. "As much as I hate to admit it, I think the art world is still very sexist, because the general belief seems to be that men are more talented and more capable than women. I know I was not considered for several large-scale projects because people presumed that I would be incapable of doing them. However, I don't let that upset or annoy me too much; my stint in the music business taught me that if you want to be taken seriously, you've got to prove that you can work as hard as any man. So that's what I'm doing while actively trying to encourage other artists to do the same," she claims.

Nonetheless, she is tormented by a misgiving: "From time to time, I wonder what my creative career would have been like had I been born a man; I know it would have been quite different."

RHUBARB AT THE CUSTARD FACTORY, Digbeth, Birmingham, UK

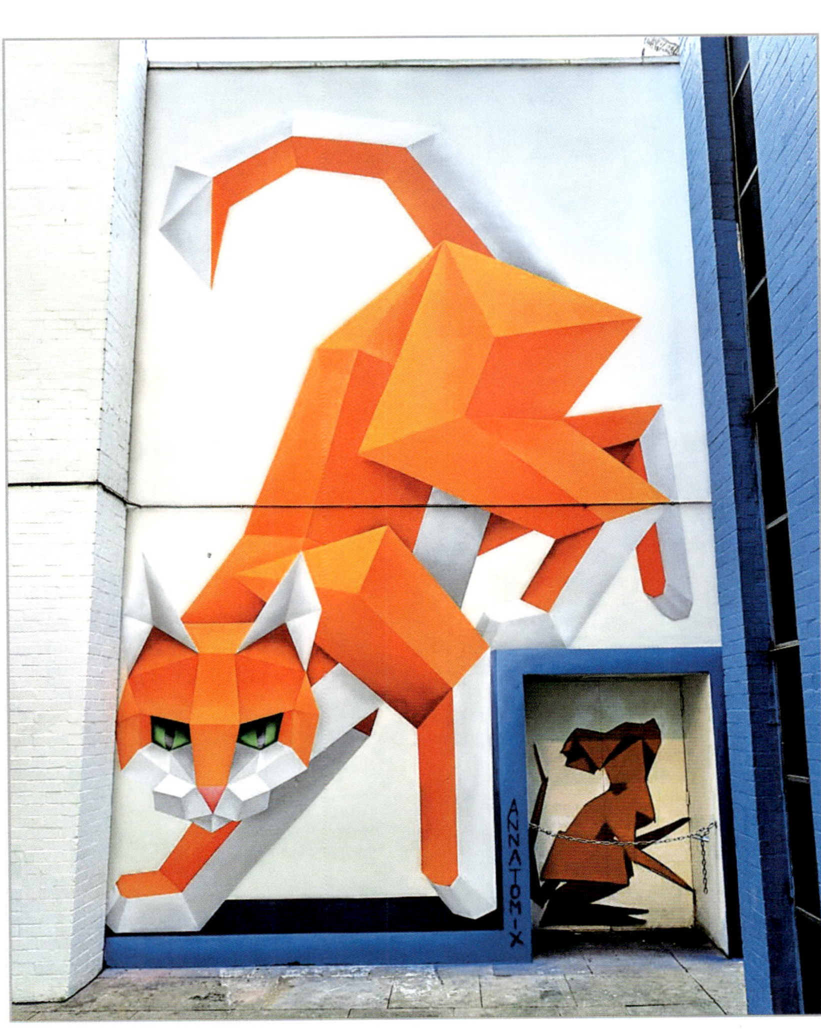

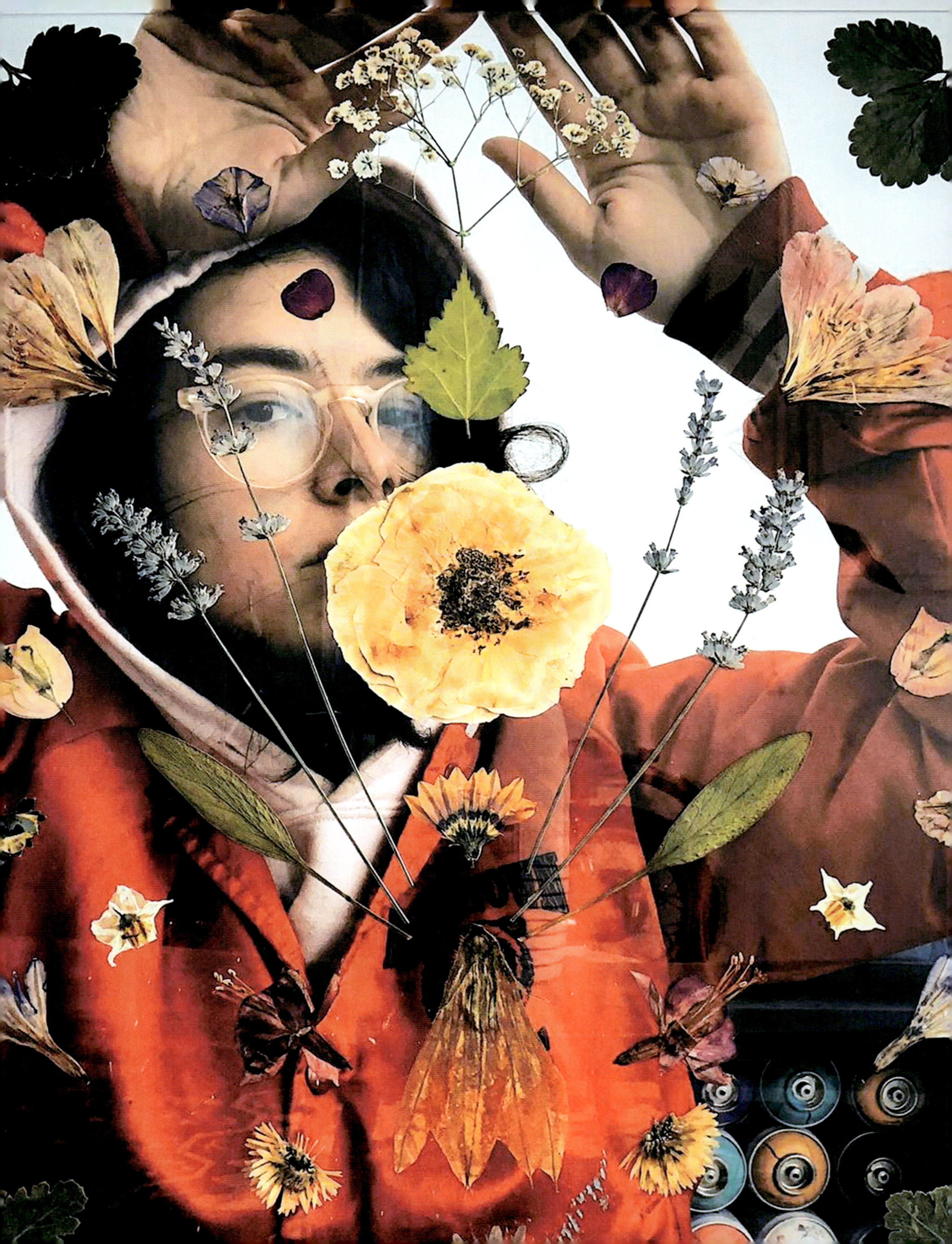

KRUELLA D'ENFER

THE WIZARD OF COLOR AND MYSTERY

*"I began painting with male artists, who always gave me
an opportunity to join them; but from the beginning, I set
limits that I never tried to overstep: don't go painting
at night or on a train, and never put myself in danger.
This was by my own choice."*

She was born on a stormy Halloween night. She believes this has affected all her art, which revolves around a unique and wonderful microcosmos of surreal, complex, bizarre creatures and themes, on which her ideas float as if on an ocean racked by steep unpredictable waves. Angela Ferreira chose a stage name—Kruella d'Enfer—that precisely evokes this: a mystical, mysterious, and bewitching spell that leads the viewer to the discovery of her art and soul. "I was born in Portugal, in a teeny village. My family was very religious, and the presence of superstitions and beliefs was quite strong. Also, I think that celebrating my birthday on Halloween sparked my interest in the mystical stories I had been told, and which, from the moment I began drawing, became some of my favorite subjects," she recalls.

Exotic and distant places are another irresistible reference for her: "I have lived in Lisbon for a long time. I felt the urge to leave the village where I had been born because I wanted to discover new universes. But, actually, adapting to life in a big city was anything but easy. At age twenty, I moved to Thailand for work and spent six months there, but in the end I willingly returned to my peaceful Lisbon: the chaotic cities of that country were definitely not my thing! Since then, I have lived happily here. Lisbon is a fantastic city; it brings me joy, peace, and a sense of equilibrium, as well as the possibility of hanging out with my friends whenever I want. Perhaps in the future I will return to the countryside and the way of life that marked my childhood. Deep down, my heart pushes me there, but right now my place is here, in Lisbon," she admits.

Destiny also led Kruella d'Enfer to the decision to devote herself to art. "My passion for art began in high school, when I was about fifteen. At the time, I certainly didn't think that I would become an artist, but it was in that period that I began going to museums and exhibitions, and coming into contact with numerous artists. At the time, I was studying interior design but felt utterly unmotivated, to the point that I decided to stop after a year and pursue an artistic career while staying put in Lisbon, a city that for me was full of stimuli," she recalls.

Her discovery of street art likewise dates back to this period. "I started painting with spray cans in abandoned factories, following friends who were already doing so. It was then that I came up with my stage name, Kruella, and began developing my own style. When I finally got used to working with spray paint, my desire to paint grew ever stronger, unrestrainable. I loved everything about that world: the smells, the colors, and every aspect of painting out of doors," she explains, barely curbing the enthusiasm that still animates her.

Kruella d'Enfer continued developing her surreal, abstract style, with figurative elements such as animals and plants, motifs drawn from fantasy and the underground, with constellations, galaxies, musical themes. . . She devoted herself to experimenting with brightly colored patterns, mixing these with drawings and black-and-white shapes and a nearly obsessive dedication to detail. "For me color is fundamental, as is the instant joy that it brings. The subjects that animate my works are related to nature and animals: they are harmonious in a surreal way; they are mystical, fantastical. It's all very bound up with my childhood and, curiously, with that distant, very intense, emotional, mystery-packed world," she relates.

What fascinates and inspires her is a complex variety of worlds, which merge and integrate in her art. "I'm really attracted to botanical tables, scientific illustrations, as well as those that emanate from the infinite universe of fantasy. The geometric forms that make up my creatures also draw ideas from architecture in their regular and harmonious alternation," she explains. "I also like the aesthetic of tattoos and what they represent in different cultures; I'm really fascinated by their symbolism. Astrology, too, intrigues me; I am attracted to the unknown and fascinated by the powers of the universe. This is the way my life acquires meaning; not having answers to everything, I realize that we find ourselves before an incommensurable mystery, simply beautiful and infinite."

Even the choice of surfaces on which she works or with which she interacts is never accidental: "Of course, a lot depends on what I'm working on, but I like to experiment and change things around. I like exploring digital art, because it

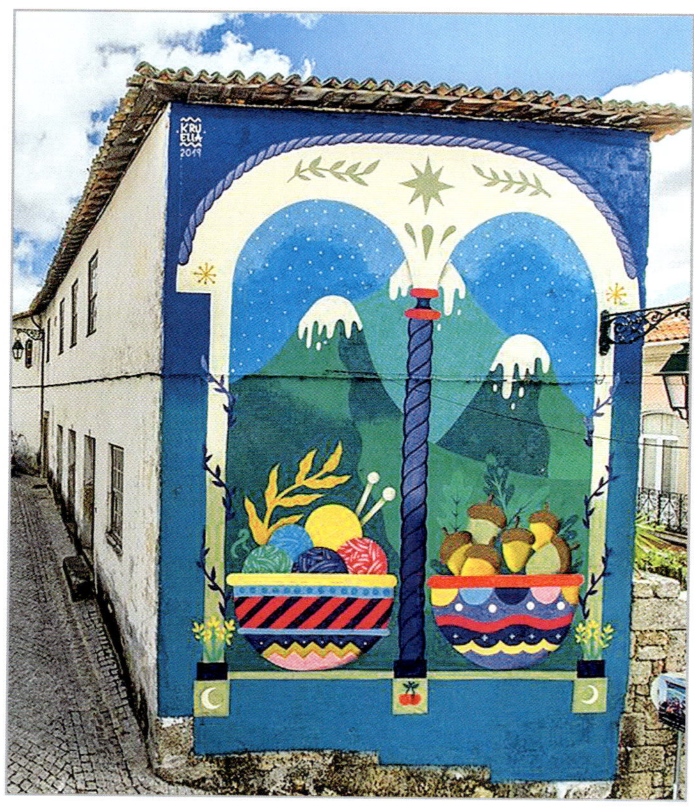

VISTA PARA A SERRA, for WOOL Festival 2019, Covilhã Urban Art Festival, Portugal

WATER, THE CONDUCTOR OF LIFE, Digital Illustration (right)

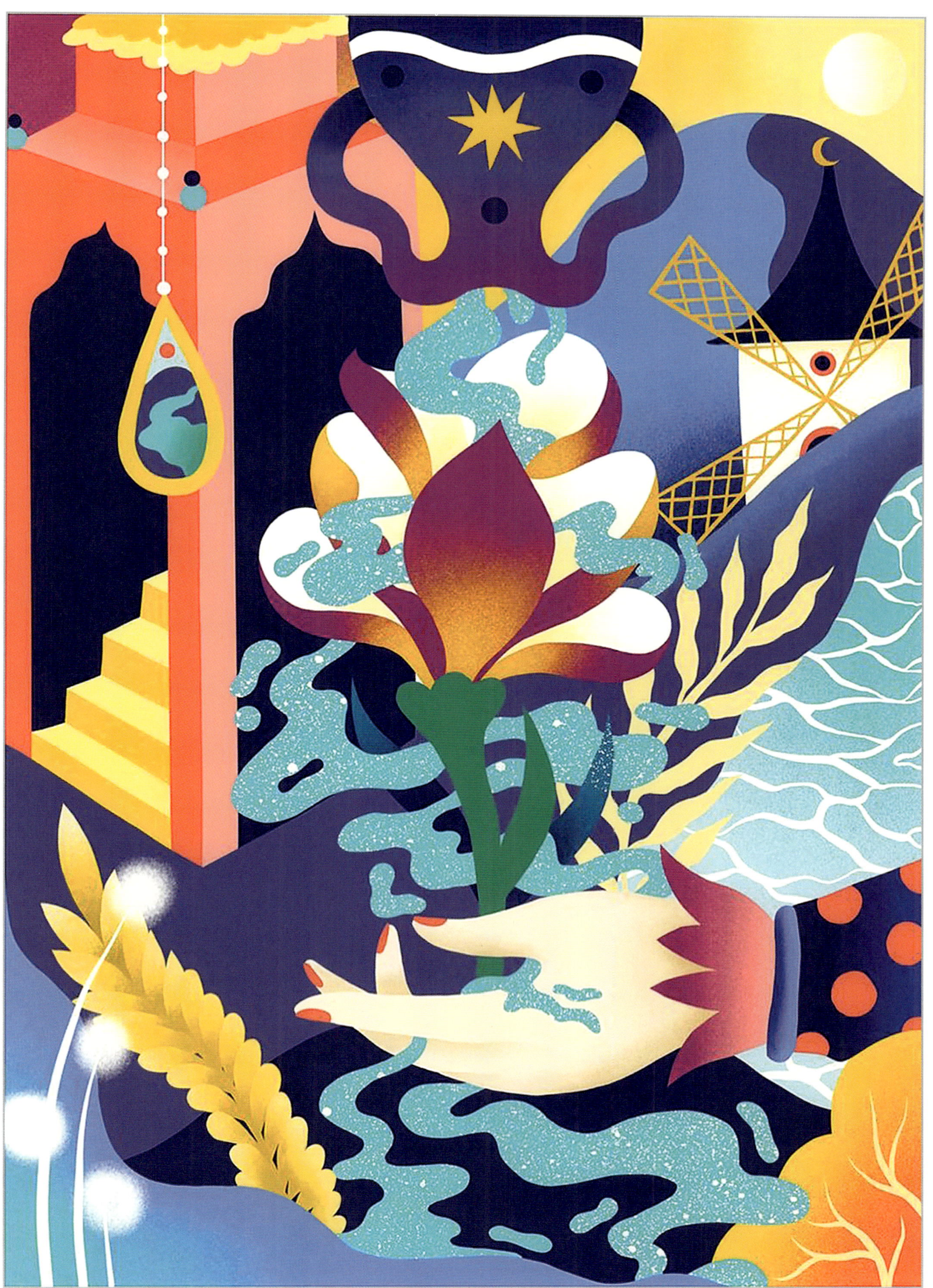

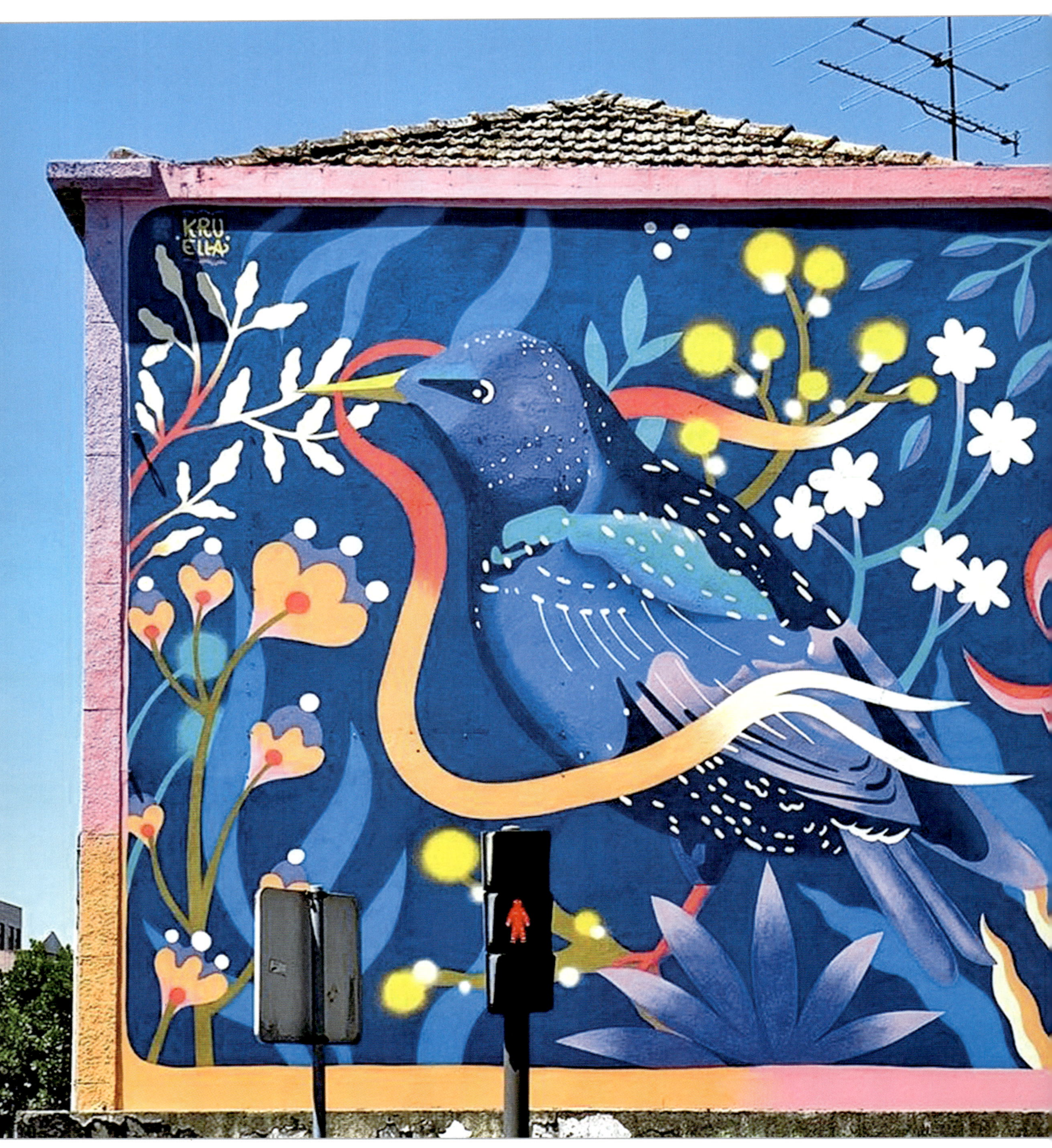

KRU
ELLA

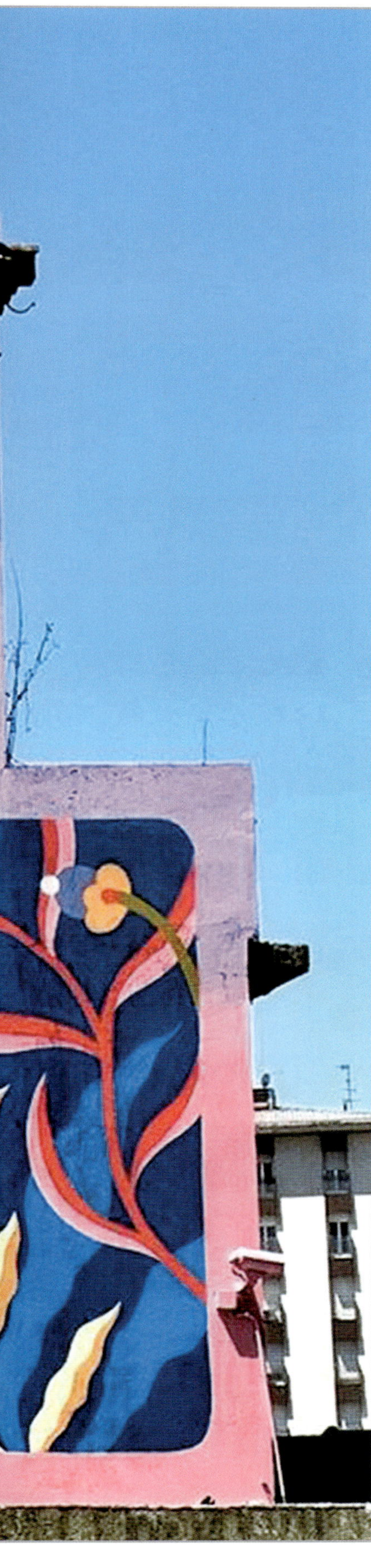

familiarizes me with new techniques and other potential forms of expression; but freehand painting is irreplaceable! I love spray paint, which allows me to do even large murals without sacrificing the power of details; but at the same time I love the delicacy of watercolor, which opens up infinite possibilities. I like to test myself with new techniques, as when working with pottery, wood, metal. . . ," she admits.

Her inspiration knows no limits and pushes relentlessly down new paths. "Traveling and learning about new cultures is a great source of inspiration; it broadens my horizons and provides me with fresh impetus. But I can find new ideas and stimuli even in a book, one possibly purchased on impulse at a flea market. Nor do I disdain the Internet, which, when used in the right way, is definitely a most valuable tool. Magritte and Dalí were the first to inspire me when I was in high school, but later I discovered an artist who completely changed my perception of reality: Jean Giraud, aka Moebius. His effect on me was so great that I was moved to tears by an exhibition dedicated to him a couple of years ago!" she recalls.

And how was your entrance into the world of street art? Did you encounter difficulties and barriers as a woman? "The moment I began participating in mural festivals was also the period when the street art movement in Portugal was exploding and open to everybody. I therefore was lucky in that sense, even if some things definitely worked differently for me—in terms of both the quantity of commissions and the consistency of monetary compensation—precisely because I was a woman. But nonetheless, I know that I enjoyed many opportunities and was luckier than others," she reflects.

To conclude, what's your secret dream? "Some day I'd like to have a gallery. I'd like to be in a position to give more opportunities to those around me who wish to start a career in art. I'd like to create a space in which everyone can share their work, interact. . . That's my dream, but I know that to achieve it I would have to make a difficult compromise between my work and a project like this, which would certainly demand a great deal of dedication and time; but I also know that my future will lie there."

O ESTORNINHO, Guimarães, Portugal

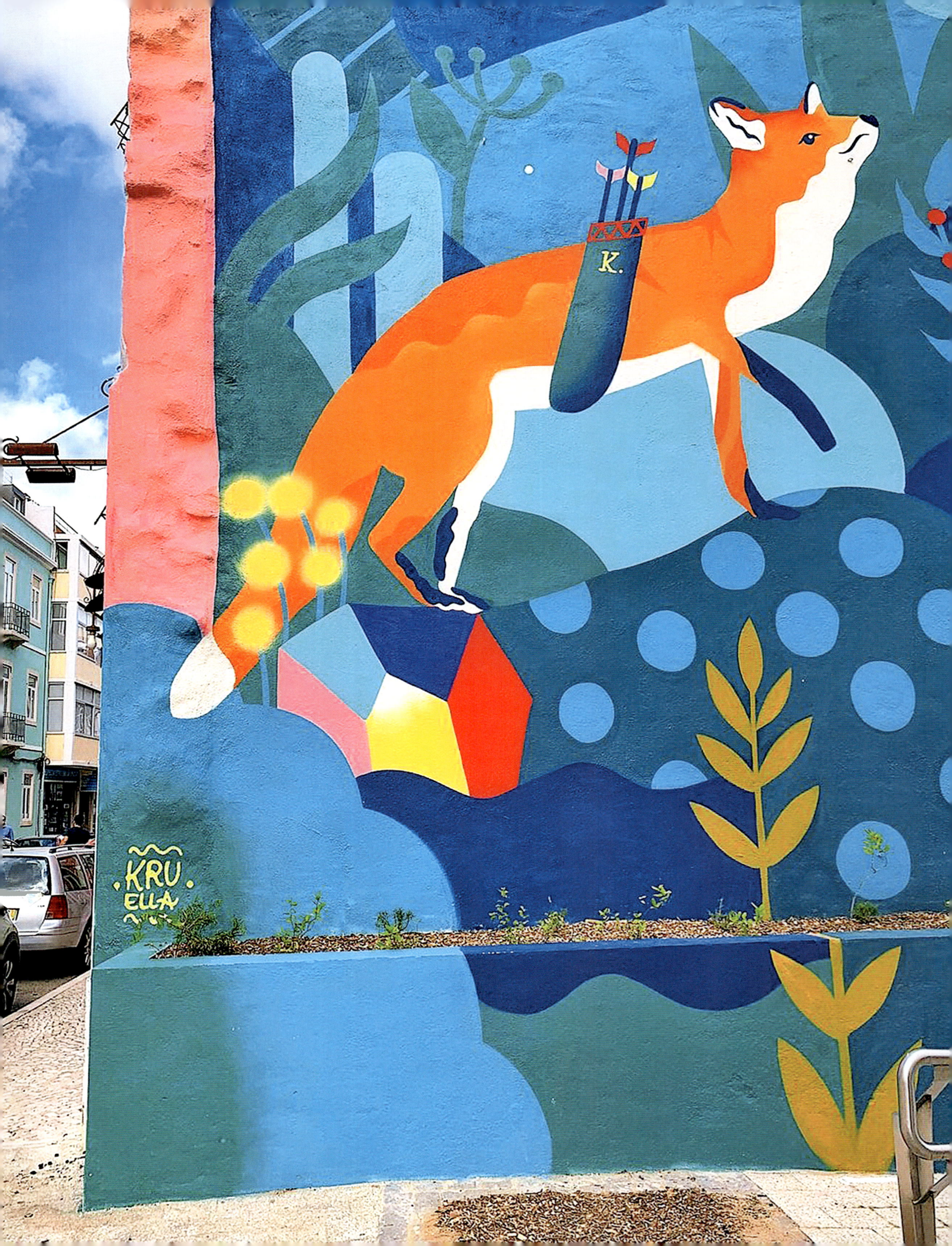

K.
KRU
ELLA

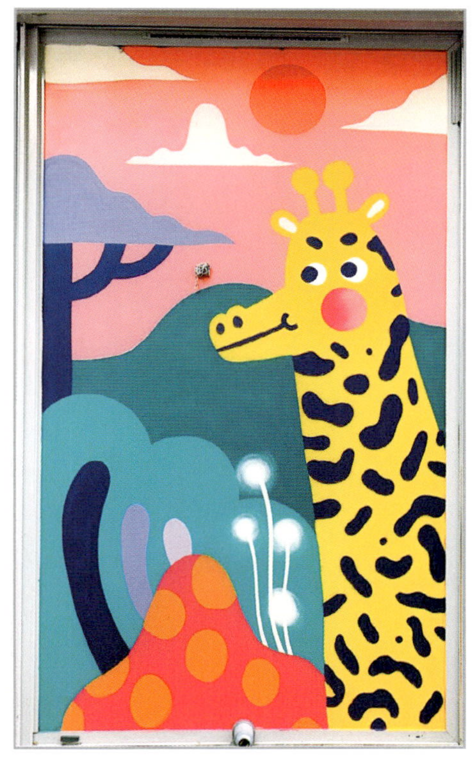
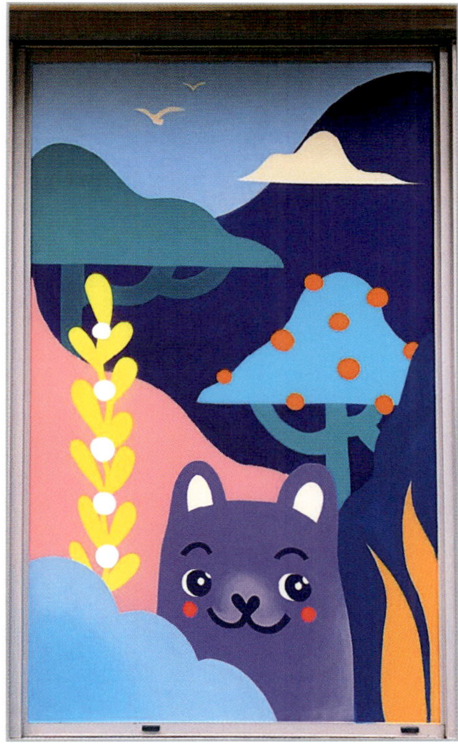
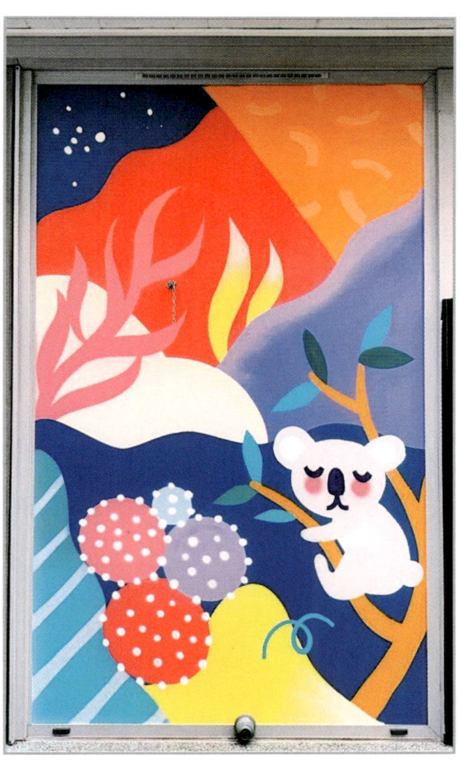
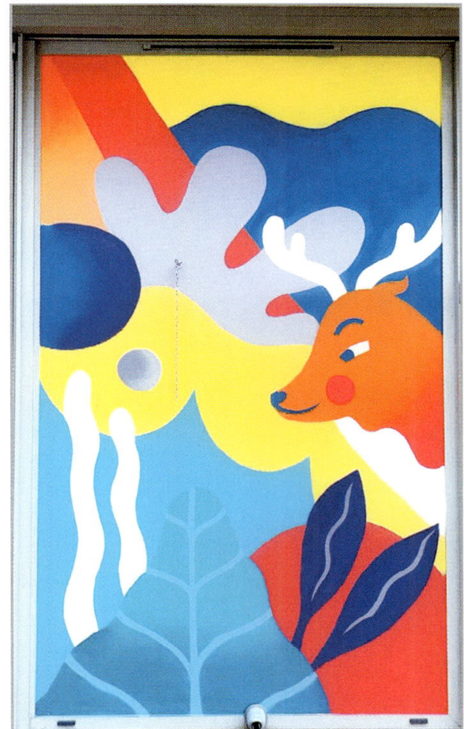
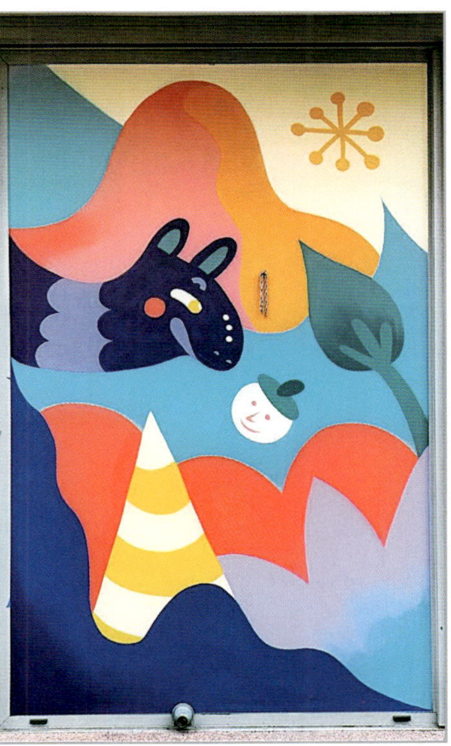

INFANT SCHOOL MURALS, Paris, France

ROMANCE DA RAPOSA, Alvalade, Lisbon, Portugal (left)

ELLE

THE LADY OF THE STREET

"On the street there's no different role for one sex or another, but it's the responsibility of art galleries, collectors, and society to ensure that everyone is equally represented and supported if they're creating equally beautiful and important work."

Her art exudes femininity and sensuality, fierce strength and courage, a desire to go beyond the surface and fearlessly explore even the darkest side of existence. "I chose Elle as my name because in French it means 'she,' and when I began working out in the street, there weren't as many women doing murals or graffiti. . . I did many works illegally; I had to remain anonymous, but I wanted a pseudonym that made it clear that I was a woman," says Elle. Tall, with bright blue eyes that evoke what's revealed in her artwork, she exudes passion and ardor in her words. She admits that she discovered street art only after arriving in New York: "I'm originally from California. I've painted and drawn since I was a child. After earning my BA in Fine Arts and Studio Art at UC Davis, I dropped out of a painting program at Brandeis University. I wasn't enamored with academia and the art world connected to it. . . I decided to move to New York and accept a job as a barista in order to start all over again."

However, one day while walking down the street in Chelsea, she had a revelation: "I saw works of street art and graffiti for the first time; I was instantly struck, and fell in love with them at first sight. It was then that I began a new journey. . . What was really wonderful was the fact that street art was accessible to everyone: a gift left on the street. It attracted and excited people who knew nothing about art, people who would never dare enter a gallery; it invited passersby to ask themselves questions, to observe, to feel involved!"

With her art, Elle likewise began entering deeper and deeper into her personal universe, exploring herself as well as the world around her, as if inside a magic kaleidoscope where shapes and sensations are constantly evolving.

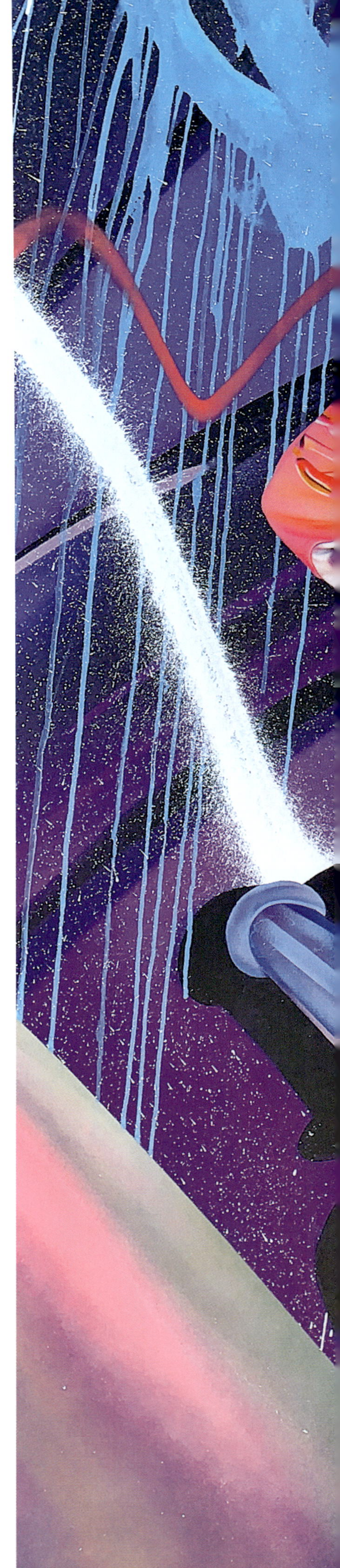

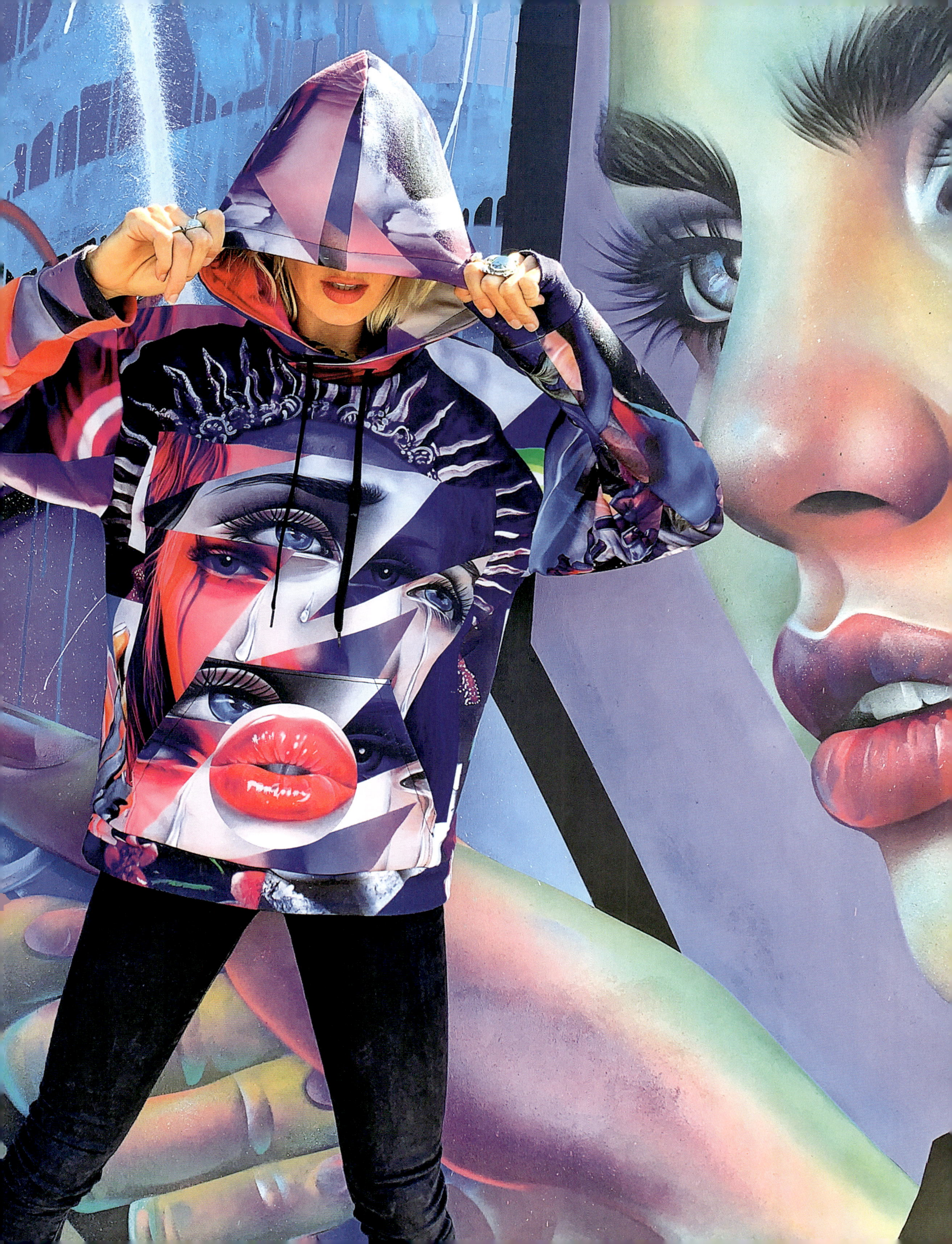

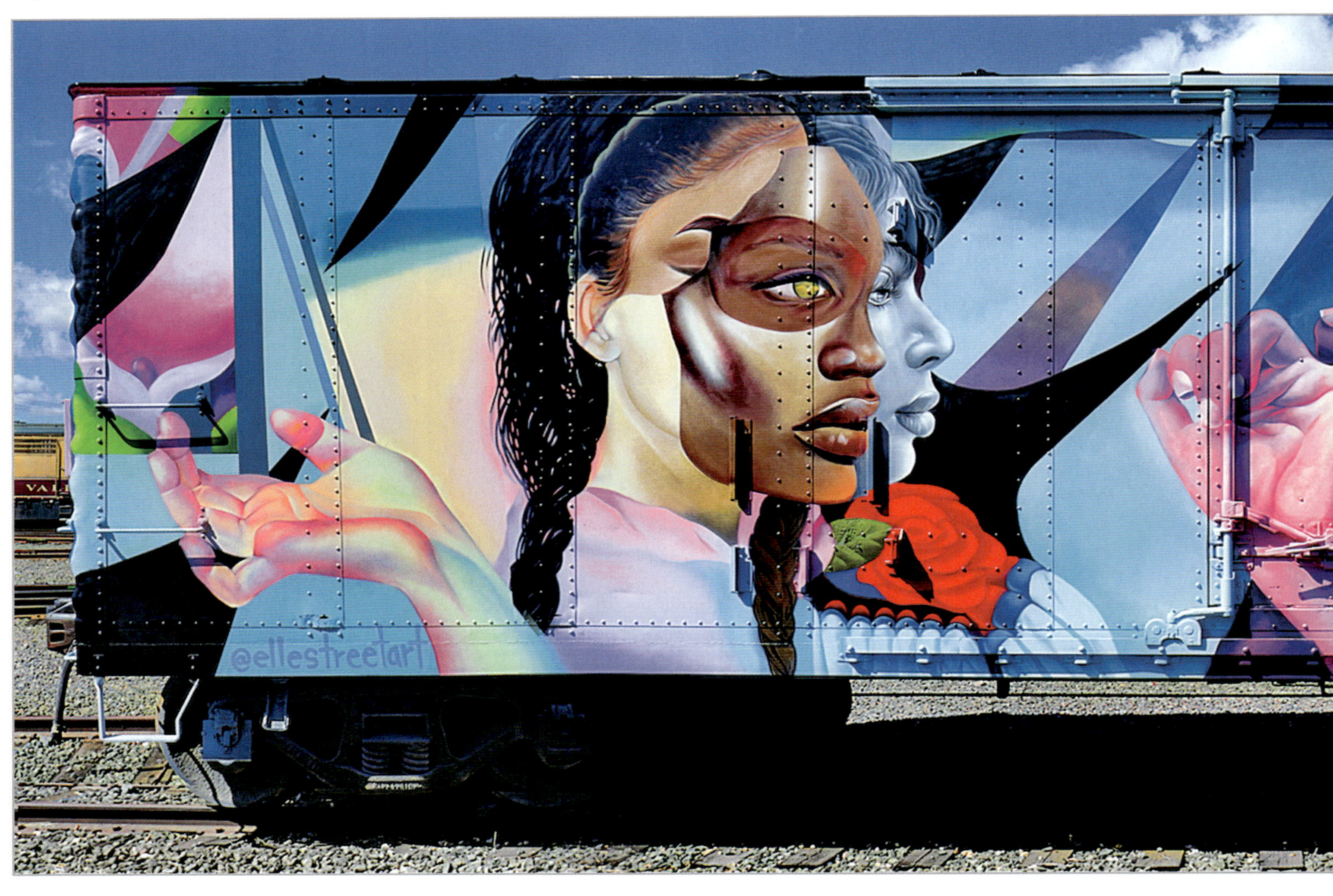

"Color has always held much meaning for me. I'm practically bewitched by it. I like to juxtapose bright and fluorescent shades with old paint, torn posters, dull-colored walls," she admits. "I basically taught myself how to spray-paint, though I've had friends like Bishop203 and Sye5 who initiated me into the technique. At first, I spent days or weeks painting on large sheets of paper that I then attached to walls with paste, but I soon became attracted to graffiti. I could do it quickly and in large quantities. . . Like me, it was wild and uncontrollable. When Liquitex, a spray paint company, sponsored me, I decided to ask people whether I could paint their walls. I soon developed a genuine obsession with spray-painting, an incredible tool for me. . . I left my barista job for good after IKEA asked me to design a poster that would be used globally. Since then, I've never had to look for another job outside of art!" the devotee confesses.

In her vast output we can see a profusion of women: animal-like women and women with two or three faces. "Much of my inspiration comes from nature: from the jungle, the water, the wind, Mother Earth. For me, the collages I create are poetry. I like when people scrutinize and derive different stories from them, interpreting them in their own ways. In a world largely dominated by men, my female figures are strong warriors,

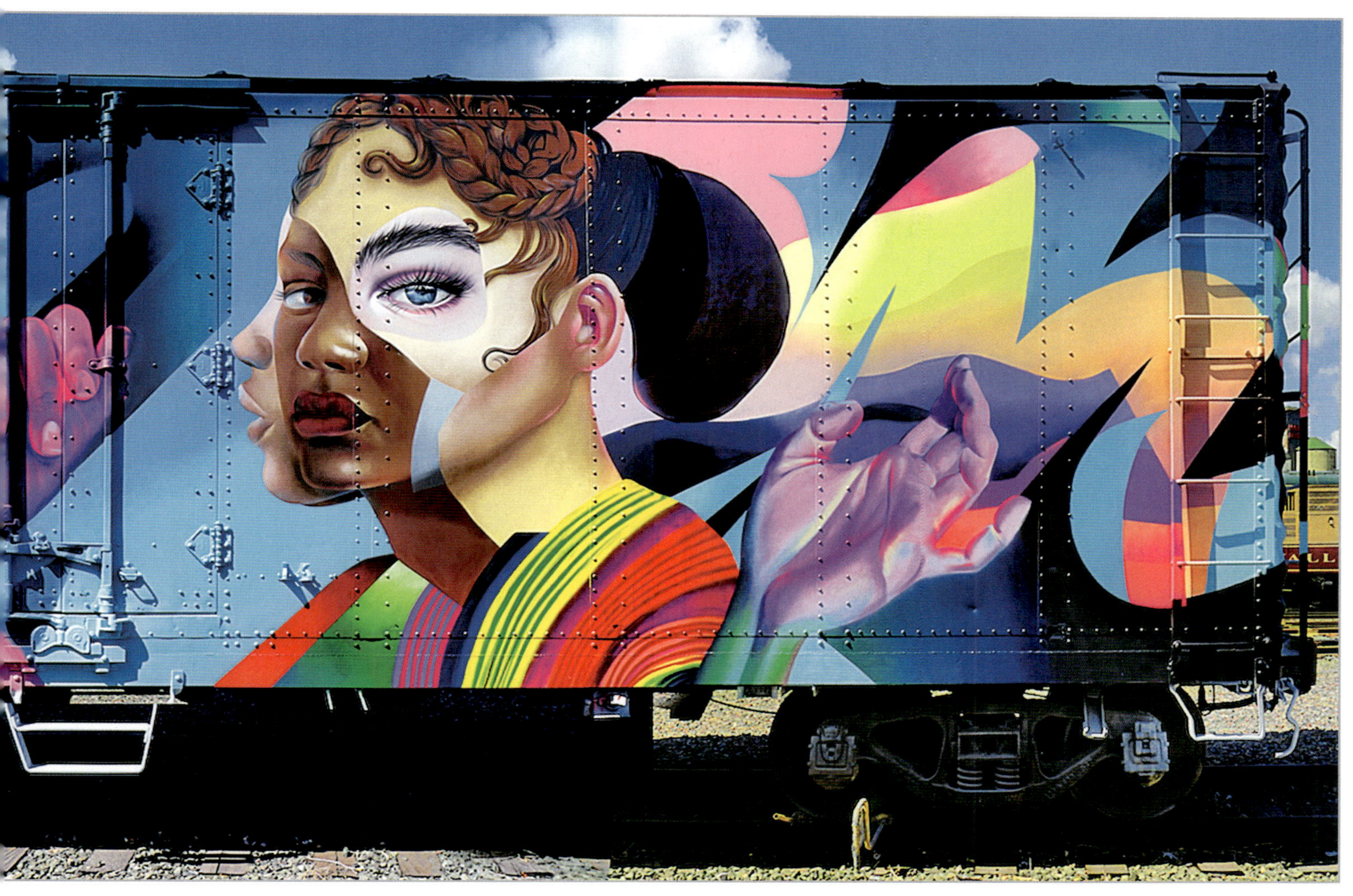

often accompanied by a sort of animal spirit. I regard them as spiritual guardians," she discloses.

Elle was invited to be the artist-in-residence in the Rialto Towers precinct in Melbourne, Australia, where, in 2018, she held her first solo exhibition, *A Space for Sinners*. Since then, she has never stopped, working on street walls as well as on canvas, illustrating the themes dear to her that portray her women, scintillating colors, slinky, disquieting, sensual snakes. . . Elle's works have been exhibited, among other places, at the Saatchi Gallery in London, the Urban Nation Museum in Berlin, and the New Museum in New York City. Her graffiti is featured in the *Tom Clancy's The Division* video game. Elle likes to experiment and constantly reinvent herself, availing herself of her unique talent for distinguishing herself with her unmistakable style, which, like her, is wild, powerful, irrepressible, energetic, and vibrant. She has thus collaborated with huge internationally renowned brands like Reebok, Nike Melbourne, and Kanye West's creative agency. She also joined Steve Aoki as the headliner of the ASICS "I Move Me" campaign. In the case of Samsung, she took part in the production of a truly unique high-tech virtual reality project: "It's as if one were entering my painting and, at the same time, my brain. One can see three-dimensional figures moving around. It's

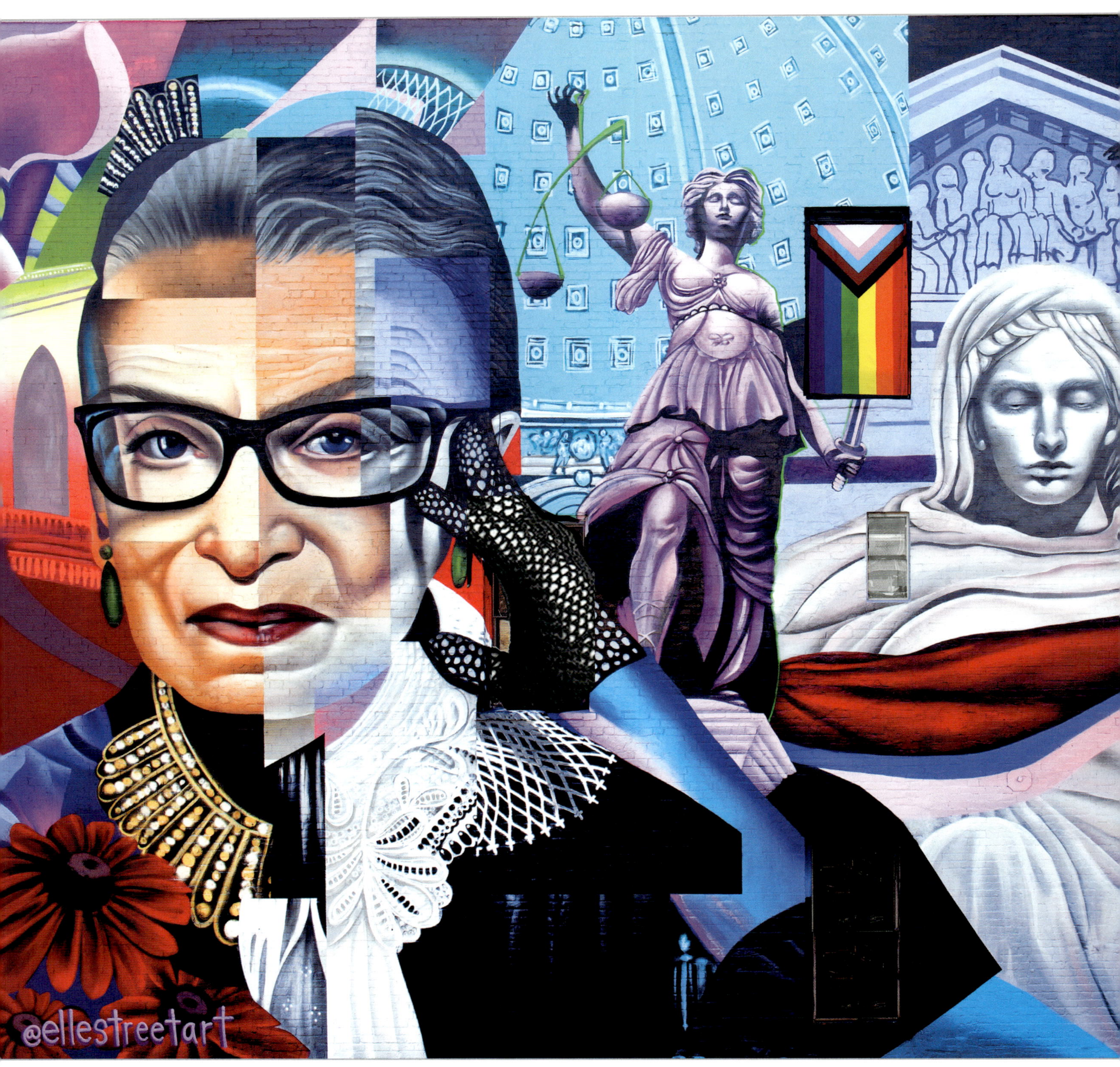

RUTH BADER GINSBURG, New York City, New York, USA, 2020

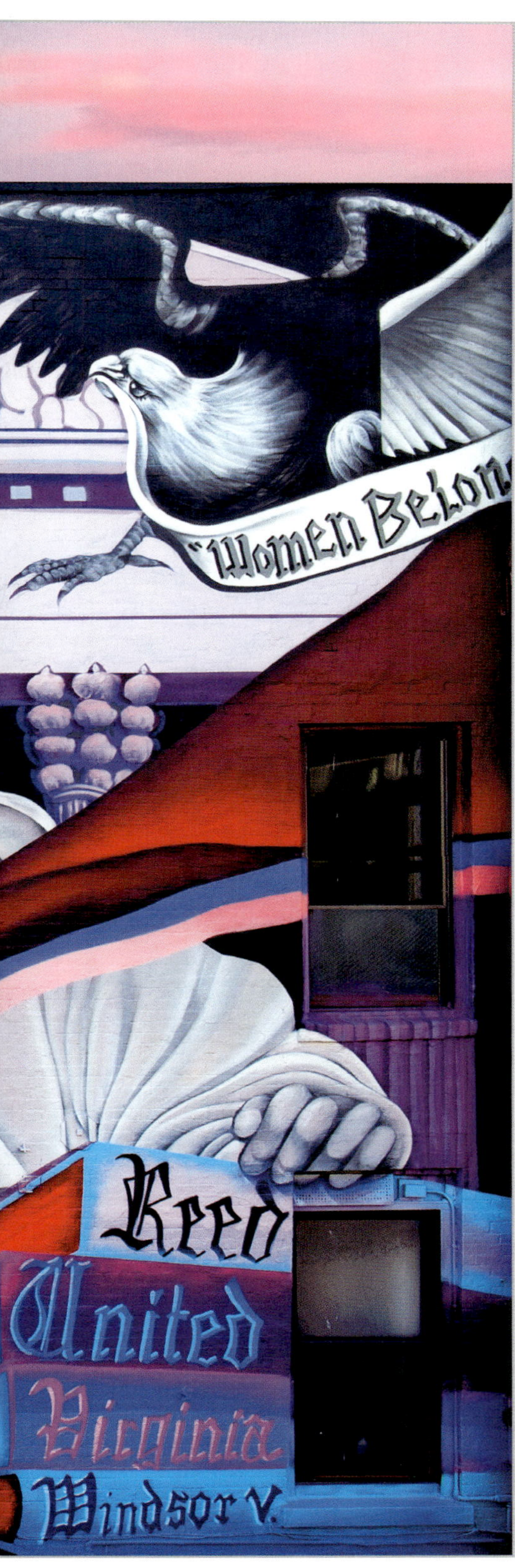

something really special! With ELLExReebok, on the other hand, I paired my street style with leggings and a yoga collection."

Endowed with innate elegance and grace, Elle has also created a line of fashion and accessories imprinted with her works that she sells from her website. "I would not say that, technically speaking, I follow fashion, but rather that I love confronting many brands. The interesting thing about art is that it can be applied to various surfaces, be they cups, textiles, shoes, bags, buildings, anything. I love new challenges, which is why it's always fun to try to apply my art to something different and unusual. But the brands must share my ethics, because I do not compromise. Otherwise I refuse the of-fer," she argues with conviction. In 2020, Elle undertook many jobs in New York, where she dedicated a great deal of attention to female figures: "I've always devoted much space in my work to figures of women, because it seemed to me that they're not rep-resented enough on the street, in graffiti, in murals, or in public art. Today, I think that other artists have followed this example and that the presence of women in the world

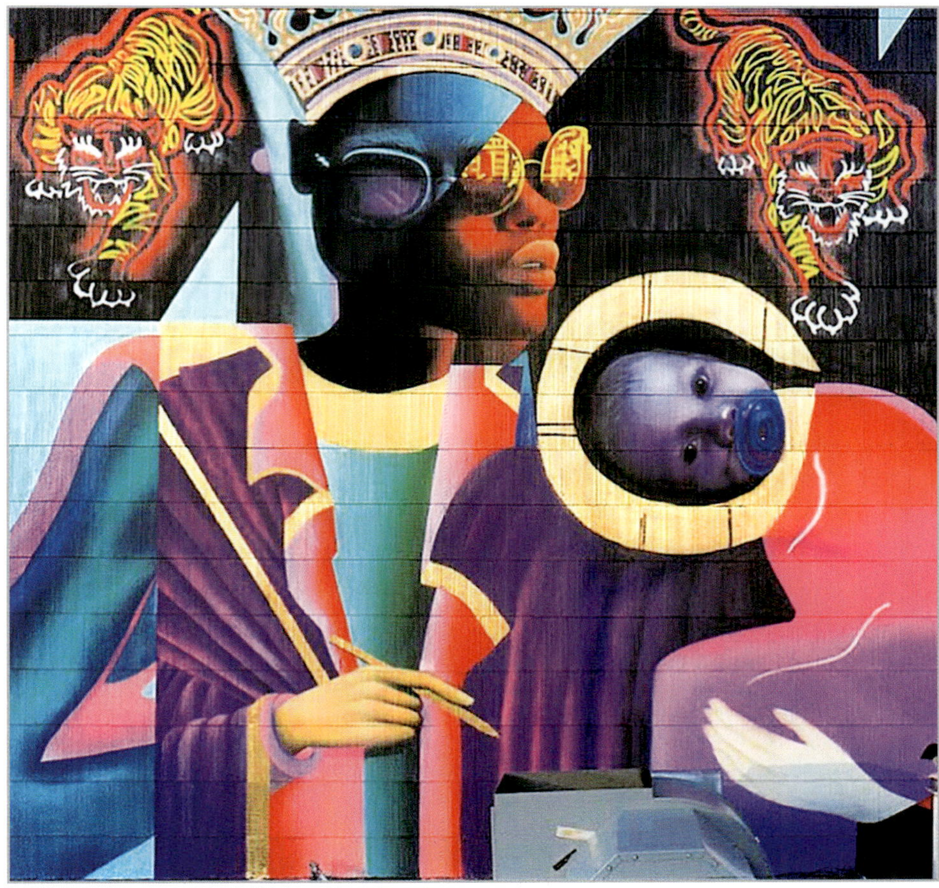

DENALI, San Francisco, California, USA, 2018

of street art has grown decidedly greater," she reflects. "Working on the street—even in the middle of the night—I've had to face strange situations. . . The most disturbing ones? One time, in Miami, a man approached me while I was working and asked me for my shoe size. The reason? Apparently he wanted to chop off my feet! Luckily, I had my bike nearby; I hopped on it, pedaled like crazy, and sought refuge in a store, where I asked for help. . . On another occasion, one of the policemen who arrested me for painting illegally asked me out while they were taking my fingerprints," she recollects.

"Aside from some personal safety issues, however, I've never felt that it was hard or that I was at a disadvantage compared to others, when it came to the world of street art; instead, it was more difficult for me to gain acceptance in the environment—mostly illegal—of those who work with spray paint. But I didn't give up and continued my work with determination, following the lead of other women active even back then, such as Miss Reds, Honey, 17, and Utah. In those days I was especially inspired by Judith Supine, Swoon, and Gaia, while today I closely watch the work of contemporary artists like Wangechi Mutu and Saya Woolfalk," she says.

"The pandemic has 'granted' me more time to work in my studio and to reconsider my plans and my desires. In short, for me, as for everyone else, this has been a period of profound reflection. I've wanted to devote myself to sculpture for a long time, and now I know that that's what I'll do next. After all, my path is one of continuous evolution: for example, in 2020 I began experimenting with colored glass, and learned the art of molding it from Meryl Pataky, a fantastic artist and incredible woman.

GIRL POWER, for Blink Cincinnati, Ohio, USA, 2019 (right)

MALALA, Los Angeles, California, USA, 2017

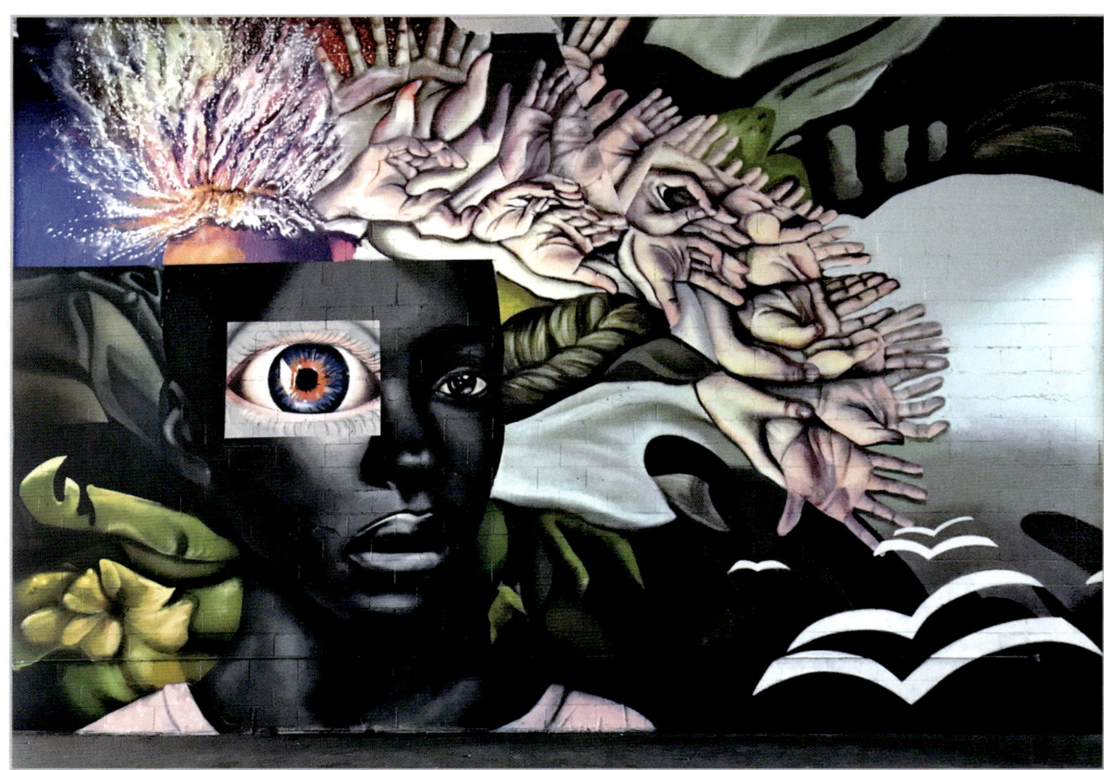

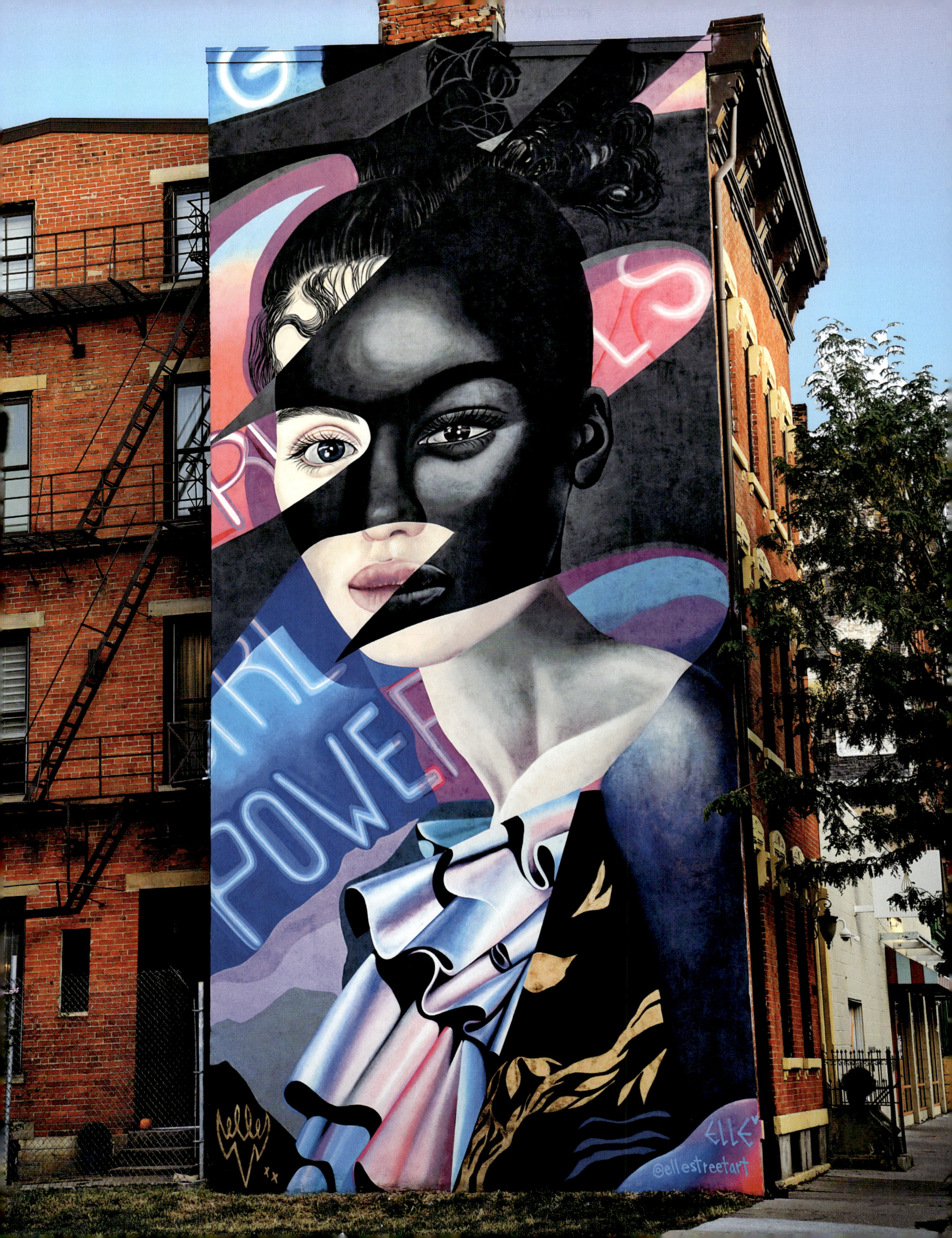
GIRLS
GIRLS
GIRL
POWER
ELLE
@ellestreetart

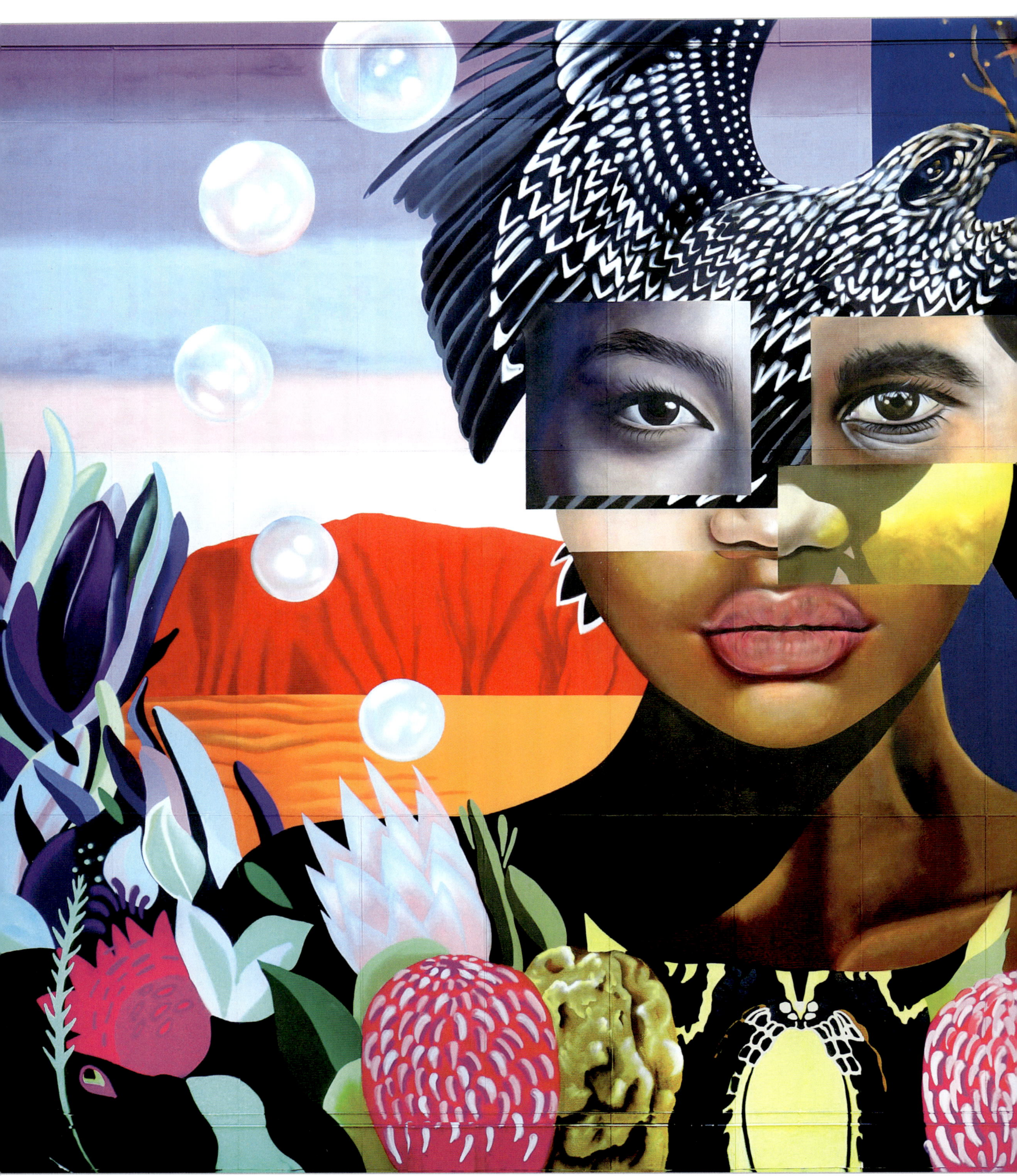

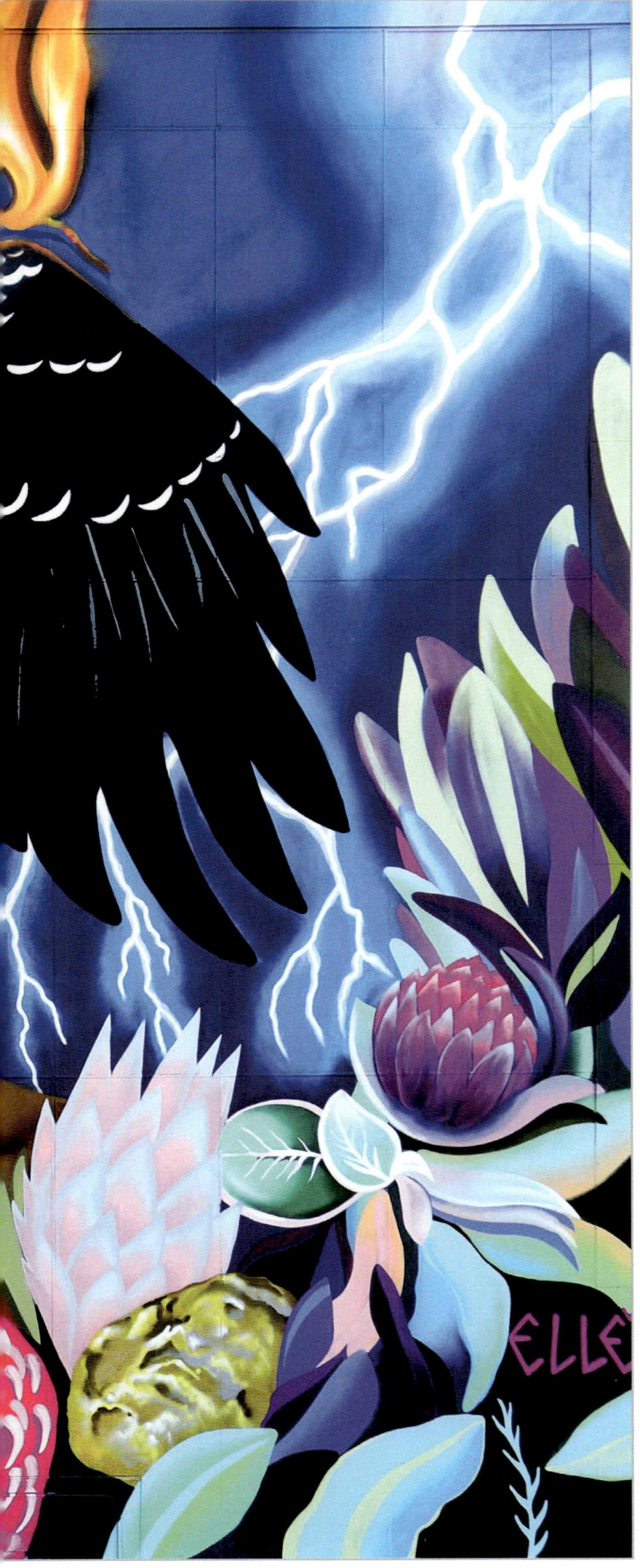

Even if my deepest passion remains anchored in color, I like to explore various media in order to figure out what can best represent the idea I'm having at a particular moment. I try not to limit myself, even if it means scouring the beach for sticks, for example, and trying to create something abstract with them. All street art correlates with the place where it's born. I take into consideration the ethnicity, culture, and language of the people who live around the places I paint. I want them to identify with my artwork and regard it as a gift to them and their neighborhood," she adds.

Your favorite places to paint? "Right now I'm living between Brooklyn and New York [i.e., Manhattan] and California and . . . other places. I'm always on the go and travel a great deal. Some day I'd also like to have a studio in Bali and Sydney. I've never been a person who loves planning everything in advance, and I go where I'm called or where I feel like going at that precise moment. I can advise other artists never to give up, to persevere at what they do, because ultimately they'll see results. My mission is to try making my work even more authentic and effective," she concludes.

DARANIKI MYALL, Austin Lane, Darwin, Australia, 2018

FAITH47

THE EXPLORER OF THE FACETS
OF HUMAN NATURE

*"I'm interested in finding a language for exploring my inner self.
We're all human and therefore share a common experience of
what it means to be human."*

Her origins are closely bound to her existence; triumphant, rugged, passionate, they rise from her art, just as her country has. "South Africa is the home of my soul. Its sky and soil are in my bones. It's at the center of my heart. My mother took us to meet the mountain and the ocean. The Earth is inside of me. I am honored to have such a rapport with this rich and multi-layered place. It has taught me everything," Faith47 notes while reflecting.

"I was born in a nation dominated by a cruel apartheid regime: I remember the old 'WHITES ONLY/*NET BLANKES*' signs, when trains, like beaches, bathrooms, and schools, were all subject to the unjust laws of racial segregation. . . The country's wealth was built on extreme exploitation. I witnessed the change in government, and I remember reading people's testimony at the hearings of the Truth and Reconciliation Commission (TRC)," she relates. "The realization of how deep we went to cause pain and suffering is something that will never leave me. That experience made me understand how easy it is for a society to consciously and cruelly go astray if there are no appropriate controls to put an instant stop to the process. The stencils and slogans of the resistance on the walls of metro stations are the first type of public art I remember. All of this has influenced my work, even when it's not always overtly political, and has led me to construct a particular perspective," she adds.

Faith47 is a completely self-taught artist and is proud of it. "I learned everything I know from trial and error, pushing myself in directions that drew my interest, with no technical know-how. But one can learn a great deal when one's inspired and deeply motivated," she says.

Her art is devoted above all to the social reality of Cape Town and South Africa, which she confronts in the streets on a daily basis: the promises of a better life for the "New South Africa" that stand in contrast with the harsh everyday reality. Faith47 began painting in 1997, three years after apartheid came to an end.

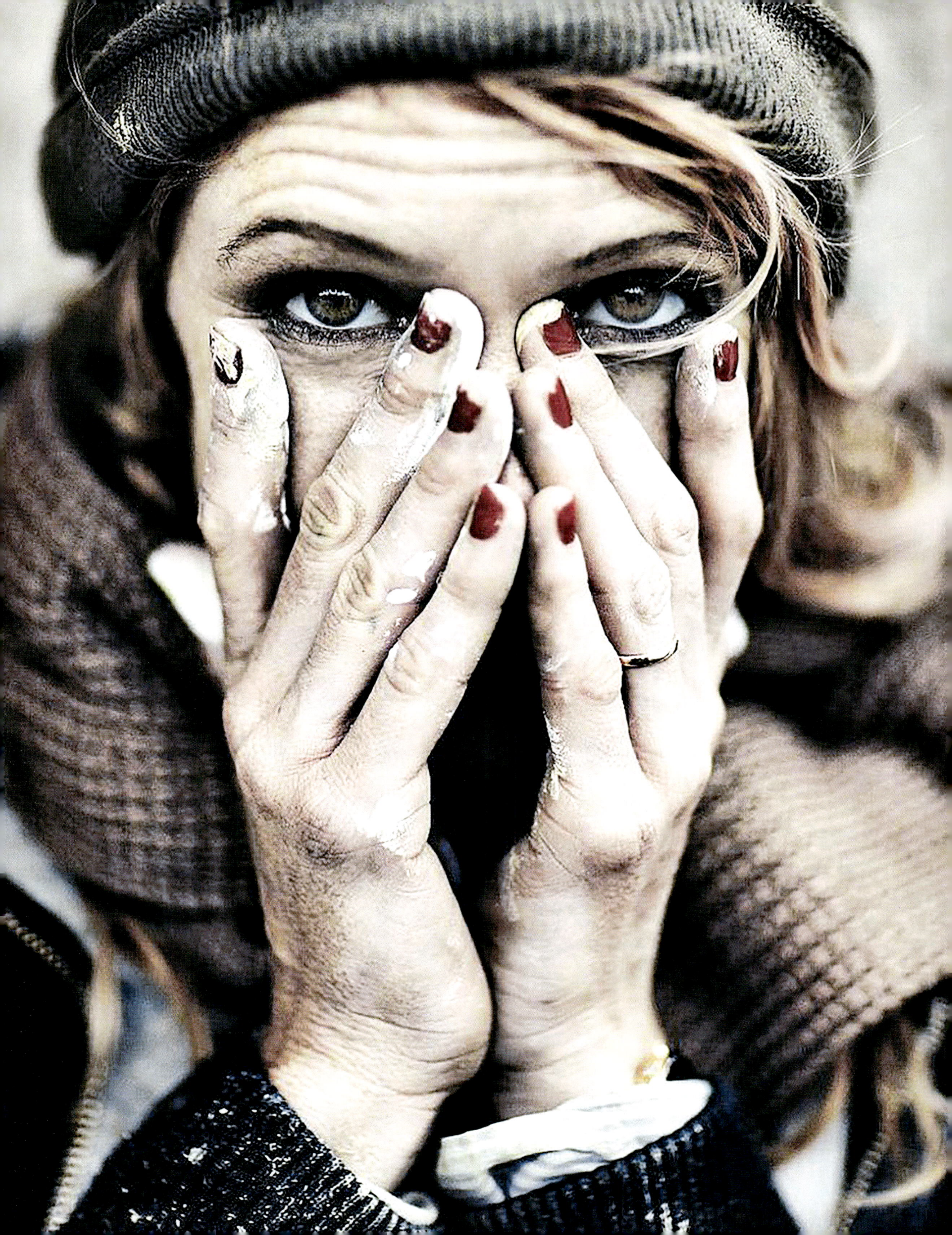

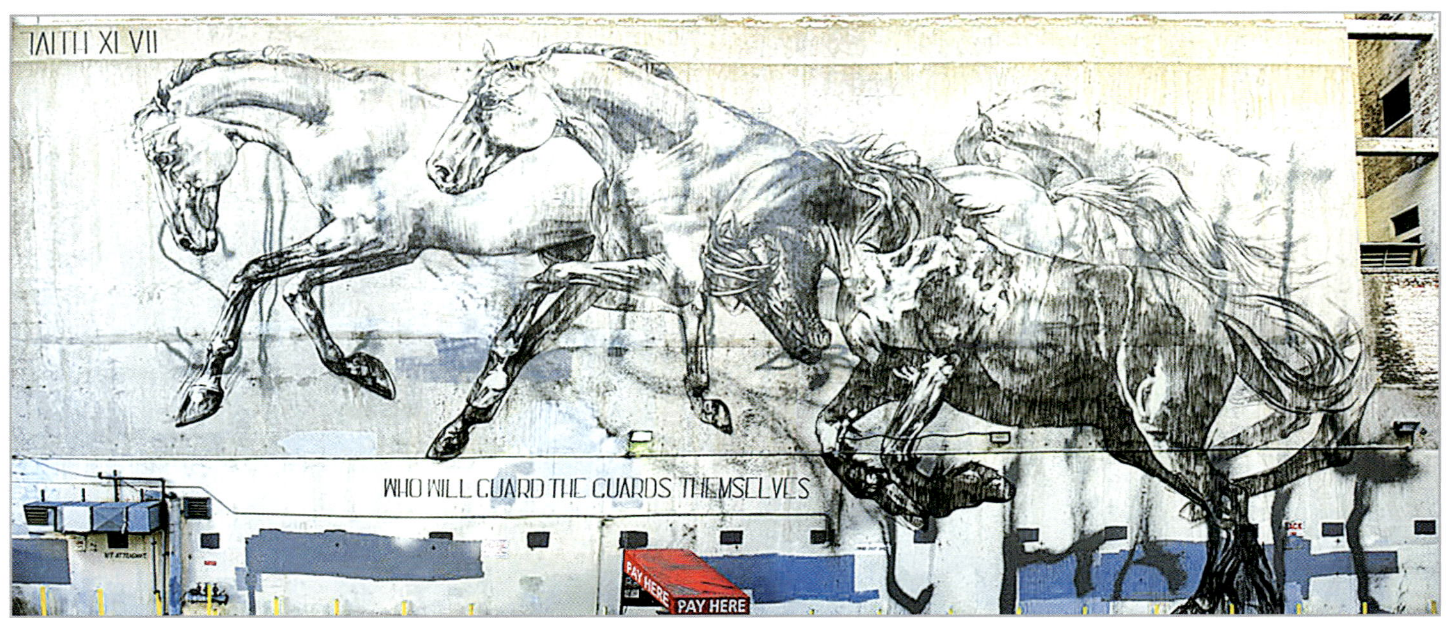

Her early works focused on economic inequality and poverty, but with time her attention also turned to nature and its spirituality, toward endangered animals and the negative impact of man. Her female figures speak of emancipation and inequality. "I became a fan of mural and public art thanks to my roots in graffiti. It was a natural progression. Today my art is decidedly multidisciplinary; I'm interested in sculpture, tapestries, painting, in media. Each medium offers a different way of speaking, of expressing oneself; visual language expands and is constantly enriched by new nuances," she notes.

Her mission is quite clear: "I am interested in humanity and human beings. How can we speak about them metaphorically, through color and visual clues? Can we open new spaces in our hearts and minds? Can we help each other with our journeys? Art, music, theater, and prose. . . they've all contributed to my artistic development in a decisive way," she explains. Then come the women who inspired her and whom she admires in particular: "Patti Smith, Marina Abramović, Hilma af Klint, Emma Kunz, Swoon, Käthe Kollwitz, Lady Skollie, Aldous Harding, Karin Dreijer; but, above all, my mother."

All her work reflects her soul, but the essence of her mindset is captured by one work in particular: "*The Human Cause* is an ode to the Peace Manifesto, a scream, an invocation to put an end to hostilities and hatred, wherever and however these manifest themselves. In conjunction with this manifesto, we did a large mural with multiple depictions of the White Flag on the UC Hastings College of Law building in San Francisco."

And she has another more recent piece which is very dear to her because it evokes themes of the past and present: *The Land War*, an installation launched in 2019: "The idea that inspired it takes concrete form in a mural, a bronze sculpture, and an installation in the Fluctuart gallery in Paris. *The Land War* installation is now part of the MUCA collection in Munich, Germany. The image of a rearing horse, bridled with fluttering reins, signifies a powerful animal subjugated by humanity.

WHO WILL GUARD THE GUARDS THEMSELVES?, Los Angeles, California, USA, 2016

THREE METHODS FOR WORKING WITH CHAOS

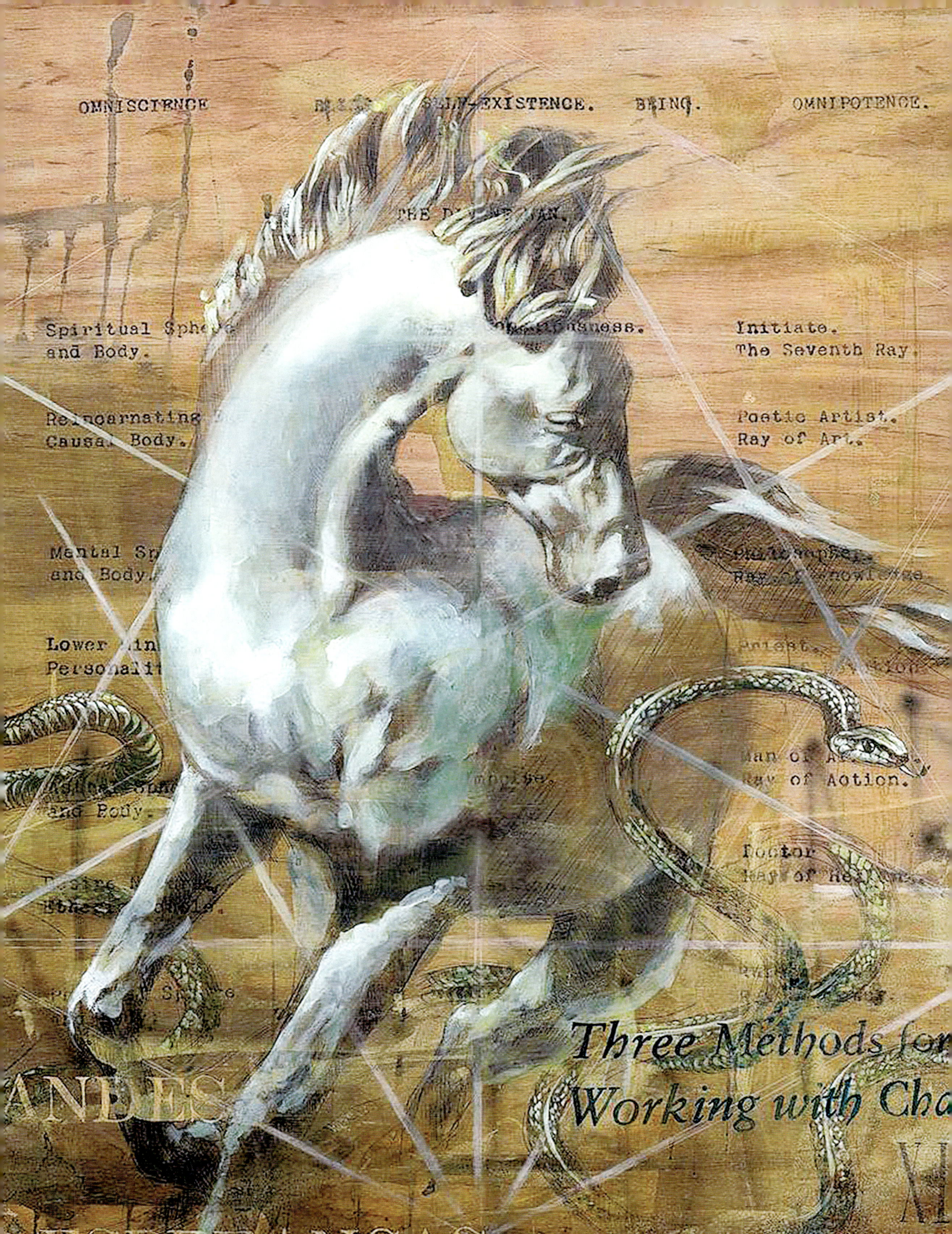
OMNISCIENCE.
SELF-EXISTENCE.
BEING.
OMNIPOTENCE.
THE DIVINE MAN.
Spiritual Sphere
and Body.
Initiate.
The Seventh Ray.
Reincarnating
Causal Body.
Poetic Artist.
Ray of Art.
Mental Sphere
and Body.
Ray of Knowledge.
Lower Mind
Personality.
Man of Action.
Ray of Action.
and Body.
Doctor
Ray of Healing.
Three Methods for
Working with Cha

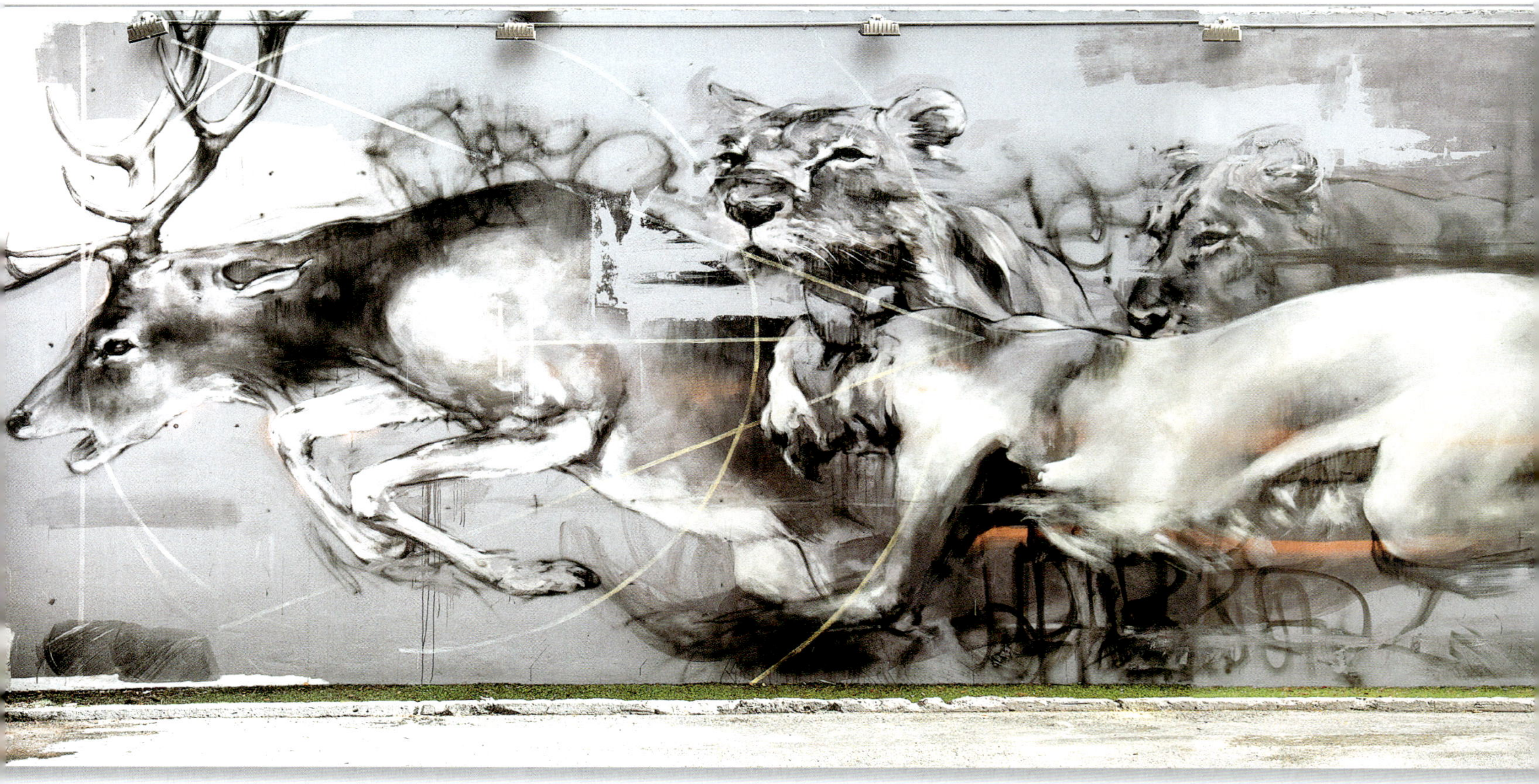

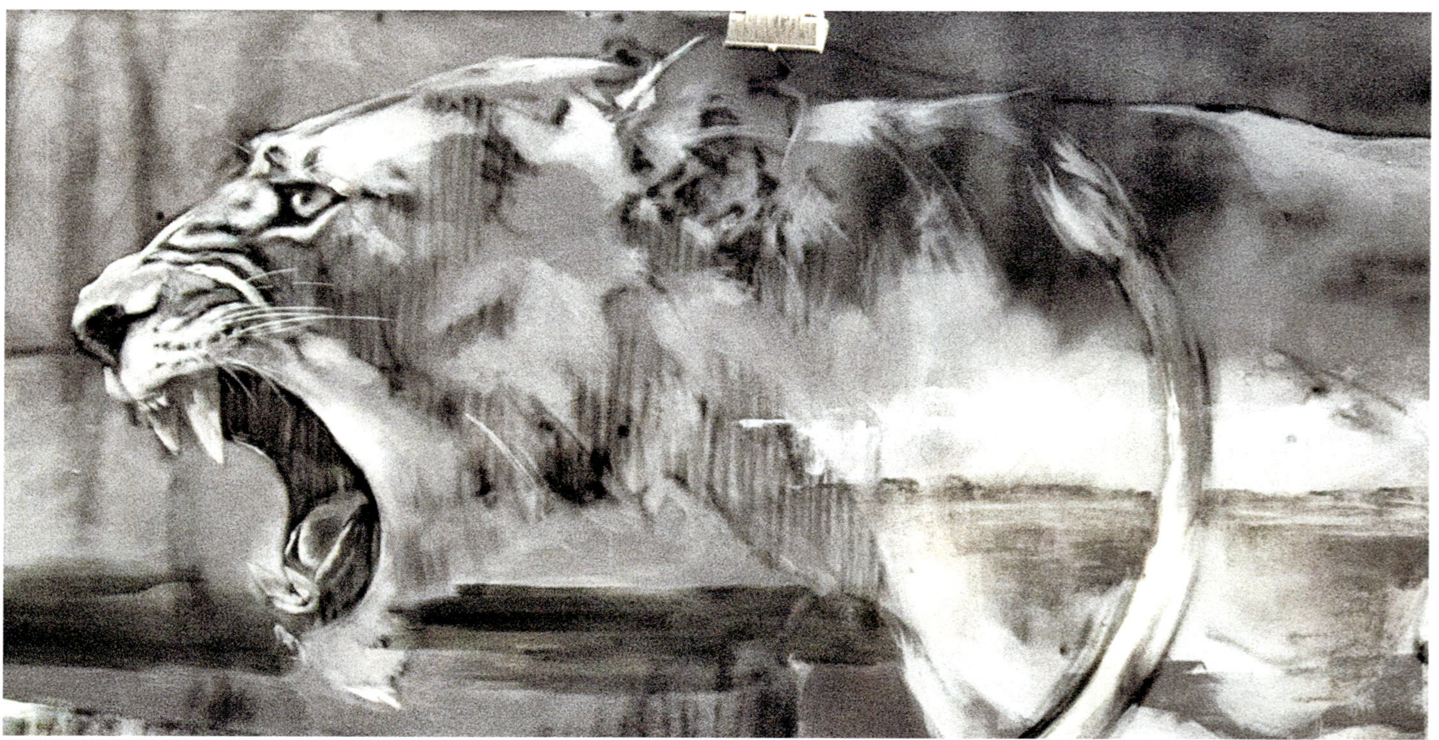

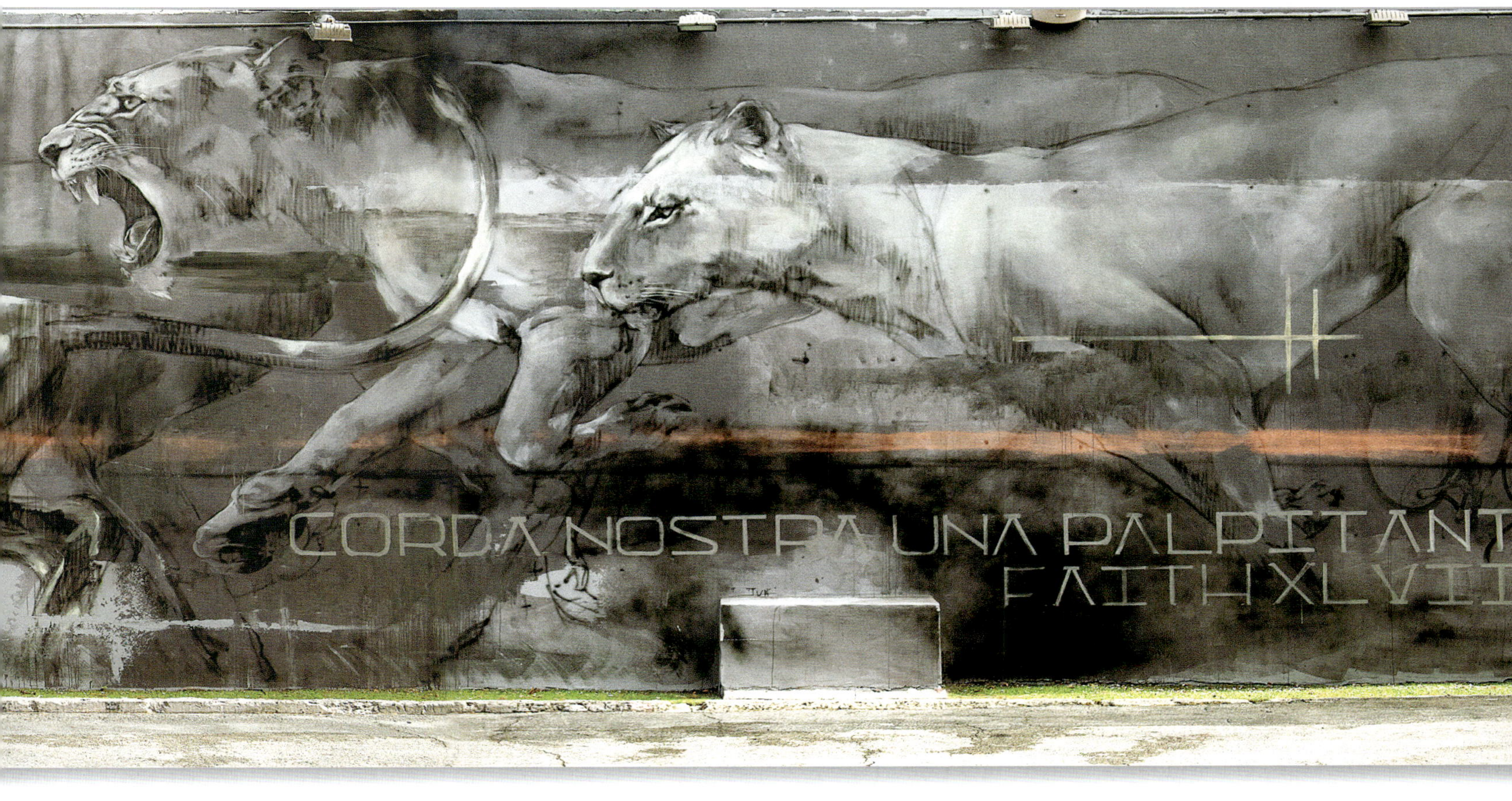

CORDA NOSTRA UNA PALPITANT, Miami, Florida, USA, 2016

"Invariably majestic and elegant, powerful, and vigorous, horses possess an inherent sense of nobility. The image of the horse carries with it the weight and valor of nationalism and patriotism, and is often associated with memorials and statues of statesmen and 'heroes.' Historically, horses have been the creatures that men bring to war, to fight and loyally perish alongside them. The figures in *The Land War* evoke feelings of resistance and revolution, and, at the same time, our ability as individuals to resist absolutist domination and totalitarian authority," she explains emphatically.

Her worldview reflects similar principles: "The world is clearly out of sync and the situation is so obvious, so dramatically real that at this point it's impossible to ignore. We live in a world that's been shaped by colonialism, racism, male domination, religious dogma. We're dealing here with a deeply macho reality, and women have fought and must still fight tooth and nail for their rights. Much work remains to be done, but until we find balance within ourselves and our communities, things will not change. This is why I want to promote and underscore things such as female strength and the power of intuition, of empathy, its connection with birth and death, with care, its tight connection with the earth," she says.

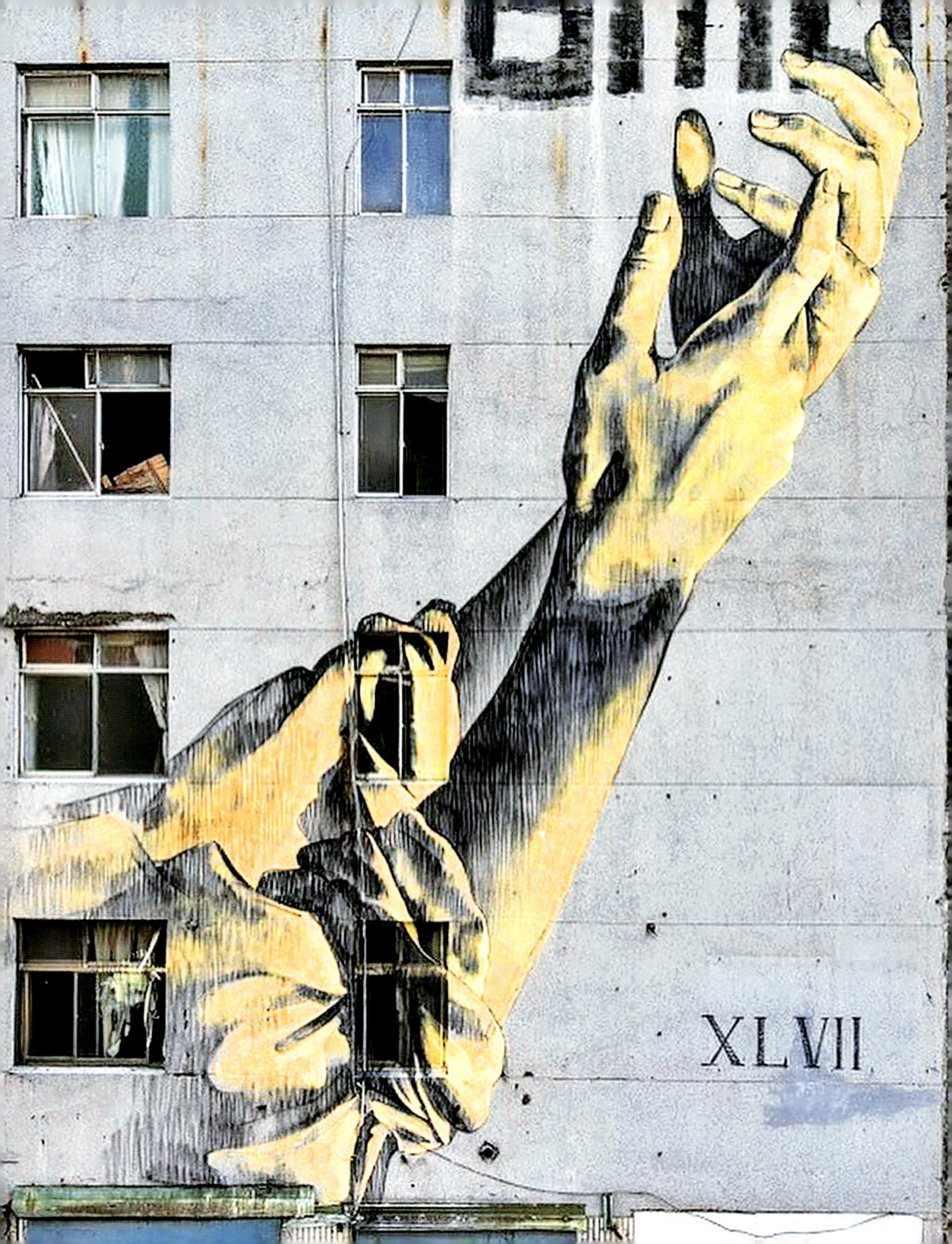
XLVII

She remains skeptical about the future, albeit without losing hope. "Honestly, I don't see the world situation getting better. I know there are a great many people who are taking things seriously, but the political and economic interests and forces at play are incredibly powerful. Noam Chomsky's words come to mind: "Optimism is a strategy for making a better future." And I believe that this is what we must cultivate and nurture within us: optimism, faith, the hope of being able to go on trying and fighting for a better world, love, empathy, sustainability, cohesion, understanding, even as we confront the most horrifying prospects. *A luta continua!*"

Humanity's progress lies hidden in the new generation. Faith47's son, Keya Tama, born in 1997, is likewise an artist. Both moved to Los Angeles in 2018. "I had Keya quite young, so we basically grew up together. He came with me to the graffiti jam; and when I took part on international projects, I always gave him a wall on which he could paint. He spent many of his days drawing in a studio while was at work. . . So he developed his own style and sense of ethics from an early age. It's been amazing to watch him grow and become such a beautiful person," she admits with pride, and with great hope in her heart.

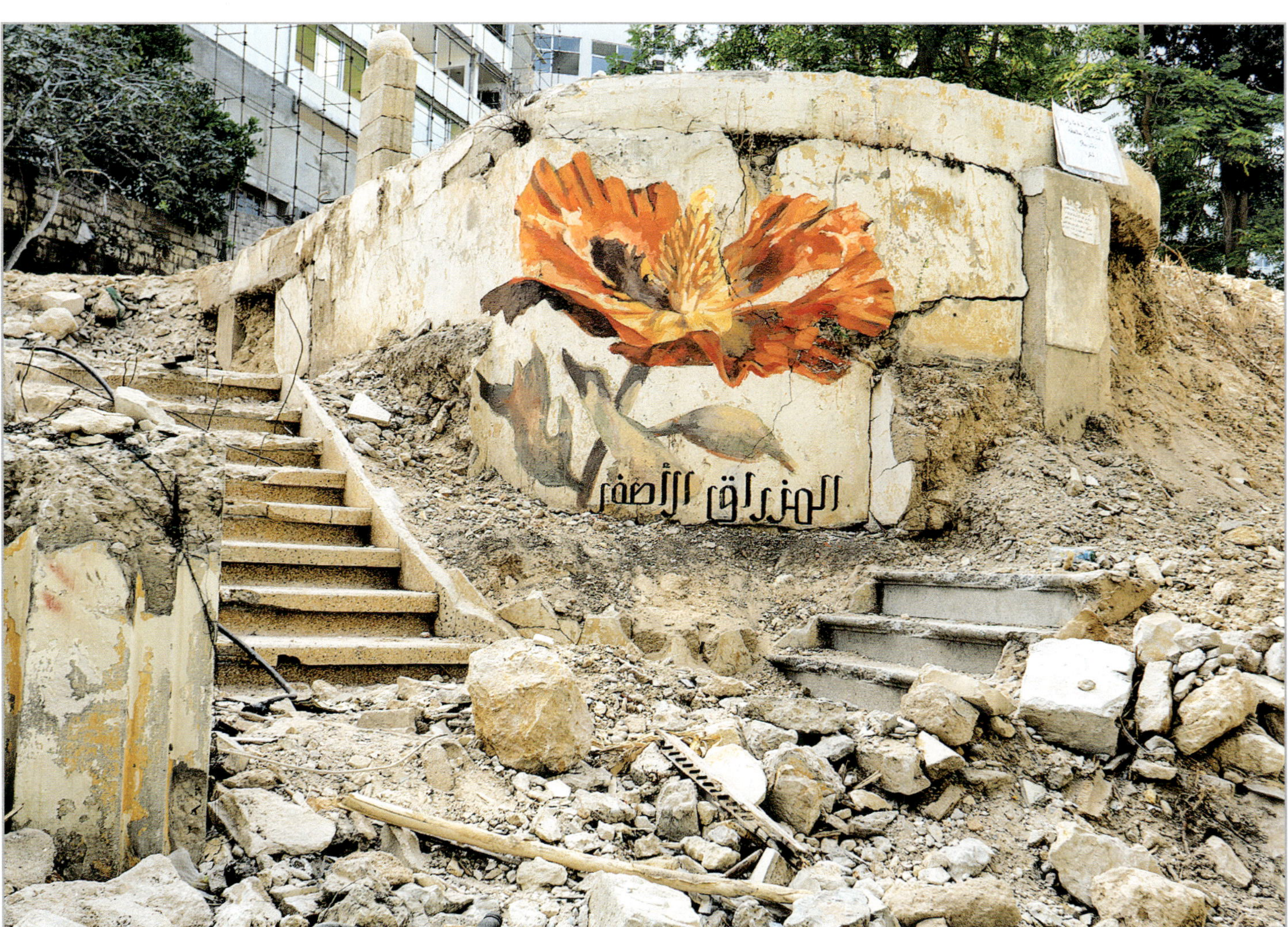

MY HANDS AND YOUR HEART EXIST ONLY IN A FRAME OF UNDERSTANDING PARTICULAR TO ONE'S OWN ILLUSION, Taipei, Taiwan

MEDICINAL FLOWERS OF LEBANON, Beirut, Lebanon, 2021

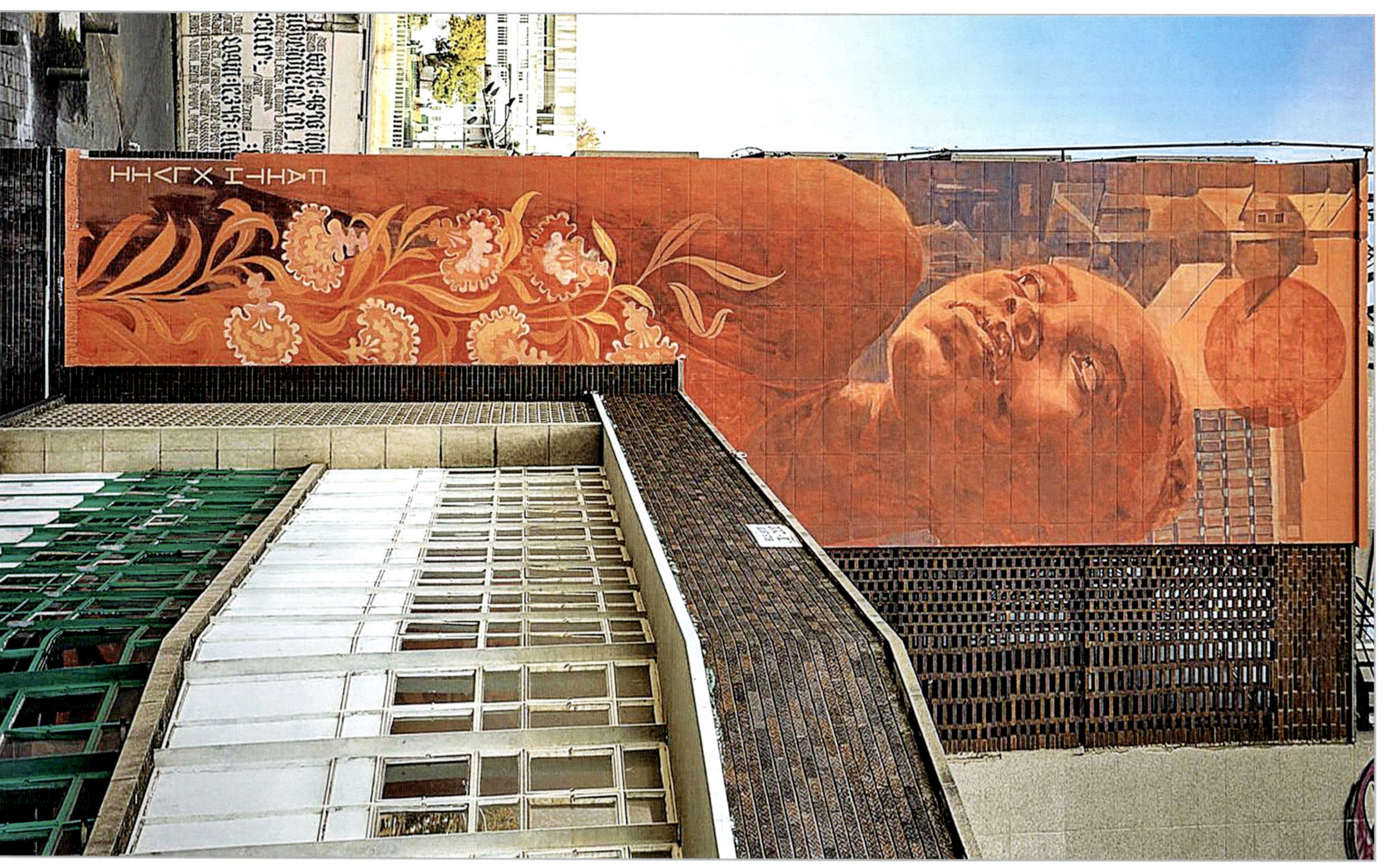

GOLD DUST, Johannesburg, South Africa, 2021

THE SILENT WATCHER, Philadelphia, Pennsylvania, USA, 2019

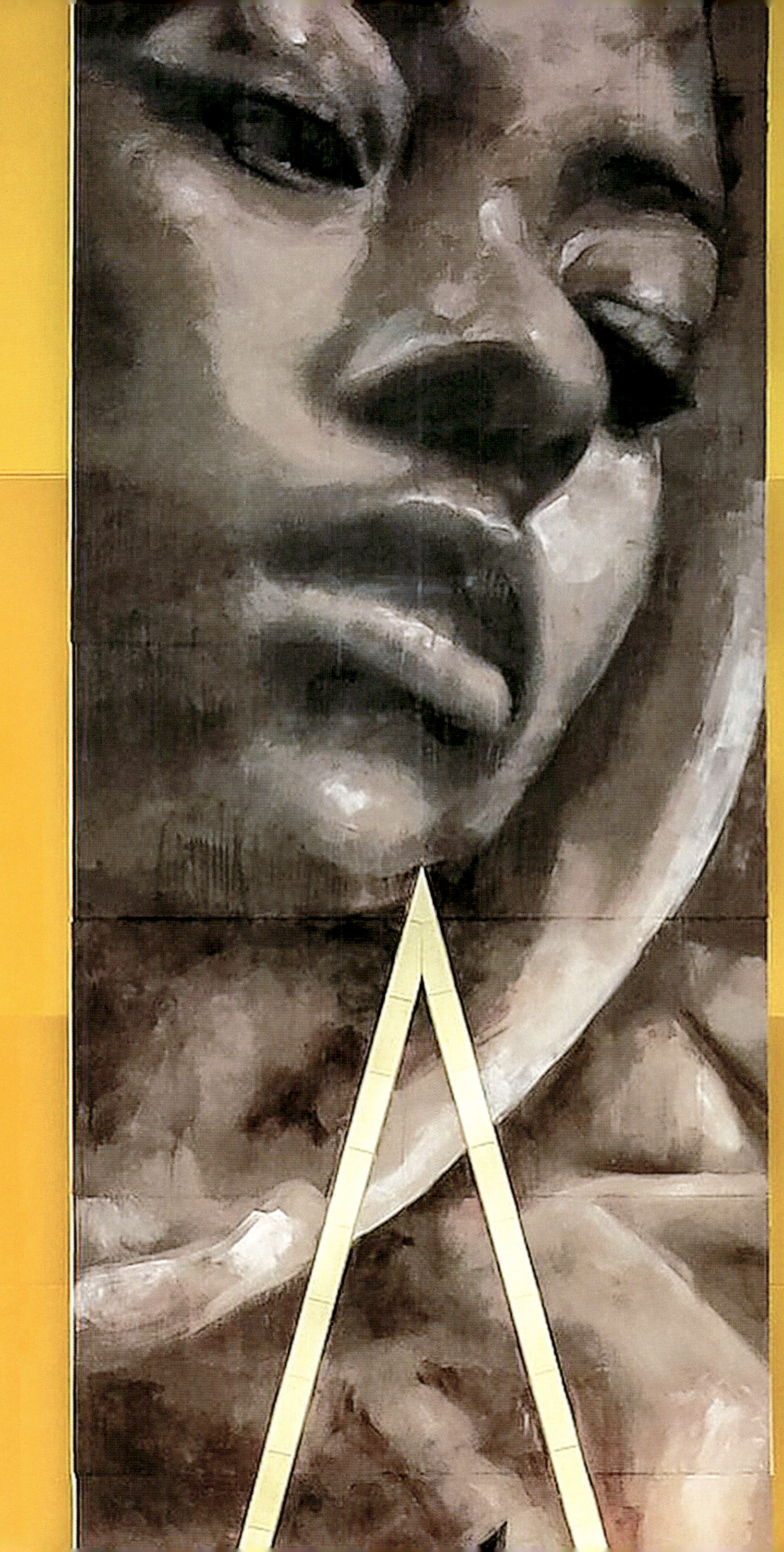

CAMILLA FALSINI

THE WOMAN WHO LOVES SIMPLE SHAPES AND COLOR

"I haven't suffered discrimination in the world of art, but, unfortunately, what happens in society at large occurs here too, since women earn less and are less present. What's more, when a woman creates a work, the fact that it's done by a woman is underscored, whereas this is not the case for men."

"Every artist has a preferred color palette," says Camilla Falsini. "Choice of color is definitely highly personal. I use colors that attract and envelop the viewer with their intensity. Red or yellow, for example. I've never been interested in pastels. I think there were books that appealed to me when I was a child, especially one by Gianni Rodari, illustrated by Bruno Munari entirely in very simple, essential red, green, and black forms."

"Next, I think of Altan's figures, like his dog, Pimpa, with its red polka dots," she admits. Born and raised in Rome, she stands out for her use of minimal and stylized forms, her clear lines, bright colors, and unique characters—some monster-like, others feline. "I've always liked drawing cats and tigers," she notes.

Camilla also does a lot of work as an illustrator: "My childhood was full of images of art—in illustrated books, magazines (such as *L'illustrazione Italiana* and *L'illustrazione dei piccoli*), and exhibition posters, like those by Picasso or Matisse, whom I admire tremendously, and Magritte and Kandinsky. I was constantly surrounded by visual stimuli, and this had an indelible effect on me," she relates.

Camilla wanted to attend an art-oriented high school, but her parents steered her toward a classical lyceum, after which she earned a diploma in illustration at Rome's IED.

She started making murals around 2007. "I grew up in the '90s. I was a little girl in a Rome invaded by graffiti: I saw it on the walls of the social centers where I was hanging out at the time, or in subway stations or trains. I began painting the walls in the company of an artists' collective called Serpe in Seno, then moved on to doing large walls on my own. I was drawing anything and everything, and I found combining technique and color amazing," she says.

PORTRAIT, Rimini, Italy, 2018

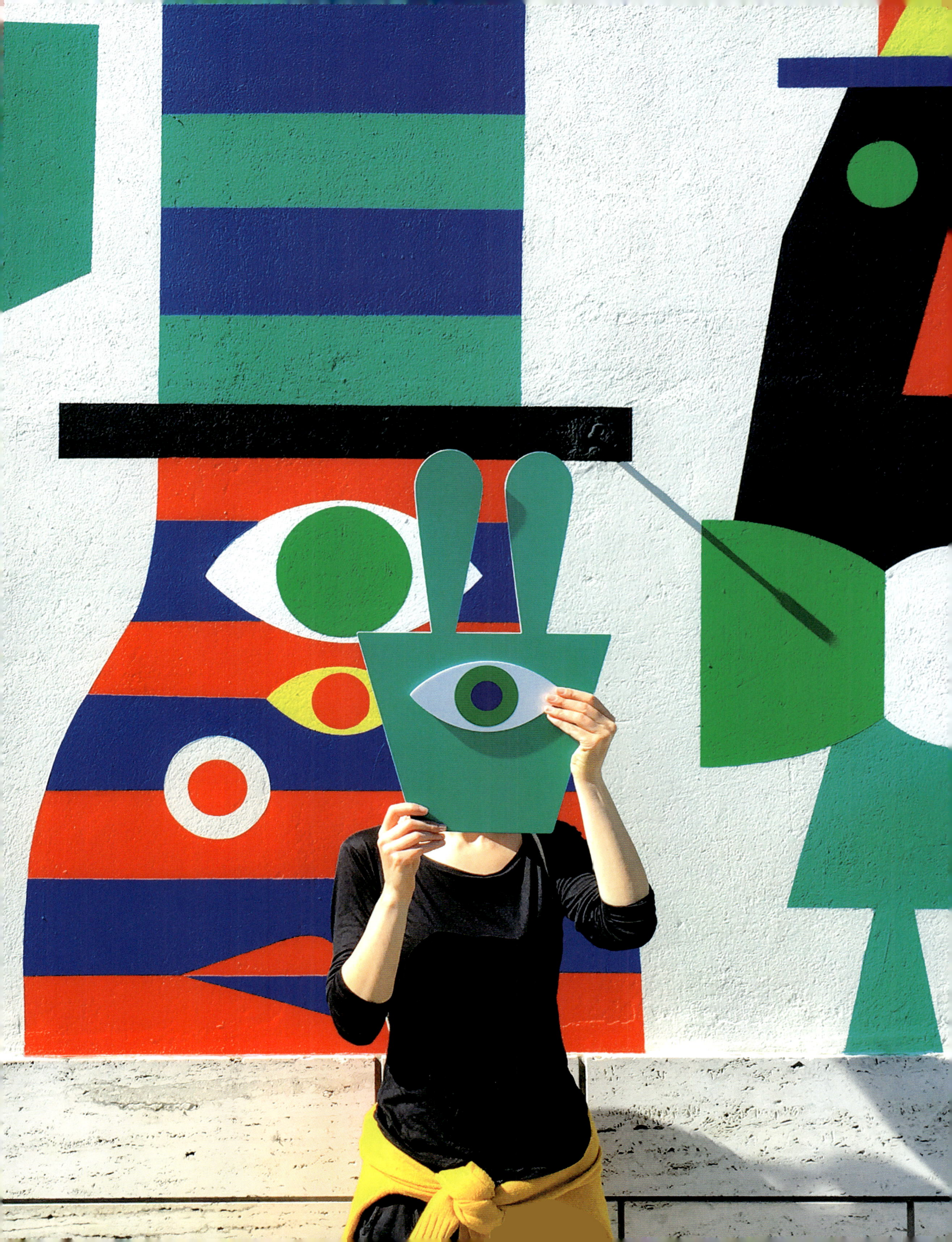

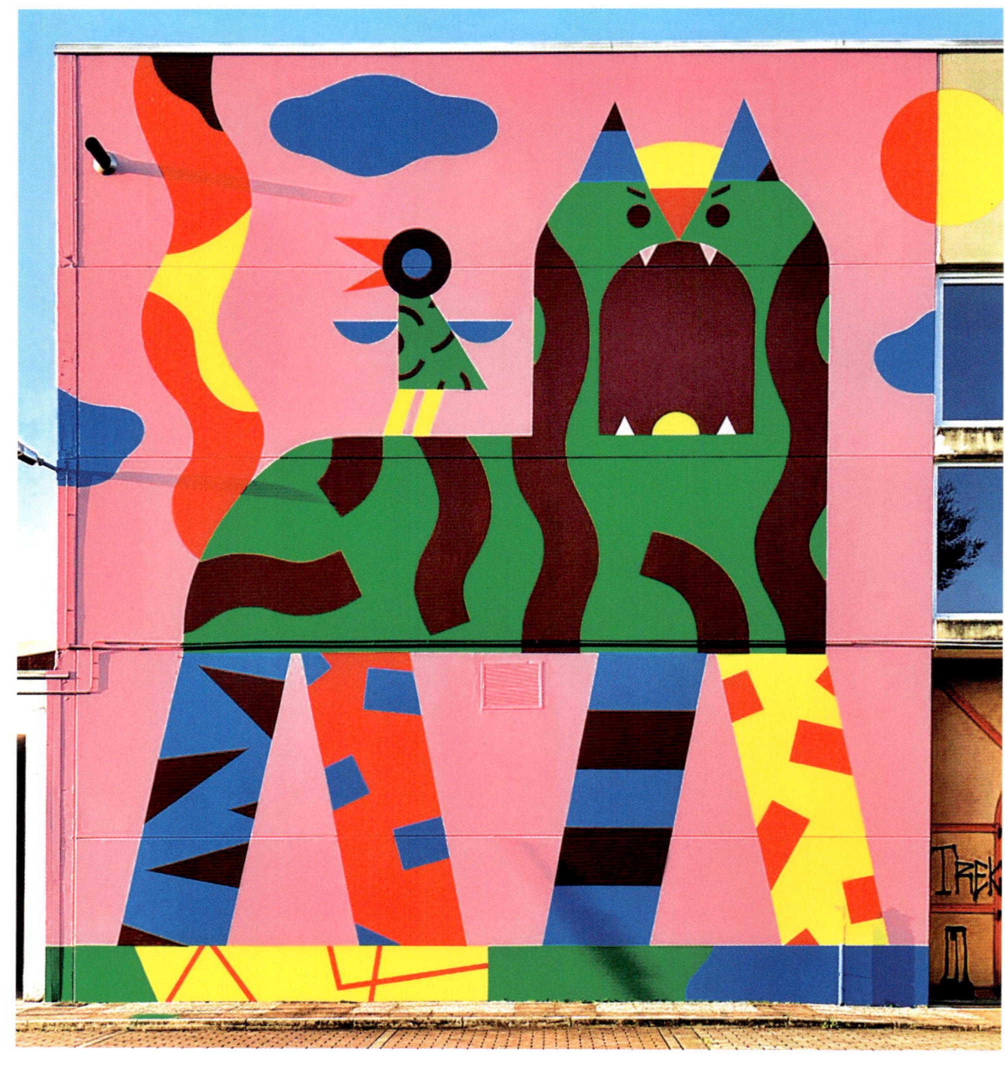

"Today, I work a lot for publishing houses, companies, agencies, public entities and organizations, but it was tough in the beginning. I certainly prefer painting characters and creatures in landscapes, but I have no particular vision. I don't think of art as something sacred, rather, I think more of a kind of applied art that is deeply rooted and embedded in day-to-day life. I don't feel as though I have to teach anything with my art, but rather communicate a message related to a project, or create something for the viewer that is beautiful or moving," she explains. "I want my art to make sense out of things. I like dealing with a text, a product, an idea, and not the inspiration that I wake up to in the morning. In addition, my style is minimal and simple, often surreal, but descriptive, and I leave its interpretation up to the viewer. The images are not didactic, and I hope people will see things in them capable of evoking a memory or arousing an emotion," she adds.

FOR IMMAGINARIA, Modena, Italy, 2021, Photo Sergio Silvestri
FOR ZALANDO, GAY PRIDE, Milan, Italy, 2021, Photo Artkademy (right)

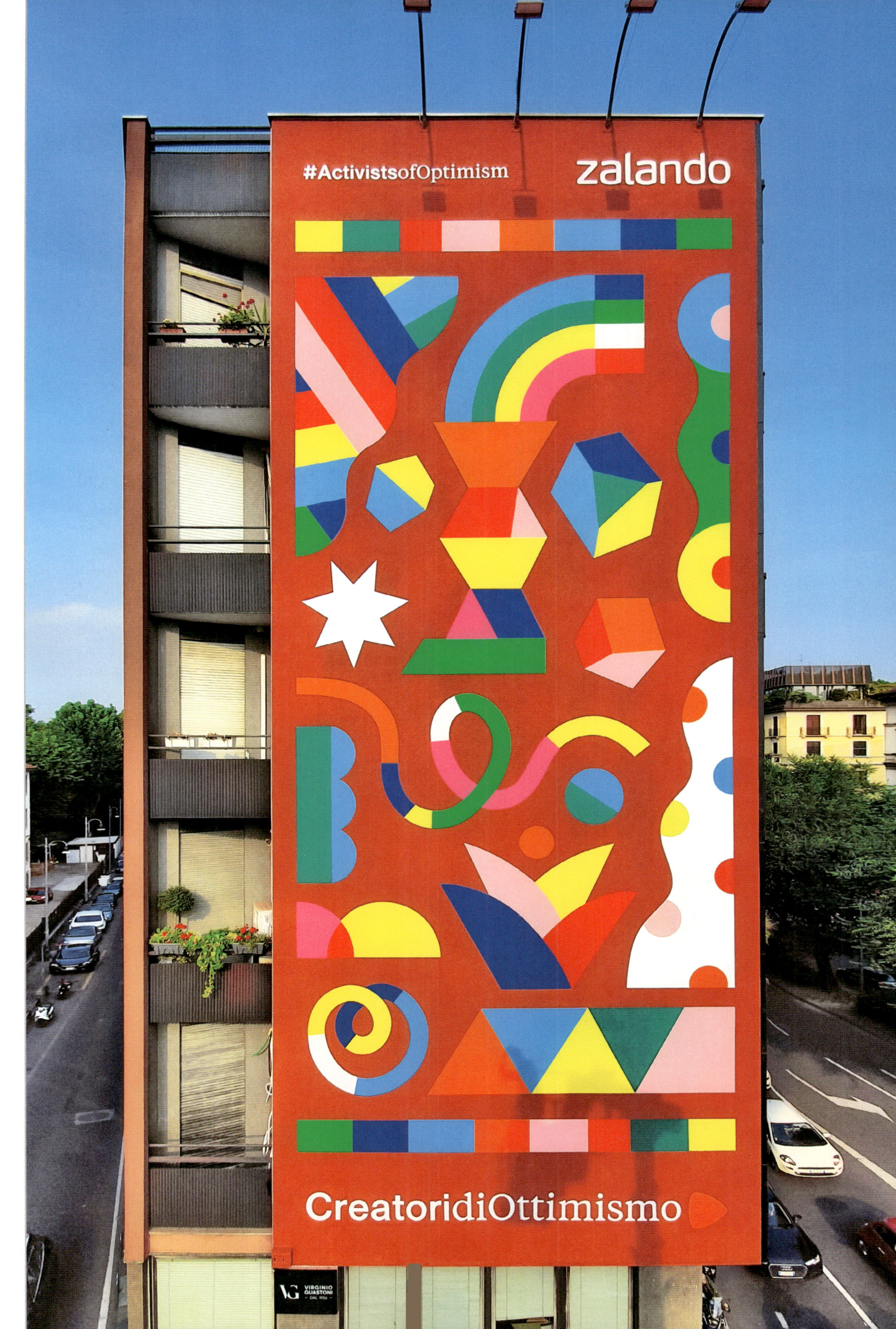
#ActivistsofOptimism
zalando
CreatoridiOttimismo
VIRGINIO GUASTONI
DAL 1956

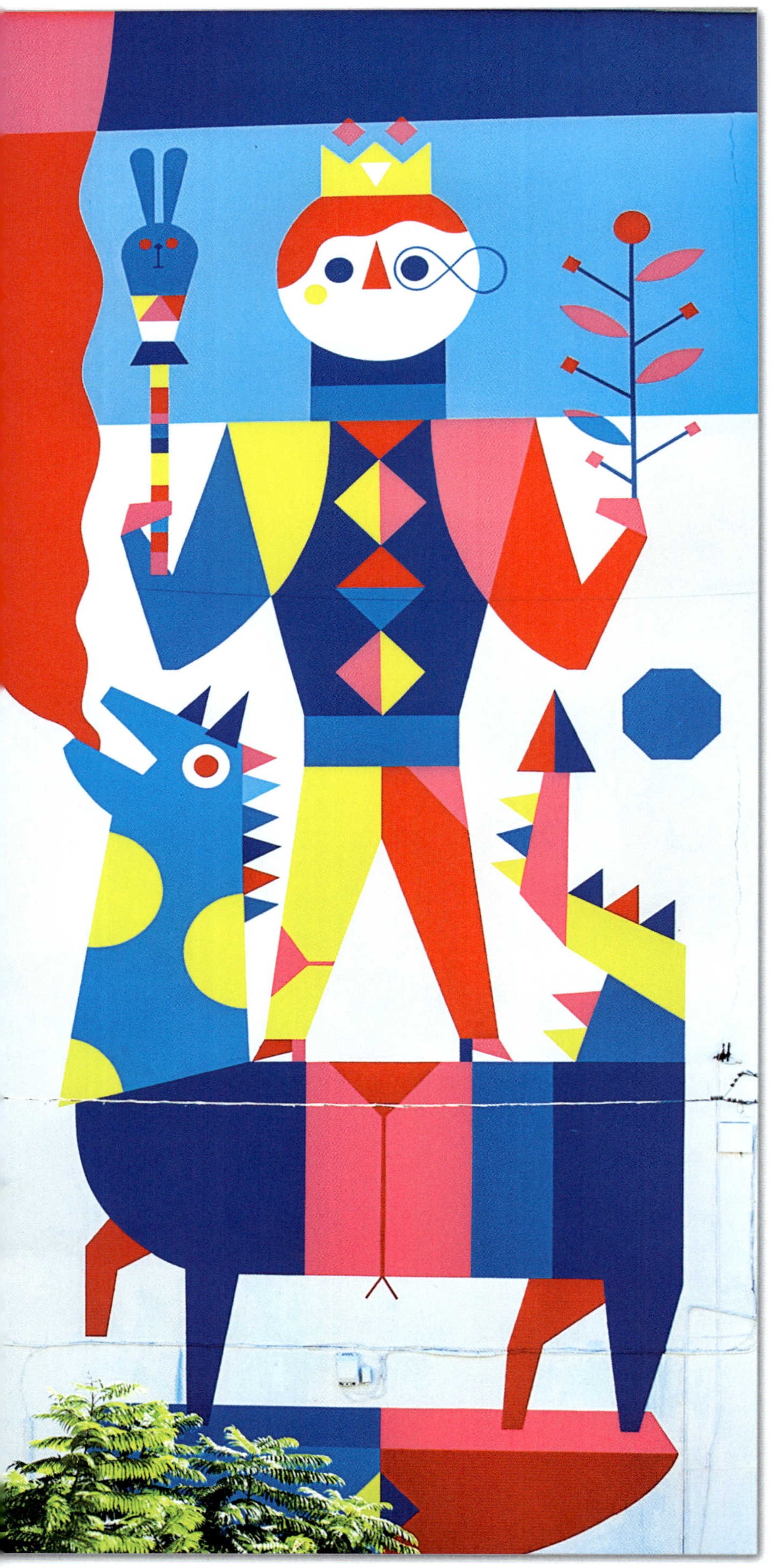

Camilla believes her inspiration comes from the millions of things that she has seen and continues to see: an exhibition, a book, a person—a bunch of different influences. "Street art came to me spontaneously, without questions. I love its public-art dimension, the fact that one creates a work that is then offered at no cost for all to see. I think it's definitely better than ads and has a special place in the community," she claims. "But I do not like to think of it as a solution to the problems that exist in many cities and neighborhoods, because it's not."

As an artist she likes to interpret a vision, and a work that left a deep impression on her was one promoted by Lavazza, *TOward 2030*, in which a select group of street artists was entrusted with the task of interpreting and representing the United Nations' Sustainable Development Goals. "They asked me, as a woman, to portray gender equality. Christine de Pizan (born 1364), the first professional female author and one of the first feminists in history, immediately came to mind.

"As a woman, I haven't suffered any particular discrimination, but it still bothers me that when a woman has a successful career, especially in professions that were previously occupied solely by men, she's often asked how she reconciles work and family. A man is never asked these questions, and now is the time to change society's view of the role women play," she maintains.

NICO, Manifesta 12, Palermo, Italy, 2018, Photo Rori Palazzo and Sonia Lo Nero

CHRISTINE DE PIZAN, project by Lavazza, Torino, Italy, 2018, Photo Lavazza (right)

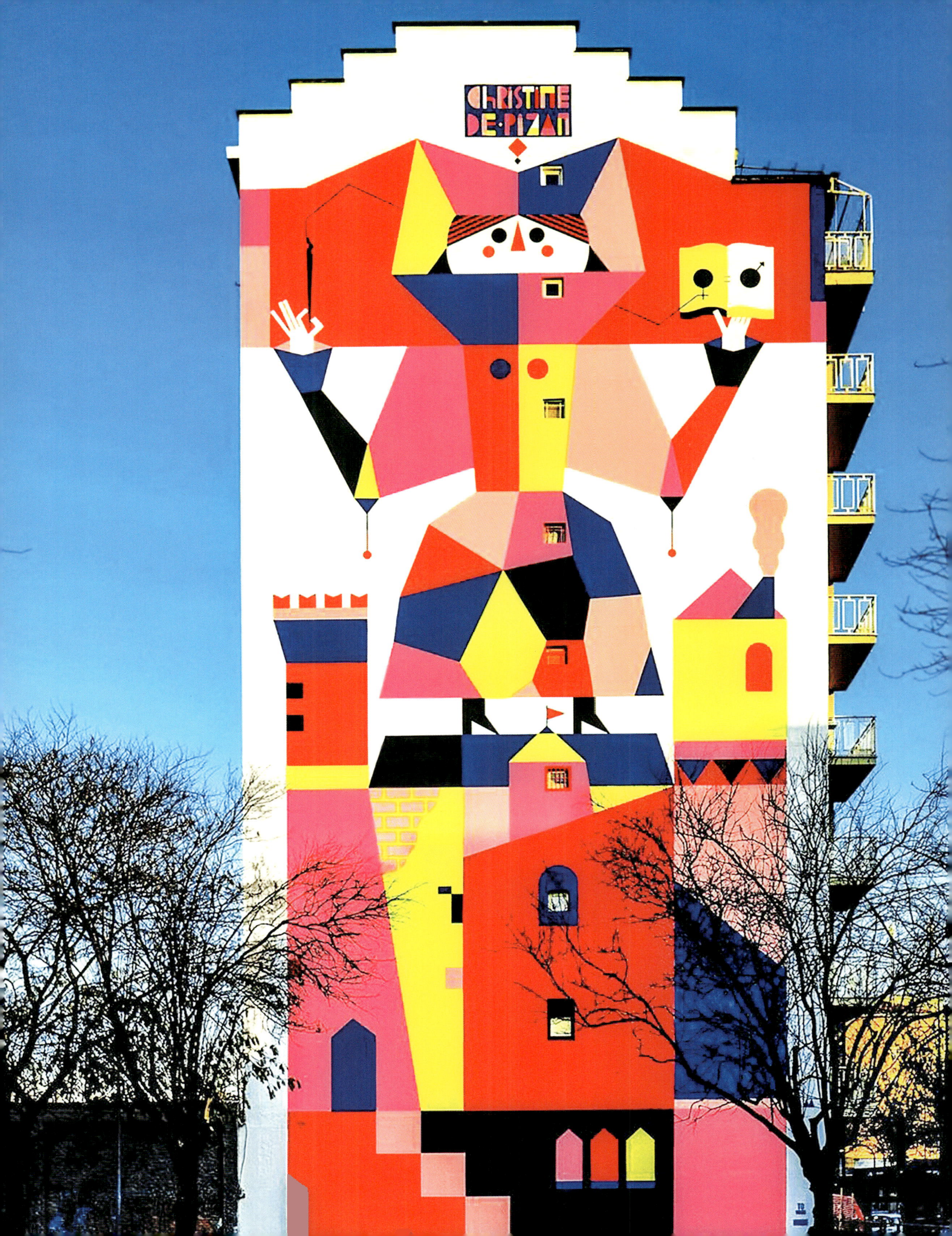
CHRISTINE
DE·PIZAN

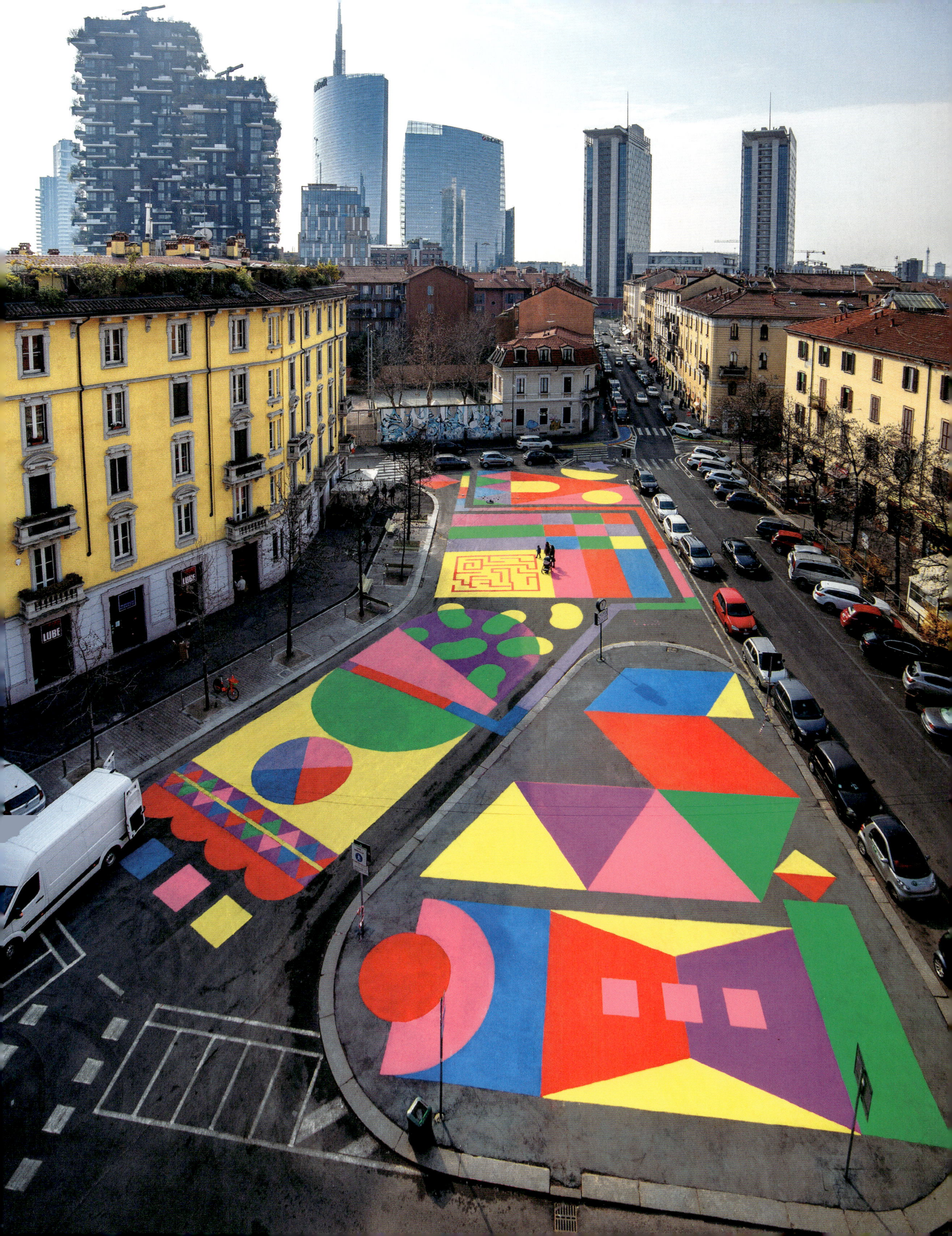

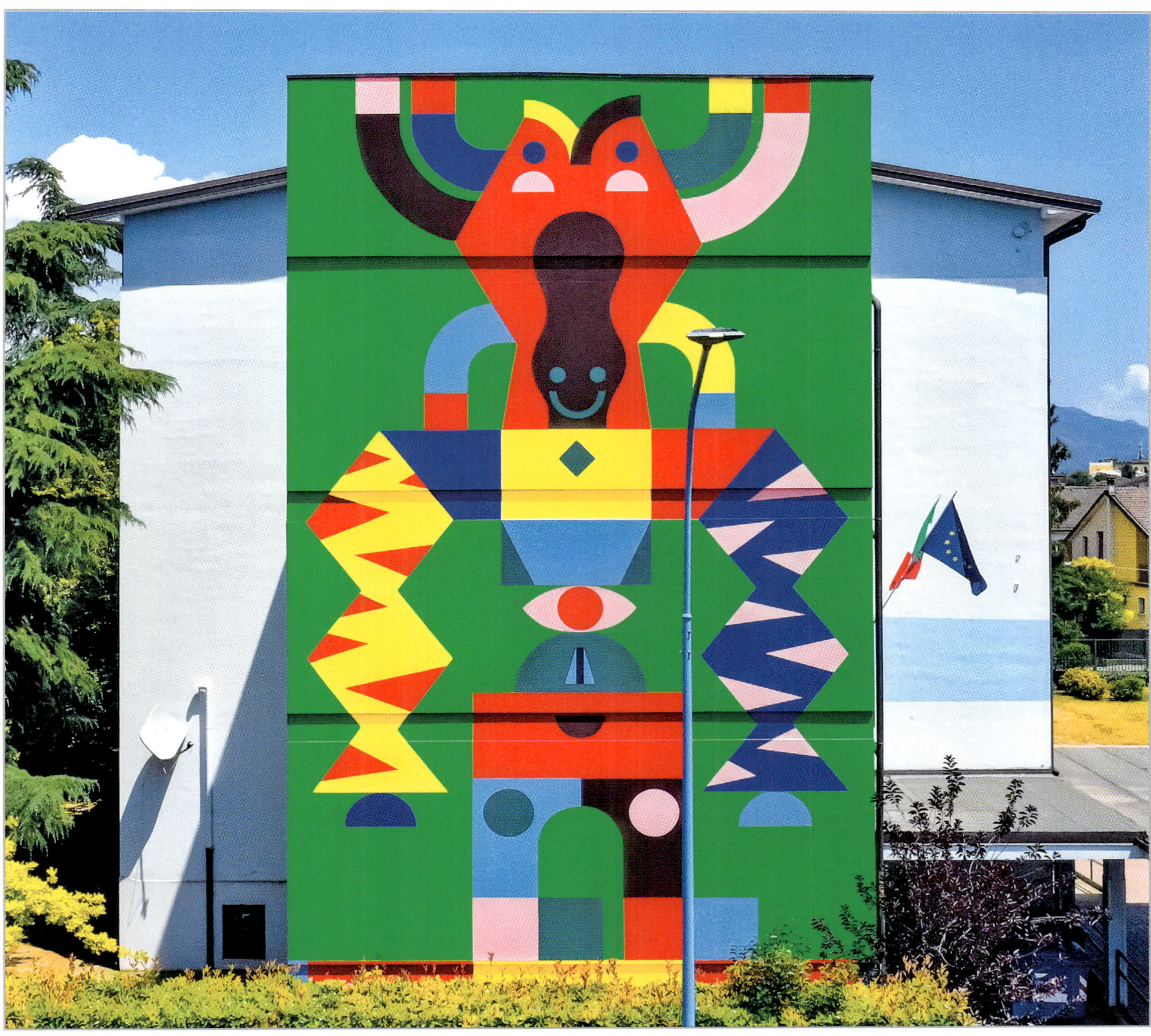

Camilla always likes exploring new ways of doing street art. In 2021, for example, she took part in Piazze Aperte, an urban redevelopment program promoted by the Municipality of Milan in collaboration with the Jungle agency. "The project involved a change in the 'look' of two squares in the Lombard capital: Piazzale Loreto and Piazza Tito Minniti.

"It was fun to fill them with deep, bright colors and a kaleidoscopic effect, especially when seen from above," she notes.

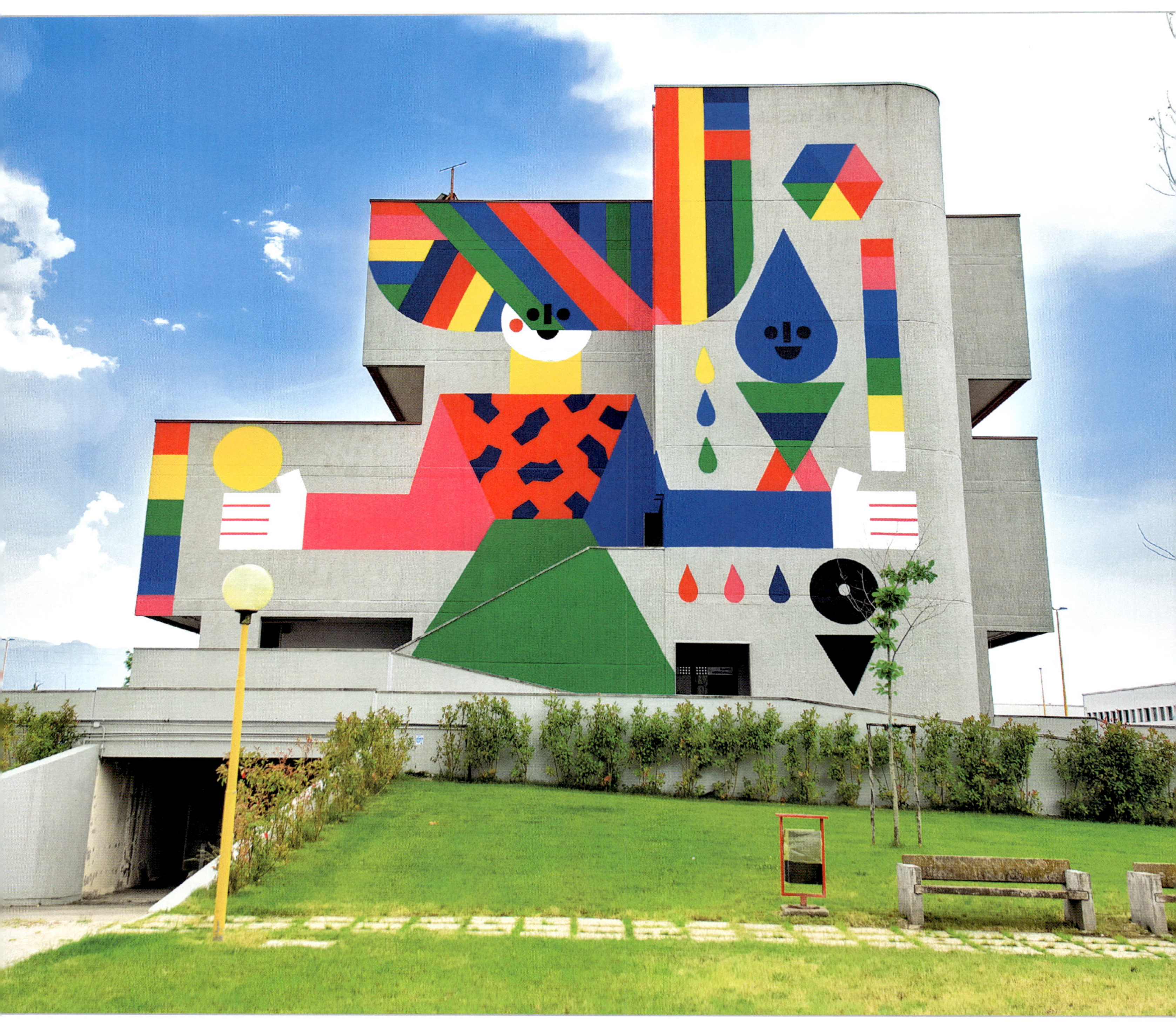

In the future, Camilla plans to direct her art eastward as well. "I will soon be collaborating with Korea and am fascinated by Asia. I'm interested in cultures that are very distant and different from my own. I would like to spend some time exploring something unknown in order to develop my art further and grow on a personal level," she concludes.

LUCE + ACQUA, Naples, Italy, 2021, Photo Bereshit
LOVE, Fidenza Village, Fidenza, Italy, 2019 (right)

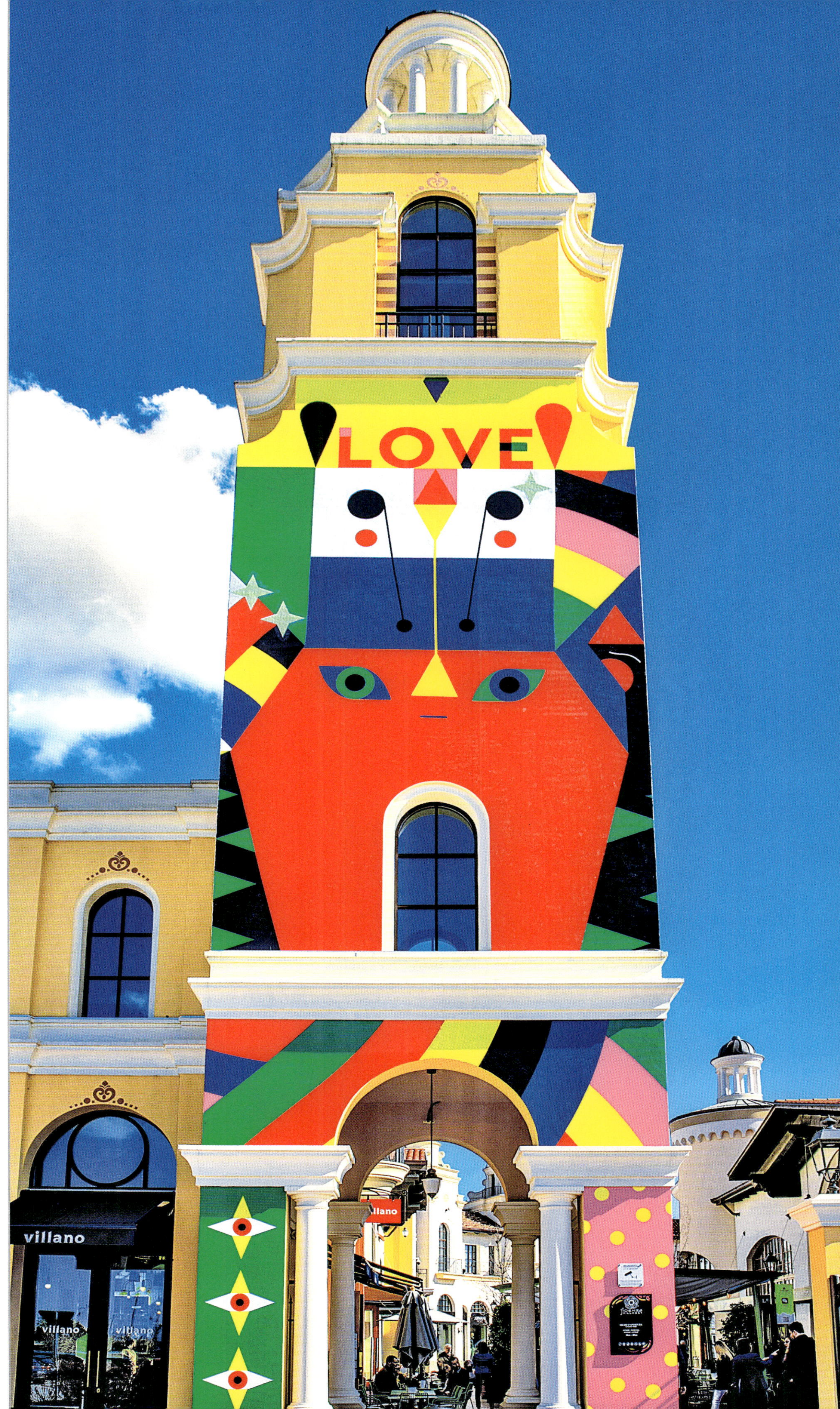
LOVE
villano

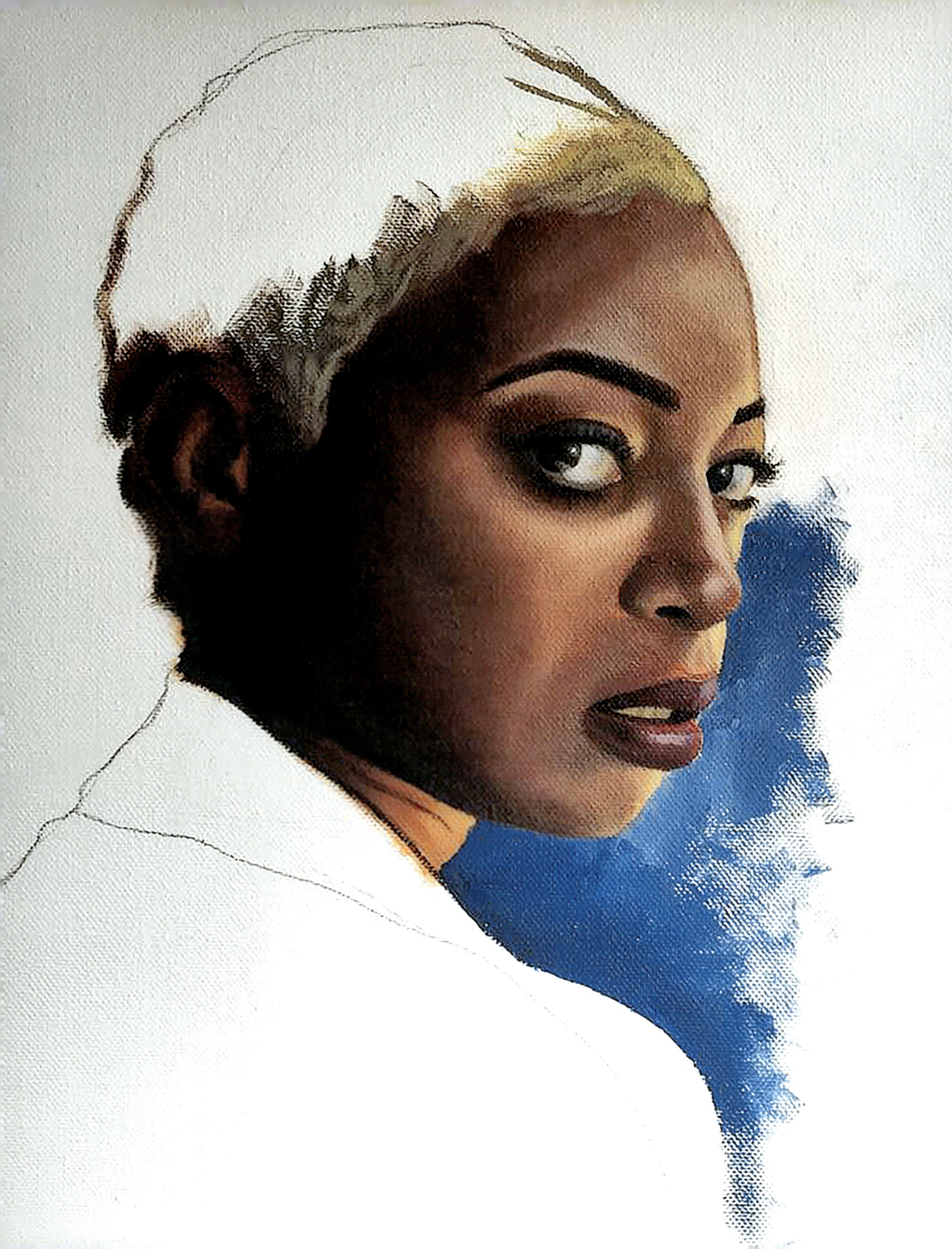

TATYANA FAZLALIZADEH

THE REVOLUTIONARY STRUGGLE FOR THE RIGHTS OF AFRICAN AMERICAN WOMEN AND ALL GENDERS

"Being Black, being a woman, being queer—for me, this is very important, as is the right for the identities of all genders to be heard."

"America is Black, She's a native. She wears a hijab. She is Spanish-speaking. She's a migrant. She's a woman. She's been here. And she's not going anywhere," Tatyana Fazlalizadeh proclaimed when responding to the 2016 US presidential elections. And it's here that her mindset is encapsulated. Her portraits tell stories. The eyes of her characters express the strength of simply being themselves, in all their intensity. Heroic figures, rendered with powerful realism, they project from the walls victorious. More often than not, they are images of African American women, still underrepresented in the universe of street art. Like them, Tatyana is astonishing and magnificent, with passion in her eyes, the temperament of a hero, with a voice that expresses courage, a soul that emanates rebelliousness and resilience, and an irrepressible desire that drives her will to change the world. She rose to distinction with her Stop Telling Women to Smile campaign, in which she tackled the difficult issue of gender-based street harassment. The project assumed the form of a series of posters portraying women whom Tatyana had met and who had spoken to her about their dramatic experiences with abuse, intolerance, and violence. The campaign started in Brooklyn in the fall of 2012, and from there embarked on a long journey around the world, resulting in hundreds of posters condemning harassment and making people reflect on the works pasted on walls and in public spaces.

"My goal, first and foremost, is to tell stories. I like to combine images and texts. This is why I have specialized in portraits of people whom I have personally interviewed so that I am well acquainted with them before I depict them. The black-and-white posters attracted lots of attention, so, over time, I decided to broaden the range of people with whom I meet and also portray queer and transgender ones of various nationalities, cultures, and backgrounds, in order to represent more experiences and be able to offer an even more authentic panorama," she notes.

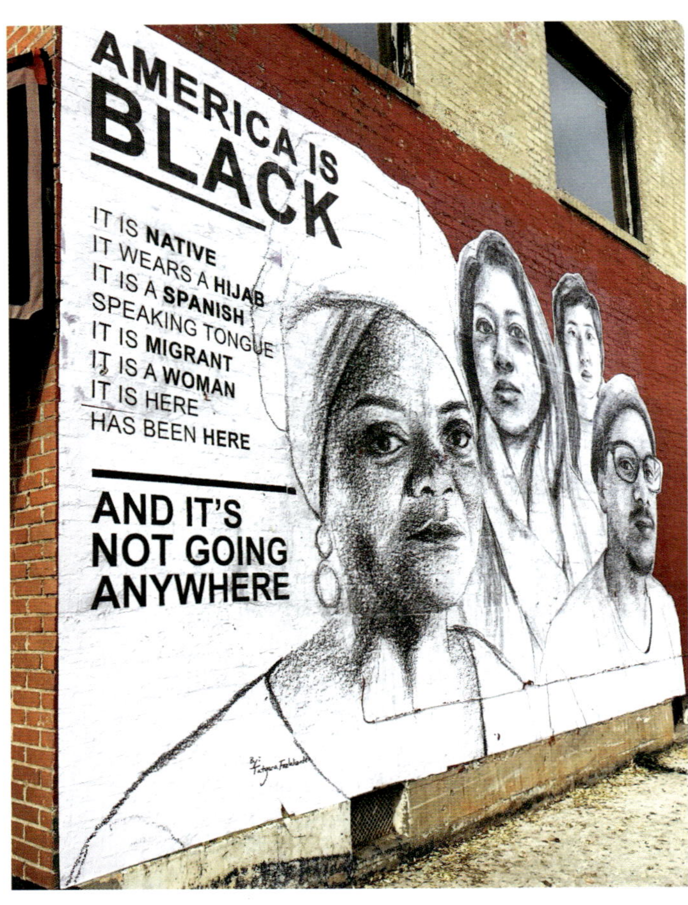

Oklahoma City, Oklahoma, USA, 2016

STOP TELLING WOMEN TO SMILE, 2012 (right)

But her mission is constantly evolving and growing: "I want my art to make people understand how individuals live in the world. I want those who see my work to be able to identify with what I portray. I want them to understand how, in their day-to-day life, they themselves can be victims of bullying and oppression. My hope is that in the world of the near future, women as well as people in general will be able to walk the streets without fear and without risking harassment and humiliation," she states emphatically.

"I wanted to give a voice above all to those who, until now, have never been able to make themselves heard, and also tell their stories on the walls of cities. These are African American but also many other women, who have long been represented more for their looks than for their merits. My women are real, with weaknesses, fears, but also with strength and the firm will to stop violence and bullying. That's why they don't smile, but look you straight in the eye," she adds.

Tatyana is convinced that the #MeToo movement has had a very important impact on the history of feminism: "Women now know that they have a platform from which they can make their voices and experiences heard, where they can say, 'Yes, that also happened to me.' For years, they lacked the courage to speak up, or could not do so, knowing full well that no one would believe the charges they made."

Similarly, she sees the Black Lives Matter movement, which she has dealt with in several of her works, as a revolutionary event: "Social justice is becoming an increasingly topical issue as the road to resolving this aberration is still long and difficult. The United States, in particular, is experiencing the tragedy of racism and discrimination; sexism is still deeply rooted here, and, unfortunately, it's a bit like this all over the world. This is why protests and the demand for vindication are fundamental to the attainment of equality. They're also a great inspiration for art in general, whether in the form of literature, film, or street art. They goad people to change their way of thinking, encourage them to voice their frustration and discontent, and to denounce anything that is unfair or does not work as it ought to."

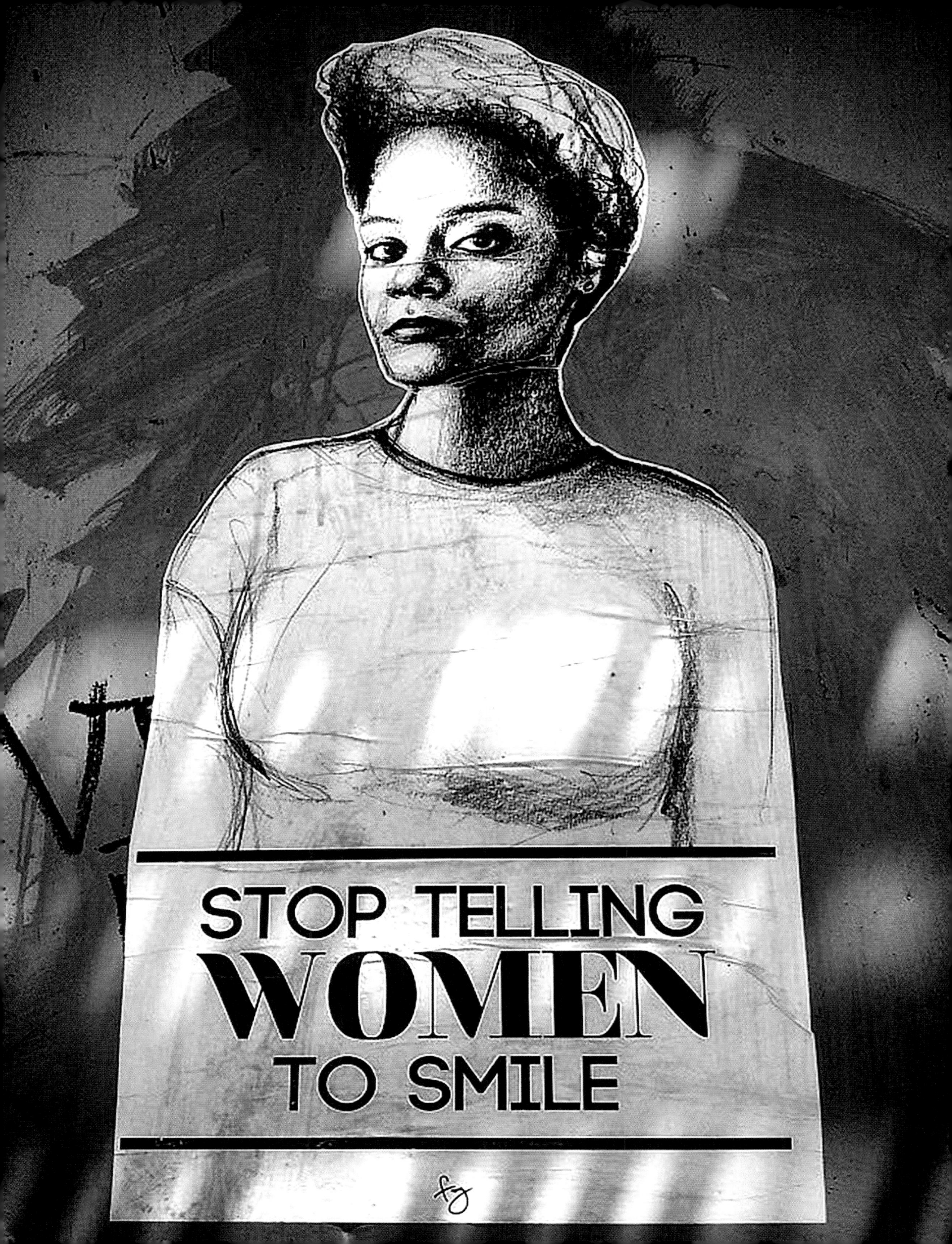

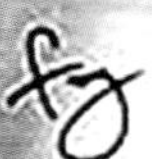

STOP TELLING
WOMEN
TO SMILE

Tatyana has been a diehard activist since her youth. Of African American and Iranian descent, she was born and raised in Oklahoma City, Oklahoma, a deeply conservative state. She later moved to Philadelphia to study Fine Arts at the University of the Arts. "My mother was an art teacher and had an incredible influence on me. Art already fascinated me when I was a child, but back then I couldn't imagine it ever becoming my profession. I only realized this when I was in art school and started going to museums and galleries. My interest immediately turned to public art. I was fascinated above all by its ability to touch the community directly and influence and engage viewers. I started doing it between the age of seventeen and eighteen, even though I was focusing mainly on oil and canvas paintings at school. There are no limits to spreading a message down a street or in public spaces: I soon understood this and was profoundly affected by it," she recalls.

Working on the street is not easy, especially for a woman, and Tatyana has gotten a direct taste of this on several occasions. "I was black, and I was a woman. And I was queer. The harassment was often sexual and verbal. Since it was intolerable, I decided to reveal all this on the walls of the city so that it would not remain hidden or ignored. When I began putting up the first posters, the reaction of other women, who had suffered the same humiliation, was incredible—not only in the United States, but all over the world. And this allowed me to extend the boundaries of my campaign," she says, reflectively.

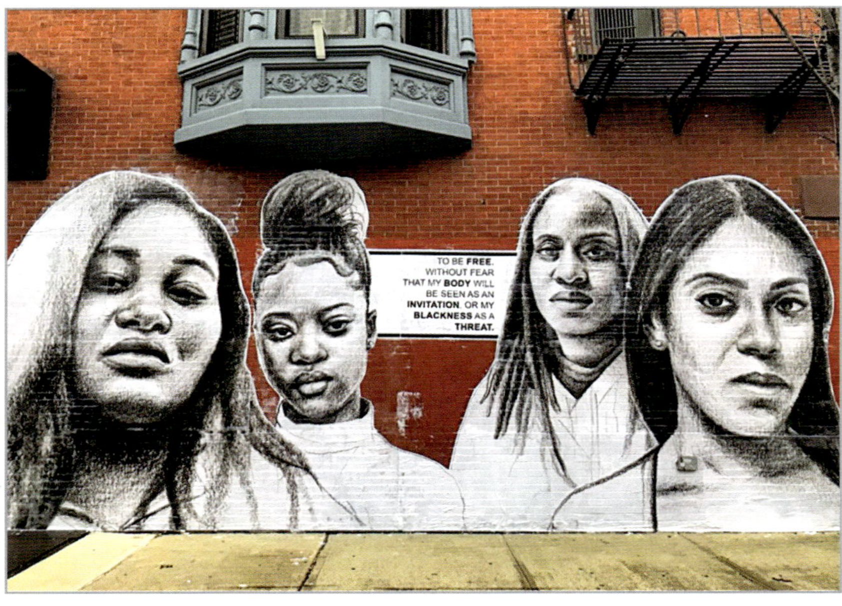

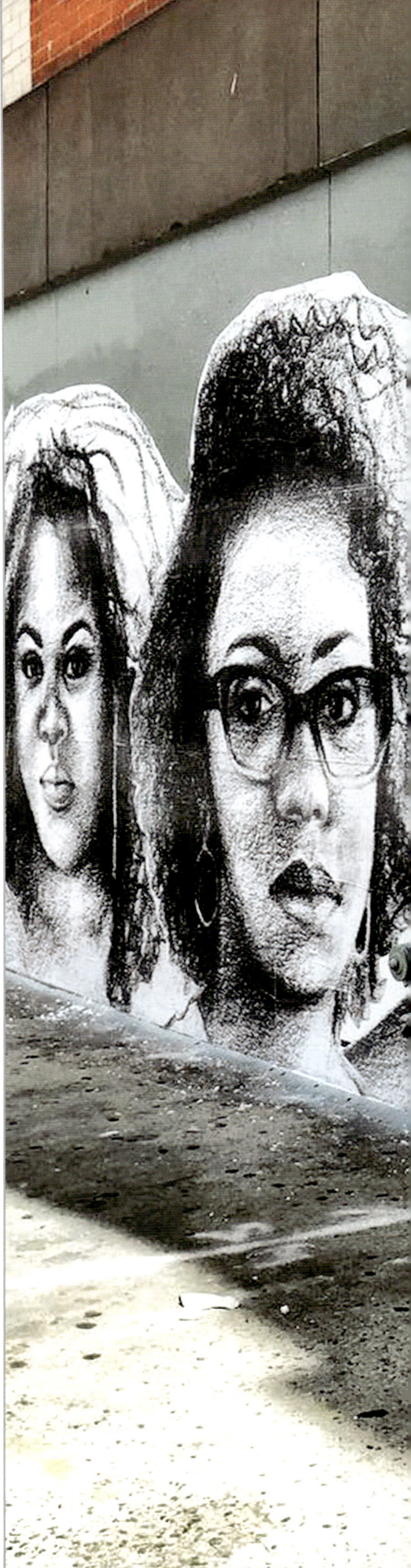

Oklahoma City, Oklahoma, USA, 2016

New York City, New York, USA, 2015 (right)

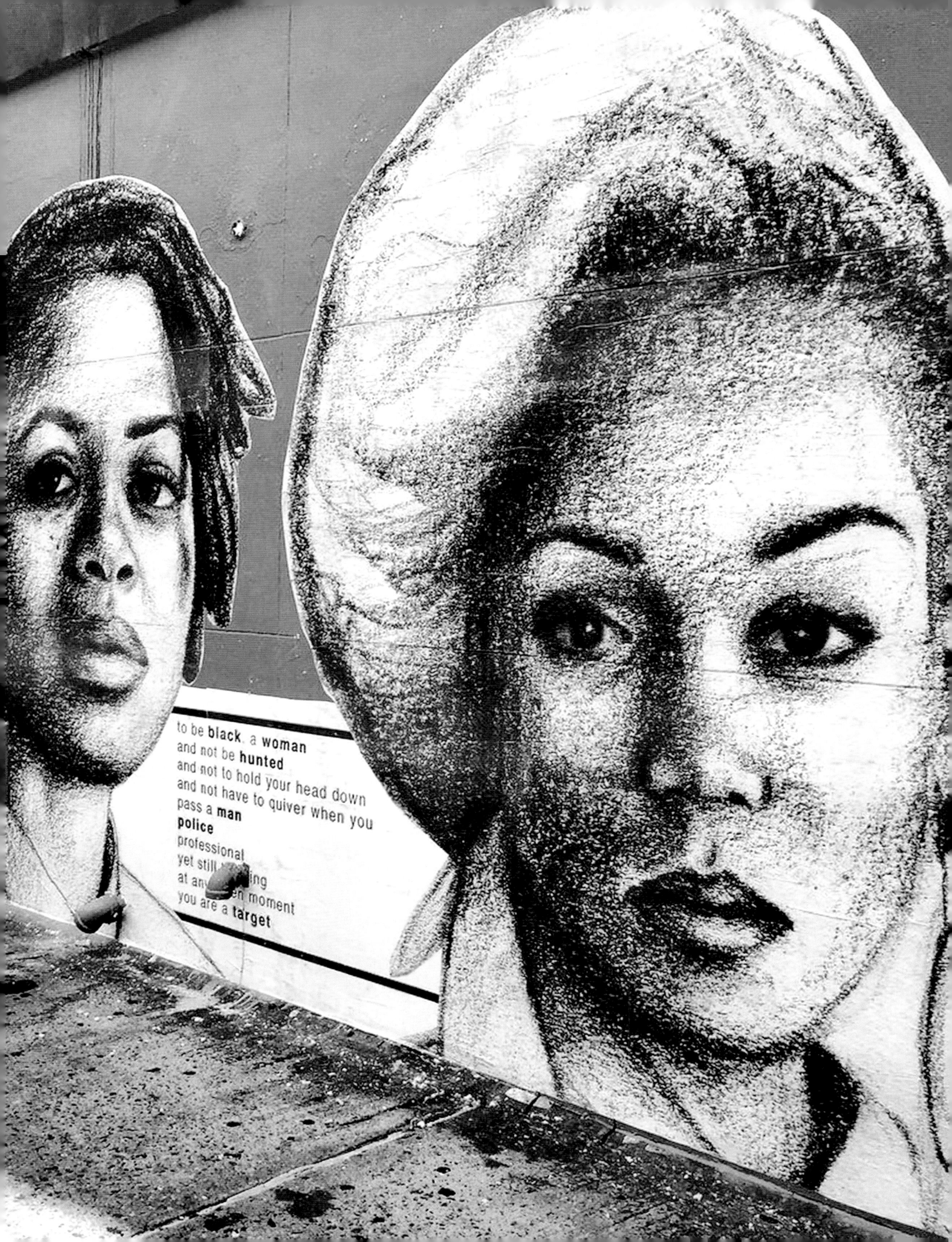

to be black, a woman
and not be hunted
and not to hold your head down
and not have to quiver when you
pass a man
police
professional
yet still trembling
at any given moment
you are a target

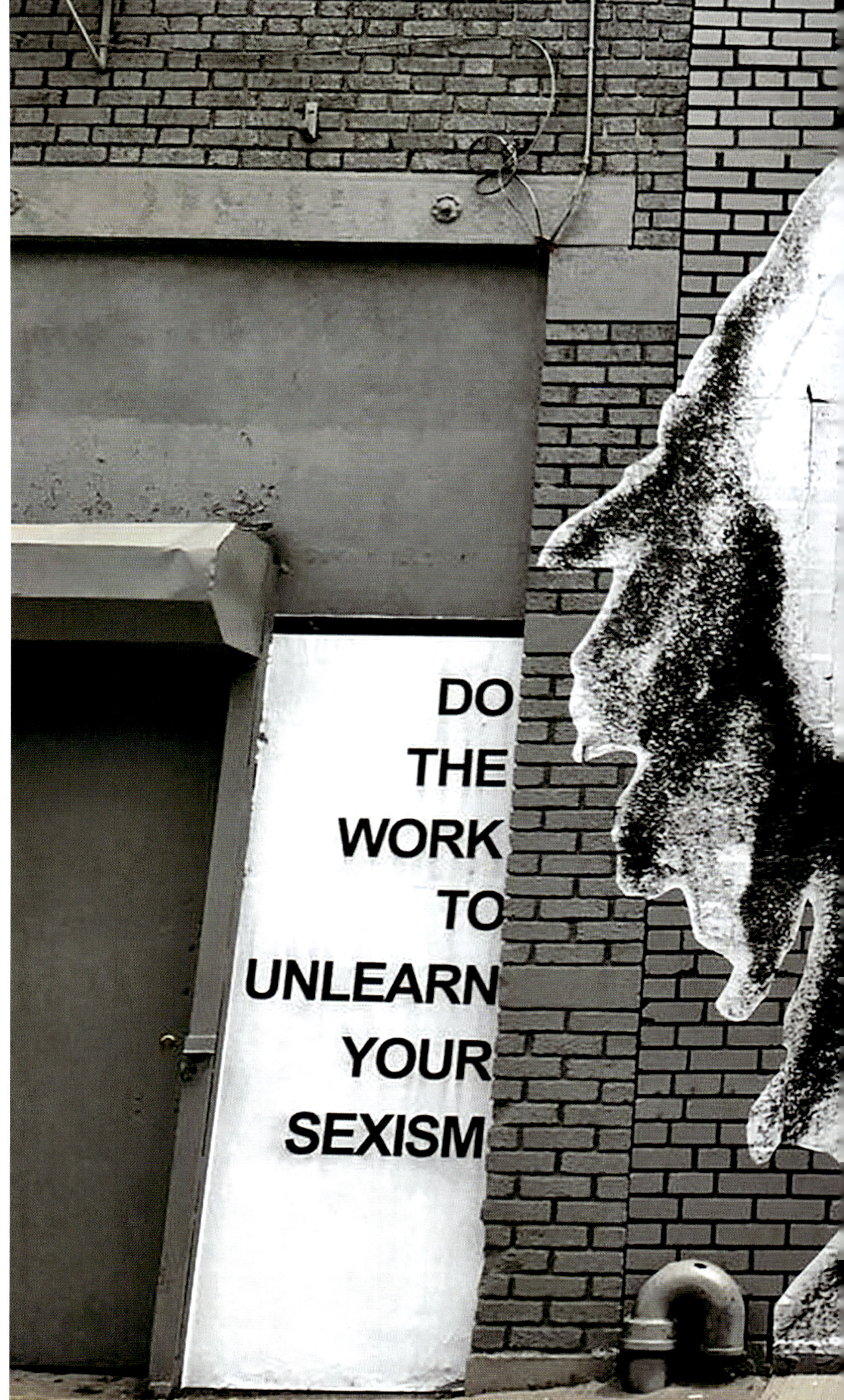

Brooklyn, New York City, New York, USA, 2017

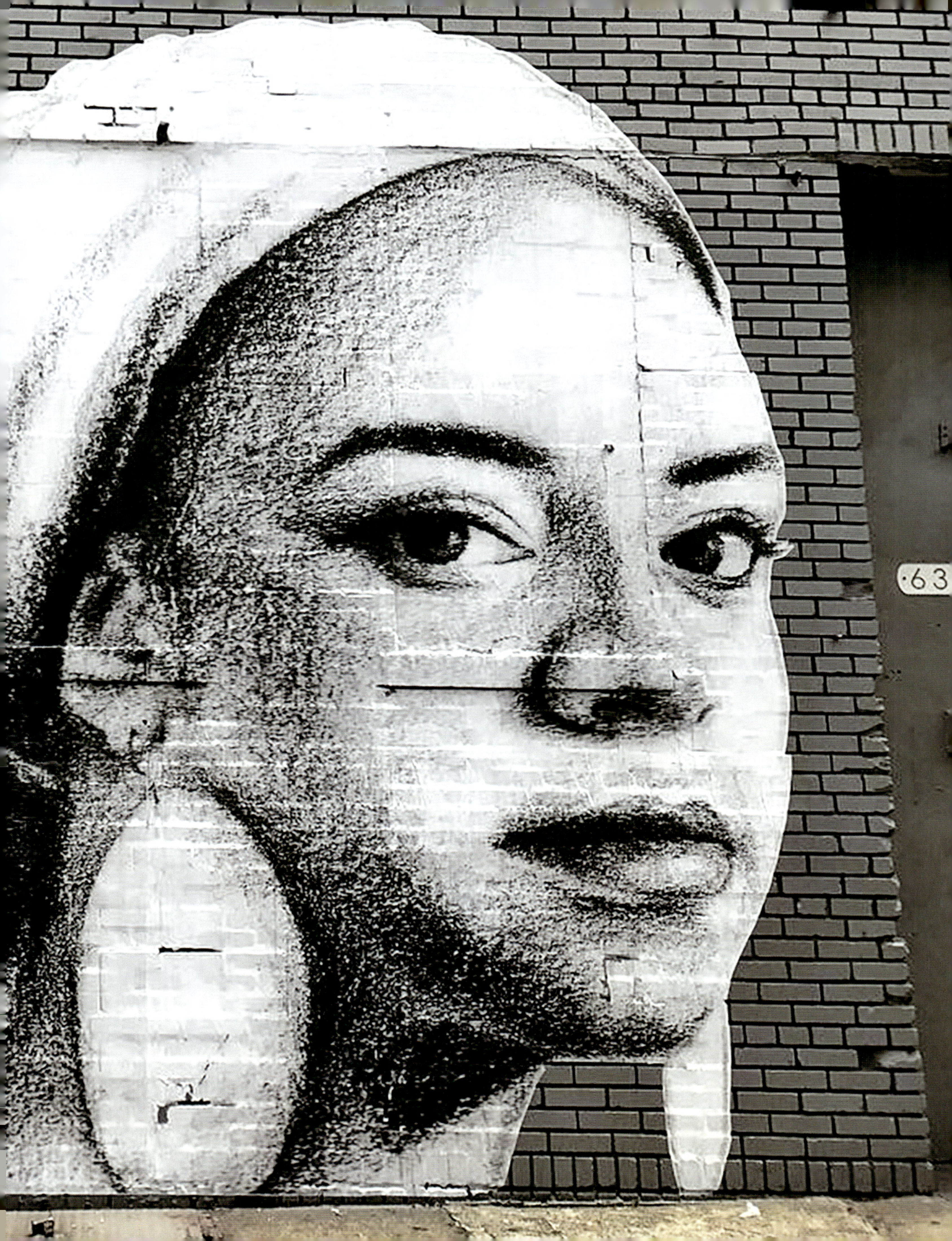
·63

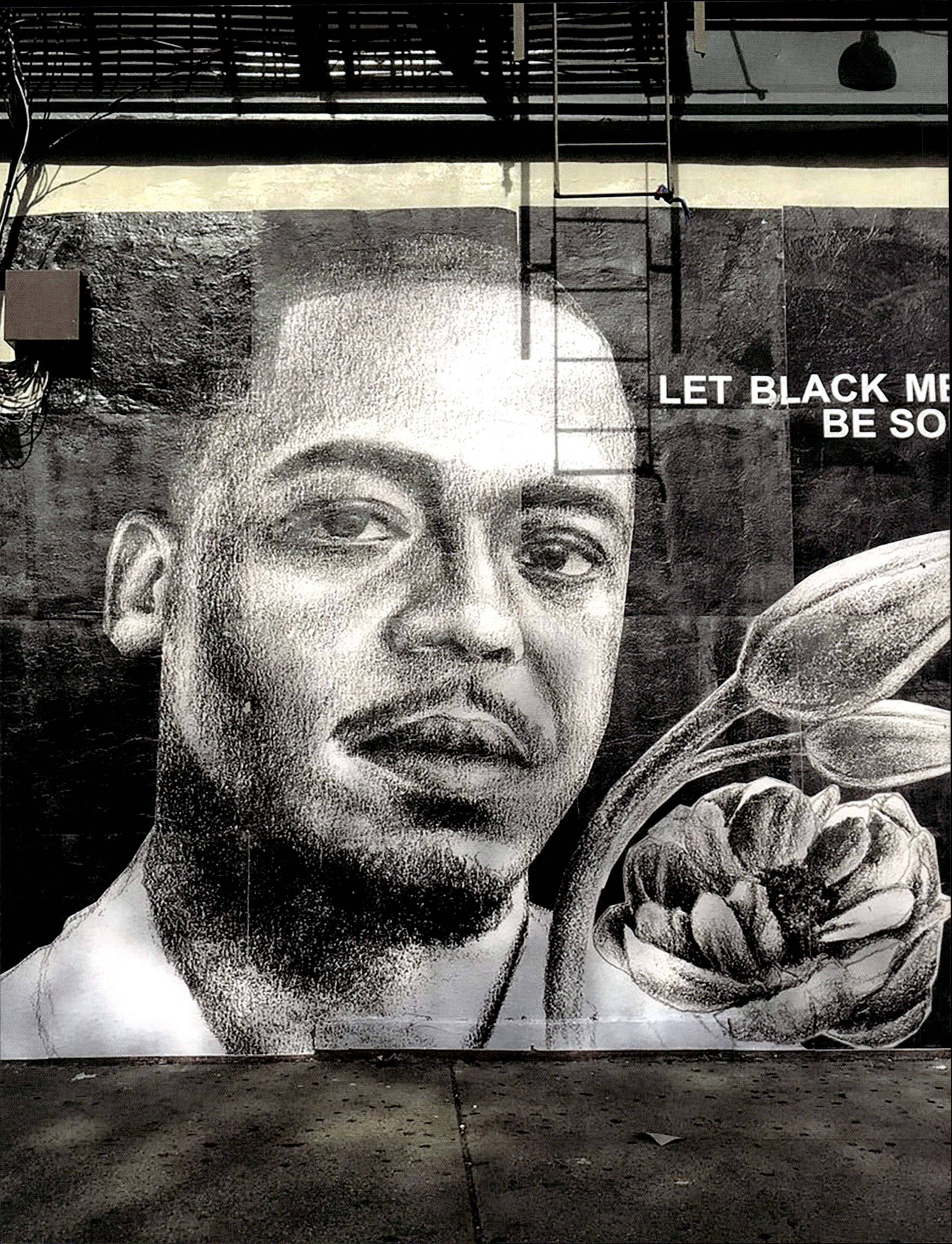
LET BLACK ME
BE SO

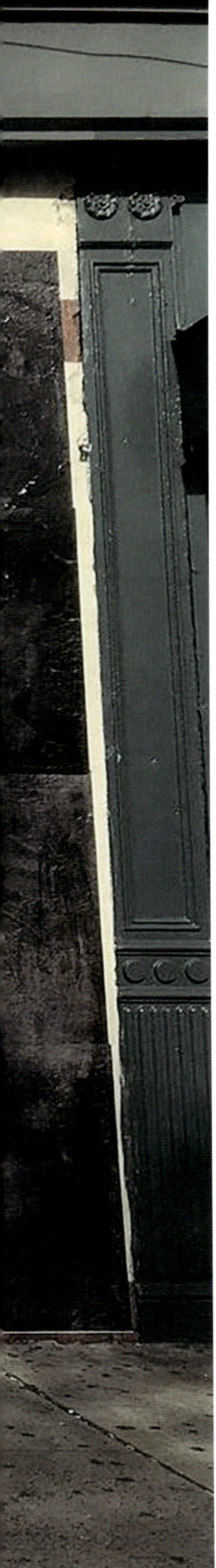

"The constant and unjustified discriminatory attitude toward me has made me even stronger and more determined to devote myself to art and employ it as an instrument of activism and social responsibility. Back then, the world of art was dominated primarily by white men, who had more opportunities and were held in greater regard; but I didn't let myself be discouraged and I was able to come up with my own style and distinguish myself from everybody else. I worked hard; it was a really intense challenge, but I'm really proud that I made it, which is why I want to encourage other women to do the same."

Tatyana is actually quite positive about the future. "I am sure that feminist movements, like those struggling for equal rights, will continue to fight for everyone, indiscriminately. The individuals most vulnerable today will be granted greater protection, and we'll finally see the triumph of some of the principles for which we have fought. Separatism will begin to disappear, as those who have wronged and harassed others will be forced to account for their actions. Things are changing, albeit still slowly; but if I think back ten or fifteen years, I realize how far we've come," she says with conviction.

New York is a city that continues to inspire and drive her in her mission. "I've wanted to come here since I was quite young, because it's the best place to pursue a career in the arts and meet other artists with whom to share experiences. I believe there's room for everyone in New York, and that everyone here can be whatever they really want to be. That's not to say that there are no problems or inequities, but in New York you can make your voice heard," she points out.

Music is extremely important, a constant source of inspiration for Tatyana. "I'm fascinated by how music is able to express ideas and feelings, how it can harmonize perfectly with art. It inspires me in my work. I especially love Black music, jazz, R&B, hip hop; my preferences change according to my soul's emotional state," she says.

Tatyana loves to experiment and is attracted to the infinite possibilities offered by new technologies: "I believe that these, like NFTs [non-fungible tokens], are the new frontiers of art's future. What interests me above all is the possibility of 'transferring' street art, so that instead of being destined to disappear or be defaced, that is, to being temporary, it can exist forever. Moreover, though artists once had to be represented by a gallery to sell their works, they can now enjoy total autonomy in this respect as well. It's a new world that certainly deserves to be explored. After all, street art itself was a pioneer."

New York City Commission on Human Rights Public Artist-in-Residence, New York City, New York, USA, 2015

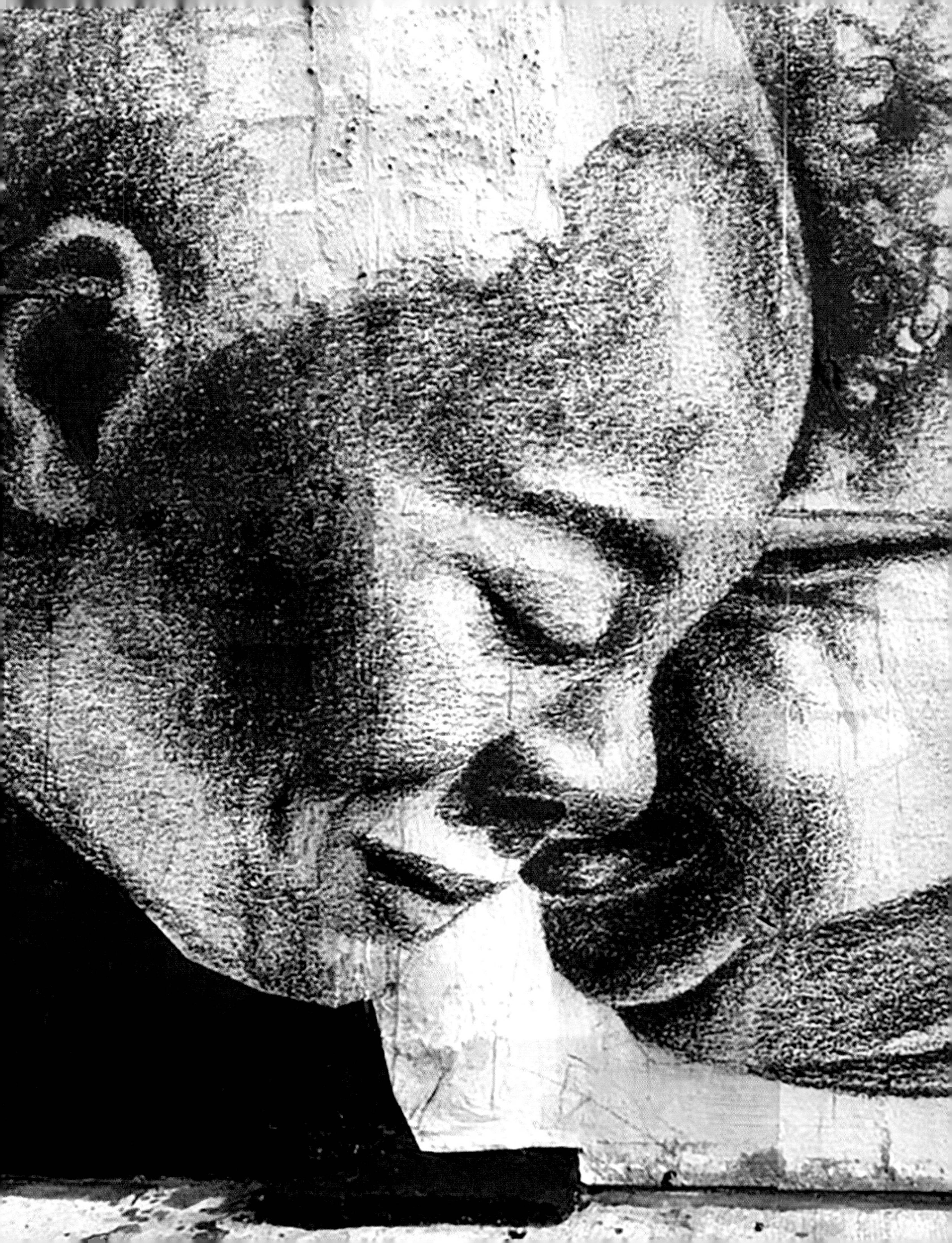

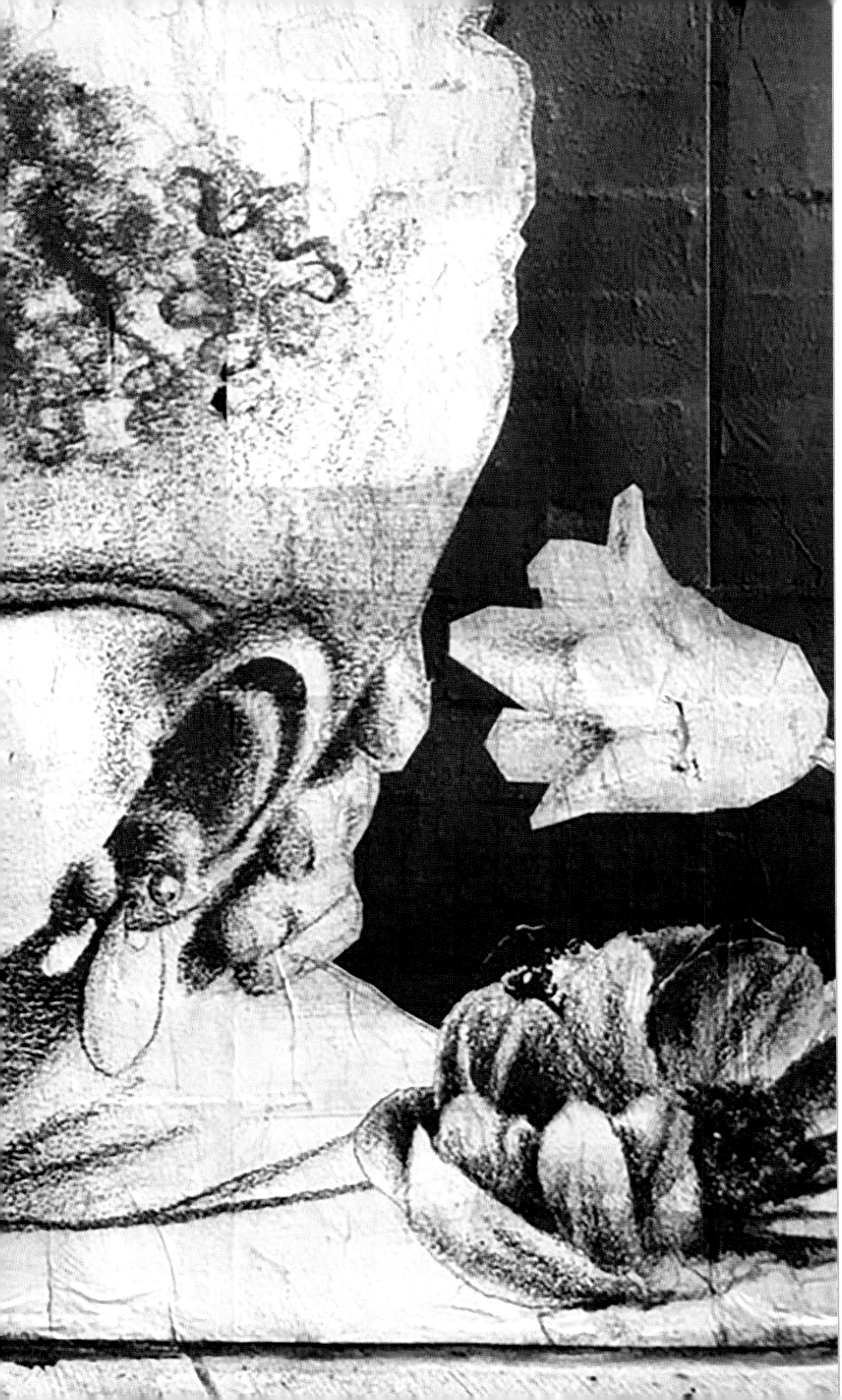

New York City Commission on Human Rights Public Artist-in-Residence, New York City, New York, USA, 2015

LULA GOCE

THE POET OF LANDSCAPES AND HUMAN NATURE

"It's generally hard to make it as an artist. But being a woman makes everything more complicated. You have to work twice as hard and constantly prove that you're good. There are times when people even try to belittle your success, precisely because you're a woman. Parity must govern the way artists are treated and regarded when it comes to opportunities, exhibitions, and projects."

Lula's art is characterized by lively colors and strong expressivity, by human beings who blend perfectly with landscapes and nature, evoking poetry and a vivid imagination. The female figures who are rediscovered in her art are particularly strong and proud, striking in their eye-catching charisma. "For me the sense of nature is always present; indeed, the poetry that springs from the beauty of the landscape is itself a metaphor of our consciousness of self, of our personal identity, of our self-acceptance. This means having to deal with our 'monsters' and our deepest fears until we know them through and through, until we can make peace with them," she reflects, revealing the real meaning behind her works.

"I was born in Galicia, in a small town on the Atlantic coast. My art has always been inspired by the sea, by the gray clouds and the power of the elements. I grew up free and in close contact with nature, well aware that it was my responsibility to take care of it," she says. "From the time I was a child, I always enjoyed creating and building things with whatever I could find, and drawing. . . From that point on, what I wanted to do was clear: I wanted to be an artist," she recalls with a touch of emotion and even, perhaps, a certain melancholy.

Lula spent five years studying Fine Arts in Salamanca, where she specialized in painting, but from the outset her passion was murals. "I've always worked on the idea of rendering space as part of the artwork. I wanted to study, learn, experiment. Afterward, I went to Barcelona, where I earned a Master's in Fine Art Creation and followed that with a PhD in Fine Arts at the University of Barcelona. I also studied illustration at the Escola de la Dona and graphic design at the Pauta Formació because I wanted to experiment with different styles and techniques, explore another universe," she says with emphasis.

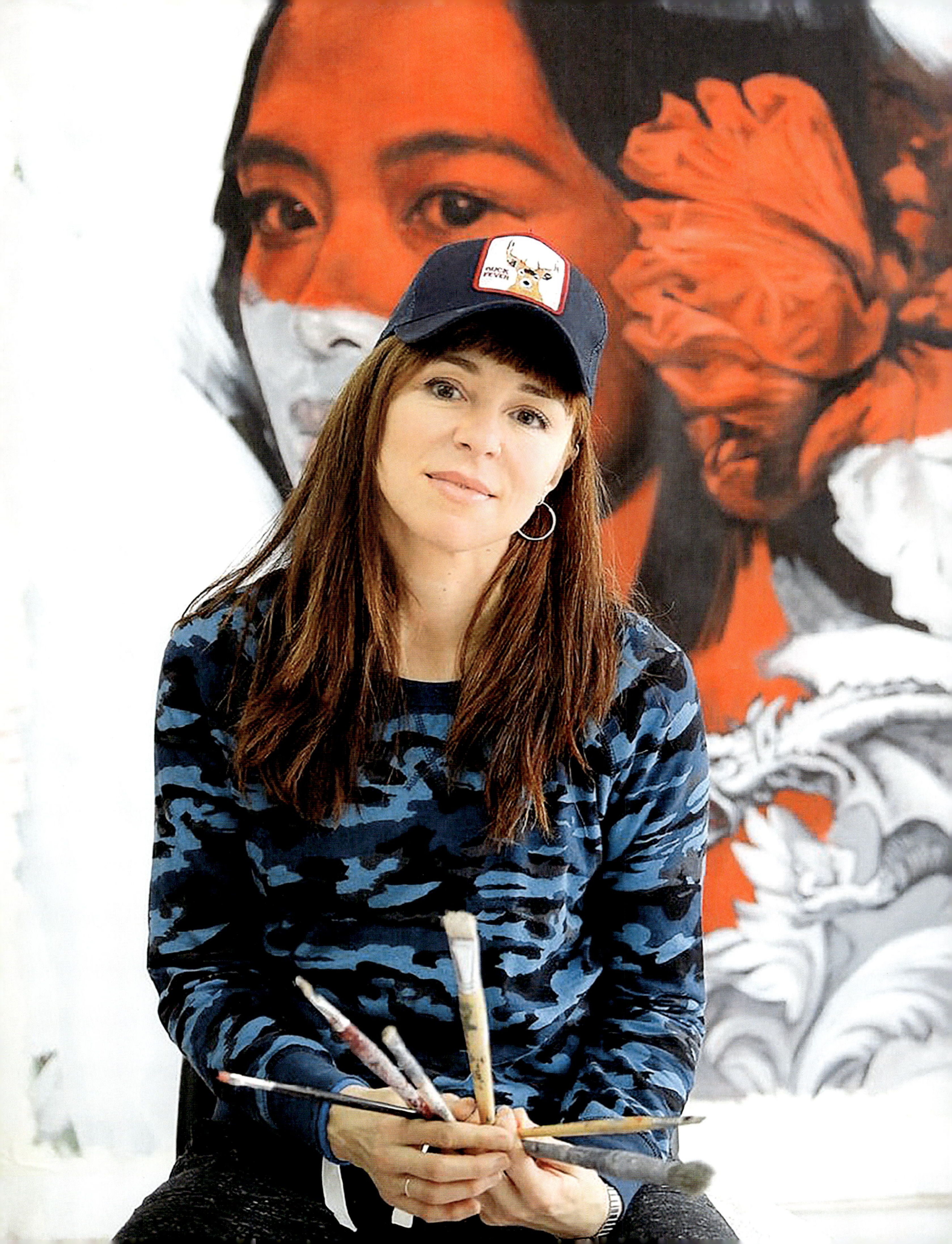

Her training has provided her with the proper tools for best expressing herself: "This combination of different disciplines and techniques has become the knowledge underlying my artistic creation and has made a profound mark on me, helping me stand out, evolve, and develop my unique style."

Her breakthrough came precisely in collaboration with other artists: "I shared a space in an independent artist workshop in the Poblenou neighborhood of Barcelona with twenty artists from different parts of the country. This was truly a fantastic moment in my life: the exchange of knowledge, the synergy, the projects we created, inside and out. While there, I had a chance to meet many street artists: we painted in the streets of Barcelona and made some murals for museums and art centers, such as Arts Santa Mònica and CCCB Barcelona, yet without disdaining gallery shows in and outside the country." But Lula had street art in her blood. "I had always worked outdoors since my teens, experimenting. In Salamanca, I painted walls with my friends and used cheap materials, such as ropes, metal foil, and paper, to make urban installations. In Barcelona, I curated an exhibition with artists like Zosen, Lolo, Sergio Mora, and Kafre. In 2015, Arne Quinze invited me to paint at the North West Wall Festival in Werchter, Belgium. There I made my first truly enormous mural. Since then, I've never stopped: I began traveling and painting large walls around the world!" she recalls.

She has a unique story to relate about each of her works; all are tightly bound up with her life or some part of it, but there is one memory that sticks in her mind: "The first mural that I painted in Vigo was a unique, magical moment for me: a girl and a boy with flowers and a green heart in their hands."

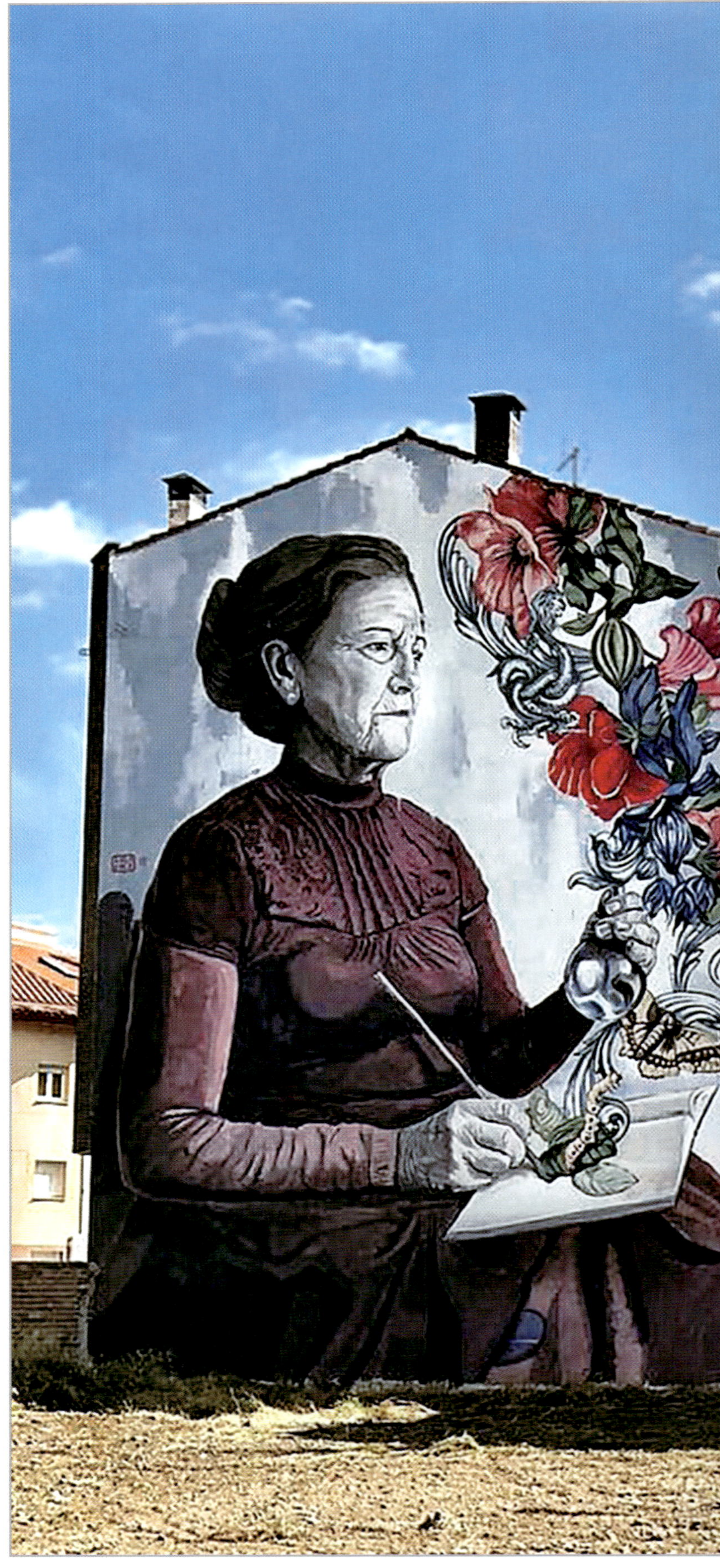

GROWING, Belorado, Spain, 2018

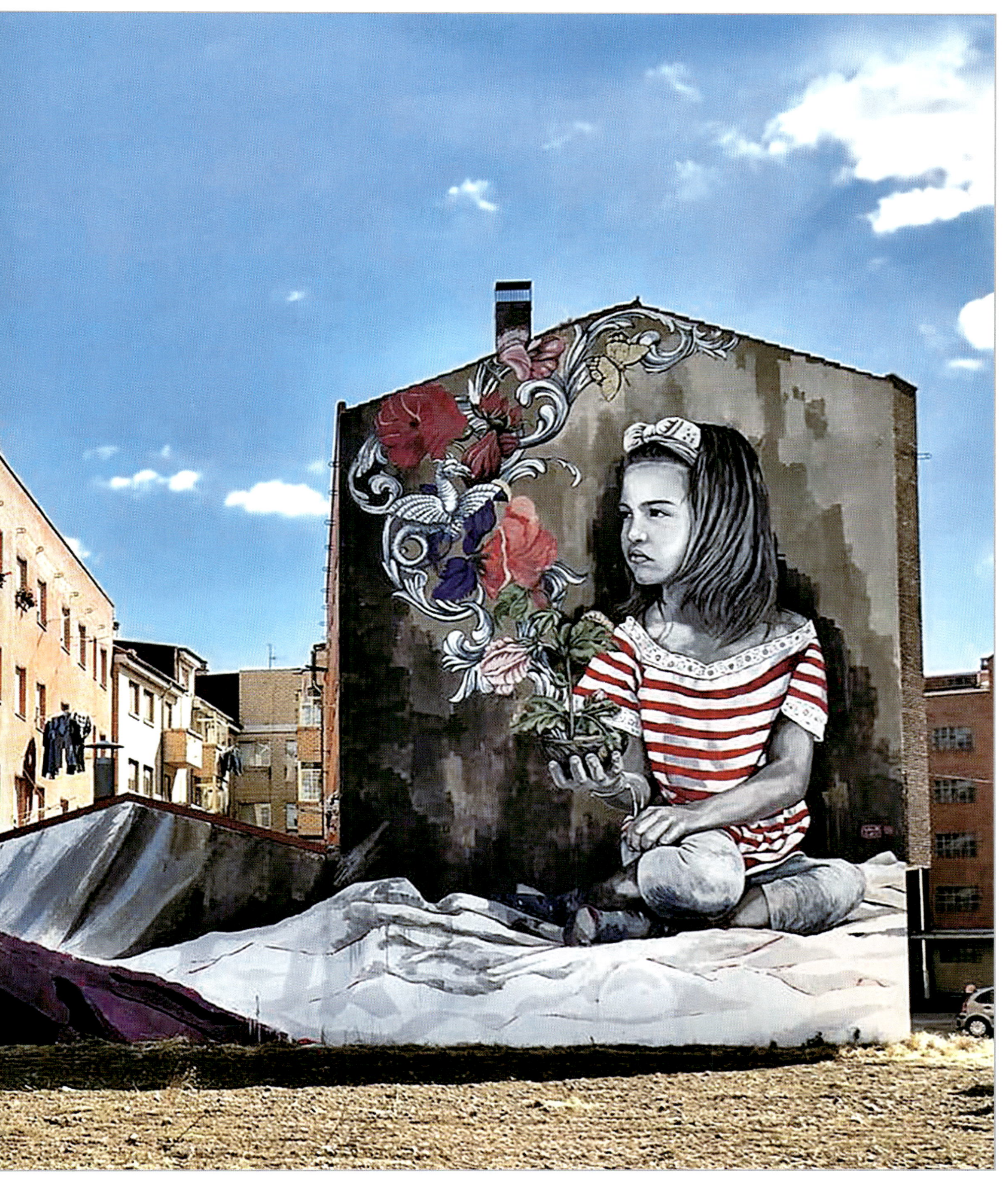

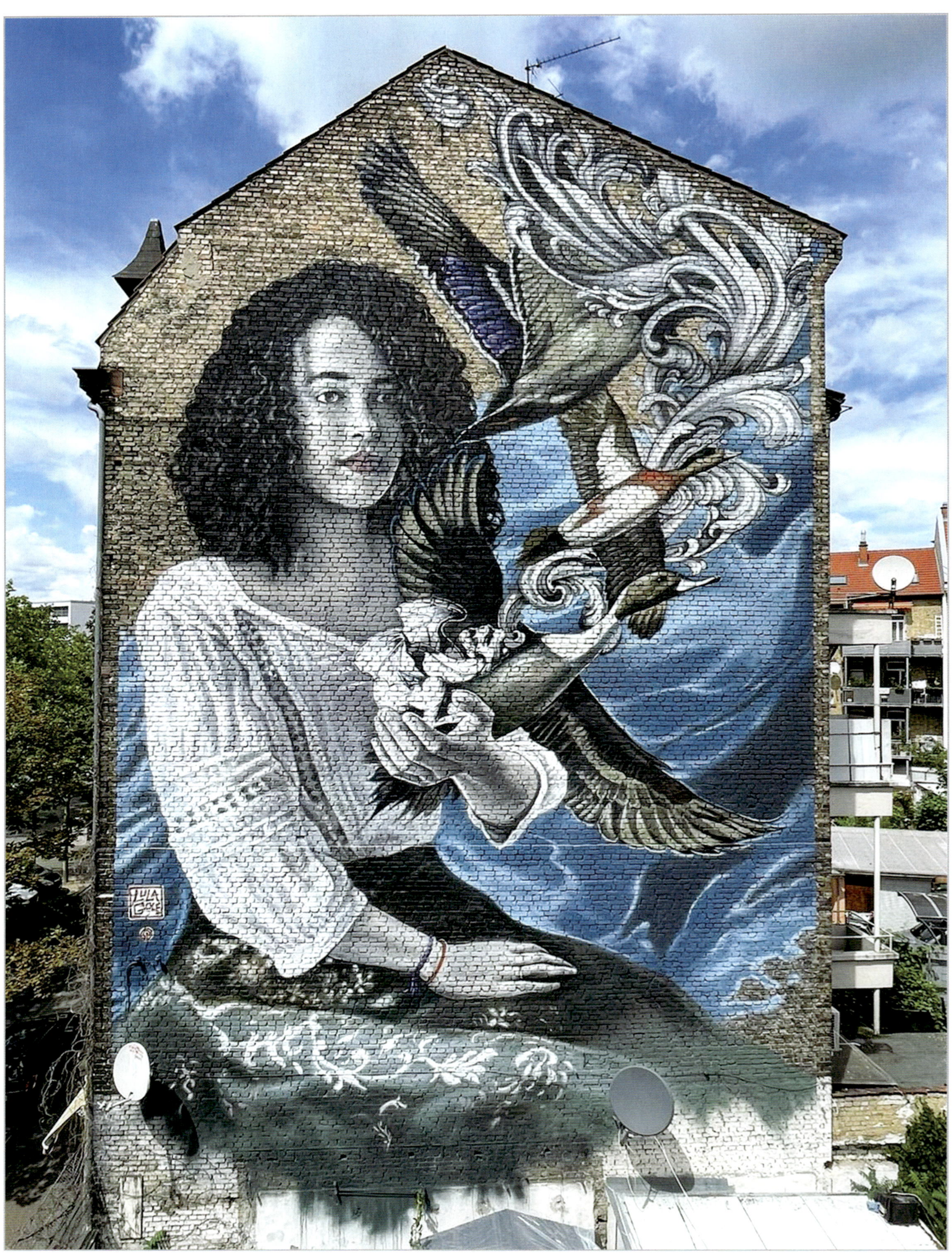

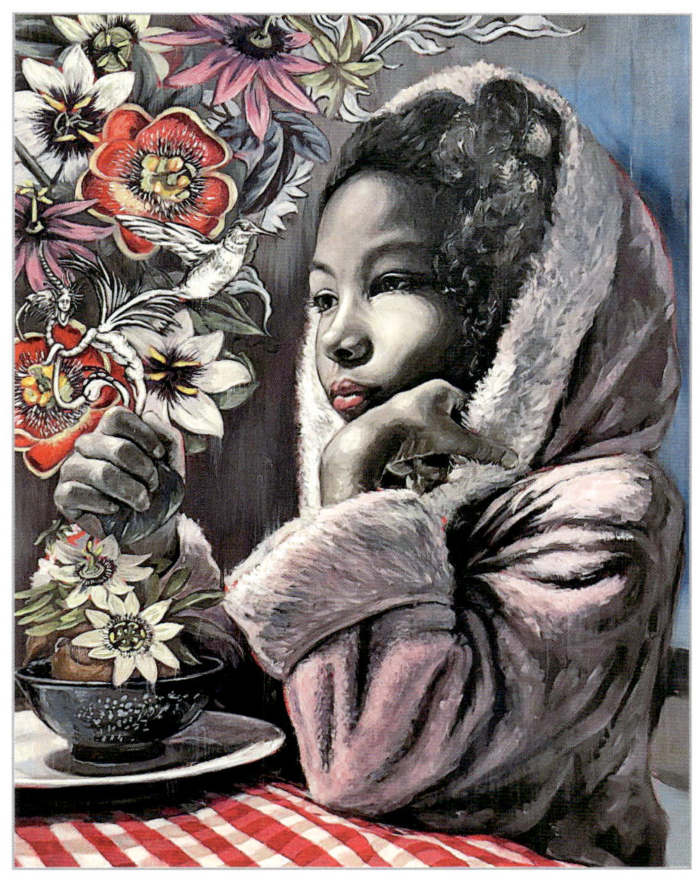

"I collaborated on it with the Neighborhood Association of Curva de San Gregorio in Vigo, which was promoting the construction of a park on a building lot. Unfortunately, the initiative was unsuccessful, and now a large building at the site has 'buried' my mural. . ." The fact that she is a woman has certainly made—and still makes—it more difficult for her to assert herself and be successful, but this is not what weighs most on her. "I believe that establishing a difference between being a woman and being a man—be it in terms of creative projects or job opportunities—rouses negative feelings of separatism, of useless antagonism. For me, equality means working together and respecting each other, regardless of gender or skin color," she asserts.

What are your main sources of inspiration? "Since I studied various disciplines and have a complex background, my art is quite eclectic. At first, I was especially drawn to classical art: I'm thinking, for example, of Michelangelo, Leonardo da Vinci, Goya, and Bosch. When it comes to contemporary art, however, I am particularly fond of the work of certain women, including Marina Abramović, Barbara Kruger, and Louise Bourgeois. In street art, I admire above all the work of Paola Delfín, Faith, Iota, and Helen Blur. . . I also adore Ron and Guido van Helten's art. The truth is that, in the end, I love any street art that has the power to move me and inspire strong feelings in me," she admits.

Lula is an inquisitive and responsible person who knows how to look reality unhypocritically in the face: "I can't deny that I am worriec about what's happening in the world; indeed, I must confess with sadness and anger that the current situation is a veritable disaster from every point of view! But this is the reality in which we live and in which we must do the best we can with the possibilities afforded us."

KNOWLEDGE II, Ludwigshafen, Germany, 2021

AMINA, Vilanova i la Geltrú, Spain, 2018

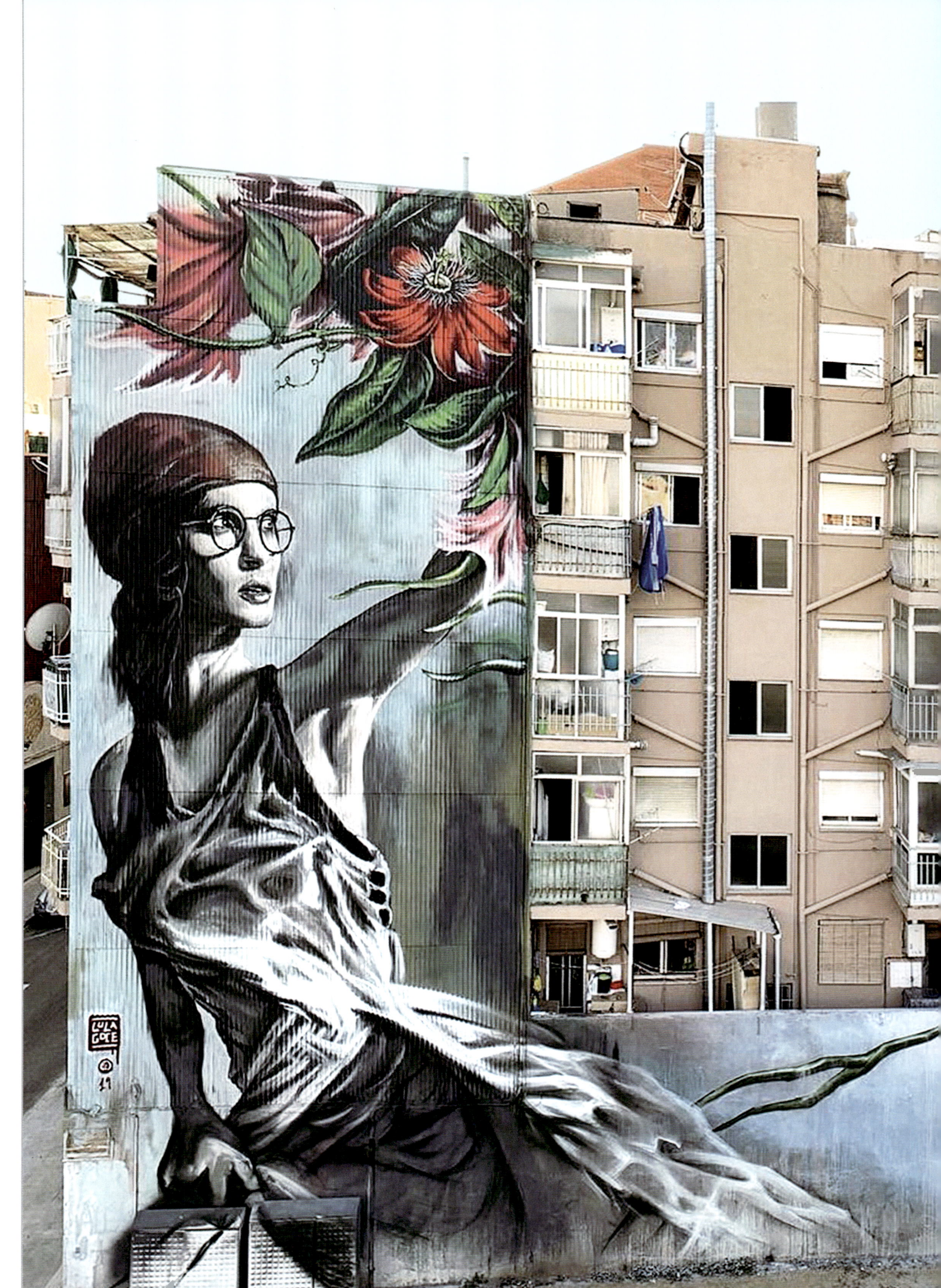
LULA
GOCE

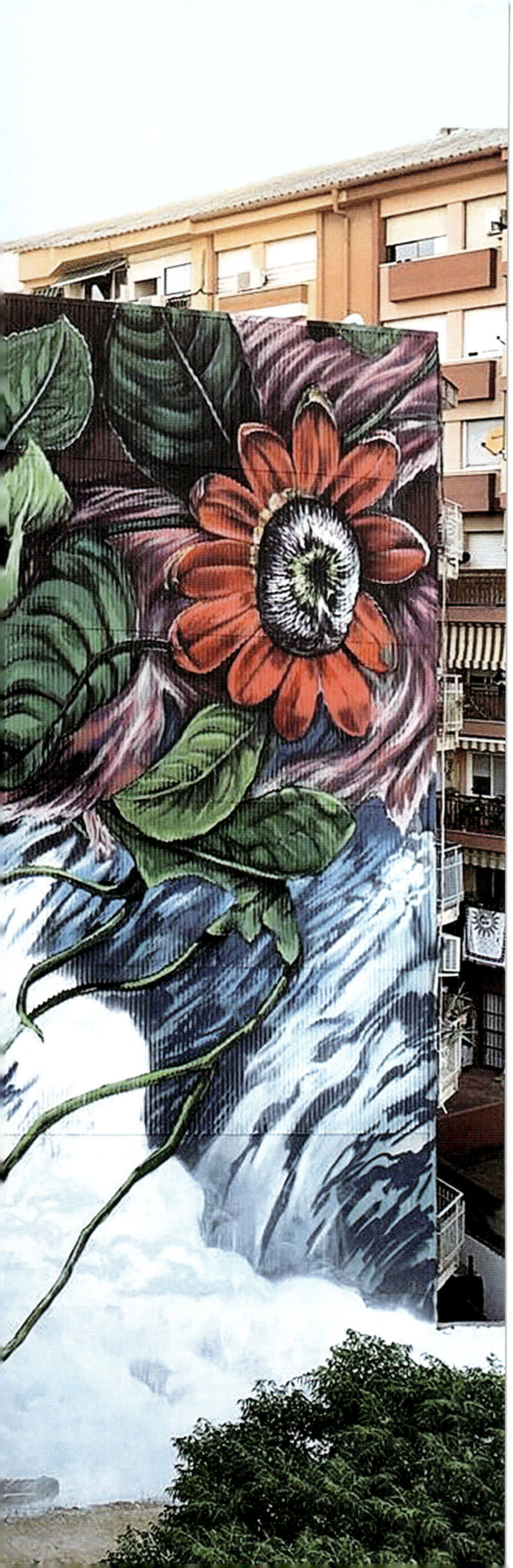

"I'm an artist, and it's with my works that I can try to contribute to change. I love graphic design and illustration and the way in which they are able to express a great deal and quite deeply through simple messages that have the power to reach everyone." She pauses for a moment before resuming with conviction: "I think that love and empathy are the preconditions for a better world. What we need is more of a connection with nature and ourselves. We must stop, learn, and get to know each other; we really need to understand what we're like, what others are like, what our environment is like, and how this is affecting us. I want women to have the same opportunities, the same freedom to choose the way they live and control their existence. I want equality for everyone. Nothing more, nothing less."

GAIA, Terrassa, Spain, 2019 (left)
ALCHEMIST, Viseu, Pcrtugal, 2019

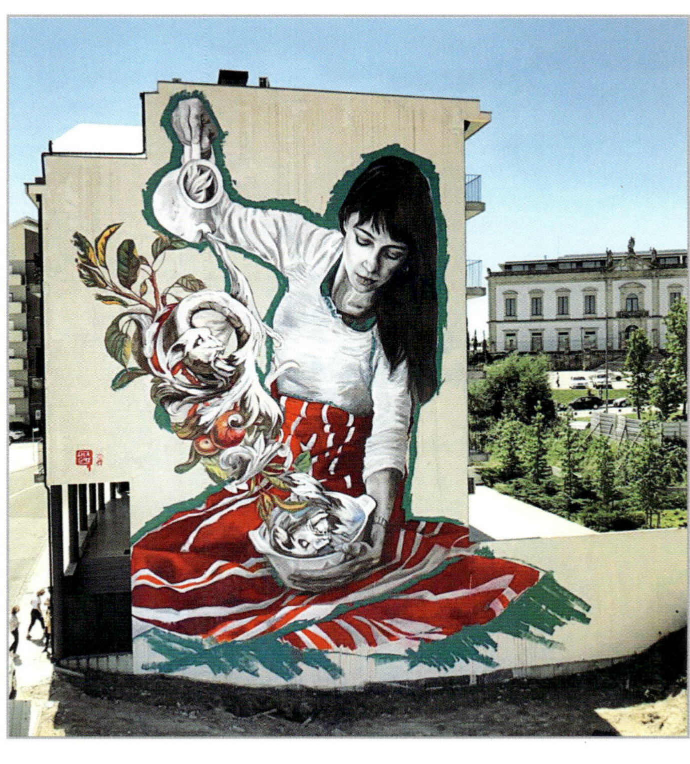

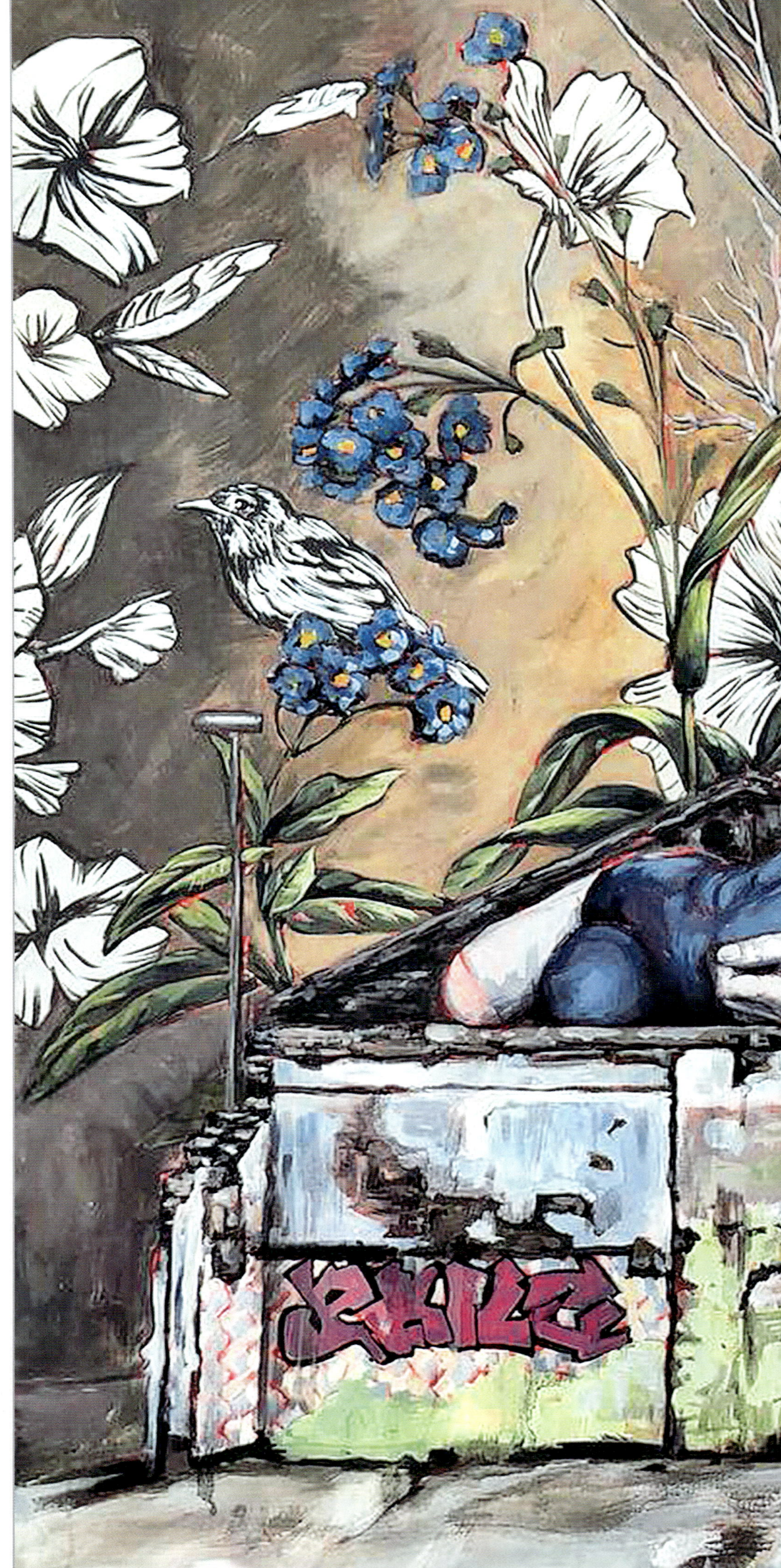

VALENTINA, *NFT Sleepers Series,*
2021

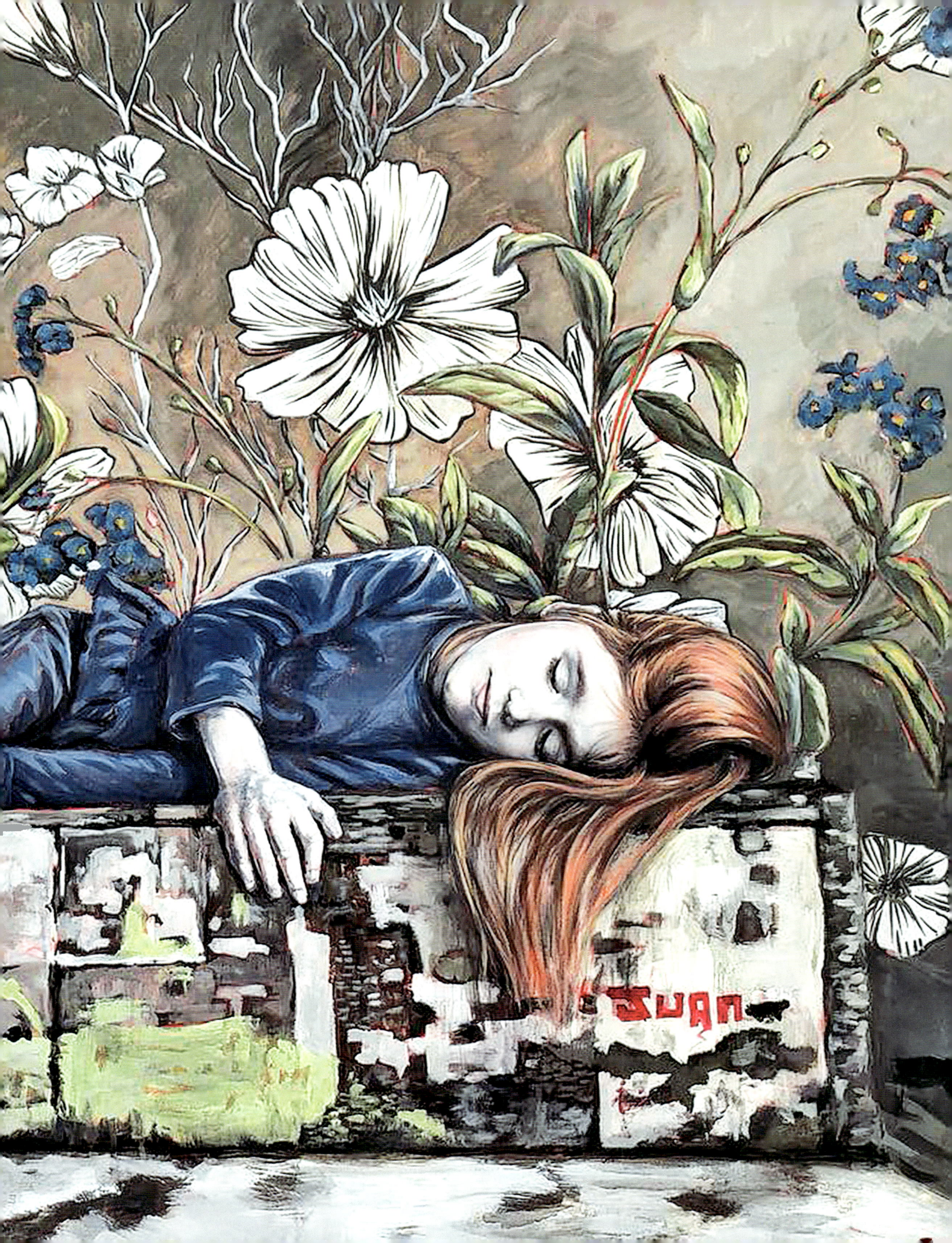

suan

MAYA HAYUK

THE AFICIONADO OF COLOR, FORM, AND SPACE

"I have no idea whether it's easier or more difficult to be a woman than a man. Are men ever asked this question? I'm pretty sure my work is loved for its merits and not the type of sexual organs I have. I would love to hear this question posed to a male artist. Perhaps this is the one major difference: female artists are constantly asked to prove that they're 'as good as' men."

She stands out for her unique style, its intricate and colorful geometric patterns, its intertwining lines, and shapes that play with each other even on murals of vast dimensions. For Maya Hayuk, the charm of existence lies hidden in geometry. "Geometry is a means and matter of organizing colors, shapes, and spaces. I like the imperfect symmetry created by a human being because it's closer to nature and far more interesting and evocative than something made with a computer. Human beings are genetically coded to prefer the imperfect simply for the sake of survival. In any case, for me beauty is more beautiful when it's not perfect. I often find myself reflecting on the fact that all ancient civilizations created works based on incredibly complex yet extraordinarily similar schemes, so much so that one wonders how this was possible before the rise of telecommunication. I actually see it as further proof that we're an enormous sentient being that has grown collectively," she muses.

Her path as a woman has been influenced by travel, art, regional crafts, spirituality, sexuality, and the concept that everything is part of a single whole. And she expresses her ideas and thoughts through her incredible symbolism.

PORTRAIT (STUDIO VIEW), Photo Lauren Silberman

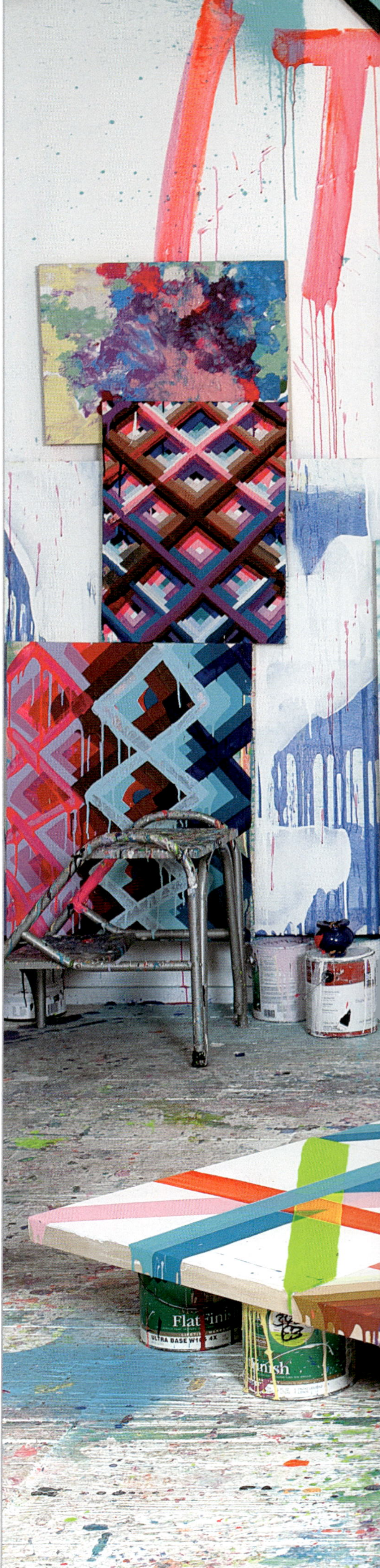

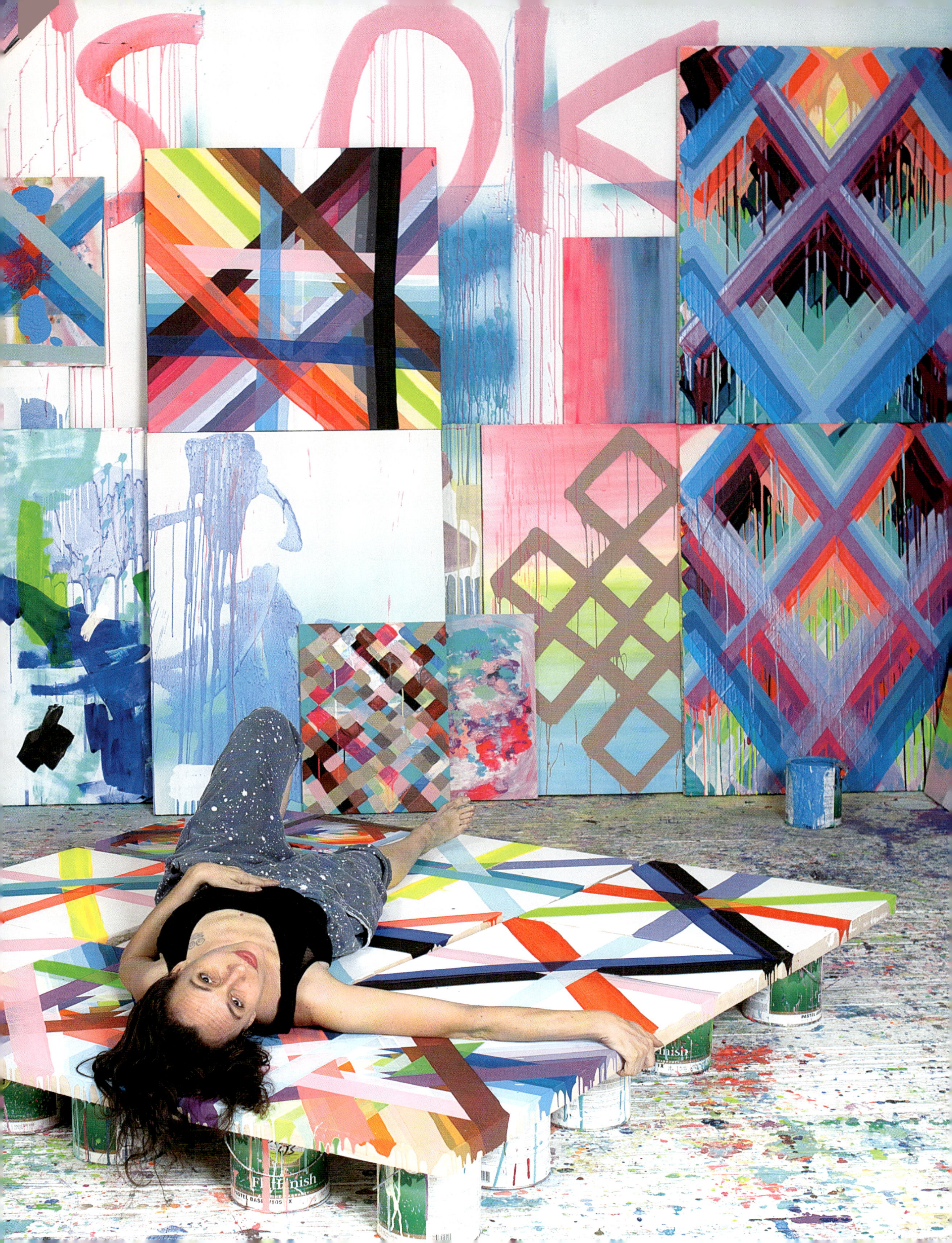

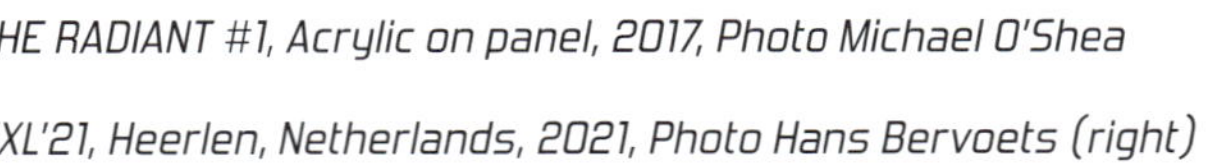

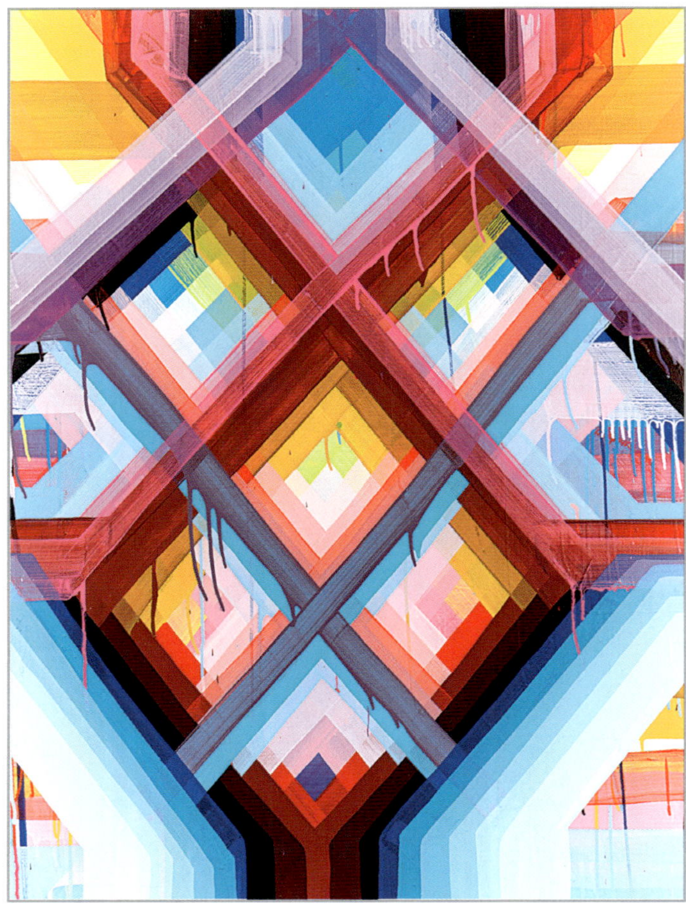

"Geometry and mathematics have their own languages, far more universal than words. I'm really inspired by the kind of work women have done anonymously since the dawn of history. Work that has generally received very little recognition and been deigned unworthy of belonging to the world of art because it's purely decorative and bound to the domestic sphere."

"Actually, such work is expressed in a universal language, one used all over the world, but which, from country to country, takes on particular characteristics so that it can be easily identifiable and recognizable," she explains. An especially significant example for her are Ukrainian Easter eggs. "They're really beautiful! Their origins go far back in time, to the pre-Christian era. They symbolize birth and fertility, so the designs that adorn them refer to different aspects of life. Or think of the Gift Drawings of the Shakers, a type of greeting card made solely by women, which families in that religious community exchange," she continues.

Colors are another really intense aspect of her art. "Color can be charged with meaning and emotion, of course. Colors can be as political as they are poetic. I am fascinated by synesthesia, the brain's ability to correlate various disparate senses: that's why colors have a sound, a smell, or a taste. I could deliberately group really 'ugly' colors together in the hope of achieving a delicious result. One way of perceiving colors is to imagine them as electric sparks that disturb frequencies through powerful cacophony," she claims.

What colors do you prefer? "I love a broad spectrum, and I like the alchemy of color. I love shades like lavender that evoke a smell as well as a color. I like the fluorescent pink and brown of sunburned skin, and I adore the colors of nature that seem impossible to reproduce in a painting or photograph, like the violet of an overcast sky right before a thunderstorm," she says.

Born in Baltimore, Maryland, and the daughter of two university professors, Maya has had a chance to travel extensively since her childhood, and thus to be inspired by different styles of art, traditions, and local cultures. She has lived in Richmond, Boston, and San Francisco in the United States, in Toronto, Canada, and has now settled in Brooklyn; in addition, she studied at the Massachusetts College of Art, the Ontario College of Art and Design in Toronto, Odessa University in Ukraine, and the Skowhegan School of Painting and Sculpture in Maine. "As a child, I traveled a lot with my parents, especially in Europe and throughout that vast nation that is the former Soviet Union. My parents, both from Ukraine, were immigrant refugees, and they felt that traveling was the best education they could give me. My father was a professor of geography, and my mother organized educational tours for him. I thus spent a great deal of time in museums and historical sites in the UK, France, Belgium, the Netherlands, Spain, Greece, Egypt, and today's Ukraine, Georgia, Armenia, Azerbaijan, and Russia," she recalls.

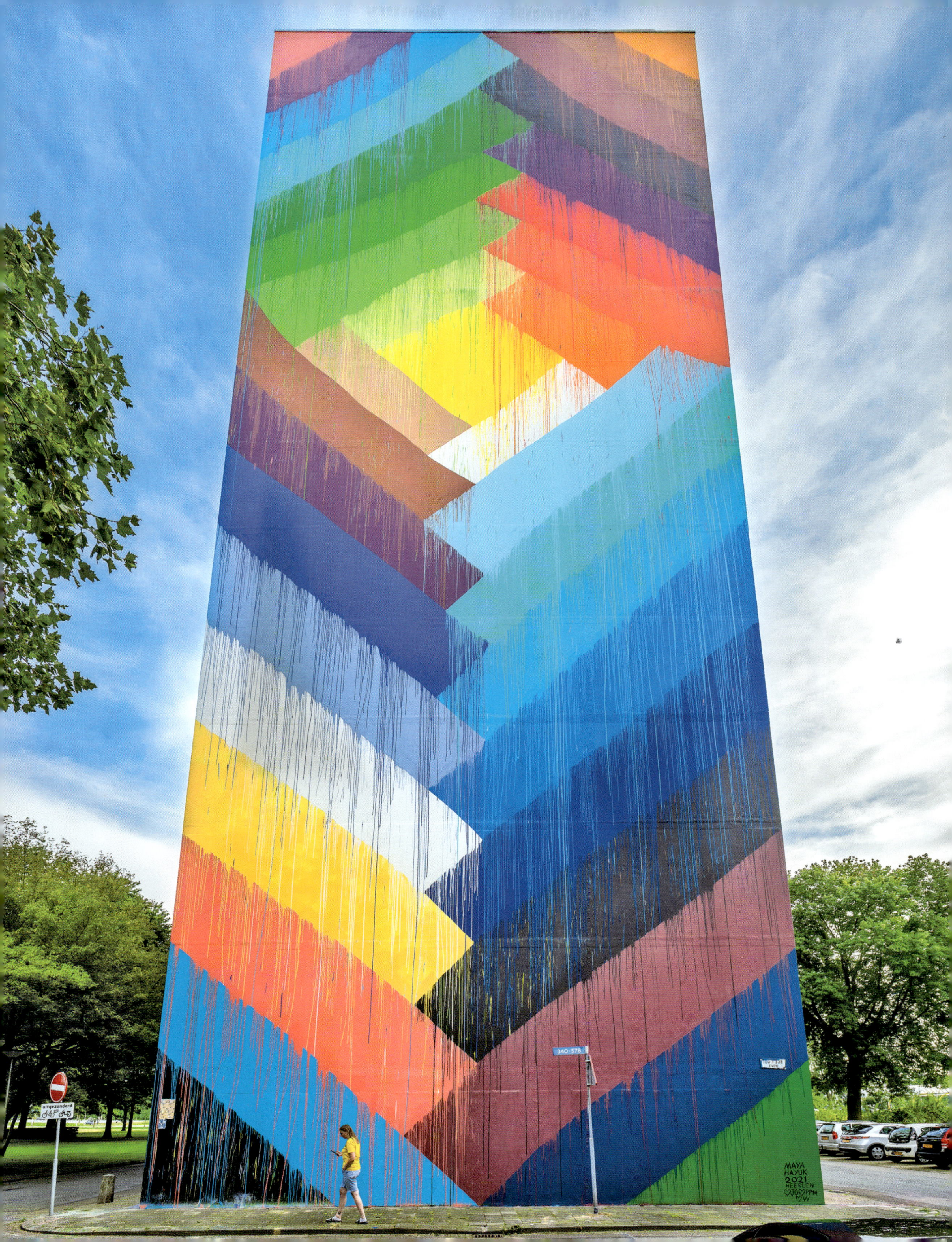
uitgezonderd
340·578
MAYA
HAYUK
2021
HEERLEN

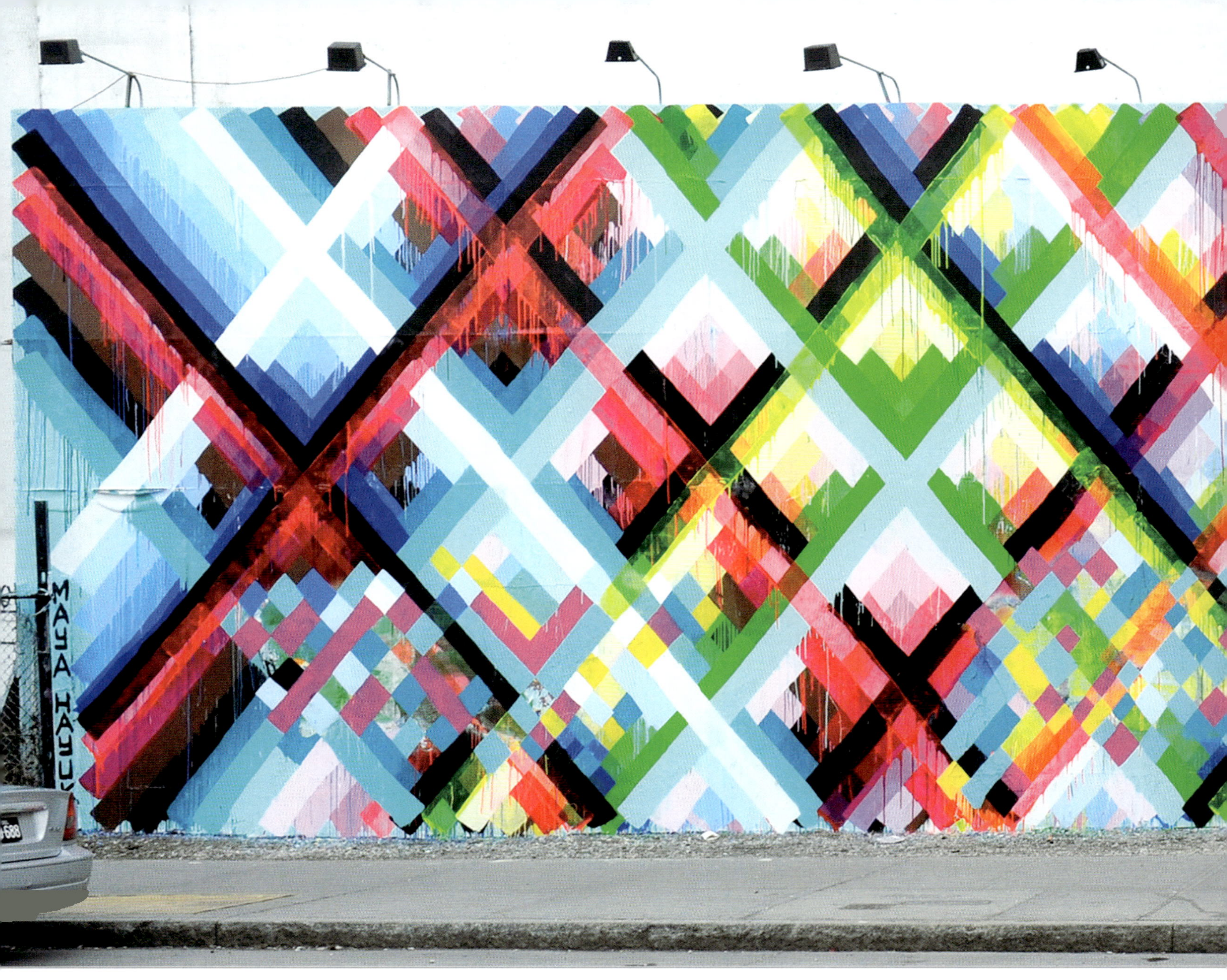

"I've always made travel a priority, and my art has served as my passport. Before I was commissioned to create murals, I was a photojournalist and dealt primarily with music, skate culture, and graffiti, settling for makeshift accommodations, and often sleeping on floors and trains. Over time, I've discovered an extraordinary network of artists and free-thinkers around the world, who make me feel at home wherever I go," she notes, reminiscing about her life as an artist.

"As a child, I realized that I liked drawing more than anything else. I was obsessed with my dreams and time travel. I wasn't allowed to watch TV, and I didn't have many friends. Drawing was a way to create what I wanted. My parents argued a lot, and wearing headphones with loud music and drawing was my best escape," she recalls.

"I moved to San Francisco in the early '90s, right around the time of the renaissance of outdoor painting: it didn't have a name yet, but the kind of art I saw was different from graffiti in terms of style, form, and message. It was fascinating, innovative, full of surprises, and inspiring.

"I was drawn by the love and concern that went into making art anonymously and as a public gift. I later discovered that most of the work was done by women: Alicia McCarthy, Ruby Neri alias

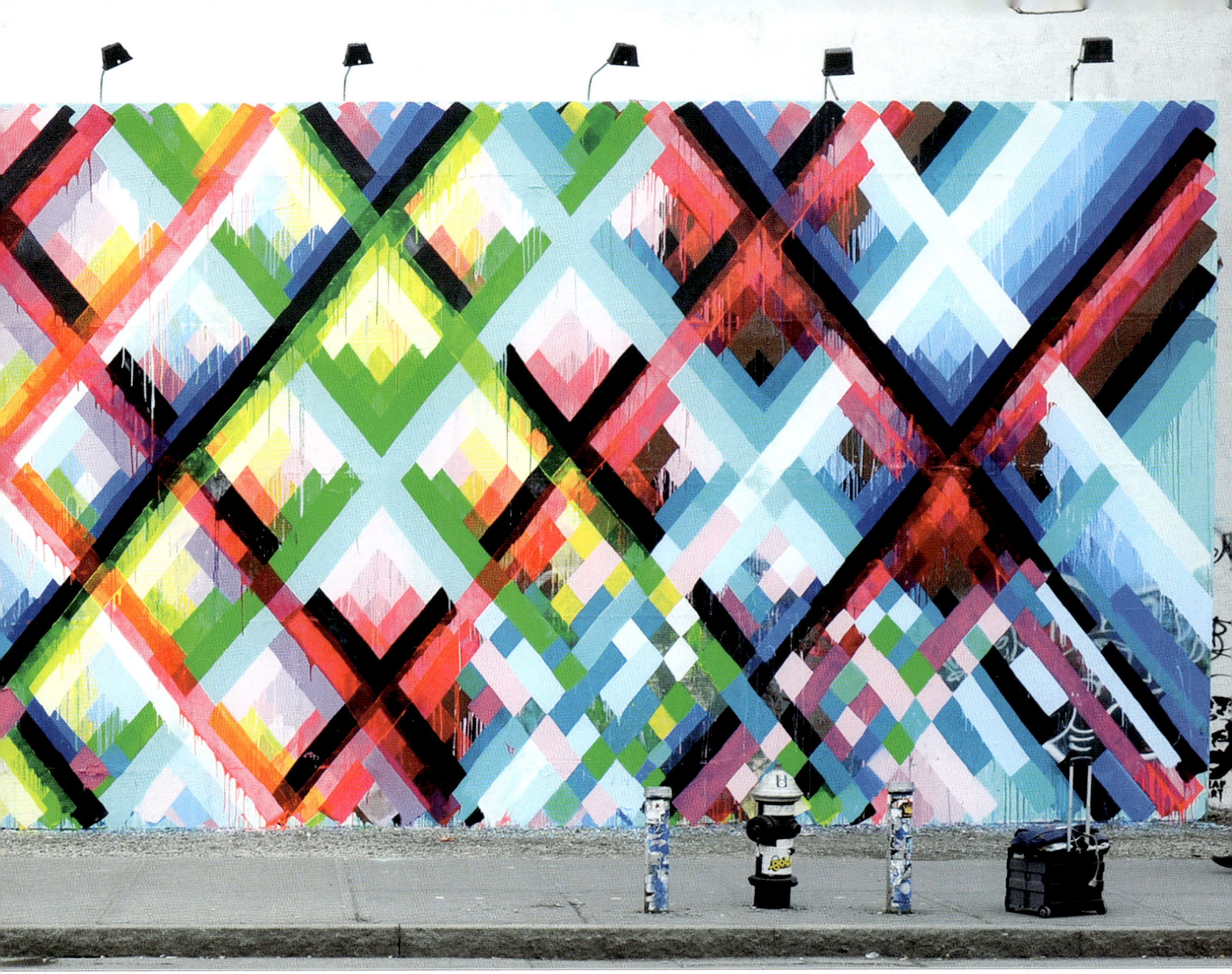

Reminisce, Margaret Kilgallen, and Carolyn Castaño. I realized that the streets were a space for equality, but the people who write history often forget that," she notes with emphasis.

"One of the best things about outdoor art is that most viewers don't think, 'Wow, that's a really nice painting for a woman,' or 'Obviously a man did it,'" she says.

When confronted with art, Maya seeks that special poetic sensation, somewhat intangible, that makes her notice that it has been created with love, passion, obsession: "On a larger scale, art can serve as testimony of a culture, either ours or that of other places or different eras."

CHEM TRAILS, THE BOWERY WALL, New York City, New York, USA, 2014, Photo Martha Cooper

SEE WEED, Acrylic on panel, 2021, Photo Michael O'Shea (overleaf, left)

HIDRA #6, Acrylic on panel, 2021, Photo Michael O'Shea (overleaf, right)

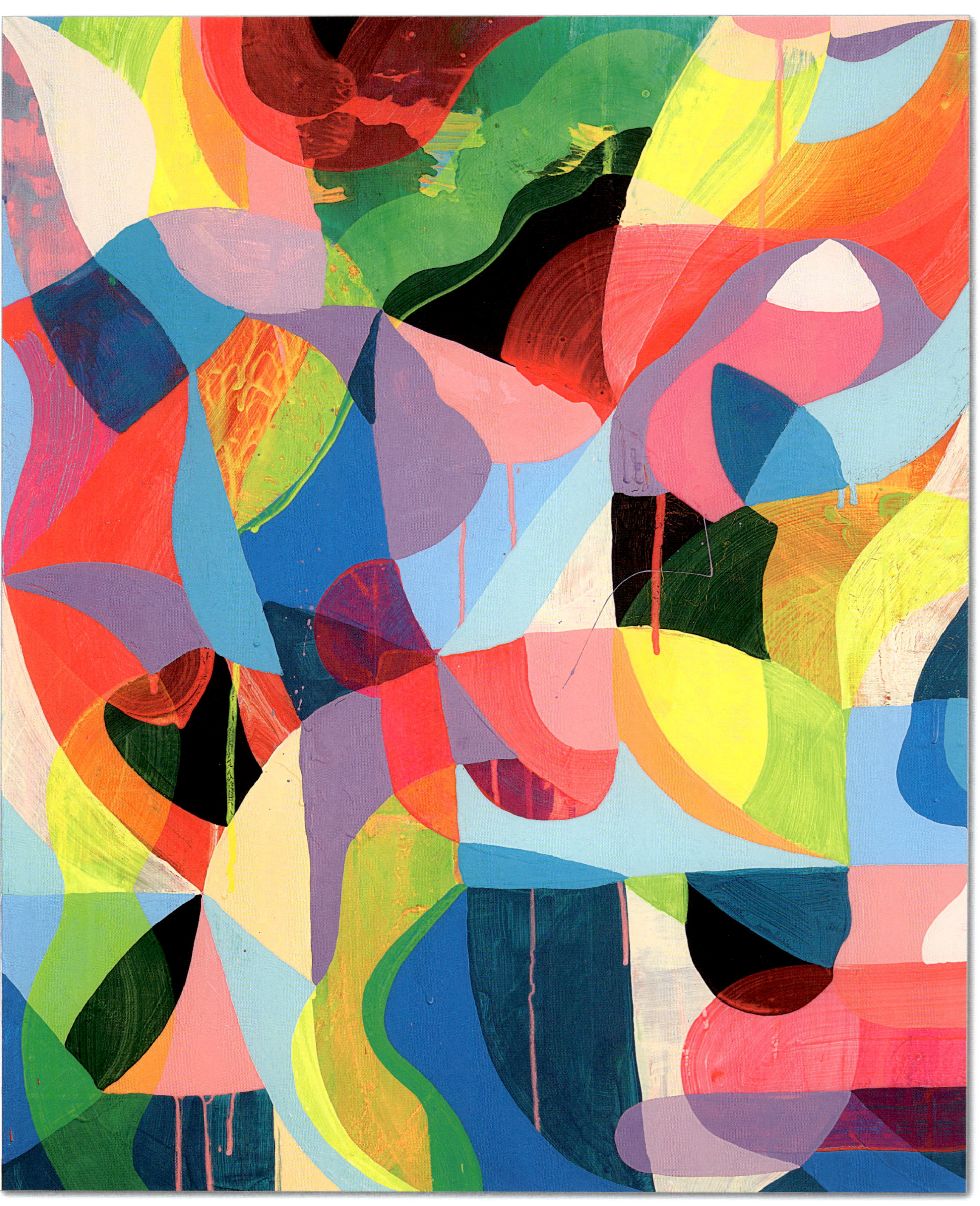

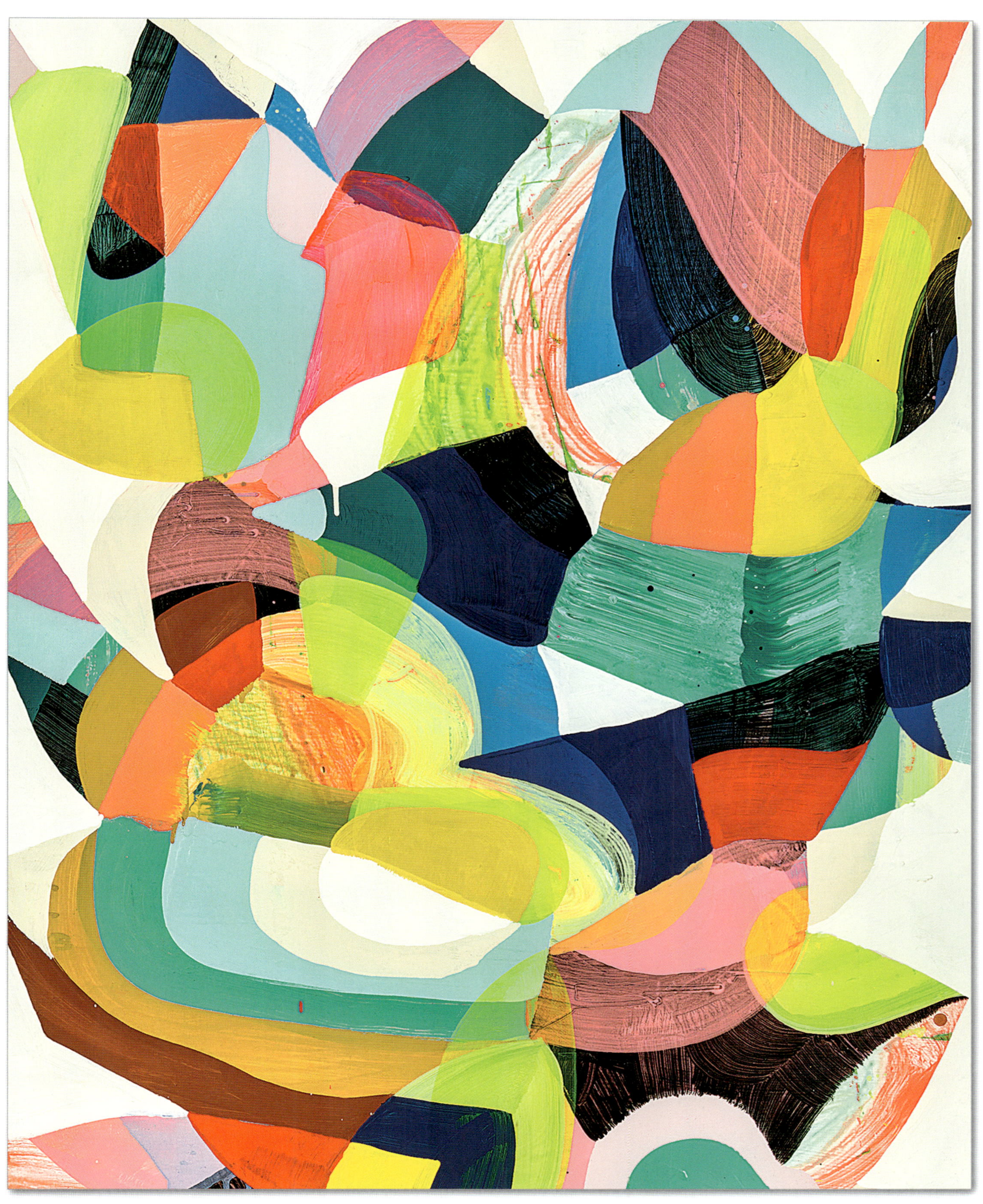

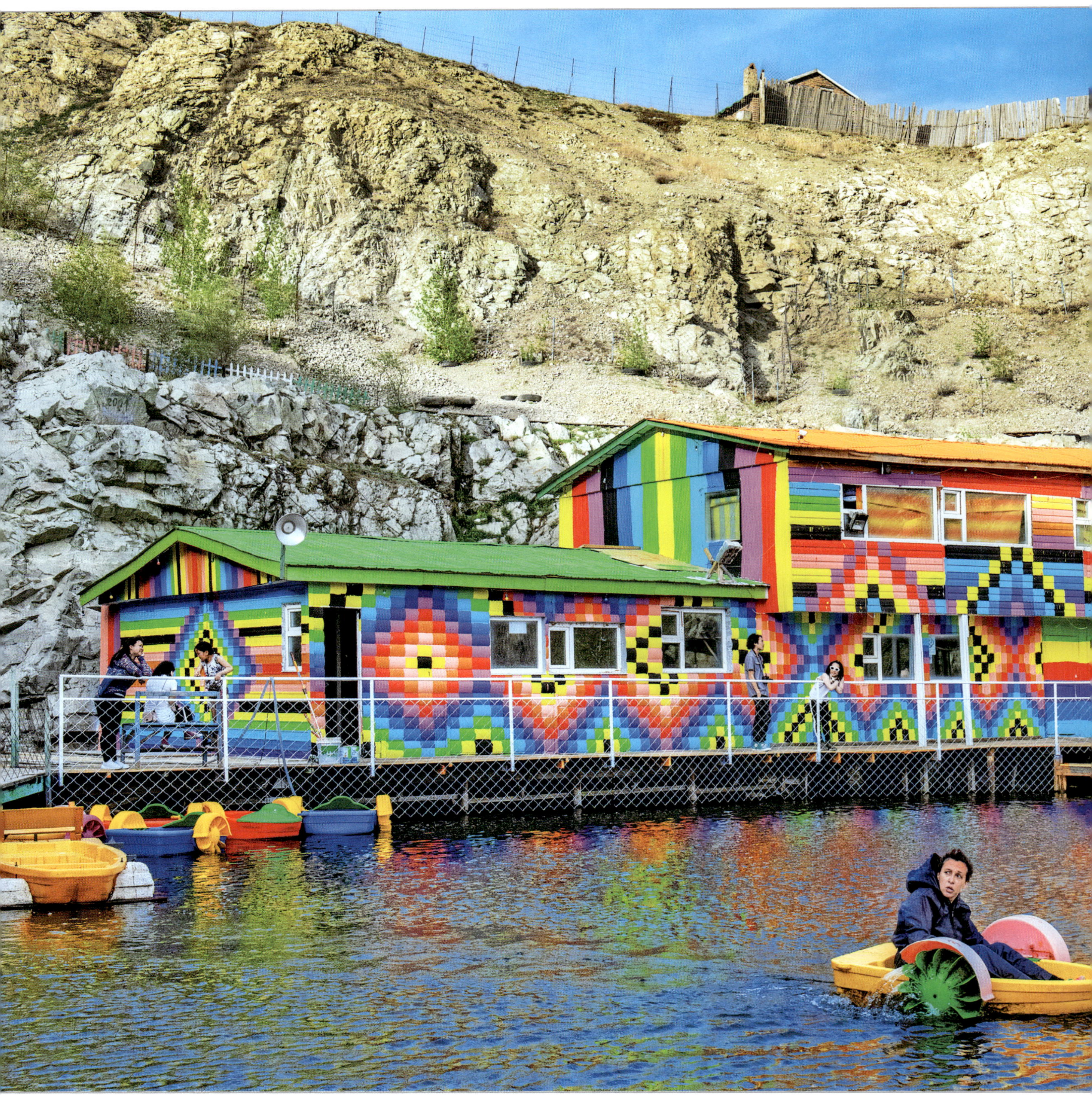

Ulaanbaatar, Mongolia, 2019, Photo Martha Cooper

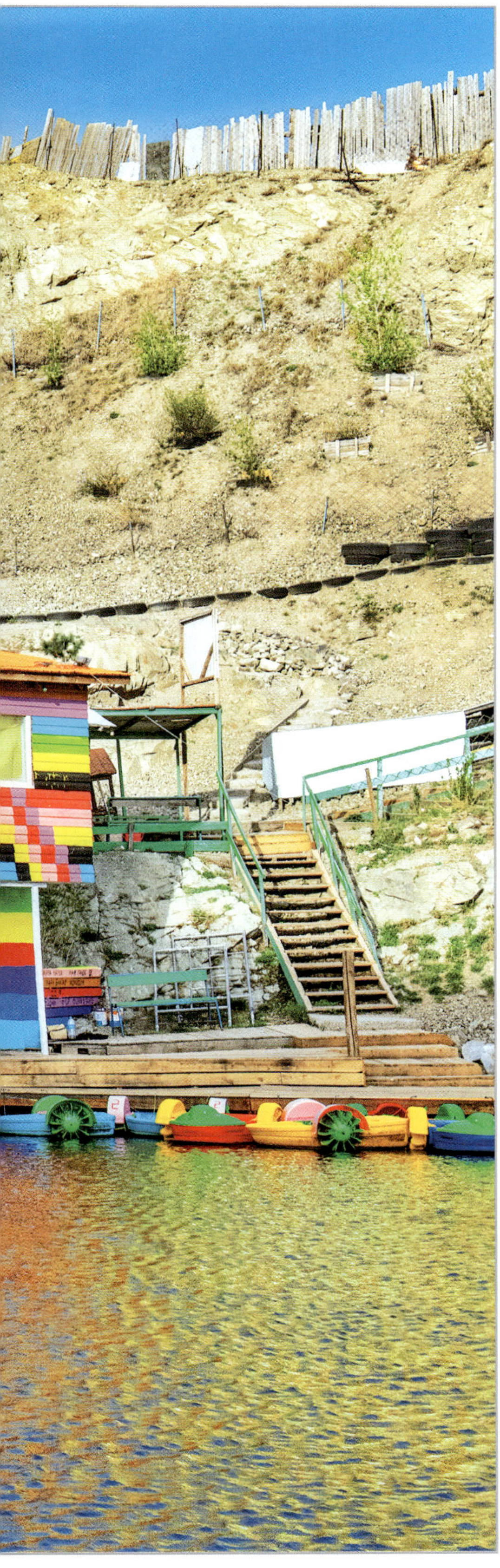

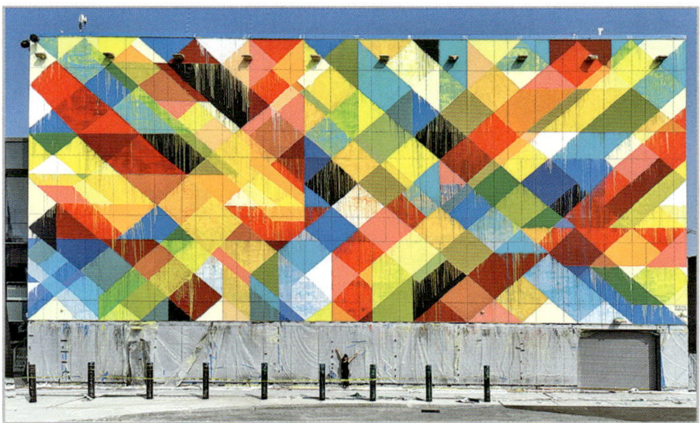

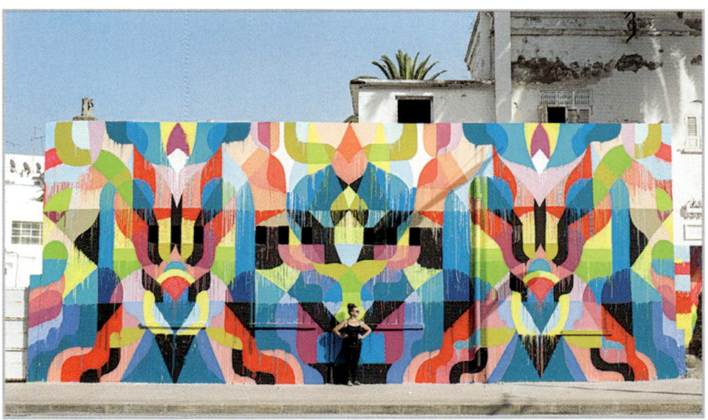

"Art is the lens through which we look to attain greater awareness. Art asks many questions but doesn't always provide answers. Art can shake your belief system and change your perspective. Art often tries to reflect an ideal truth in our imperfect reality," she muses.

What's the meaning of your art, what's its purpose? "I view my artistic production as my mission to give something back to the world. I prefer questions to answers. I like puzzles and mistakes and the adventurous voyage of 'making art,' especially when I'm not quite certain what I'm doing. When I was a child, I wanted to be a time traveler or a parapsychologist. . ."

In the future, Maya hopes to continue evolving throughout that passionate artistic journey into which she has transformed her existence. "I hope to work more with large-scale architecture, collaborating directly with designers, the community, and the natural environment. I want to deepen my visual grammar. The world is a mess, but here and there I see glimmers of hope. I'm always amazed at what the younger generations are coming up with," she concludes.

Albright-Knox Art Gallery, Buffalo, New York, USA, 2021, Photo courtesy of the artist (above)

Rabat, Morocco, 2021, Photo Zakaria Latouri (below)

SHAMSIA HASSANI

THE VOICE OF AFGHAN WOMEN

"Sometimes, while I'm working, people approach and harass me, annoy me. In fact, they don't think that in an Islamic culture a woman has the right to stand in the street and do graffiti."

"Art can't be expressed in words. . . Art must be felt. Art must create a bond with mankind," claims Shamsia Hassani, who is convinced that art can change people's mentality, and that through art people can change the world. In her works, she portrays Afghan women in all their intensity, as iconic symbols of a society almost completely dominated by men. She provides women with a face, a voice, and an existence in a world that wants them to remain invisible. In her art, she offers hope and inspires other Afghan artists, who now know they're no longer alone in their struggle for emancipation.

Shamsia's path has certainly not been easy, but she has never given up. "I was born in Iran, in 1988, to Afghan parents. In Iran there's no law that allows you to become a citizen, so I remained an Afghan. As a child, I didn't realize that there was a clear-cut difference between me and my Iranian friends with whom I played outside. At the time, I had nothing to hide; but once I started school, I understood the importance of not letting others—Iranians—know that I was Afghan. I didn't know why; but I realized that if they knew the truth, things wouldn't be easy for me. Unfortunately, at least twice a year the school administration rounded up the Afghans and asked them to show their documents and permits to study in Iran, and thus our nationality became clear to everyone," she relates. "Years passed, and I got to high school: I was so excited because I thought I was going to study art at school, but I was wrong. Sadly, I was told that, being Afghan, I was not permitted to do so and was encouraged to take up other subjects, such as math, physics, environmental sciences, accounting. . . ," she continues.

BIRDS OF NO NATION, Shamsia Hassani's Studio, Kabul, Afghanistan, 2016

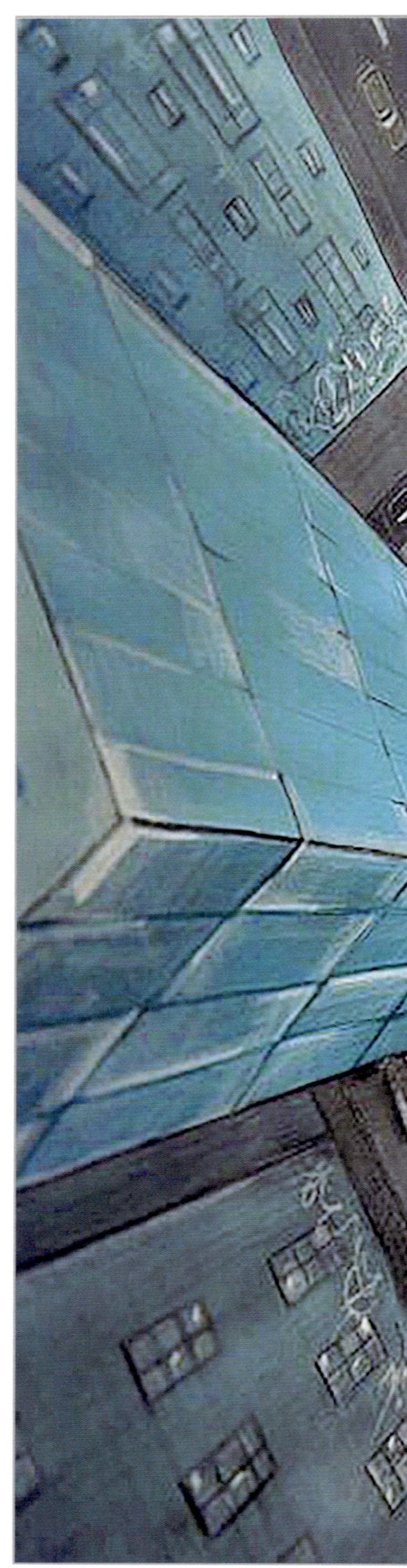

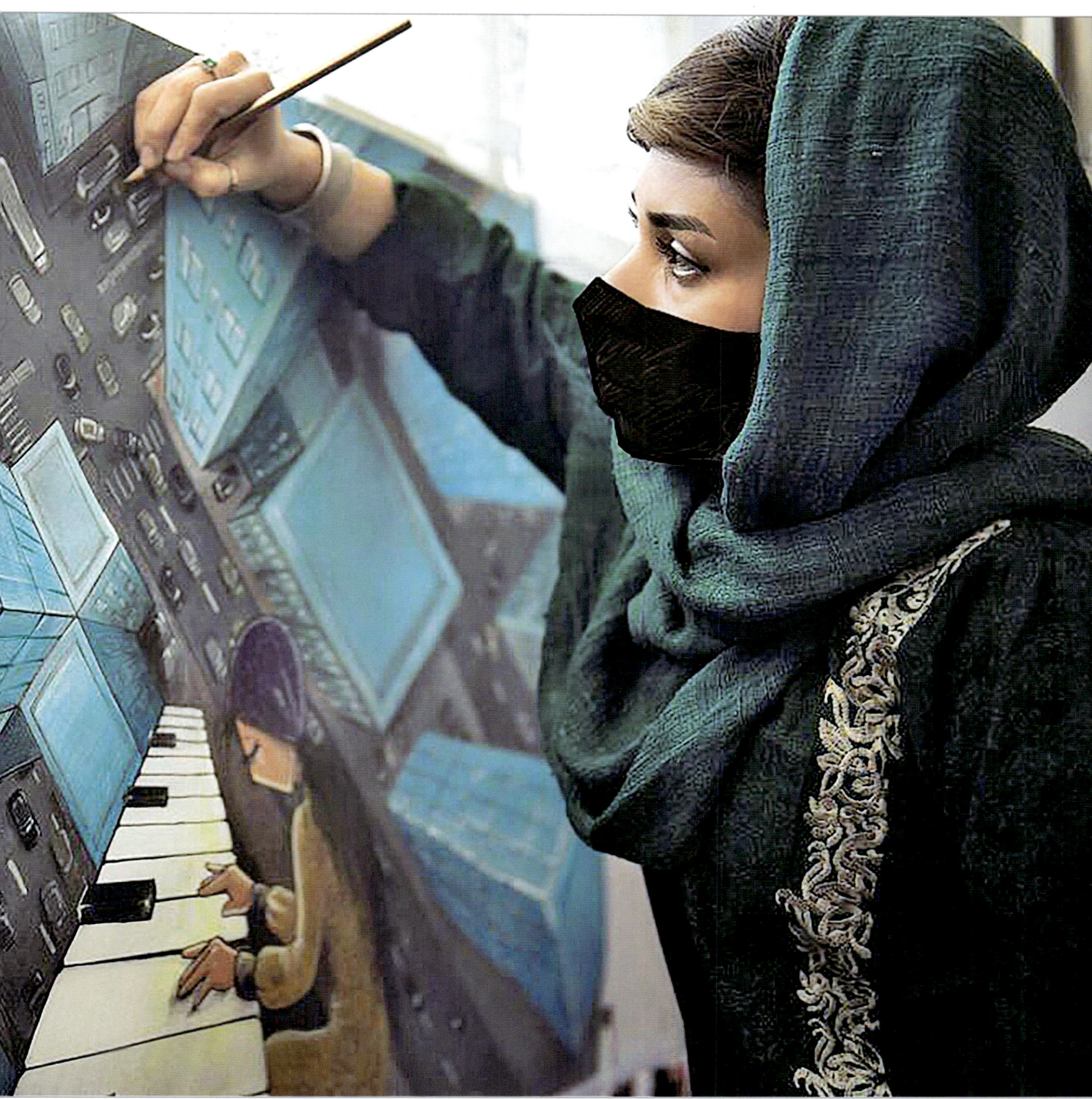

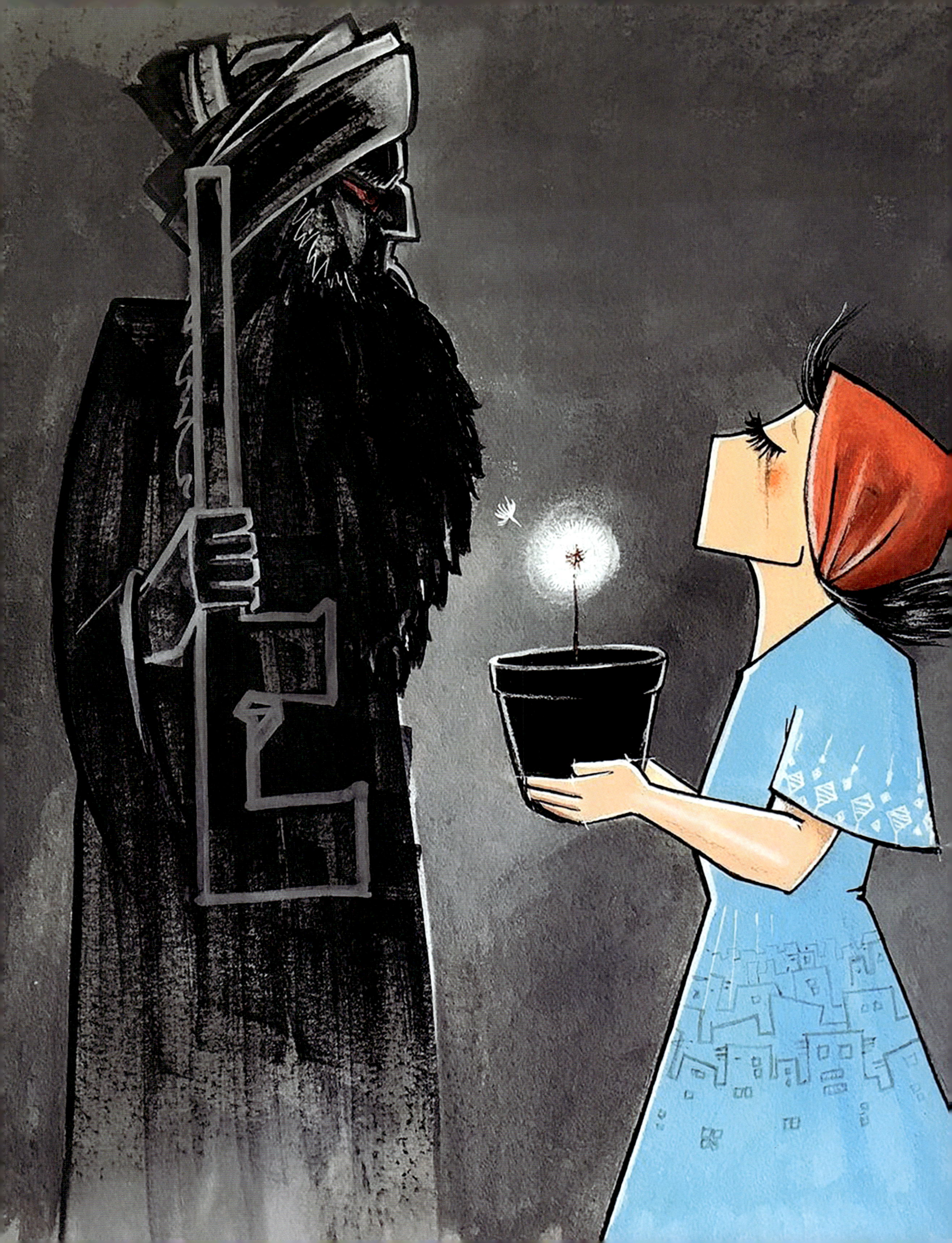

Shamsia, however, did not give up and became not only one of the most successful artists in her country and a professor of Anatomical Drawing and Drawing at Kabul University, but also one of the founders of the Berang Arts Organization, which promotes culture and art in Afghanistan.

But it was the street that, above all, enabled her to realize her dream. Shamsia discovered street art while attending a workshop at the University of Kabul held by the British artist Chu. Thereafter, she began doing colorful graffiti, which, aside from exalting female figures, hoped to mitigate the dire negativity caused by the war. "I wanted Afghanistan to be known for its art, not for the war," she says. For Shamsia, in fact, images get more results than words do and offer the best means of fighting peacefully for ideals. As a woman in Afghanistan, however, she has suffered a great deal of discrimination: "It was extremely difficult and dangerous for me to go out in the street and do graffiti, both because of the general situation and the conditions of women in the country; I was often insulted and threatened. Another major problem was the lack of space for my works, as no one wanted graffiti on their walls; and if by chance they gave me permission, they did so only on the condition that I depicted what they wanted. Whenever I painted in public spaces, I felt insecure and most of the time was forced to leave after a few minutes, without any possibility of completing my work. I eventually realized that I could not complete works that were overly complex, and instead had to focus on simplicity."

MAYBE IT IS BECAUSE OUR WISHES HAVE GROWN IN A BLACK POT. . ., 2021 (left)
DEATH TO DARKNESS, 2021

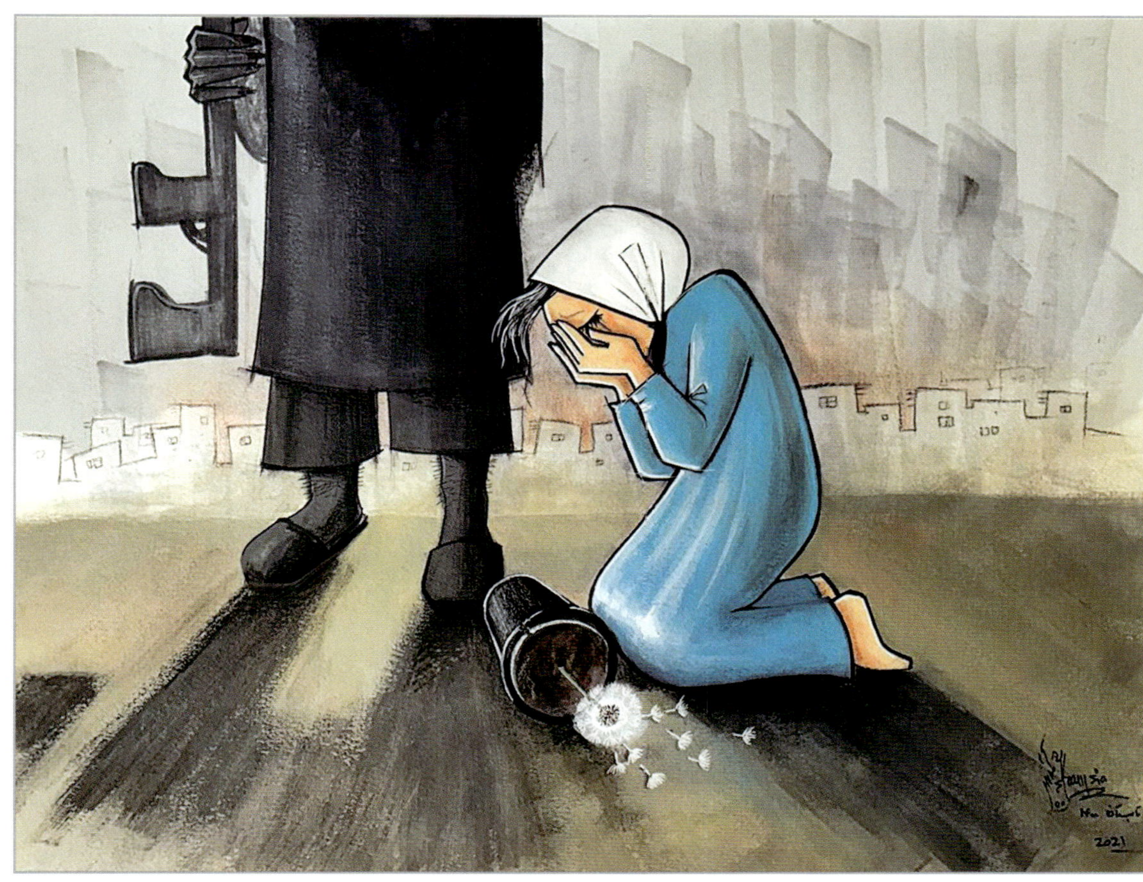

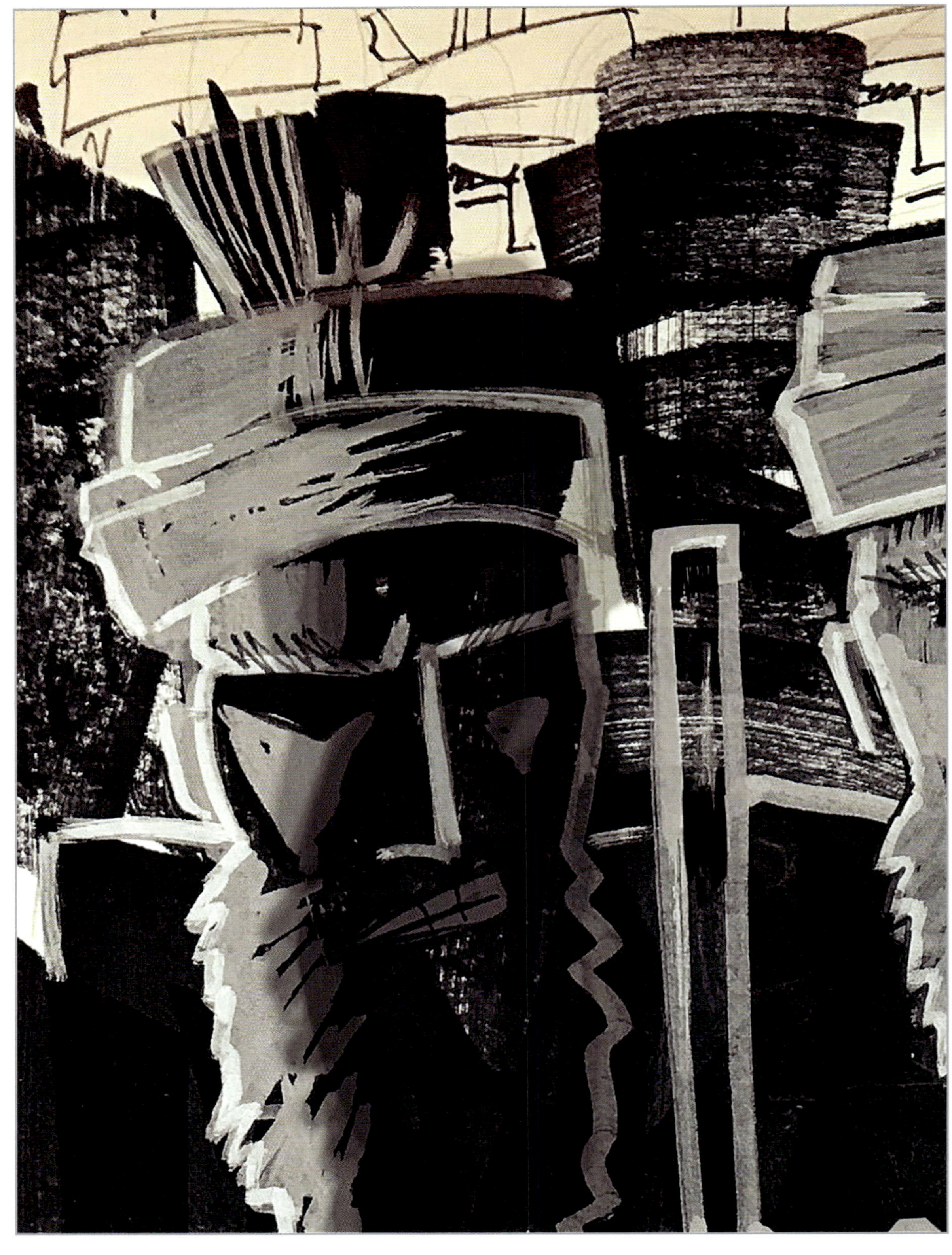

NIGHTMARE, 2021

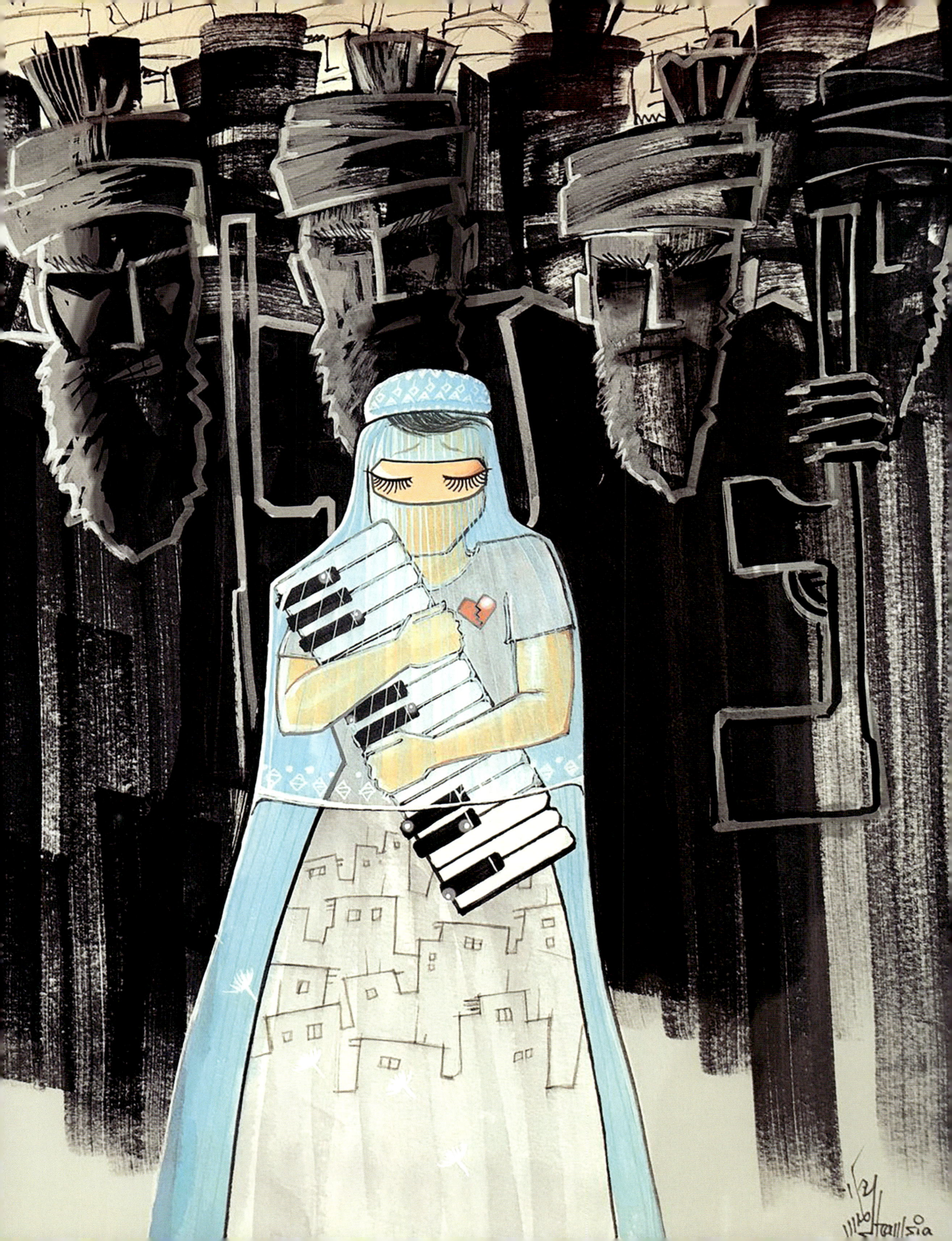

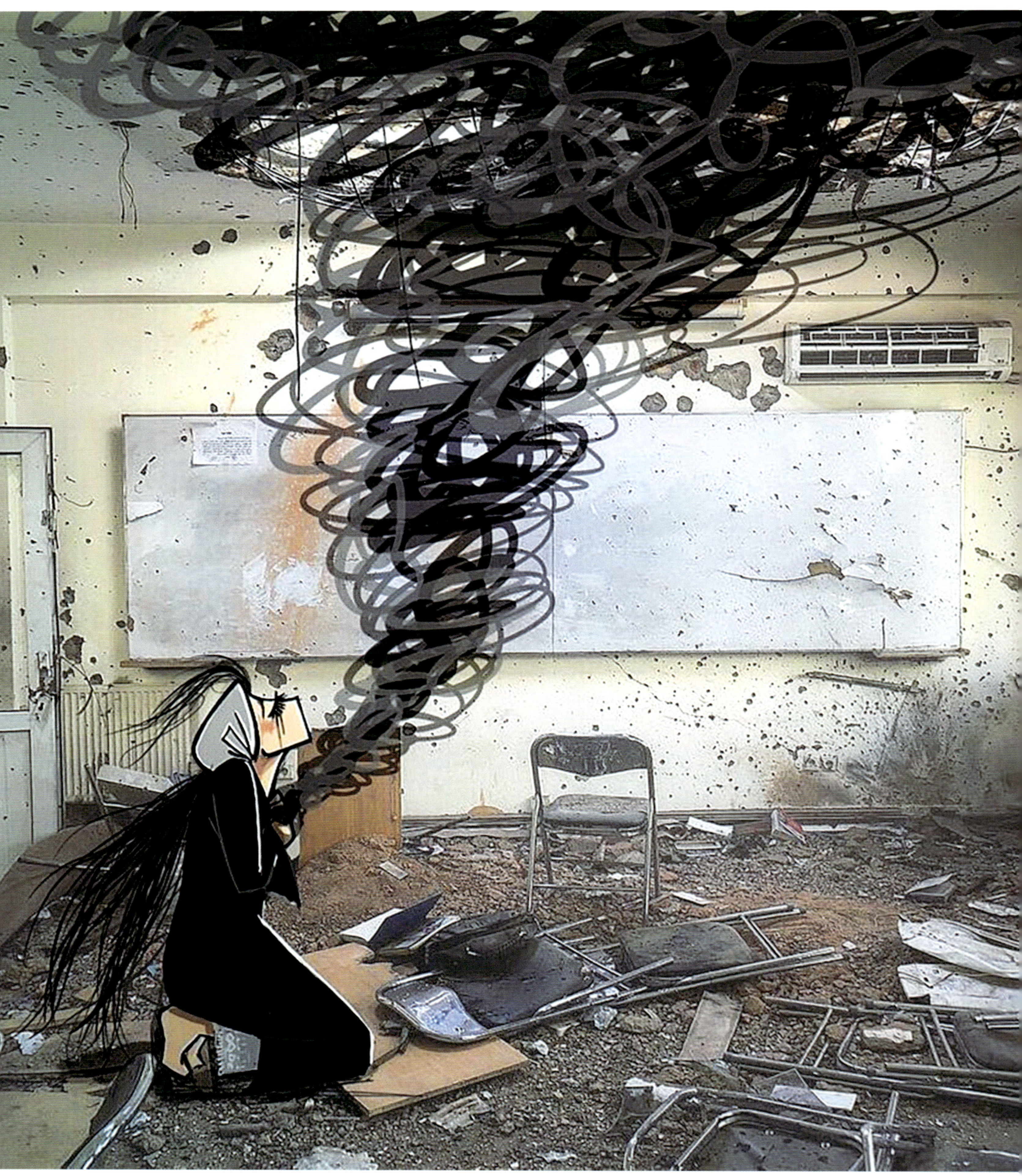

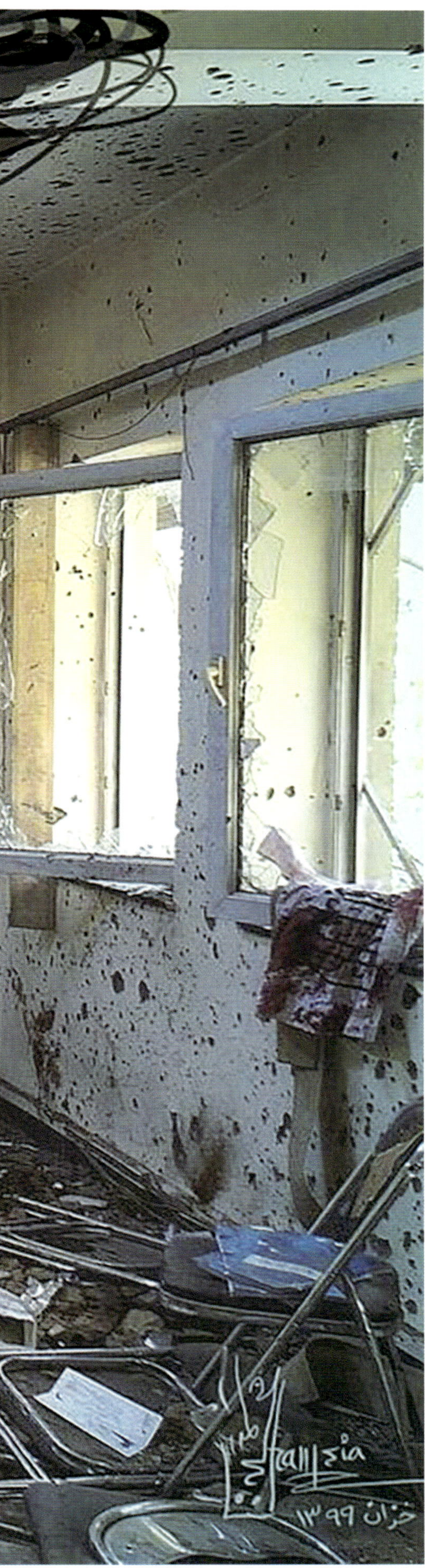

But perhaps it was for this very reason that her women became so unique and special. "The subjects of my paintings have well-defined character, with clearly presented and straightforward feelings, aspirations, and messages. Through them, I want to give a voice to all the women in my country who don't have one; I want to give them hope and strength. My woman has her eyes shut, as she believes there's nothing good to see; she wants to ignore everything, feel less pain. My woman has no mouth, but the misshapen musical instrument that she holds in her hands grants her the power and confidence to speak and make her voice resound with strength. She's a patriot who loves her homeland and fights despair," she states with emphasis. She still recollects her earliest work and the character she chose at the time to serve as its protagonist. "My first images showed a woman in a blue burqa: in terms of form, she was dynamic and looked much stronger than real women. I thought this might give courage to women, but my message was misinterpreted; many thought I wanted to reaffirm the tradition of the burqa. Actually, I wanted to show that eliminating it would not solve our problems, as the virtues and strengths of women are not bound up with that item of clothing, or any other.

"In short, the removal of the burqa in itself would not resolve any problems for women in Afghanistan, and so their situation would not change. In the end, seeing that people did not understand and couldn't go beyond appearances, I decided to eliminate the burqa from my paintings so that my message could be more easily understood. But if I changed their manner of dress, I wanted to depict them with their eyes closed and without mouths in order to underscore and express their discomfort living in a society in which they cannot speak, cannot study or receive a decent education, cannot make decisions," she clarifies. "My women have their eyes closed not because they're blind, but because they can't see their future and hope that something positive will eventually happen," she emphasizes.

At this sad moment, Shamsia is pessimistic and seeks refuge in art, in the hope of overcoming pain and finding new energy. "Unfortunately, I don't see anything good in the foreseeable future; my heart aches from all the years we have worked so hard to win peace and freedom in Afghanistan. Change takes decades, but it only takes a second for everything to fall apart," she admits. "The fall of Kabul had a disastrous impact on my mind and spirit: since that day, the world has changed for me. The sorrow of losing my homeland tortures me each moment, so much so that I can no longer think about the future. I live from one day to the next, in the immediate present; I don't want to think either about the past or the future," she confesses, demoralized. "I want to tell the people of the world that they should appreciate every moment of their life. Today peace, tranquility, and freedom are taken for granted in many countries; but when these are lost, life no longer makes sense."

UNTITLED, 2020, Photo courtesy of Najiba Noori

UNTITLED, Istanbul, Turkey, 2018 (overleaf)

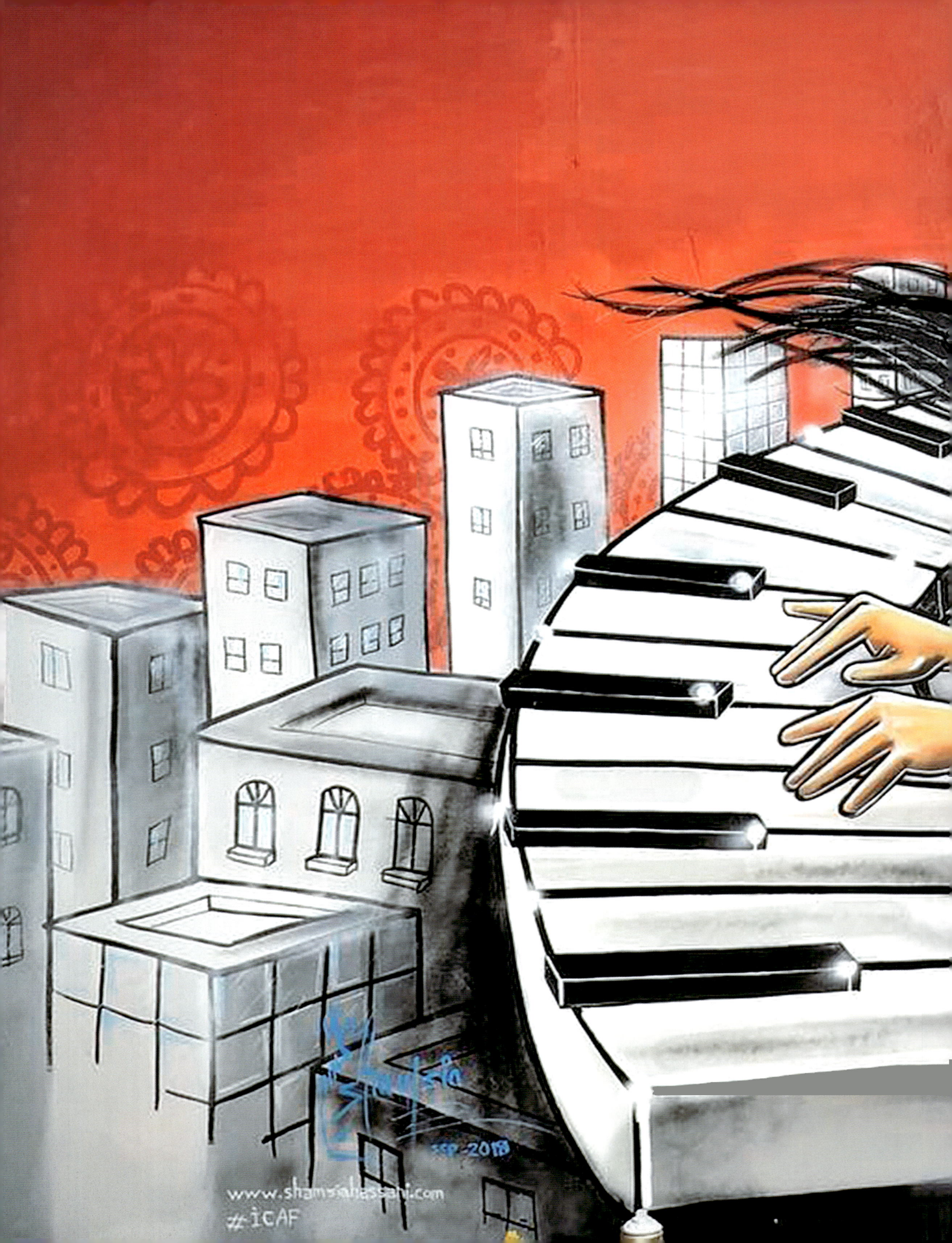

www.shamsiahassani.com
#ICAF

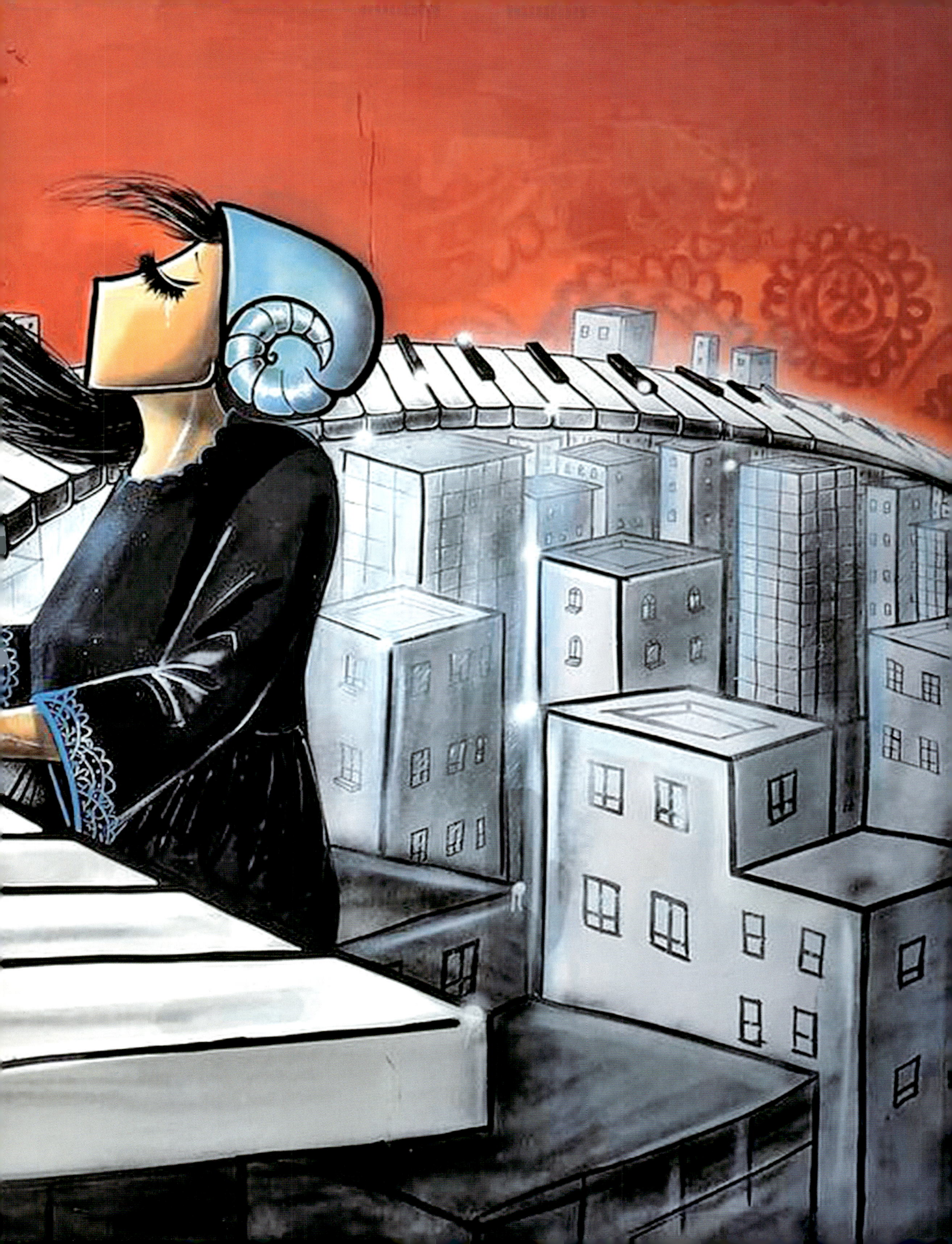

HERA

THE FAIRY OF SYMBOLISM AND MELANCHOLY

"One day as I was finishing a painting of a girl who, like me, was holding a spray can, a couple of men walked past and made a comment that I didn't like at all. So I had my character repeat it on the wall: 'Look at that girl; she can't even hold a spray can in her hand!' And I promised myself that from that point on, I would show everyone who I was."

The eyes of her creatures have the power to capture the soul of whoever looks at them. They are present, intense, touched by a certain melancholy, albeit always full of hope. Bewitching and intriguing, they pique curiosity but also agitation. "Fairy tales and children's books have always inspired me, because I want my images to be easily understood by everyone. This is why I often depict animals, easily decipherable symbols, such as wolves, foxes, rabbits . . . and whenever the characters I portray wear costumes or headdresses that represent them, they interact with that same animal spirit. I don't use strong colors, because my art doesn't need to be aggressive. I love drawing. At first I was inspired by Egon Schiele, then OSGEMEOS; despite their originality, both were always in sync with their world," she claims.

Jasmin Siddiqui, aka Hera or Herakut, was born in Frankfurt to a Pakistani father and a German mother. At the moment, she lives between Berlin and Frankfurt with her dog Frida, whom she rescued in Greece and whom she named after one of the artists who has profoundly inspired her. "When my parents met, they were of very different backgrounds: like yin and yang. My father, who held two doctorates from the university, was Jewish, a man with a mild and gentle disposition. My mother, who came from a protestant, conservative family, was a rebel, a Pippi Longstocking-type character. She too was a really intelligent woman and the one who taught me how to navigate through life early on," she recalls.

"I grew up in a noisy and foul-smelling building, full of people: I hated the place, and my parents taught me how to escape reality by reading books they found at flea markets, and through which I satisfied my insatiable curiosity. I knew how to draw every kind of animal, even

HERA PAINTING, Paris, France, 2021

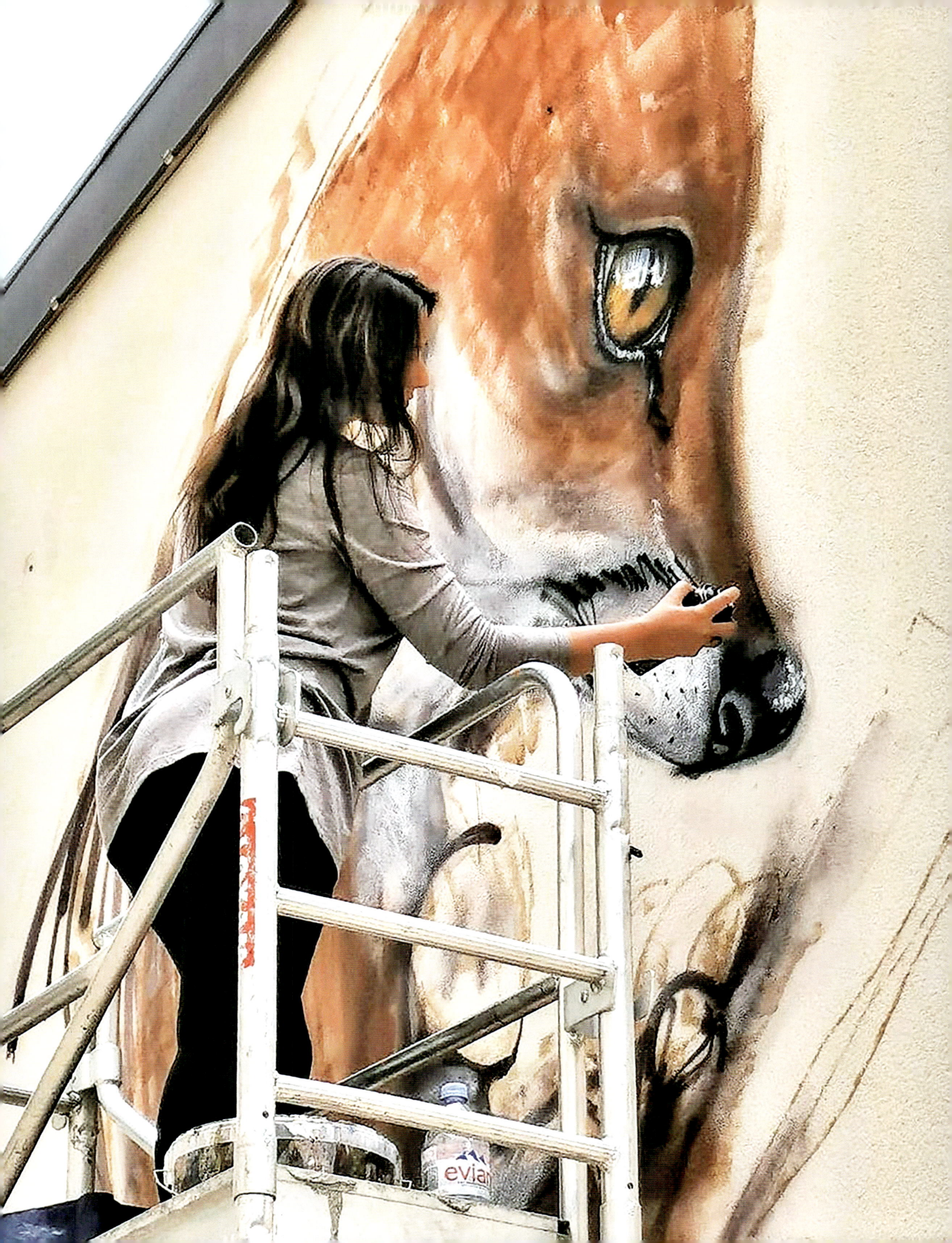

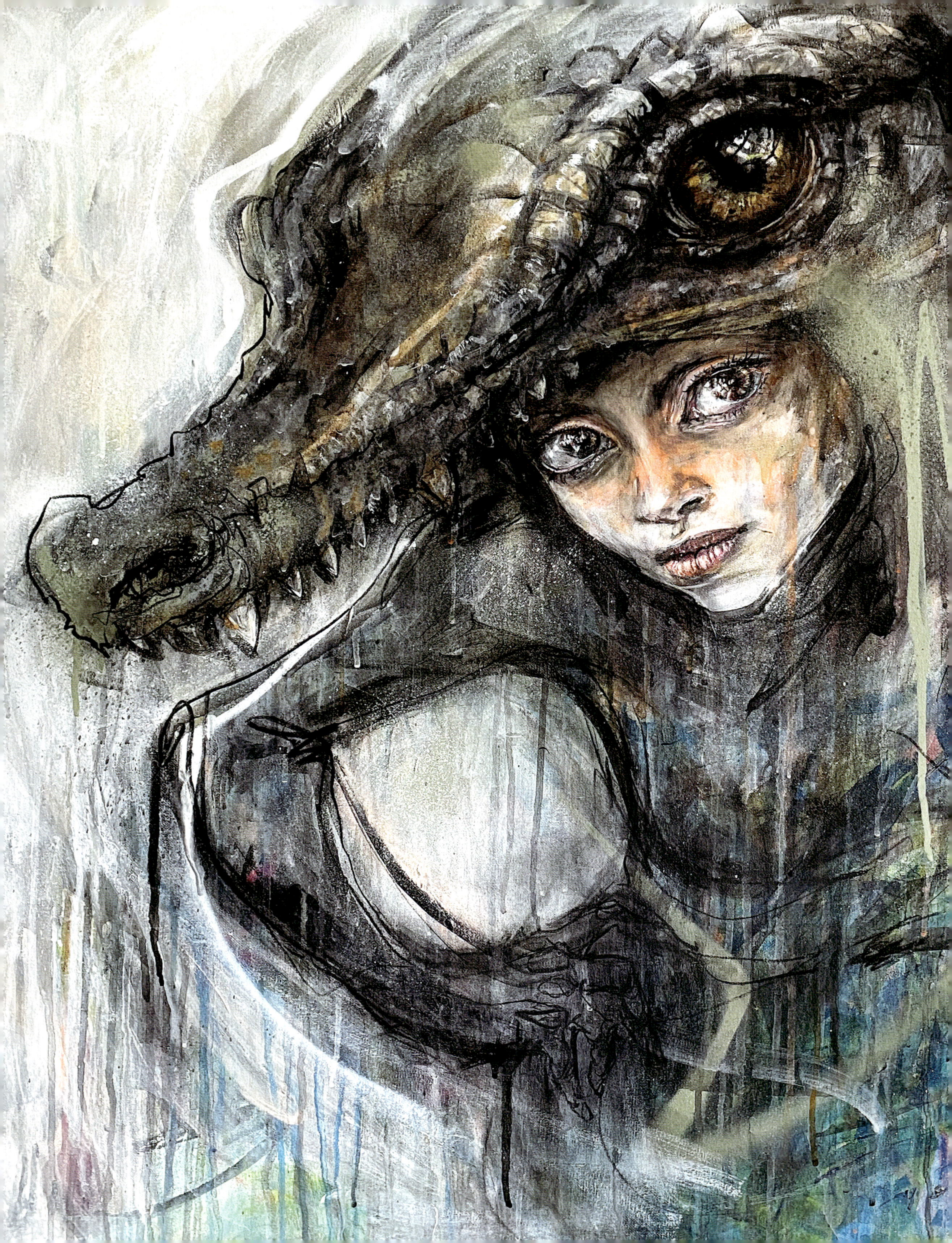

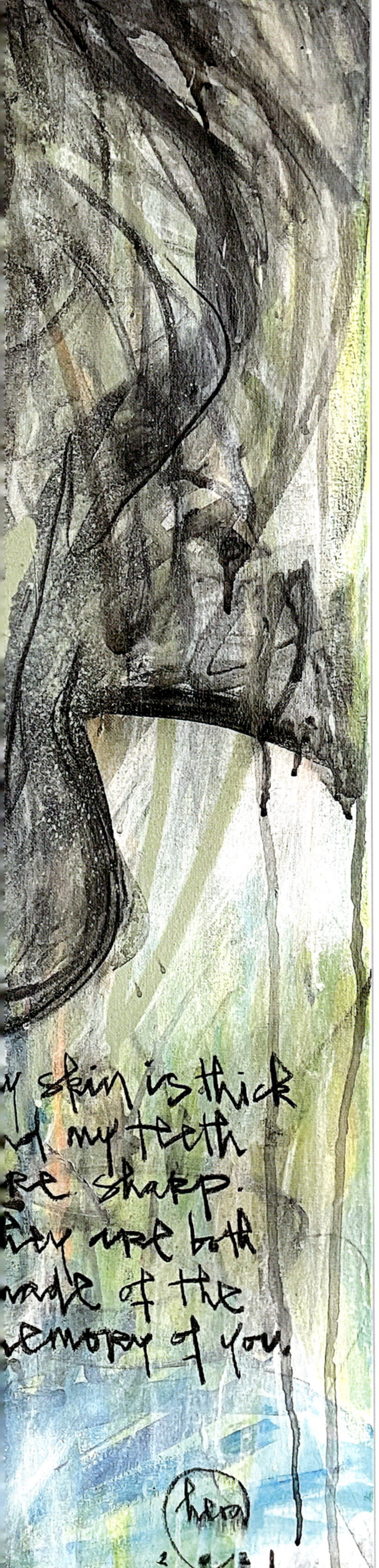

if I had never seen it in real life. I was particularly keen on art history books because I could learn different styles from them; even back then, I was already trying to understand the secrets of the language of symbols. We didn't have much money, but my parents would save up all year so they could take cultural trips and round out my education," Hera reflects. Drawing up memories, she continues: "When I was in elementary school, the teachers noticed that I had a particular talent for drawing. So, to encourage me, my parents got me a private teacher—an elderly lady who hated people and who specialized in portraits so realistic that they looked like photographs."

"I took lessons with her from the age of eight, and was in complete shock when she died, completely alone. I decided that it might be better to look for a safer line of work: artists certainly didn't have an easy life. At the beginning, I enrolled in graphic design, and took on various jobs as a salesgirl or bus driver 'to pay for school.'" Temperamentally speaking, Hera could not stand humoring the system: she wanted to create art in her own way. So one day she offered to paint a mural inside a shoe store in exchange for a pair of shoes. This marked the beginning of her career. First she was discovered by Nike, then by Carhartt, and then by an artist who organized street art festivals around the world. "I entered a community of artists who painted together with me . . . and found my path," she admits.

She also found a new stage name: "Jasmine doesn't sound good in German; it doesn't end with an A, like other female names do. . . And jasmine is a very hardy flower that grows everywhere, but it's really tiny. . . I was fascinated by Greek mythology, and *Hera* evoked a warrior, exactly what—more than anything else—I felt I was at that time."

In 2004, Hera began a long collaboration—for over sixteen years—with the graffiti artist Falk Lehmann, aka Akut, with whom she traveled all over the world to work on large murals.

THICK SKIN SHARP TEETH, 2021

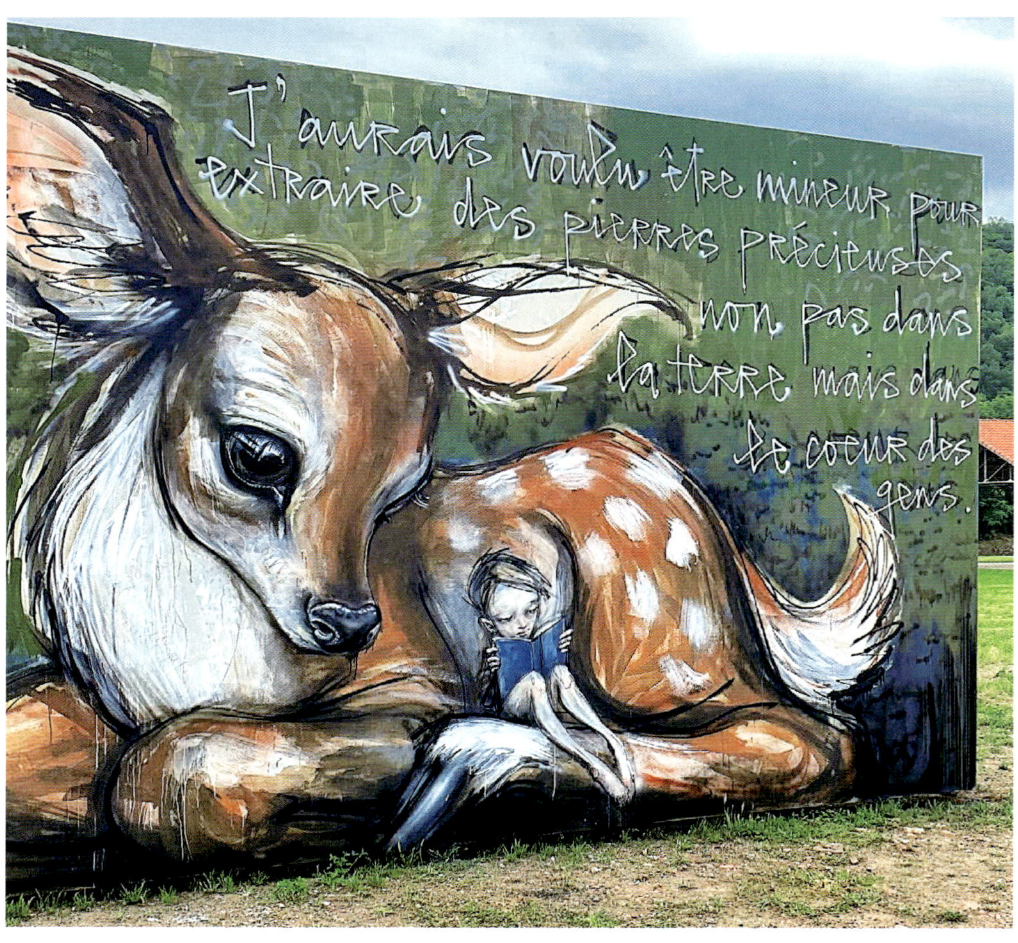

Together they became famous as Herakut. By combining their styles, they created something unique: imaginary worlds and original characters set in environments that oscillated between melancholy and the art of storytelling. "Akut was less driven than I was, and when he became a father, he decided that he didn't feel like traveling that much anymore, so our collaboration came to an end. But there's always an 'open door' between us; so, who knows, in the future. . . ," she notes. During the Herakut period, Hera discovered her true artistic calling, which she then applied to all her work. In 2015, the NGO aptART invited them to paint a series of murals in Jordan.

"We were supposed to make these with Syrian children from the Al-Zaatari refugee camp. Seeing the light in the eyes of these children and people as they collaborated with us, or simply watched what we created, made me realize that I had found the right path and that I was proud of being a street artist," she recalls with a mixture of emotion and enthusiasm in her voice.

With Akut, Hera also discovered the harsh reality of racism: "When we participated in a project in East Germany, people asked me if like the *Wessis* (West Germans), I wasn't worried about taking jobs away from the *Ossis* (East Germans). . . Or they asked me about my surname, which was clearly not German, and joked a lot about how difficult it was to pronounce. . . We decided not to place any weight on this and to focus solely on our work, and that was the right decision. I also came up with the idea of creating a youth club and inviting young people to collaborate with us. It turned out to be an excellent initiative to unite and bring people together. This experience also made me aware of how important it was to work with future generations in order to change the world," she declares.

Decazeville, France, 2021

Goch, Germany, 2021

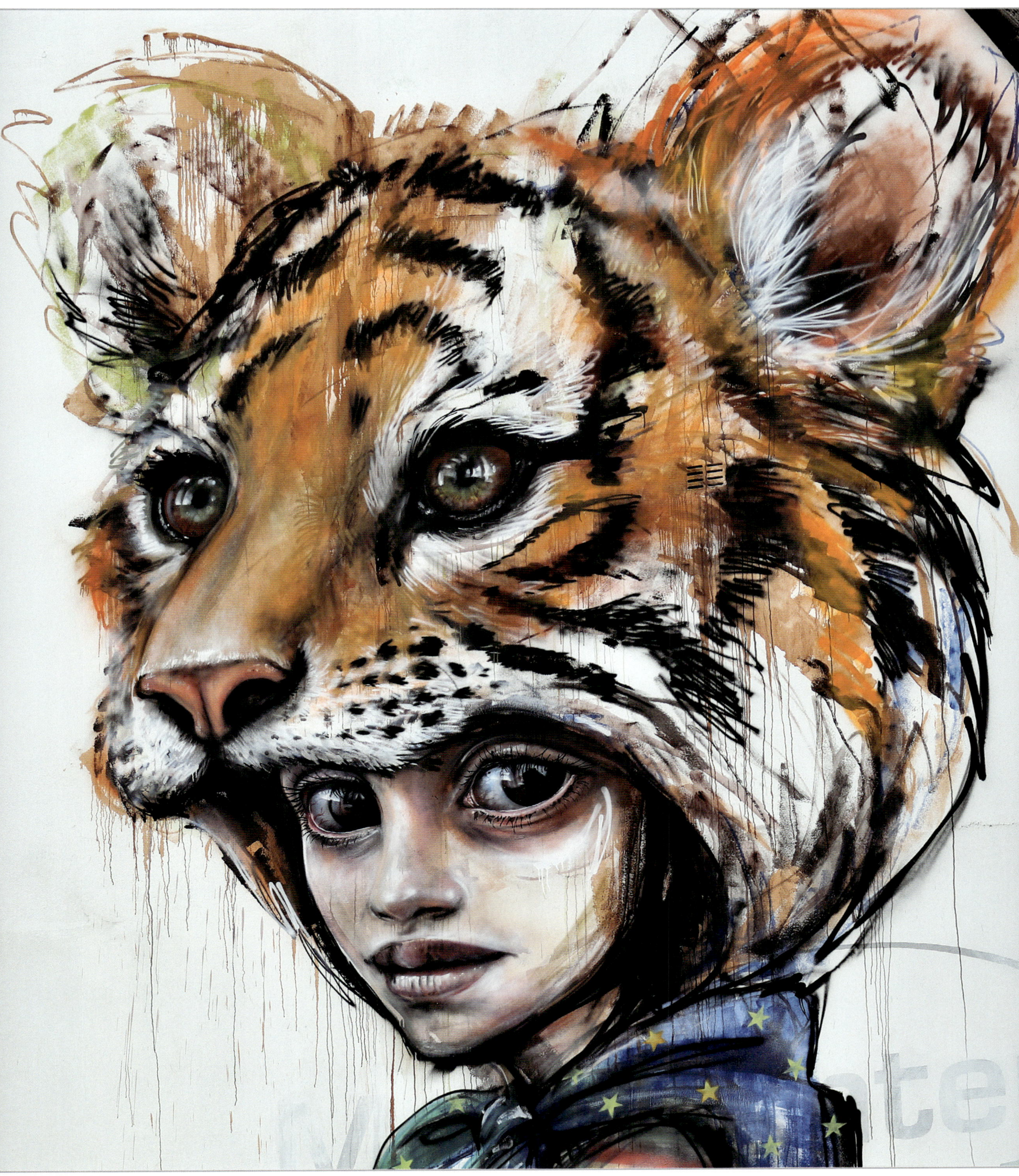

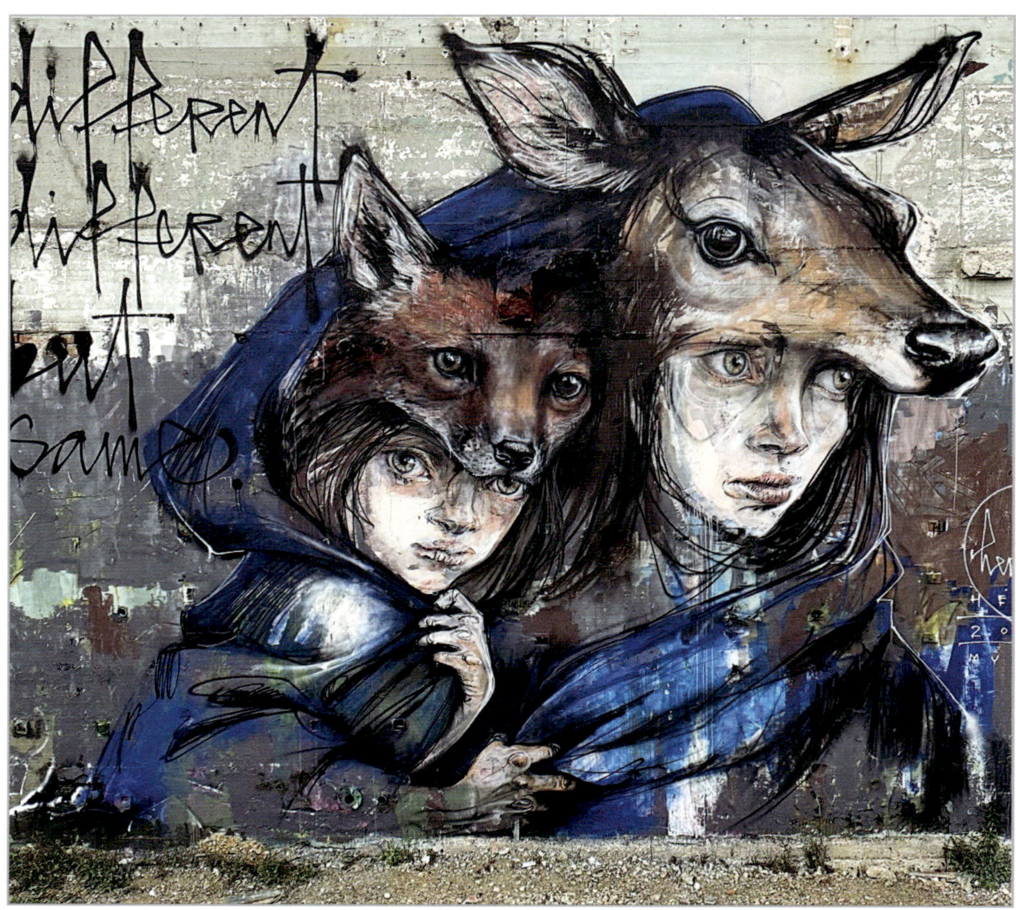

In this respect, Hera admits that she was greatly influenced by Mexican muralists during the time that she lived in Los Angeles, where she had done her studies: "It was art in the streets that fell within reach even of those who couldn't read, who were conditioned by religious beliefs and political propaganda."

When it comes to this, Hera's mission goes much further: "I like to inspire and direct young generations toward art, which is why I organize various workshops and often involve children in my installations and works, and I want to continue doing so. At the same time, I want to help other female artists establish themselves in a world that has not always been accesible to them."

Hera wants to use her art to spread a powerful, universal message of respect, tolerance, and humanity: "My mantra is to create something better, something that comes close to perfection, a surprising union of elements that is in dialogue and harmony with nature."

Munich, Germany, 2020

Næstved, Denmark, 2021 (right)

Teufelsberg, Germany, 2021 (overleaf)

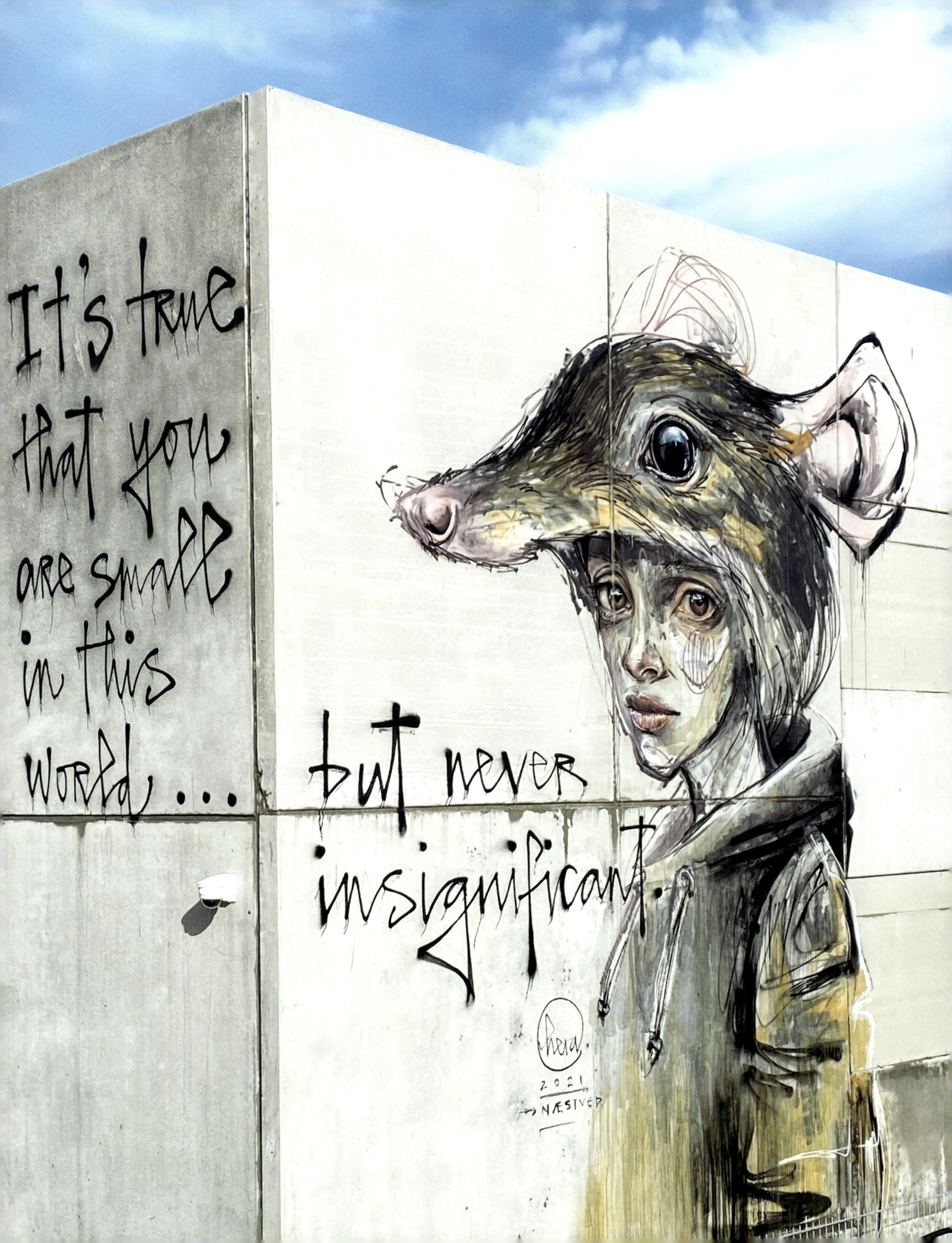

It's true that you are small in this world ...
but never insignificant.
hera
2021
NÆSTVED

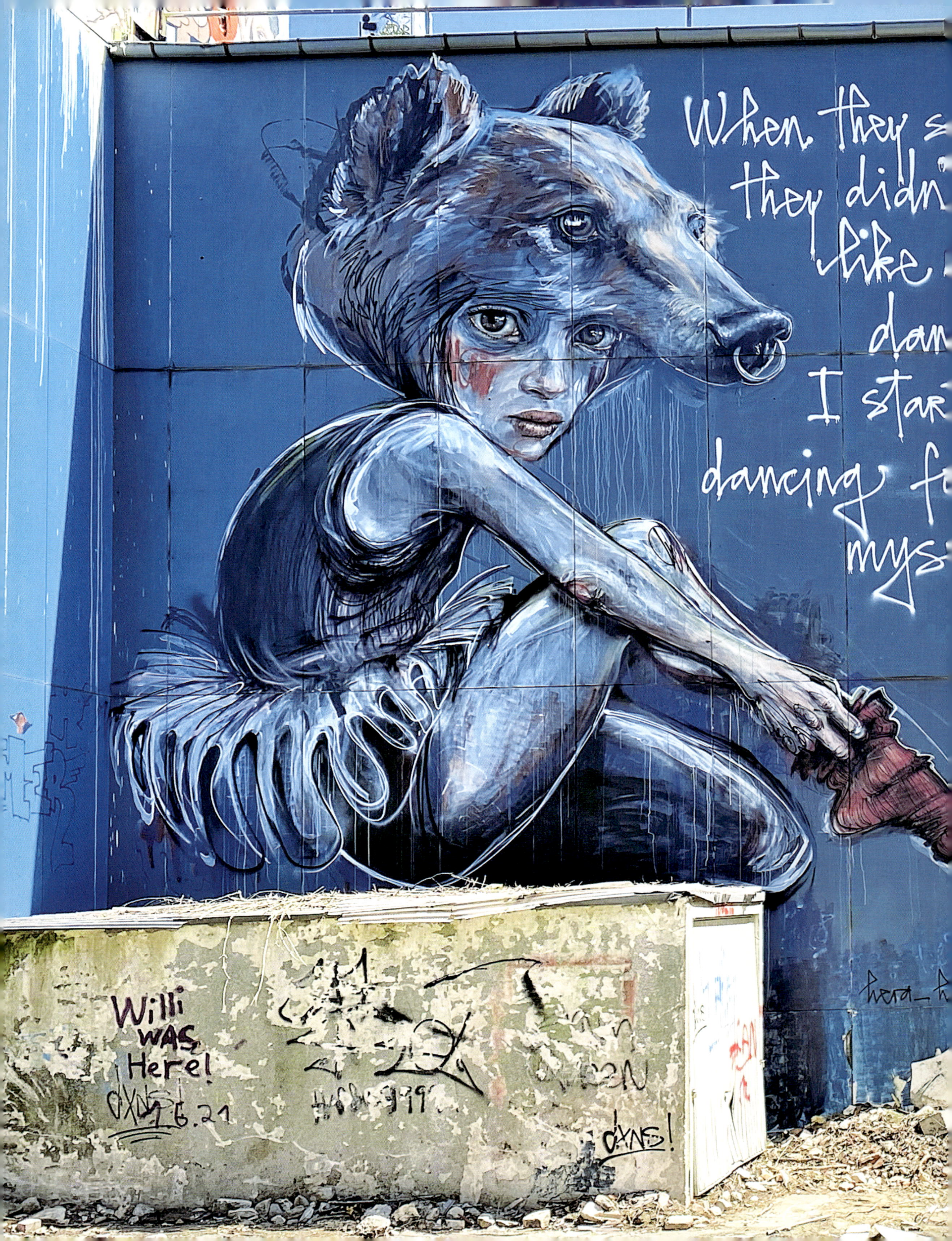

When they s
they didn'
like
dan
I star
dancing f
mys
Willi
WAS
Here!
6.21

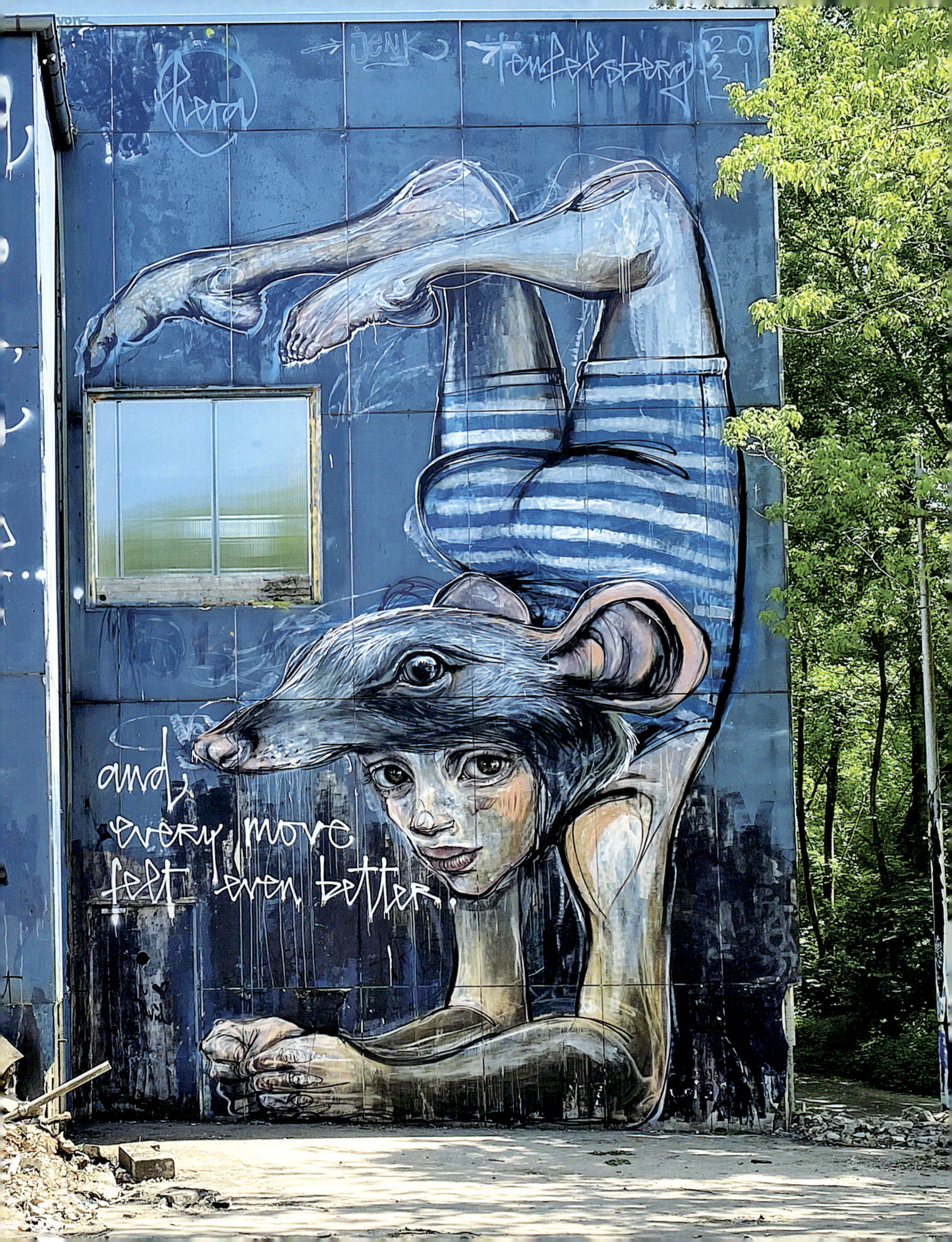

and
every move
felt even better.

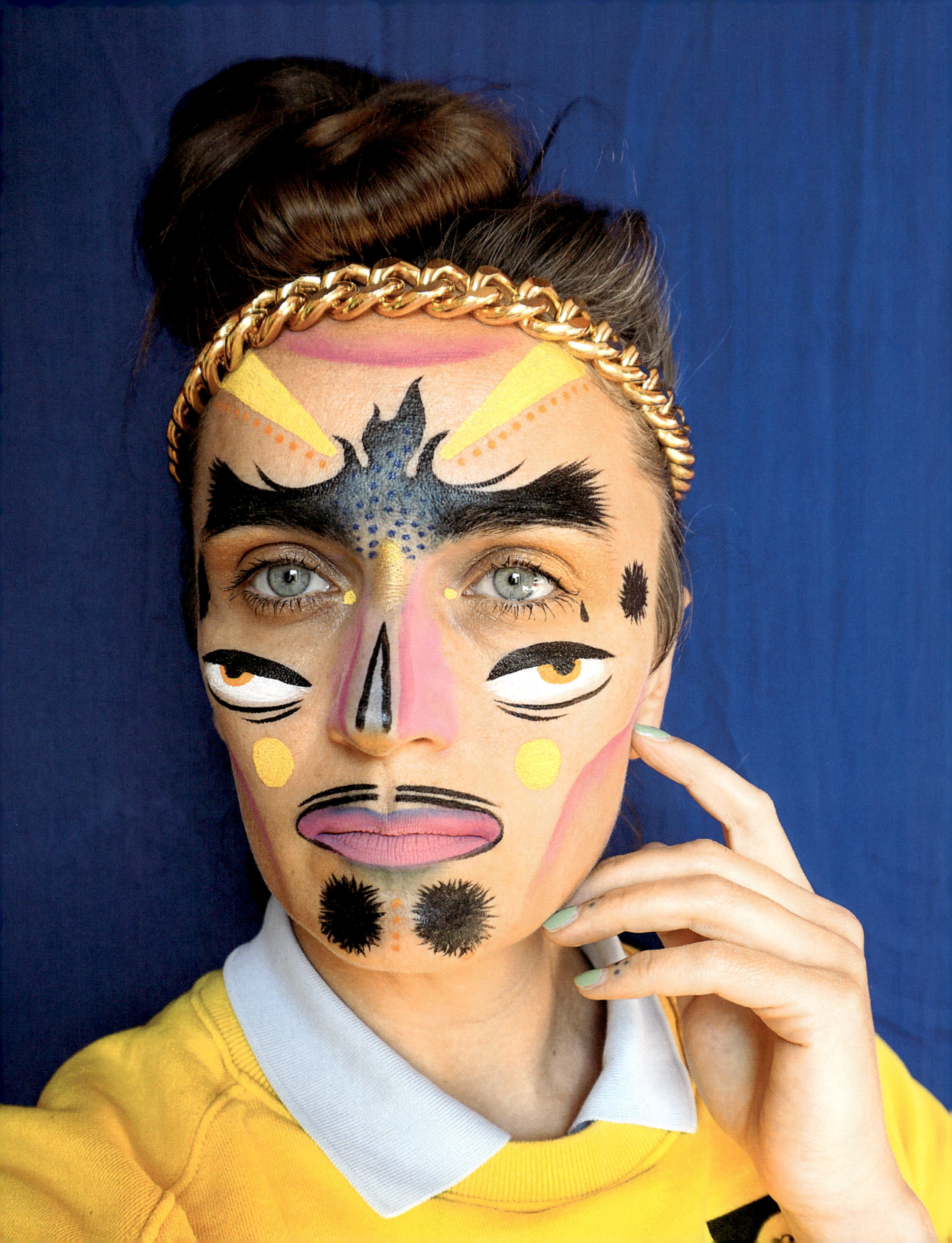

KASHINK

THE REVOLUTIONARY OF STYLE

"Just like any form of art, street art is also challenging for women artists. It's easy to name ten male painters who marked art history, but much more difficult to name a few women painters, for example. Street art is the same. Women artists face the same problem of visibility."

"Art means challenging normativity to me. The role of an artist is to share their vision and give a different perspective of the world to the public. As an artist, you can question what seems to be normal to people, what seems acceptable, or not. I'm not interested in art that is made to be pretty or decorative. Art has to have a purpose and a meaning," claims Kashink.

Her style is unique, revolutionary, provocative, to the point that it can shock even the world of street art. Her brilliant colors reflect her magnetic and intriguing personality, as do her weird, unexpected, unusual, and symbol-laden characters with their multiple eyes. In the art world, Kashink stands out for her ability to be an outsider in every respect. "My work is about identity and questioning aesthetic codes. I'm trying to share a different vision of what's acceptable about faces, bodies, and identities. My goal is to celebrate the diversity of humanity," she explains with pride.

French by birth, Kashink lives in Paris but has a global vision of the world and of art, which has marked her since her childhood. "I've always been creative. When I was a child I loved to draw or create little collages, or experiment with all sorts of material. But I wasn't considered 'gifted' or great at drawing, for example. . . My parents were not really supportive, even when I decided to travel for street art opportunities," she recalls. "When I started painting on walls, I never thought I could make money with my art, even in my wildest dreams. No one in my family is an artist, so I didn't really have any role models around me either. It was very difficult to make it in the art world. I worked very hard to get the visibility I have today. For years, I traveled to paint walls around the world, using my own money; I wasn't invited anywhere. But little by little, I started getting

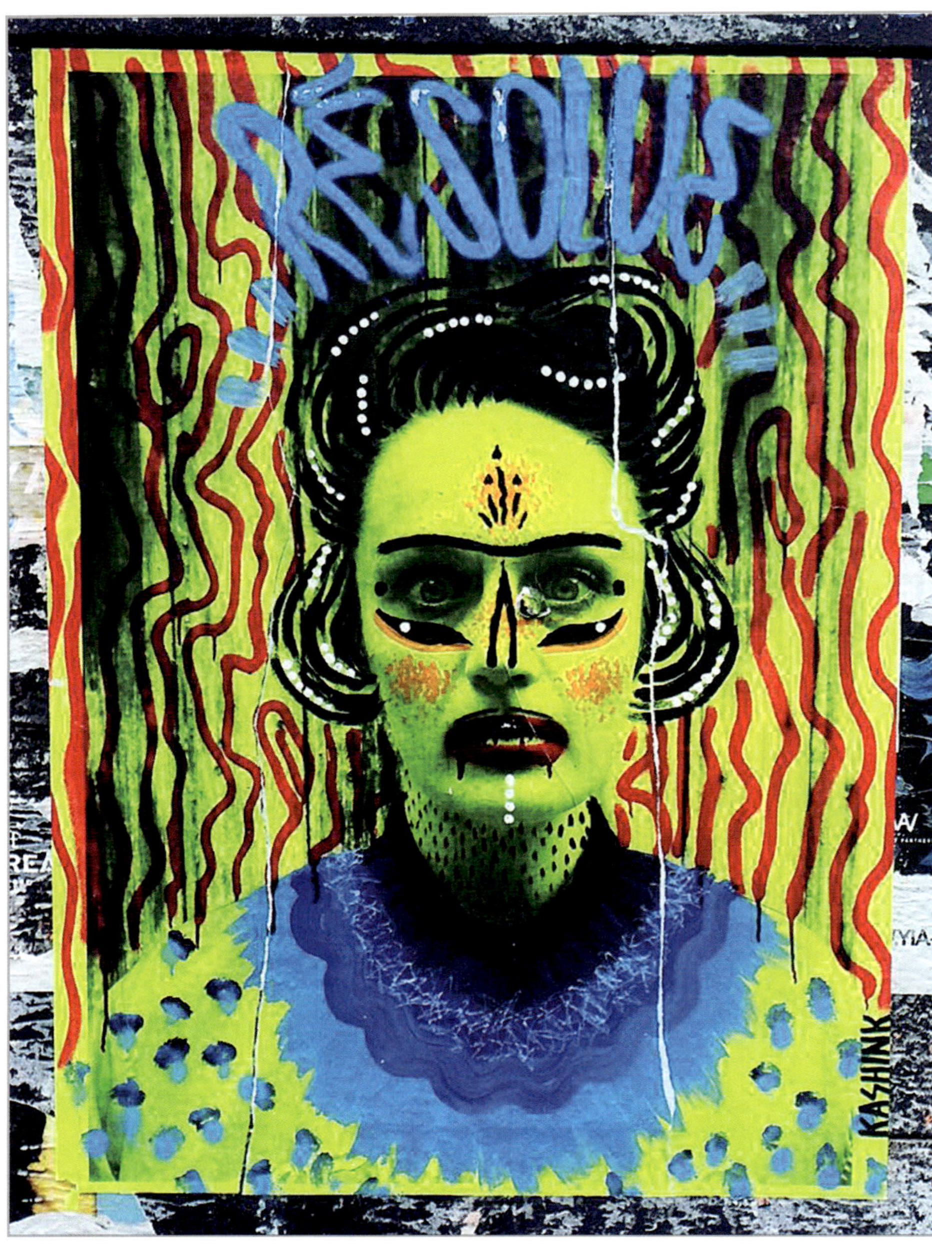

RESOLUE — GENRE LIBRE, Los Angeles, California, USA, and Paris, France, 2017

attention, also because my style was very different from that of other street artists and the message I was trying to communicate was strong and global. And also, because I'm an activist and I have a lot to say, I started getting invited to many cultural events, such as university conferences, around the world."

But it was always in the street that Kashink recognized her own universe, the artistic means through which to express herself. "When street art started to get more attention and be recognized as a real form of art, I had already been painting for several years. Before that, I never thought I would be a full-time artist, and I did many other jobs to support myself," she still remembers.

Throughout her evolution as an artist, Kashink has always tried to deconstruct aesthetic codes and the norms that define gender, beauty, standards, and the common concept of freedom; she identifies herself as a non-binary feminist, and remains outside of any conceptual framework.

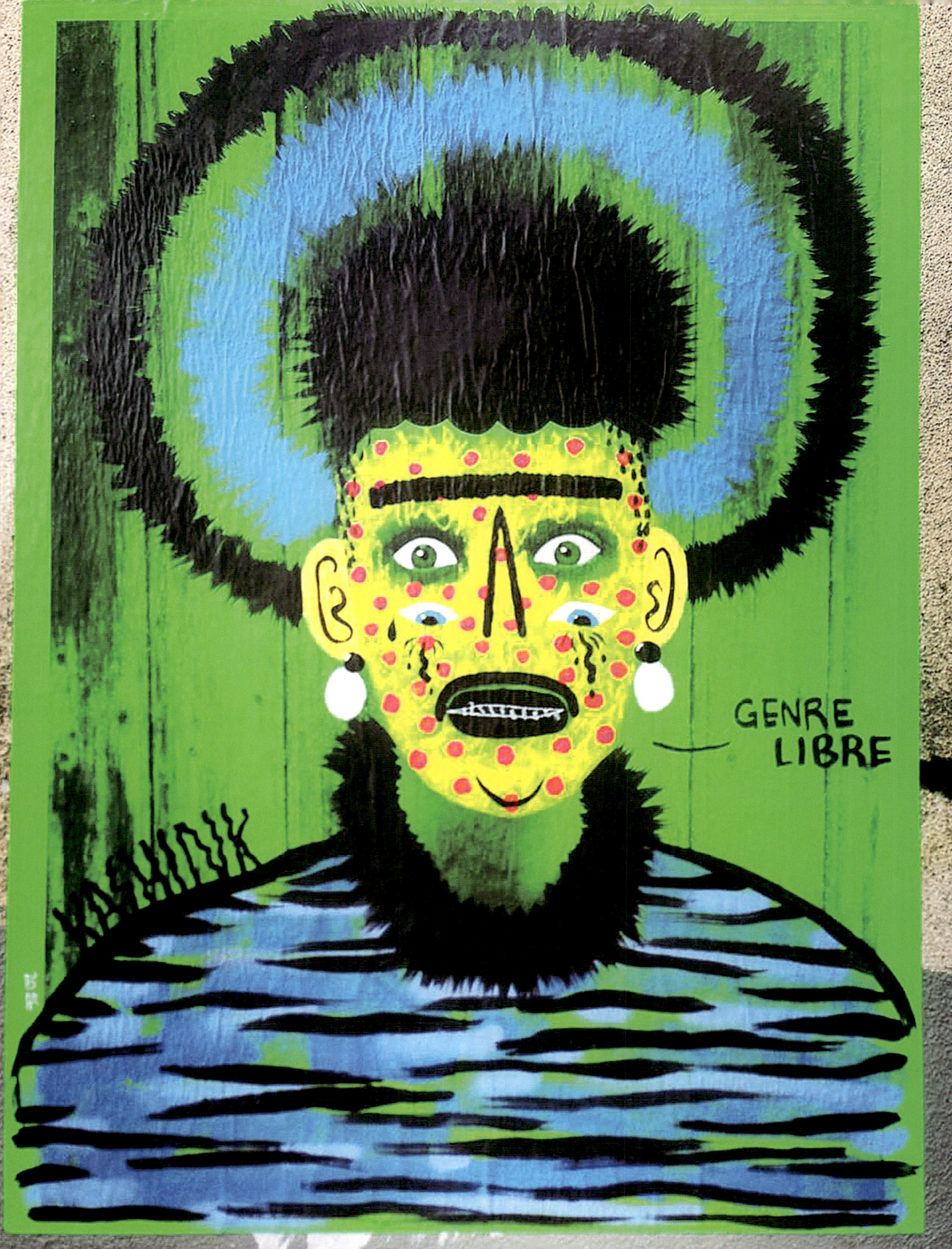

GENRE
LIBRE

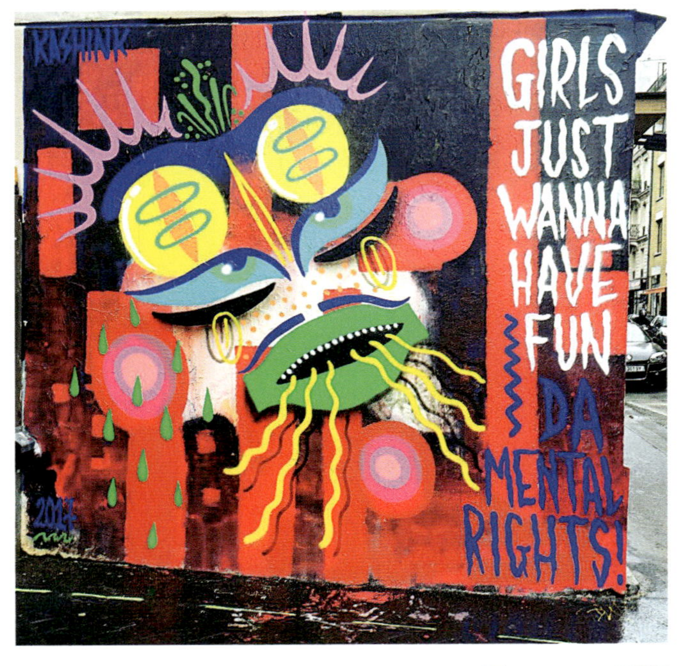
KASHINK
GIRLS
JUST
WANNA
HAVE
FUN
DA
MENTAL
RIGHTS!
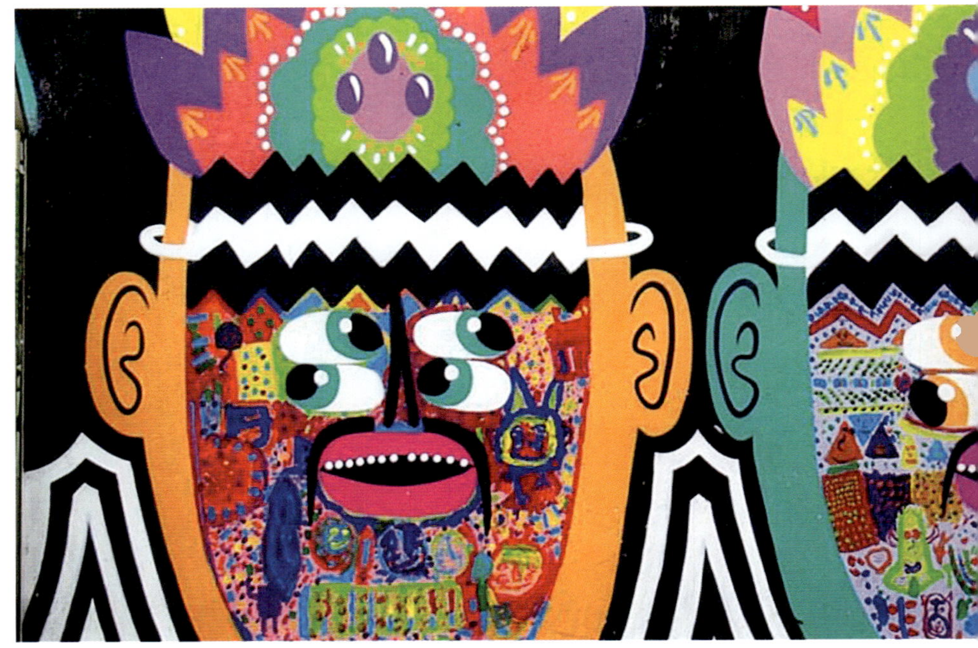
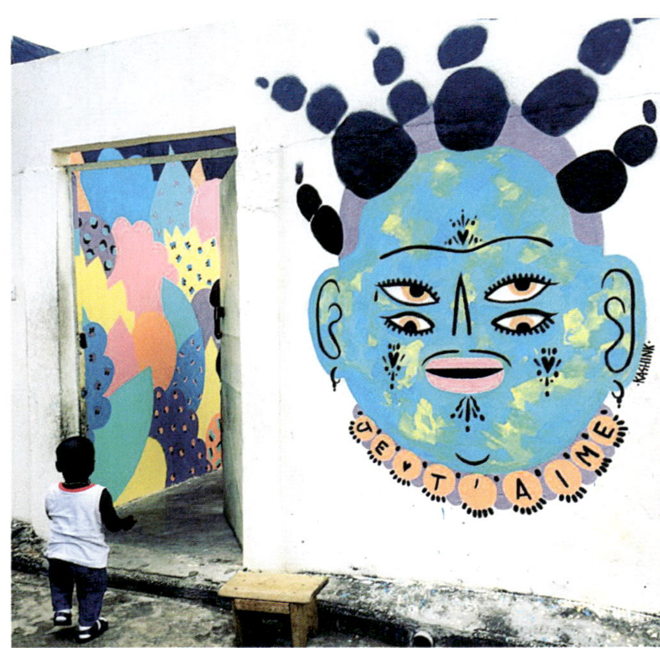
JE T'AIME
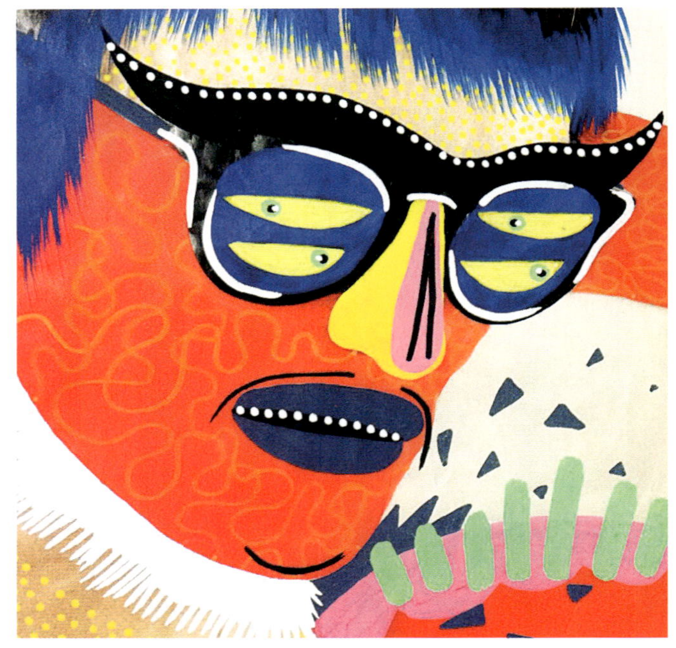
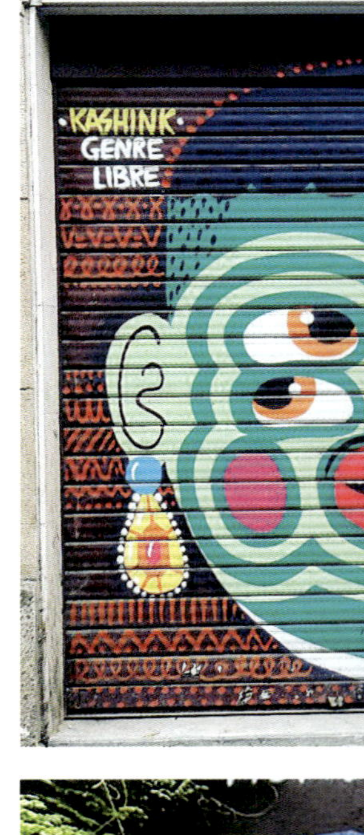
KASHINK
GENRE
LIBRE
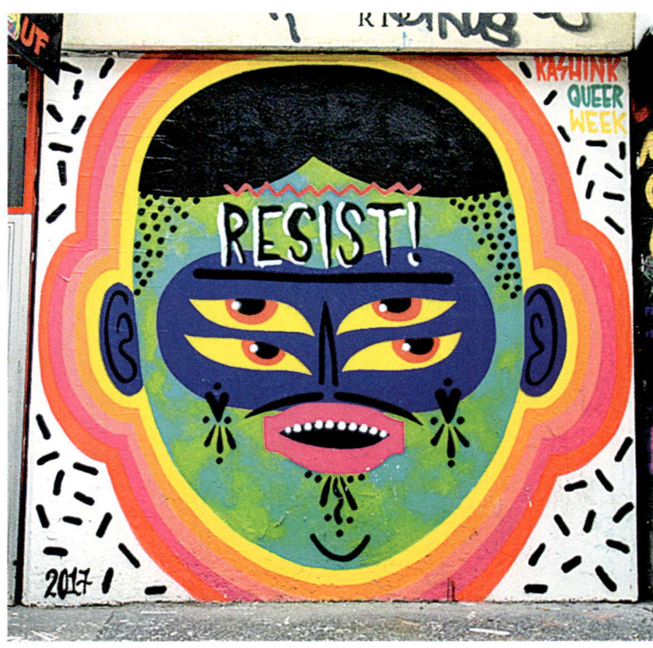
KASHINK
QUEER
WEEK
RESIST!
2017
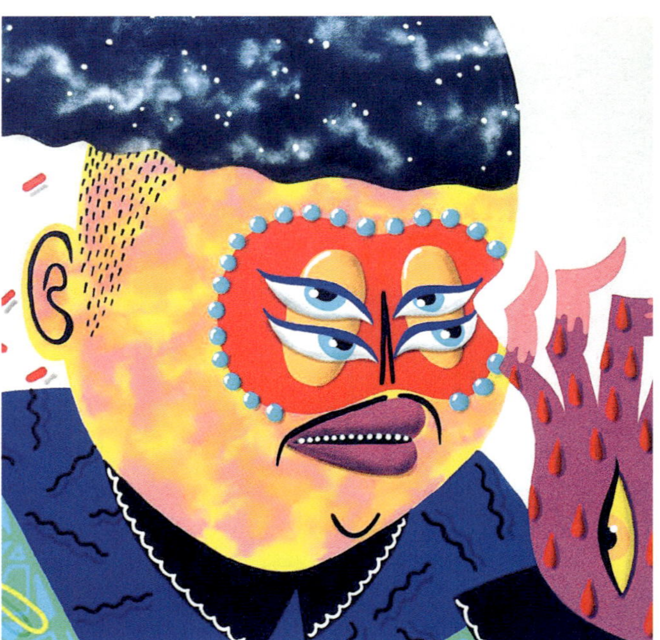
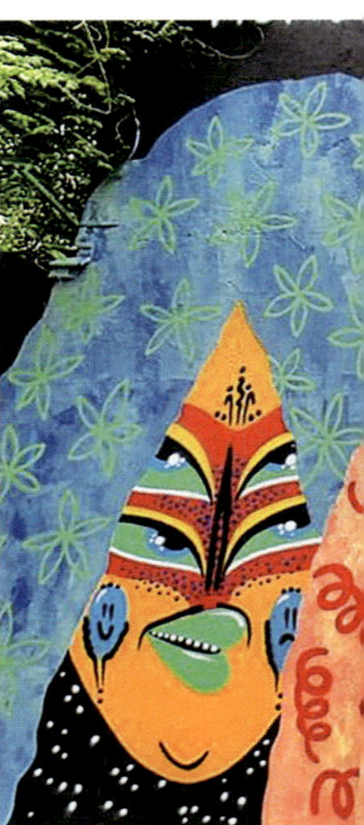

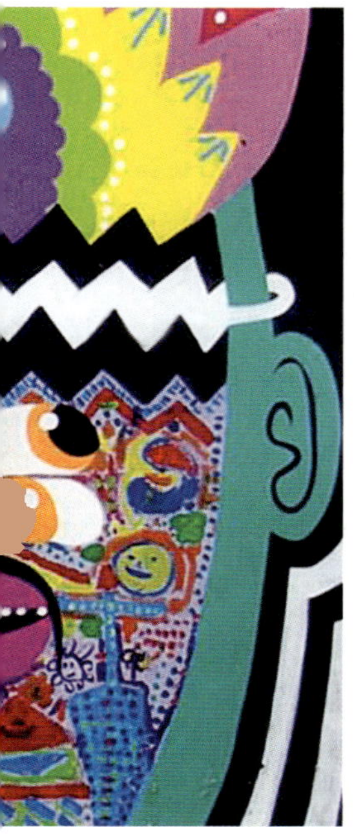
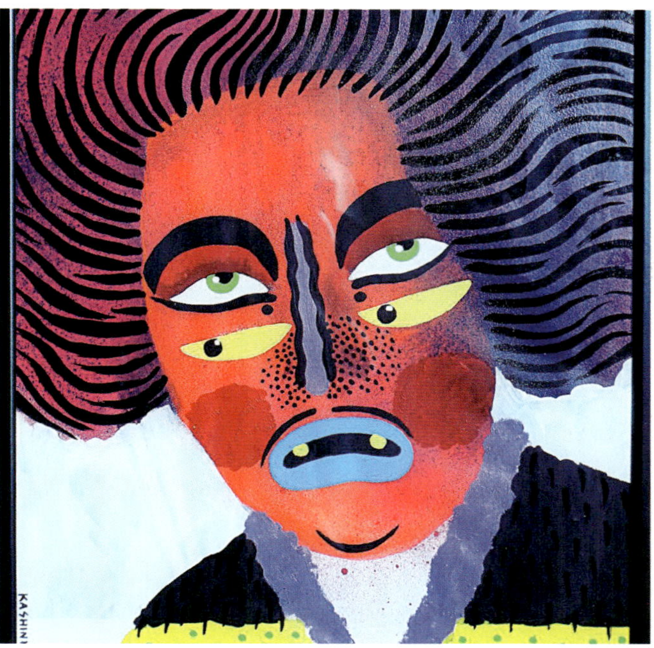
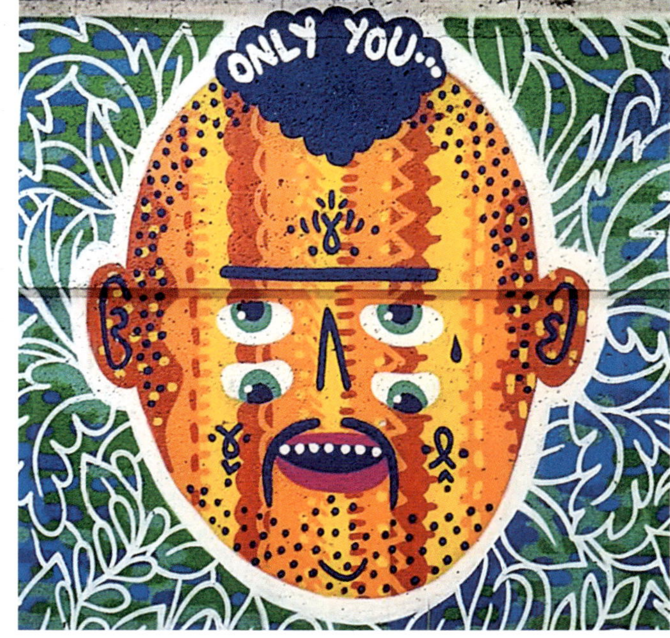
ONLY YOU...
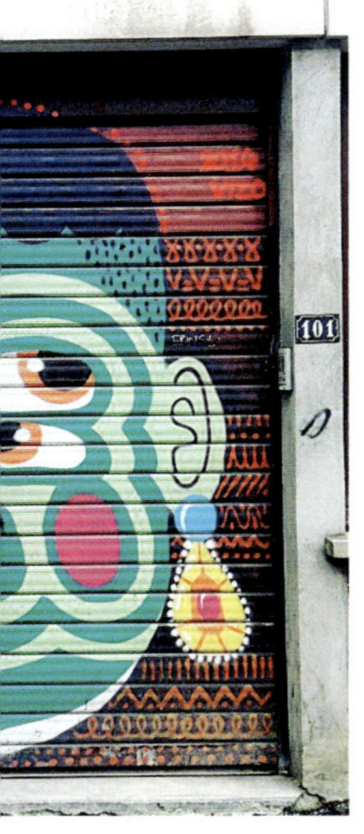
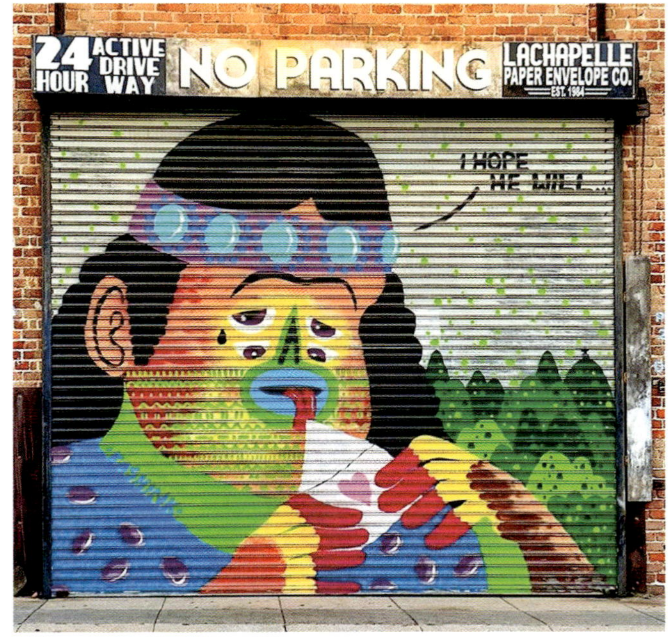
24 HOUR
ACTIVE DRIVE WAY
NO PARKING
LACHAPELLE PAPER ENVELOPE CO.
EST. 1964
I HOPE HE WILL...
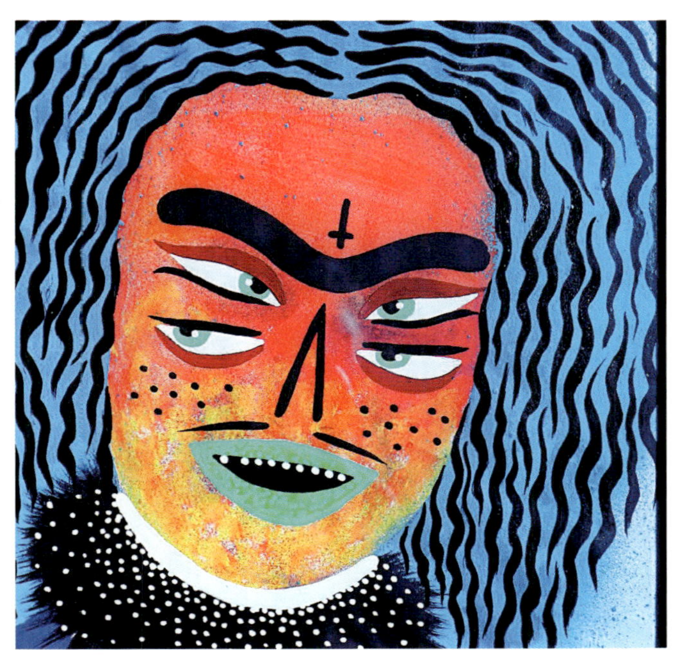
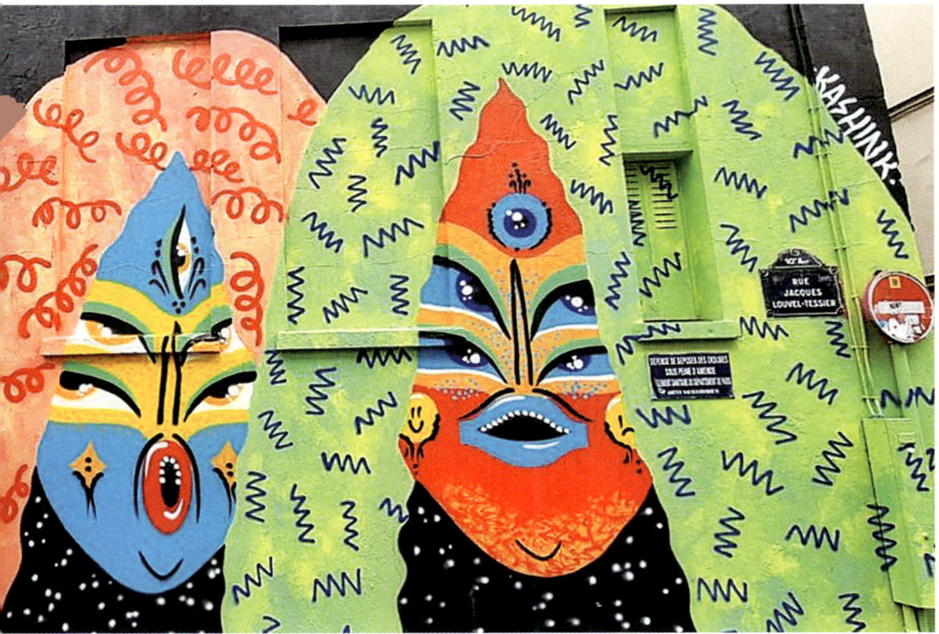
KASHINK
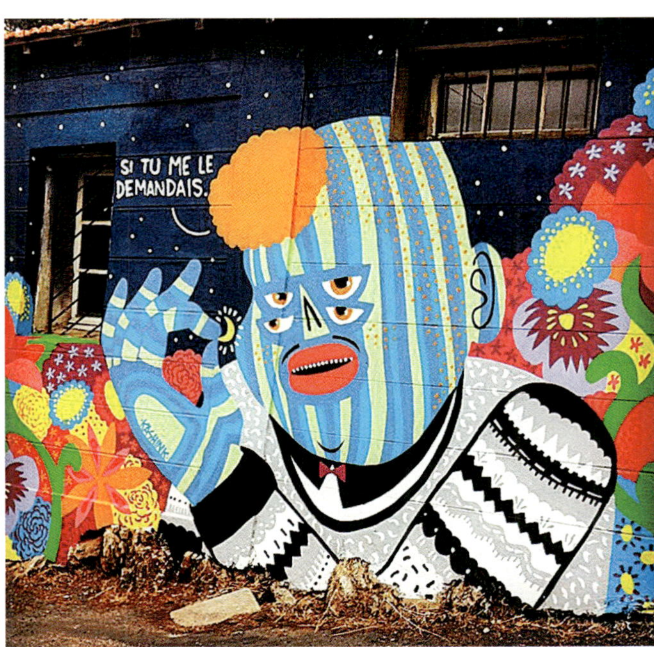
SI TU ME LE
DEMANDAIS.

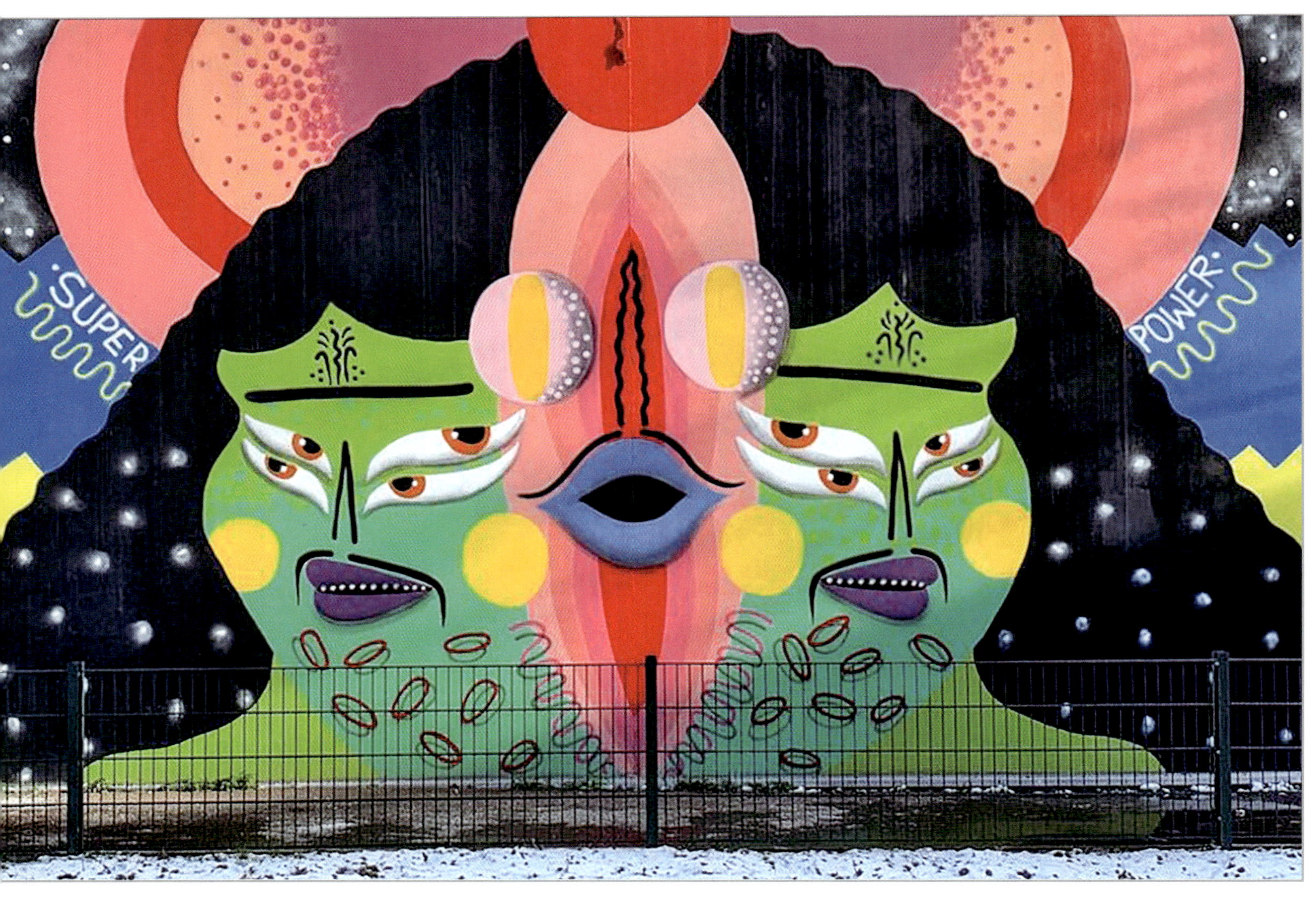

Since 2013, she has used eyeliner to draw a mustache on her face and regards this gesture as a stance and a sociological experiment. She paints enormous murals and tests out the paintings on her own face, creating amazing characters that arouse curiosity, capture the eye and mind, and make people ponder. And she's constantly experimenting: "I've been working on films and music, and I'm really excited to be able to complete my artistic practice with different approaches. I'm also currently writing a book about my experience; it's like a journal, or an essay, that I started writing in 2013, and I'm very excited to be able to share my journey as an artist and an activist."

Kashink concludes with a reflection on her most recent experience and with a glance toward the future: "The first lockdown gave us an opportunity to focus on ourselves, our priorities, what we really want to do with our lives; it showed us how fragile we are, and how important the people around us are, but it also brought conflicts and divisions. Yet, I also think we are at a crossroads in history. This extreme situation that we are experiencing is new and already has a lot of serious consequences on many levels. Let's hope we can all cope with that and move on toward a better future, taking into consideration what we've learned along the way."

SUPER POWER, Malakoff, France, 2018

50 CAKES OF GAY, Art Basel, Miami, Florida, USA, 2013 (overleaf)

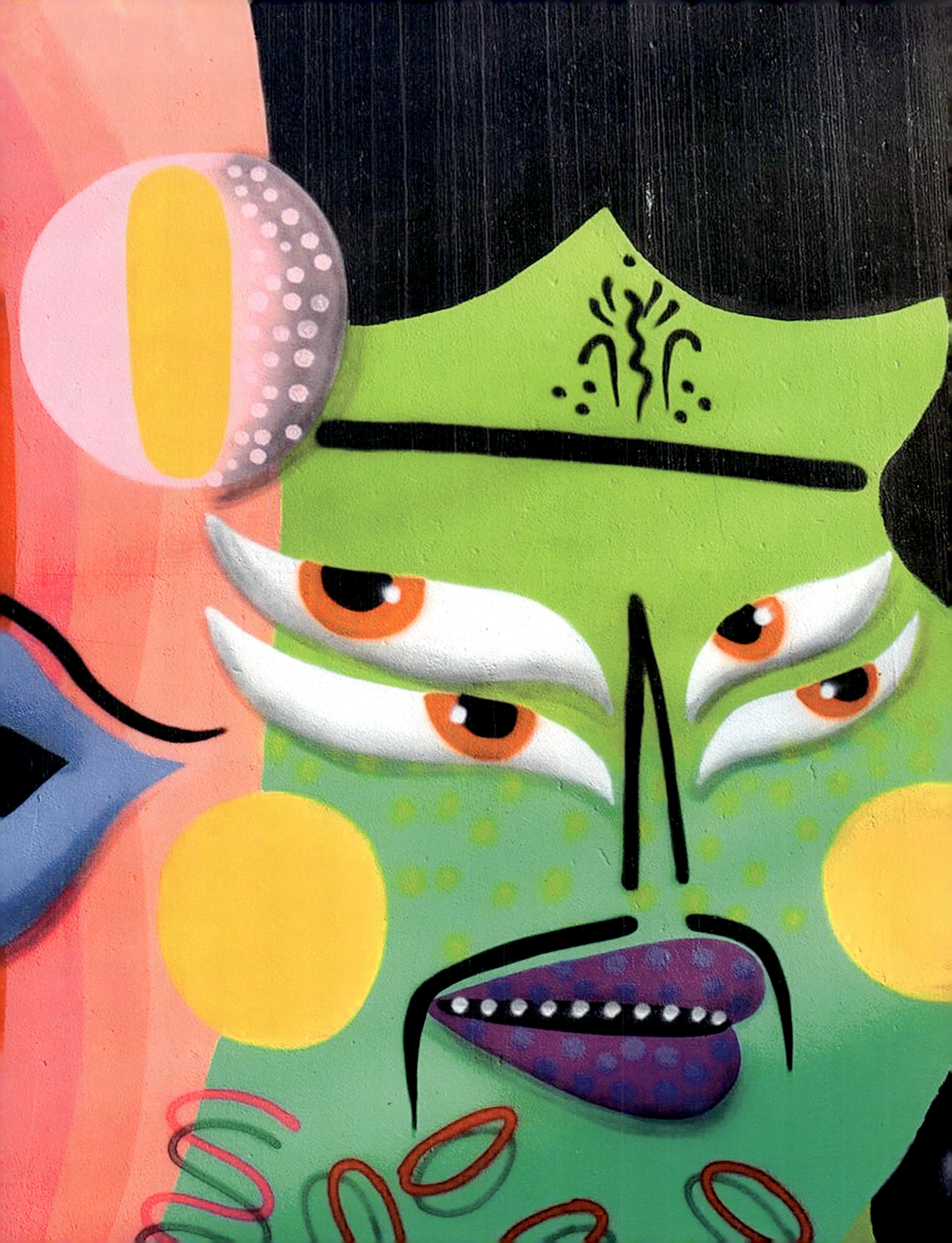

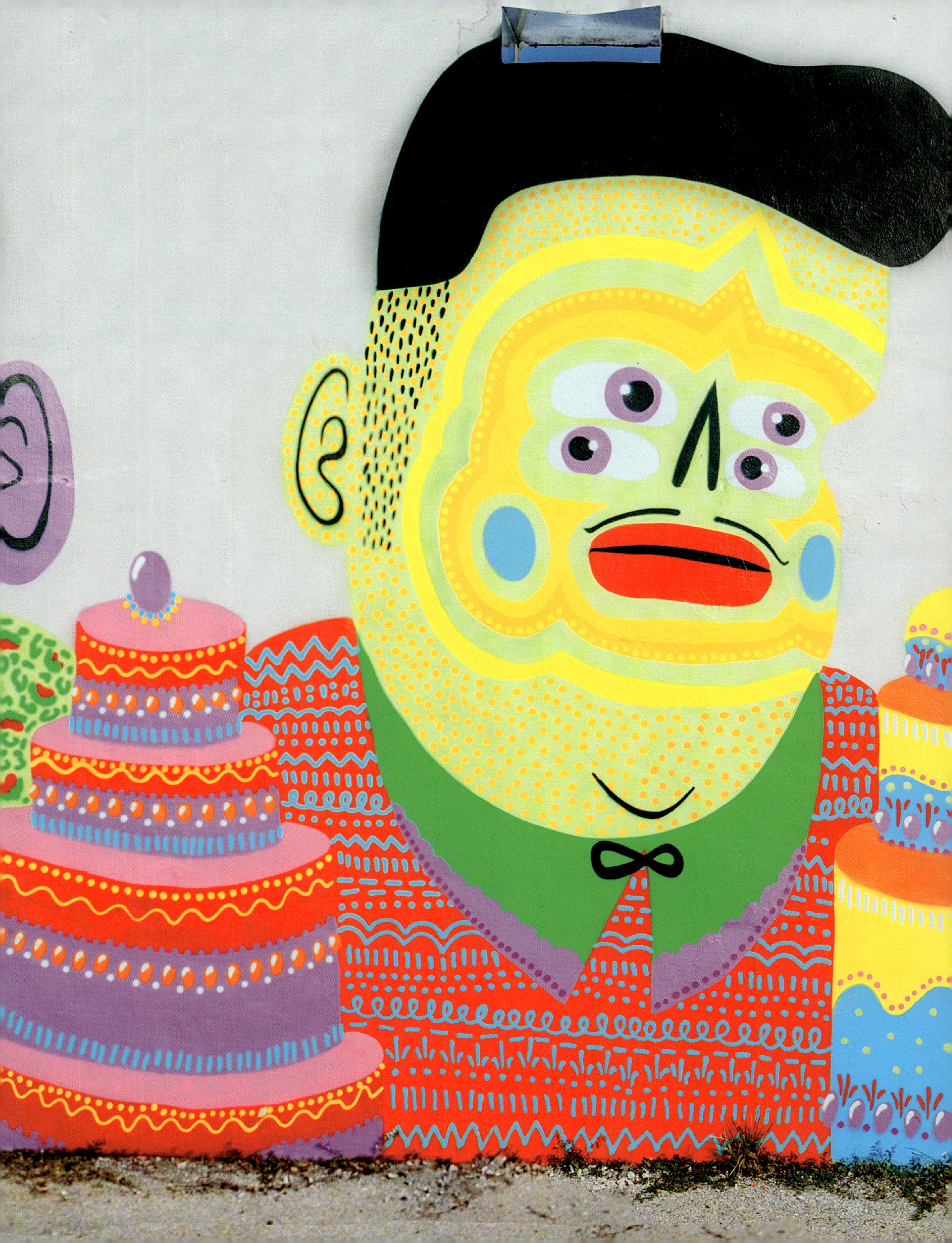

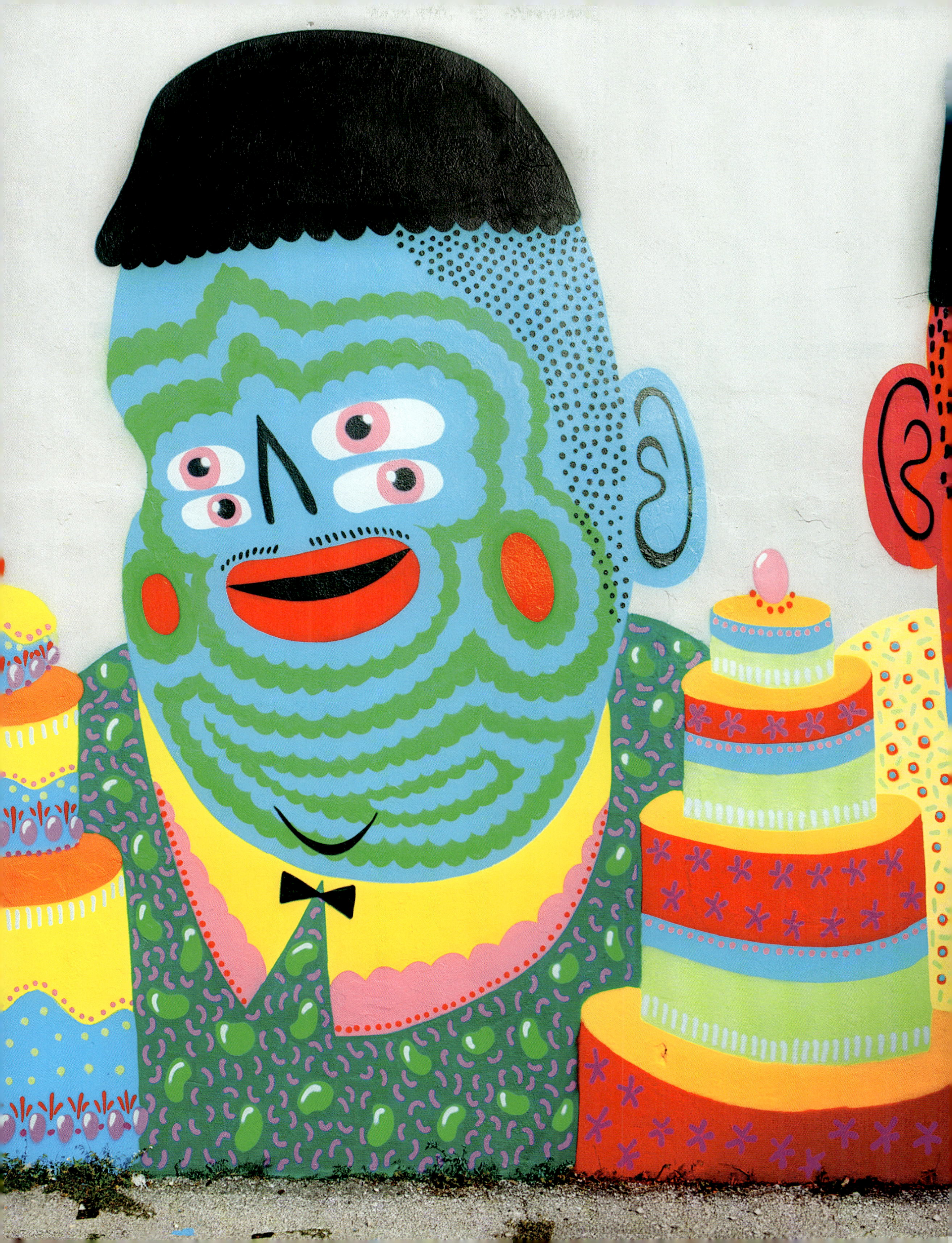

LADY PINK

THE PIONEER IN GRAFFITI
AND WOMEN'S EMANCIPATION

"Strong sexist and hostile attitudes still exist in the world, and being a woman can prove extremely difficult; yet strong feelings of acceptance and tolerance exist as well. Writing graffiti is a tough and special art form that requires a great deal of physical labor. It's not for everyone, but certainly doing what one loves always brings great satisfaction."

She lives in a forest a few hours away from New York City, in an unspecified location that she does not feel is important to mention. Her life revolves around her art, which she produces incessantly, as if it were a vital necessity. Lady Pink, Sandra Fabara, is a graffiti world veteran and a feminist pioneer. "Some have said that I was the first woman to do graffiti, though actually there were other women like me in the '70s when I started. . . The artists of my generation called themselves 'graffiti writers'; the term 'street art' came later, in fact, and arose from our movement. In those days we worked mainly in the subways," she explains.

Born in Ecuador, she came to New York with her family when she was only seven, and went to live in Astoria, Queens. "I have very few memories of that time. My mother worked hard; she was hardly ever at home, which allowed me to run free on the streets until she returned. I began drawing when I was five; at school, I had great teachers, who saw my talent and helped me prepare a good portfolio for the High School of Art and Design, and also encouraged me to exhibit my works," she recalls.

Only seventeen at the time, she was already traveling the world for her work, hanging out with Andy Warhol, Keith Haring, and Jean-Michel Basquiat, and never turning down an opportunity to venture out with her friends and paint the cars of the New York subway.

LADY SHIVA, Welling Court Mural Project, New York City, New York, USA, 2014

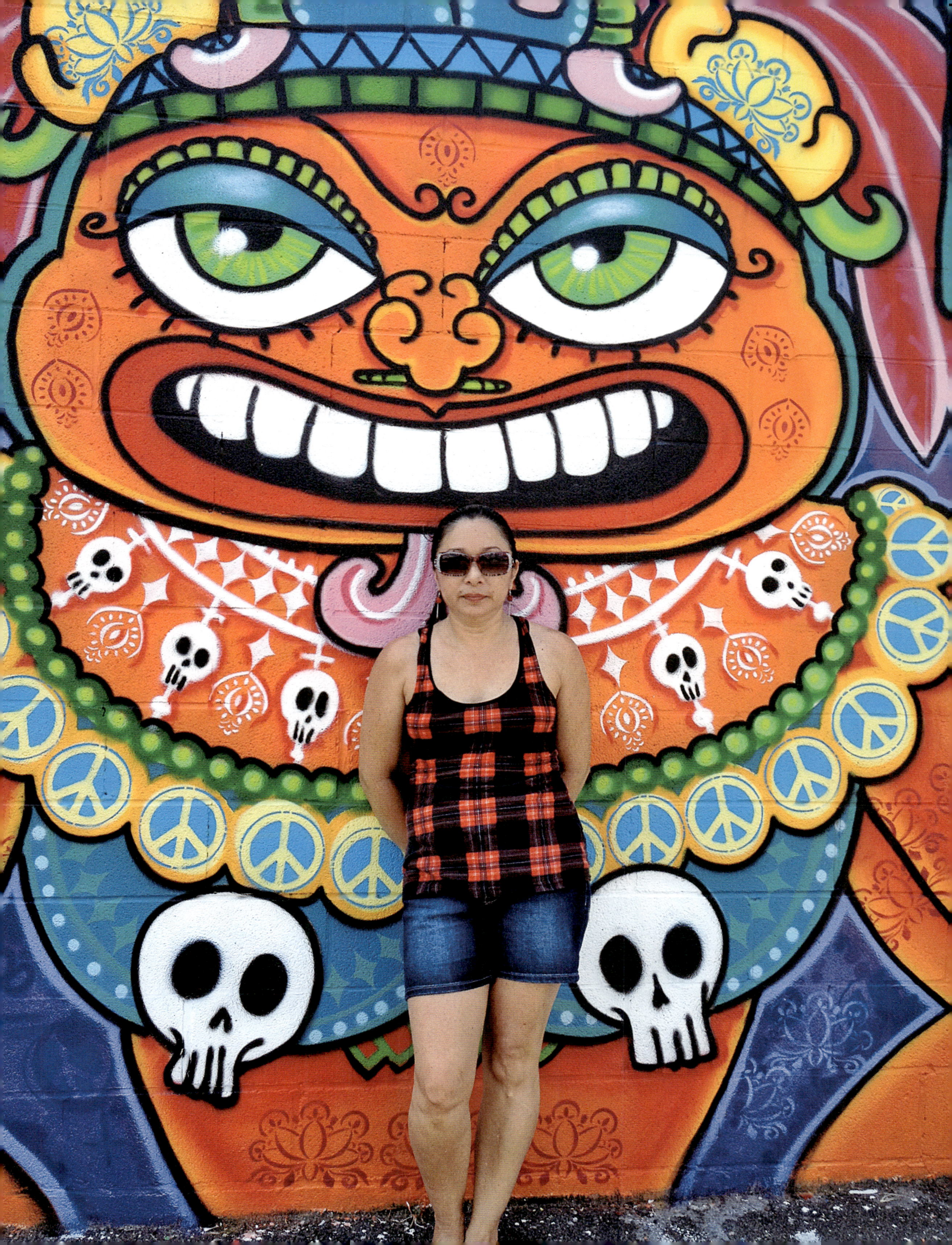

Lady Pink began doing graffiti in 1979 and went on painting trains until at least 1985, distinguishing herself through her style so much so that she was asked to star in *Wild Style*, Charlie Ahearn's 1983 film about hip hop. From 1993 to 1997, she painted freight trains with her husband, graffiti artist Smith. Lady Pink soon earned international fame and became a leading figure and point of reference in the hip hop subculture. "For me, painting trains with other graffiti artists was an exciting adventure. I love bright and vibrant colors. My favorite has always been purple: I just like it, for no particular reason," she notes.

"At the beginning, I had a hard time getting accepted into the graffiti scene because I was quite feminine, even in the way I dressed, but I also knew how to play the 'tomboy' and didn't find it difficult to totally change my style whenever necessary. So, in the end, I managed to persuade my friends to take me along.

GYM IN SALEM, Massachusetts, USA, 2020 (right)
SCHOOL IN SAINT-DENIS, Reunion Island, France, 2021

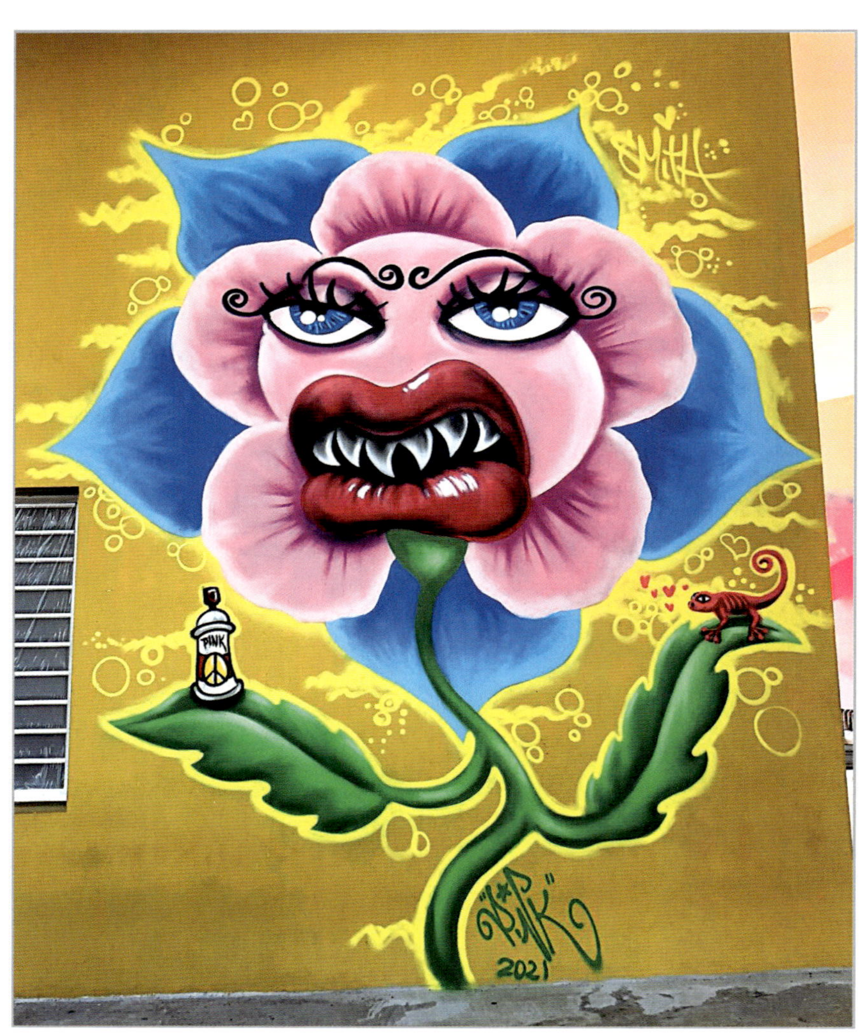

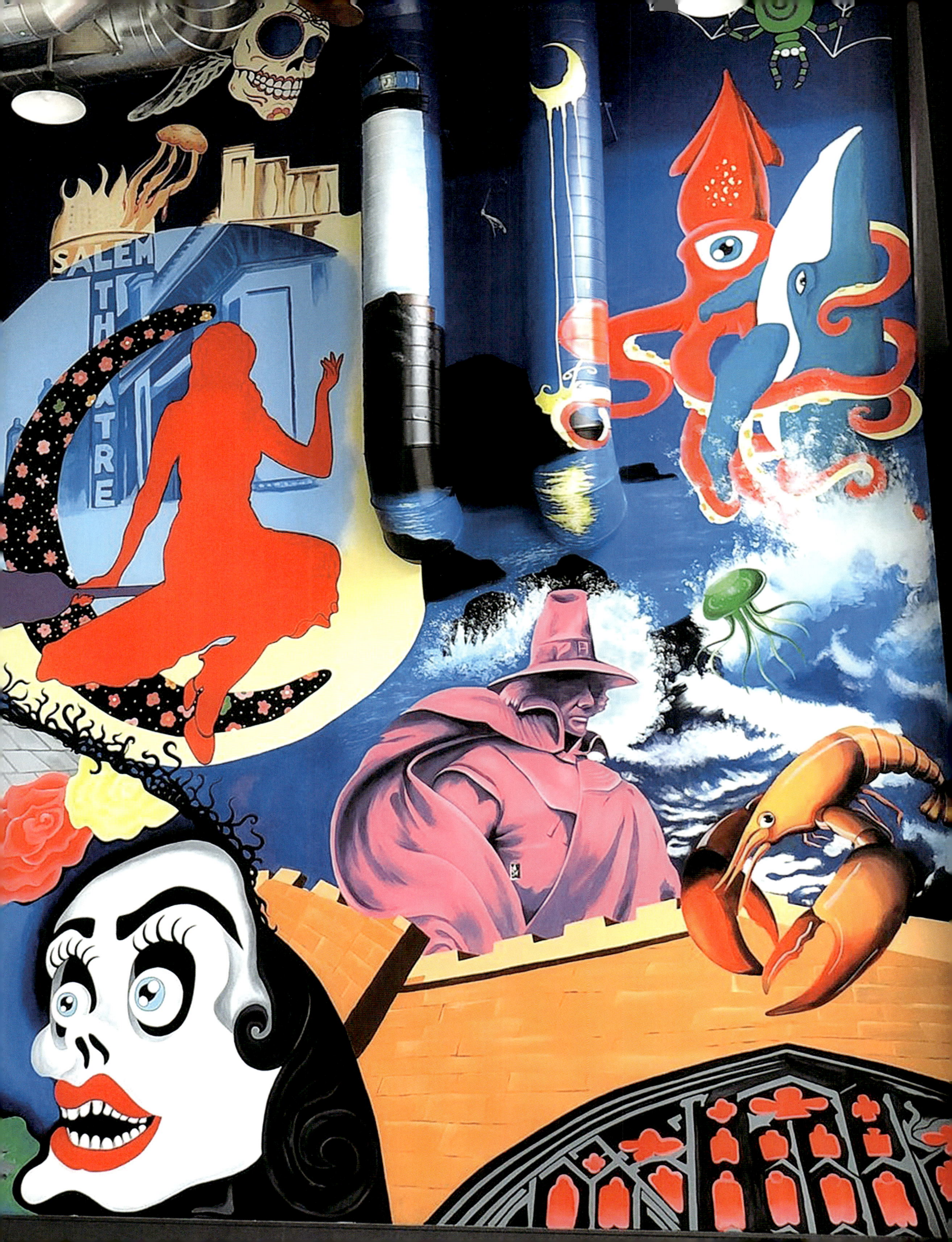

SALEM
THEATRE

It wasn't easy; there were all sorts of difficulties, like problems with the police because we were painting illegally, the bitter cold of night, the effort required to carry heavy bags of equipment, the stress caused by the need to be quick."

"I was almost always one of the few women among groups of guys; I often felt fierce hostility directed toward me, but also support and acceptance. I was proud of being a woman, which is why I wanted a feminine name. It was a friend of mine, Seen TC5, who first called me Pink, and we liked the letters when written together, one after another. I have always loved reading, and at the time I was reading a book on European aristocracy, whose characters were dukes and duchesses. I also had a special passion for England and the Victorian period. One of the books I loved most, that I read when I was twelve, was Barbara Cartland's *Love Conquers War*. So, to complete my name, I thought about something related to romance, to that fantastic period and its history: Lady Pink seemed perfect!" she explains.

In the 1970s, the feminist movement was on the rise, and it also profoundly marked Lady Pink—a teenager at the time—and her vision of the world and things. "I didn't let myself be influenced by anyone; I knew what I wanted and did my own thing. Back then, I was not aware of the fact that I was one of the first feminists. . . There was a lot of talk about the equality of the sexes in those days;

Welling Court Mural Festival, New York City, New York, USA, 2016 (right)
GRAFFITI GARDENS in the Wynwood neighborhood of Miami, Florida, USA, 2019

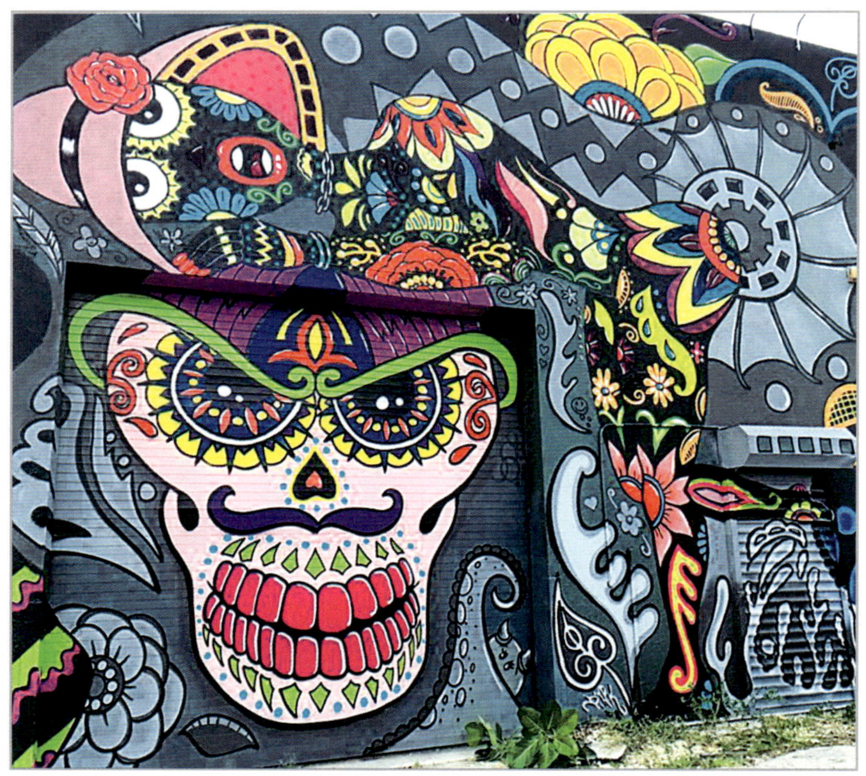

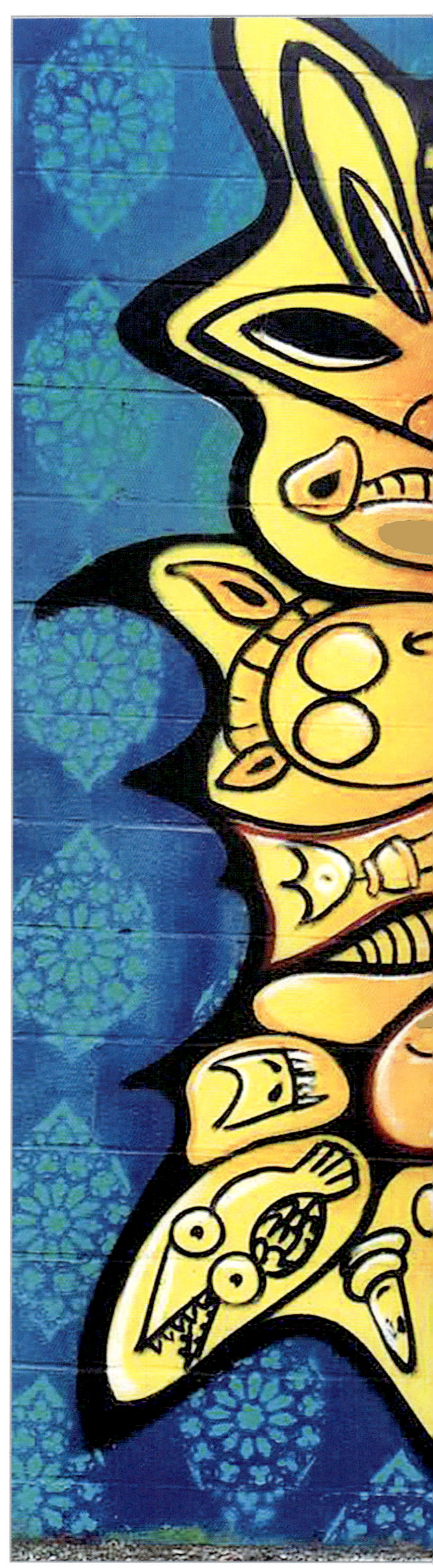

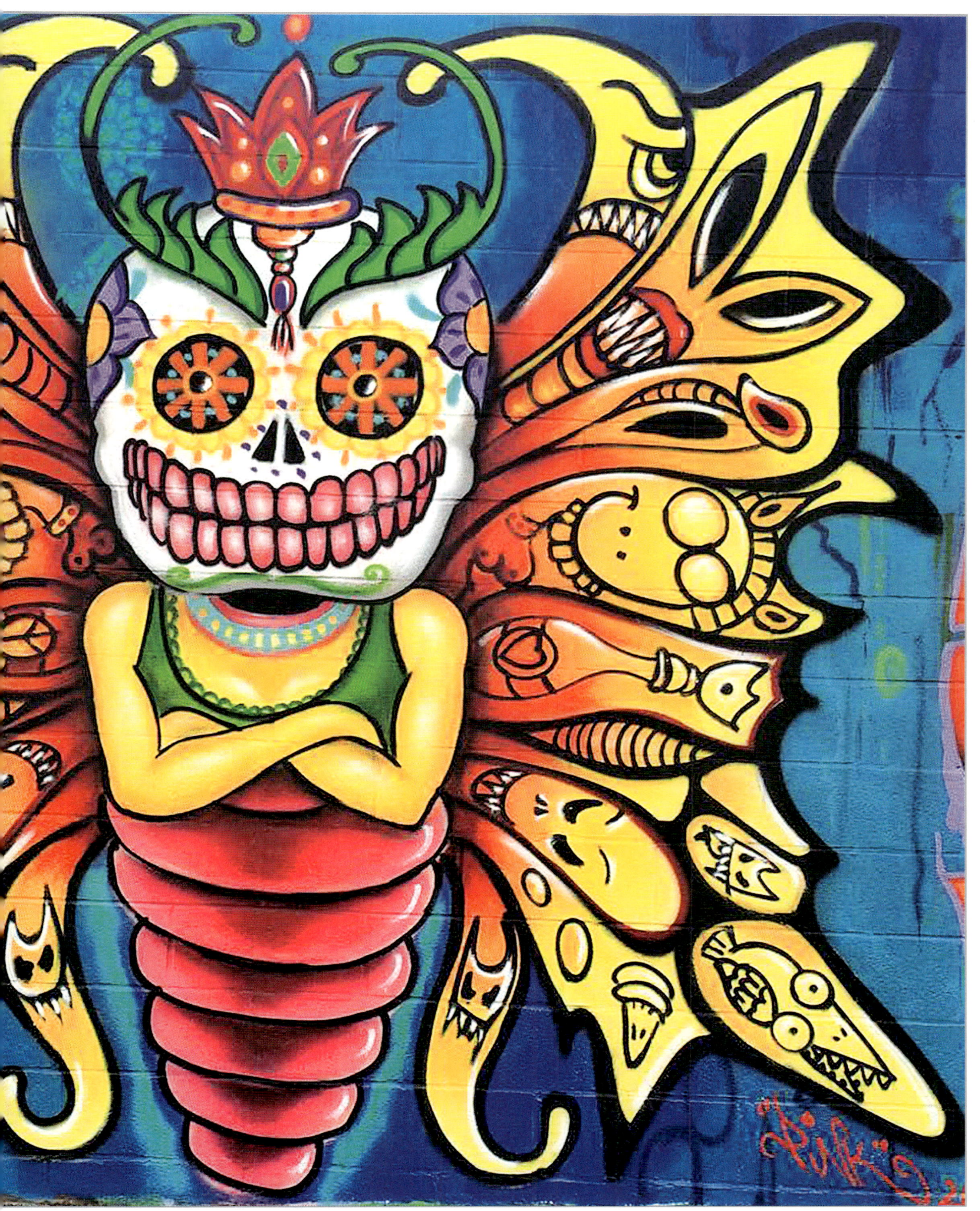

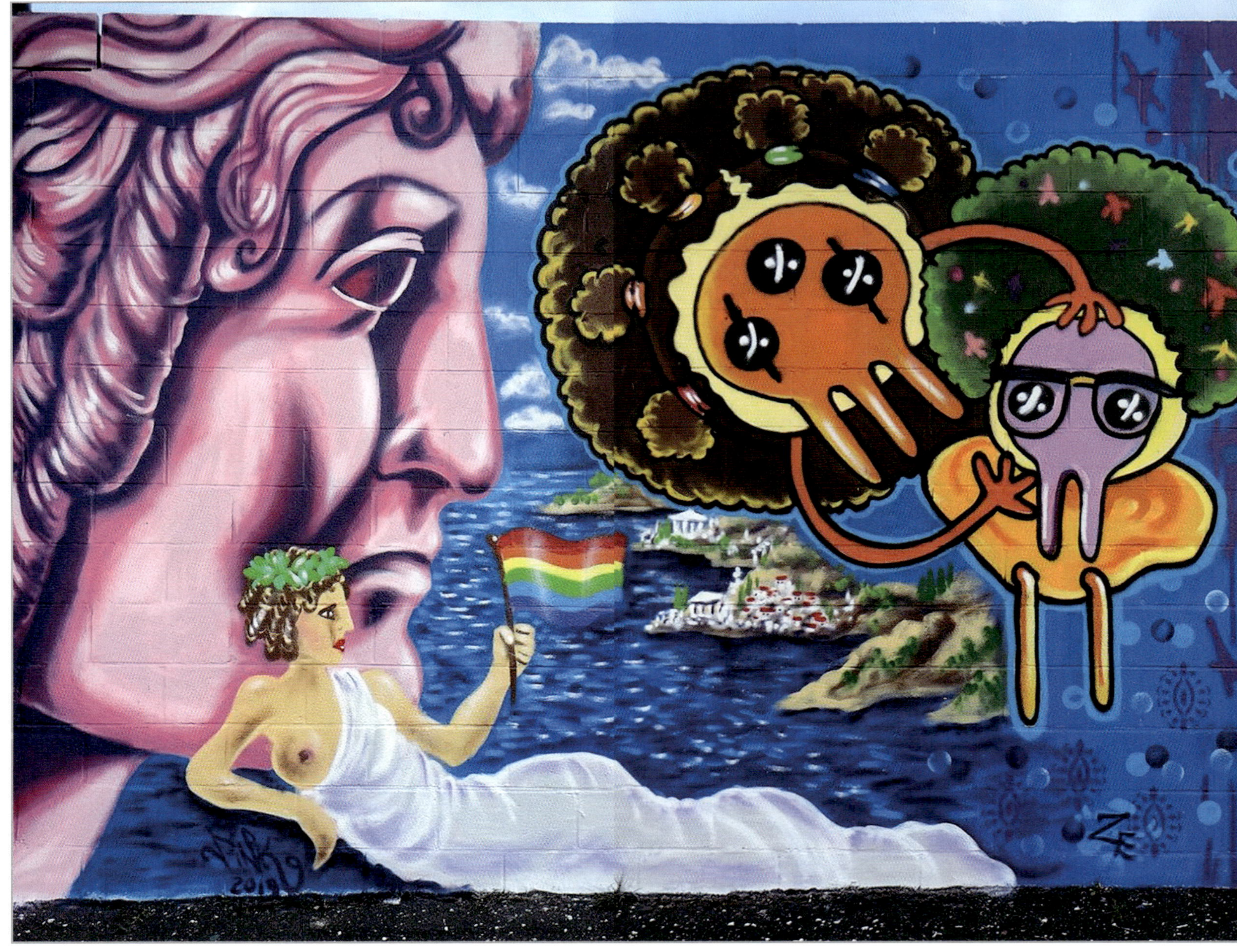

there was a real struggle for emancipation, and I was totally involved in it. That period certainly marked and deeply influenced my entire repertoire," she recalls.

When Lady Pink began painting murals as well, she tried to work on stories with themes and symbols related to love, social justice, political issues, social rights, equality, and Latina women such as herself. "My oeuvre is rich in images of females because I think I draw them better than I do men. The themes of my works have definitely changed over time; after all, I draw inspiration from everything that surrounds and affects me. One needs to constantly evolve, both on a personal and artistic level, and social media certainly helps. This is why I follow the artists whom I love and who inspire me, and I think that staying connected and continuously discovering new stimuli is critical," she says with conviction.

Her creativity is indefatigable and richly varied, her commitment unfaltering: "I've made some murals for Black Lives Matter, for example, and lots in support of women's rights. Other times, I've depicted animals or natural elements," she points out. A particularly important work for her is *When Women Pursue Justice*, which she executed in Brooklyn in 2005. "I was one of the more than thirty female artists who painted portraits of women who had contributed to the struggle for human rights throughout history. This was an extremely meaningful experience for me, and also made me reflect on how I could contribute as a teacher at mural workshops oriented toward youth.

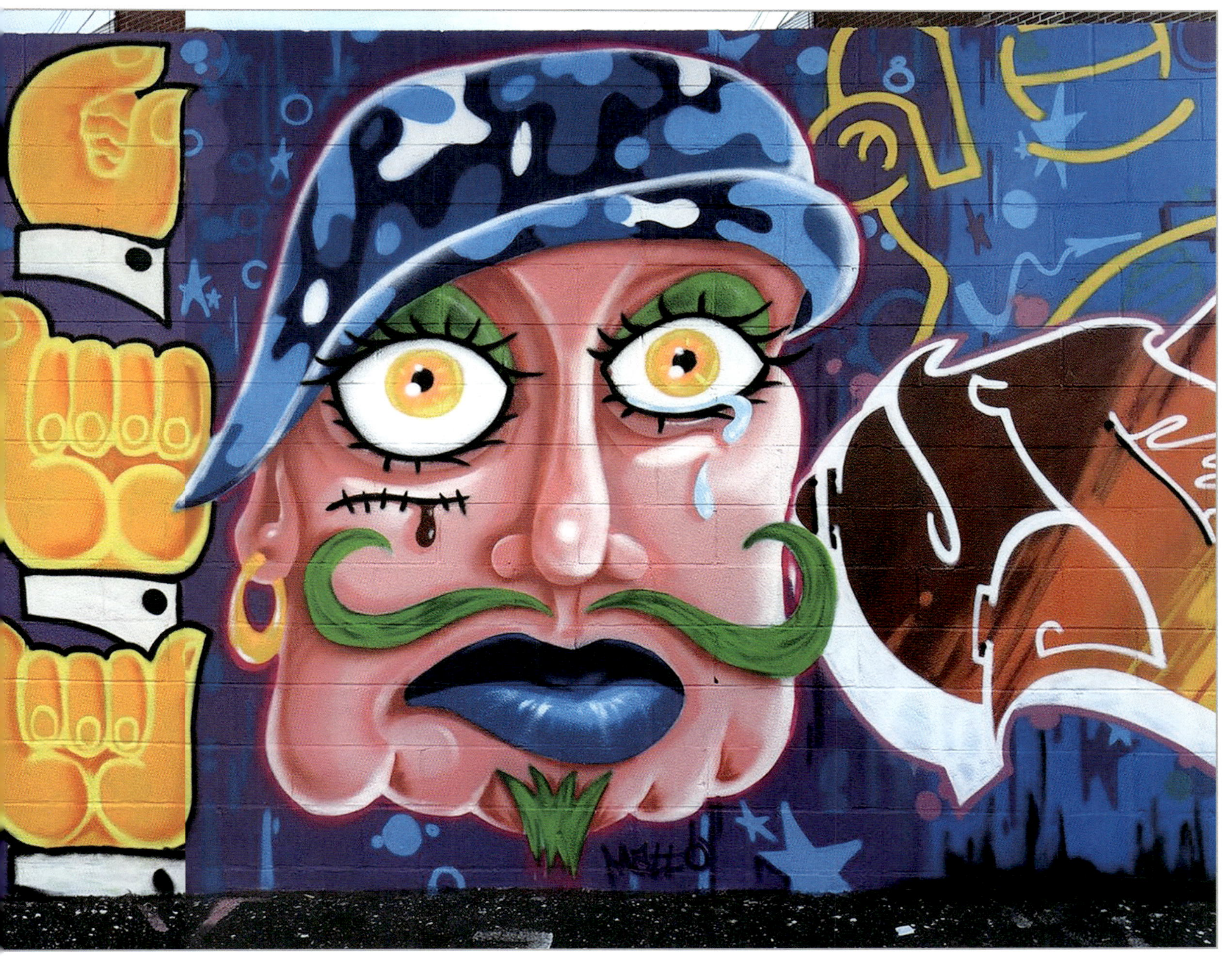

I have no children, but I want to be a mentor to young artists and start working with them while they're still children—just as my teachers helped and encouraged me. I know they need guidance and security; I know that studying in America costs a bundle and that they need help obtaining scholarships. This is the focus of my work at the Frank Sinatra School of the Arts," she states.

Lady Pink knows how essential it is for an artist to have solid mentors. "Artists often have fears and insecurities, and it's important for them to feel strong if they are to be successful. I've had so many people who supported and helped me, and I haven't forgotten that," she concludes.

LGBTQ PRIDE, Welling Court Mural Festival in Astoria, New York City, New York, USA, painted by Lady Pink (left), Zelinette Estrada (middle), and Matt O'Connor (right), 2019

#LEDIESIS

THE ANONYMOUS SUPERHERO

"Who we are is not important; what matters is the content we wish to convey in our works. We are not actors or a band's frontgirls; we are artists, and what we express lies in our work. We like to think that our superpower rests precisely in our invisibility because it makes us far more free."

Their women are iconic and powerful. They are marked with the S of Super-woman, as if they were multiple heroes deployed under that name. They peer out from windows, smiling, inspiring reflection, standing up for themselves and entire generations; they are symbols of the past, the present, the future. Beautiful and strong representations of female characters from history or the world of pop culture, they embody all the greatest models of the female planet. They indicate that times have changed and are still moving toward ever greater equality, toward a generation of young women who are by now well aware of their superpowers. The artists who did them? Lediesis. They are two women who wish to remain anonymous and about whom until recently absolutely nothing was known. Because, to them, it's the message, above everything else, that matters. "We two are friends: one with an academic education and the goal of living with art; the other from the world of communications but who has always been involved in exhibitions and shows," they disclose.

"Our strength lies precisely in joining these two worlds, art and communications, seemingly distinct, to create something unique as a pair. What unites us is a similar vision of life and of the path we wish to follow. We share a similar desire to communicate an important message in a lighthearted way without taking ourselves too seriously," they add.

Their choice to remain anonymous at all costs is quite explicit: "Since street art is still largely illegal, anonymity is not only a requirement, it is also, above all, of value. Remaining in the shadow is a way of protecting our privacy, but it's also

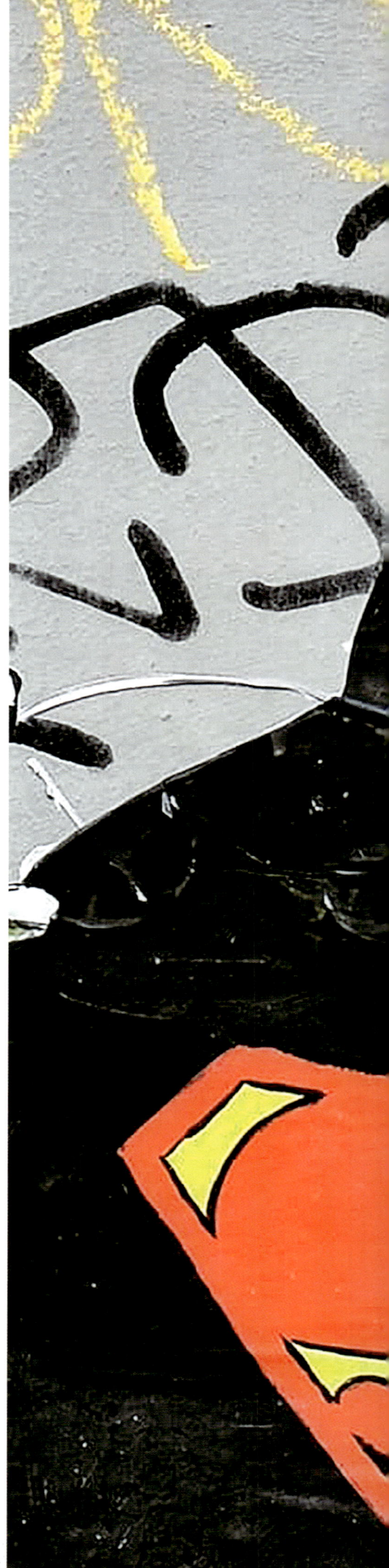

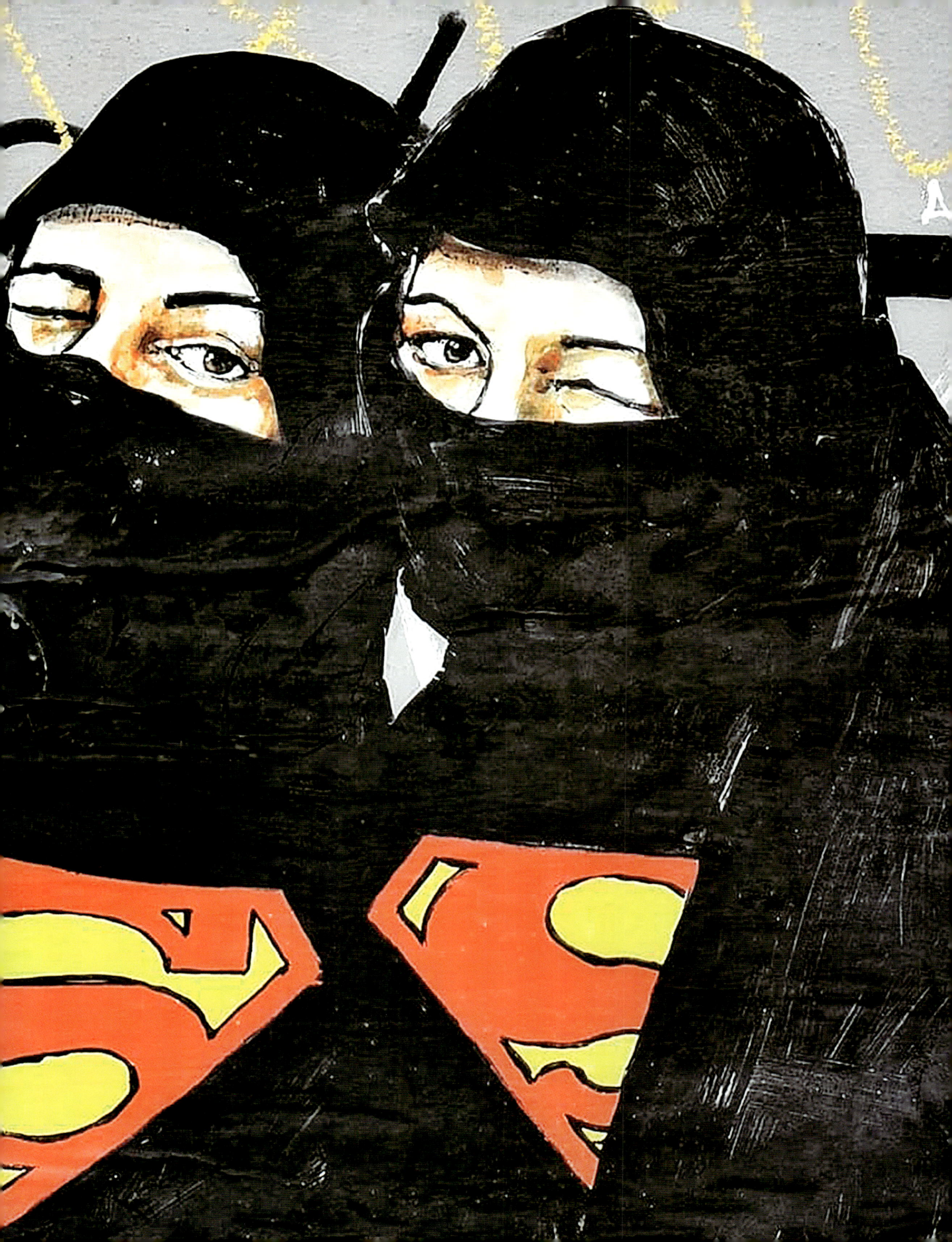

a means of highlighting what we do. We are not interested in revealing who we are: that's irrelevant to what we create."

How did they get their name? "#LeDiesis emerged as a play on both social and musical lingo. The word 'Lediesis' is a cross between 'ladies' and 'sisters,' between the great ladies of history and the many anonymous sisters in the world. Diesis is also the interval in the ascending semitone of a bass note. Our pursuit of change is thus reflected in the name, in the painting, and in the choice of characters that we portray, all represented with the 'S' of Superman, a symbol attributed to a man—and, why not—even to a woman!" they explain.

Is their message feminist? "If by feminism one means an awareness of a woman's capabilities, we are absolutely feminists. What inspires us is touching people's hearts, provoking emotions. Our dream is to change the vision of the world and of minds through art," they state with conviction.

They claim that they have not encountered any particular obstacles while emerging as women in the world of street art: "In art, there are no genders. Even if historically speaking we live in a patriarchal society, this doesn't mean that this is always the case. We feel that we are in the midst of a reawakening of women's conscience, an awareness of our potential that is growing stronger by the day. This doesn't necessarily mean that we must collide with men: there's room for everyone! The space of women in the structured world of art is directly proportional to the awareness that each woman, or, rather, each person, has of her or himself. The appropriation of a space within it is the consequence of this personal effort."

Adhering to these principles, they have chosen their subjects with particular care, as if they had conceived their project for the sole purpose of granting power to femininity in all its nuances. "The idea of the Superwomen originated in January 2019, during a visit to the Arte Fiera in Bologna. We wanted to create something that would draw attention to women. This was a completely natural and instinctive decision, without any expectations," they recall. "In choosing characters, we follow our instinct: they are liberated and enlightened women who convey a positive message, one of individual growth that is also reflected in the spiritual growth of society. This is why they are depicted with the Superman 'S' while winking complicitly at passersby, so that everyone can reflect on and discover their own superpowers," they explain. "There are some subjects that inspire us in particular, such as sora Lella, Madam Mim, the niqab girls—who are actually our self-portraits—or Barbie, who goes shopping like a regular housewife in Rome's Campo de' Fiori. Some, such as Margherita Hack and Rita Levi-Montalcini, we selected for their commitment to science, or to art, as in the case of Anna Magnani, Maria Callas, Alda Merini, Marina Abramović, and Frida Kahlo. We've also portrayed men who have played with role reversal, like Manuel Frattini in *Priscilla* or Freddie Mercury as a housewife in the *I Want to Break Free* music video," they explain.

SUPERWOMEN, Florence and Rome, Italy, 2019 (previous page, right, and overleaf)

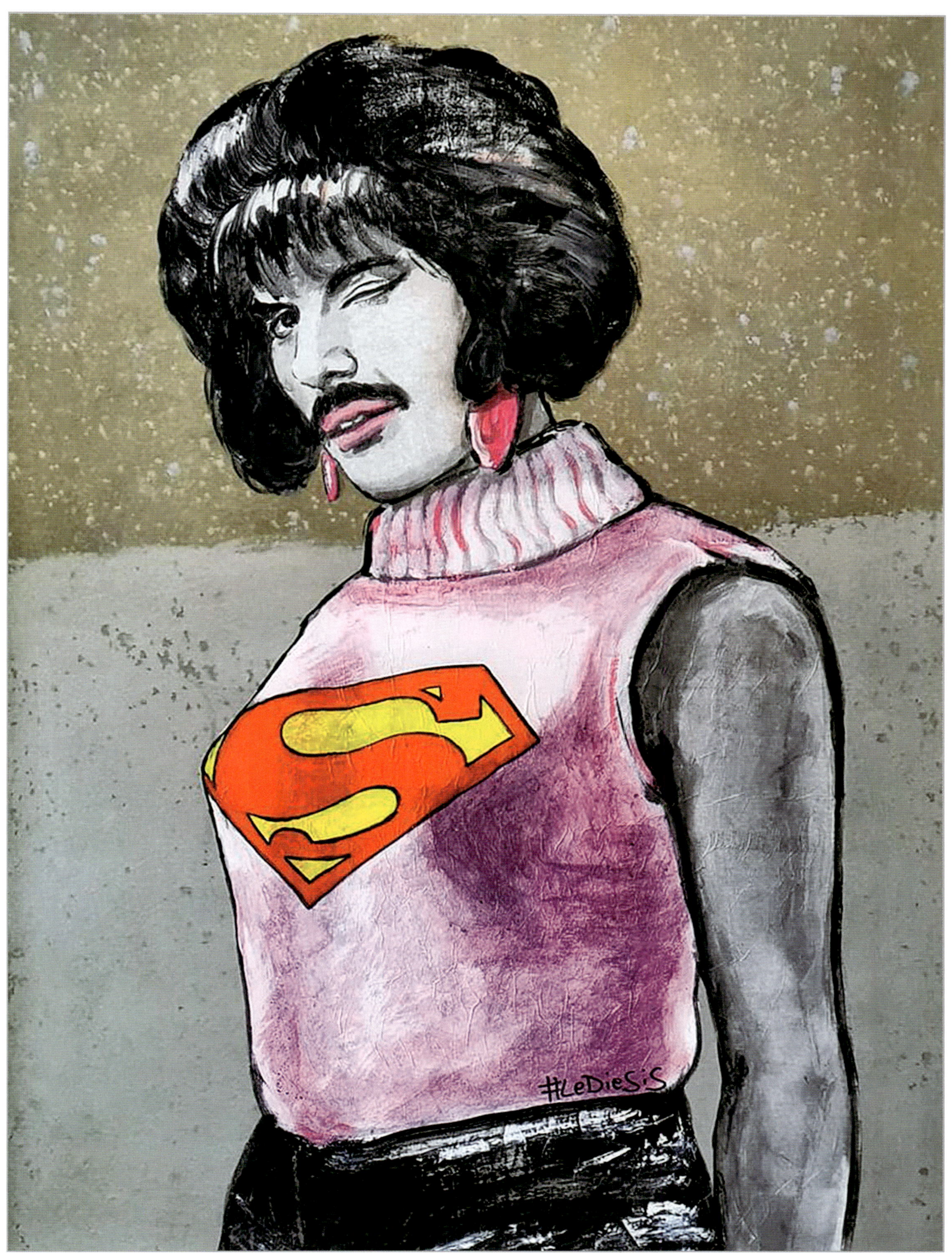
#LeDieSiS

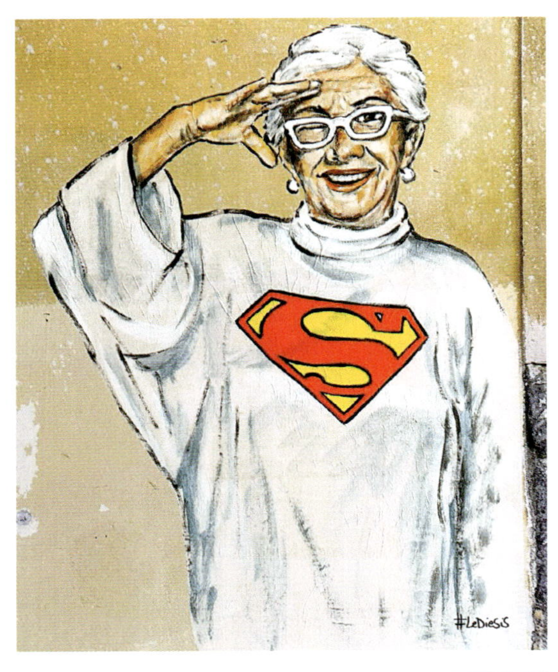
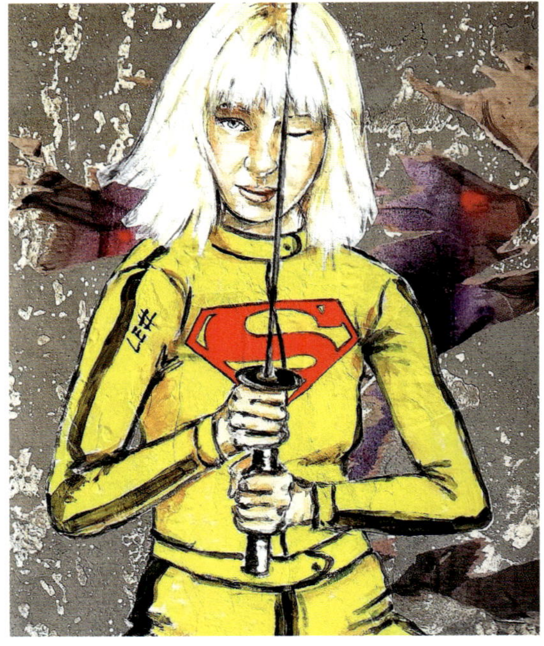
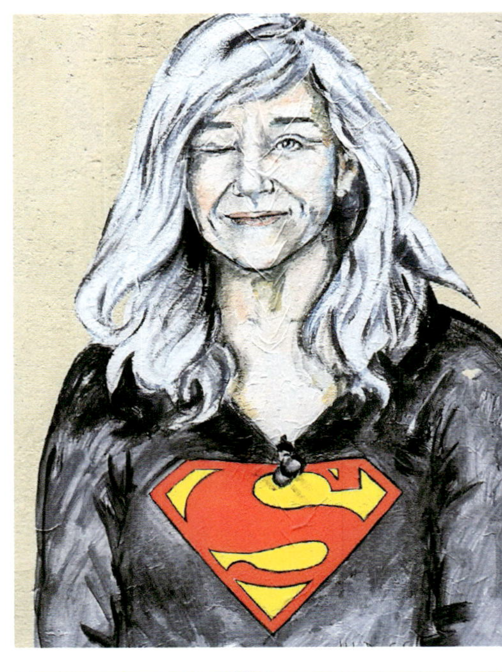
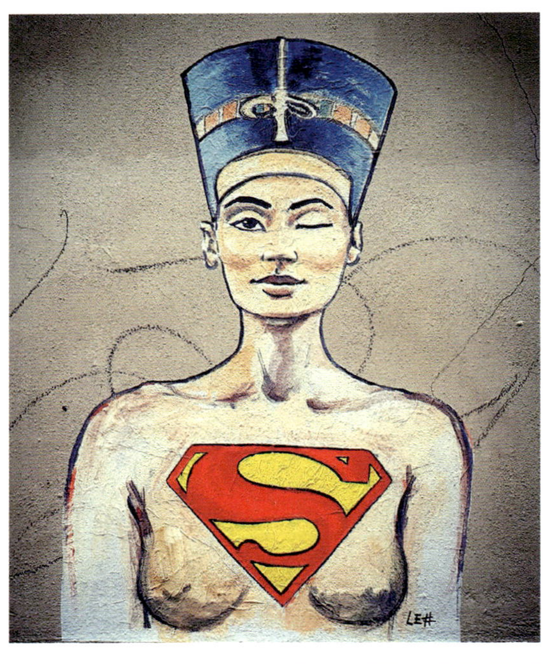
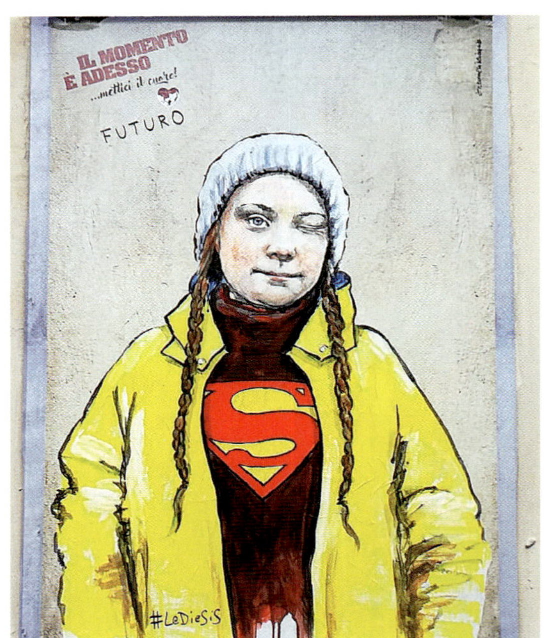

IL MOMENTO
È ADESSO
...mettici il cuore!
FUTURO

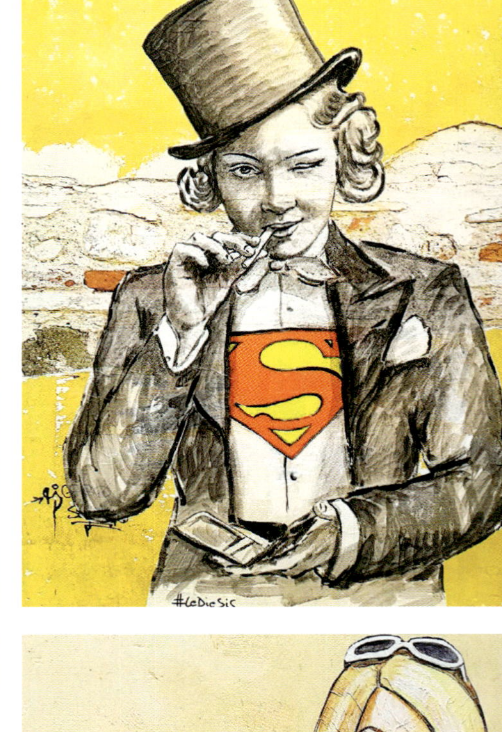
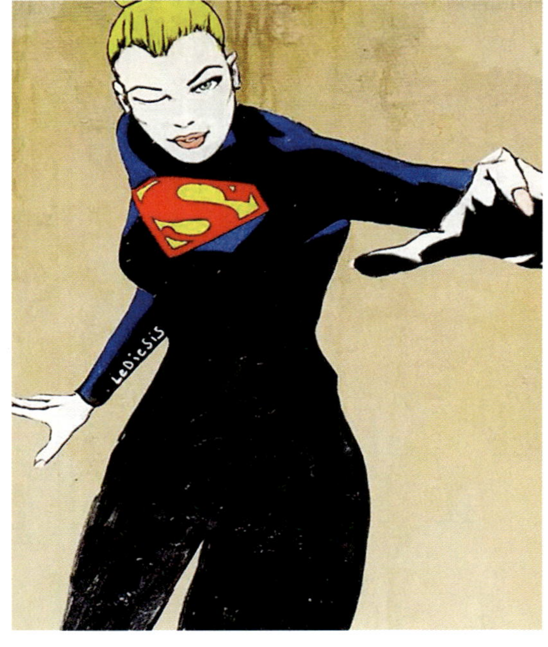
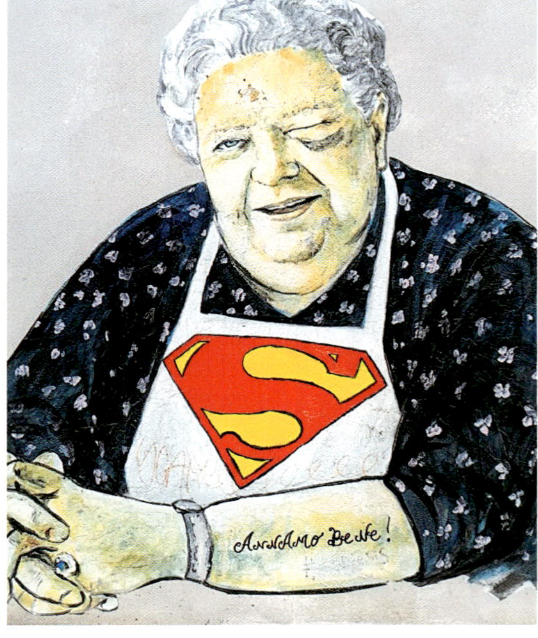
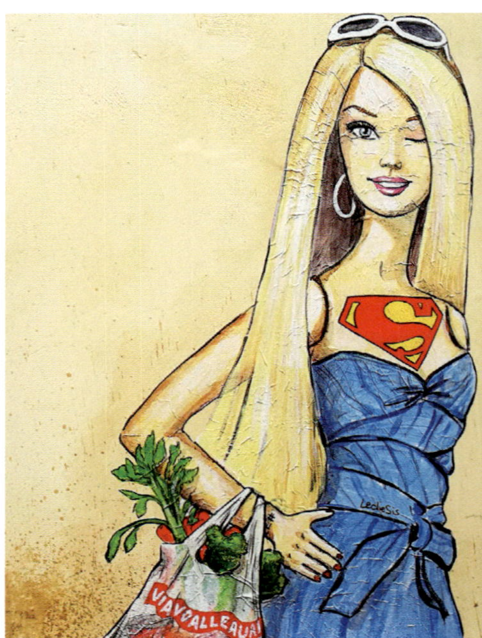

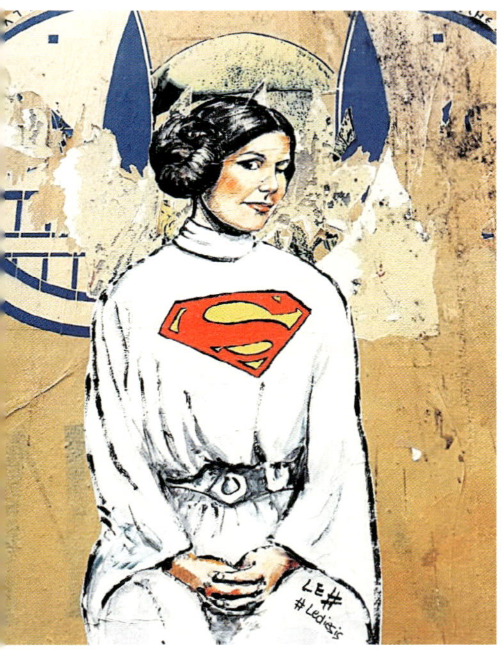
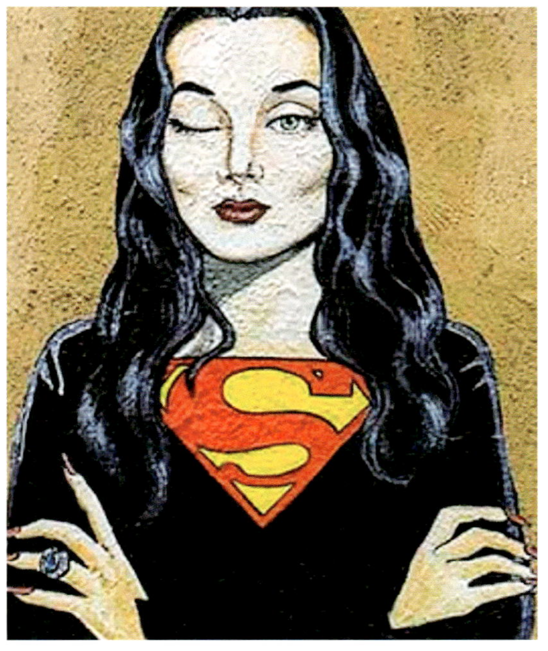
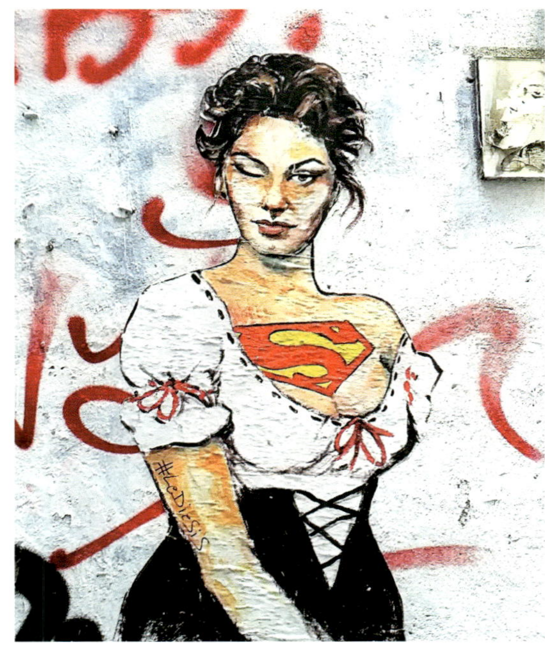
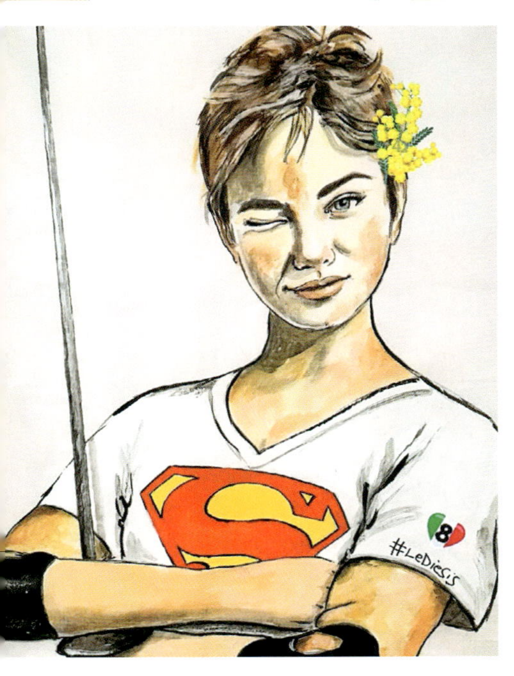
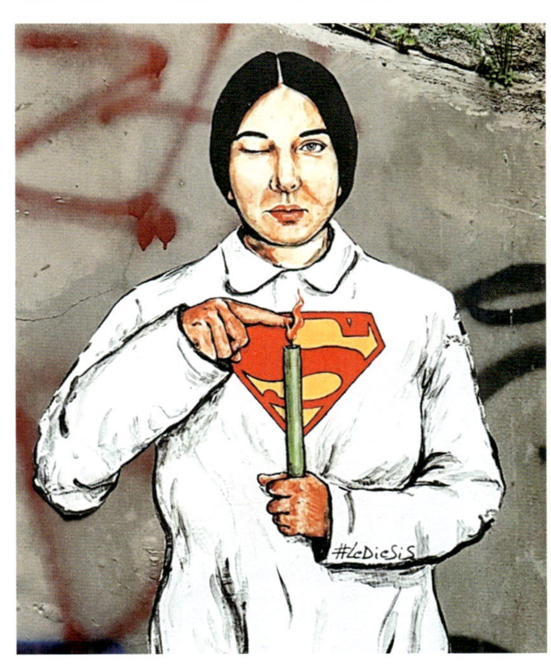
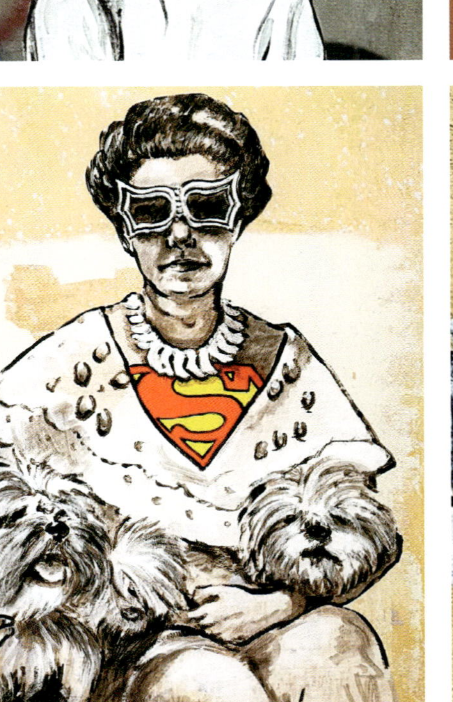
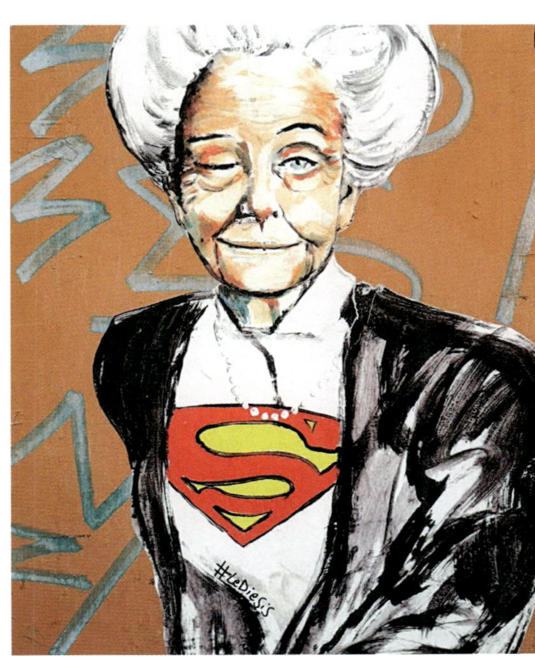
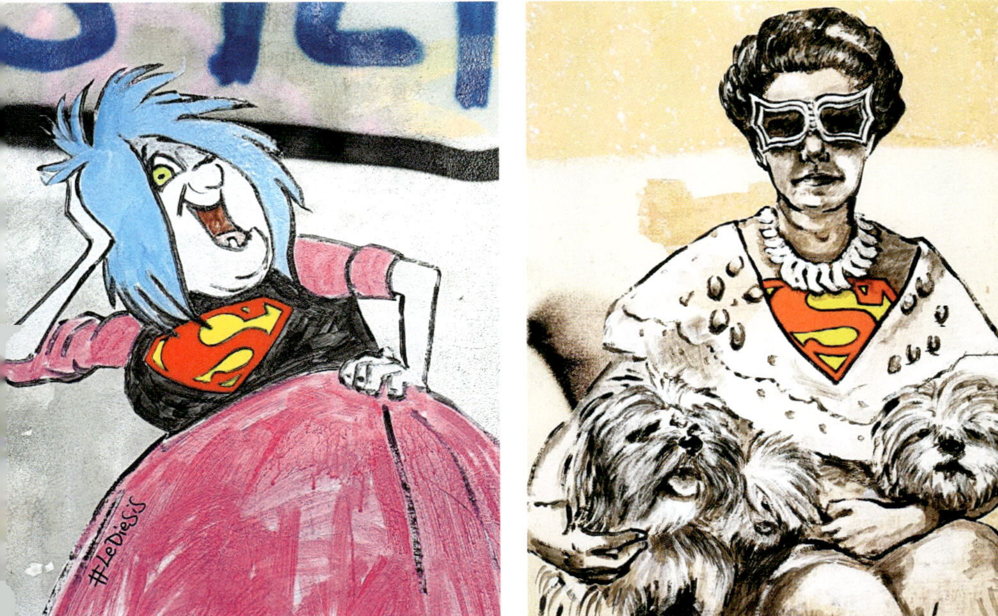
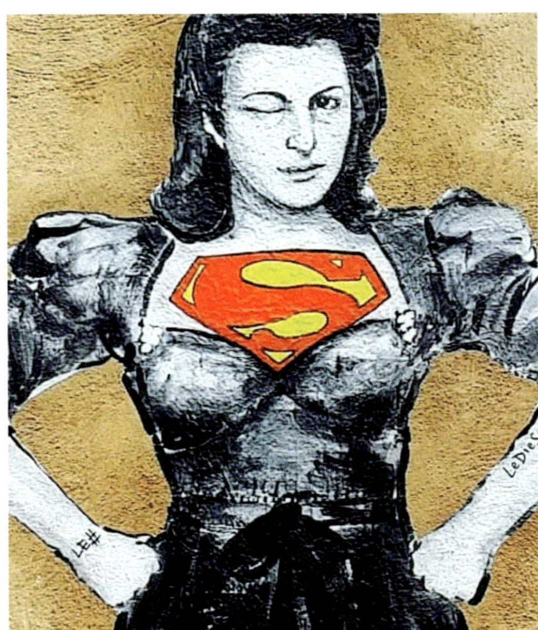

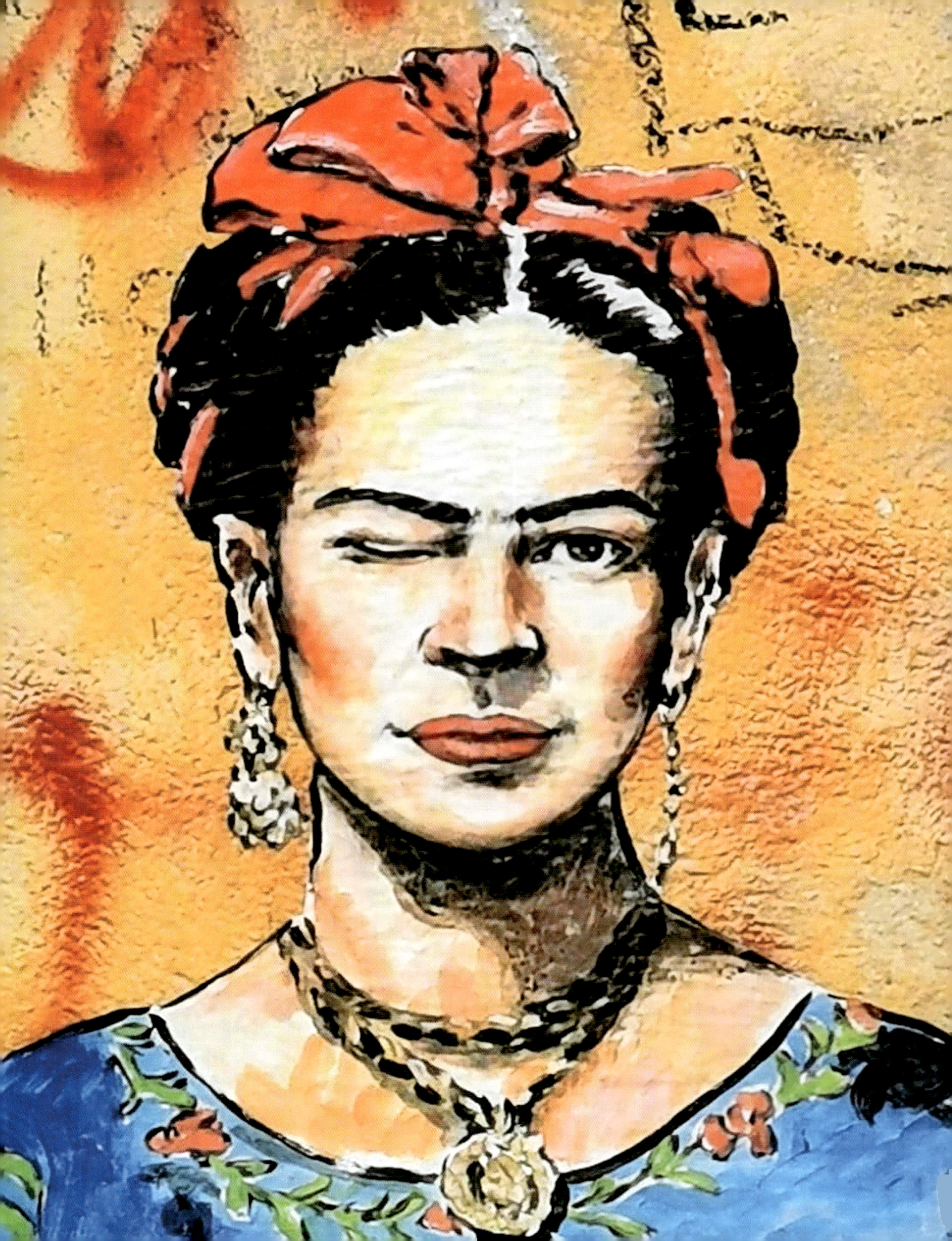

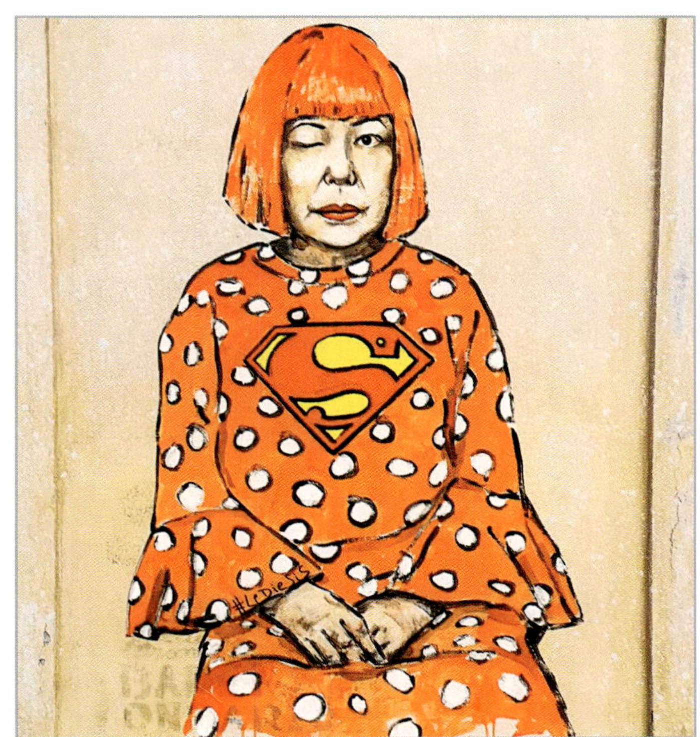

Their vision is closely bound up with social and humanitarian endeavors, with the dream of a better world, which they can already envision: "Art means grasping the change of our times, foreseeing the future. This is why artists are often revolutionaries who oppose the many stereotypes of the era in which they live."

"Today, more than ever, art cannot disregard social, popular, and educational objectives," they claim. "For us, getting into street art was more of a natural consequence than a deliberate choice. We are Florentine, and, in recent years, Florence has become one of the top cities for Italian street art thanks to artists such as Clet and Blub. This is why our first foray was in our city, on March 8, 2019. We pasted eight icons of women on some shuttered windows in the historic center, simply to share them and provide a moment of reflection for everyone. Street art is an incredibly energetic means of communication. The fact that it takes place on the street is yet another reason for transmitting positive messages," they openly admit. "By now street art is completely accepted in the Italian and international art scene, yet it still retains some of its essential features due to its more direct, informal, and daily contact with the viewer, but also its greater creative freedom and expression. Street art dares to go where most traditional artists seem afraid to venture," they state with conviction.

Their intention is also to travel around the world and take their message everywhere, as they have done through social media, where they have now gone viral. "Italy continues to regale us with thousands of emotions and thousands of ideas, but we are also working abroad, at Lugano's WopArt and in Barcelona. . . We can't wait to travel even more because we constantly need new stimuli," they point out. "During the pandemic, we came up with a graphic series, *Superblack*, in which iconic symbols, from the Statue of Liberty to Queen Elizabeth, exorcise people's fear of COVID. Now we are trying to break free from the 'S' symbol in order to try out new messages: for example, we portrayed the soldier Nicole Gee, a victim of the attack on Kabul airport, without the Superman symbol, and Victoria of Måneskin with the word 'Boss,'" they say. "For us the lockdown was a really creative moment because we had time to focus on our personal path and on our goals and future artistic choices. During the pandemic, women showed that they were more resilient—even physically—than men. They are more capable of adapting to new situations. Women are growing increasingly aware of their potential and will certainly bring about many positive changes in the world," they conclude.

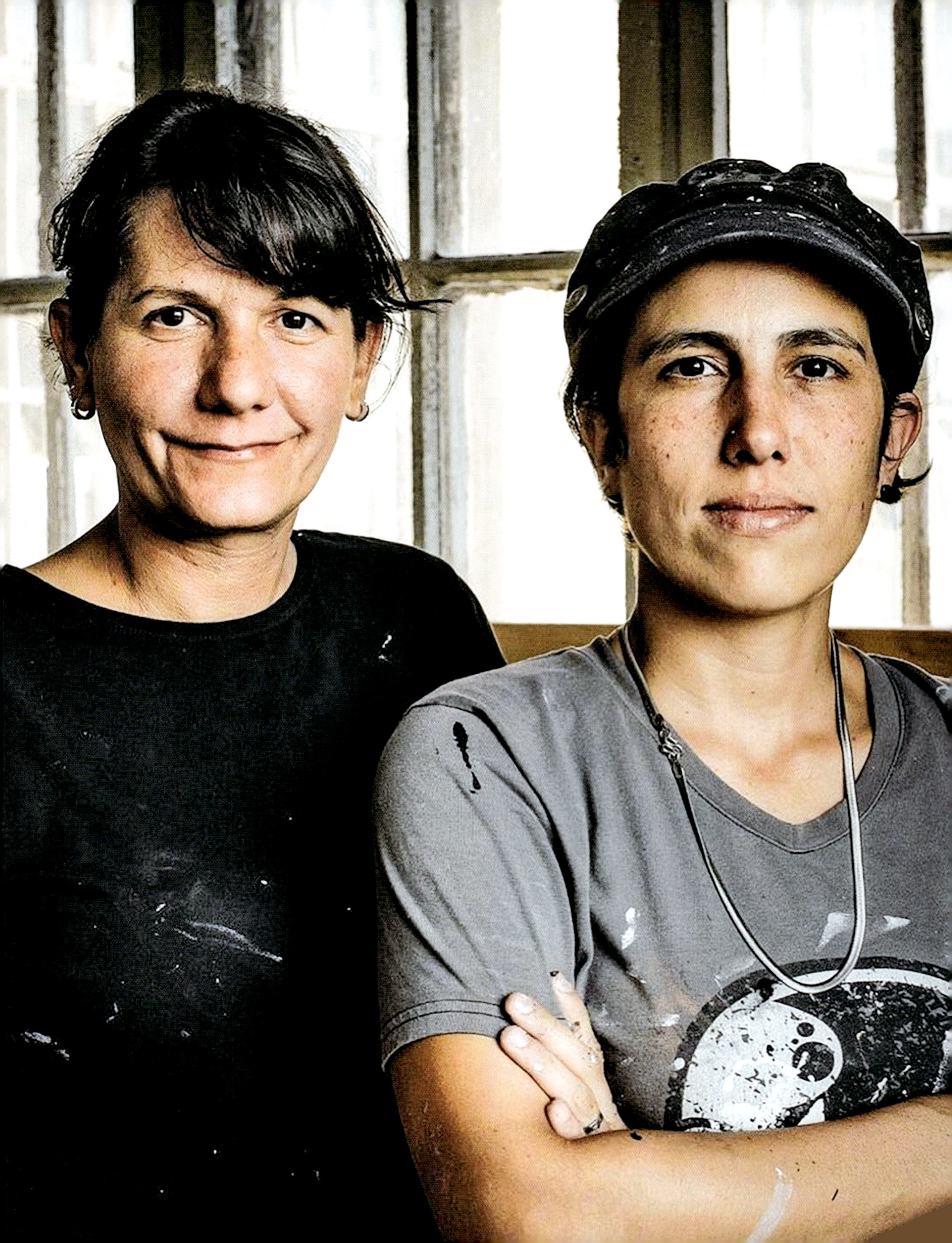

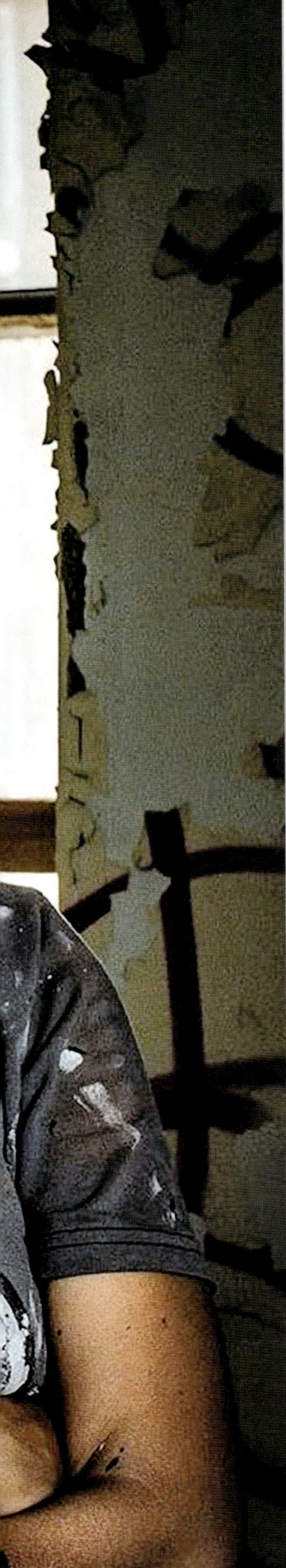

MEDIANERAS

GENDER-EQUALITY
AND PUBLIC-SPACE ACTIVISTS

*"On various occasions we were the only women
in groups of men who painted on the street.
This posed no obstacle to our calling."*

They are known as Medianeras. Vanesa Galdeano and Analí Chanquía have made large murals that pay particular attention to Ibero-American cultures and are characterized by their intensity and the contrast between their warm, bright colors and black and white. In their works one discovers realist portraits, the faces of ordinary people, proud and courageous, icons symbolizing something deeper. Medianeras wish to change the way in which spaces are perceived, and intend to alter the urban landscape of the street with impactful messages. "We are a couple in both life and art, and thus our day-to-day existence and our projects capture our mutual growth. We called our duo Medianeras because we cherish the concept and idea of sharing. In Spanish, this means 'party walls,' which are those dividing partitions shared by neighbors. There's a difference between walls whose function it is to separate spaces, and such walls, which, conversely, join them. We maintain that public art, aside from making cities more attractive, proclaims the idea of a place shared by all the individuals who pass through it. We teamed up with the idea of conceiving and creating public art together. At present we are dedicating ourselves to mural painting, but we have also worked on collective mosaic interventions in public spaces," Analí explains.

The Medianeras vision is also tightly bound to gender equality. "Our murals center on the representation of gender in its vast diversity. Although the works vary according to where they are located and how they are viewed, one of their standard features is faces, whose gender is not necessarily distinct. Our theme corresponds closely to our way of thinking about gender. Throughout our education, we are taught what a man does and what a woman ought to do. However, in both our case as well as that of a broad range of human beings, gender is something that can change and is often unable to adapt to this binary imposition," she continues.

"We want our works to convey the message of a broad concept of gender. We believe that once the rigorous distinction between men and women comes to an end, we will see the development of freer social relations and generations of people who are less concerned with what they should be and more attentive to what they could be. In other words, we believe that by breaking these rigid and constrictive molds, we can overcome certain forms of discrimination, as well as roles imposed on us from the outside. Our works reflect individuals, poetically and visually transformed, who often struggle to break out of the molds in which they find themselves. We also like to do a trick using anamorphosis. From one angle, one sees images of faces while, from another, one sees the distortion of these faces— the images reveal that they are illusions, something we believe are real, but that are not necessarily so," she clarifies. This is why Medianeras study the area around as well as the points of view from which the wall will be perceived: the image is conditioned both by the wall on which it will be displayed and the environment.

In general, they find that it is difficult for women to be recognized as equals in activities that are conducted mostly by men. "We are now somewhat appreciated for our work, but it's been a difficult road for us. So many talented women have

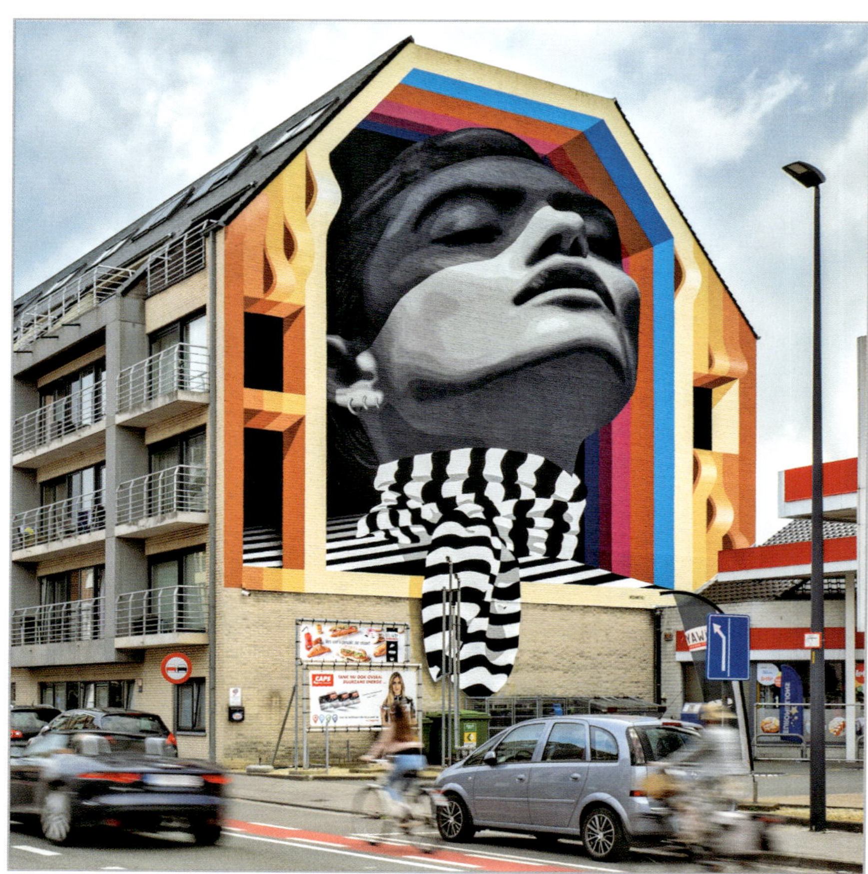

THE CRYSTAL SHIP, Ostend, Belgium, 2021

Vancouver Mural Festival, Canada, 2019 (right)

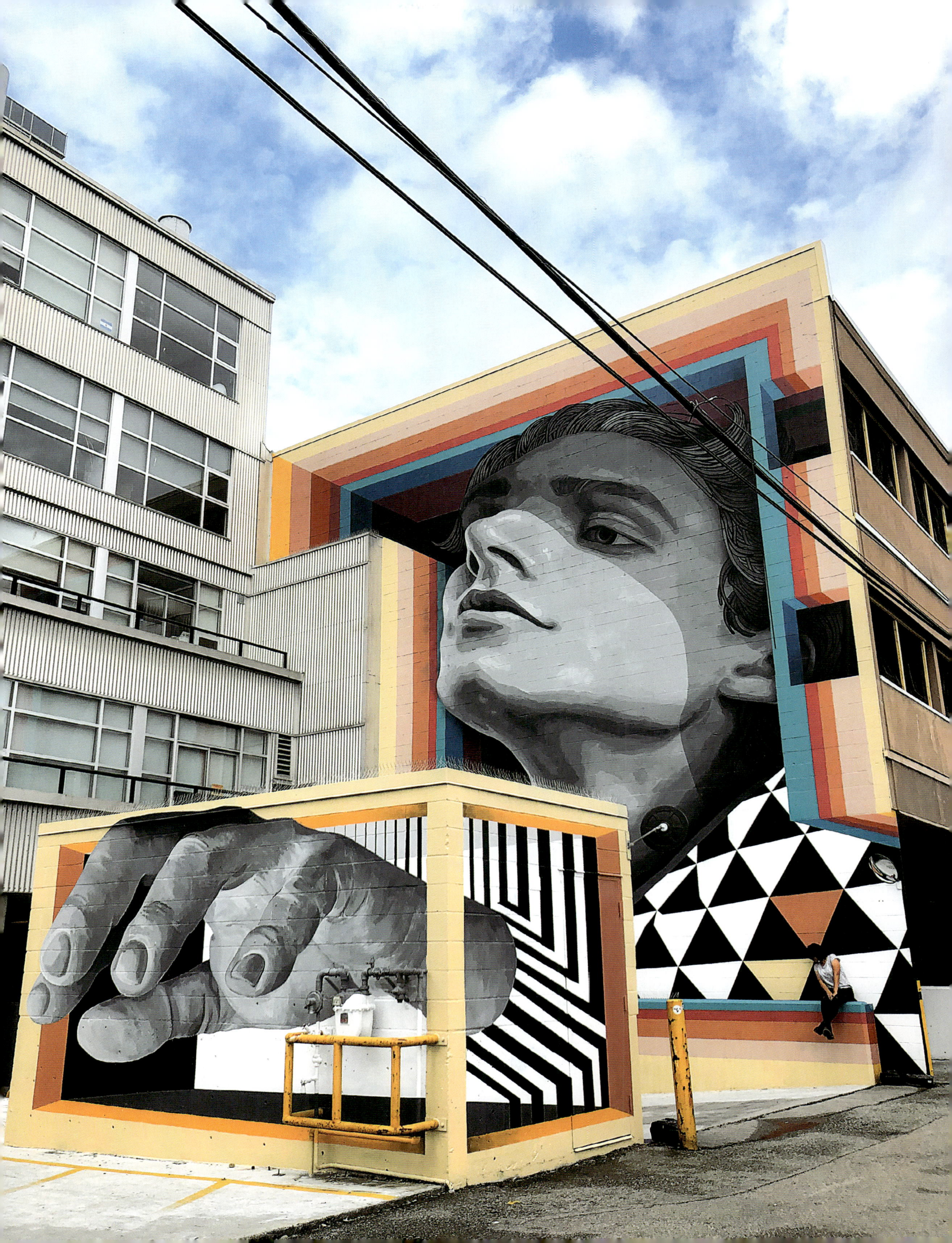

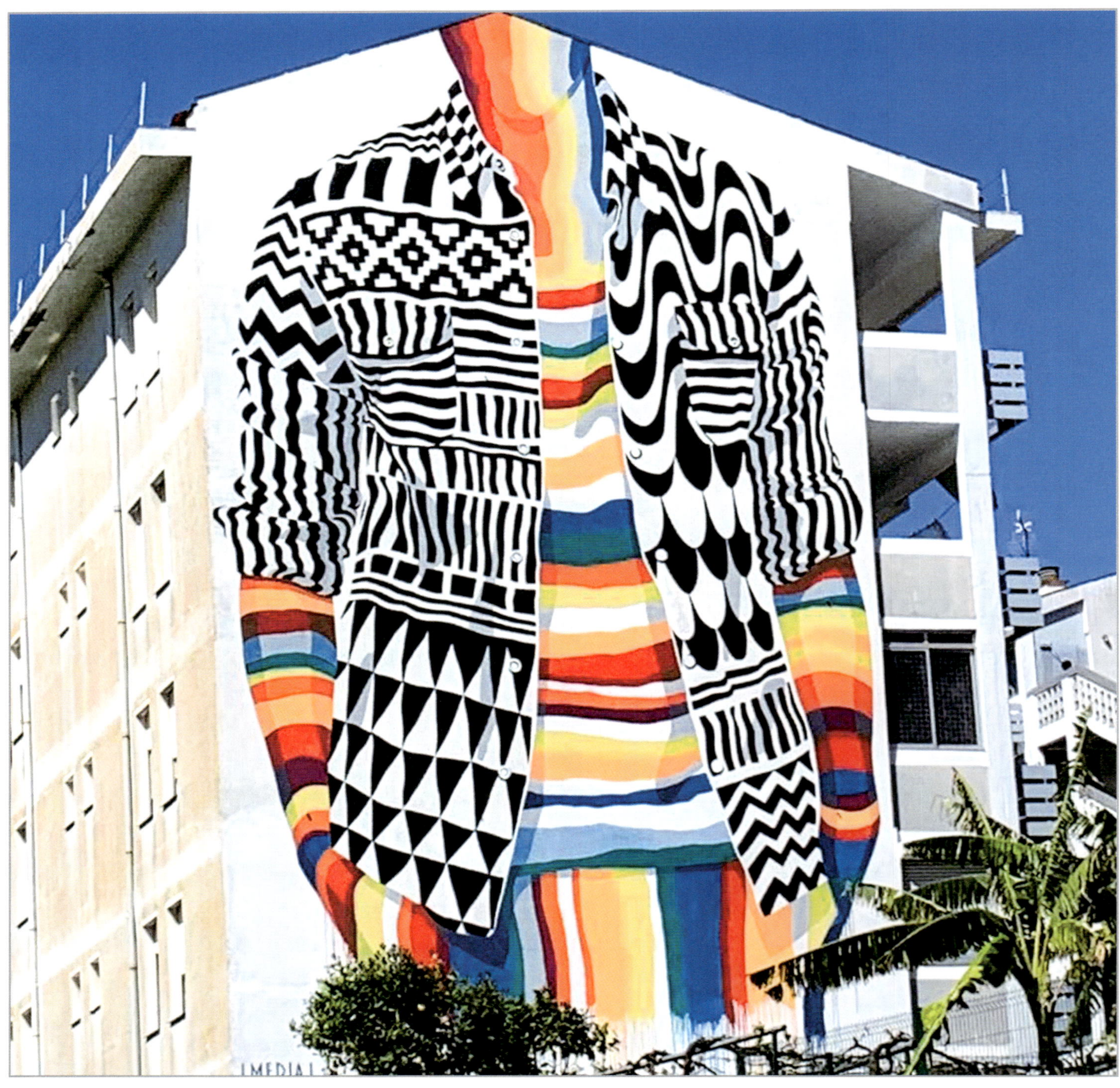

been painting on the street forever, but many of them did not have the visibility they deserved until a few years ago. Larger walls have gone primarily to men. We believe that this has to do with the prejudice toward women in stubbornly patriarchal societies. This situation has been changing in recent years, and now we are meeting more and more women who have been given an opportunity to grow with their works of art and the space to communicate their own vision," says Vanesa.

Medianeras are both Argentinian, raised in Rosario, a city near the Paraná River. "Our country is incredible and beautiful, as well as unstable and unpredictable. This forces its inhabitants to adapt to constant changes, be these economic, political, social, or other. Consequently, Argentines are quite creative when it comes to facing

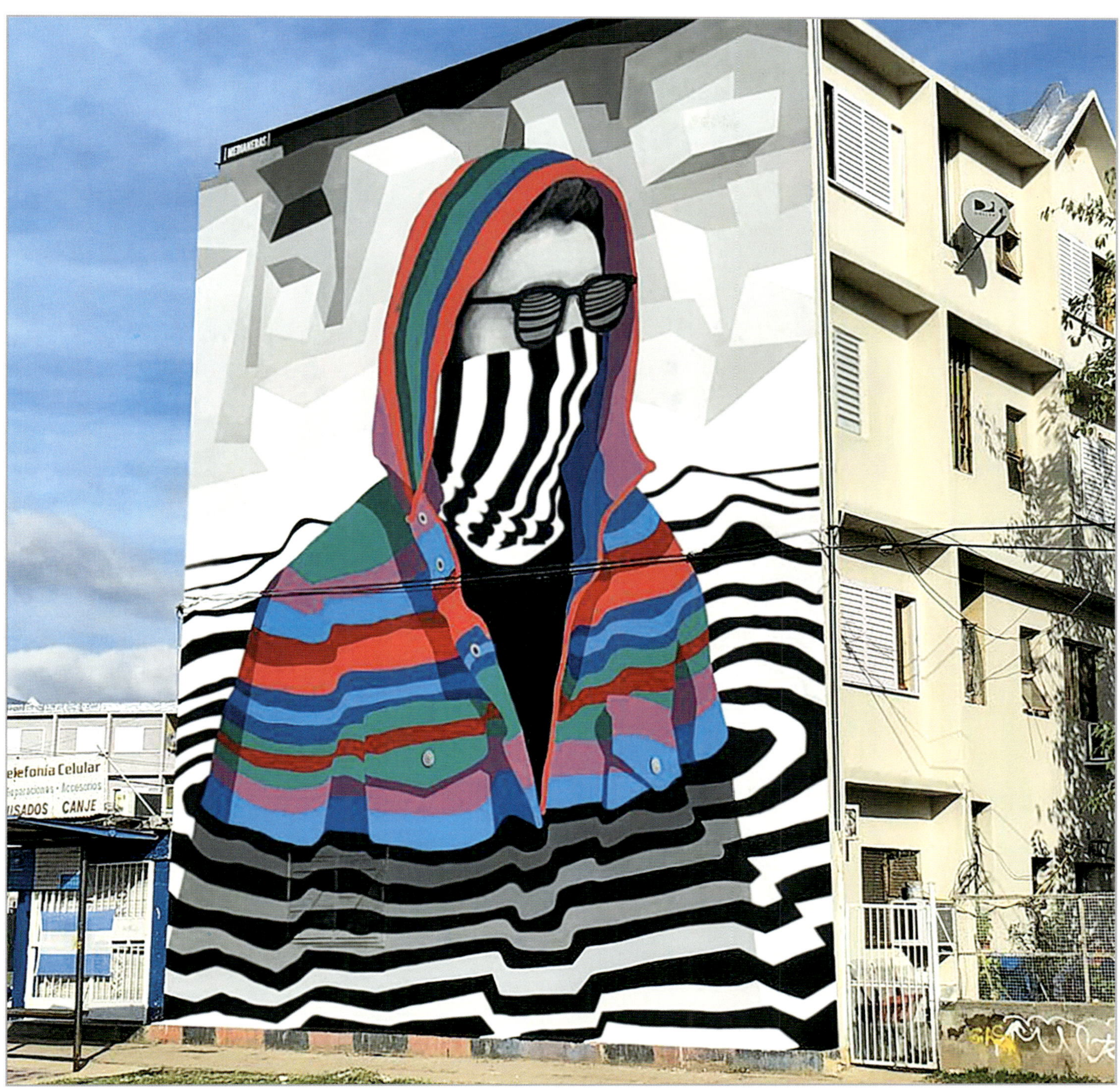

difficulties: indeed, we are a society accustomed to improvising and quickly adapting," she adds.

"As a child, I loved to make things, draw, invent new items. I attended several art workshops and studied art at the National University in Rosario, during which time I completed several murals," Analí recalls.

"I studied architecture and fine arts," says Vanesa. "I've always had a general predilection for urban planning, but I started engaging in collective urban interventions while directing a mosaic workshop after completing my studies."

MURO, Urban Art Festival, Lisbon, Portugal, 2017 (left)

Festival Triangulo, Rosario, Argentina, 2019 (above)

MAAANSO ENCUENTRO, San Juan, Argentina, 2018 (overleaf)

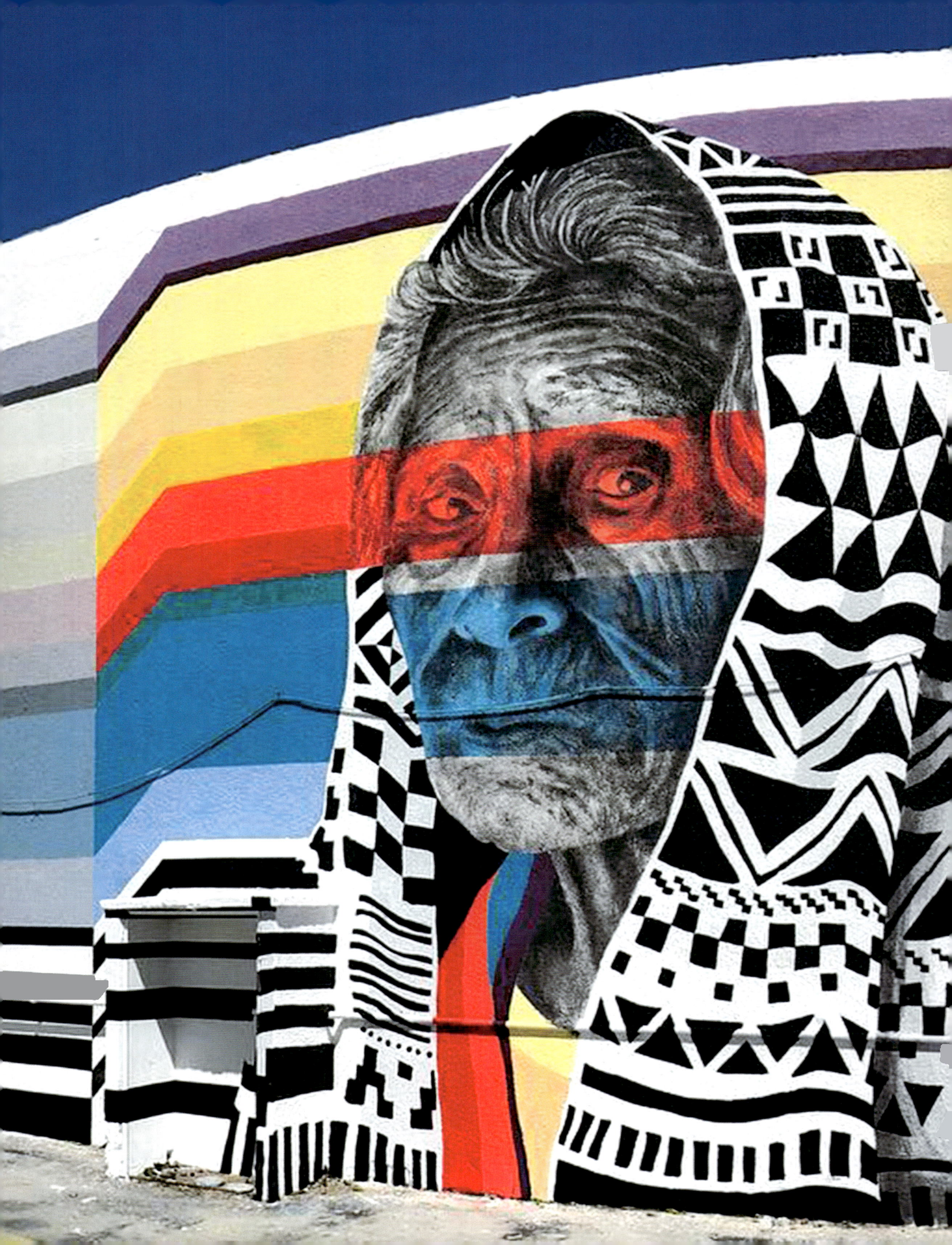

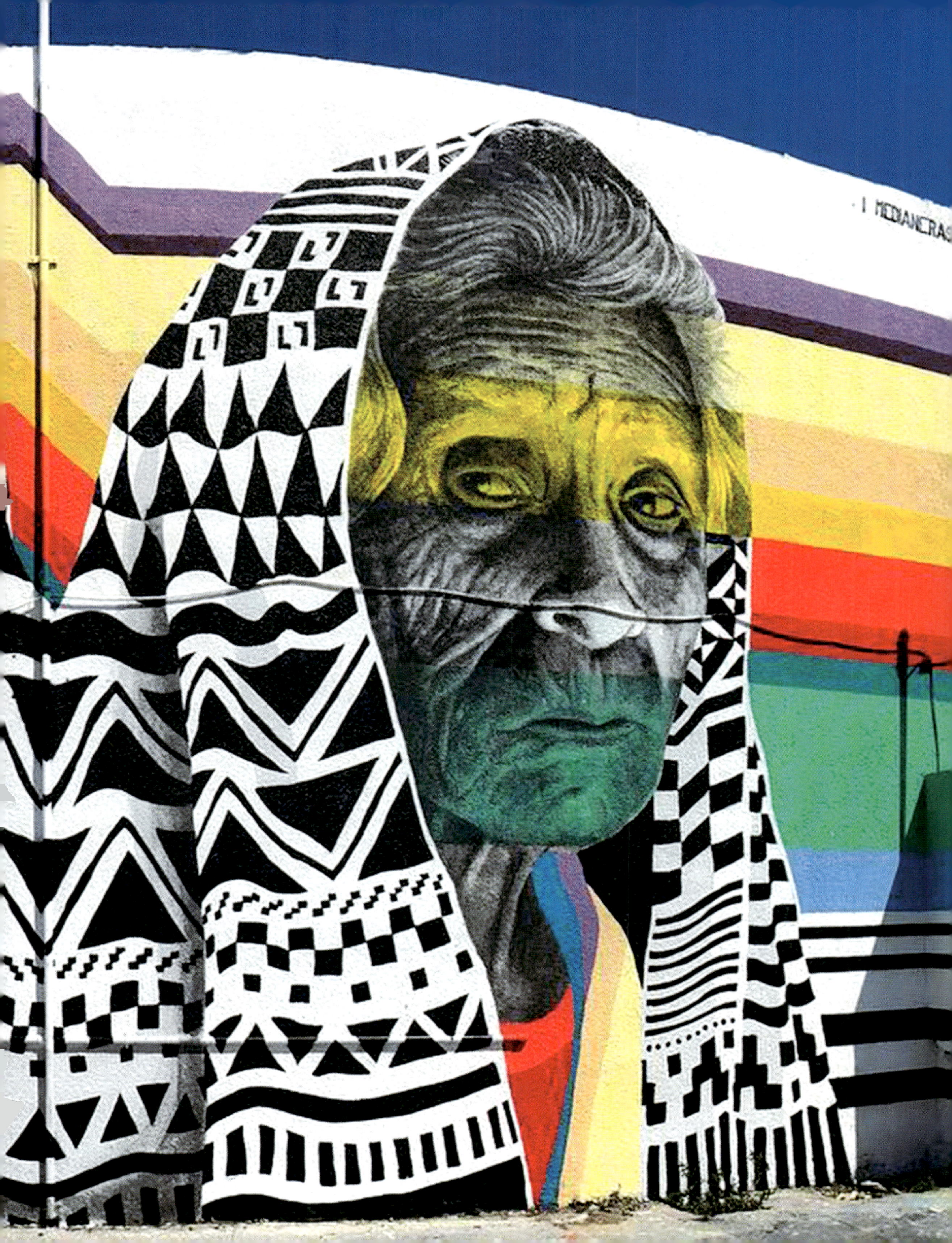
MEDIANERAS

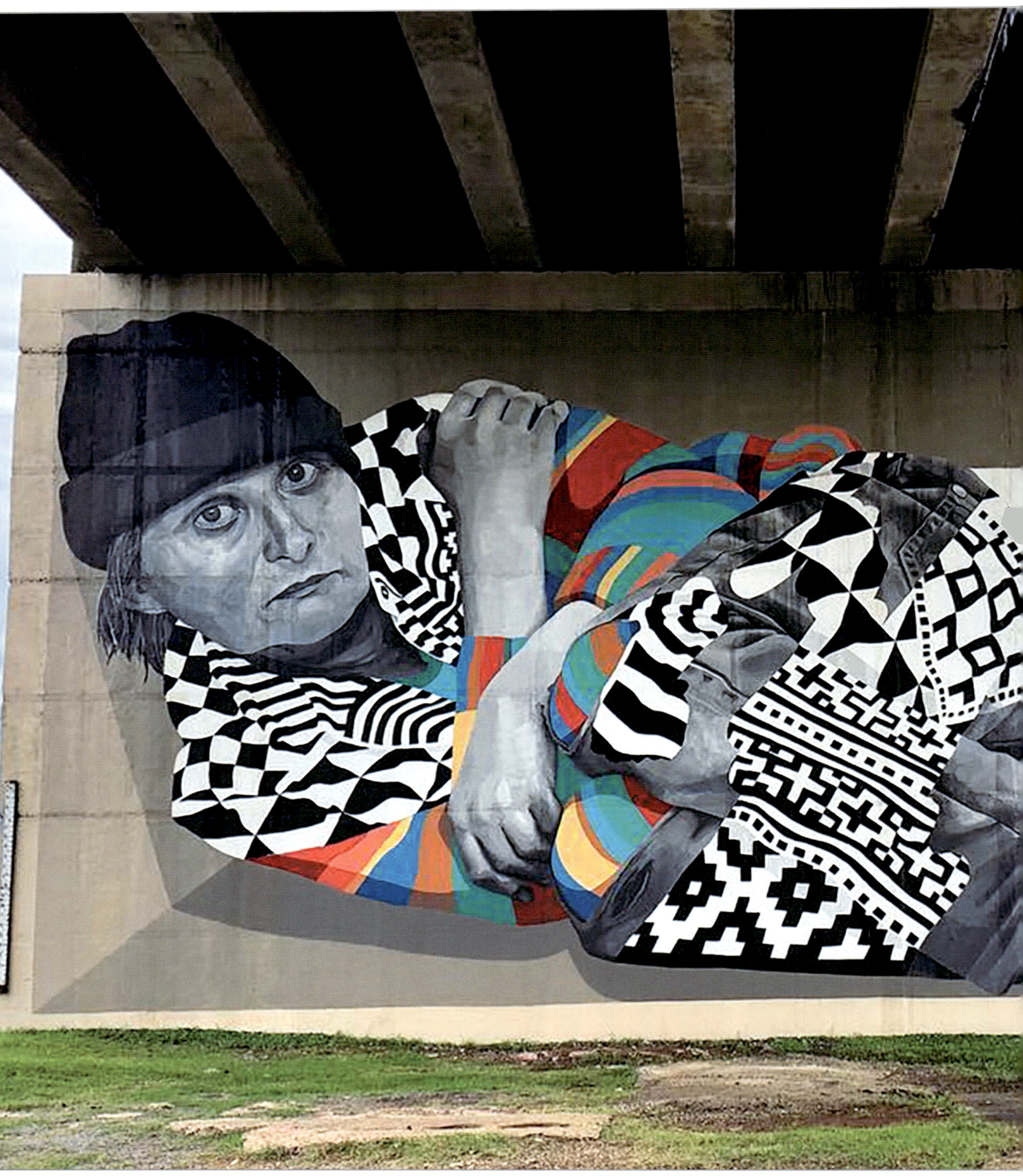

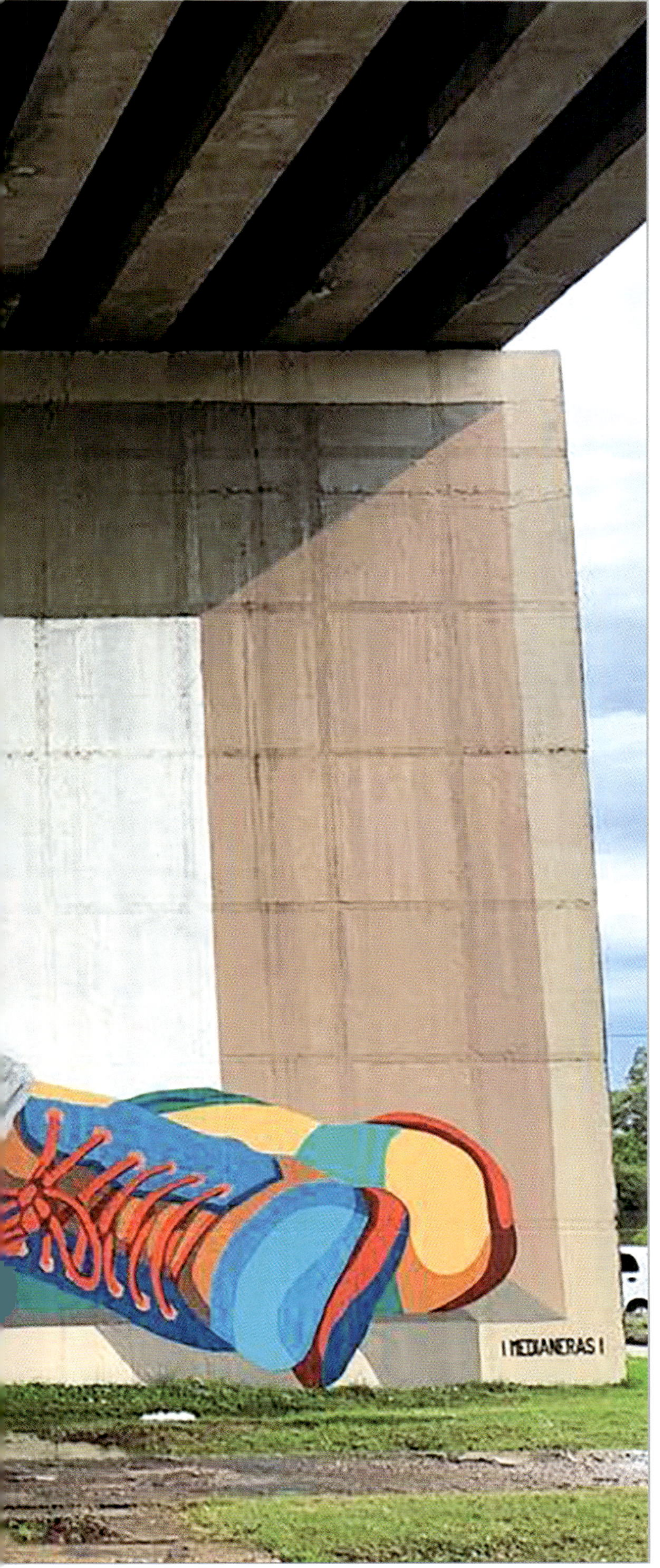

"There's always been something driving us to make public art; we even met while working on the street. The goal that we've always shared is to make street art for everyone—be those murals or urban interventions—because we believe it's the right place for us as well as the right means for our expression. Public art is the most honest way for us to create works that anyone can access. It is art for everyone," Analí asserts.

Medianeras met in 2012 in Rosario at precisely that mosaic workshop directed by Vanesa, who had contacted several graffiti artists regarding a mixed-media collective work of art. "We fell in love and started a life together full of love and art. And together we continue to grow," says Analí.

Their sources of influence are quite varied; they're interested in a bit of everything and in all kinds of art. "We've studied many critical moments in the history of art and have focused particularly on the Mexican murals of the twentieth century, as well as contemporary art. We look at many works by urban artists from different parts of the world, but we are also inspired by the creations of architects, writers, and artists from different disciplines. We like theater, film, music. Female figures have always been our guides, above all, because they've had to fight tenaciously to reach their goals—from our mothers who raised us while holding jobs, to all the other women who have come to occupy the visible positions they deserve," Vanesa explains.

"We like the fact that in street art, an artist need not pursue a career or be selected by a jury or institution to display their works to people. The important thing about urban art is that it expands this offer, making it accessible to everyone and democratizing access to culture. The main goal is to live the experience of creating a public work, of engaging a community. That's what we're looking for and what fully gratifies us," Analí concludes.

33 GRADOS FESTIVAL, Mercedes, Uruguay, 2019

MINA MANIA

THE GRAFFITI MYSTIC

*"Everything one does with passion requires a vision, a strong will,
and tireless motivation to serve as guides. In a certain sense,
it's been difficult to work in a man's world, but the passion has
always been strong enough to prevent me from getting distracted
from my goals. An optimistic attitude enables you to focus more
on the positive aspects of your work and on the unique gifts
that life bestows."*

Graffiti and art have always been her creed. "I've got lots of good memories from my childhood, in which I love letting my memory roam. I spent plenty of time in nature; I was really adventurous and imaginative; I wasn't afraid of anything, and I often enjoyed dressing up. I braved tests of courage in the forest with my older brother and his friends, but I also enjoyed playing with dolls with my little sister or sewing their clothes. I've had much variety in my life, but drawing, painting, and being creative have always been a constant feature," says Mina Mania. Her family contributed in a decisive way to nurturing all her passions. "I was lucky to grow up among very strong characters who provided my sister, my brother, and me with the security that allowed us to follow the right path. A sense of freedom has always accompanied me, and my imagination had no limits. From the time I was a child, I set my ideas and my experiences in drawings; pen and paper were always my main means of expression. I started painting on canvas at age twelve because I had always admired my aunt's paintings on the walls of my grandparents' home, a place that was a kind of 'cabinet of curiosities' full of collectibles and art objects from around the world," she recalls.

Mina was born and raised in Munich: "I'm a genuine 'Münchner Kindl,' as they say in Munich. Bavaria is my home; my existence is rooted there. I have a strong bond and inexhaustible love for my family and friends, for my homeland and Bavaria's rich culture, for its delicious food and beer, authentic dialect, and typical humor."

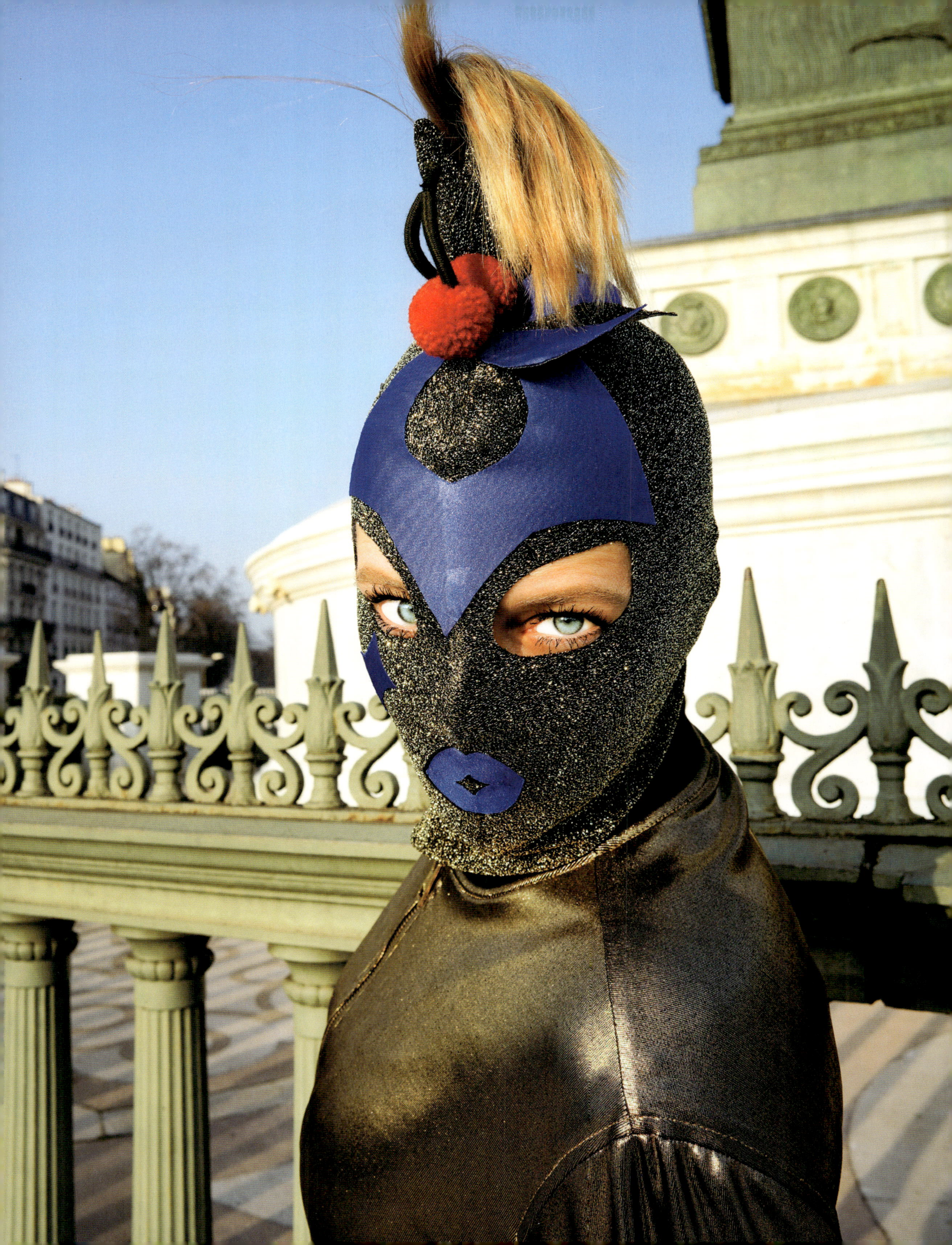

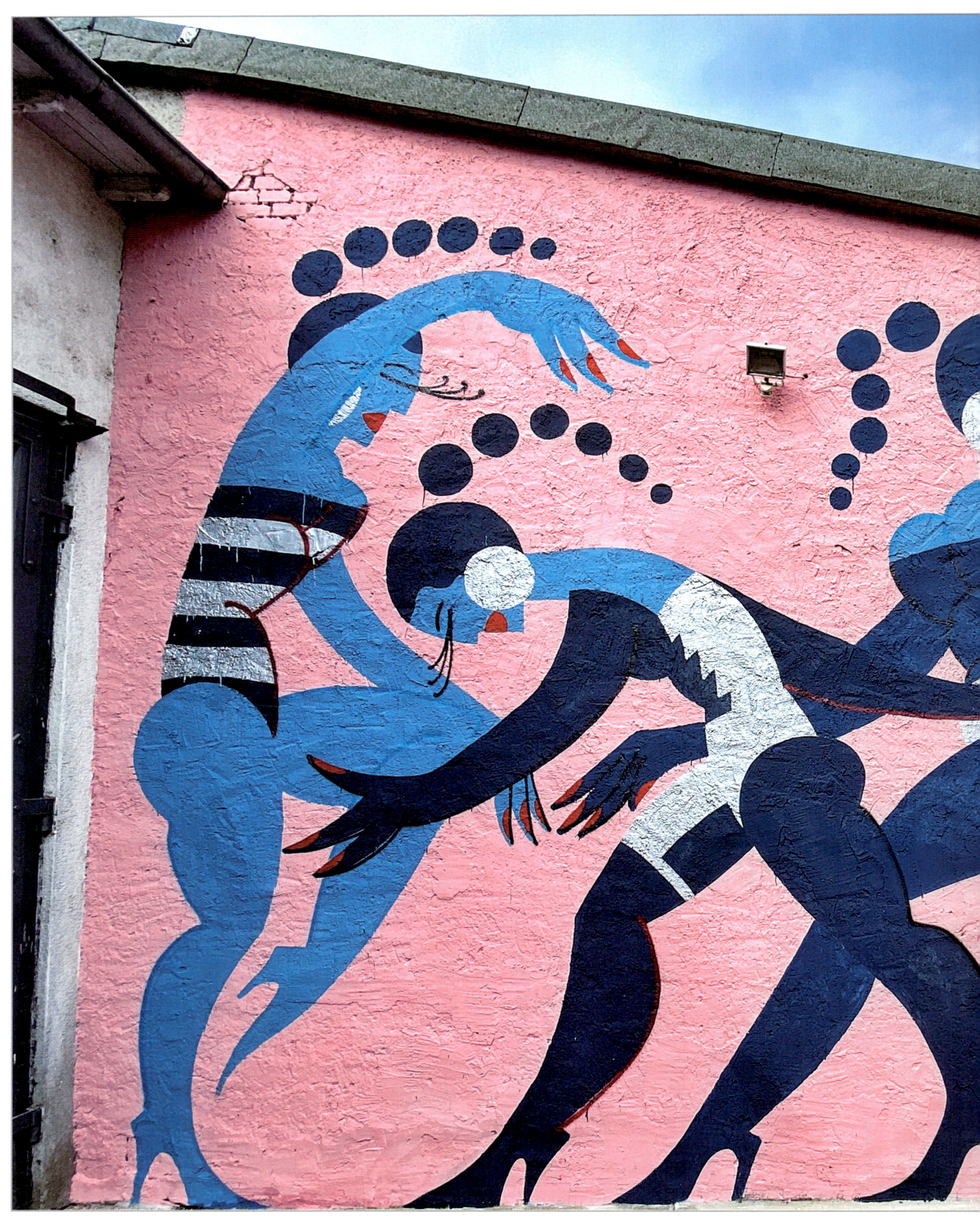

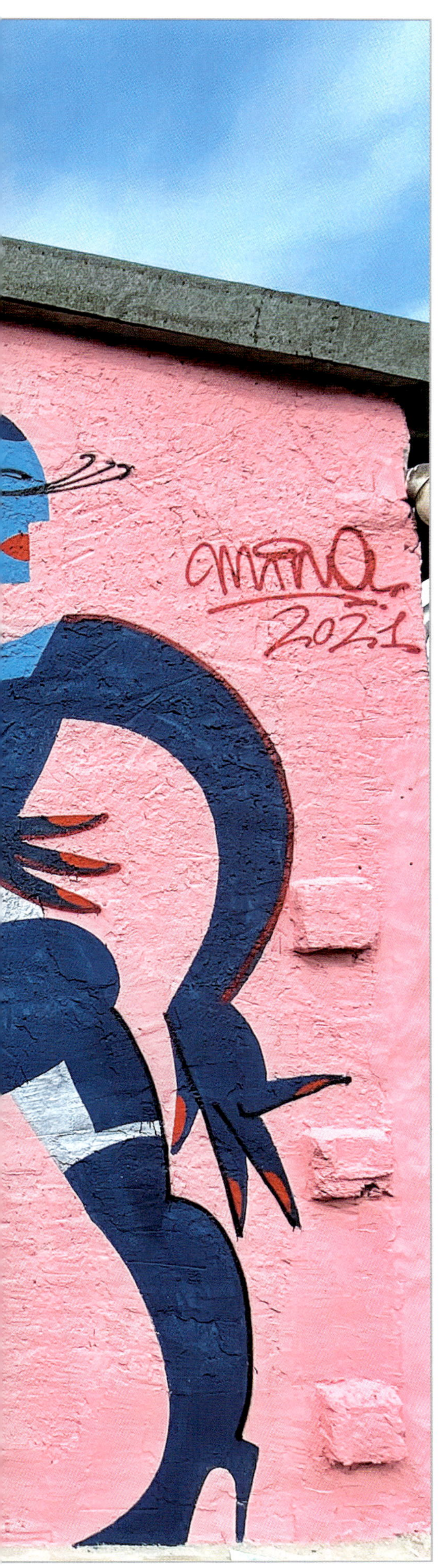

"Nonetheless, I must say that all the places in which I've lived have helped me grow and enriched my soul. I spent several years in Hamburg and Paris before moving to Berlin, a city that I love and which I feel is mine; I feel at home in my neighborhood, surrounded by interesting and inspiring people. The sense of freedom that I feel here has become essential to me; diversity in every form, which the city is so good at welcoming, enriches me. Life in Berlin is a constant source of inspiration for me," she reflects.

Mina began doing graffiti when she was only fourteen. Near her home was a notorious abandoned industrial site: "It was located between my best friend's house and mine. Our curiosity soon piqued, we began exploring it together. The

BREAK FREE, Sprungturmfestival, Darmstadt, Germany, 2021, Photo Mina Mania (left)
GRACE JONES, Kunstlabor 2, Munich, Germany, 2021, Photo Mina Mania

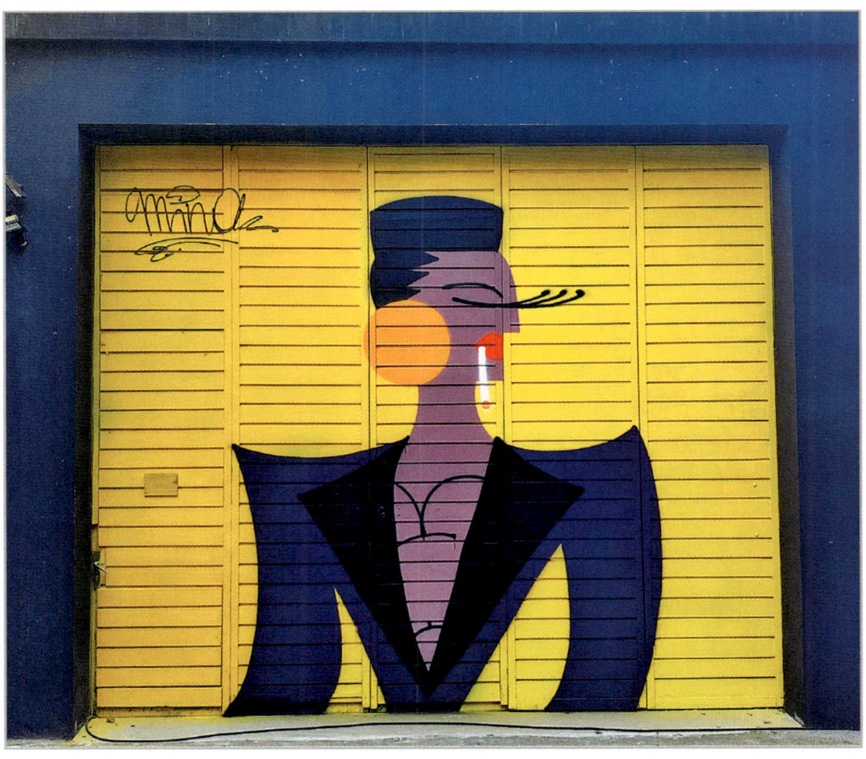

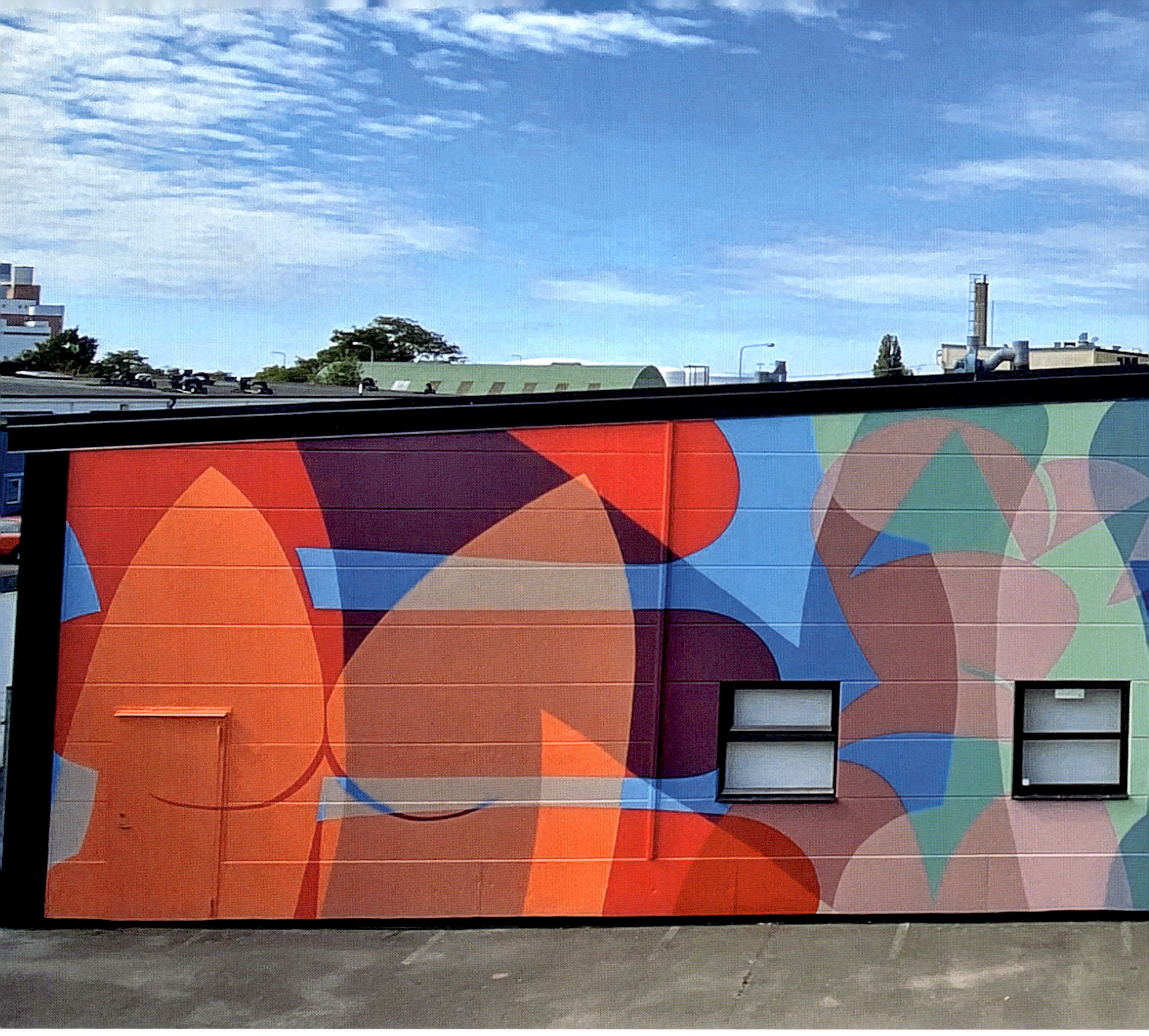

attraction it exerted on us was so strong that it became our usual meeting place. I recollect all the colors, the mystical ambience, and the charm of the forbidden. And the graffiti, above all, the graffiti! I still remember when we found ourselves before a mural by OSGEMEOS: we couldn't believe our eyes! A magic moment, one of many, I should say. The dimensions and colors of the graffiti impressed me so much that in the end I too wanted to start painting on walls," she continues, recalling the past.

Her path is full of memories that have left indelible marks. "When I was thirteen, my father gave me a book about Frank Frazetta: I practically immersed myself in his paintings. SatOne put the first spray can in my hand. I really admired his art, just as I did the murals of OSGEMEOS, WON ABC, and Loomit. MODE 2's style utterly amazed me. Usually I couldn't decode wildstyles, but I did enjoy copying them from the few graffiti magazines that I owned. Today, I've had the good fortune to meet many of the artists who served as my role models. Stohead, who's become a good friend and crewmate, is one of them," she reveals.

Mina immediately stood out in the street art world for her bubble letters and characters. She even created her own iconic

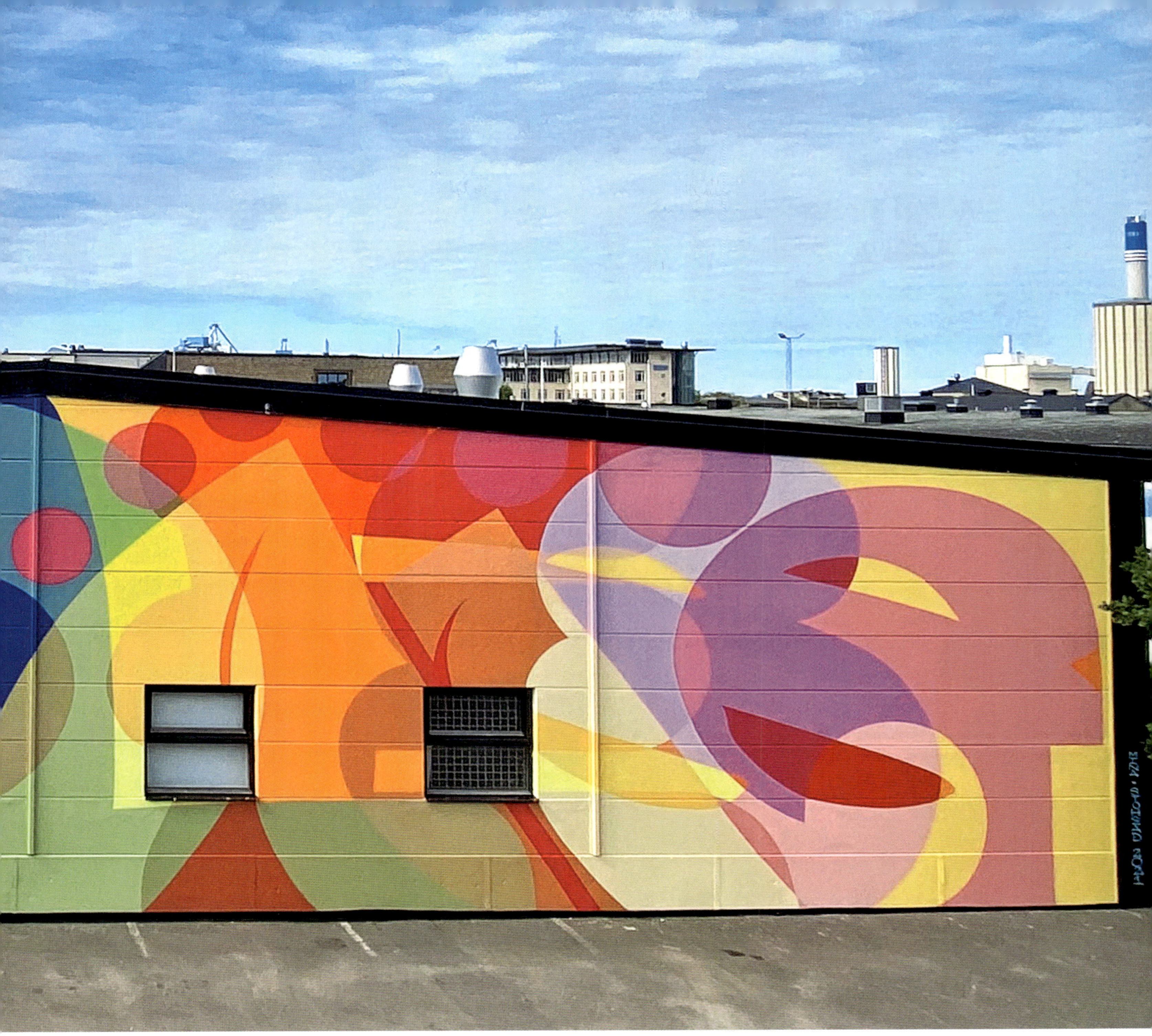

ENDLESS SUMMER, Mina Mania and Stohead for Pow Wow, Helsingborg, Sweden, 2021

female character, Nana—an open-minded, brave, and confident woman, a symbol of female power: "Some years ago I was working a lot on abstract compositions constructed out of letters. I was interested in expanding and deepening my formal vocabulary. I focused on the four letters of my name: M I N A. 'Nana' came out of my pen by accident at a moment when I was relaxing. "At first, I didn't attach any meaning to her, but soon my sketchbook was filled with variations on her lively figure," she explains. It was one of her artist friends who persuaded her to draw Nana in all her facets on walls. "I had three colors

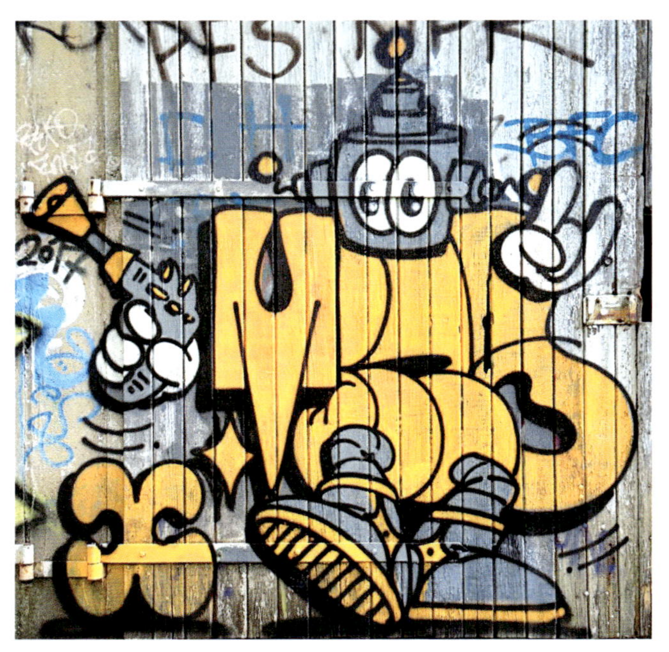

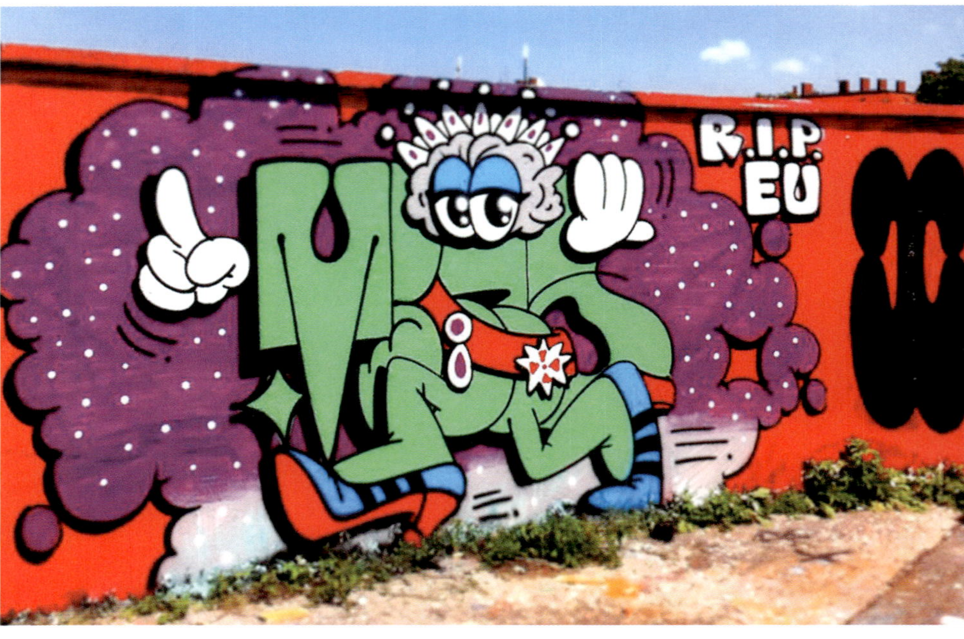

R.I.P.
EU

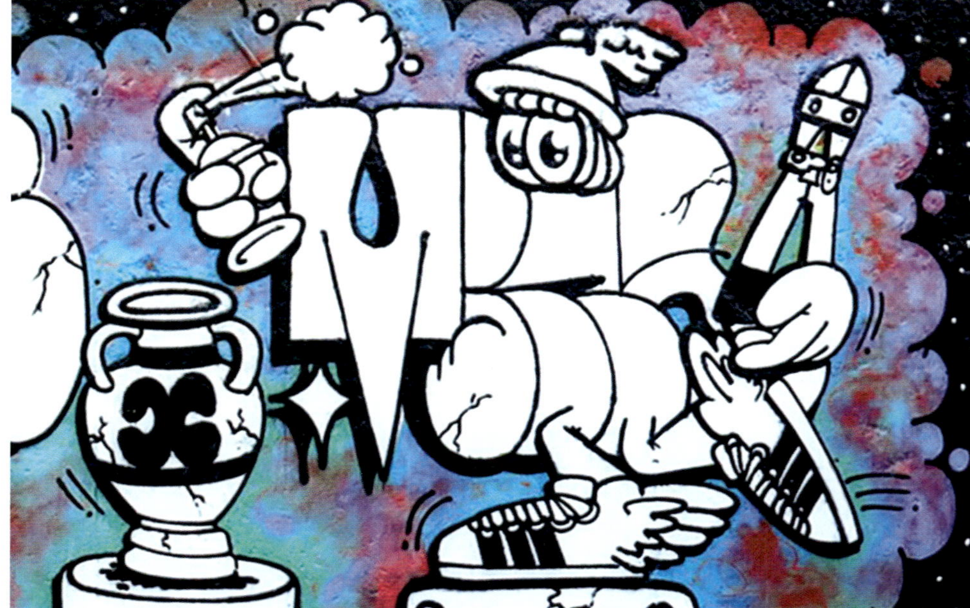

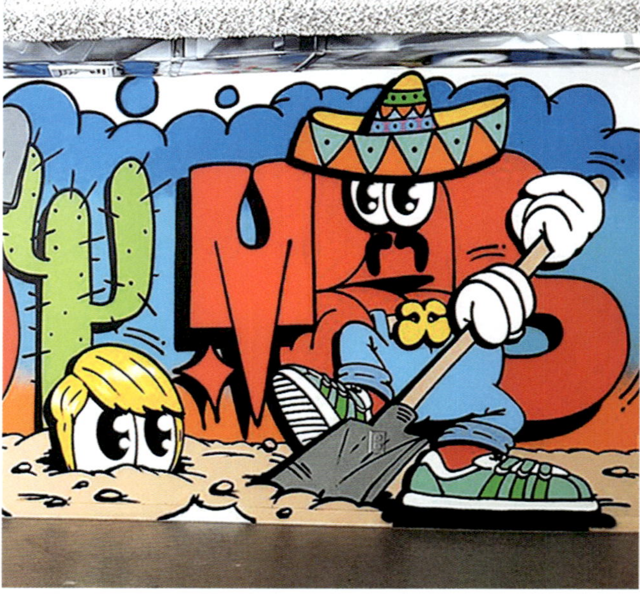

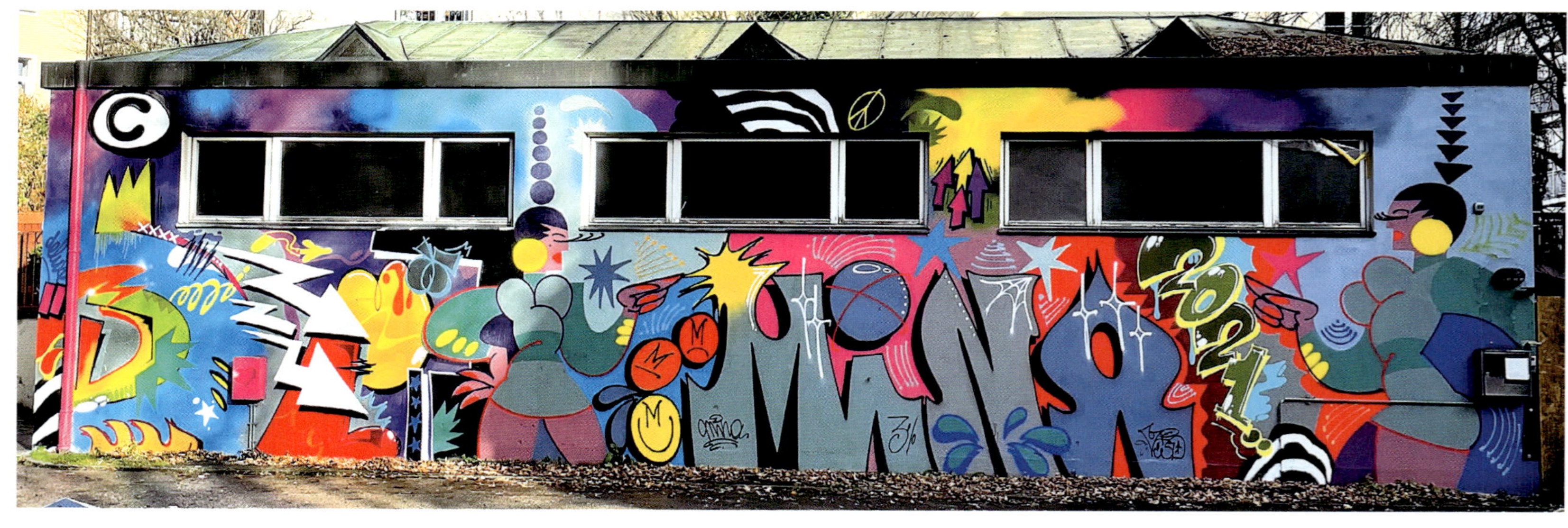

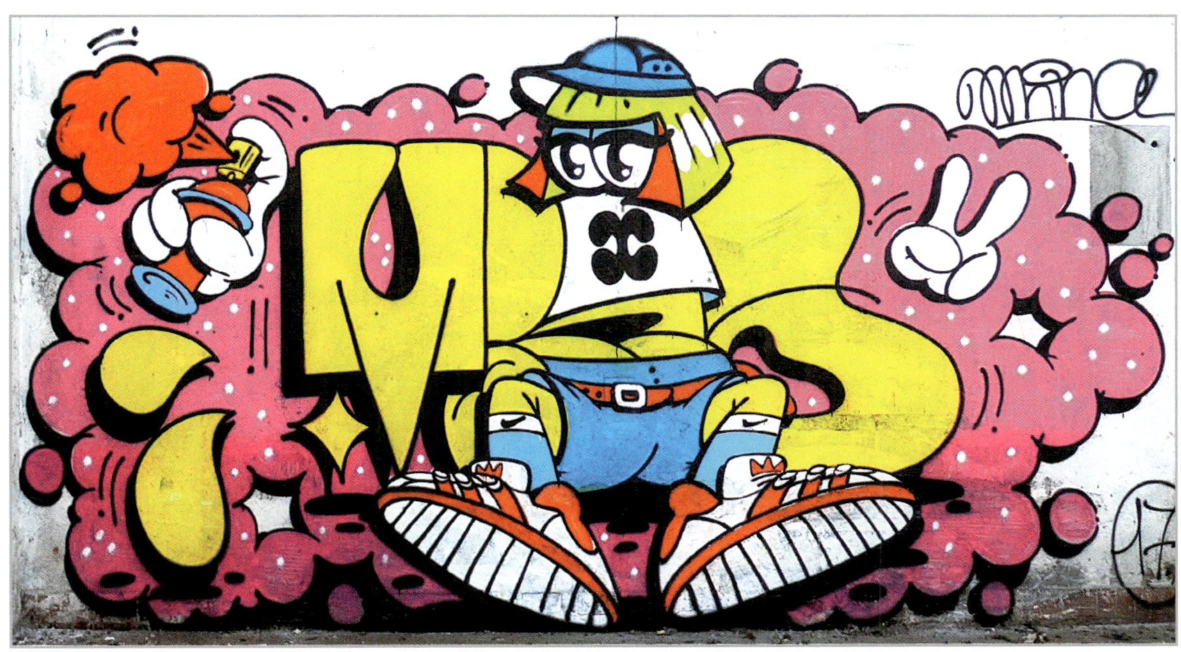

in my bag: black, white, and orange. I decided that this would be her color code. So I began painting Nana on canvas as well, and my first work, exhibited at a French gallery, immediately sold. Nana occupied me more and more, to the point that I ended up identifying with her," she says in reflection.

Mina, who had always been fascinated by the world of fashion, directed her creativity in this direction during the pandemic: "I had been making masks for a few years. At the beginning of the pandemic, when the supermarkets were empty and the panic was brewing, a colleague and I had the ironic idea of sewing protective suits against Coronavirus out of old shopping bags and giving life to a unique upcycling project. Equipped with all the necessary accessories, including, obviously, a bottle of disinfectant, they turned out much better than we had initially imagined. The suits were the first step toward our *LOCKDOWN Welcome to Yolo Land* series. After all, as a child I had been fascinated by Karl Lagerfeld's fashion designs and Coco Chanel's creations!" she confesses.

Another fundamental source of inspiration for her artistic creations is music: "Musicians know how to touch people deeply and generate strong emotions in them. As a painter, I wish at times I could get a musician's immediate opinion on my work."

Mina's vision is to transmit powerful, motivational, and euphoric energy, just as a piece of music does. "As an artist, I don't see my work as a mission, but rather as an offer by an outstretched hand to enter my universe. For me, art provides an opportunity to create an individual space in which everything is possible, in which I can express my feelings and offer food for thought on certain issues. The effect varies depending on the viewer. Not everyone recognizes the message between the lines. What's left, therefore, is the offer to look more closely and read on a level other than that of aesthetics. Free to interpretation," she says.

JUST CHILLIN', Milan, Italy, 2017, Photo Mina Mania (above)

MINA BROBOT, Berlin, Germany, 2017, Photo Mina Mania • GOD SAVE THE QUEEN, Munich, Germany, 2016, Photo Mina Mania • HERMES, Berlin, Germany, 2016, Photo Mina Mania • FUCK TRUMP, New York City, New York, USA, 2017, Photo Mina Mania • DELUXE MINA, Samy Deluxe & Mina Mania, Kunstlabor 2, Munich, Germany, 2021 , Photo Boris Schmidt (facing page, from left to right and top to bottom)

MISS VAN

THE WITCH OF SENSUALITY AND EROTICISM

"Expressing myself and my identity in the works I make has always been very important to me; it doesn't matter if my women are imperfect, I know they must be mine, in tune with my style and my personality."

Her characters with naked breasts and bodies are highly sensual women unafraid to display themselves in all their femininity. They assume burlesque poses and expressions and wear corsets, petticoats, brassieres, and tutus that float in an interlude of time suspended between past and present. Fitted out with animal heads, there's something tribal or folkloric about them. Or else they wear disconcerting and eclectic masks, some of warriors, others of dancers or parade participants, and yet others of the kind used in ceremonies. Then there are those representing animals, deer, rabbits, foxes. . . They are all endowed with magnetic and charming allure. Miss Van confesses that she is obsessed with their hair, which hides or frames their faces and shapes, exudes eroticism by conforming to every curve, and is either flaming red or white with the melancholy passage of time.

"When I was very young, at the beginning of my career, I called my women poupées or dolls, but today I say they are my muses because, possessing a spiritual and independent soul, they have evolved with me. They all arose naturally. I never created them according to a specific plan but generated them from pure instinct. Sometimes I've been criticized for making them too much like female sex objects, but to me it's not important to please or gratify. It's through them that I want to express myself and my intimate vision of femininity," she explains.

To Miss Van, or Vanessa Alice Bensimon, these women are intriguing, mysterious, and ambiguous beings—just as she and all of humanity are, at heart. "I have a twin sister, Natacha, a writer and poet, who is absolutely *unidentical* to me. I've always been more shy and introverted, plagued by feelings of inadequacy, an outsider, in search of my identity. For me, drawing and painting were a way of expressing myself, and isolating myself in a parallel universe, separate from the real one. Art has always been a kind of therapy for me. Despite our differences in character, my sister and I are quite close and have many interests in common. We are both fascinated by the female universe and sometimes carry out projects together," she says.

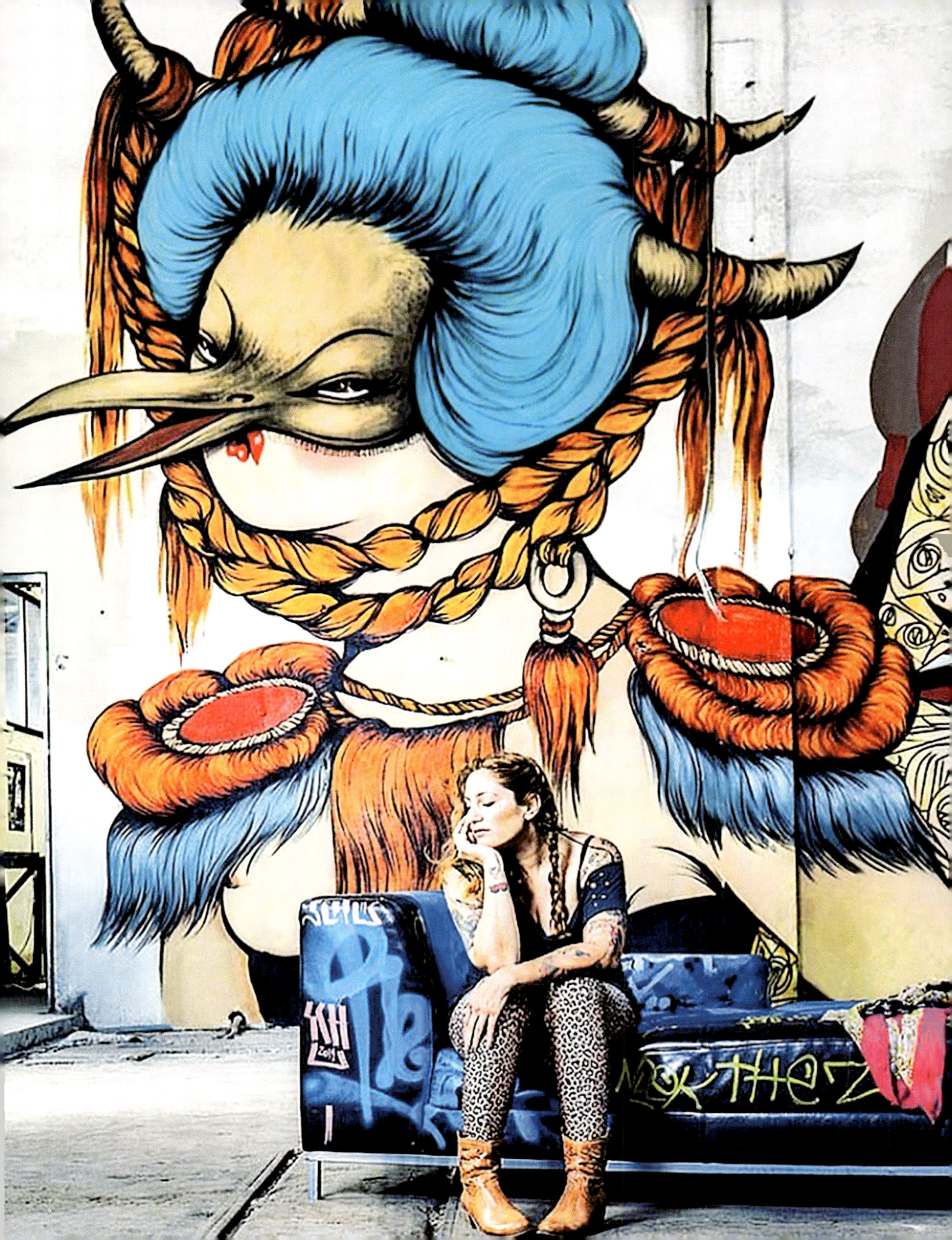

Miss Van's women are unique in the street art world: they represent a powerful rejection of male supremacy, a cry of revenge and triumph, of irrepressible, aggressive, and sometimes even slightly dark sexuality. They have evolved over time to become more elegant and intriguing, symbols of femininity in all its ambiguity and complexity.

Miss Van began painting on the streets of Toulouse, where she was born and raised, when she was about fifteen. "As a child I drew constantly; I needed to do so to escape the real world, and it was in this way that I developed my personality. I studied art at university, then met many other artists with whom I could share my opinions and ideals in the world of graffiti and street art. We had our own language, and it was an act of provocation against the status quo to write our names on walls. I confess that the sense of doing something forbidden was intoxicating!" she recollects. "I was a rebel, and perhaps I really needed to make art illegally in order to express myself, but I was sure of one thing: from the beginning I wanted to represent femininity in all its nuances, all its eroticism, even exploring its boundaries with fetishism," she continues.

Miss Van did not allow herself to be intimidated by the fact that she was surrounded by a mostly male environment. "I had lots of energy; I was opposed to the system; creating art made all my fear disappear, made me strong. Many of my friends, male street artists, likewise supported and encouraged me. I didn't care

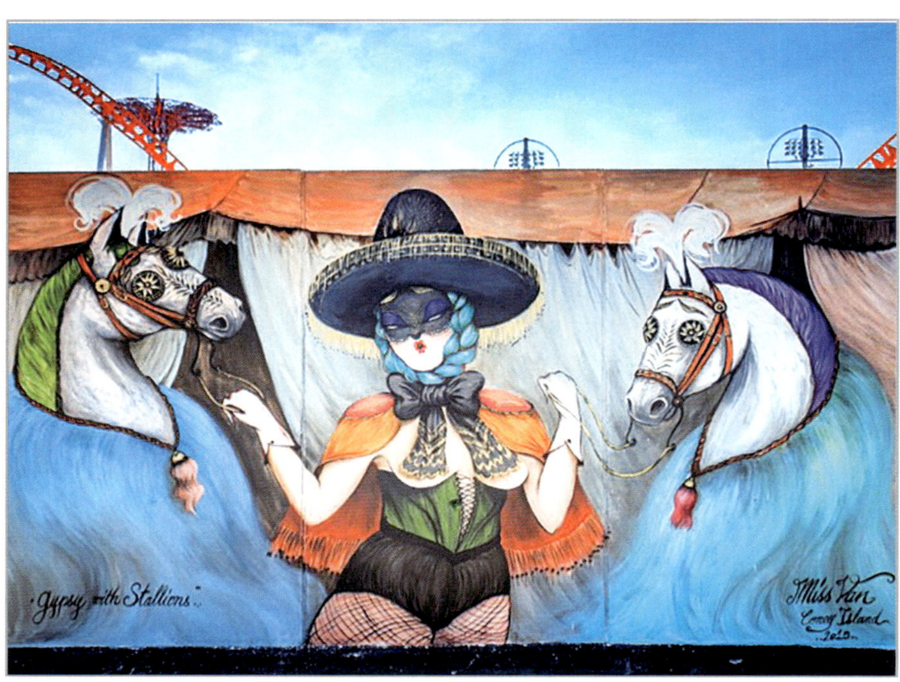

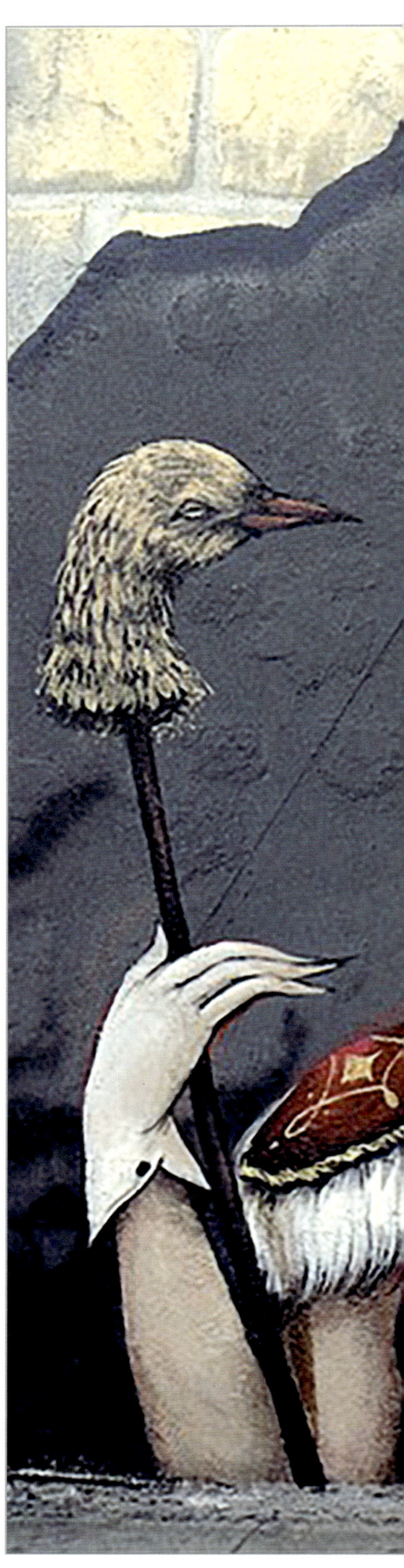

Coney Island, New York City, New York, USA, 2015

Palace Costume, Los Angeles, California, USA, 2015 (right)

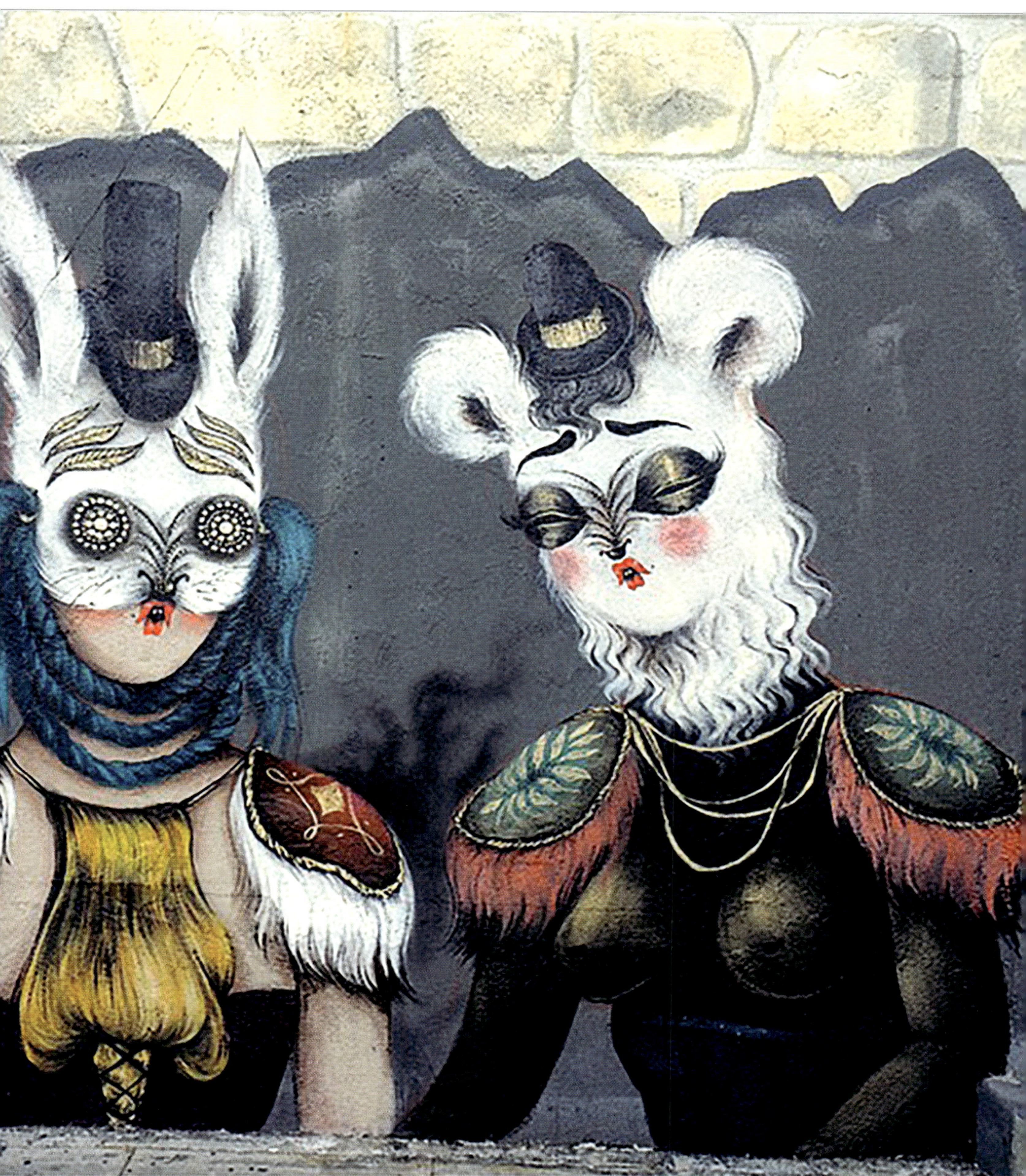

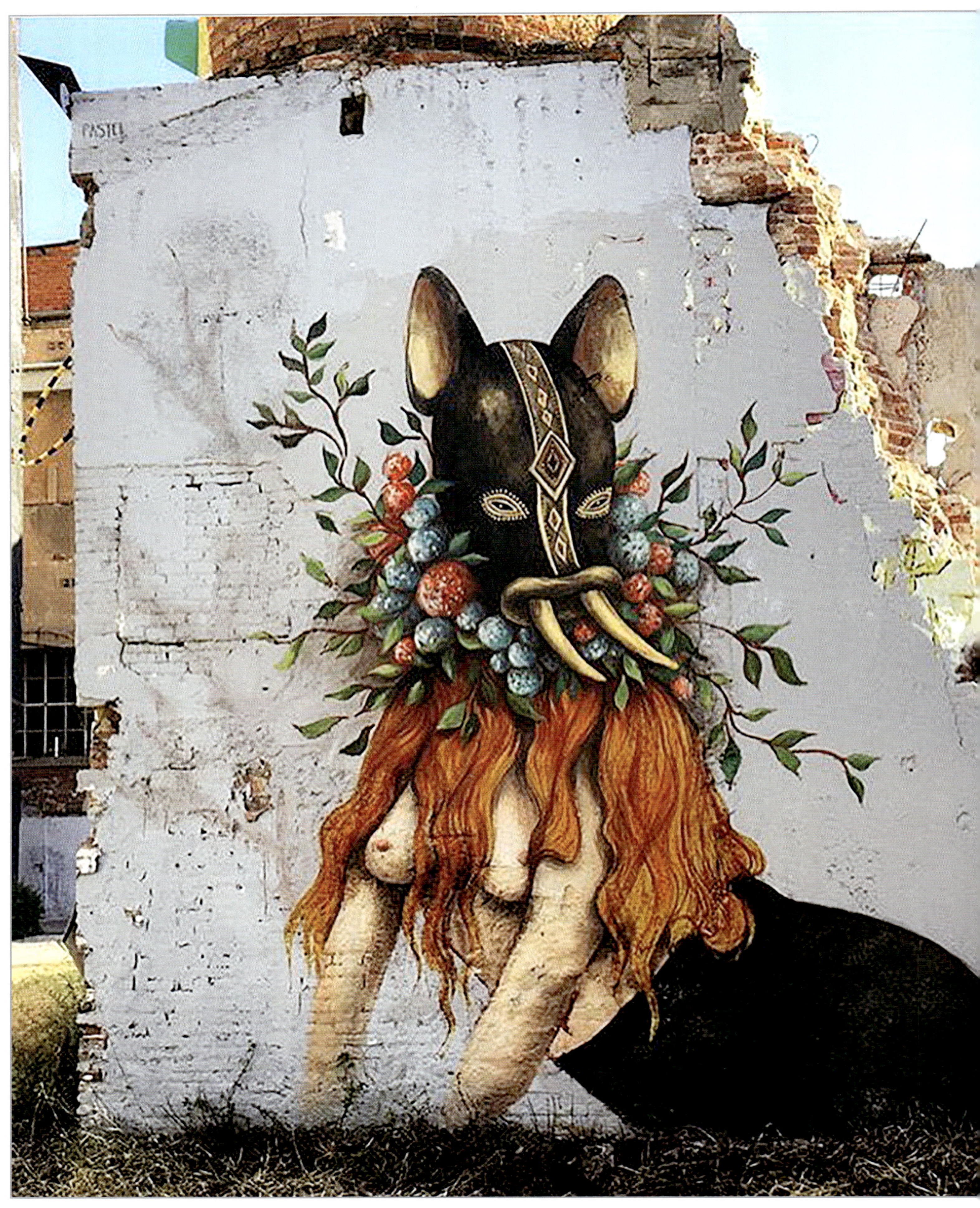

PASTEL

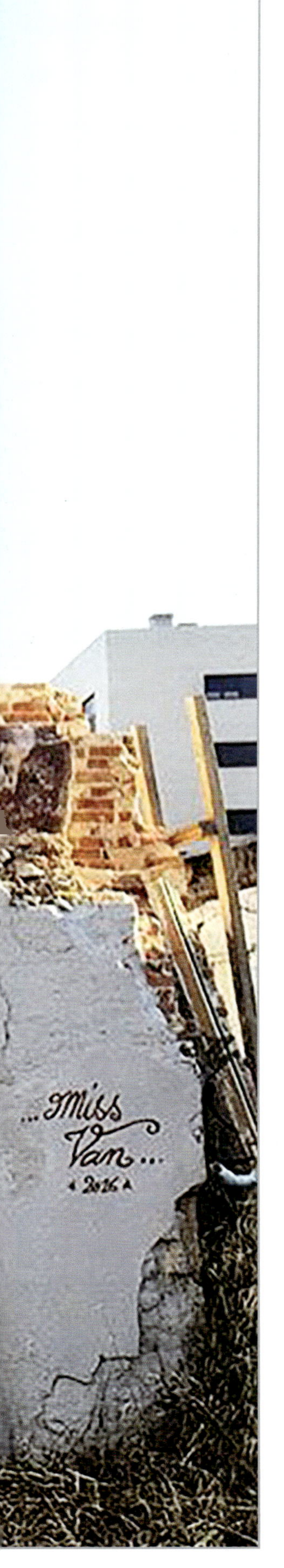

about anything that anyone said or did around me or about what other people thought: I was completely absorbed by my passion for art. When I started painting in the streets, I immediately realized that I wouldn't ever be able to stop. There's always been a provocative quality and ambiguity to me," she notes.

When graffiti and street art stopped being tolerated in Toulouse and was removed from walls, Miss Van decided to move to Barcelona.

"I knew Spain well, because my parents had moved to Ibiza, and Barcelona was a super-liberal and open city. I've been living there for over twenty years at this point, and it continues to be a source of inspiration, though I've also spent lots of time in the United States," she admits. "My art has grown with me and become more intimate and mature. Today I devote myself only to large walls that are really special to me, and spend more time working in the studio and on canvas. Various things inspire me: sometimes these are photographs, at other times they're books or films or people I meet; but in the end, when I paint I have to isolate myself. Sometimes I close my eyes and let the work develop from my vital energy that moves practically autonomously over the canvas or wall. I try to imagine the feelings and emotions that I want to translate into my language so that I can convey them to others; then I paint: for me these things are more important than technique. In the end, my artistic career continues to be an infinite search for myself," she concludes.

FESTIVAL DE MURALES DE LA ESCOCESA, Barcelona, Spain, 2016 (left)
AVANT GARDE TUDELA 2020, Tudela, Spain, 2020, Photo Fer Alcalá

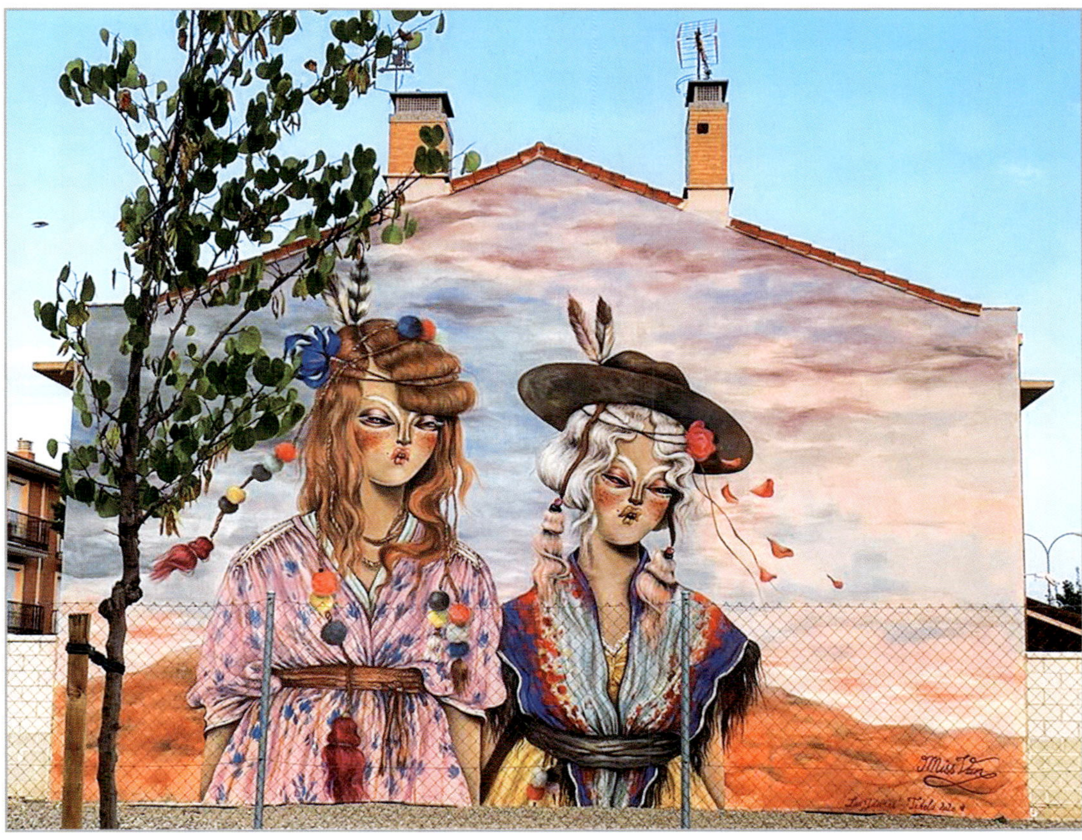

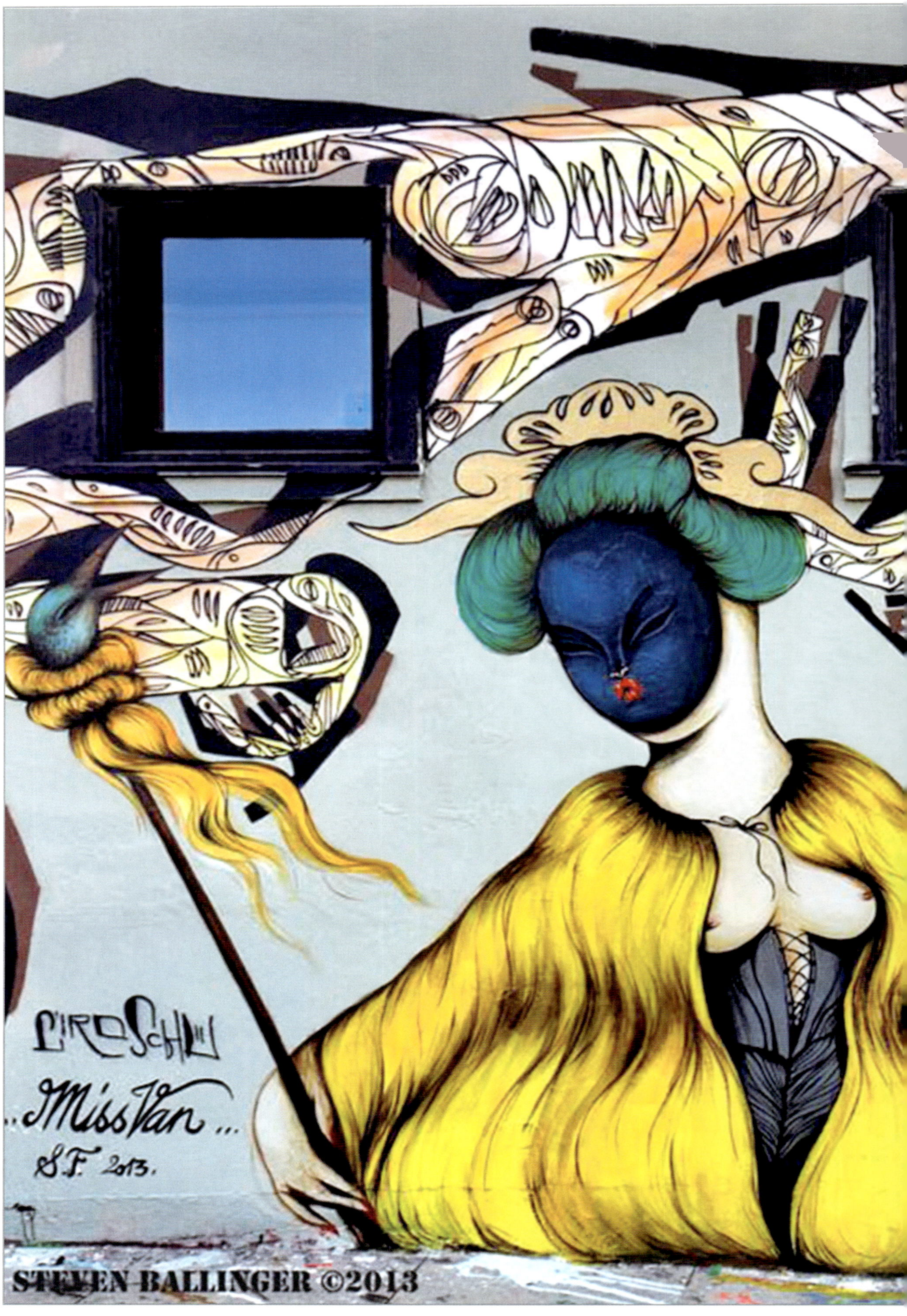

MissVan & CiroSchu — San Francisco, California, USA, 2013, Photo Steven Ballinger

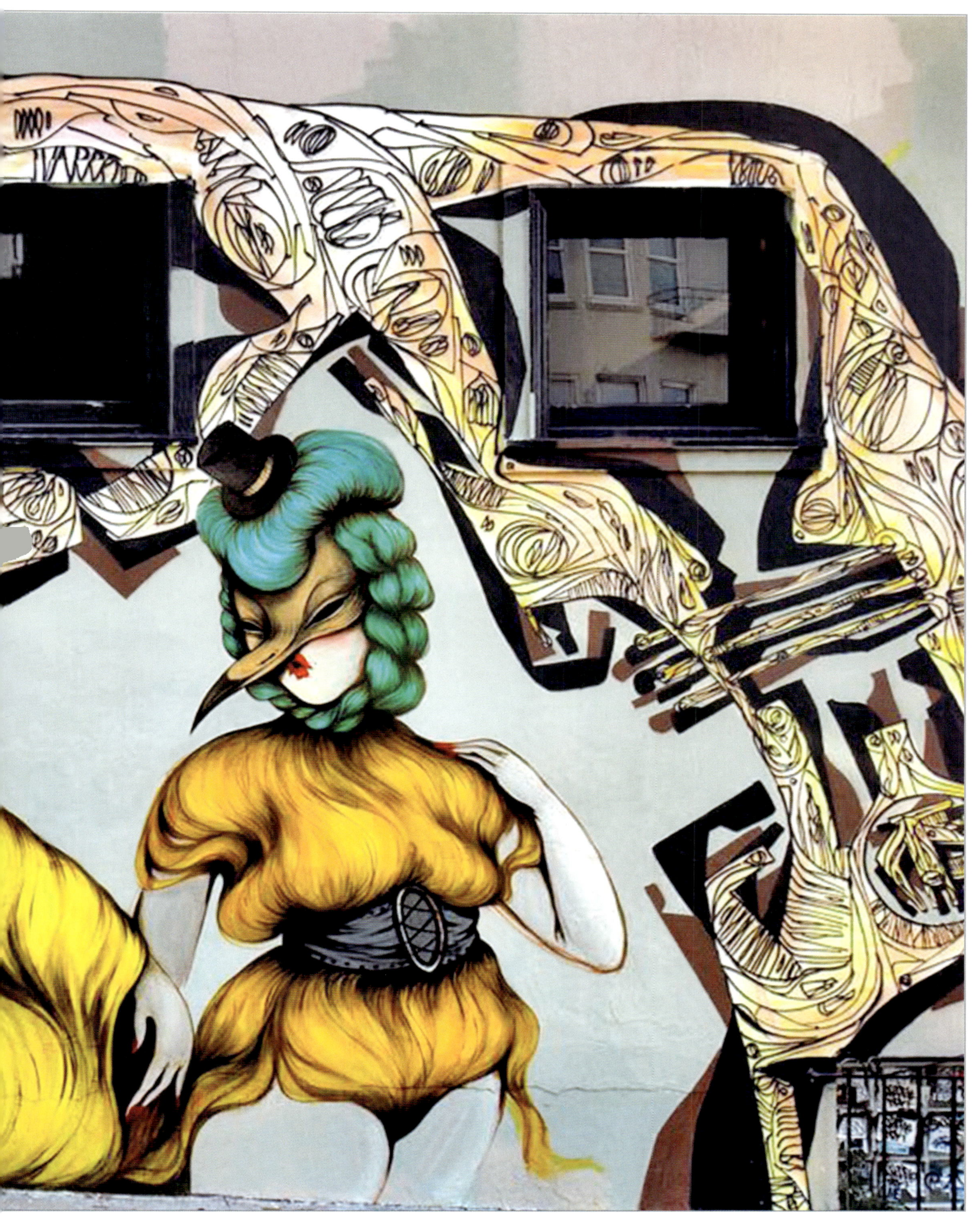

ALICE MIZRACHI

THE CUSTODIAN OF ANCESTRAL BEINGS
AND WATER

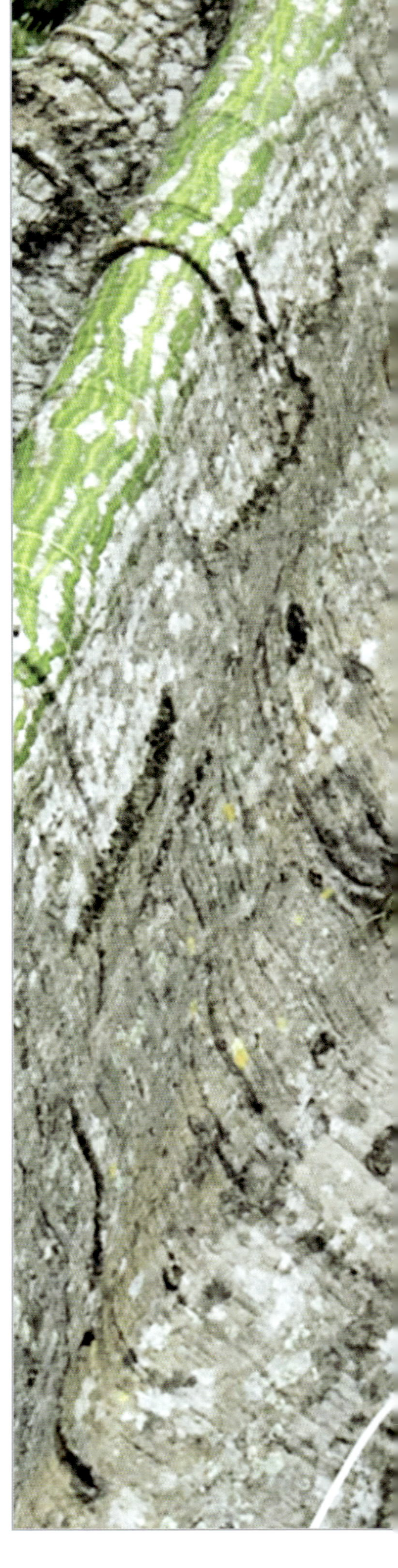

"I am a stalwart supporter of gender equality in every field, not only art. I am convinced that we must focus on who we are and who we want to be, rather than complain about what doesn't work. If I feel that I'm not accepted for who I am, I continue, resolute, on my way to new possibilities."

"Water is our body; we are closely, intimately connected to water, we are surrounded by water, and all the movements of our body depend on it. Water is the first thing we experience in this world. For me, water is also the means that brought me to America, since my parents crossed an ocean to get here. Water, accompanied by the image of the moon, often surrounds divine female energy. The initials of my name, as well as those of my sister and brother, lead back to water as they spell the word SEA. I also used that for the title of an installation. . . I frequently insert symbolic geometry into my works, which people often fail to see, but which refers to this close bond," states Alice Mizrachi.

Her entire life has been an incredible adventure aimed at discovering her roots, her origins, her ancestors. Her large-scale murals show powerful women, mythical female figures, ancestral beings, and female divinities associated with Earth and nature. A first-generation American with Sephardic-Israeli roots, Alice often uses art as a tool for exploring concepts such as community and family. "I grew up in New York, in Queens, in the Dutch Kills neighborhood. Now, with my husband, the graffiti artist TRAP, I also spend a lot of time in Miami, another city on the water, like Tel Aviv and New York."

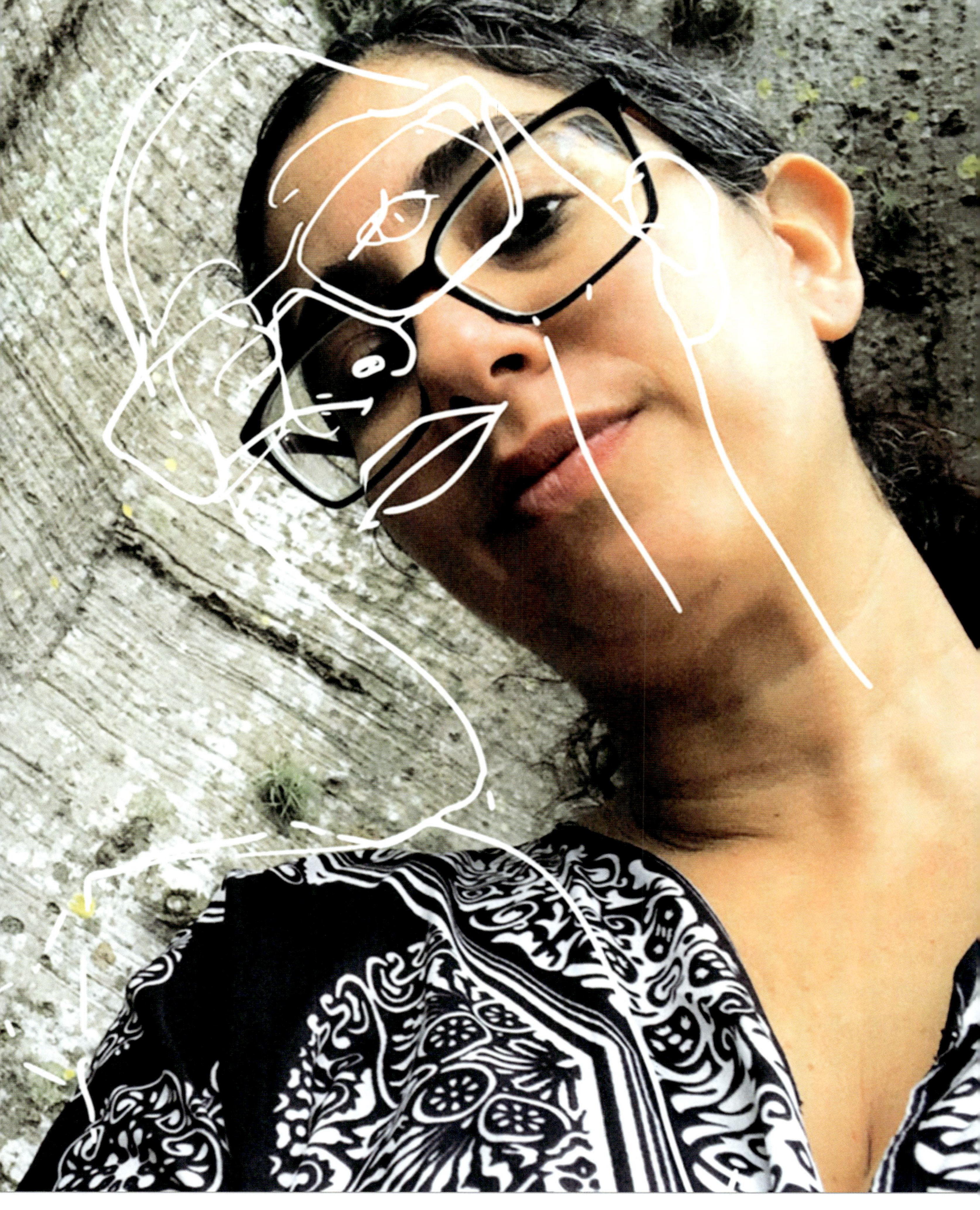

Alice is deeply attached to her Israeli origins, as these have left their mark on her entire artistic journey of self-discovery. "My parents came from Tel Aviv, Israel, and brought up my brothers and me according to the values of that country: our ancestors and their values are deeply rooted within us, in the individuals we are today. I grew up immersed in two cultures that differed a great deal and were antithetical in various respects: it wasn't easy. My brother was the one who introduced me to hip hop culture. I was particularly fascinated by graffiti, which I first saw at the age of eight," she recalls.

It didn't take long for Alice to find a community into which she could integrate and with which she could interact. "When I started high school, I found myself surrounded by many other kids with similar interests. I was also lucky to have a great art teacher, and I soon learned to work with different materials and put them to full use."

Alice later attended Parsons School of Design in New York, and soon established her reputation not only as a muralist, but also as an artist, well represented in museums and art galleries. "Admittedly, for a long time I felt like an outsider and viewed the United States as a foreign country. Even the food that the other kids ate differed from mine, which came closer to Mediterranean cuisine. I had a decidedly more holistic approach to life, closely bound to the culture of my ancestors and origins, which I respected. I am convinced that all this has had a great influence on my art," she adds.

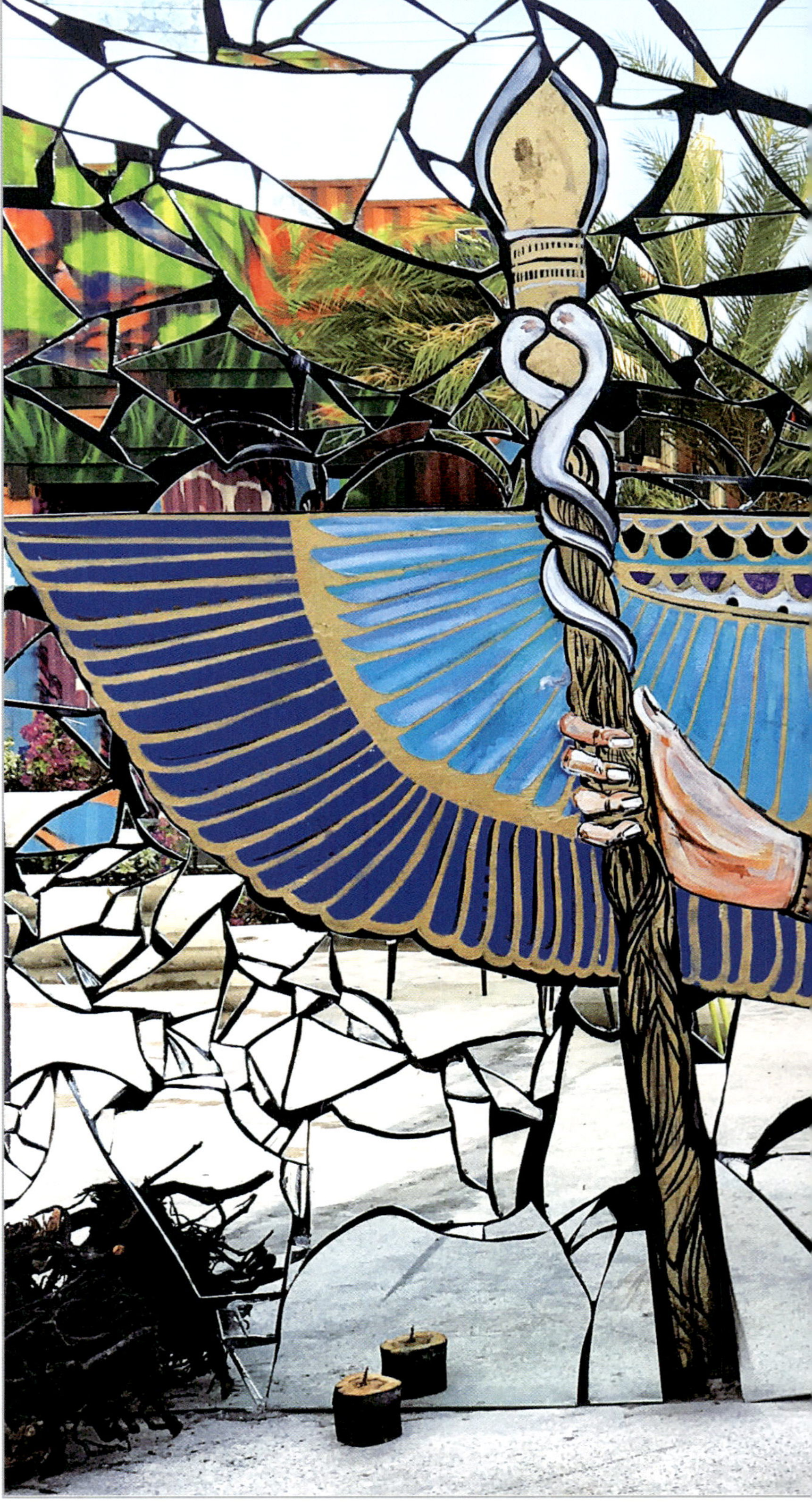

GODDESS MA'AT, Graffiti Gardens, Miami, Florida, USA, 2017

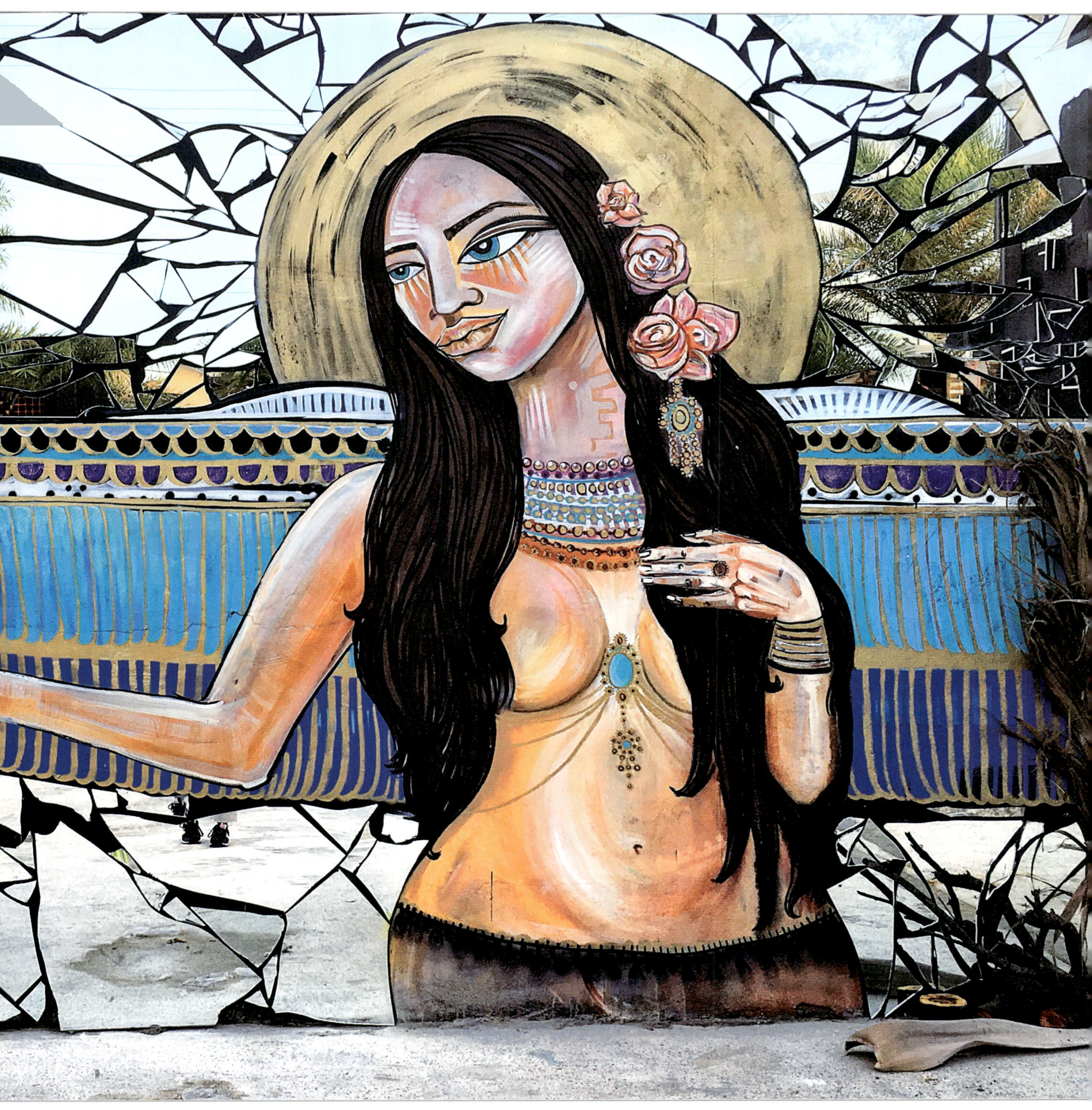

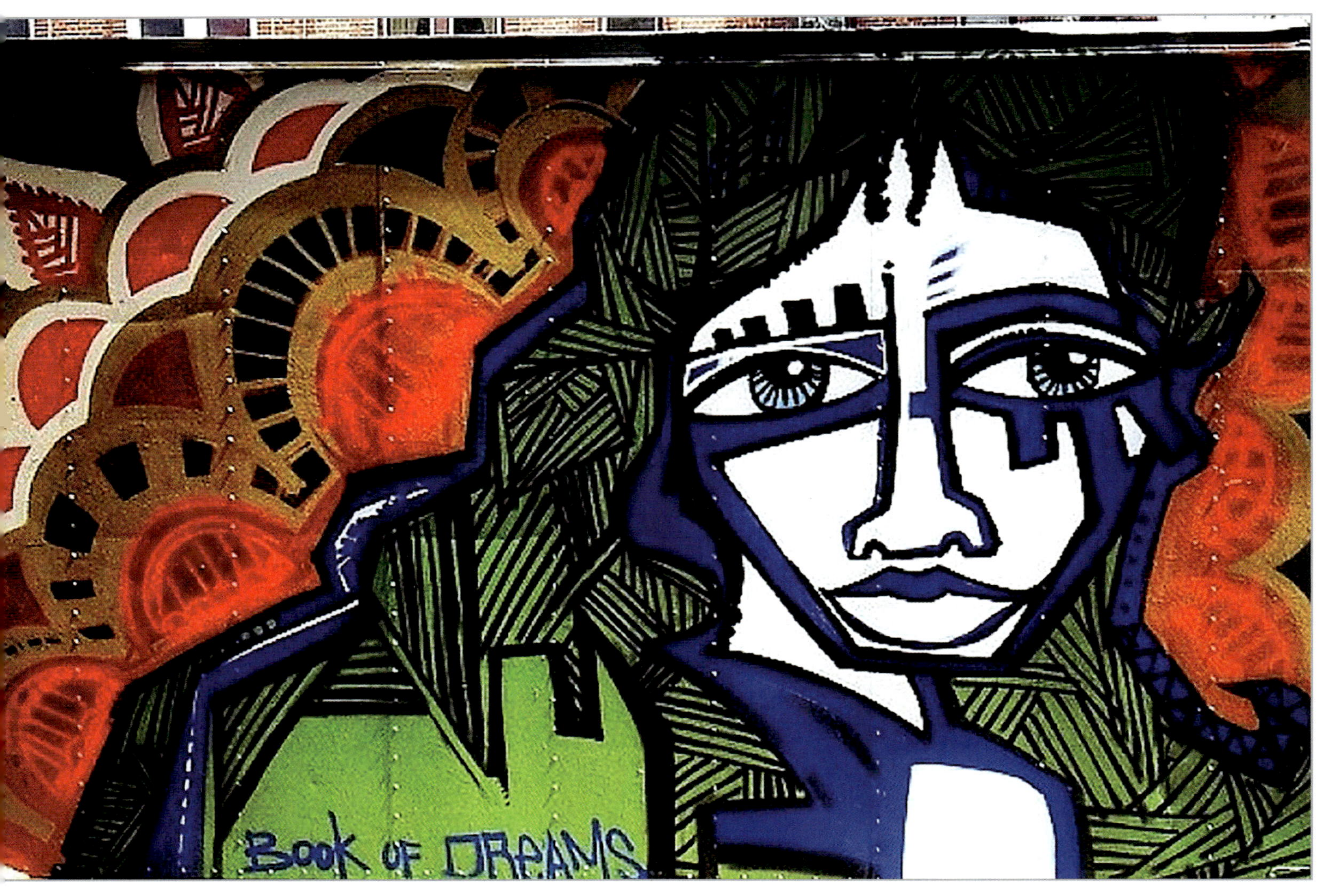

BOOK OF DREAMS, *Truck Mural, New York City, New York, USA, 2014*

In her works, Alice pays particular attention to women who struggle or who have fought in the past to enable today's generation of women to demand their rights and place in society. "Feminism has played an essential role, charting the path that has led to emancipation, fighting for all women, even those who could not take to the streets to protest since they had to work hard to support their families and raise their children. My mother was one of those, as were my forebears, my grandmother and my great-grandmother," she explains. "Today things are certainly easier than they were back then, even in the workforce, but we can certainly not say that full equality has been reached. I too have experienced this, both as an artist and as a woman. Despite living in New York, a very open-minded city, I've often met with sexism; but since I'm in a large metropolis, I've been able to choose the people with whom I wish to associate. I've set a general principle for myself: not to talk about what didn't go well or the rejections I've received, but rather to think while working about all the

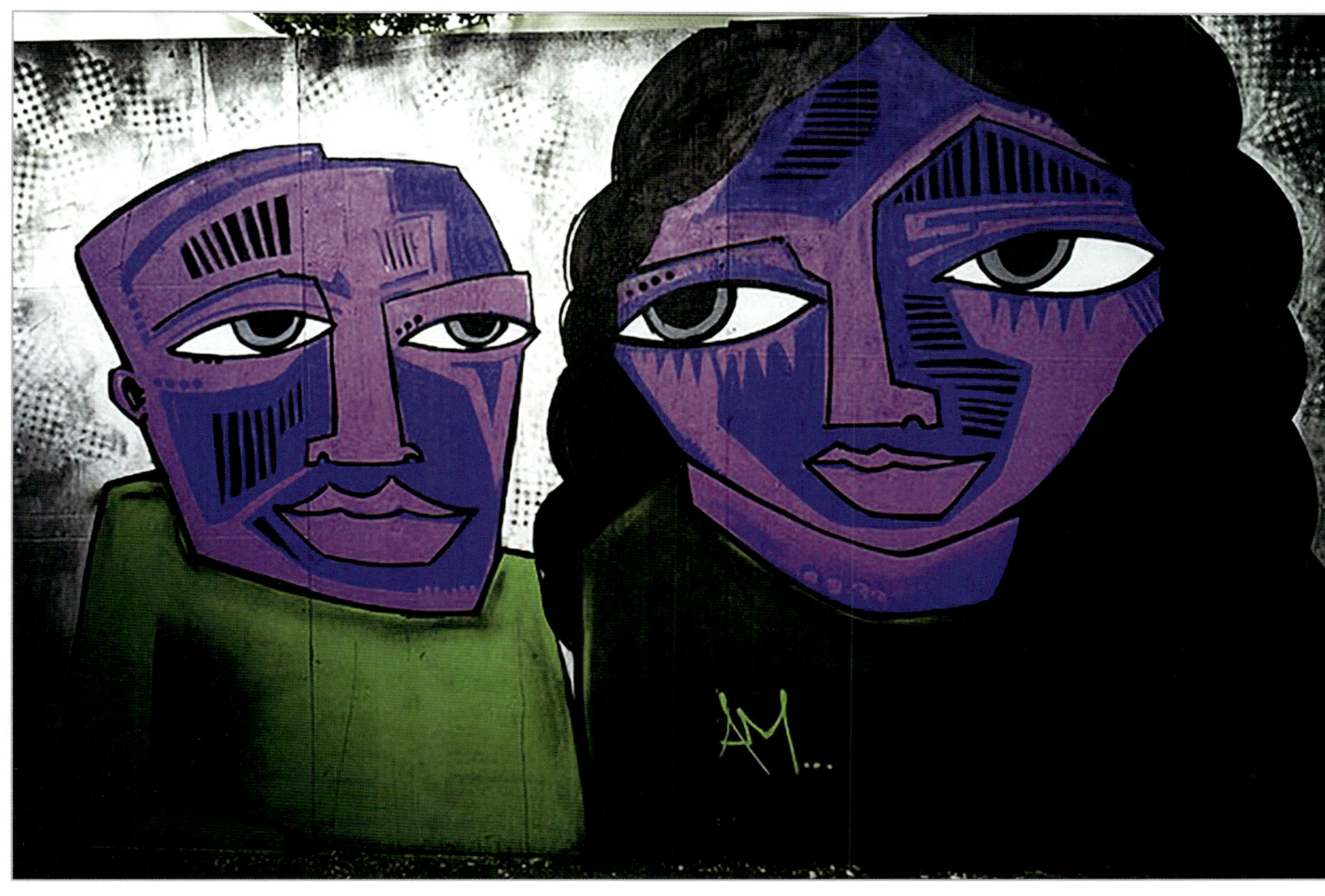

positive things surrounding me. Even now, were I to succumb to negativity, I would get depressed and would no longer be able to create," she notes, underscoring her sharp sensitivity.

Alice loves the universal concept at the basis of street art—its ability to reach everyone—and is moving toward more multidisciplinary techniques, such as sculpture and installations. "Whenever I do public art, I always try to make it relate to a community or a neighborhood. I want it to affect the environment in which it's inserted. My aim is never to occupy a space if it's not relevant and hasn't got any meaning," she claims.

As for the future, Alice plans to work more in her studio, always remaining open to experiment. "The art that I produce in my studio is moving toward greater introspection. My inspiration comes from the people with whom I'm in contact, whom I see or who appear in my dreams or waking moments," she says. And this

AFROPUNK FESTIVAL, Brooklyn, New York City, New York, USA, 2014

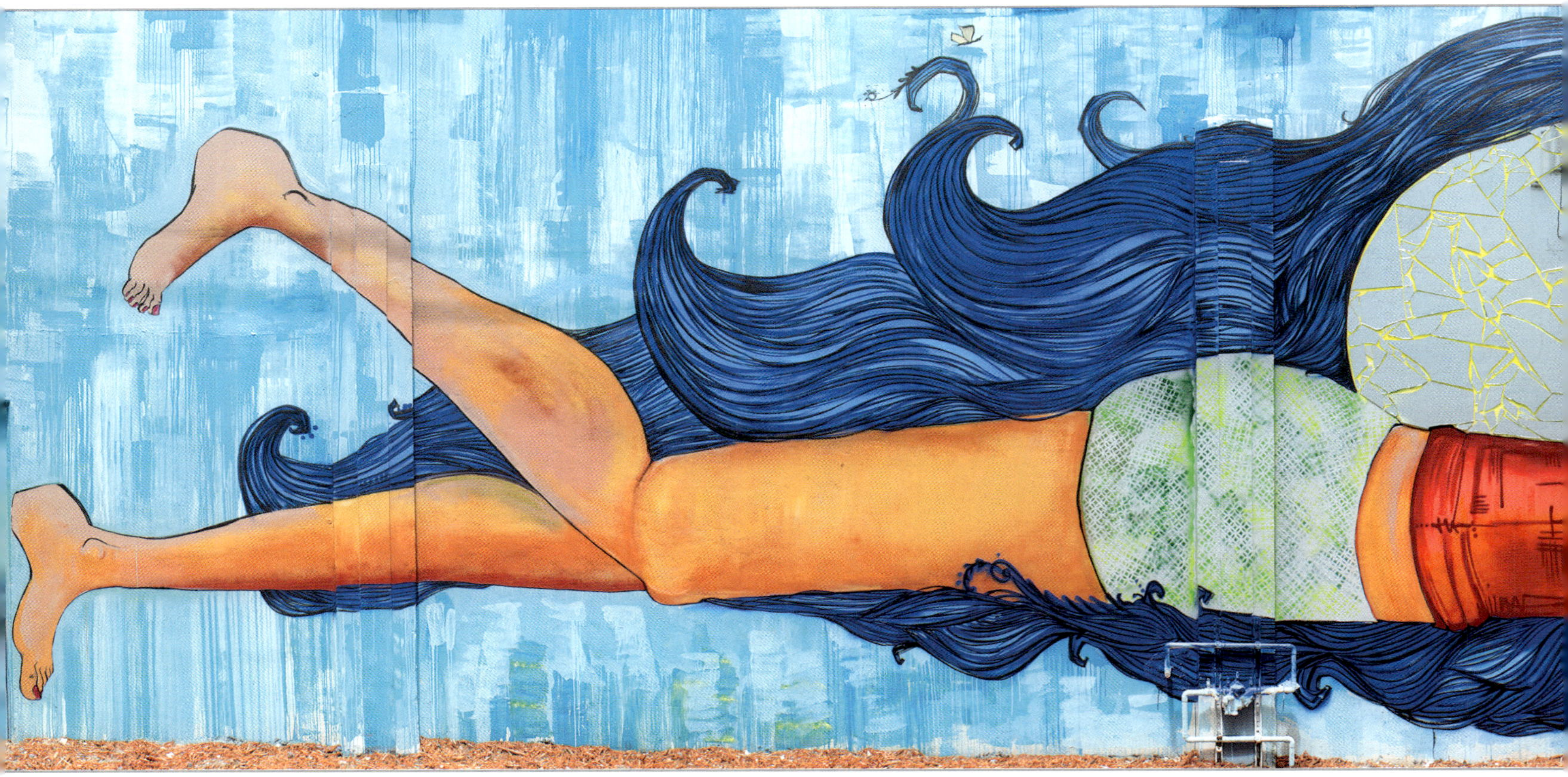

MOTHER SUN, MOTHER MOON, Downtown Hollywood Mural Project, Florida, USA, 2018

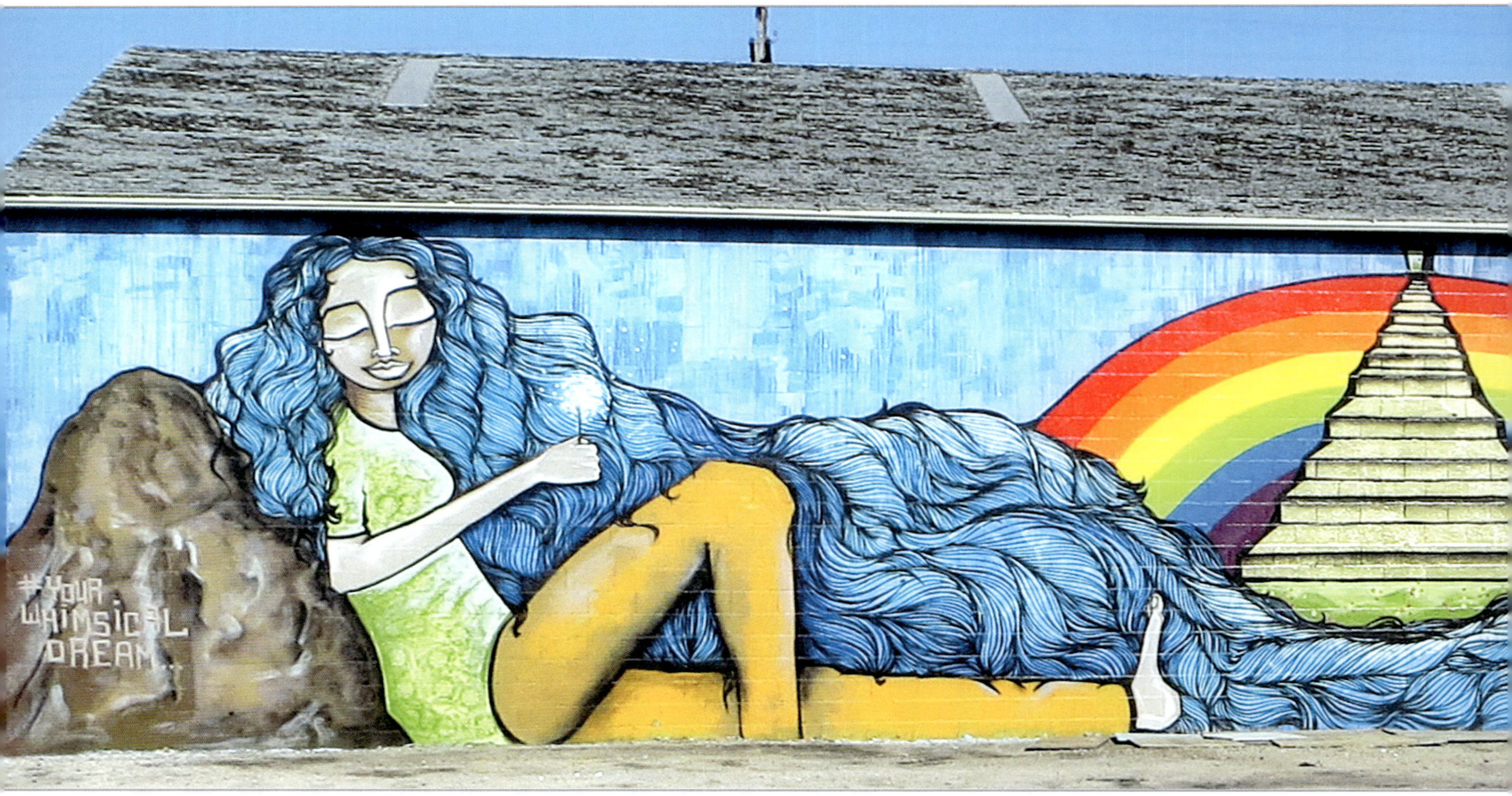

YOUR WHIMSICAL DREAM, The Railroad Museum, Greeley, Colorado, USA, 2016

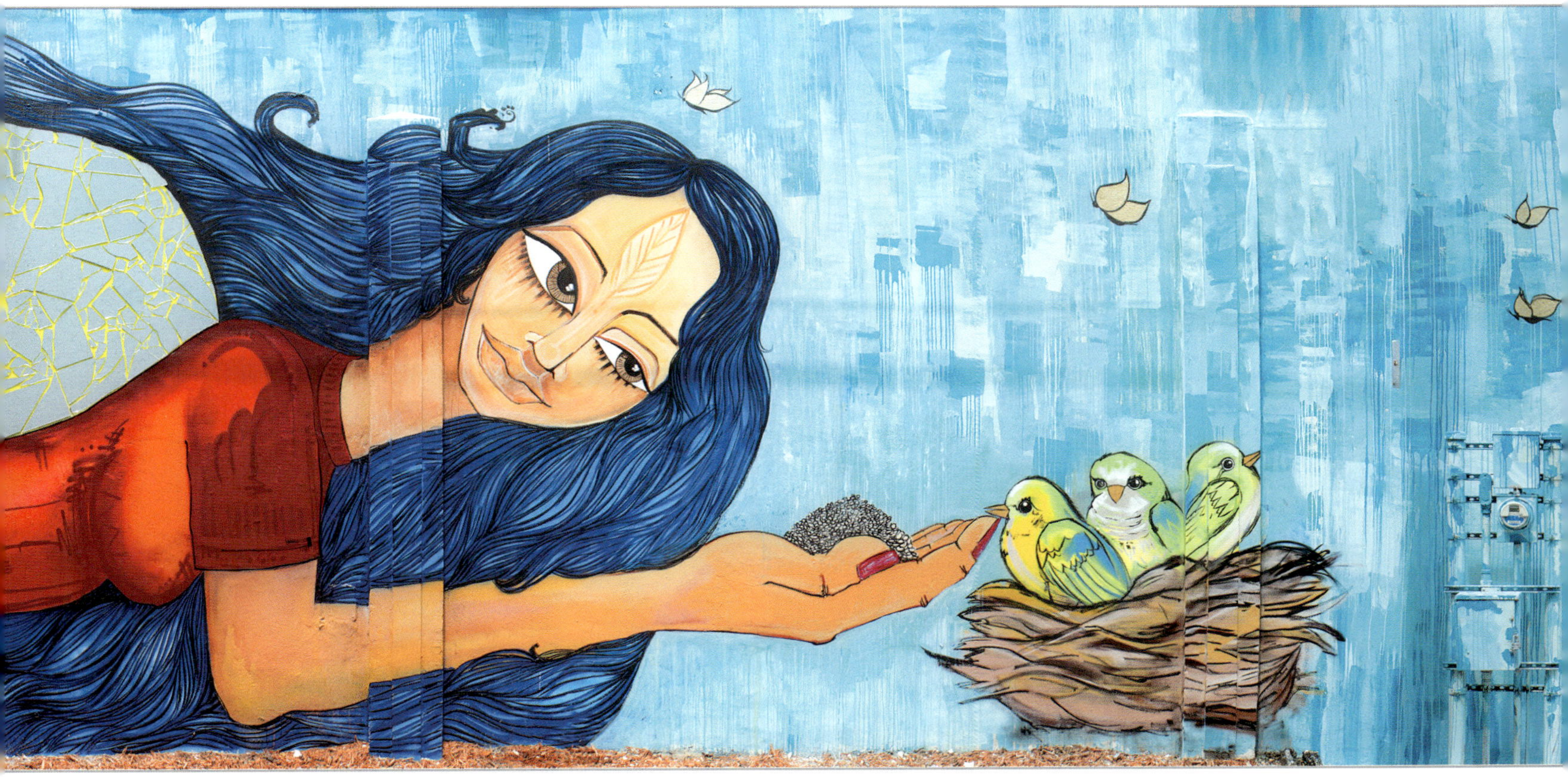

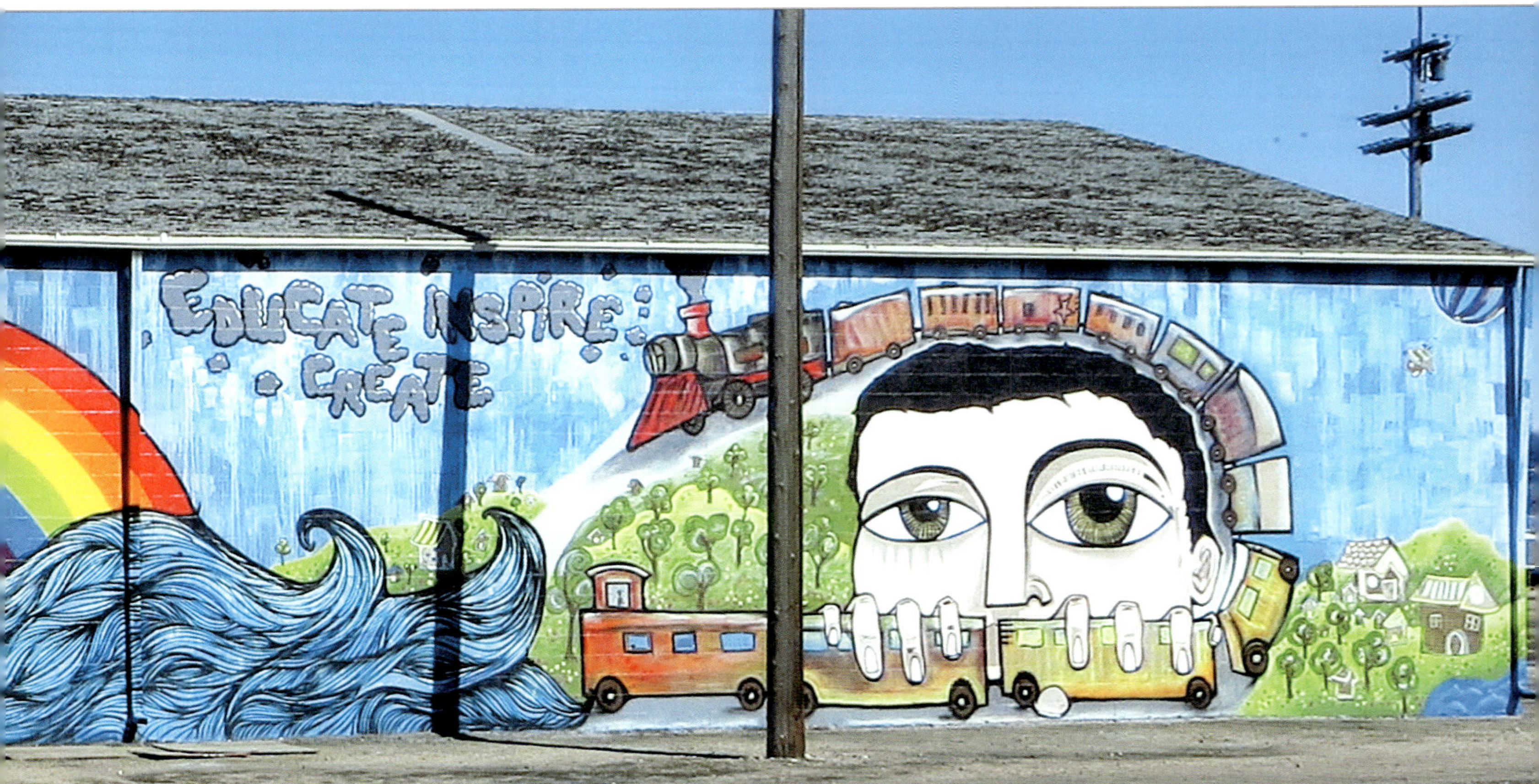

EDUCATE INSPIRE
CREATE

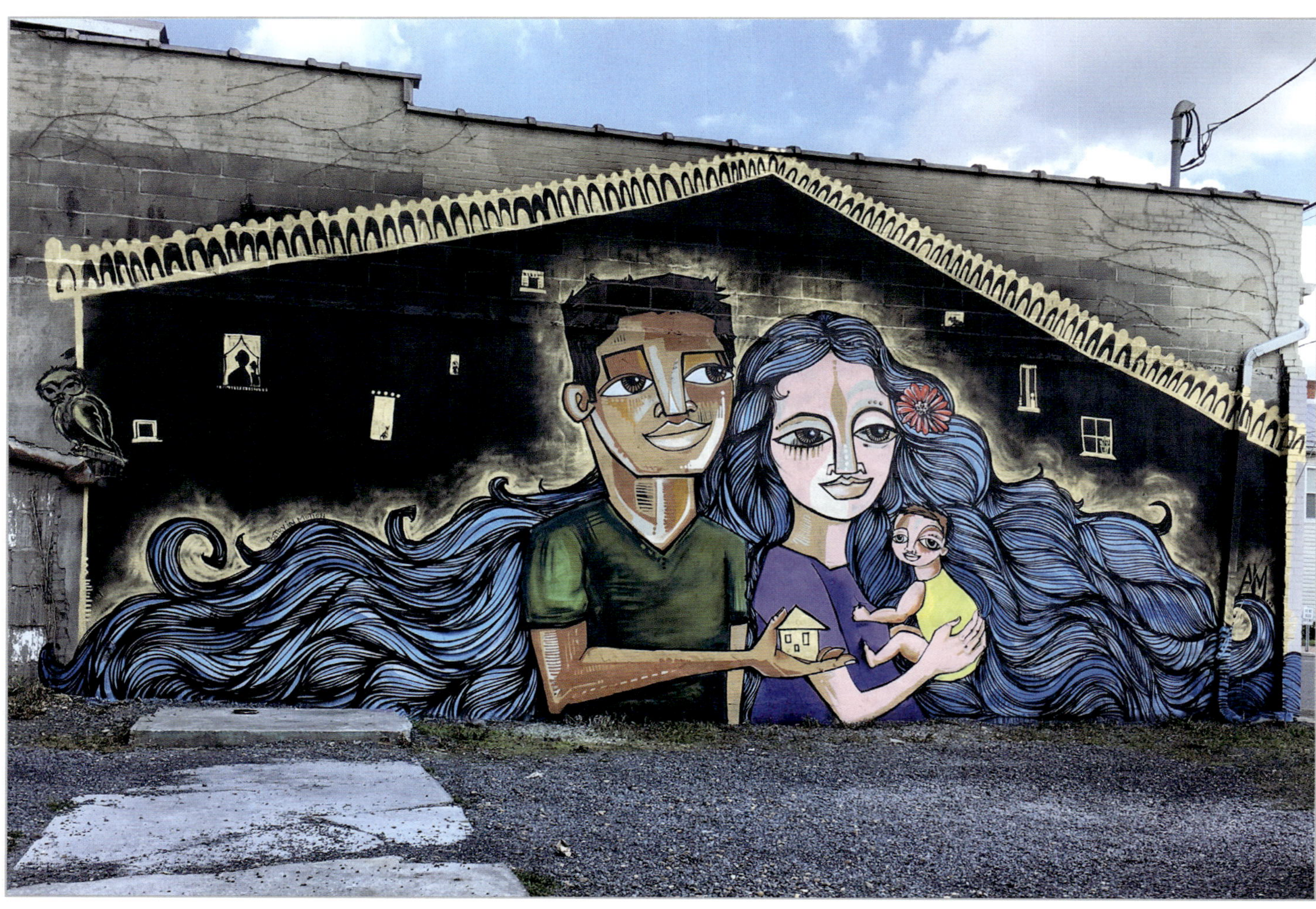

is why it's really important for her to work as a teacher who is particularly keen on providing women with opportunities and strength. "I care a great deal about my job as an educator in Harlem and the Bronx. Sometimes the teenagers and children I meet inspire me with their ideas and their passion more than I do them. I enjoy spending time with them because it offers me a chance to gain a new and fresh perspective. As a teacher, I've learned how to listen, something I consider fundamental in life. And I've learned to ask questions when something isn't clear," she admits.

Alice also works as a show and exhibition curator. "In this role, I try to promote emerging artists in the world of graffiti and street art," she explains.

"I always like to grow with my work, to be fluid, to accept all forms of expression as needed. . . I did a statue in Harlem, of which I am very proud: *Renaissance Women*. It's my first public art sculpture and is meant to honor the women of the Harlem Renaissance. It's normal to evolve, to experiment; it's normal to reflect on things and make decisions, and also to take new paths," she admits.

POETRY IN MOTION, Staufferstadt Artist-in-Residence, Strasburg, Virginia, USA, 2016

FAMILY FIRST, Atlantic City Arts Foundation, New Jersey, USA, 2019

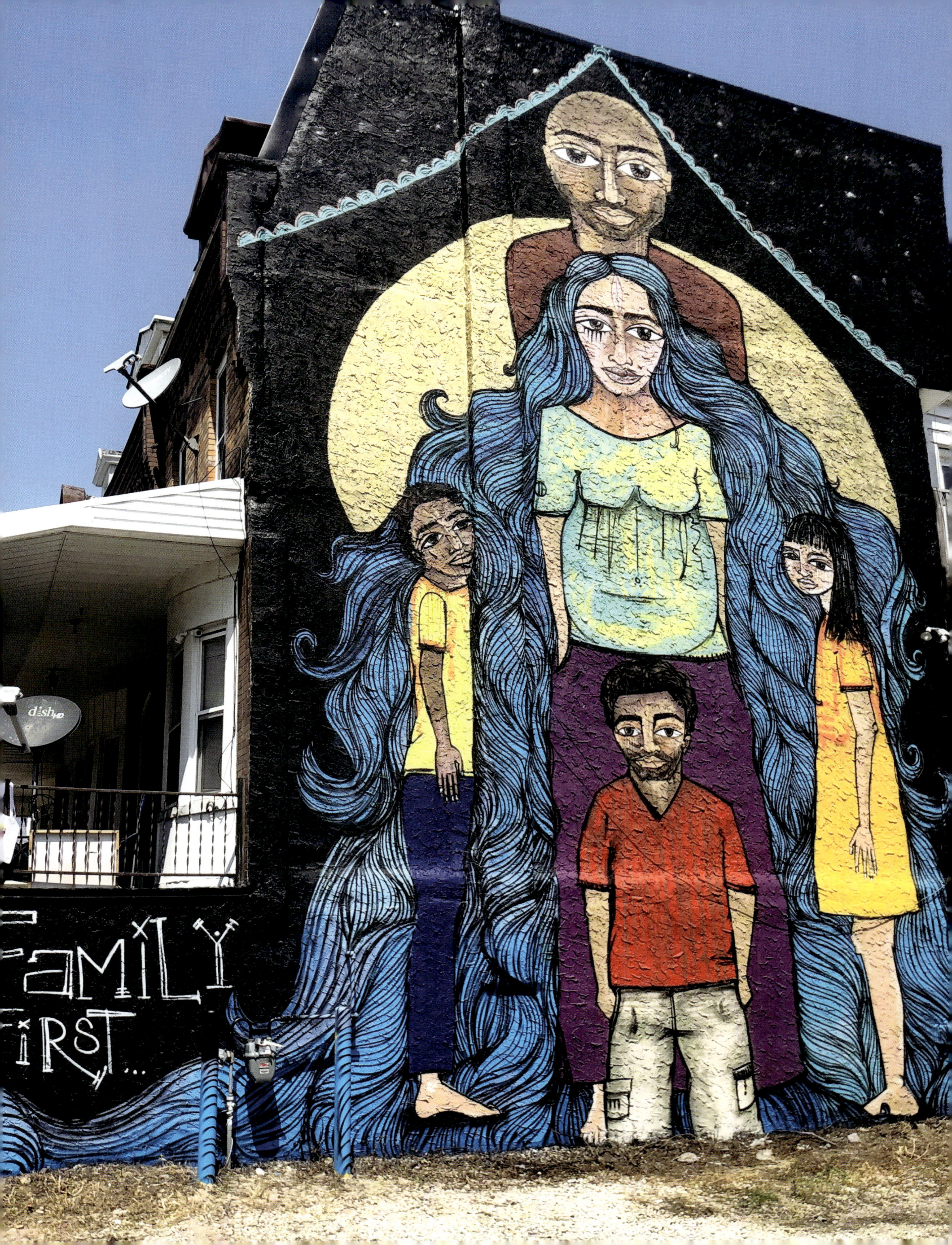

FAMILY
FIRST...

KELSEY MONTAGUE

THE DEVOTEE OF INTERACTIVE ART

*"I wish there were more women in the world of street art,
because our art and our perspective need to be represented.
Our point of view is valuable. The work of women is
underrepresented in museums around the world. Our
voices are important and essential to the accurate
retelling of the stories of our time."*

Kelsey Montague creates interactive murals on streets around the world—ones that offer people a chance to enter straight into her work, become a living piece of art, and share their experience online. It could be a butterfly, a flock of birds taking flight, a bundle of balloons floating up into the sky, a pair of headphones for listening to music, or a phantasmagoric procession of soap bubbles. . . Kelsey believes in art's power to bond people and make them relate to each other.

A native of Colorado, she has lived and studied art in Florence, London, New York, and Los Angeles. "I've had the good fortune to live for a bit in lively cities all over the world. While in college, I studied in Florence, Italy; that period really provided my art with a foundation. Architecture, and the opportunity to visit some of the world's best museums, opened me up to new perspectives on art. Then I moved to London to complete my studies: there, I had world-class teachers and a chance to see the importance of street art as a means of expression," she recalls. After receiving her degree, she moved to Los Angeles to work in the movie business, and from there to New York City. "It's still the place that inspires me the most in terms of creativity. It's there that I had the opportunity to do my first interactive piece, a pair of wings in Midtown Manhattan, and New Yorkers instantly fell in love with it!" she recounts.

For her, art is a veritable experience that must be created with others: "What interests me most is art that insinuates itself into everyday life. It's the kind that proliferates in public spaces and invites people to interact with it. I want people to experiment with art, not admire it from a distance in a detached manner, but rather become part of it, feel an intimate, personal connection with it. This is why I invite people to 'enter' my works, complete them, in the hope that this will make them feel strong, beautiful, powerful, fabulous."

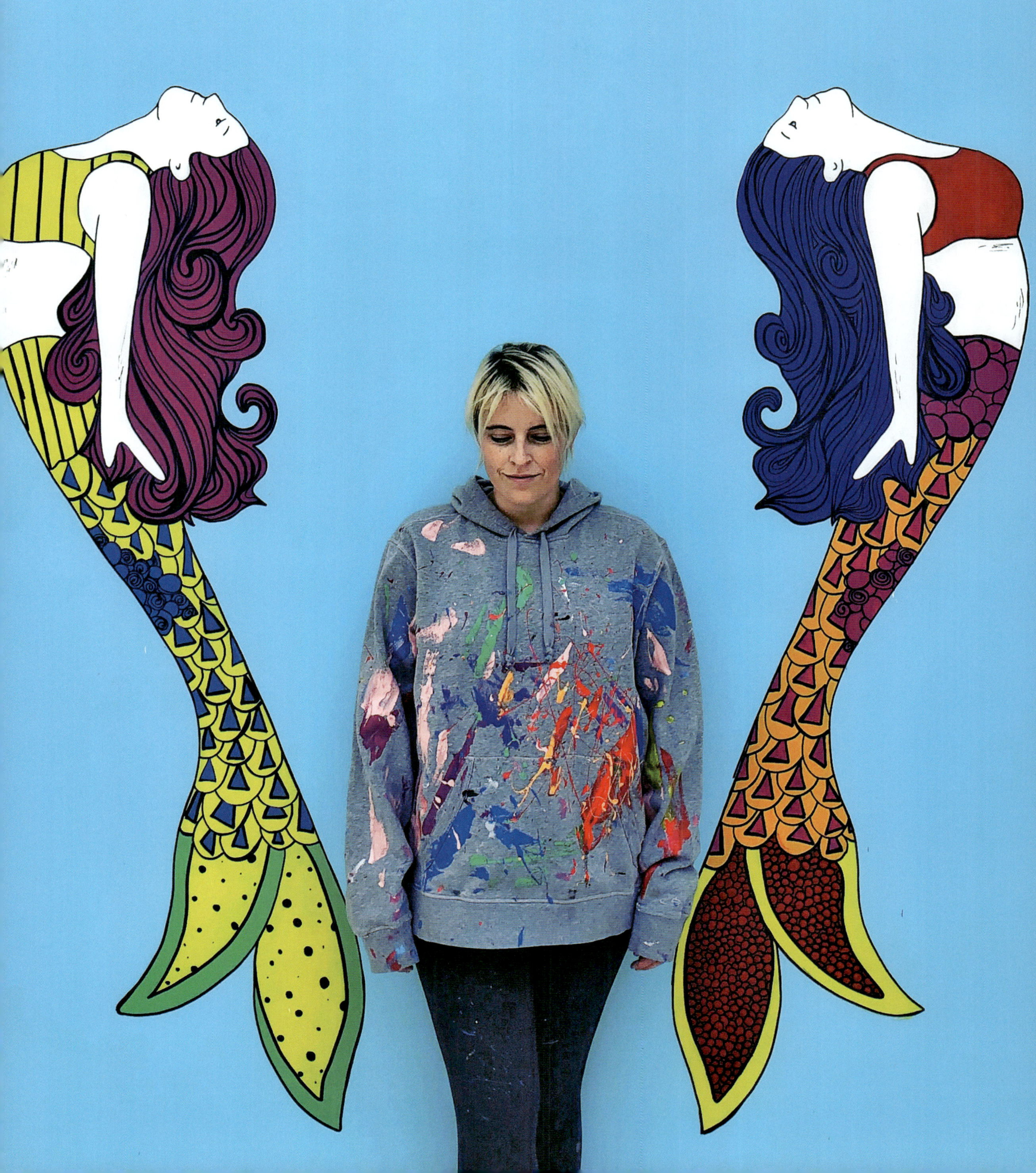

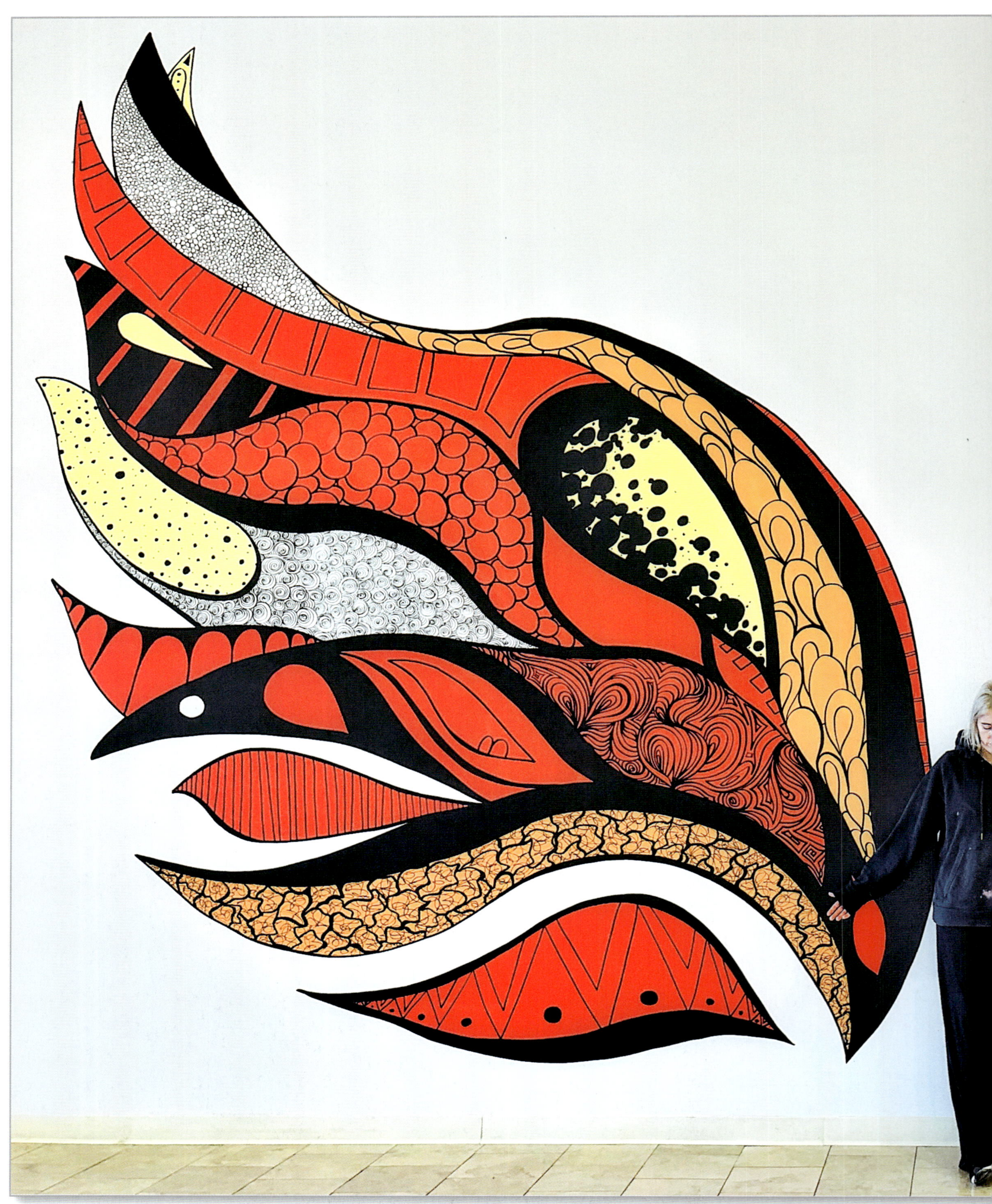

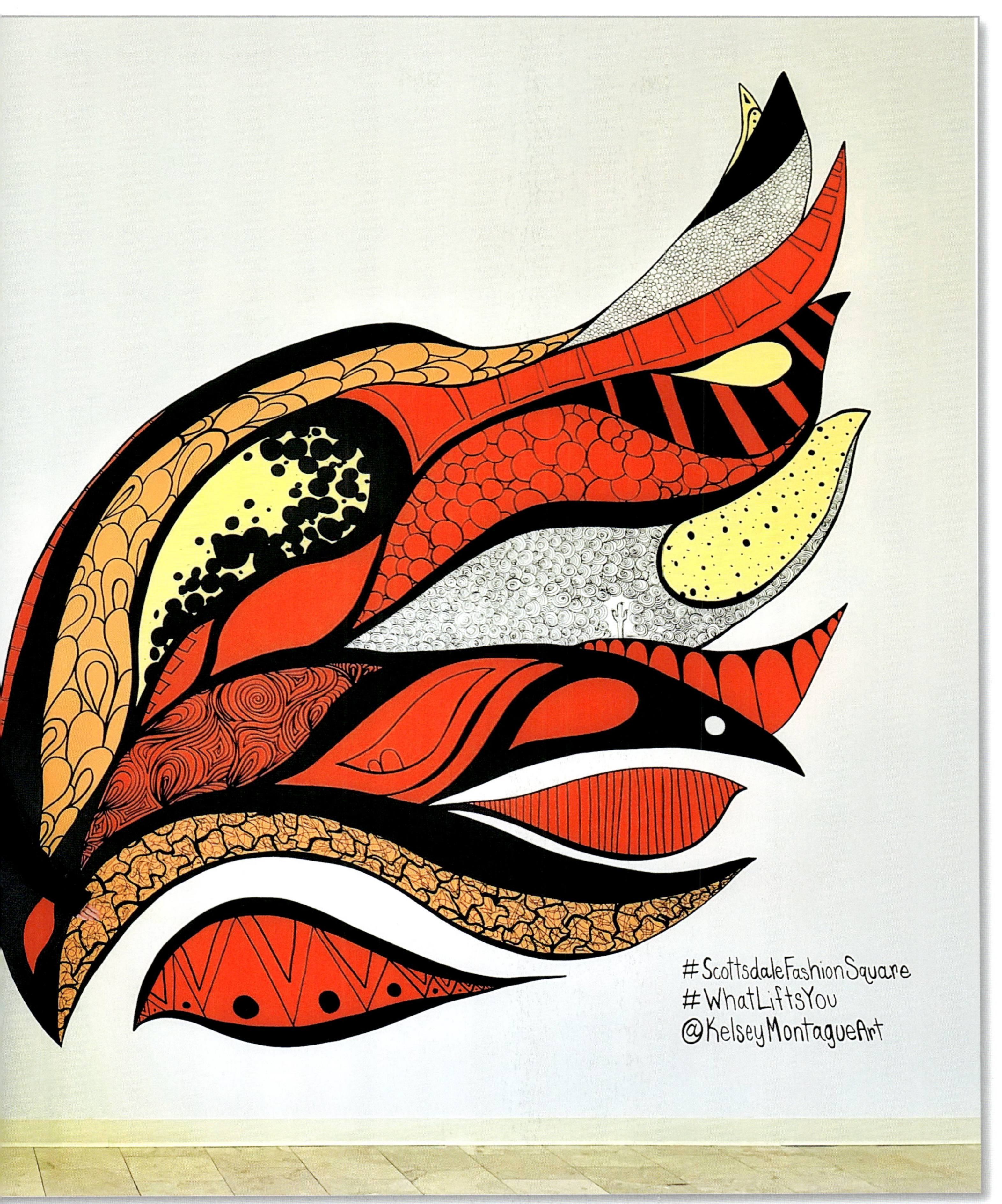
#ScottsdaleFashionSquare
#WhatLiftsYou
@KelseyMontagueArt

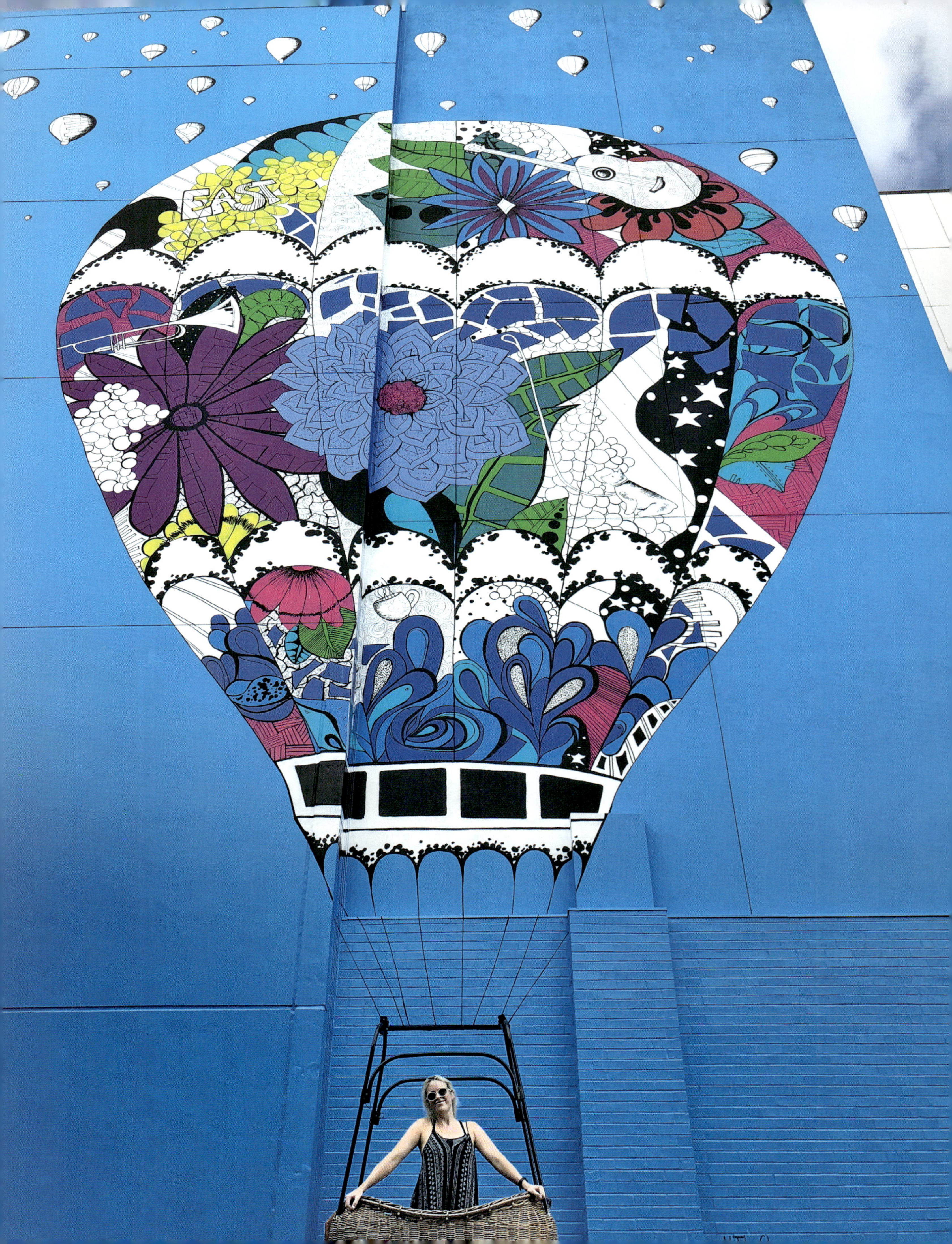

EAST

And it was precisely the #WhatLiftsYou campaign, conceived by her for this very purpose, that brought her success. "After my interactive street art piece—the pair of wings—went up, the campaign quickly attracted a great deal of attention. Celebrities like Vanessa Hudgens and Taylor Swift spoke about it, and from then on my work quickly took off."

But why did she choose wings for her first work? "My mother is a watercolor artist, my grandfather was a painter, and my uncle teaches art. Even my great-grandfather loved to paint, so I come from a long line of artists. My grandfather, and above all my mother, have served as sources of inspiration for me and have always encouraged and supported me. And wings and birds have always been an important aspect of my family's art," she explains. "My grandfather painted a bird in every one of his pictures: he did it as a way of representing God and spirituality. And birds were also one of my mother's favorite subjects. The idea of using wings in my early works thus came to me naturally; also, I love what they represent: freedom, rebirth, strength, and magic," she says.

Social media is a fundamental means of transmitting and conveying her artistic message. "Social media can be used in good or bad ways. When I began working in the interactive art space, I wanted to create situations in which people could become living works of art. I attached a hashtag to my first winged piece just to encourage people to take a snapshot and share #WhatLiftsYou on social media, because I don't think we're asked often enough 'What's the most important thing in life? What do you cherish?' My real hope is that my art helps put social media to better use," she says wistfully.

How does she see her art evolving in the future? "I want to make even larger interactive art installations around the world. I'd also like to focus on works meant for an art gallery. But I have so many ideas! My main goal for the future is to figure out how to make them all happen!" she admits.

SCOTTSDALE PHOENIX WINGS, Arizona, USA (previous spread)

NASHVILLE HOT AIR BALLOON, Nashville, Tennessee, USA (left)

SAN DIEGO FLOCK, building mural, San Diego, California, USA (below)

VENICE DRAGON, Los Angeles, California, USA (overleaf)

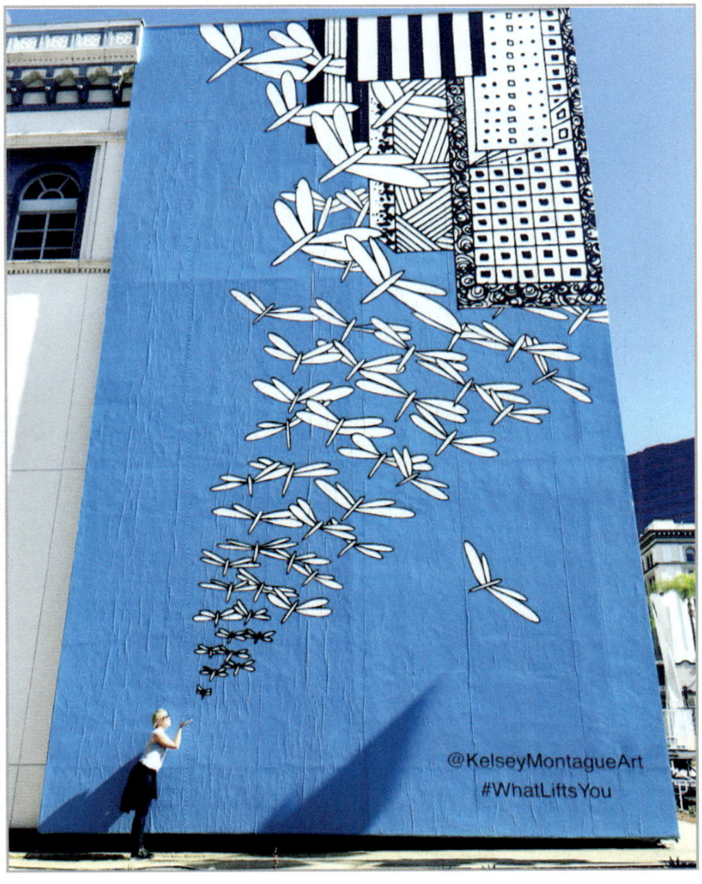

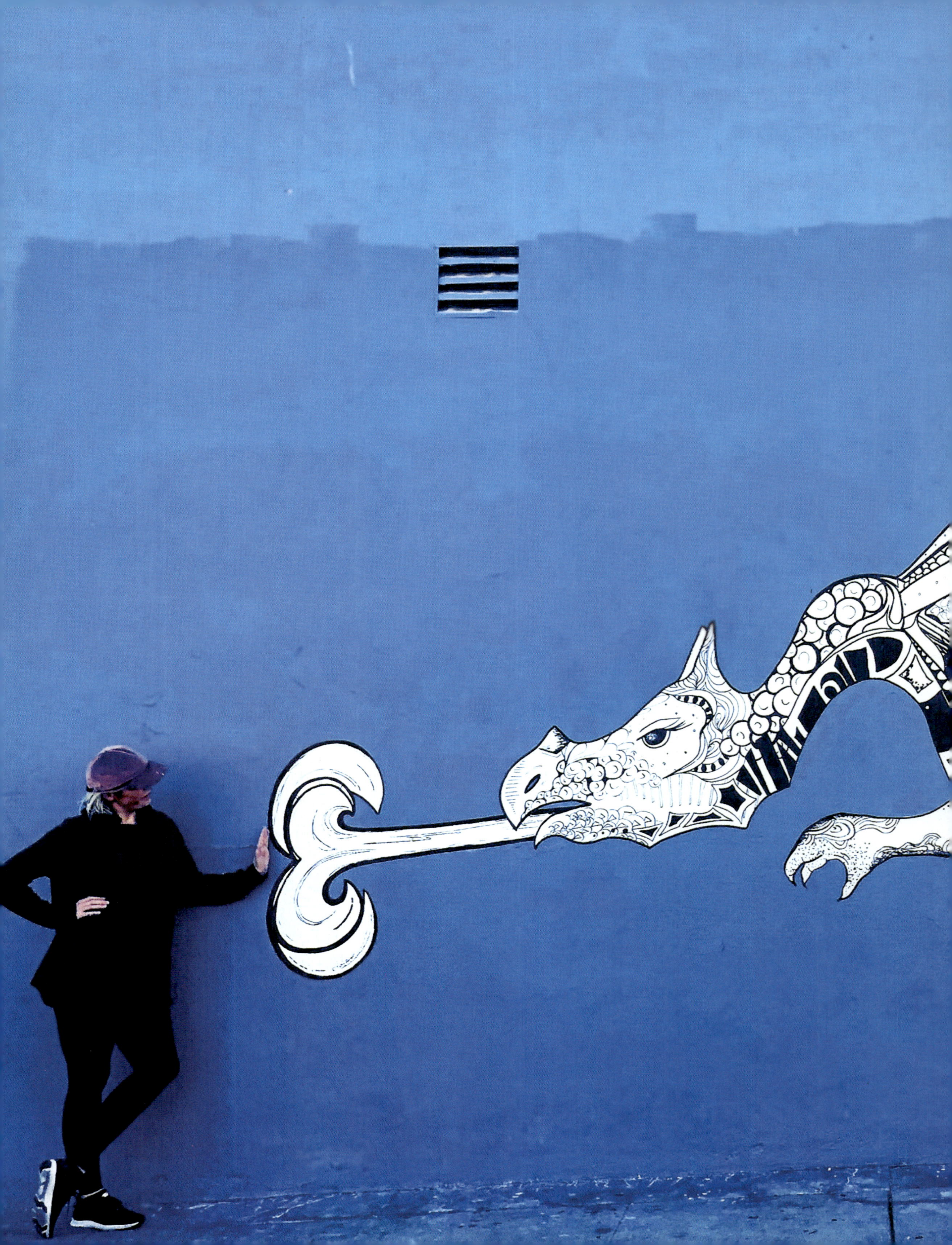

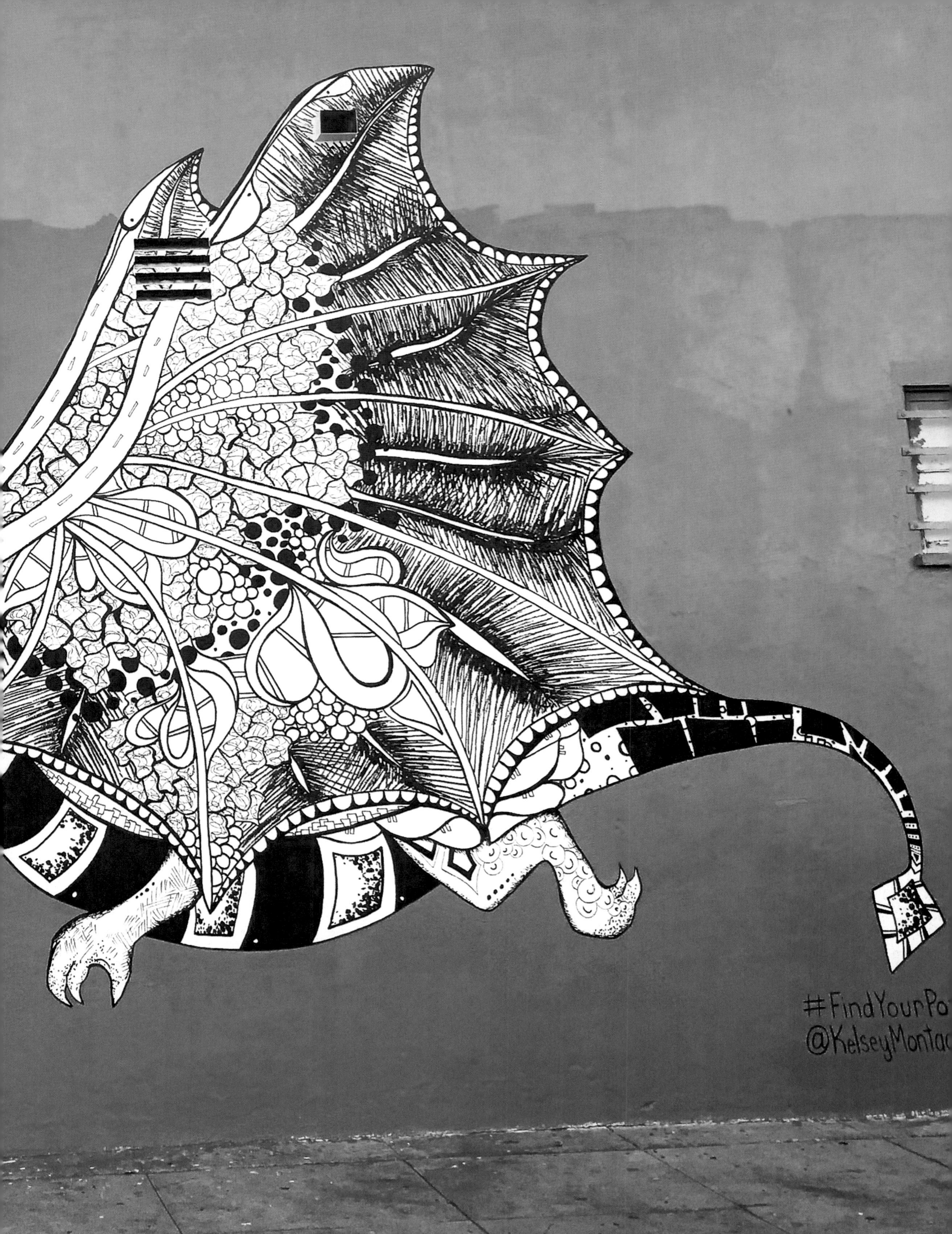
#FindYourPo
@KelseyMonta

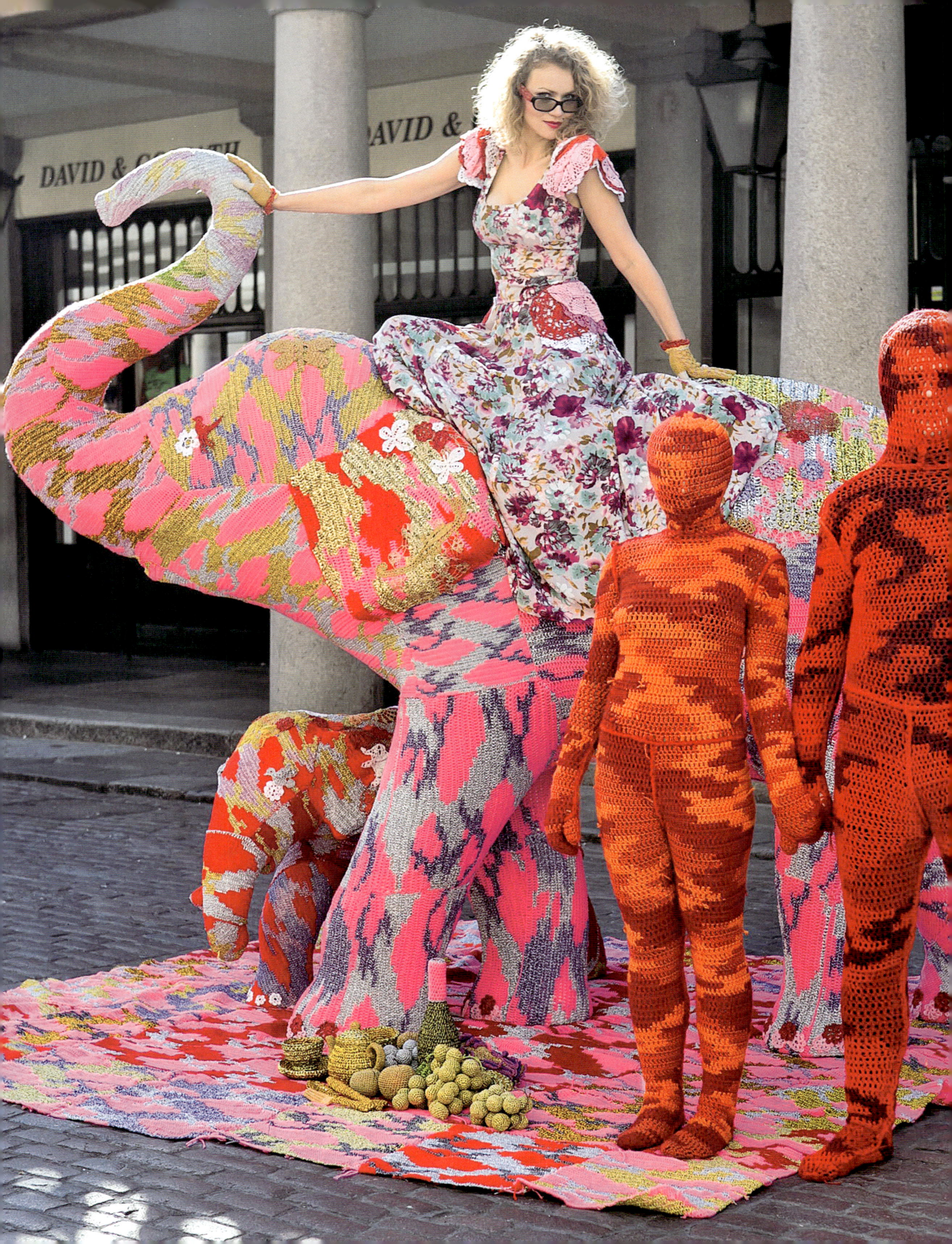
DAVID &
DAVID & G

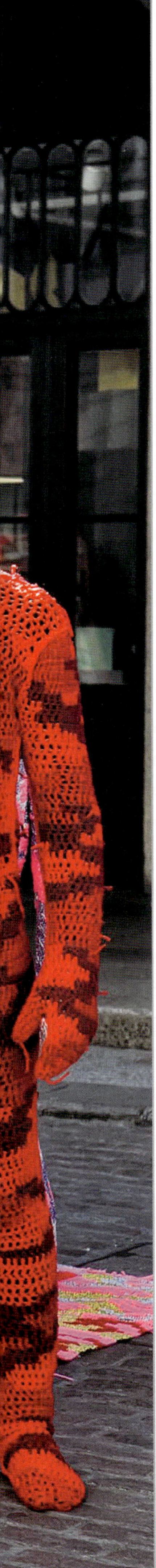

OLEK

THE SPIRIT OF CROCHET AND THE ART
OF FIERCE ACTIVISM

"2020, like a perfect vision, was the year I clearly saw the world around me and the reasons for my existence in it. I understood why I had moved to the USA, and why I needed to escape the golden cage. We come here to be spiritually awakened thanks to the culture, art, and sacred ceremonies of the Native Americans. The spirits of this land told me who I am. The artist, the whole persona manufactured by the system, is just a mask that they ripped from my face. There is no gender, no race, no age, no nationality. My soul was freed and my body followed".

Olek's works include buildings, sculptures, bicycles, people, even a scuba diver, cars, obelisks, an apartment, a locomotive, and the *Charging Bull* of Wall Street—masterpieces covered in crocheted fabric strips and yarn, highly original and weird sculptures, inflatables, and installations, to which hair, audiocassettes, and stuffed animals are occasionally added. "It is nearly two decades that I have employed my crochet hook, this old traditional tool, as my contemporary brush, as my language to transform my thoughts, dreams, and desires into reality. The same hook took me to various places around the world; it connected me with diverse communities, cultures, religions. I understood we are all one soul constantly searching for the footprints of our past roads," Olek relates. "Be a voice, not an echo," says Einstein; for Olek, this phrase has been a continuous source of inspiration.

"My life is a dream story. With every breath I take, I'm grateful for choosing the path I did. Now I believe we choose this life, the moment we come to life, and even our parents. Our consciousness is infinite, and it chooses the soul and the body. We come here with one purpose, and I am finally getting to understand all the steps that brought me here. The more I know, the more I realize I know nothing. I choose to live in the present moment and enjoy the now. Now never ends," Olek claims.

Olek and their team for ELEPHANT FAMILY, charity event in London, UK, 2013, Photo Jeff Moore / Alamy Stock Photo

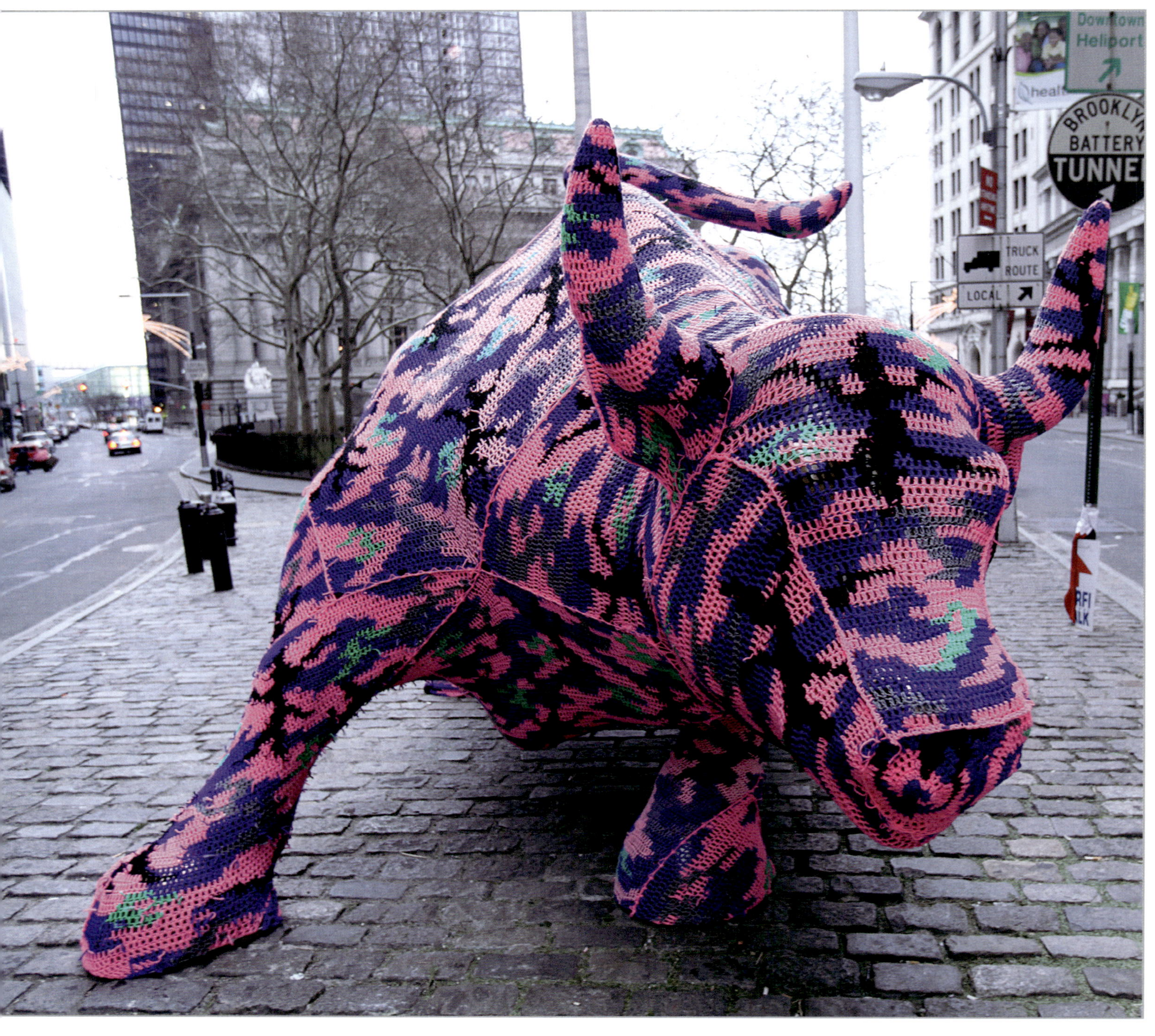

"Every story can be told in the literal way, and the metaphorical way that our soul understands when it crosses to the other side. Die before you die. Trauma is a portal, and it opens the gates to the infinite knowledge of all times," they profess.

Olek is originally from Poland. "In 1977, as an endless energy flying freely in the universe, I decided to come back to Earth in a human body and chose really amazing parents, Bogumila and Henryk Oleksiak. Their pure love brought me to life. I was born Agata Oleksiak, on April 5, 1978, in Staszów, Swietokrzyskie, in communist Poland, a country that was just rebuilding itself from wars, partitions, and many occupations over the centuries. I always thought I grew up in a place that was very stingy with possibilities and granted us no eccentricities. But now I know that land made me such an amazing, strong, talented, beautiful inside-out unbreakable soul," they recollect.

"I grew up between an industrial Silesian city and a tiny rural village where I had to work in the fields. Creativity came to me as a necessity. We had to make our own clothes, as no one had any money and the department stores were empty. This forced me to create my own wonderland. I was always a creative kid

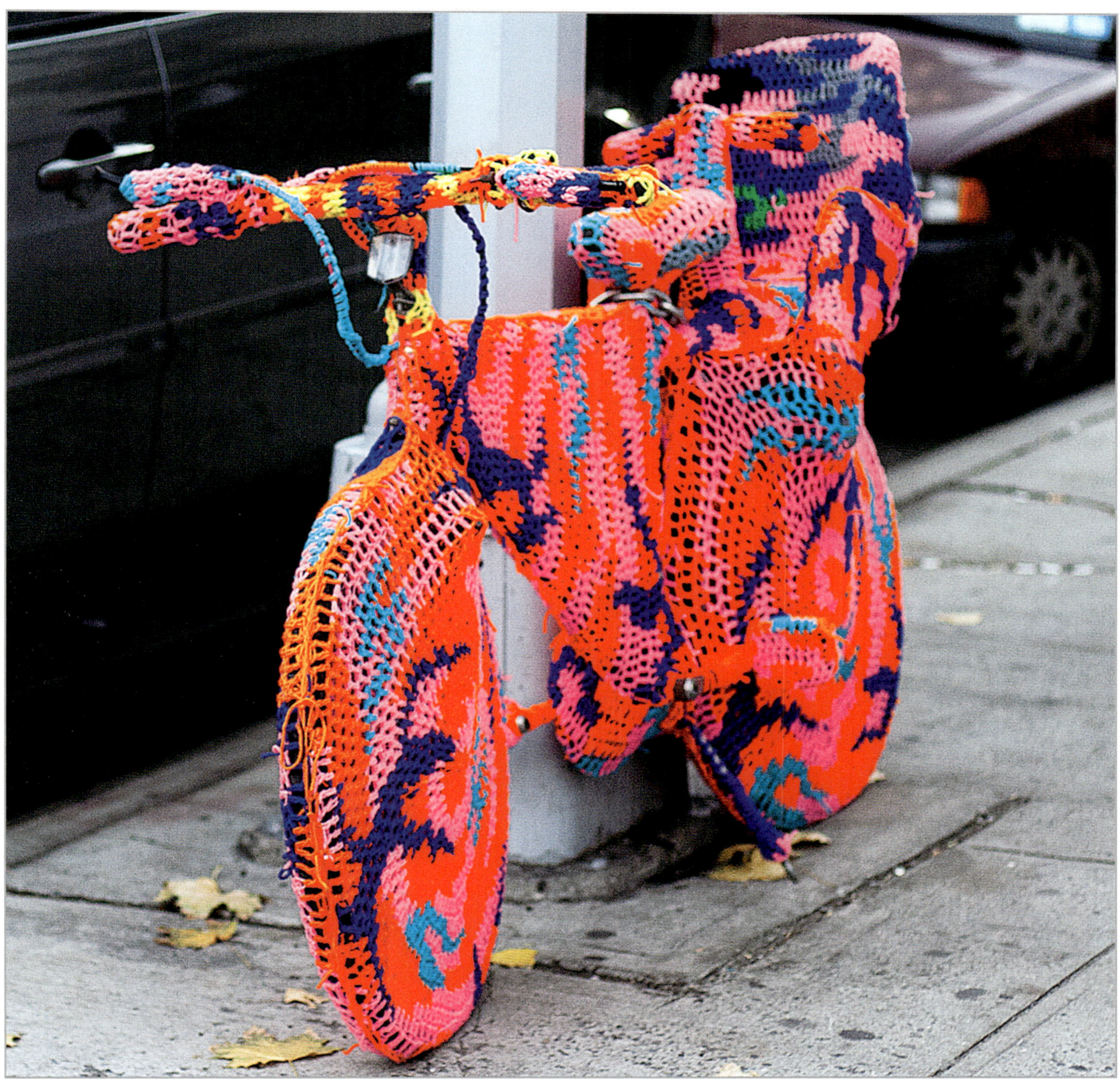

who made things constantly; I created things out of air, fantasies, and dreams, whatever I could get my hands on. I'd save the colored tops of tins, then make Christmas decorations out of a year's worth of savings.

In elementary school I won all art competitions, dreaming of a very competitive art high school. Unfortunately then, though fortunately now, my dreams were smashed when my drawing became the subject of my first art argument. My teacher did not write the necessary recommendation to get me into the school. Communism collapsed, the border was opened, and my art education instead was based on hitchhiking around Europe to sneak into the most prominent museums and walk through the streets once touched by artists like Van Gogh, Picasso, and Dalí," they continue.

CROCHETED BIKE created for the 2 Days in New York *film directed by Julie Delpy, New York City, New York, USA, 2011*

CHARGING BULL, Wall Street, New York City, New York, USA 2010 (left)

"In 2000 I culminated my university studies at the Adam Mickiewicz University of Poland with a thesis on 'The Symbolism of Costumes in the Films of Peter Greenaway.' Studying his art masterpieces not only allowed me to complete a very successful thesis, but—what is even more valuable—it gave structure to my own experiments and artistic desires."

Olek first used crochet to make art in 2003, captivating audiences and critics alike. They had moved to the United States a bit earlier, in 2000, at the age of twenty-two. "My teachers and friends encouraged me to leave Poland for New York City, where I first worked as a costume designer and made a living cleaning houses, working on a factory floor, and babysitting. Faced with concerns about my legal status in the United States, I enrolled at LaGuardia Community College. During my studies, I met Professor Brooks, who encouraged me to take his class. He suggested I should incorporate my love for fabric and create something out of yarn, rope, and twine, and connect it in any way I wanted. While experimenting with my first sculpture, I rediscovered my crochet skills, which I had learned as a child and had used occasionally over the years. I knew immediately that it was the right sculpting method for me, and Professor Brooks agreed. He said, 'This is what you're going to be doing for your entire life,' and christened me 'Olek,'" they explain.

Olek discovered their ideal universe in America, where they could experiment and give free rein to their artistic creativity. "New York City became my home, my spiritual home, where I had the freedom to express myself fully in a cultural dialogue and a malleable exchange of ideas. That is why I created the crocheted camouflage pattern: to transform the human form into a new species. Once a person enters the crocheted skin, their race, color, ethnicity, and sexuality become irrelevant, camouflaged. They are transformed into citizens of Olek's world where these identifiers don't matter and everyone is free," they say, clarifying their vision. "I think crochet, the way I create it, is a metaphor for the complexity and interconnectedness of our body and its

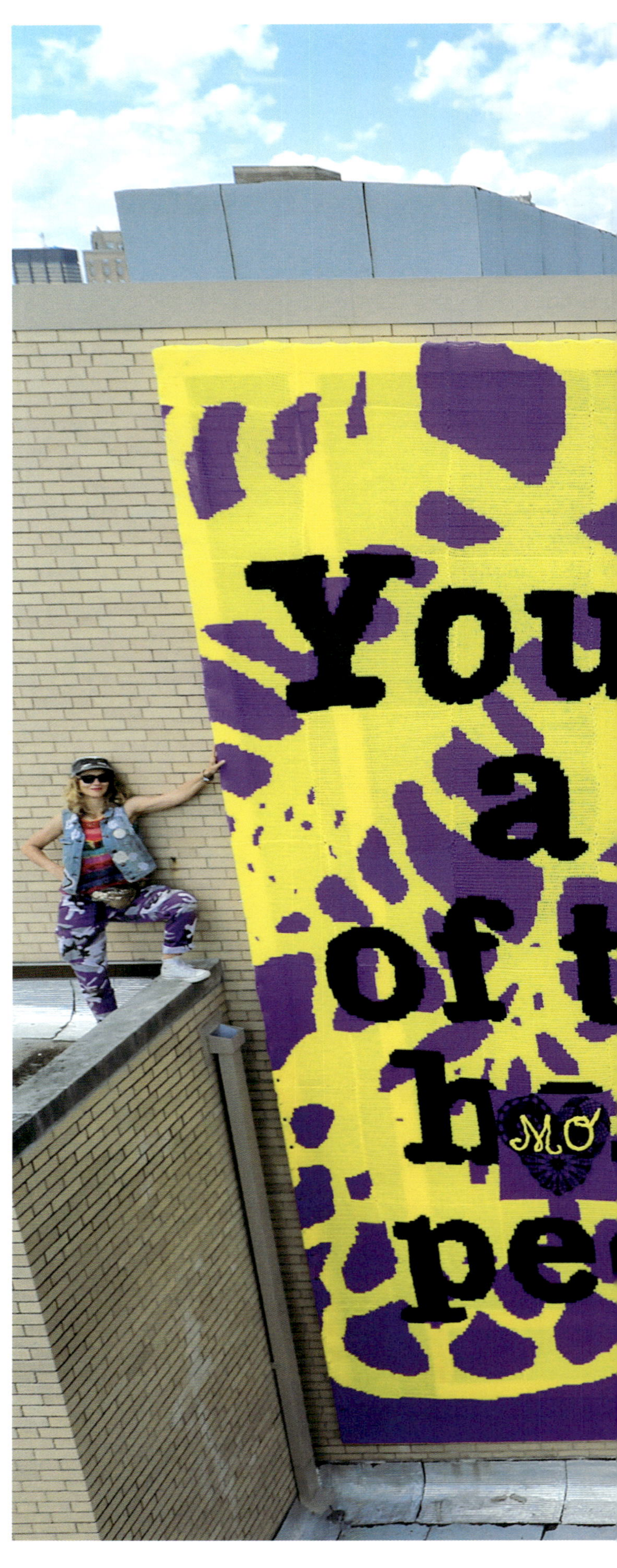

YOU LOSE A LOT OF TIME HATING PEOPLE, community based project, Love Across the USA with the Barnes Foundation and Mural Arts, Philadelphia, Pennsylvania, USA, 2018

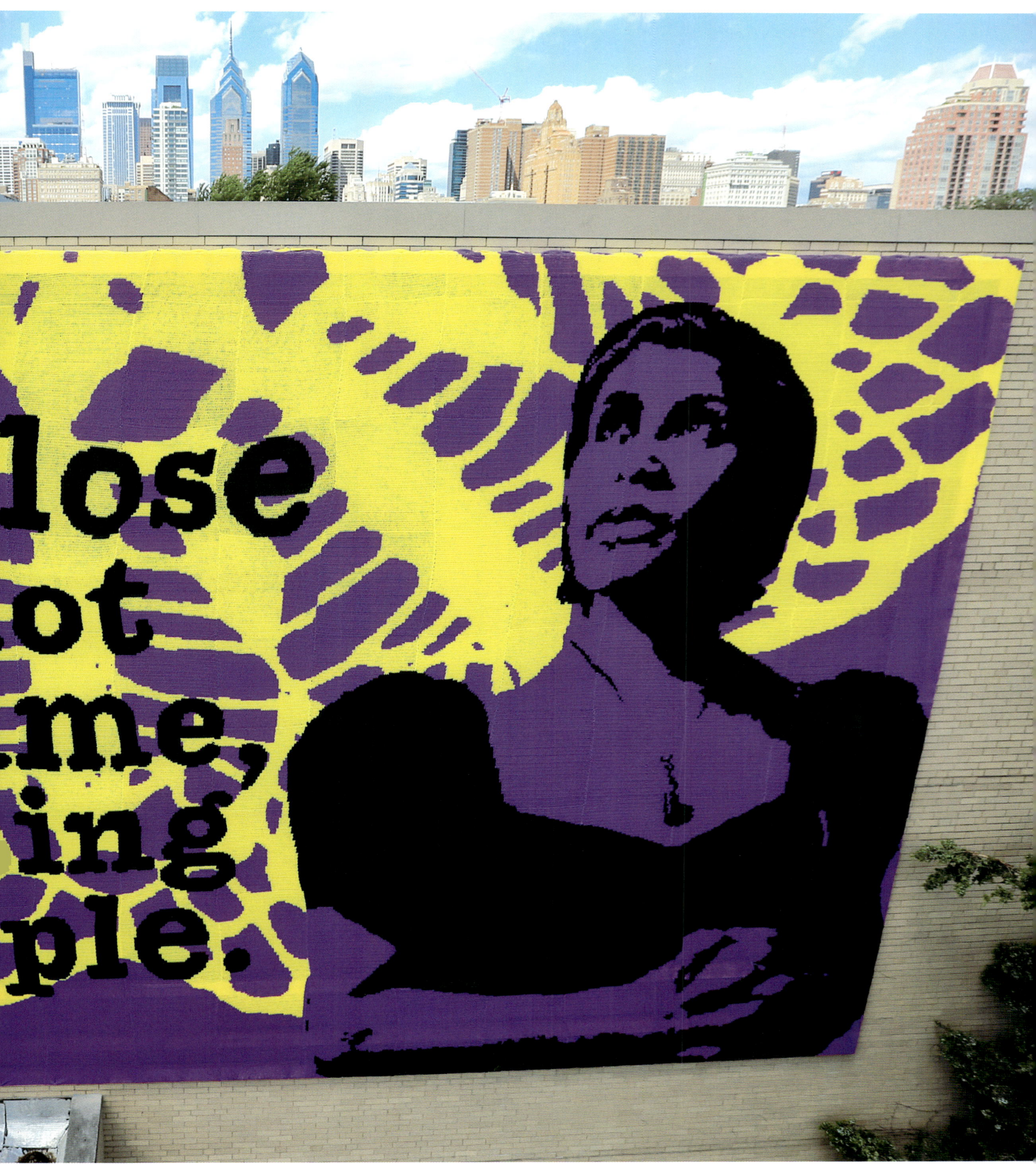
lose
ot
me,
ing
ple.

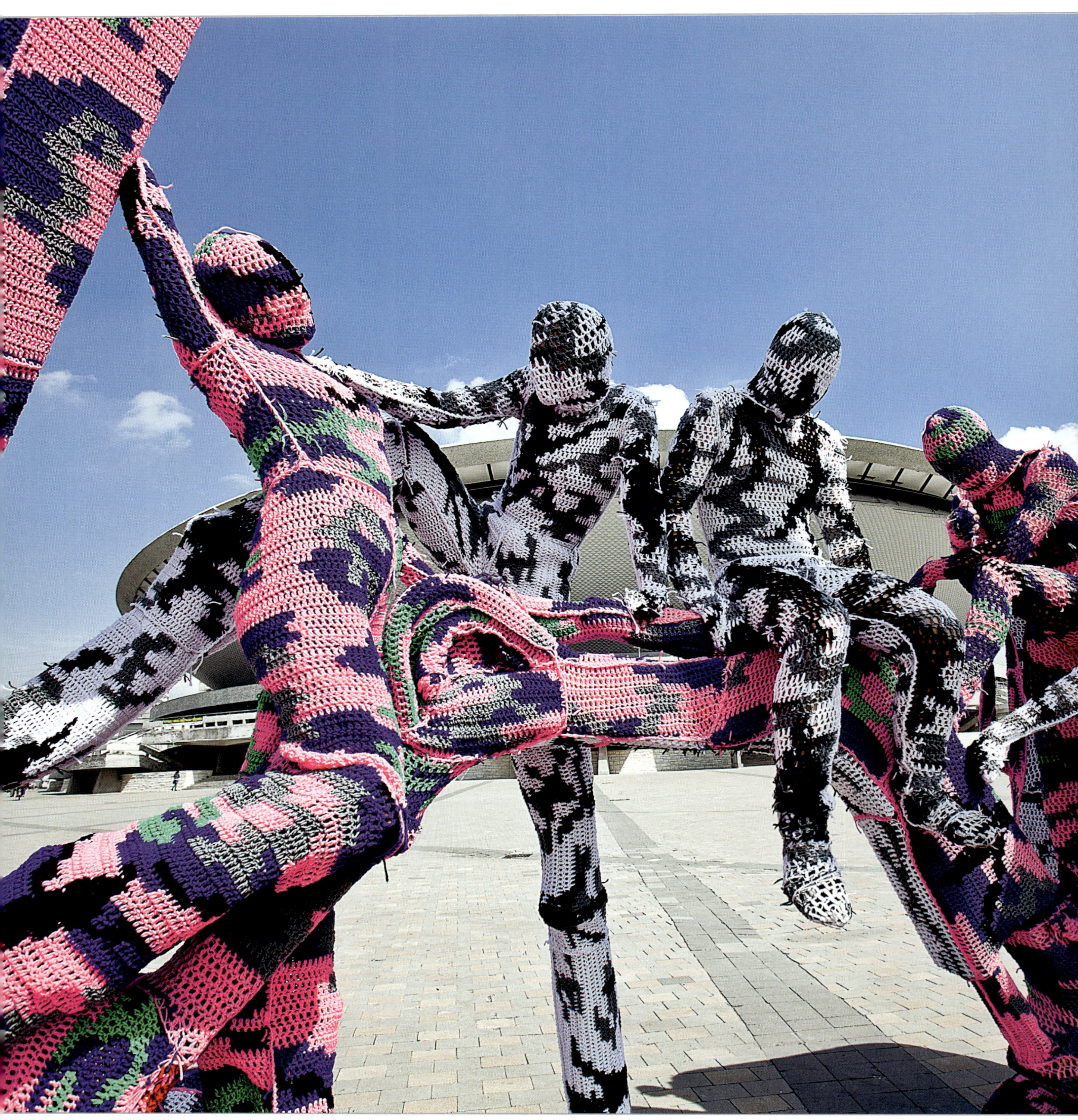

Team Olek on *CROCHETED EXCAVATORS*, Katowice Street Art Festival, Katowice, Poland, 2018

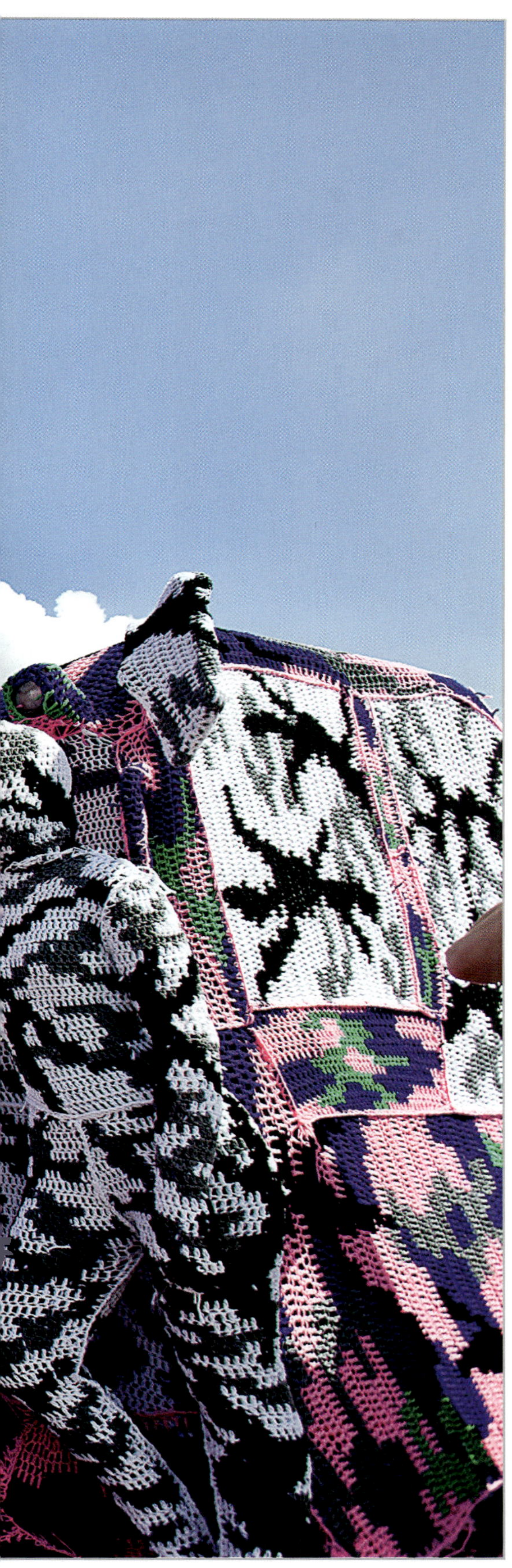

systems and psychology. The connections are stronger as one fabric, as opposed to separate strands; but if you cut one, the whole thing will unravel. We are stronger together."

For Olek, art is first and foremost a mission. They actively support the rights of women and the LGBT community, gender equality, and freedom of expression; they work on behalf of the rights of artists and writers, showing solidarity with those stifled by oppressive laws around the world. At the same time, Olek's work always conveys color and life, energy and astonishment, positivity and hope, irony and empathy, but without ignoring political and cultural criticism. Olek is constantly evolving, changing the materials they use and experimenting with other artistic media, which include film and virtual reality. One thing is for certain, they never stop creating, because art and life are inseparable. They love reading books and listening to audiobooks, even while crocheting. They love nature and dedicate many of their projects to the environment and the pressing need to preserve it from ruin.

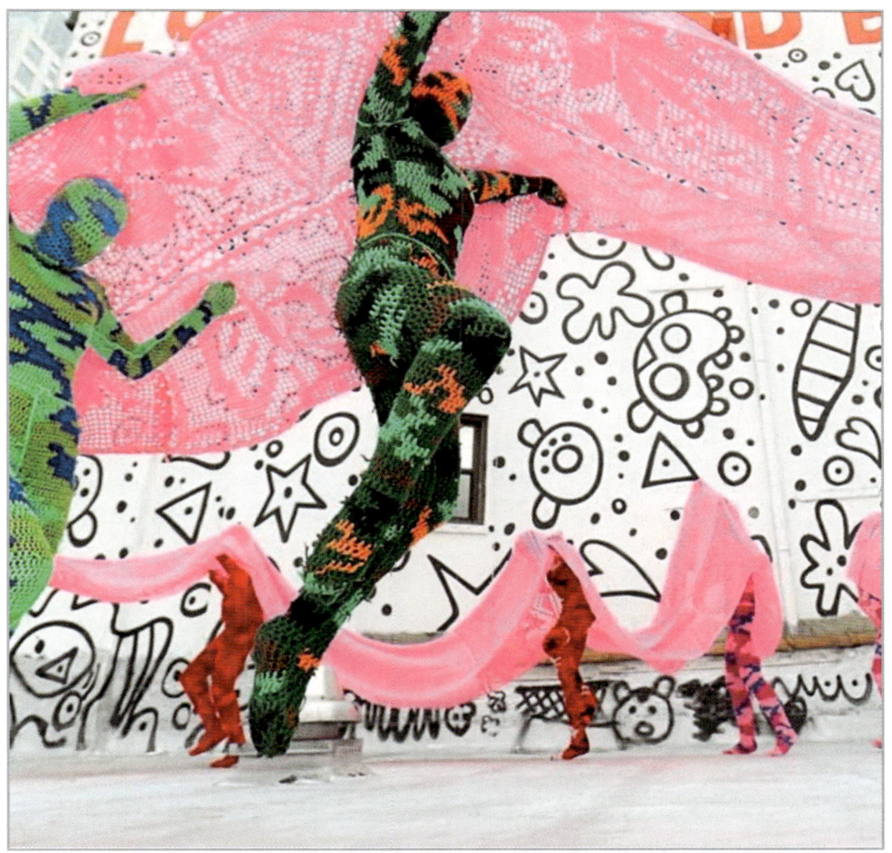

LOVE BEYOND BORDERS, performance, New York City, New York, USA, 2016

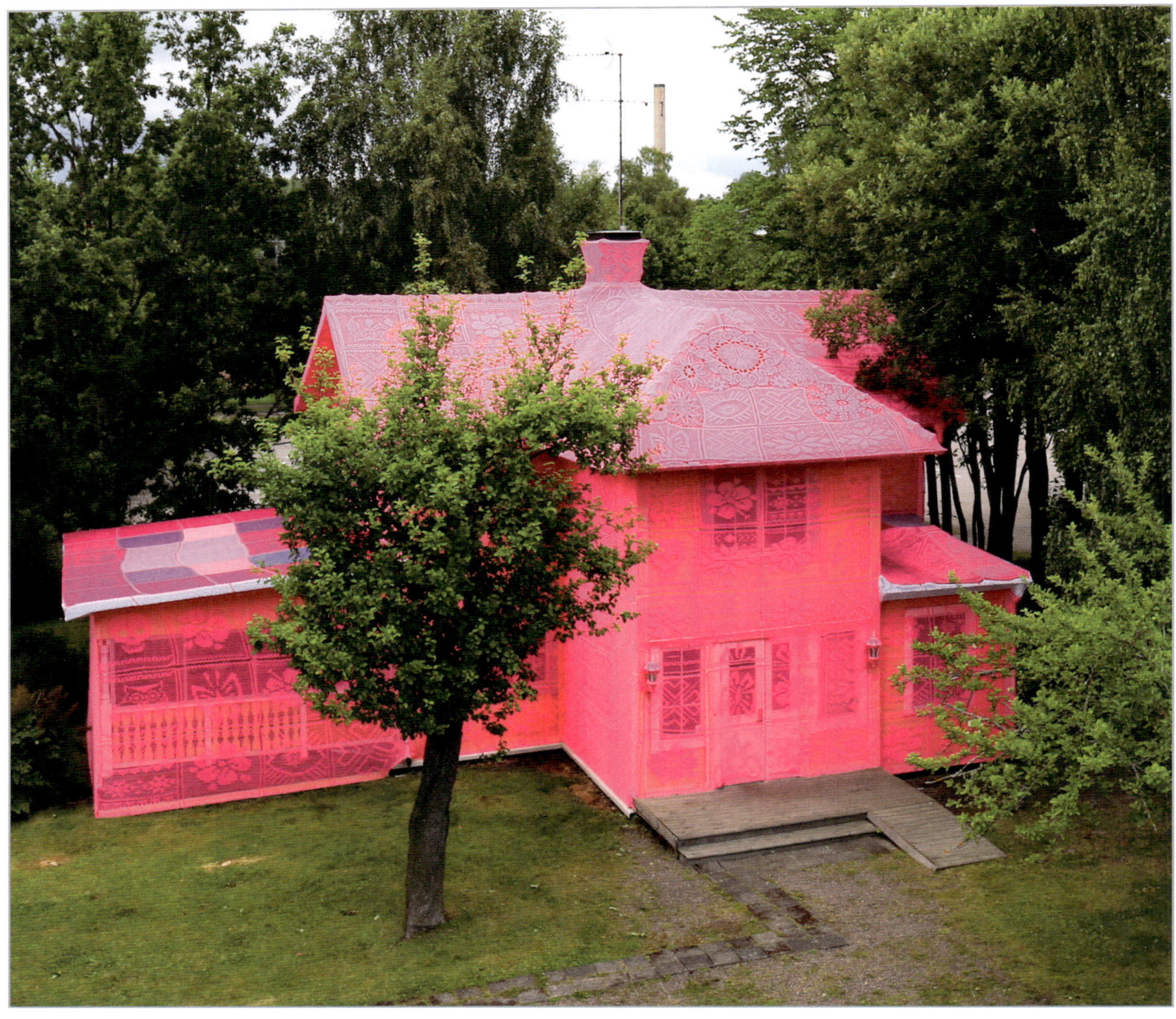

Talking about themself, Olek recalls one of the fundamental, greatly illuminating moments of their life. Years ago, while incarcerated in London, they met a woman condemned to a lifelong sentence and by then resigned: she would never again swim in the ocean or climb a tree, never again know freedom. All the experiences of that period changed Olek as a person and artist, made them realize that that they had to direct their art toward a greater purpose, that they should no longer limit themself to using their skills and talent merely to decorate something, but to fight for the rights of those who cannot stand up for themselves. They thus began taking an active interest in public and street art, which has now assumed an extremely important meaning for them: "I love the fact that public art can speak to everyone, even people who would not normally enter a museum or gallery."

During the pandemic in 2020, Olek discovered what, according to their experience and feelings, would be the art of the future: "I found the potential of the art that came knocking on the doors to my creative consciousness. I connected to the spirit of virtual reality. The whole world paused so we could enter new dimensions. I pressed the reset button on the world. I created a new technique called 'cropainting.' I crochet paint inside virtual reality with the Google Tilt Brush as my virtual crochet hook. The viewers can get lost in enormous crocheted painted

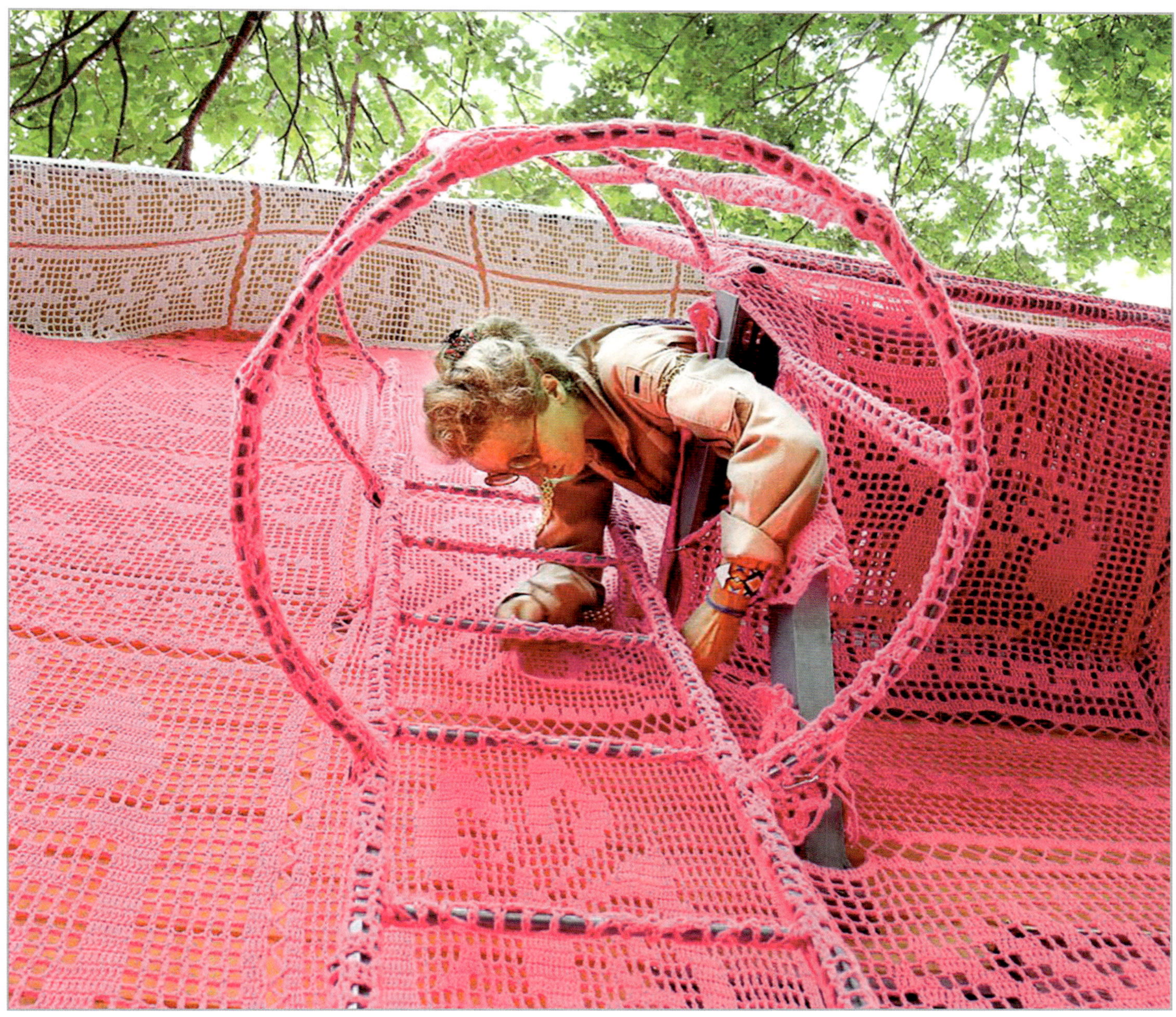

installations that flow freely inside the boundless room. I know I started something really unique. This new, contemporary form brings endless possibilities for creativity. Crochet and VR are a flawless marriage of old and new, tradition and innovation. This is the future of our creative space, and I am grateful for having discovered it at this particular time. Two of these pieces were installed on a Chinese satellite that is actually orbiting the Earth now. My work has a selfie with our beautiful planet in the background!"

About virtual reality, Olek says, "I think in the future we won't need the equipment. Everything is energy. You just need to wake up to see it".

OUR PINK HOUSE, community based project, Avesta Art Museum, Avesta, Sweden, 2016

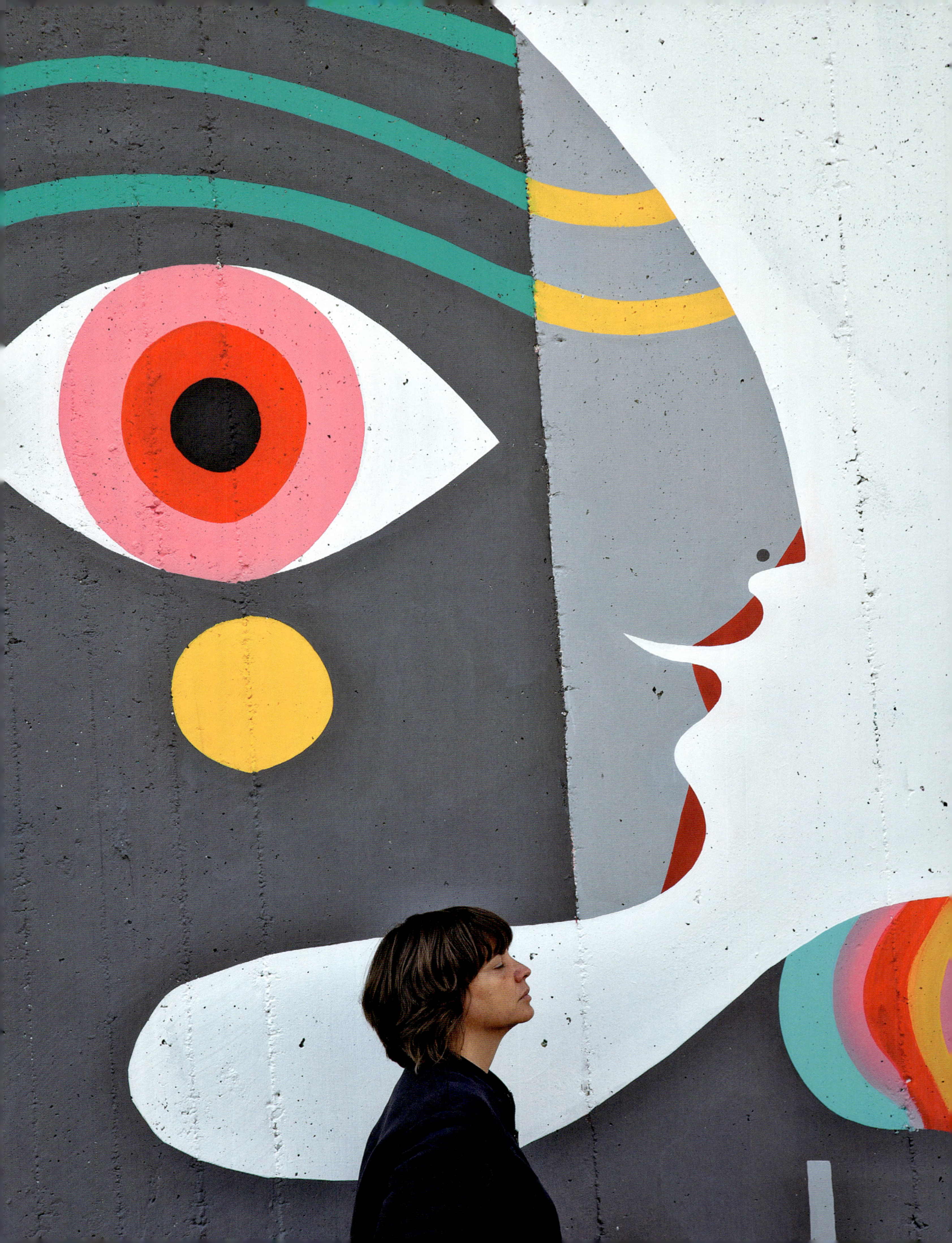

GIO PISTONE

THE MASTER OF IMAGINATION
AND OF EXTRAORDINARY CREATURES

"As a woman, it was not in the least difficult for me to emerge in the world of street art. Fortunately, street art falls outside of that dynamic, or at least that's how I've perceived it. I think that one way around this lies in not distinguishing artists by gender at this historical moment in which different genders, transgender, and no gender exist."

Gio Pistone's paintings, drawings on paper, and murals are populated by strange, fascinating, magical, and bewitching creatures born of her imagination. Some have names like Albino, Olione, and Collatesta. They move in a surreal atmosphere full of meaning, colors, eyes, shapes. . . Possessed by a nearly hypnotic power, they are charged with irresistible visual charm, as if casting a spell. Her inspiration comes from her love of nature and animals, books, mystery, and surreal universes: "Art is a form of personal communication; it's the vision of reality that passes through the lens of those who produce it. It is a particular worldview."

"In order to succeed in saying something, an artist must live, study, read, observe—otherwise, they'll have little to communicate. The outline and idea of a form, even a simple one, are the result of highly structured thought," claims Gio Pistone. "I've always chosen not to explain my drawings. I can describe what inspired me to do a project, but not an individual drawing, since it is practically impossible to explain an image in words without sounding banal. Freedom of interpretation is what makes a work of art mysterious, personal, and precious," she adds.

"What I'm looking for is an off-balance formal equilibrium; perhaps only poetry could serve as a language for making an image comprehensible in words, but it too would end up incomprehensible," she ponders. The colors of her art are strong, intense, and preponderant; they unfold in her paintings practically like an incredible musical melody.

"I use color a great deal, and I apply it as if its tones were musical notes. I know that red is a strong note, and I use it in small touches; indeed, today I am playing with half-tones more and more, in contrast to what I did in the past when everything seemed to echo the key of the triumphal march in yellow, red, green, blue," she says.

IN GIOCO, Street Alps Festival, Pinerolo, Italy, 2016, Photo Riccardo Ten Colombo

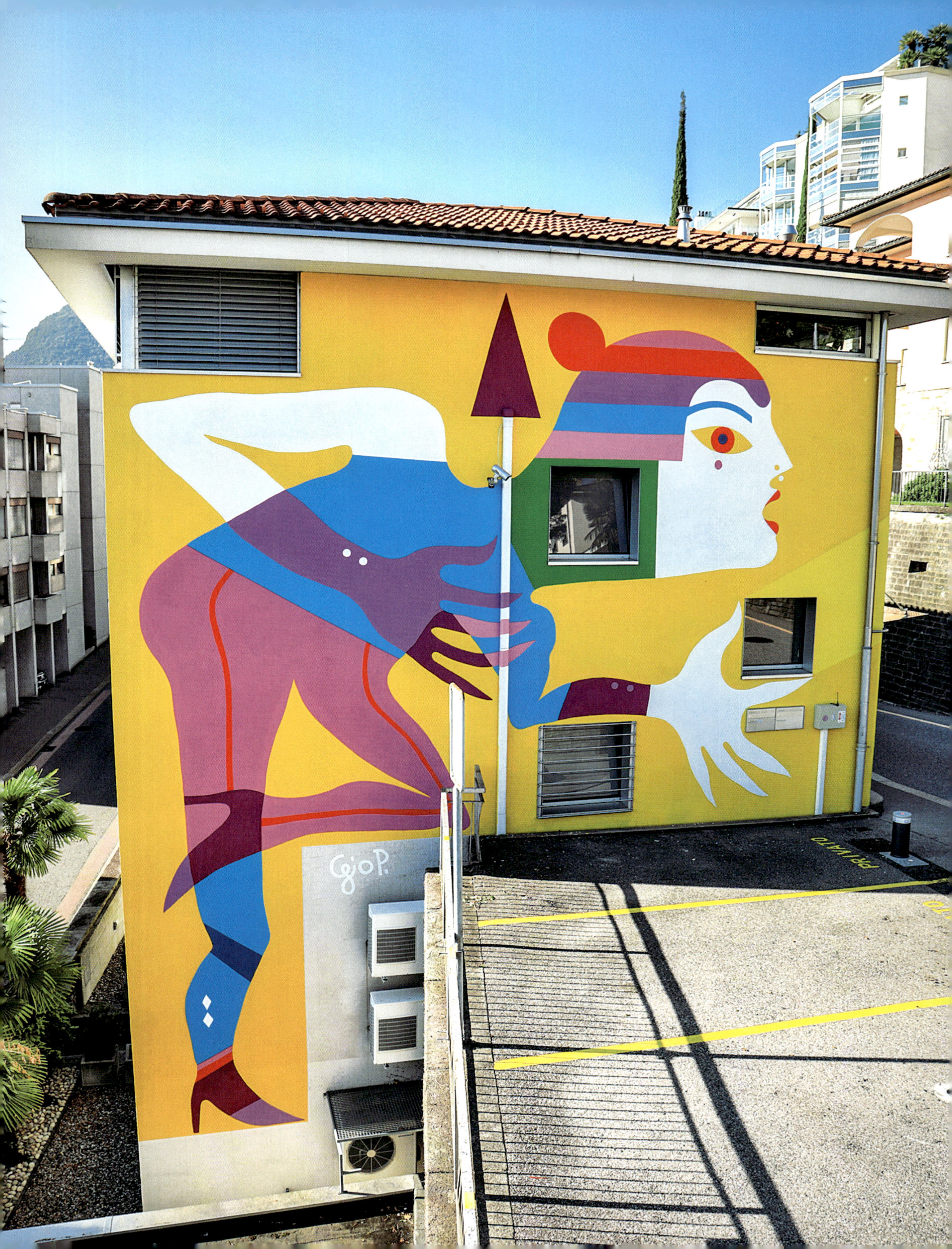
GiOP.

As a woman, Gio has not faced particular difficulties in the world of street art; nonetheless, she feels that it's of vital importance that distinctions in, and separations between, genders not be made. "This type of discrimination clearly exists in the world, and how! I did a themed project called Witch that focused on the woman's body with regard to some historical processes that I had been observing for a while. In the working world especially, the distinction between genders is more obvious than ever, in terms of both remuneration and the availability of opportunities. It's absurd! In Italy, we've been voting since 1946 and, little by little, have acquired nearly all the rights of men; yet having to say 'nearly' even today makes no sense to me at all.

"I take part in the struggle for the rights of 'Non una di meno' [no one left behind], but we've still got a long way to go because gender-based violence, as well as violence against women, have not only failed to diminish in recent years, but have even grown," she reflects with bitterness. Gio grew up in Rome, in a free-spirited, anarchic, revolutionary, and highly stimulating environment: "I was born in Rome in the winter of 1974. My parents were very young revolutionaries. I remember colorful, non-violent demonstrations, faith in a future that would be reorganized from scratch, a house always full of friends, music, art, and dance. I remember the joy of going to school—a Montessori one—of doing sports, theater, dance, and ending the day falling asleep while inventing stories in my head and amid drawings of dreamt-up monsters."

GENESI DI UN INCANTESIMO, Lugano, Switzerland, 2020, Photo Igor Grbesic (left)

DEADIANA for Galleria Uovo alla Pop, Livorno, Italy, 2018

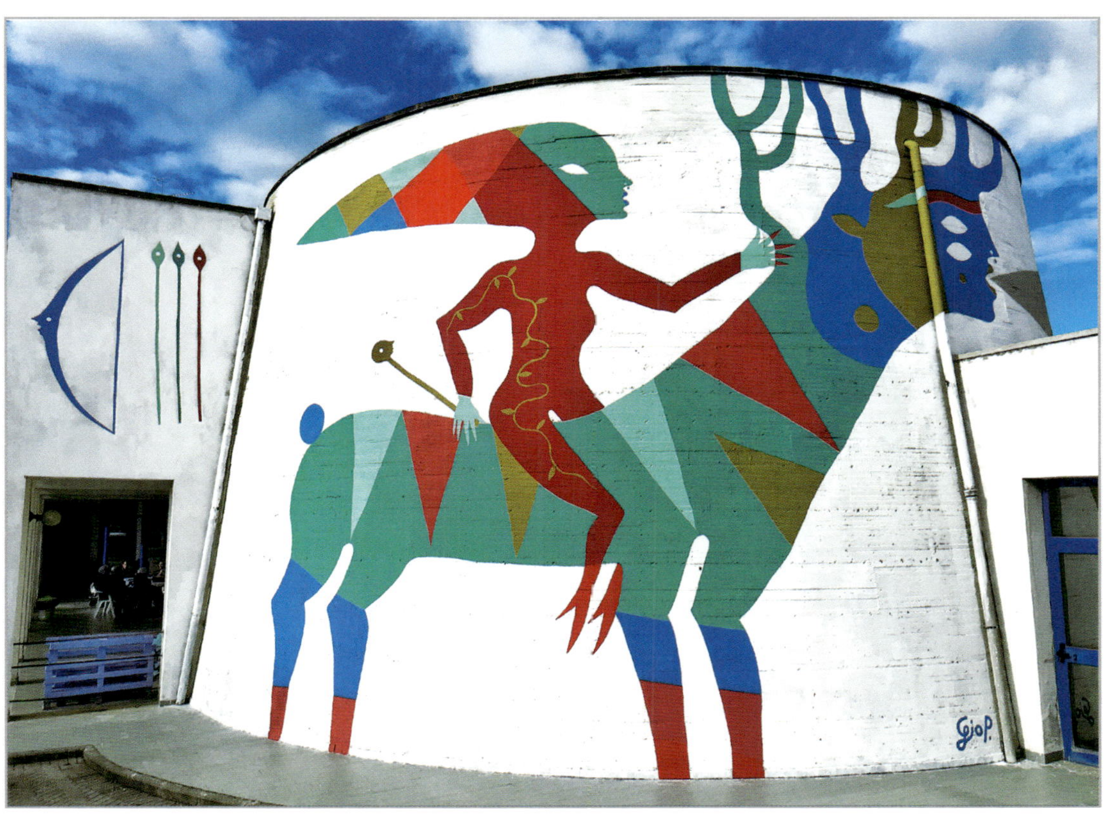

A feverish passion for art has consumed her ever since her childhood. "I chose drawing as a second language from the earliest years of my life, meaning that I spoke while drawing. I studied by making illustrated diagrams. My notebooks were full of large colorful drawings. I was definitely inspired by the many illustrated books I owned and by characters like Munari and Rodari, who accompanied me as I grew up and who are still a source of inspiration in my life. At the age of six, I became crazy about engraving. My father worked and ran a printing workshop in the Jewish Ghetto in Rome. Here I learned—in my own way—some engraving techniques and met people who only later I recognized as great masters: Pino Zac and Jean-Pierre Velly," she recounts.

"When I was around thirteen, something amazing happened to me. I saw walls covered with posters and playbills full of multi-colored letters designed by artists inviting people to participate in various initiatives. Although they definitely caught my attention, I had no idea of what they were promoting. At the time, they seemed to me simply mysterious abbreviations; I didn't yet know that they would later become my language. This period coincided with the creation of the social centers in Rome and the birth of the countercultural movements of Punk and Hip Hop. I got involved in the early forms of TAZ, in the illegal parties of 1994 held in abandoned factories on the outskirts of cities. This entire world was fundamental to my growth as an artist and predisposed me to take a broad-minded perspective of the world. I questioned any concept taken for granted by the dominant moral code and developed critical thinking skills. Thanks to the vision of the world that I constructed for myself, thanks to all these factors, I have grown quite aware of my power to change my manner of living whenever I so desire, and to take ownership of my life. To have the courage to build a work out of crazy ideas: this is what lies at the base of my thinking. Then again, reality is often something else: it's frustrating and scary, but basically there's a small engine inside me that doesn't give up," she admits.

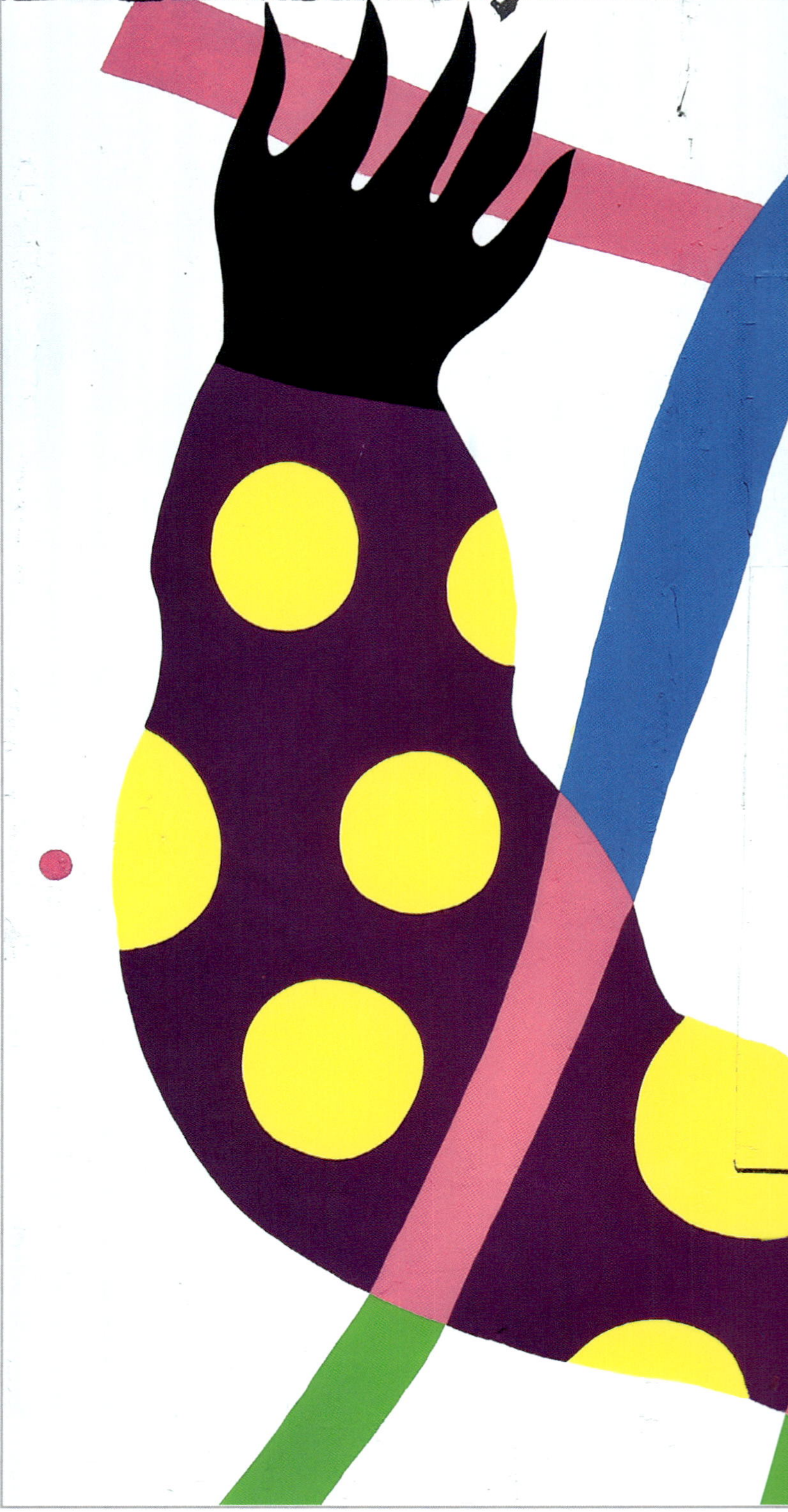

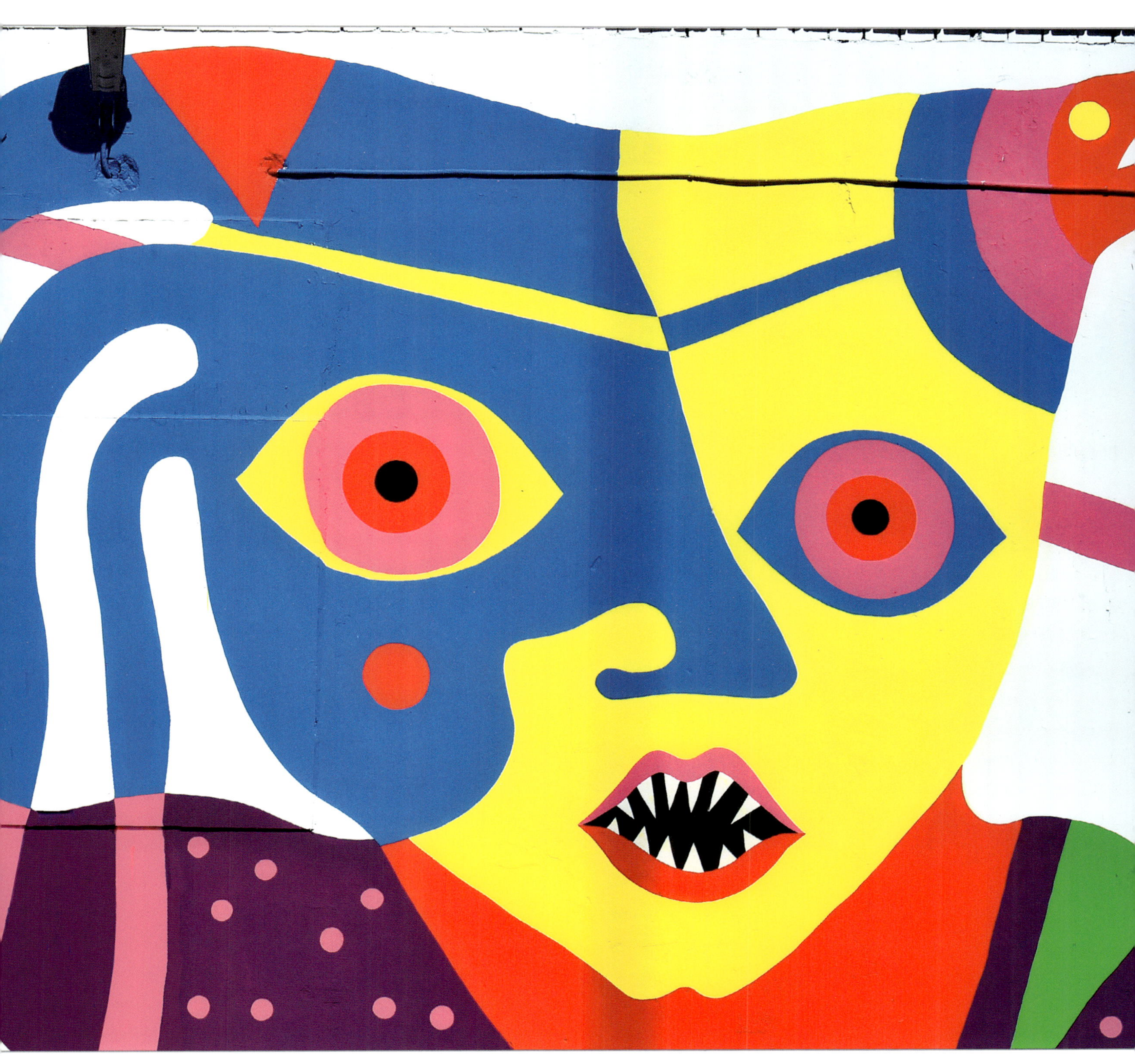

OUDEIS, Street Art Museum of St. Petersburg,
Russia

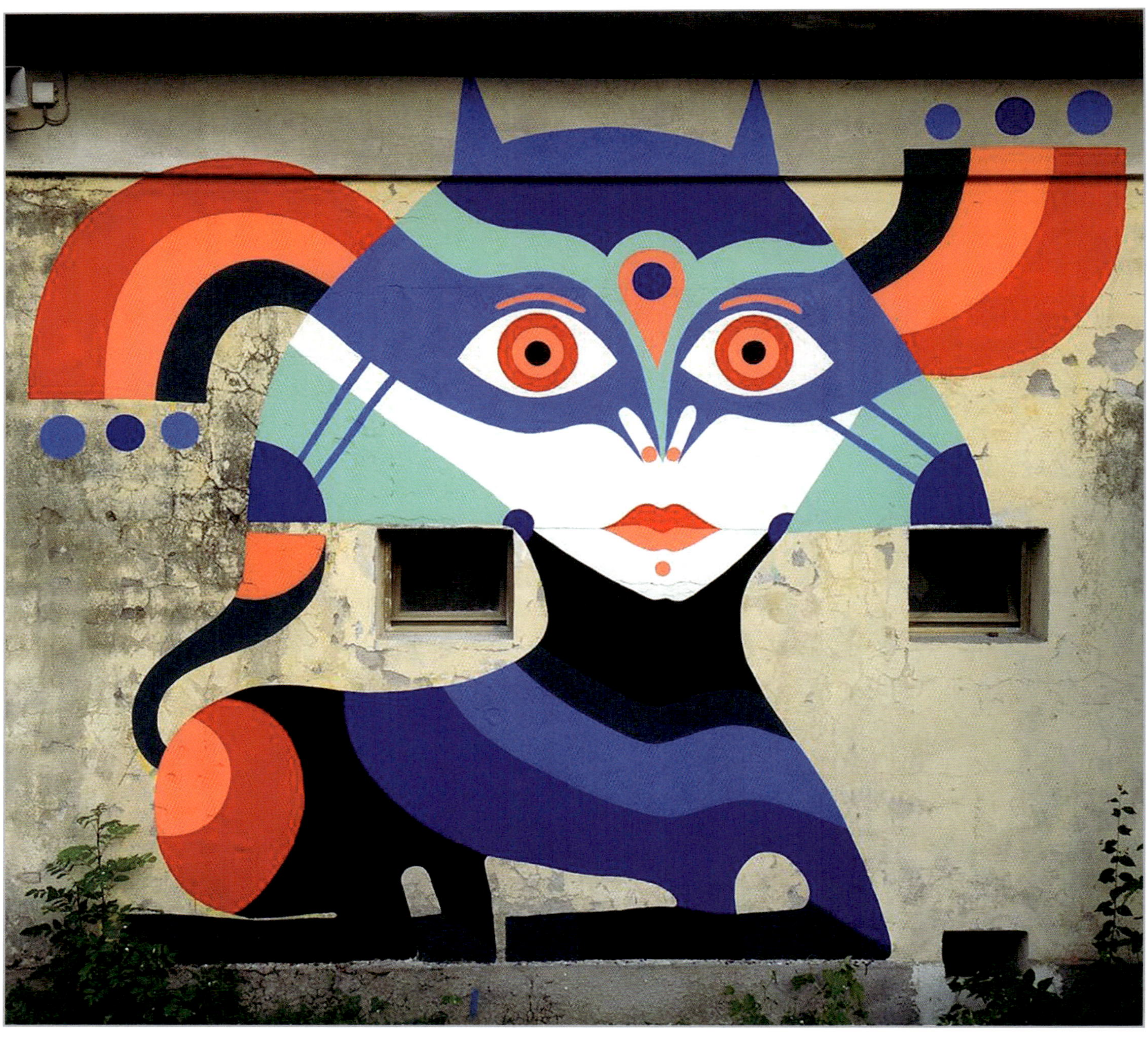

LA SFINGE DEL TERNE, Belluno, Italy, 2015

L'ASSASSINIO DI DAVIDE LAZZARETTI, Grosseto, Italy, 2014 (right)

Street art came naturally and instinctively to her. "I've always drawn large. My mother used to draw; my father is a sculptor, painter, and engraver. I've been inspired to work in this direction from the time I was in the cradle! I was allowed to draw on the walls of my room; then I moved on to the walls at school, abandoned factories; and later, when I was about twenty, I happened to take part in a legal *murata* [wall competition], organized in a neighborhood in my city. From that moment, I slowly began getting calls to paint: first on small walls, then on bigger and bigger ones, and, best of all, on different surfaces, small structures, boats, abandoned ruins—which I love. These are interesting supports for my work because I hate a big blank wall," she confesses.

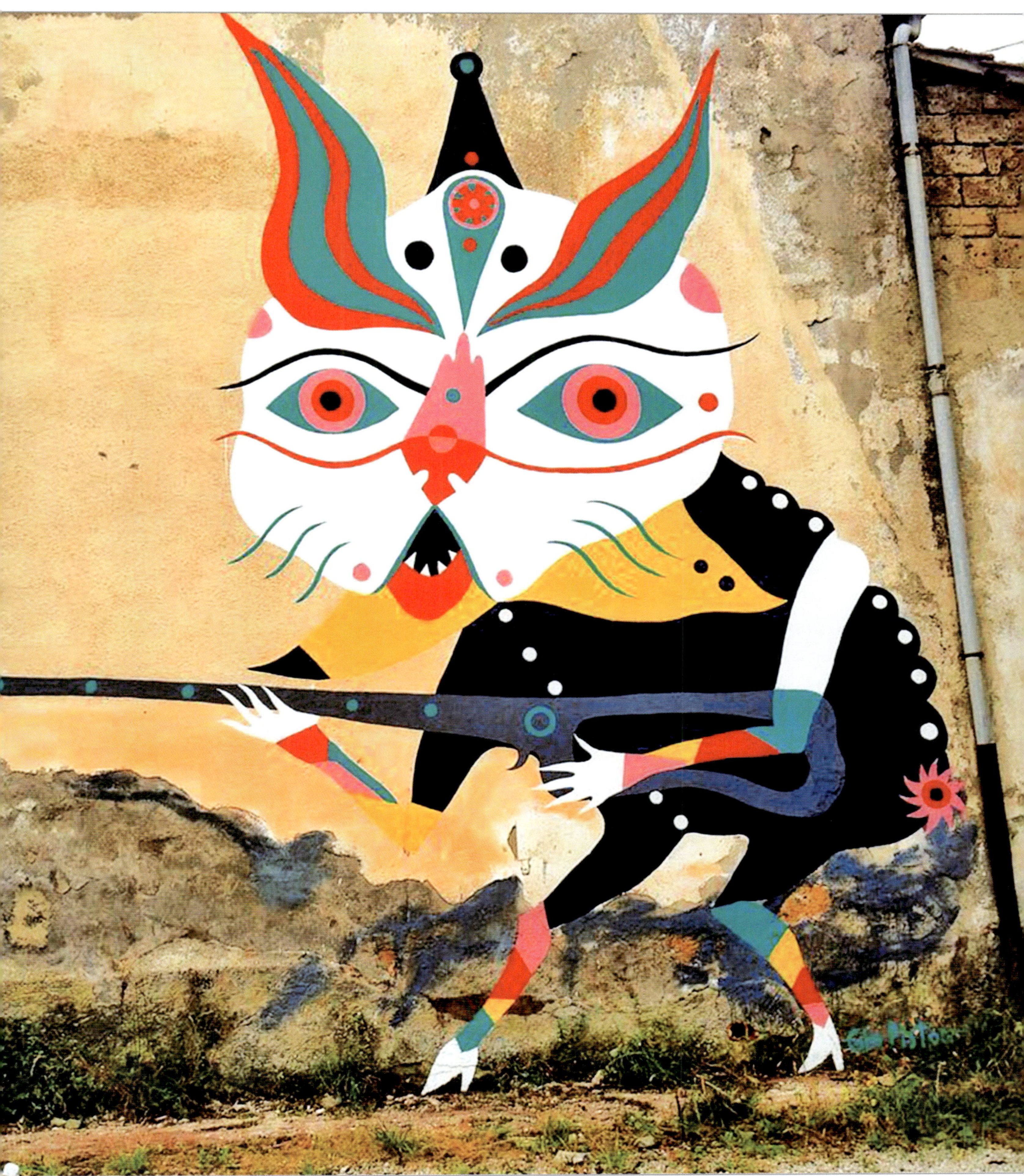

"What interests me most about this type of art is what fascinated me at the very beginning: having full autonomy over one's
lifestyle, the power to leave one's mark on cities, the ability to be
recognized even from millions of kilometers away, the fact that
it's a public and quite democratic form of art. The possibility that
anyone can admire, comment on, like or dislike it without feeling
inept," she points out.

When she's in front of a wall or any other surface, Gio sees
the light and its effects on it and initiates what appears to be a
direct dialogue. "Of course, I do a drawing before I paint a wall;
but at the moment of drawing, which is the most delicate stage of
a mural, I prefer to improvise a bit, work freehand, guided by my
silent conversation with the wall as it explains to me its critical
features; and I respect these by proposing a form that is as harmonious with them as possible," she explains.

Her vision for the future is a hope of sorts, which periodically
shifts: "I want to be able to express what I wish to say calmly and
in a simple manner, because I often realize how overloaded we
are with superstructures that distance us from what is essential." In what kind of form? "Right now sculpture, but also drawing,
though at this stage I prefer working in the third dimension. I did a
series of very large sculptures representing the modern Muses,
the bearers of today's ideas and dreams, focusing on their matri-
ces and body structure."

"My brain is active and continues to travel and dream…
Therefore, I very much hope to be able to bring into being what
is now merely a giant lump of soft clay," she admits." I would like
a place in which people reflect and also work towards a common
good from multiple angles, where their concern for themselves
and their children is equal to that which they feel for the children
of others. And, I would like more empathy for everyone," she says
longingly.

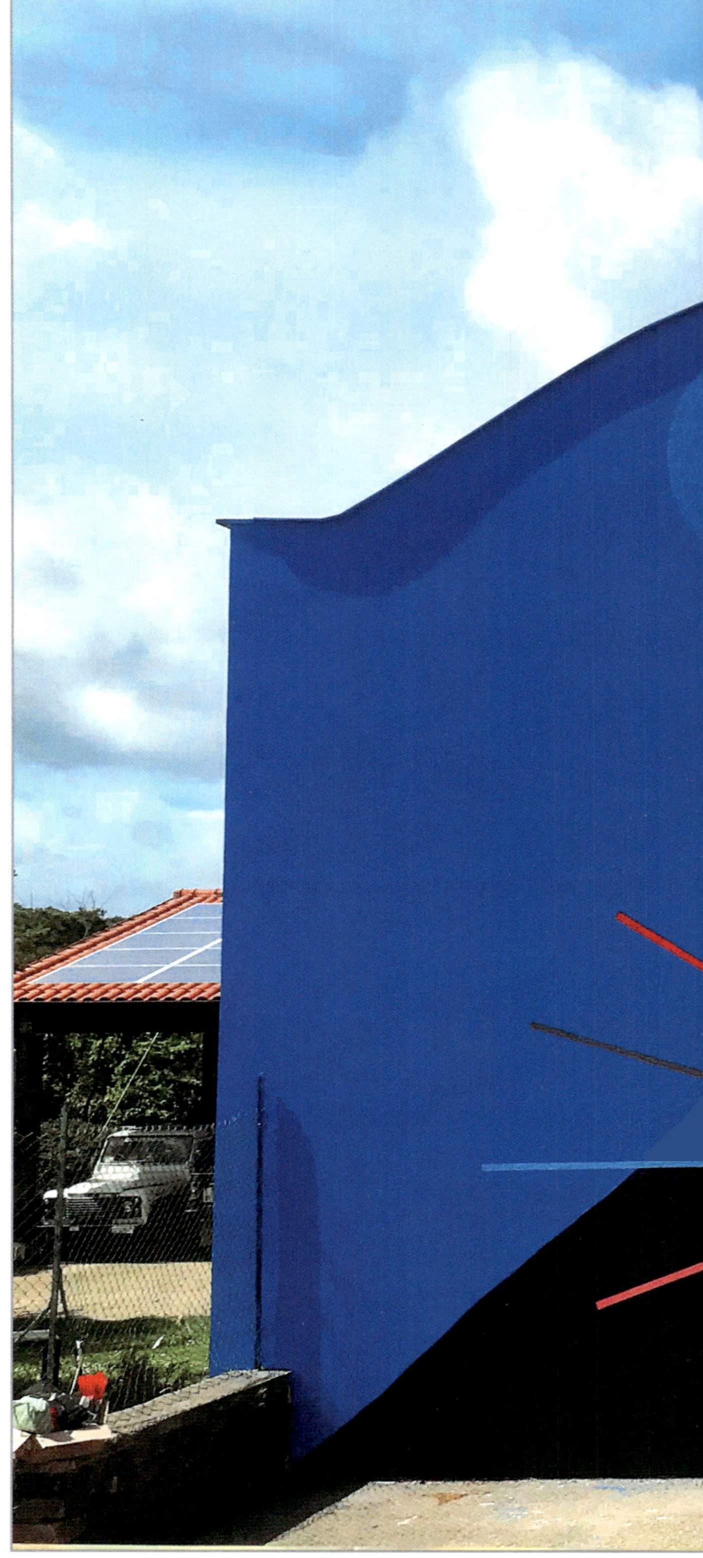

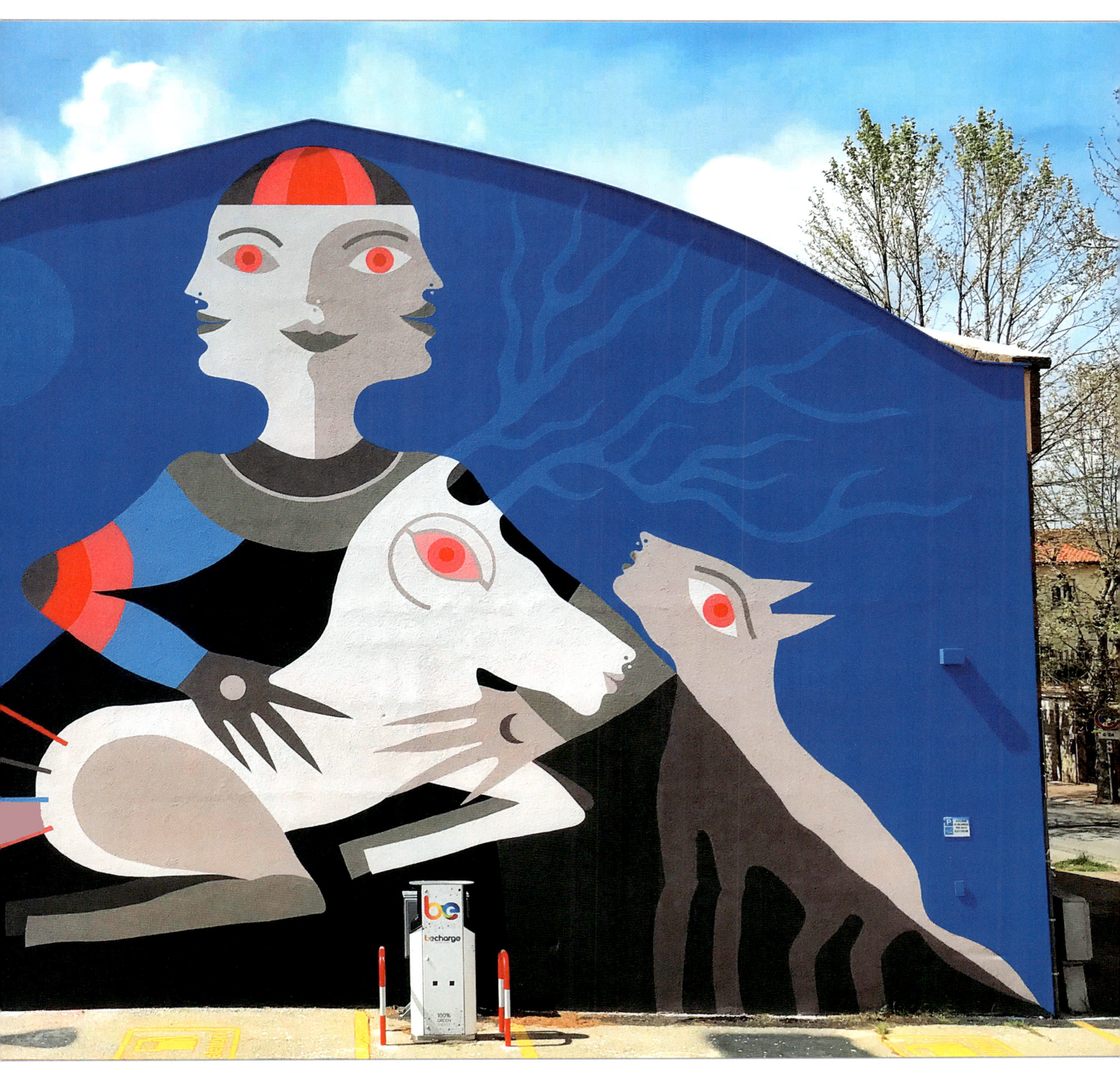

FERONIA, Parco Regionale Marturanum, Barbarano Romano, Italy, 2021

SWOON

THE VOICE OF WOMEN'S AND HUMANITY'S DIGNITY

"In my art, I've always tried to portray and draw women as they really are, in and of themselves. Over the years, I've come to realize more and more that I want to serve as a spokesperson for their rights."

Swoon was one of the first street artists to achieve international fame in a world of men. *Swoon* refers to a strong emotion, one so intense that it causes fainting. It was for this reason that Caledonia Curry chose it as her professional name, after it came to her friend in a strange dream. Similar sensations are evoked by her works, in which women are often portrayed with great dignity and pride. Heroines of the past, present, and future, they project from the walls but at the same time are charged with a subtle realism that conveys their human fragility, their tenacity in conflict, their need of recognition, their boundless courage, and their indomitable will to overcome all adversity. Swoon also devotes her attention to sculpture, stop-motion animation, and film, and creates immersive and magnificent installations. She focuses on the transformative power of art, its catalytic power and ability to heal communities in crisis from within.

Born in Connecticut and raised in Daytona Beach, Florida, Swoon was brought up by parents who suffered from drug addiction and mental illness. When she was ten, her mother, recognizing her talent in art, enrolled her in some art courses for retirees, and she was practically adopted by this group of eighty-year-old painters who taught her how to paint. "Thanks to them, I gained a sense of security and determination; they encouraged me and appreciated my works. I needed all this, and, above all, stability. And thus, the serious and precocious child that I was, I began concentrating ever more on developing my art, which meant everything to me," she recalls.

At nineteen, Swoon moved to Brooklyn to study painting at New York's Pratt Institute. In 1999, feeling that the world of conventional art and museums, as well as galleries, was not the environment in which she wanted to distinguish herself, she decided to start pasting paper portraits of herself on walls.

CALEDONIA CURRY/SWOON, Photo Adrian Buckmaster

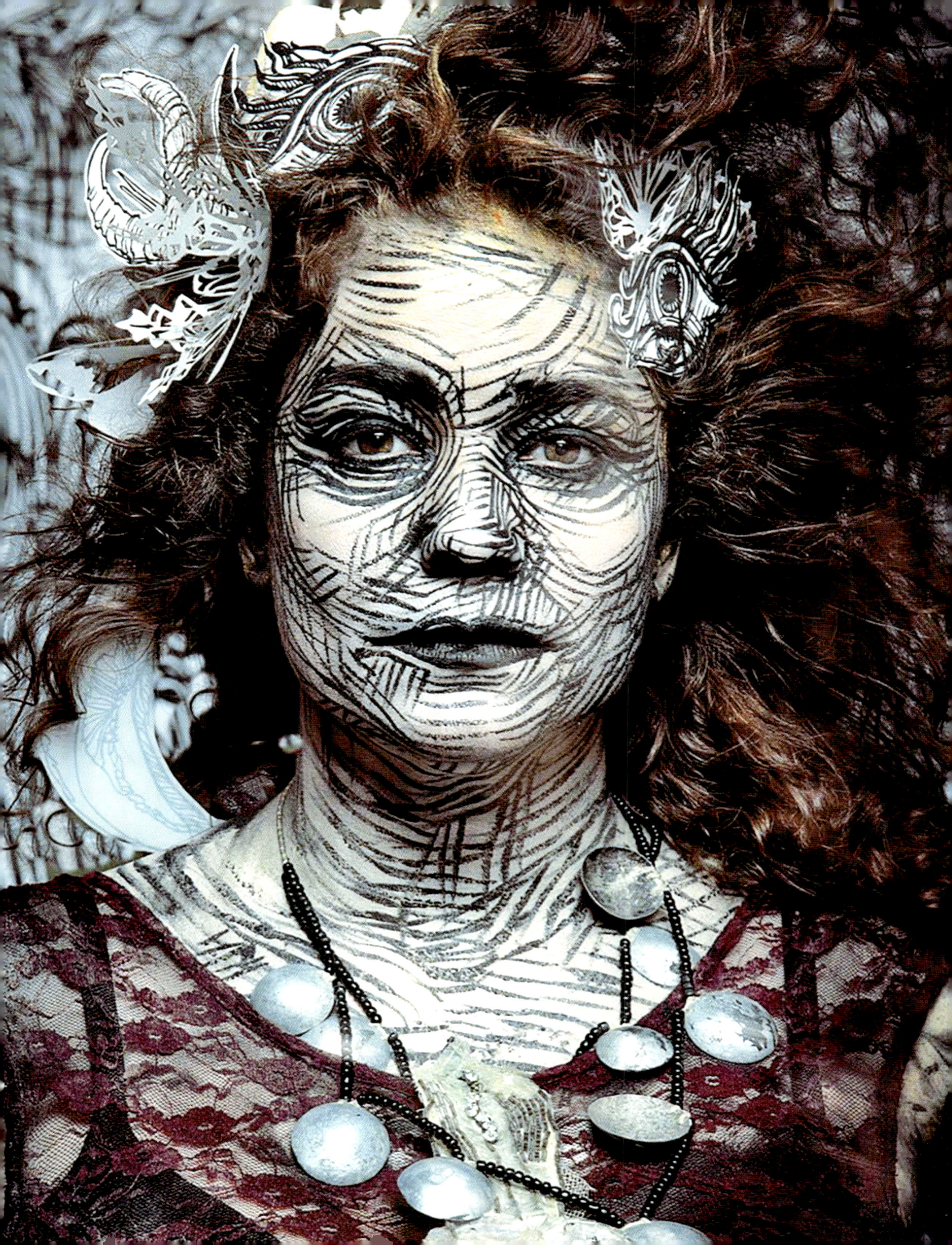

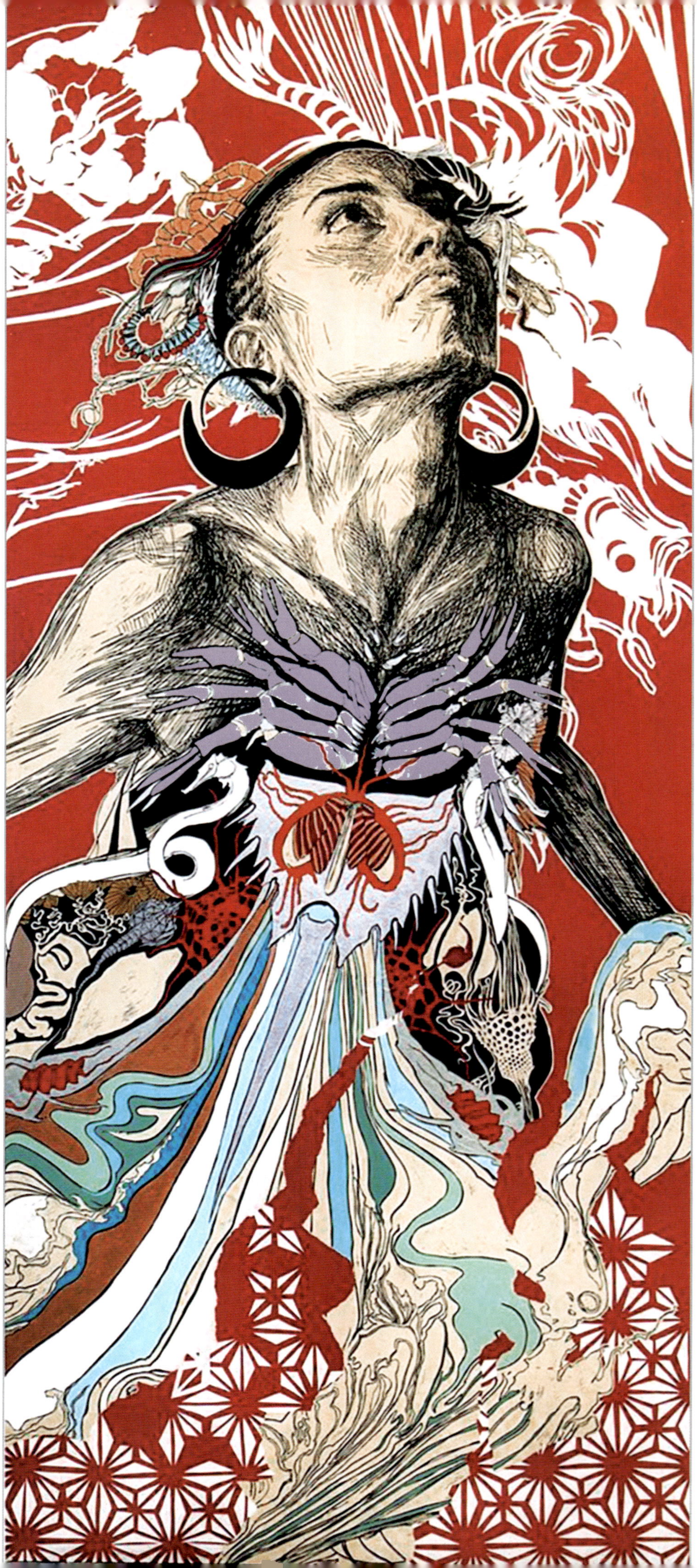

THALASSA, silkscreen, cut paper, and acrylic gouache on paper and wood, 2021

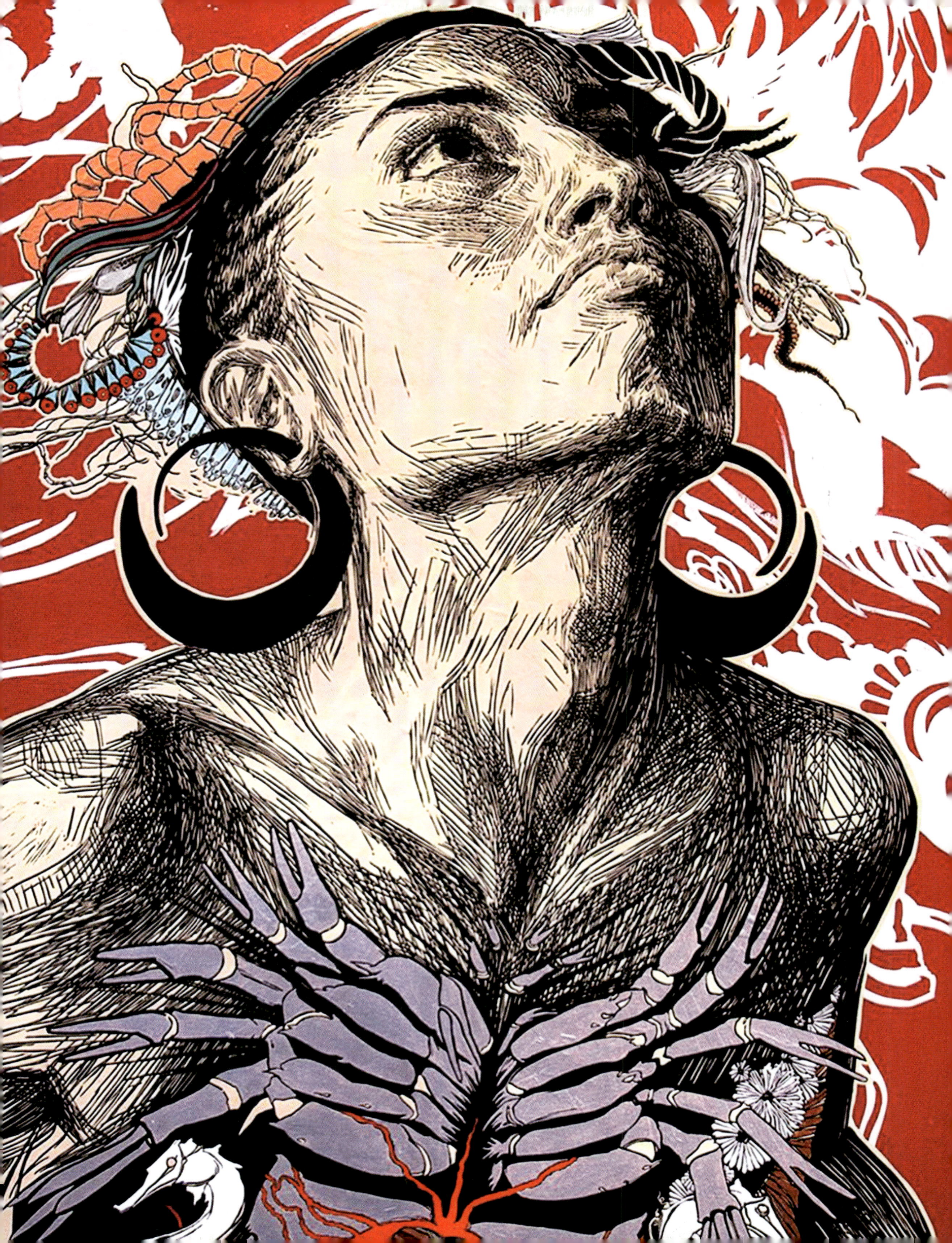

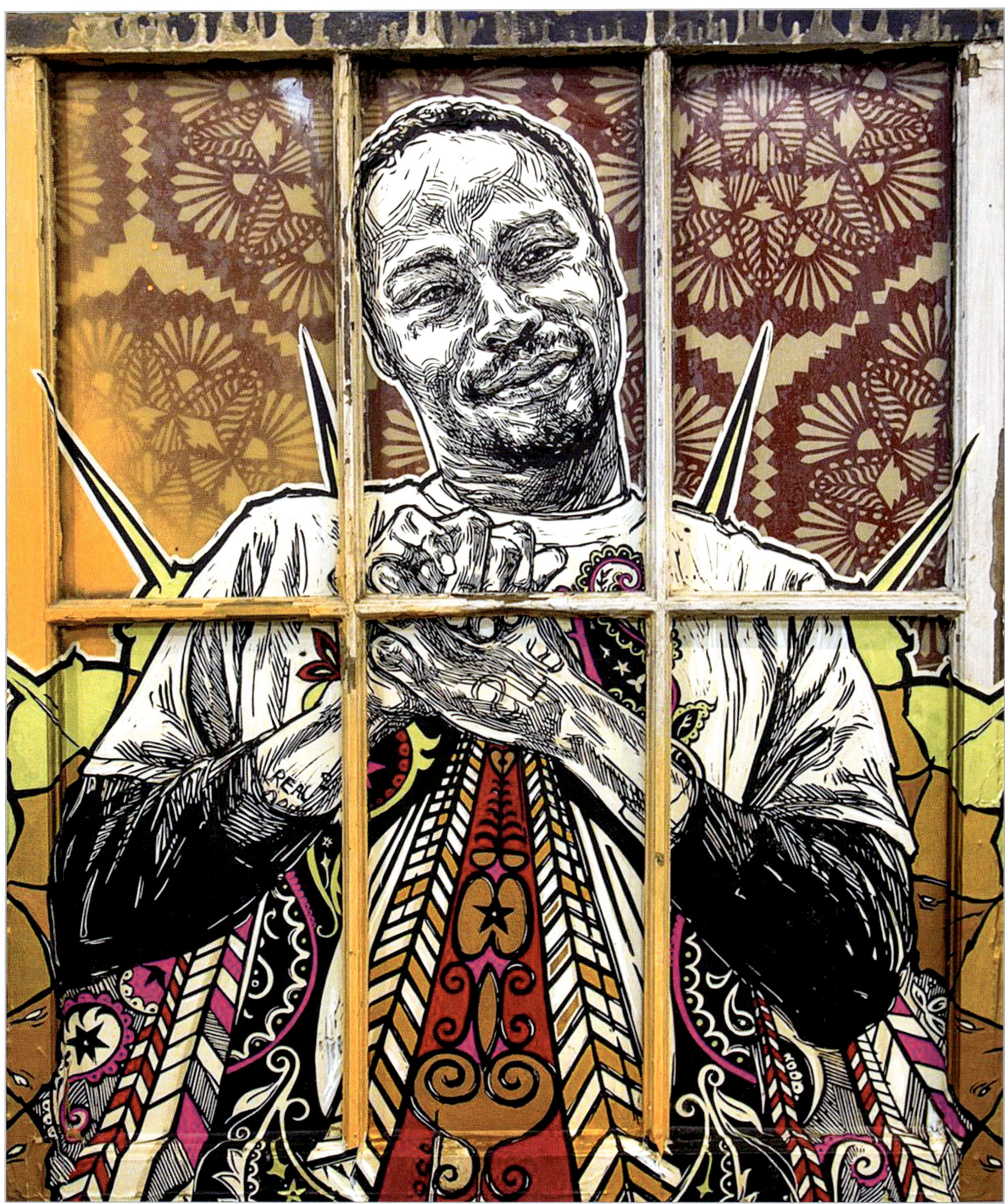

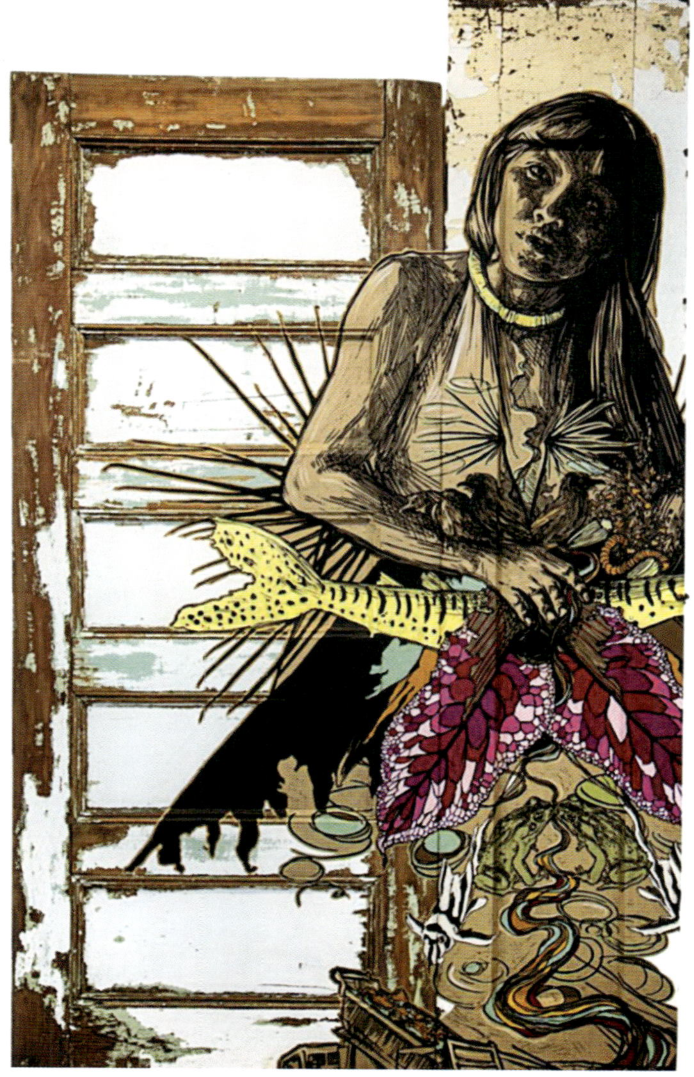

Soon afterward, she became involved in the feminist movement Toyshop Collective, a theater run by women who organized secret events in New York. Her first exhibition took place in 2005 at Deitch Projects, a space belonging to Jeffrey Deitch. Since then, Swoon has continued working on ever more ambitious projects for which she has finally received well-deserved international recognition. In 2017, Fredric King made a documentary about her titled *Swoon: fearless*.

"When I was younger, I wanted to be on an equal level with men and constantly produced art. I wanted to smash 'the glass ceiling'—as we say in English—that unacknowledged obstacle to professional advancement which affects women and minorities, in particular. As I worked on increasingly important projects, I found myself having to deal with various forms of sexism, and, sad to say, I realized that I was accepting certain aspects of this as if it were normal. It's still a tough struggle, and the end of this absurdity is still a long way off," she adds.

Swoon was deeply affected by the environment in which she spent her youth, one fraught with problems, tension, and insecurity: "I grew up among women who had survived domestic violence, who had been forced to complete pregnancies even when they didn't want to, who had suffered all kinds of abuse. That's why I decided from the outset to devote myself to making portraits of women: I wanted them to see themselves as they really were, as possibly no one had ever seen them before because they had been invisible. Whenever I portrayed a woman in this way, I felt revitalized, as if I myself had grown through this experience."

Swoon is glad that things are changing now, even if slowly. "I'm very active in the world of cinema, and it makes me happy to see that in recent years more and more space is given to female directors. The art sector and every other field has seen a real explosion of female talent. US politics is witnessing a battle over women's autonomy, and I am very proud of the activism

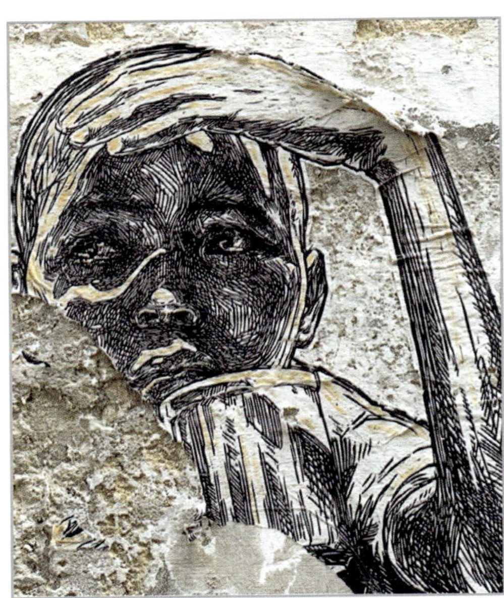

of the previous generation, as well as my own. The #MeToo movement subtly encapsulates what I've gone through in my career as an artist. And the new generations now have a strong voice, which they are not afraid to make heard," she boldly stresses.

Swoon also believes that street art is very open to this attitude. "It was not difficult for me to make my way into the world of street art. Initially I maintained my anonymity; but when people discovered that I was a woman, they urged me on, so I felt no discrimination. What can prevent female success is a society that is still too frequently full of prejudice, a closed and blind culture. But street art promotes equality with conviction: get on the street and spread your ideas, regardless of whether you're a man or woman," she claims.

One needs determination, discipline, and tenacity to succeed in the art world, and Swoon knows this well: "You've got to work much harder than everyone around you, devote yourself completely to your art, not allow yourself to get distracted, aim for big goals. You've got to follow that sense of eternity, which you discover within yourself and that propels you forward. It's also important to be in the right context: things become culturally important when they develop in an environment that is sensitive to them."

Swoon recalls her first steps in the street art world: "I started working on the street in the late '90s. Street art was still illegal back then, kept in check, a bit vague, mysterious. It invited participation, and no one knew who made it and how. Even now, I love that erratic and spontaneous side of it. When I came to New York, I participated in all the happenings, in performances, and in the various forms of expression of various artists, which have always served as sources of inspiration and points of comparison for me. I saw the rise of different art forms, which left their mark on me and pushed me to create large installations. I wanted to remain who I am, but at the same time become part of the City,

TUMAINI, Grottaglie, Italy, block-print paper pasteup, 2013

MILTON II — DIOGENES, silkscreen, watercolor, and acrylic gouache on fabric mounted to wood, 2020 (right)

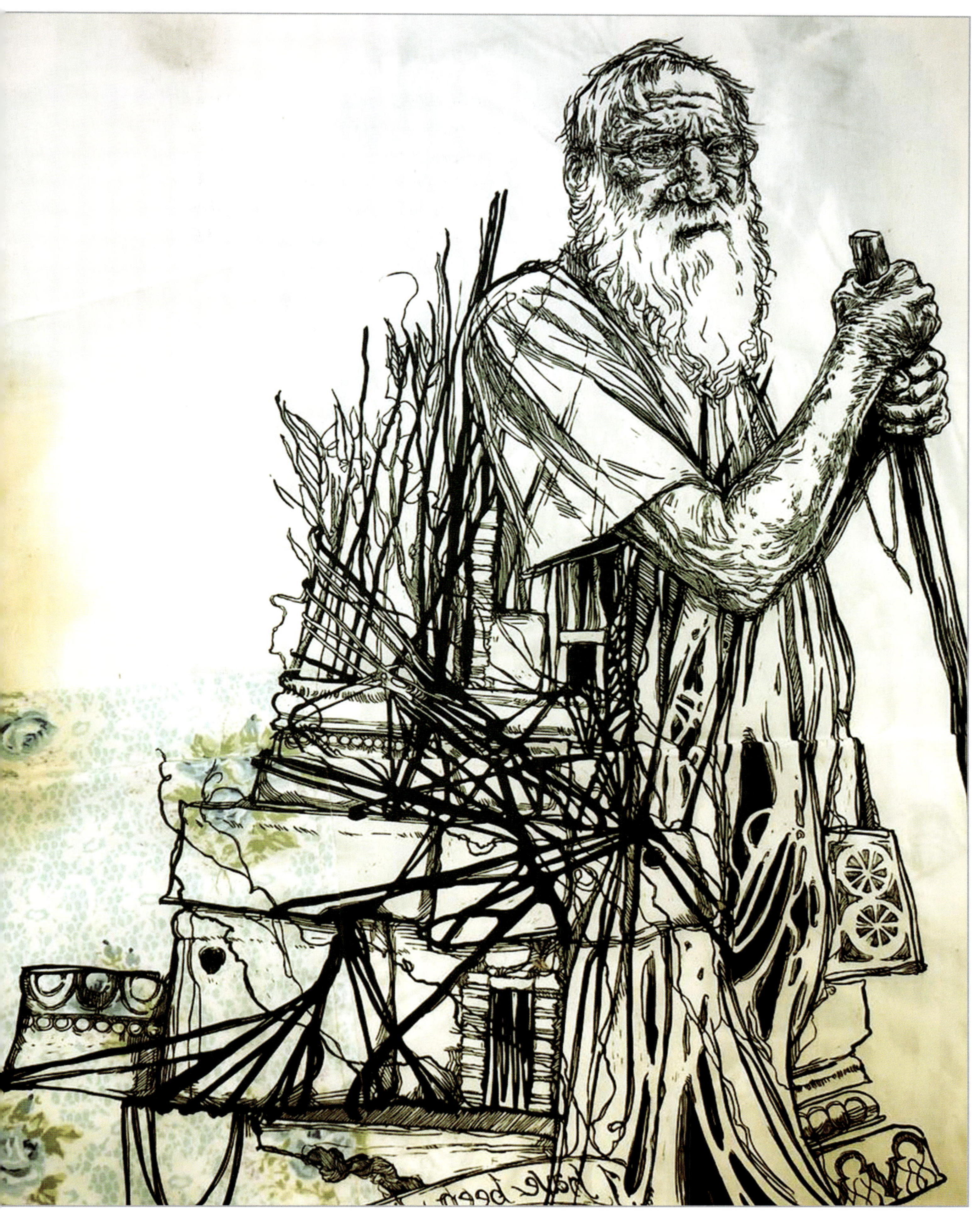

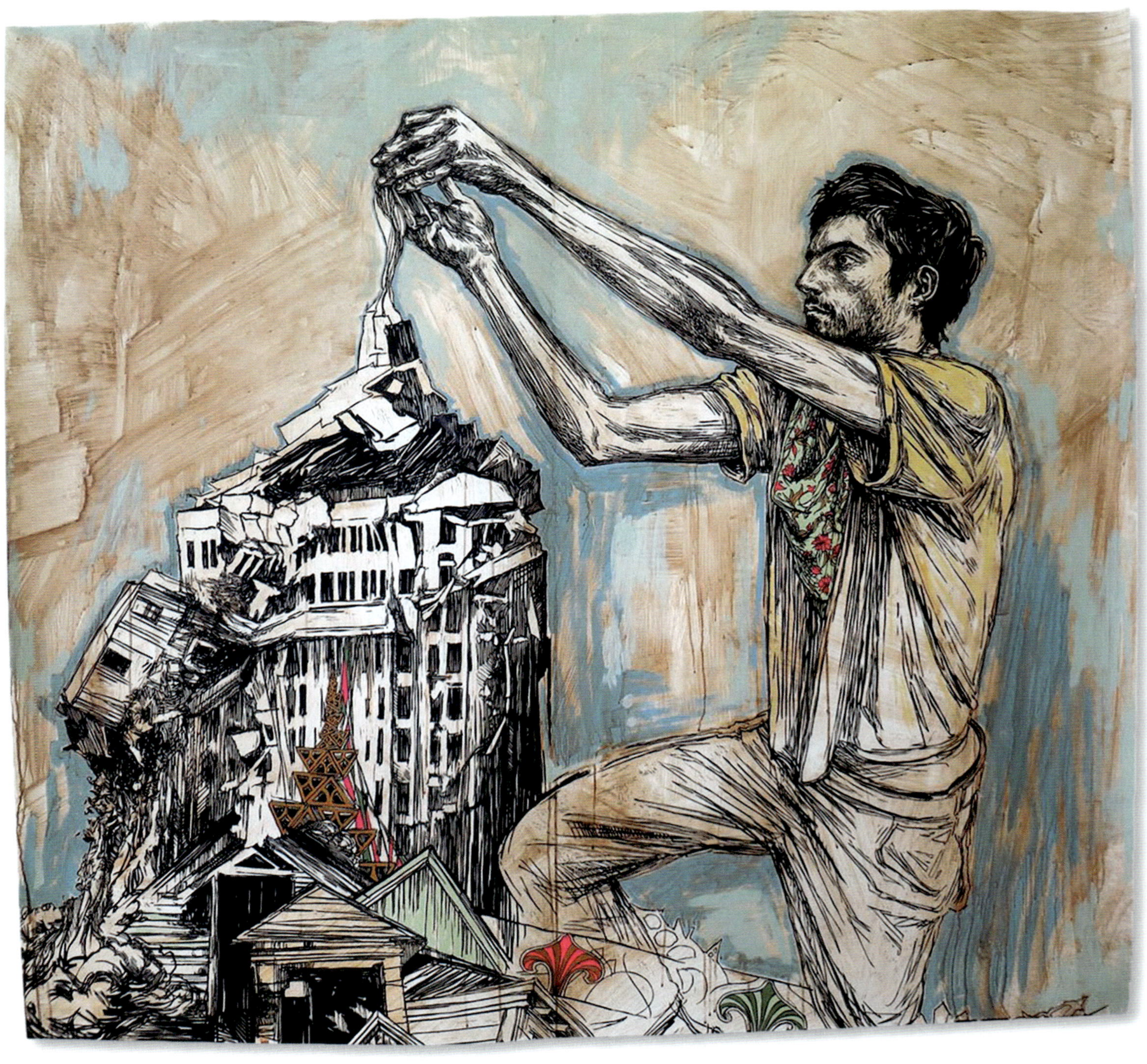

capable of better, understanding everything that was happening around me."

Her vision was clear from the outset: "The portrait and a regard for humanity have stood at the center of my work from the beginning, and everything still revolves around them. I'm also interested in architecture, mythology, storytelling—all roots that feed the tree of my art. Working in the street has made me realize how much people can do as a group. As an activist, you don't merely paint a portrait on a building; you can help construct a new building, create better residential spaces, like the ones in the projects I worked on after the Haiti earthquake, or when I participated in the construction of a safe home, a space of hope, for former convicts and the homeless."

Swoon sees her art as steadily evolving and, like her, constantly growing richer. "I see many experiences, full of meaning and promise, emanating from my art. When you've created art your entire life, it changes with you: it's a tirelessly evolving path. People often think that artists seek inspiration from a muse capable of capturing ideas from universal consciousness, or from some other evocative force. For me, everything

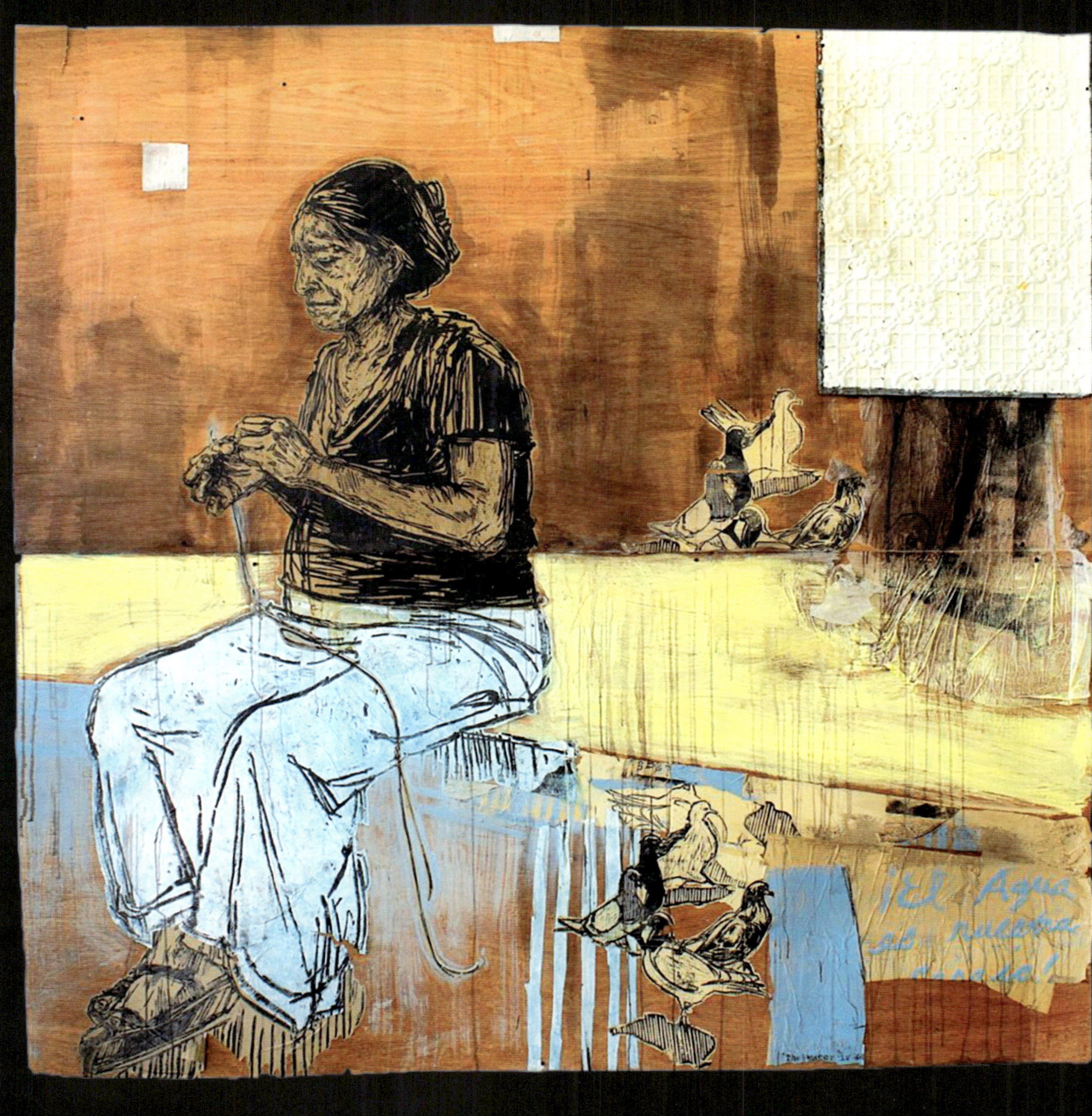

HUAHUAPAN, mixed media woodblock print and collage, 2007

BEN, hand-painted block print on mylar, 2012 (left)

arises from the power of nature, the spark of life, which is forever compassionate, generative, and loving, never tractable, but believes in the goodness of people and in the right of everyone's existence. I want this to be felt in every piece I do. The longer I work, the more precise my goal. Over the years, I, like everyone, have had to deal with the pain of losing many people dear to me, beginning with my parents. . . Pain is something that changes you profoundly, and, at a particularly difficult moment, as I was undergoing the process of spiritual healing, my tone, and also my work, was altered by meditation," she confesses.

As for the future, Swoon is aiming at something different, though equally and closely connected to nature and its multifaceted character. "I'm learning to work with actors as a director because I want to make films and tell stories. I'm convinced that I can pool all my talents in film. The 2020 pandemic helped me reflect on and reinvent myself; I drew a lot, I continued working with other artists, discovering new ways to collaborate; I saw how New York, my city, responded to the emergency with compassion, how people cared for each other. I'm very optimistic about the future," she concludes.

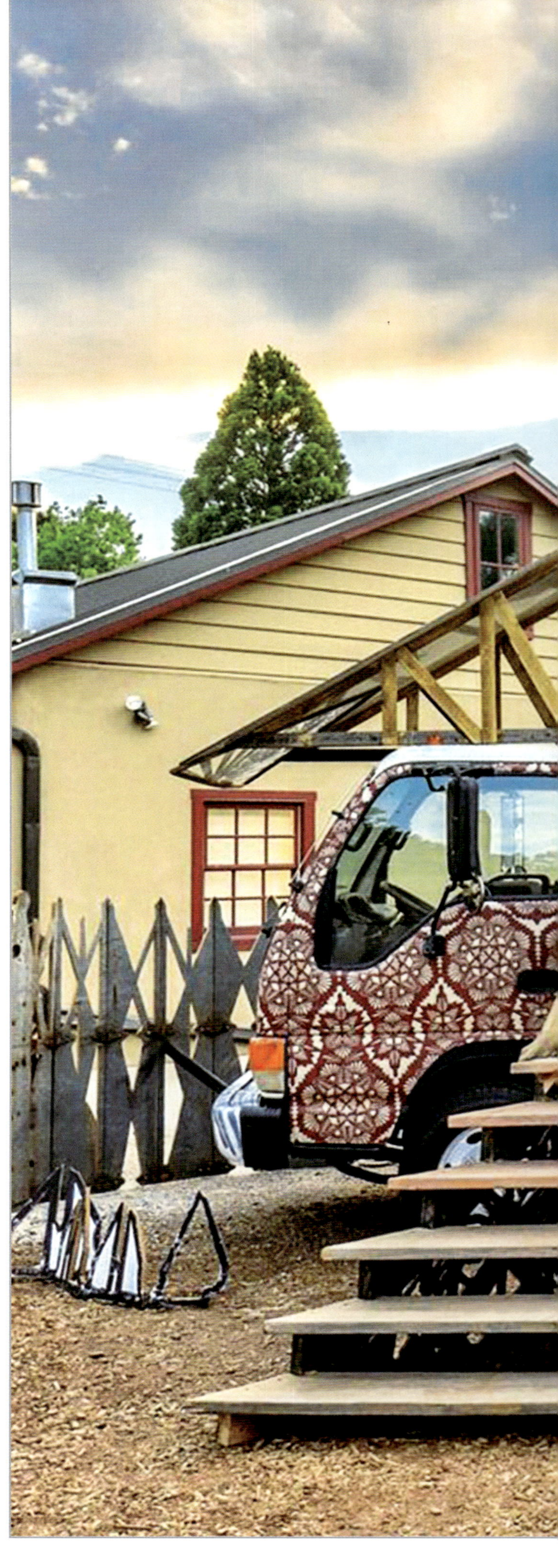

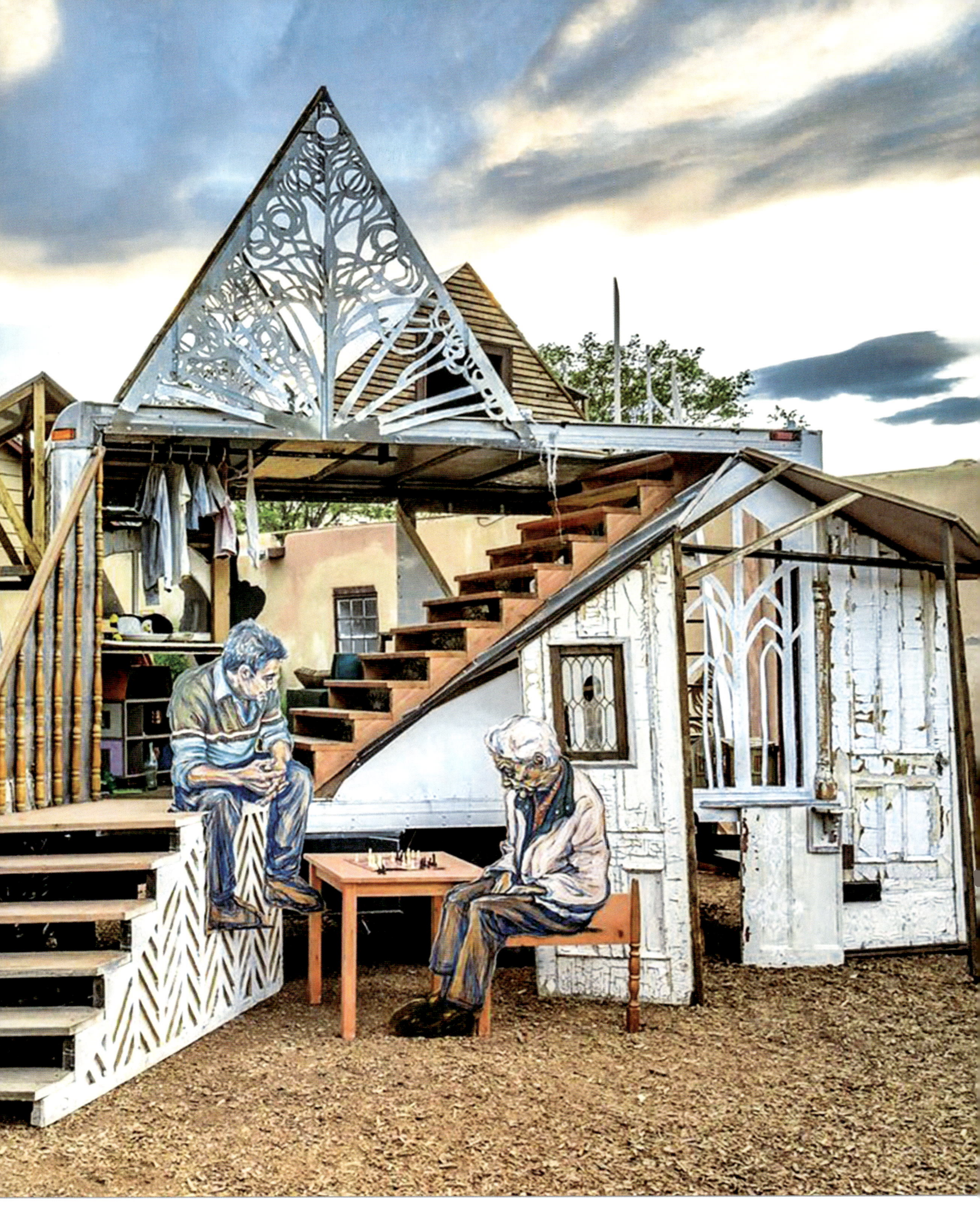

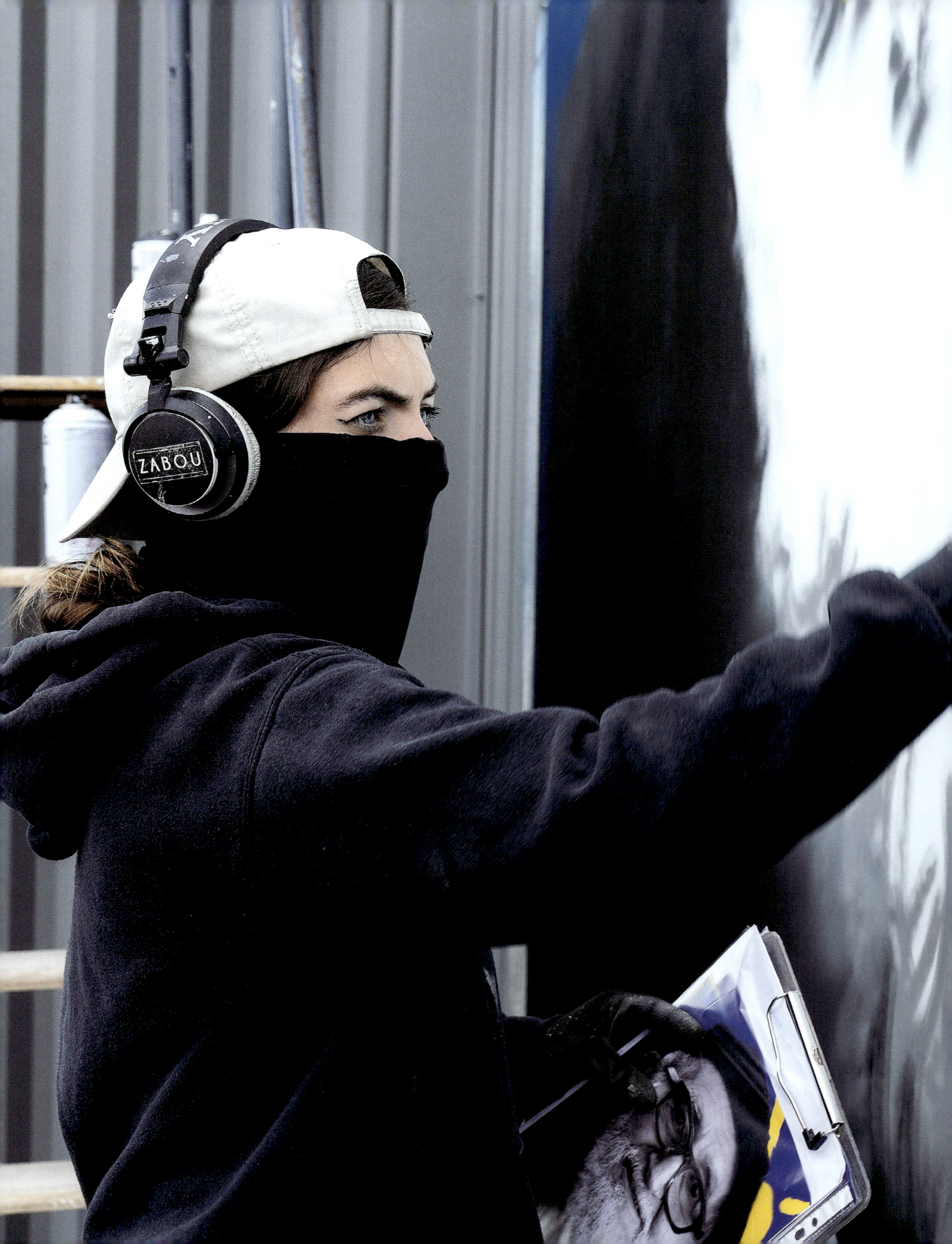

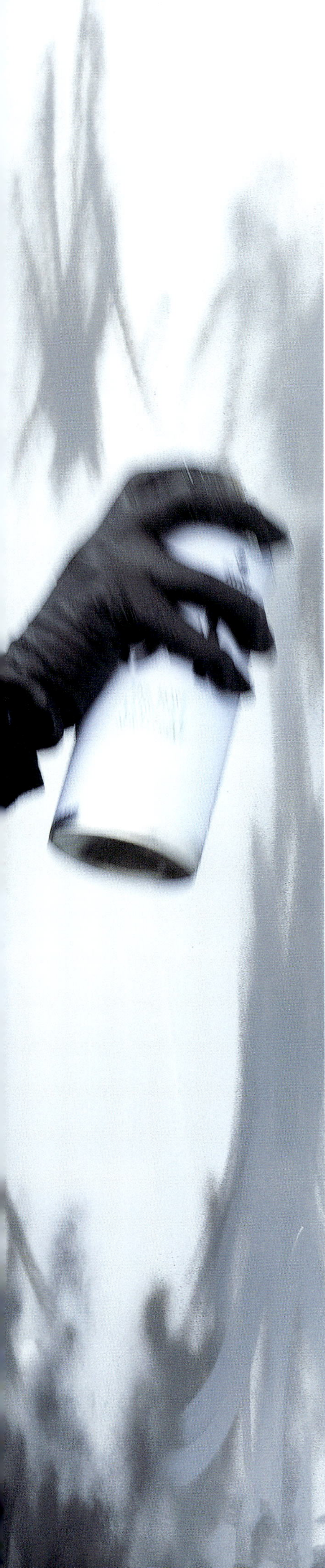

ZABOU

THE MASTER OF REALISM AND SOLIDARITY

"Personally, I did not meet with discrimination when I started, and I felt really welcomed by other artists, but unfortunately I know many women who have had a different experience."

Zabou's art offers a vision of infinite generosity and compassion, of love, tenderness, hope. In some cases, we recognize the faces of famous artists, such as Charlie Chaplin or Salvador Dalí; in others, scenes from films; but what more often dominates her works are regular people, caught in moments of everyday life, while protesting, or completing tasks. "I think that art is a way of connecting with others; it's the beginning of a dialogue. It's one of the marvels that make life a little less boring. I want my works to convey emotions to those who look at them—perhaps by surprising viewers, making them wonder, smile, or grow sad. . . My works speak of that which makes us human. Even if I stick my own vision or a message into them, I want people to feel free to interpret them based on what they see and feel," Zabou explains.

French by birth, she fell in love with London, a place where she finds inspiration and manages to express herself to the fullest. "London is a city that never sleeps: things are always happening—things to do, to see, to experience, people to meet. It's exciting and amazing, but it can also be terribly stressful due to the energy it demands and the not inconsiderable financial burden it poses: living in London, as everyone knows, is extremely expensive!" she admits.

Zabou is connected to her origins, but at the same time loves change, adventure, discovery. "I grew up in Saumur in the Loire Valley, in France. It's a beautiful and peaceful city with a rich history, but short on contemporary urban culture. I've been drawing and painting ever since I was a child: this has always been my passion. I've always known that I was born to be an artist!" she says reflectively. "I moved to London in late 2011 to study. I immediately felt a deep connection with the city and realized that it was the right place to set a new course, one that has made its mark on my entire artistic development," she continues, recalling the reasons behind her decisions.

ARTIST PORTRAIT, Saumur, France, 2020, Photo Sylvie Moreau

For her London meant the discovery of urban art. "Graffiti and street art have always fascinated me, but I didn't know much about them. . . In London I finally discovered and experienced them in person. First, I learned to spray-paint, then to work on walls; finally I was overcome by 'wild' enthusiasm. After a few years, this unexpectedly became my full-time job."

What, in particular, does she love about this world of hers? "I adore the fact that street art and graffiti allow artists—and anyone who wants to try it—to express themselves, to 'invest' in colors, ideas, opinions, figures, personalities, public spaces, to share their art for free and let everyone experience it. They brighten up our gray streets and people's day a bit," she notes.

Zabou has developed her own technique. She often photographs her subjects, focusing on the expressions and emotions she sees on their faces. She works primarily in spray paint and likes depicting her characters in black and white against colorful backgrounds, full of the play of light and shadow, and thus challenging spatial boundaries.

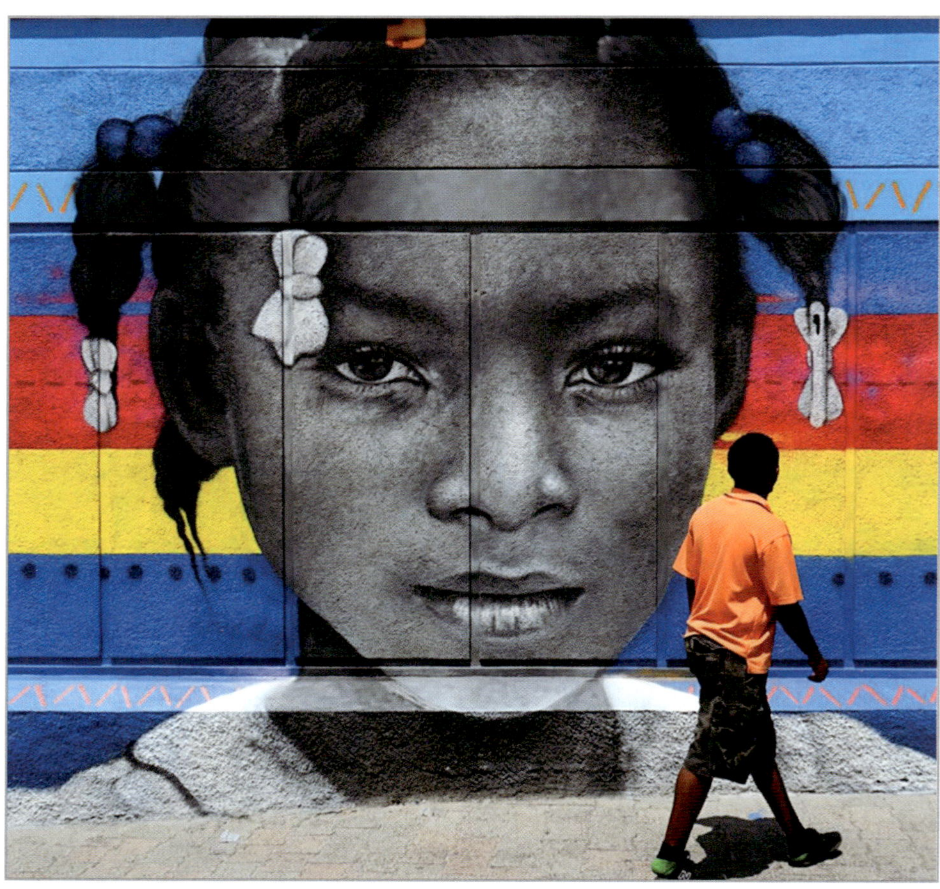

IN THEIR EYES, Port-au-Prince, Haiti, 2019, Photo Zabou
RACISM IS A VIRUS, London, UK, 2020, Photo Zabou (right)

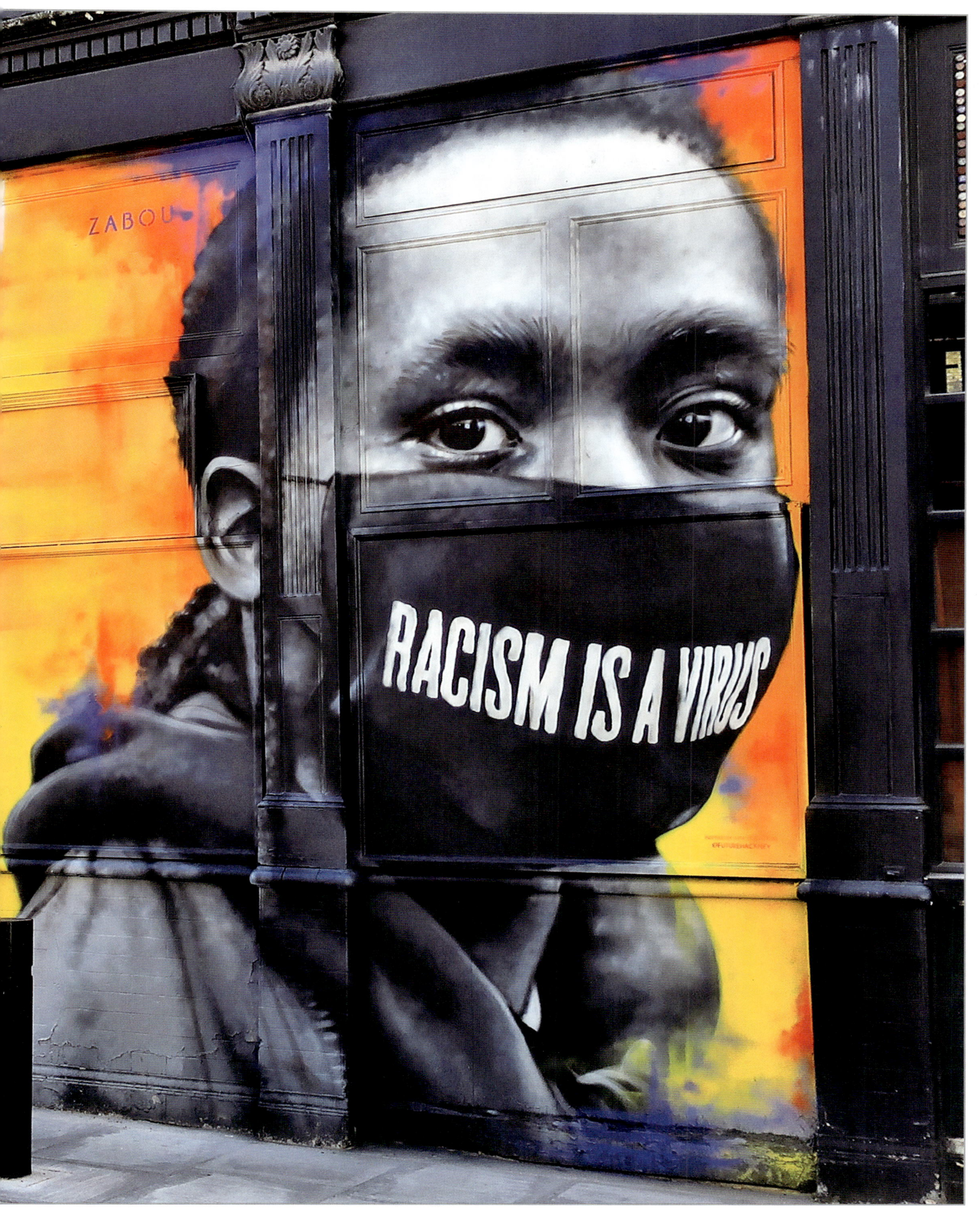

ZABOU
RACISM IS A VIRUS

It seems as though Zabou wishes to examine humanity in all its facets, searching for the essence of life itself. Her inspiration, moreover, knows no boundaries: it can come from art or everyday experiences, her surroundings, or particular situations.

"I started taking photographs for my murals in 2018 because it helps me with my work, with the composition as well as the choice of light, and makes me think about how much I want to capture and how I want to portray it. My subjects vary: sometimes they have links to the place where I'm painting or to famous celebrities, such as a musician or actor, for example, or they're 'normal' people who inspire me in their own way. I have so many stories that I can't simply choose one. I want others to make my art speak, as I never get tired of pointing out," she reveals.

Zabou has an extraordinary ability to infuse her art with a particular type of realism capable of touching the soul: "Portraits and the human figure fascinate me: it's an infinite subject. I'm deeply inspired and influenced by the reality surrounding me—by people, stories, and current events. The pandemic, for instance, has changed me profoundly. Everything was a bit crazy, an inconceivable challenge for everyone. Personally, I've changed many of my habits; I spend a lot more time at home and am a bit less sociable. Unable to travel, I was also forced to cancel or postpone most of my jobs." Yet all this has led to something unforeseen and positive: her first solo exhibition at London's Saatchi Gallery.

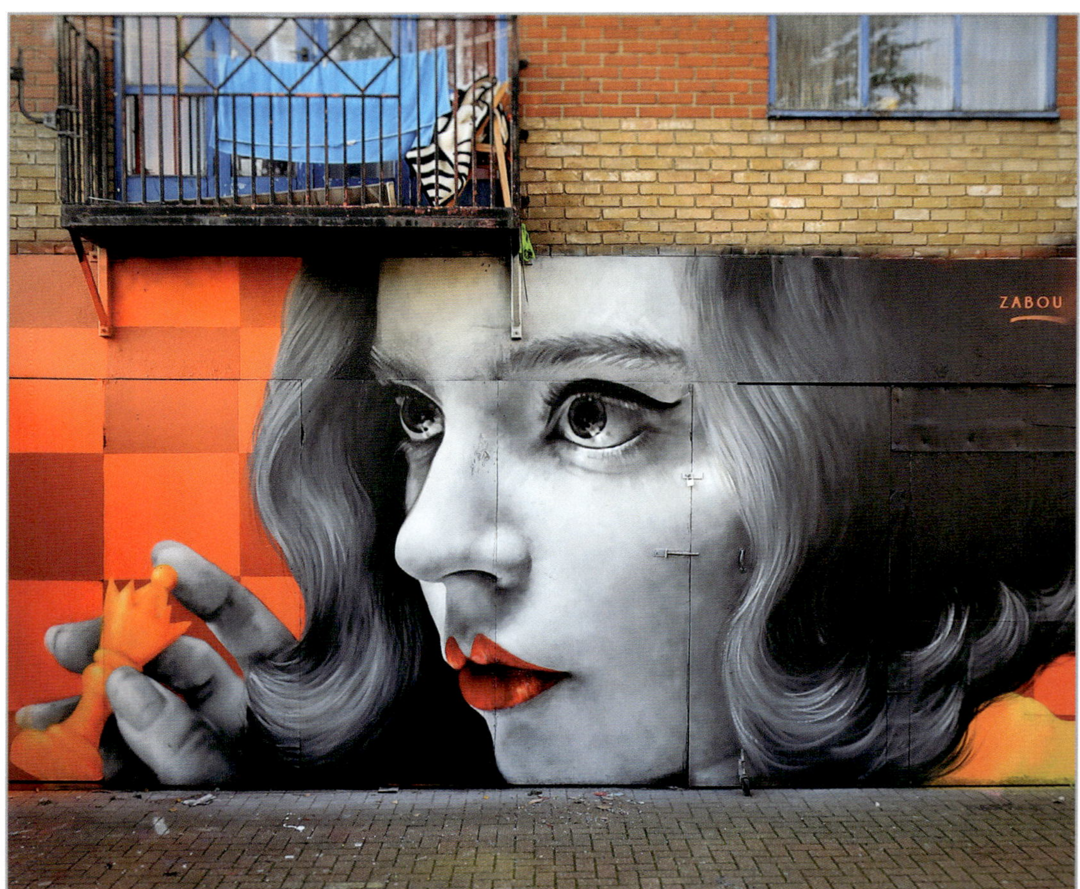

QUEENS GAMBIT, London, UK, 2021, Photo Zabou

MUM, Saint-Quentin, France, 2020, Photo Zabou

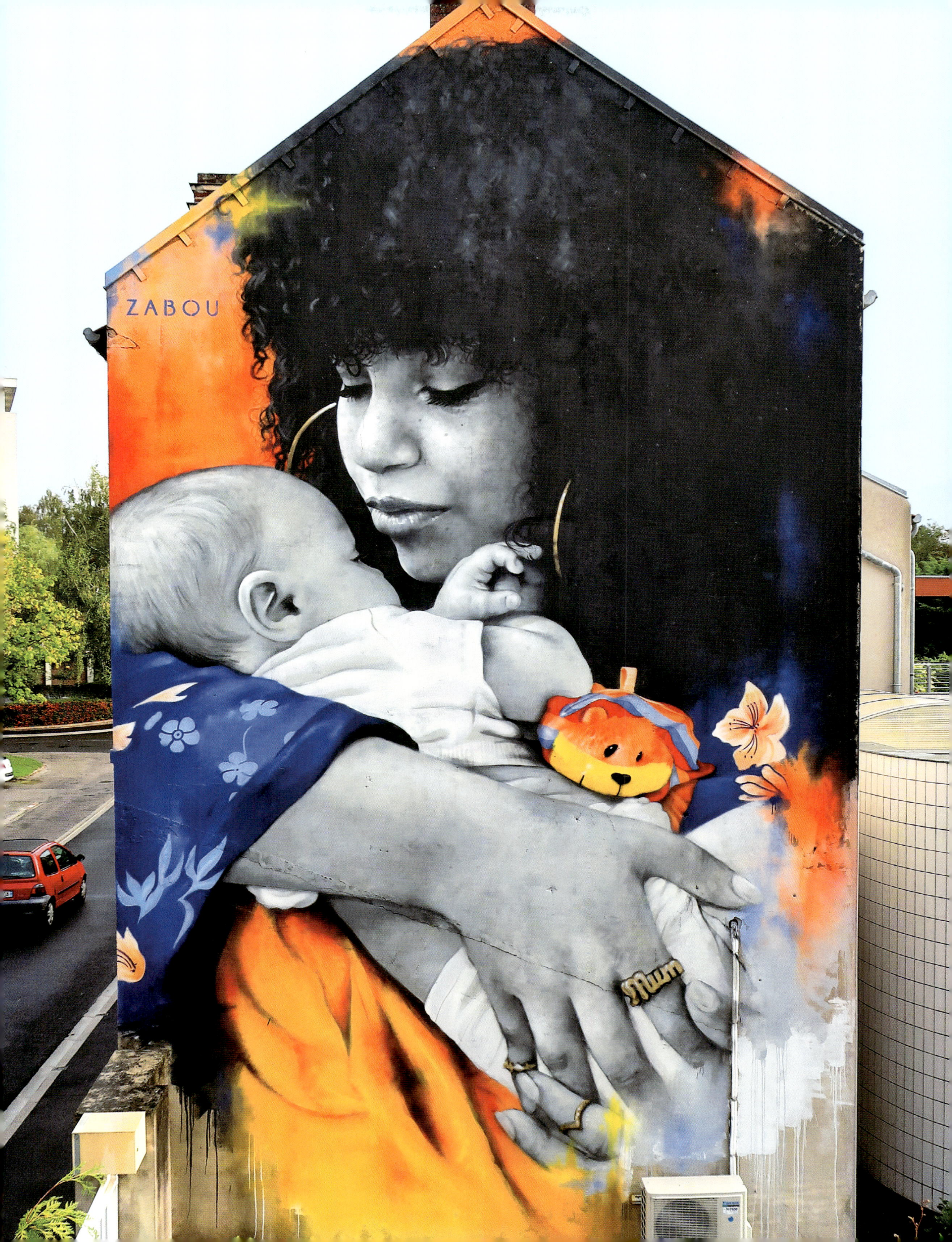
ZABOU
Mum

"I hope my work can strengthen and inspire anyone who is touched by it, and, of course, the women and the many artists like me. The last decade has seen a tremendous increase in the number of female artists in the street art scene. Plenty of talented women out there have been illuminated and inspired, and that makes me happy. We hope that others will let themselves be inspired and join us in the coming years," she concludes, full of enthusiasm.

HERE FOR YOU, Patras, Greece, 2021, Photo Zabou (right)
SLIM, Bristol, UK, 2021, Photo Zabou

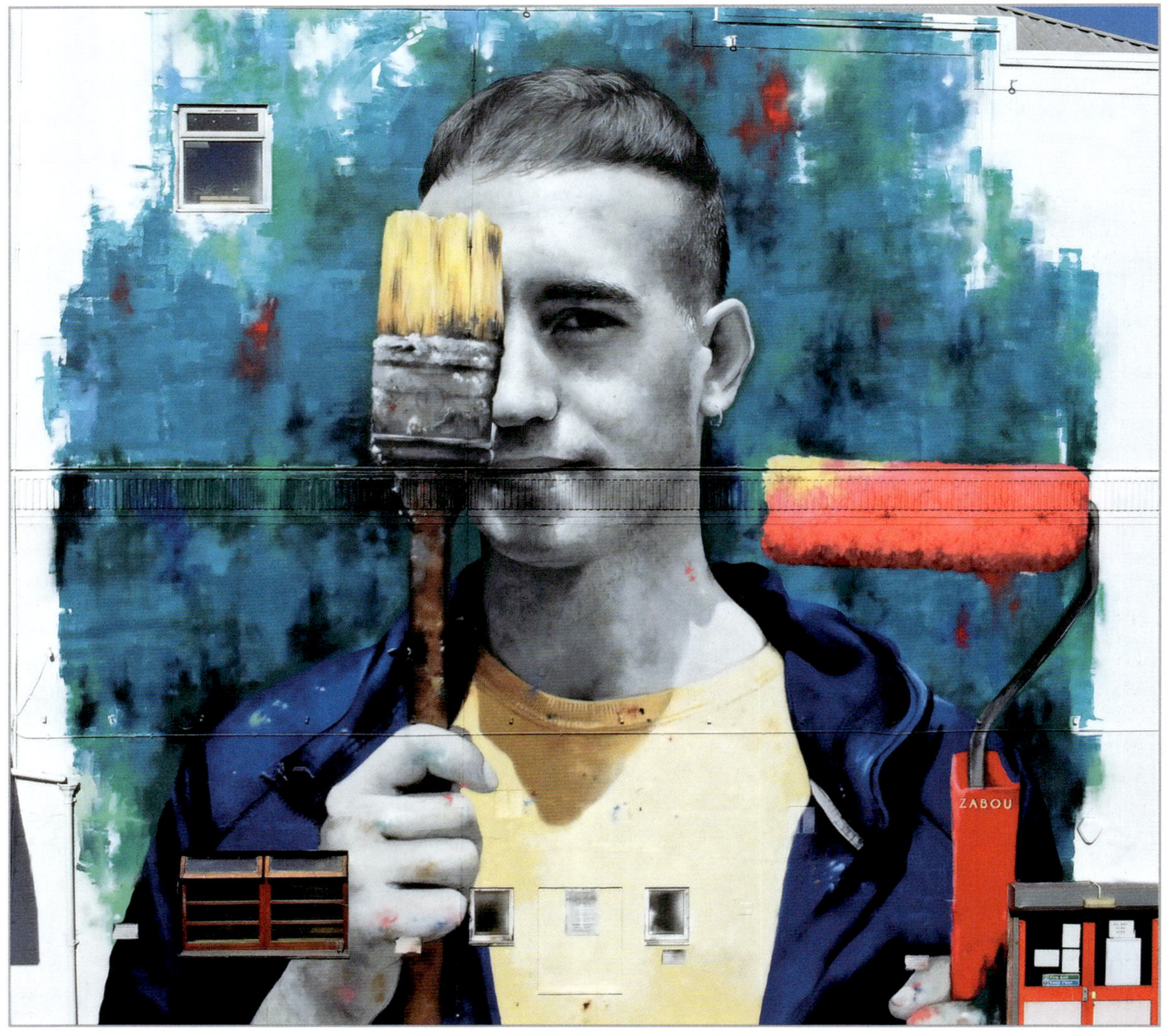

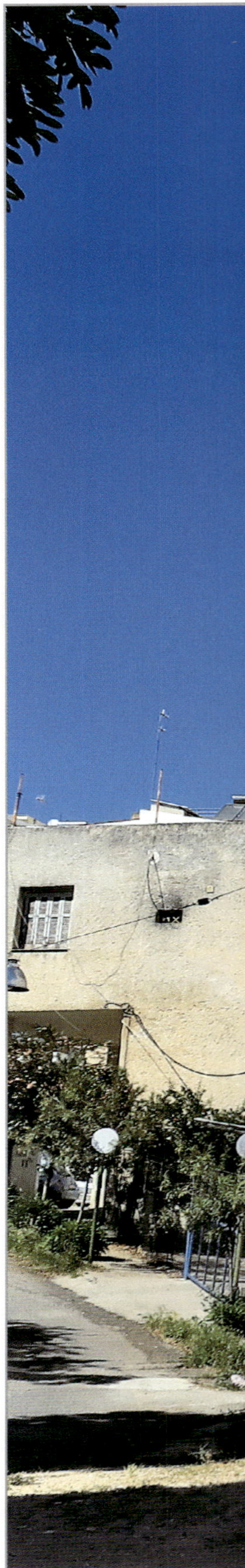

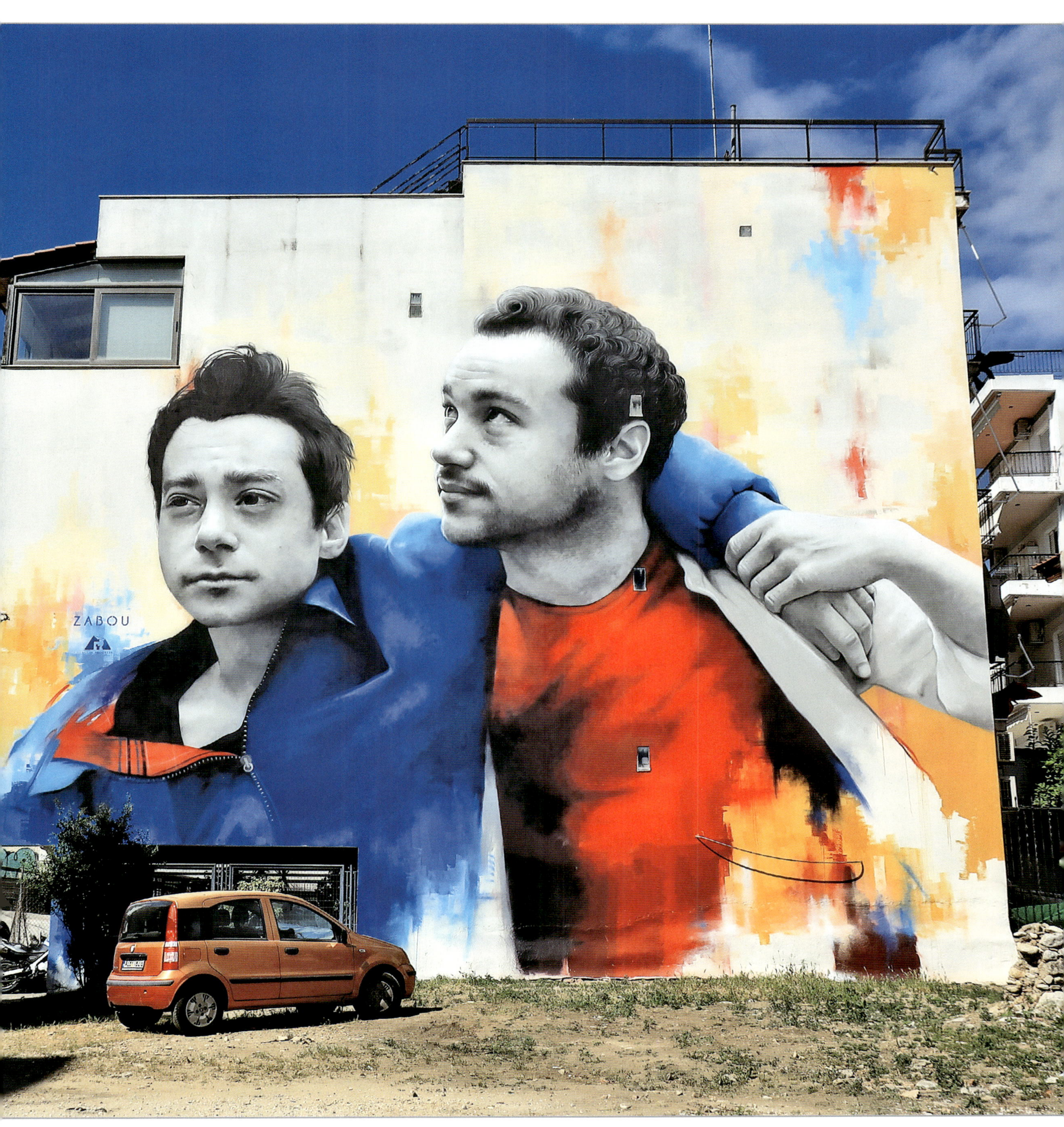

ZABOU

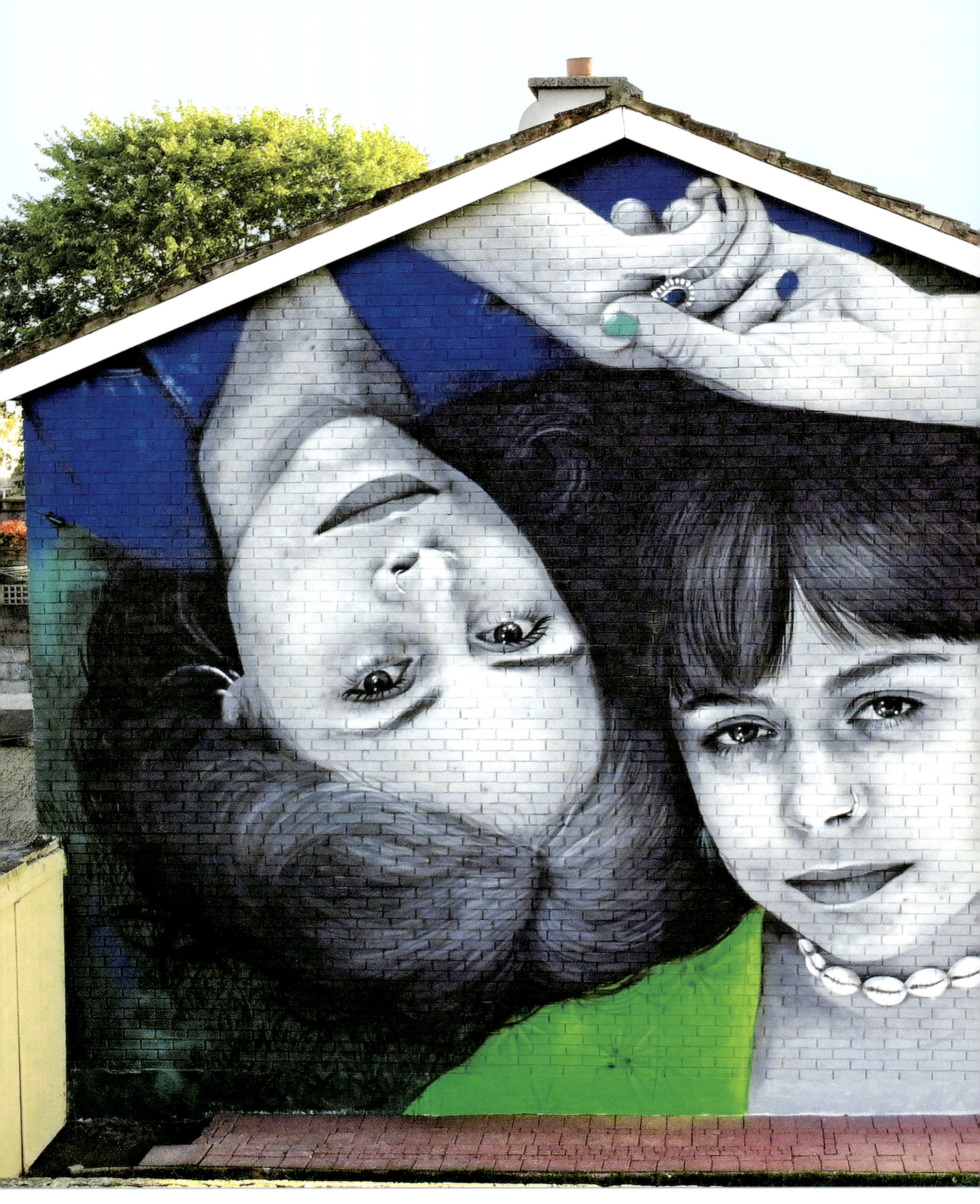

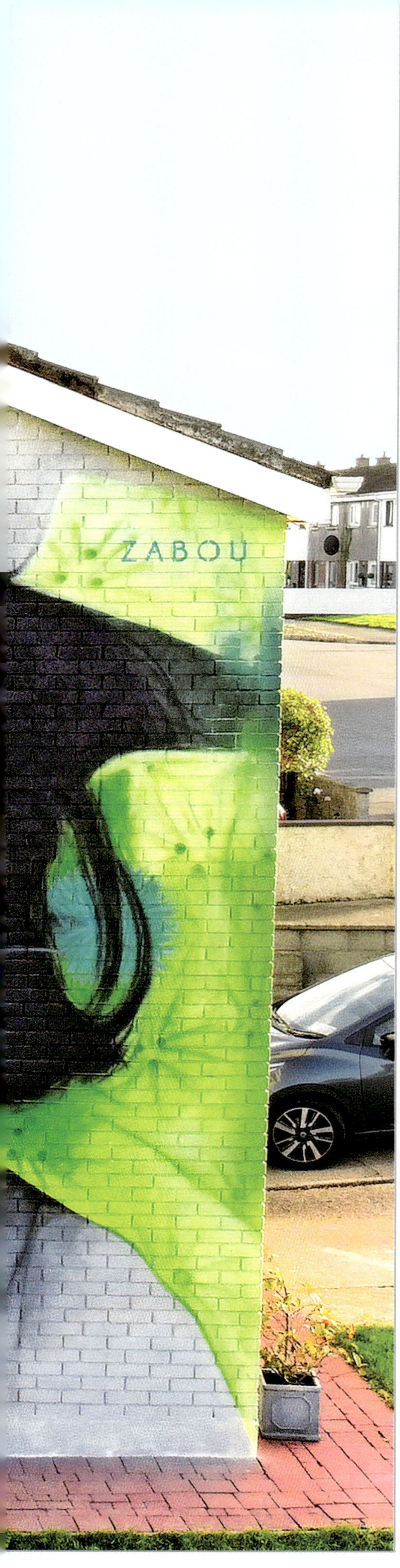
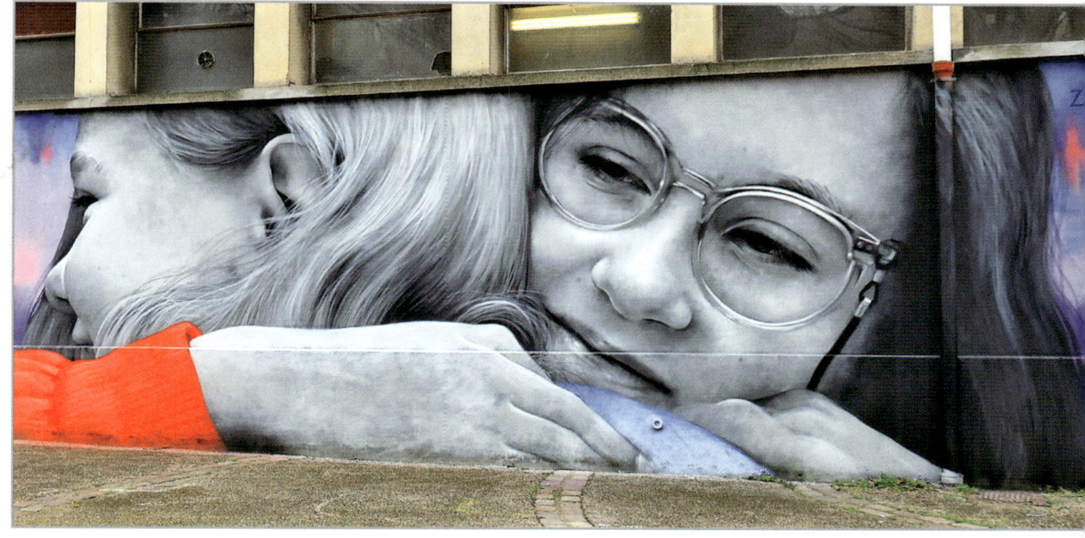

I'VE MISSED YOU, Paris, France, 2021, Photo Zabou

SAME BUT DIFFERENT, Waterford, Ireland, 2021, Photo Zabou (left)

ALESSANDRA MATTANZA, author, screenwriter, and fine art photographer, has lived in New York, San Francisco, and Los Angeles for a number of years. At the moment, she is a contributor and writer for several publishing houses and magazines, among them *Cosmopolitan* and *Elle*, *Vanity Fair*, *Forbes*, *F* and *Natural Style*, *ICON*, and the *Financial Times*, and collaborates on interviews and mini-documentaries for Studio Universal and other television networks.

She is also the author of novels, screenplays, illustrated travel books, and tourist guides. In 2014, she came first in the Personality Profile — International Journalism category of the Annual Southern California Journalism Awards in Los Angeles, and, since then, has won several additional awards and has been nominated every year in the Journalism and Nonfiction Books categories at the SoCal Journalism Awards in Los Angeles. For White Star she has published: *Wonders of New York*; *Australia: The New Frontier*; *My New York: Celebrities Talk about the City*; *My Paris: Celebrities Talk about the Ville Lumière*, *Street Art: Famous Artists Talk about Their Vision*, *C215: #christianguemy - Stencil Art*, *Banksy*, and *SOS Planet Earth: Voices for a Better World*.

Except where expressly indicated,
all images have been provided
by courtesy of the artists themselves.
Cover images: Tatyana Fazlalizadeh (front) and #LeDiesis (back)

First Published in Italian by
WS White Star Publishers®, a registered trademark property of White Star s.r.l.
© 2022, White Star s.r.l., Piazzale Luigi Cadorna 6, 20123 Milan,
www.whitestar.it

English edition
© 2022, Prestel Verlag, Munich · London · New York
A member of Penguin Random House Verlagsgruppe GmbH
Neumarkter Strasse 28 · 81673 Munich

In respect to links in the book, Verlagsgruppe Random House expressly notes that no illegal content was discernible on the linked sites at the time the links were created. The Publisher has no influence at all over the current and future design, content or authorship of the linked sites. For this reason Verlagsgruppe Random House expressly disassociates itself from all content on linked sites that has been altered since the link was created and assumes no liability for such content.

Editorial direction Prestel: Claudia Stäuble
Project management: Andrea Bartelt
Project handling: VerlagsService Dietmar Schmitz GmbH, Heimstetten
Translation into English: Irina T. Oryshkevich
Copyediting: José Enrique Macián
Graphic Design: Maria Cucchi
Production management: Corinna Pickart

A Library of Congress Control Number is available;
a CIP catalogue record for this book is available from the British Library.

Printed in Poland

ISBN 978-3-7913-8895-3

www.prestel.com